The Growth of Multinationals

The International Library of Critical Writings in Business History

Series Editor: Geoffrey Jones
Reader in Business History, Department of Economics, University of Reading

1. The Growth of Multinationals
   Mira Wilkins

Future titles will include:

Government and Business
Steven W. Tolliday

Mergers and Acquisitions
Gregory P. Marchildon

Regulation and Anti Trust
Giles H. Burgess Jr

The Growth
of Multinationals

Edited by

Mira Wilkins

Professor of Economics
Florida International University, USA

An Elgar Reference Collection

Published by
Edward Elgar Publishing Limited
Gower House
Croft Road
Aldershot
Hants GU11 3HR
England

Edward Elgar Publishing Company
Old Post Road
Brookfield
Vermont 05036
USA

British Library Cataloguing in Publication Data
The growth of multinationals. – (International library of
  critical writings in business history, 1).
  1. Business enterprise
  I. Wilkins, Mira II. Series
  338.88

Library of Congress Cataloguing in Publication Data
The Growth of multinationals/edited by Mira Wilkins.
      p. cm. – (The International library of critical writings in
  business history : 1) (An Elgar reference collection)
    Includes bibliographical references and index.
    1. International business enterprises. I. Wilkins, Mira.
  II. Series. III. Series: An Elgar reference collection.
  HD2755.5 G77 1991
  338.8′8–dc20   91–12367
                                                                         CIP

ISBN 1 85278 370 2

Printed in Great Britain by Galliard (Printers) Ltd, Great Yarmouth

Contents

Acknowledgements

The editor and publishers wish to thank the following who have kindly given permission for the use of copyright material.

American Economic Association for article: O. Williamson (1981), 'The Modern Corporation: Origins, Evolution, Attributes', *Journal of Economic Literature*, **19**, pp.1537–68.

Banco di Roma for articles: M. Wilkins (1977), 'Modern European Economic History and the Multinationals', *The Journal of European Economic History*, **6**, pp.575–95; M. Wilkins (1986), 'The History of European Multinationals: A New Look', *The Journal of European Economic History*, **15**, pp.483–510. Reprints by Schmidt Periodicals GmbH, Dettendorf, D-8201 Bad Feilnbach 2 – West Germany.

Basil Blackwell for articles: R.H. Coase (1937), 'The Nature of the Firm', *Economica*, n.s. **4**, pp.386–405; A.D. Chandler (1980), 'The Growth of the Transnational Industrial Firm in the United States and the United Kingdom: A Comparative Analysis', *Economic History Review*, 2nd series, **33**, pp.396–410; G. Jones (1984), 'The Growth and Performance of British Multinational Firms before 1939: The Case of Dunlop', *Economic History Review*, 2nd series, **37**, pp.35–53; S. Chapman (1985), 'British-Based Investment Groups before 1914', *Economic History Review*, 2nd series, **38**, pp.230–51; M. Wilkins (1988), 'The Free-Standing Company, 1870–1914: An Important Type of British Foreign Direct Investment', *Economic History Review*, 2nd series, **61**, pp.259–82; G. Jones (1988), 'Foreign Multinationals and British Industry before 1945', *Economic History Review*, 2nd series, **41**, pp.429–53; E. Penrose (1956), 'Foreign Investment and the Growth of the Firm', *Economic Journal*, **64**, pp.220–35.

Cambridge University Press for excerpts: T. Kuwahara (1989), 'The Japanese Cotton Spinners' Direct Investments into China before the Second World War', in A. Teichova, M. Lévy-Leboyer and H. Nussbaum (eds.), *Historical Studies in International Corporate Business*, pp.151–62; E. Harris (1989), 'J. & P. Coats Ltd in Poland', in A. Teichova, M. Lévy-Leboyer and H. Nussbaum (eds.), *Historical Studies in International Corporate Business*, pp.135–42.

Gower Publishing Group for excerpts: G. Jones (1986), 'Origins, Management and Performance', in G. Jones (ed.), *British Multinationals: Origins, Management and Performance*, pp.1–23; M. Casson (1986), 'General Theories of the Multinational Enterprise: Their Relevance to Business History', in P. Hertner and G. Jones (eds.), *Multinationals: Theory and History*, pp.42–63.

Harvard Business School, President and Fellows of Harvard College for articles: J.M. Stopford (1974), 'The Origins of British-Based Multinational Manufacturing Enterprises', *Business History Review*, **48**, pp.303–35; L. Franko (1974), 'The Origins of Multinational Manufacturing by Continental European Firms', *Business History Review*, **48**, pp.277–302; M. Wilkins (1982), 'American-Japanese Direct Foreign Investment Relationships, 1930–1952', *Business History Review*, **61**, pp.497–518; M. Wilkins (1986), 'Japanese Multinational Enterprise before 1914', *Business History Review*, **60**, pp.199–231; A.M. Carlos and S. Nicholas (1988), '"Giants of an Earlier Capitalism": The Chartered Trading Companies as Modern Multinationals', *Business History Review*, **62**, pp.398–419.

Harvard University Press for excerpt: M. Wilkins (1974), 'The American Model', a selection from the Epilogue to the author's *The Maturing of Multinational Enterprise: American Business Abroad from 1914 to 1970*, par.2, p.414 to middle of p.422, and notes p.565.

Institute of Social Science, University of Tokyo, for article: T. Abo (1982–83), 'ITT's International Business Activities, 1920–40', *Annals of the Institute of Social Science*, **24**, pp.104–28.

Japanese Yearbook on Business History for article: M. Udagawa (1985), 'The Prewar Japanese Automobile Industry and American Manufacturers', *Japanese Yearbook on Business History*, **2**, pp.81–99.

Geoffrey Jones for his own article: (1984), 'Multinational Chocolate: Cadbury Overseas, 1918–39', *Business History*, **26**, pp.59–76.

Unwin Hyman Ltd. for excerpt: J. Dunning (1983), 'Changes in the Level and Structure of International Production: the Last One Hundred Years', in M. Casson (ed.), *The Growth of International Business*, pp.84–139.

Mira Wilkins for her own article: (1988), 'European and North American Multinationals, 1870–1914: Comparisons and Contrasts', *Business History*, **30**, pp.8–45.

Every effort has been made to trace all the copyright holders but if any have been inadvertently overlooked the publishers will be pleased to make the necessary arrangement at the first opportunity.

In addition the publishers wish to thank the Library of the London School of Economics and Political Science and the Librarian and Staff at The Alfred Marshall Library, Cambridge University, for their assistance in obtaining these articles.

Introduction

Once many economists assumed that the modern multinational enterprise was a post-World War II phenomenon. This was said of American multinationals when they dominated the headlines in the 1960s, of European ones as they seemed in their international expansion to follow the American pattern, and then of Japanese multinationals. In fact, the institution has had a long history, with modern British multinationals emerging before and coincidentally with their American counterparts. Part I of this collection has four survey articles covering the historical background of the modern multinational enterprise. The first essay [1] on the growth of multinationals is from *The Journal of European Economic History*. At the start of this 1977 paper, I noted that there had been a number of scholarly (archive-based) business histories of American multinational enterprises that detailed their worldwide business (the three-volume history of Standard Oil of New Jersey, now Exxon, and Mira Wilkins and Frank Hill's study of the Ford Motor Company's business abroad are cited as good examples); there had even been a two-volume general history of American multinational enterprise (Mira Wilkins, *The Emergence of Multinational Enterprise: American Business Abroad from the Colonial Era to 1914* [Cambridge, Mass.: Harvard University Press, 1970] and Mira Wilkins, *The Maturing of Multinational Enterprise: American Business Abroad from 1914 to 1970* [Cambridge, Mass.: Harvard University Press, 1974]). Likewise, there were archive-based studies of particular European multinational enterprises (excellent histories of Unilever, Courtaulds and Imperial Chemical Industries are the ones cited), but overall the history of European business abroad had been neglected by trained historians. I suggested in that article possible applications of the historical work on American multinational enterprise to research on the history of other countries' international businesses.

At once the output on the history of European multinational enterprise soared, as the second selection in the present collection [2] (published in 1986 but written three years earlier) demonstrates. The books that were referred to in that article as in process have now for the most part been published, along with numerous others. There has been an acceleration of new research, with the late 1980s producing a sizeable number of fine works including Geoffrey Jones and Peter Hertner (eds.), *Multinationals: Theory and History* (Aldershot: Gower, 1986). The session on multinationals at the International Economic History Conference at Berne in 1986 resulted in two volumes, both edited by Alice Teichova, Maurice Lévy-Leboyer and Helga Nussbaum: *Multinational Enterprise in Historical Perspective* (Cambridge: Cambridge University Press, 1986) and *Historical Studies in International Corporate Business* (Cambridge: Cambridge University Press, 1989). V.I. Bovykin and Rondo Cameron's edited book on international banking is still forthcoming, but will be published by Oxford University Press in 1991. Geoffrey Jones has edited *British Multinationals: Origins, Management and Performance* (Aldershot: Gower, 1986), and R.T. Davenport-Hines and Geoffrey Jones edited *British Business in Asia since 1860* (Cambridge: Cambridge University Press, 1989). Peter Hertner's edited volume, *Per La Storia dell'impresa Multinazionale in Europa* (Milan: Franco Angeli, 1987), has appeared. In the autumn of 1988, *Business History Review* devoted an entire issue to the history of multinational enterprise. Indeed, as the 1980s came to an end and the 1990s dawned, the many works in process demonstrated an immense interest in this subject.

In January 1988, I published in *Business History* an essay on 'European and North American Multinationals 1870–1914: Comparisons and Contrasts', reprinted as the third selection [3] in this anthology. It reflects the state of art at that time, attempting to compare the evolution of British, continental European, American and Canadian enterprise. It was in print when Christopher Armstrong and H.V. Nelles' *Southern Exposure: Canadian Promoters in Latin America and the Caribbean 1896–1930* (Toronto: University of Toronto Press, 1988) was published. This splendid archives-based study of Canadian business in Latin America, describing Canadian-based public utilities, principally those in Brazil and Mexico, adds to our knowledge and changes some of our thinking about Canadian multinationals.

In none of my articles on European business abroad have I attempted to include overall figures on foreign direct investment. The most comprehensive statistical series on the history of American foreign direct investment are in my two-volume history mentioned above. John Dunning sought to provide international figures on foreign direct investment in his 1983 article, 'Changes in the Level and Structure of International Production: the Last One Hundred Years', reprinted as the fourth [4] in the introductory section of this compendium. As Dunning himself would be the first to admit, his figures are tentative and in many cases controversial, but at least he has bravely tried to provide some guideline statistics. In short, the first section of this anthology contains four survey essays which consider the evolving state of the art on the history of multinational enterprise in the late 1970s and 1980s.

Part II of this collection, entitled 'The Pioneers', includes substantive and unique material on the evolution of multinational enterprise. The initial selection [5], from my *Maturing of Multinational Enterprise* (1974), offers a model of the evolution of the American multinational enterprise; this paradigm emerged from archival-based research on the history of hundreds of US multinational enterprises. *The Maturing of Multinational Enterprise* and its predecessor, *The Emergence of Multinational Enterprise* (1970), as noted earlier, were the first (and remain the only) overall book-length histories of American business abroad. The next two selections in the present volume [6 and 7] are by John Stopford and Lawrence Franko respectively, both of whom were students of Raymond Vernon at the Harvard Business School. In the 1960s, Vernon undertook a major project to study American multinationals; subsequently he considered foreign multinationals. Stopford and Franko became aware of the long history of such firms. Their two essays appeared in the Autumn 1974 issue of *Business History Review*, the first to be devoted to the history of multinational enterprise. Stopford and Franko's articles were the earliest attempts to provide an overview of the history of British and European multinationals. Later, Franko published a book entitled *European Multinationals* (Stamford, Conn.: Greylock, 1976), contributing further historical data. Neither Stopford nor Franko used archival sources; they depended on published histories and the data bank collected in connection with Vernon's mammoth research project. The fourth selection [8] in this section on pioneer contributions is my own on Japanese multinationals before 1914. Like the work of Stopford and Franko, this was published in *Business History Review* (but in 1986). It was the first to deal with the early history of Japanese business abroad and to show that prior theoretical work on the history of Western multinationals also had applicability to the course of the overseas expansion of Japanese business. The last entry in this section

[9] is Geoffrey Jones's 'Origins, Management and Performance' (1986), which deals with British multinationals before 1939 (the third of a sequence of articles by Jones on this subject). Since it adds so much beyond Stopford's 1974 article on the history of British multinationals, it can appropriately be put in the pioneering category.

Because of lack of space, I have not included in this section other trail-blazing studies of a particular nation's business abroad several of which, however, I thoroughly recommend: Peter Hertner, 'German Multinational Enterprise before 1914: Some Case Studies', and Ragnhild Lundström, 'Swedish Multinational Growth before 1914: Some Case Studies' (both in Hertner and Jones (eds.), *Multinationals: Theory and History*); also Gerald Feldman, 'Foreign Penetration of German Enterprises after the First World War: The Problem of *Uberfremdung*', in Teichova et al (eds.), *Historical Studies in International Corporate Business*. Likewise, the student of the history of multinationals will find valuable the articles in the volume edited by Peter Hertner and Richard Tilly, *Deutsche Auslands-investitionen seit 1870* (forthcoming Stuttgart, 1991). Harm Schröter also has forthcoming work on the history of small country multinationals which is certain to be very exciting.

Part III of the present collection is entitled 'New Perspectives'. Whereas the first part included overall surveys and the second innovative studies that provide the basic building blocks for further scrutiny of the history of multinationals from the standpoint of source countries, the third part presents a small sample of articles that have had a major impact on those studying the history of multinationals. These selections were the most difficult to make for the field has benefited from a multitude of different contributions. I will explain my inclusions and then comment on certain other influential writings that had to be omitted (some because they are of book-length).

The section opens with the 1937 essay of R.H. Coase on the nature of the firm [10]. Increasingly, students have come to recognize that the best way to view the history of multinationals is to begin with the firm; most now realize that a theory of a firm's behaviour provides crucial insights for understanding an enterprise's extension over borders over time. In this view, a multinational ought to be examined with precisely the same theoretical tools that are used to consider the business history of any firm. The major difference is that a purely domestic company faces the policies of a single national government, while a multinational operates under more than one such sovereignty. Coase's essay on why a firm expands has had major impact both on business historians and on students of the history of multinational enterprise. Although not on multinationals, it provides a basic framework for some of the recent thinking and writing about such enterprises and their growth through time.

The second contribution [11] is a 1956 article by Edith Penrose entitled 'Foreign Investment and the Growth of the Firm'. This essay had considerable direct influence since every historian dealing with multinational enterprises in the 1960s read it along with her book *The Theory of the Growth of the Firm* (New York: Wiley, 1959). Penrose subsequently wrote on the history of international oil companies in *The Large International Firm in Developing Countries: The International Petroleum Industry* (Cambridge, Mass.: MIT Press, 1968).

The third essay [12] in this section was published in 1981 by Oliver Williamson and is on the growth of the modern enterprise. It puts multinational developments in the context of the rise of the modern corporation. Williamson's work on transaction costs has been convincing to many students of multinational enterprise and their history. The fourth item

[13] in this part is Mark Casson's 'General Theories of the Multinational Enterprise: Their Relevance to Business History', which was included in Hertner and Jones (eds.), *Multinationals: Theory and History* (1986).

The next selection [14] is by Stanley Chapman on British-based investment groups. It shows the variety in British overseas investments and was very influential in the development of my own essay [15] on British free-standing companies. My research on the history of multinationals led to the discovery of an important type of British direct investment abroad that did not fit into the model of the American multinational enterprise (see selection 5). Whereas many students had assumed that the historical pattern for American and European multinational enterprise would be similar, my essay on British free-standing companies showed considerable differences.

Selection 16 is by the greatest business historian of our times, Alfred D. Chandler. In many of his articles and books, such as *The Visible Hand* (Cambridge, Mass.: Harvard University Press, 1977) and *Scale and Scope* (Cambridge, Mass.: Harvard University Press, 1990), he has written on the history of multinational enterprise. I have chosen to include in this collection his 'The Growth of the Transnational Firm in the United States and the United Kingdom: A Comparative Analysis'. Chandler has shaped the discipline of business history in the United States and worldwide. His influence on students of the history of multinational enterprise has been immense.

A second, comparative article [17] – Mira Wilkins, 'American-Japanese Foreign Direct Investment Relationships, 1930–1952', published in *Business History Review* – deals with cross-investments: American business in Japan and Japanese business in the US. The research uncovered asymmetry in the cross-investments. This is a key finding, since much of the theoretical literature on multinational enterprise, stemming from the work of economists in the field of industrial organization, has assumed symmetry in the behaviour of companies by industry worldwide. The argument for asymmetry is further confirmed in other works by Wilkins.

The final article in this section [18], by Ann Carlos and Stephen Nicholas, argues that the multinational enterprise form can be legitimately applied to the chartered companies of the sixteenth and seventeenth centuries. In doing so, it performs the useful exercise of examining what is meant by multinational enterprise.

This section on 'New Perspectives' includes only the one contribution by Stephen Nicholas, a scholar who has encouraged the business historian to become more conscious of theoretical applications, who has become committed to a transaction cost approach to business history, and who has attempted to apply econometric methods to data relating to the history of multinationals. His material has greatly stimulated business historians but is not included here since it is being republished in other Elgar collections.

Neither does this section include material on multinational enterprise and international contracts, mainly because of space constraints. However, there exist a number of books and articles, old and new, that are very useful. Of the older works, George W. Stocking and Myron W. Watkins, *Cartels in Action* (New York: Twentieth Century Fund, 1946) has not been surpassed. A new work on Du Pont, covering its joint ventures and international accords by David Hounshell and John Kenly Smith Jr., *Science and Corporate Strategy* (Cambridge: Cambridge University Press, 1988), is highly recommended. Likewise of great interest is Harm Schröter's 'A Typical Factor of German International Market Strategy: Agreements between the US and German Electrotechnical Industries up to 1939', in Teichova et al. (eds.), *Multinational Enterprise in Historical Perspective* (1986). For theoretical insights on this topic, see Mark Casson, 'Multinational Monopolies and International Cartels', in Peter J. Buckley and Mark Casson, *The Economic Theory of the Multinational Enterprise* (New York: St. Martin's Press, 1985).

Attention should also be drawn to D.K. Fieldhouse's 'The Multinational: a Critique of a Concept', the lead article in Teichova et al. (eds.), *Multinational Enterprise in Historical Perspective* (1986). In this disturbing essay, Fieldhouse made the extraordinary claim that it was widely accepted that 'multinational is merely a shorthand for a wide range of capitalist enterprises which share only one common and non-definitive feature: that beyond there is fundamental diversity under an umbrella term' (p. 26). Far from being 'widely accepted', few students of the history of multinational enterprise would agree with this assertion, as the essays in this collection demonstrate.

Also omitted from this section on 'new perspectives' have been articles (or book excerpts) by such economists as Raymond Vernon, Stephen Hymer, Charles Kindleberger, Richard Caves, John Dunning, Jean-François Hennart, Robert Aliber, David J. Teece, Edward Graham, Paul Krugman, Kenneth Arrow and Harold Demsetz, all of whom have had substantial impact in this field. (Many of the writings of these economists have been reprinted in other Elgar collections.) Moreover, the one selection from Mark Casson's work does not adequately reflect his influence.

This section has nothing on the work of dependency theorists nor on immiserizing growth. While most historians of multinationals have been concerned with their impact on the economic development of third world countries, all basic corporate archival work has shown that these particular theorists fail to add new perspectives or meaningful insights on the history of multinationals *per se*. Their contributions are more reflective of the environment in which the enterprises have operated than in understanding the multinational as it evolves through time. So while this literature has clearly shaped the thinking of many third world policy makers and in that sense has influenced how multinationals function in third world countries, these materials are purposely excluded. So too is the new work on 'imperialism'; again widely read, this literature has perhaps had more influence than that on dependency and immiserizing growth in that the problem of where the multinational enterprise fits into the weighing of metropolitan and periphery power is of considerable significance. Yet to include even a sample from the books and articles on this subject would extend this compendium more than seemed desirable.

Likewise, this section on new perspectives might have contained some of the recent work on the history of service sector multinationals, particularly banks. On this, I recommend Geoffrey Jones (ed.), *Banks as Multinationals* (London: Routledge, 1990). Jones is also writing a history of British overseas banks that will be a major contribution to the literature.

The fourth part of this anthology has several case studies of particular multinational enterprises. As pointed out above, a number of book-length business histories have dealt with individual companies' international business; many of these are cited in the notes to the survey articles [1 and 2 especially]. Included herein, however, are three essay-length case studies: two [19 and 20], those on the British rubber company, Dunlop, and on the British chocolate company, Cadbury, are by Geoffrey Jones. He has also written 'The Gramophone Company: An Anglo-American Multinational, 1898–1931', in *Business History Review*, **59** (Spring

1985), pp.76–100, which regrettably I do not have the space to include. The third essay is on the International Telephone and Telegraph Corporation [21] by the Japanese scholar Tetsuo Abo. There are numerous other case studies of individual firms that I would have liked to include, for example, John McKay, 'The House of Rothschild (Paris) as a Multinational Industrial Enterprise: 1875–1914', and Claude Ph.Beaud, 'Investments and Profits of the Multinational Schneider Group: 1894–1943', both in Teichova et al. (eds.), *Multinational Enterprise in Historical Perspective*, as well as the unpublished paper of T.A.B. Corley, 'From National to Multinational Enterprise: The Beecham Business, 1848–1945'. Space constraints are the inhibiting factor. I regret that I have no cases on the history of oil or mining companies, or on agriculture endeavours, again for the same reason.

The fifth part of this collection is on the history of multinationals in individual host countries. The first essay [22], by Geoffrey Jones, entitled 'Foreign Multinationals and British Industry Before 1945', is the most general of the group. The next two [23 and 24] are on a particular group of companies in a single country, Tetsuya Kuwahara on Japanese cotton spinners in China and Masaru Udagawa on American automobile companies in Japan. The last [25] is by Emma Harris on one company in one country: J. & P. Coats in Poland.

There have been a number of historical studies that have focused on particular host countries. Thus Wilkins, *The History of Foreign Investment in the United States to 1914* (1989) has a substantial amount on multinational enterprise in the United States. Jones and Davenport-Hines's *British Business in Asia since 1860* contains essays on British business in various Asian countries. Then there is Mira Wilkins, 'The Impacts of American Multinational Enterprise on American-Chinese Economic Relations, 1786–1949', in Ernest R. May and John K. Fairbank (eds.), *America's China Trade in Historical Perspective* (Cambridge, Mass.: Harvard University Press, 1986). M. Udagawa and T. Yuzawa, in *Foreign Business in Japan before World War II* (Tokyo: University of Tokyo Press, 1990), have assembled a worthy set of papers on the role of foreign businesses in that nation's development. Mark Mason's Harvard Ph.D. dissertation (1988), publication forthcoming, is on 'The Development of United States Enterprise in Japan'. Robert L. Tignor's new book, *Egyptian Textiles and British Capital, 1930–1956* (Cairo: The American University in Cairo Press, 1989), is an archive-based history of two British textile firms in Egypt. Alice Teichova and P.L. Cottrell provide a collection of essays on *International Business and Central Europe, 1918–1939* (New York: St. Martin's Press, 1983). Fred Carstensen, *American Enterprise in Foreign Markets: Singer and International Harvester in Imperial Russia* (Chapel Hill: University of North Carolina Press, 1984), deals with two key US companies in Russia. On American business in Nazi Germany there is the recent essay by Charles Cheape, 'Not Politicians but Sound Businessmen: Norton and Company and the Third Reich', *Business History Review*, **62** (Autumn 1988), pp.444–66. Charles Harvey and Peter Taylor, 'Mineral Wealth and Economic Development: Foreign Direct Investment in Spain, 1851–1913', *Economic History Review*, 2nd series, **40** (May 1987), pp.185–207, is in this genre. Philip Shepherd, an expert on multinational enterprises in the cigarette industry, deals with 'Transnational Corporations and the Denationalisation of the Latin American Cigarette Industry', in Teichova et al. (eds.), *Historical Studies in International Corporate Business* (1989). Lawrence A. Clayton, *Grace: W.R. Grace & Co.: The Formative Years, 1850–1930* (Ottawa: H. Jameson Books, 1986), offers a history of one of the most important American multinationals in Latin America. These articles and books are but a limited sample of recent studies that focus on the role of multinationals in individual host countries (or regions) and show the variety of multinational behaviour in different environments, including both developed and less developed countries. The literature has in the main argued that to understand the behaviour of multinationals in any host country, one must know a great deal about the multinational enterprise *per se*. Both sides of the coin are interesting to the business historian: the impact of the multinational enterprise on the host country's economic, technological, social and political history, and the impact of the host country's economic, technological, social and political history on the multinational firm.

The surveys, as given in the first part of this anthology, deal with comparisons between homes of multinationals. There is now a growing literature on the history of multinationals in different host countries and an opportunity for comparative studies of hosts to multinationals. While there have been several regional works (covering Asia, Central Europe or Latin America, as indicated above) and cross-investments studies (see essay 17 in this collection for example), and while every home country study and business history deals with the activities of the firm abroad, what is lacking are global comparisons of multinationals in host countries, with the focus on the host country. Indeed, students of the history of multinationals in third world countries have often been forced to rely on the development literature for a comparative framework, since historians of multinational enterprise have not provided any generalized statements from this vantage point.

The present anthology may seem in some ways ahistorical but this is not intentional. The historian always wants to include materials in a chronological manner. Most of the essays and books cited show change, growth and development (as well as retreats) over time. Yet to arrange the entries in this collection into pre-1914, 1914–1939, post-1945 categories did not prove viable since many individual studies move across such periods. In concluding this introduction, however, I want to stress that the essence of the historical approach to multinationals is of the firm as an evolving entity, learning from its own history and experience domestically and in foreign lands, and facing conditions at home and abroad that alter over time. Historical insights are dynamic. And while the historical approach sees certain definable institutional characteristics of the firm, it never forgets that the world in which the firm operates is always subject to changes which affect in a material way the strategies of the enterprise. Indeed, this literature's major contribution to the more general works on multinational enterprise lies in the emphasis on complexities and on the transformations that occur through time.

In short, the pages that follow provide the reader with a sample of the vast amount of research on the history of multinational enterprise – from both home (source of capital) and host (recipient of capital) nation perspectives. Hopefully, the reader will obtain from them a sense of what is being accomplished in this field.

Part I
The Surveys

[1]

Modern European Economic History and the Multinationals

Mira Wilkins

Florida International University - Miami, Florida

Books on multinational corporations proliferate.[1]   Some are historical.[2]   As research moves forward, it seems obvious that the history of European (including British)* headquartered multinational enterprise has been grossly neglected.[3]   There have been some

---

* Throughout this paper I will use the word "European" to include "British".

[1] United Nations, Economic and Social Council, *Research on Transnational Corporations,* 28 January 1976, E/C. 10/12/Add 1 contains a bibliography on published materials and work in process.   Since then, additional books have appeared, at the estimated rate of at least five a month!

[2] The authors of the history of Standard Oil (N.J.) found they were writing about multinational enterprise. See RALPH HIDY and MURIEL HIDY, *Pioneering in Big Business* (New York: Harper, 1955); GEORGE SWEET and EVELYN H. KNOWLTON, *The Resurgent Years 1911-1927* (New York: Harper, 1956); and HENRIETTA LARSON et al., *New Horizons* (New York: Harper & Row, 1971). MIRA WILKINS and FRANK ERNEST HILL, *American Business Abroad: Ford on Six Continents* (Detroit: Wayne State University Press, 1964) is a history of Ford Motor Company's international business.   For a general history of American multinational enterprise, see the two volumes, MIRA WILKINS, *The Emergence of Multinational Enterprise: American Business Abroad from the Colonial Era to 1914* (Cambridge, Mass.: Harvard University Press, 1970) and MIRA WILKINS, *The Maturing of Multinational Enterprise: American Business Abroad from 1914 to 1970* (Cambridge, Mass.: Harvard University Press, 1974).

[3] Recent pionees works that begin to fill the gap include LAWRENCE G. FRANKO, *The European Multinationals* (Stamford, Conn.: Greylock Publishers, 1976); CHARLES WILSON, *The Multinational in Historical Perspective,* in « Strategy and Structure of Big Business », edited by Keiichiro Nakagawa (Tokyo: University of Tokyo, n.d. [1976?]), pp. 265-286; and JOHN M. STOPFORD, *The Origins of British-Based Multinational Manufacturing Enterprises,* Business History Review, XLVIII (Autumn 1974), pp. 303-356.

Mira Wilkins

splendid business histories of such multinational firms.[4]   But the
surface has barely been touched.   Many questions seem to cry out
for answers.   This paper is designed to consider the kinds of
insights recent research on multinational enterprises might contribute to new studies in modern European economic history.

Students of multinational corporations emphasize that they are
not dealing with international finance, but with the expansion
internationally of enterprises.   While capital flows are involved,
there are also movements of goods, men, skills, technology, patents
and trade marks, *and management*.   The vast literature on British
capital exports, for example, is useful to the student of multinational enterprise, but it only tells part of the story.[5]   Likewise, books
on international finance, foreign trade, immigration, technology
transfer, and the international histories of particular industries are
relevant, but serve basically as grist to the mill of the researcher on
multinational enterprise.[6]   The study of the history of multinatio-

---

See also LAWRENCE G. FRANKO, *The Origins of Multinational Manufacturing by Continental European Firms*, in « Ibid. », pp. 277-302.   The research of Franko and Stopford
was undertaken in connection with Professor Raymon Vernon's project at Harvard
University, which initially studied American-headquartered international business and
subsequently devoted attention to European (and Japanese) multinational enterprise.
Both Franko and Stopford had done research on contemporary American business
abroad before they embarked on their historical studies of continental European and
British multinational enterprises.

   [4] For example, CHARLES WILSON, *Unilever*, 3 vols. (New York: Praeger, 1968);
D. C. COLEMAN, *Courtaulds*, 2 vols. (Oxford: At the Clarendon Press, 1969); W. J.
READER, *Imperial Chemical Industries*, 2 vols. (London: Oxford University Press,
1970, 1975).

   [5] The literature on British capital exports of the nineteenth and early twentieth
century includes such volumes as C.K. HOBSON, *The Export of Capital* (London:
Constable & Co., 1914); A. K. CAIRNCROSS, *Home and Foreign Investment* 1870-1913
(Cambridge: Cambridge University Press, 1953); LELAND JENKS, *The Migration of
British Capital to 1875* (New York: Harper & Row, 1973; first published in 1927);
A.R. HALL, ed., *The Export of Capital from Britain 1870-1914* (London: Methuen &
Co., 1968); HERBERT FEIS, *Europe: the World's Banker 1870-1914* (New York: W.W.
Norton, 1965; first published in 1930); J.H. ADLER, ed., *Capital Movements and
Economic Development* (London: Macmillan, 1967); MIRA WILKINS, ed., *British
Overseas Investments, 1907-1948* (New. York: Arno Press, 1977), which reprints G.
Paish's and Robert Kindersley's important studies of British capital exports.

   [6] See WILLIAM WOODRUFF, *Impact of Western Man* (New York: St. Martin's
Press, 1967); WILLIAM ASHWORTH, *A Short History of the International Economy*
3rd ed. (London: Longman Group, 1975); and A.G. KENWOOD and A.O. LOUGHEED,
The Growth of the International Economy (London: George Allen & Unwin, 1971) and

nal enterprises throws new light on these topics yet is distinctive in its own right.

" International business ", "multinational enterprise ", "transnational corporation " (I use the terms interchangeably) involve a company's making foreign investments and establishing stakes abroad that are under the control (actual or potential) of the parent firm. Multinational enterprise signifies investment that carries *control,* not investment only for financial return where operations of the business are left exclusively to others. Contemporary terminology refers to investment by multinationals as " direct " investment.[7]

The origins of American multinational enterprise go back to the colonial period, when merchants installed members of their families in distant locales.[8] The origins of *modern* American multinational corporations date from the 1850's, when technologically-advanced U.S. manufacturing companies began to establish operations in Europe.[9]

Multinational enterprise headquartered in Europe has a longer history than American business abroad. As Charles Wilson has pointed out, in the Middle Ages Italian bankers such as Bardi and Peruzzi operated in England, representing the Papacy.[10]

The Hanseatic League had certain multinational characteristics. In the sixteenth century, Italian and German bankers/merchants undertook international operations, requiring coordination of business stakes in alien lands. The trading firms of the seventeenth

---

bibliographies in each. In 1976-1977, I assembled a collection of *out-of-print* books on European business abroad for a reprint series of Arno Press, a *New York Times* subsidiary. This series of fifty-nine volumes — published in 1977 and entitled « European Business: Four Centuries of Foreign Expansion » — gives an indication of the wide range of titles that are related to Europen direct foreign investments.

7 See publications of the U.S. Department of Commerce. Two Arno Press anthologies, *Estimates of United States Direct Foreign Investment, 1929-1943 and 1947* (New York, 1976) and *Statistics on American Business Abroad, 1950-1975* (New York, 1976) conveniently collect statistics on U.S. direct investments abroad.

8 WILKINS, *The Emergence,* Chap. 1.

9 *Ibid.,* pp. 29-30, 37-39.

10 WILSON, *The Multinational,* p. 265.

Mira Wilkins

century, with their outposts directed from a British or Dutch center, fit some definitions of multinational enterprise.[11]

Modern European business abroad had its origins before the nineteenth century. Rondo Cameron's *France and the Economic Development of Europe* tells of a French company's investment in Germany, in operating a coal mine at Hagenbach in Baden in 1770.[12] This precedes Lawrence Franko's example of the English ironmaster Cockerill, who settled in what became Belgium, and then built a factory making textile machinery in Prussia in 1815.[13] After the Napoleonic wars " much British capital entered France. . . to establish textile factories and [later] to construct railroads.[14] Indeed, from the 1830s British and other direct foreign investments in railroads inside and then outside Europe expanded.[15]

---

11 Some definitions of multinational enterprise insist on "producing" stakes abroad and thus exclude trading companies (although some trading companies did processing abroad). My own definition requires a stake abroad that is part of (controlled by) the headquarters enterprise; the functions of the foreign operation can be to *produce goods* (the typical definition) or *services* (i.e. to trade, or perform other services). A splendid example of a study of XIXth century international trading and banking houses, which was published after my article was completed, is S. D. CHAPMAN, « The International House: The Continental Contribution to British Commerce 1800-1860 », *The Journal of European Economic History* (Spring 1977), pp. 5-48.

12 RONDO CAMERON, *France and the Economic Development of Europe* (Princeton: Princeton University Press, 1961), p. 372. We do not know whether the same company also operated *in France*.

13 FRANKO, *The European Multinationals*, p. 3.

14 HARRY D. WHITE, *French International Accounts 1880-1913* (Cambridge, Mass.: Harvard University Press, 1933), p. 102. See also JENKS, *The Migration*. Professor Ira A. Glazier has pointed out to me that he believes that « hundreds and probably thousands » of British, Swiss, and French firms invested in less developed regions of Europe, especially Italy, in the post-Napoleonic period. They started branches for production and trade and were important in developing export industries. They were active in agriculture and minerals in South Italy, as well as textiles. Dr. Glazier has suggested the following recent studies, dealing with specific aspects of this expansion: BERTRAND GILLE, *Les Investissements Français En Italie 1815-1914*, Archivio Economico dell'Unificazione Italiana, Ser. II, vol. XVI (Turin: ILTE, 1968), RALEIGH TREVELYAN, *Princes Under the Volcano* (London: Macmillan, 1972), LUIGI DE ROSA, *Iniziativa e capitale straniero nell'industria metalmeccanica del Mezzogiorno 1840-1904* (Naples: Giannini, 1968), MAURICE LEVY-LEBOYER, *Les Banques Éuropeennes et L'Industrialisation Internationale dans la premiére moitié du XIX siecle* (Paris: Presses Universitaires De France, 1964), and IRA A. GLAZIER and VLADIMIR N. BANDERA, *Periphery and Metropolis in Historical Perspective: Commercial Relations Between Great Britain and Tuscany in Nineteenth Century*, in « Studi in memoria di Federigo Melis » Napoli, Giannini, 1978, Vol. V.

15 WILSON. *The Multinational*. p. 269. CAMERON, *France and the Economic Development of Europe*, Chaps. 8-10. See also note 41 below.

Modern European Economic History and the Multinationals

The investments over borders of modern European-headquartered manufacturing companies appears to have accelerated in the late nineteenth and twentieth centuries.[16] This rise of multinational enterprise seems to have been directly associated with the shortening of distances by railroads and the steamships.[17] European international firms introduced new products. To reach markets outside their home nations, before 1914 Nestlé, Lever, the Dutch margarine makers, Bayer, St. Gobain, Solvay, and SKF, to give a few examples, came to manufacture in foreign industrial countries. They made baby food, soap, margarine, aspirins, glass, alkali, and ball bearings.[18] The extent of the international business interactions is barely touched on in this listing, which excludes oil, aluminum, and rayon companies with their complex multinational ties that included direct foreign investments.[19] Swiss, British, Dutch, German, Belgian, and Swedish companies participated in multinational manufacturing. Some of the same firms, and others, also made supply-oriented investment to obtain raw materials. Leslie Hannah suggests that " since Britain was less-well endowed with raw materials than the United States, her entrepreneurs' experiments in integration took an international rather than national form ".[20] This may well be, although many

---

16 WILSON, *The Multinational* and MIRA WILKINS, *Multinational Enterprises,* in « The Rise of Managerial Capitalism », edited by Herman Daems and Herman van der Wee (Louvain: Leuven University Press, 1974), p. 217.

17 Alfred D. Chandler's work on the rise of American big business has been very helpful conceptually. See his « The Beginnings of "Big Business" in American Industry », *Business History Review,* XXXIII (Spring 1959), pp. 1-31, and his *Strategy and Structure* (Cambridge, Mass.: M.I.T. Press, 1962). In « The Development of Modern Management Structure », in LESLIE HANNAH, *Management Strategy and Business Development* (London: Macmillan, 1976), pp. 23-51, Chandler compares U.K. and U.S. enterprises.

18 WILSON, *The Multinationals,* p. 278, and FRANKO, *The European Multinationals,* p. 9.

19 On oil, see MIRA WILKINS, *The Internationalization of the Corporation - the Case of Oil,* in K.E. LINDGREN, et al., *The Corporation and Australian Society* (Sydney: The Law Book Company, 1974), pp. 278-282; ROBERT HENRIQUES, *Marcus Samuels* (London: Barrie and Rockliff, 1960), and F.C. GERRETSON, *The History of the Royal Dutch Company,* 4 vols. (Leiden: E.J. Brill, 1953-1957). On aluminum, see DONALD H. WALLACE, *Market Control in the Aluminum Industry* (Cambridge, Mass., Harvard University Press, 1937). On rayon, see COLEMAN, *Courtaulds,* and JESSE W. MARKHAM, *Competition in the Rayon Industry,* (Cambridge, Mass.: Harvard University Press, 1952).

20 HANNAH, ed., *Management Strategy,* pp. 3-4. Hannah uses the word entrepreneur to encompass individual and enterprise activity.

Mira Wilkins

British firms appear to have manufactured abroad before they made foreign investments in raw materials.[21]

Studies of the history of multinational enterprise begin with data on individual firms. They consider the reason for investments and markets contemplated. They look at decisions on vertical and horizontal integration, diversification, and unrelated conglomeration on an international scale.

Research on multinational enterprises provides important additions to our understanding of modern European economic history. In this article, I will suggest eight different aspects of modern European economic history that might profit from such inquiries. Because of space constraints, the first two will command more attention here than the subsequent six.

One. Studies on multinational enterprise turn new attention to conduits — that is, to the institutions, agencies, and vehicles participating in economic change. The studies provide valuable data on economic development. There is a recognition that economic change is *not* automatic and that there are actors in the form of business organizations. Research on European (and American) multinationl enterprises offers suggestions on the means by which economic progress has spread within Europe, to Europe, and from Europe to the rest of the world. The work stimulates us to consider European nations as home of and host to international business. Most were both.[22] Multinational investments appear to have been historically asymmetrical. Thus, American firms introduced into European markets and manufactured in particular European countries differentiated products that were new to Great Britain and the Continent. European firms produced in the United States distinctive products.[23]

---

21 Lever Bros. is one example. On investments in foreign manufacturing versus raw material, see STOPFORD, *The Origins*, pp. 316-317, 325. Regrettably, the tabulations give no sequence on investments.

22 RAYMOND VERNON, *Storm over the Multinational* (Cambridge: Harvard University Press, 1977), Chap. 5, has fascinating suggestions on the conduit process.

23 This asymmetry in explored in MIRA WILKINS, *Cross Currents*, forthcoming in « Business and Economic History Conference Proceedings », VI (1977).

Modern European Economic History and the Multinationals

Writers on economic progress have tended to look at national or regional economic change, or, when they consider international economic history to do so in terms of international trade, international migration, and international "finance". The literature on multinational enterprises provides very concrete alternative, or better still supplemental, approaches to the study of the spread of economic progress.

Michael G. Mulhall in the late 1890s recorded that in 1769 the first cotton factory in Spain was built and in 1851 the first cotton mill was constructed in India. He failed to ask about the interrelationships, the investment pattern, the role of multinational enterprise. Now scholars turn more attention to the movement of individual entrepreneurs and the spread of economic progress.[24] But, the questions that the literature on multinational enterprise prompts have still to be fully explored. What were the direct *investment* connections in cotton textiles, for example, between enterprises in diverse lands?[25] To what extent were enterprises transferred over borders as well as individuals and technology? Were there "headquarters" in the home country? What is the effect on the recipient and on homeland of the stake abroad? Not atypically, William Woodruff's *Impact of Western Man, A Study of Europe's Role in World Economy* 1760-1960, deals with international economic progress, but provides no answers to questions on the role of investments that carried with them skills, technology, and management.[26] Ivan Berend can write "Foreign Capital played a determinant role in investment activity in East-Central-Europe [in the years before World War I]". Research on multinational enterprises would suggest a follow-up analysis of these investments in very specific terms. John McKay uncovered excellent evidence on foreign *entrepreneurs*

---

24 Compare, for example, MICHAEL MULHALL, *Dictionary of Statistics*, 4th ed. (London: G. Rutledge & Sons, 1899), p. 161 and DAVID LANDES, *The Unbound Prometheus* (Cambridge: Cambridge University Press, 1969) which gives attention to the entrepreneur's role.

25 JENKS, *Migration*, pp. 180-183, has some suggestive data on cotton and linen textiles and direct foreign investments. This is only a beginning.

26 WOODRUFF, *Impact of Western Man.*

Mira Wilkins

in Russia and their links with foreign investment; studies of multinational business would encourage further questions on whether these stakes were part of a larger pattern of integrated, diversified, multinational enterprise.[27] Leslie Hannah suggests that the degree of foreign influence on British business was "so great, and is located in such important growth sectors of the economy, that unfavorable inferences about British entrepreneurs are difficult to avoid".   The research on multinational enterprise can moderate and add to such conclusions.[28]

The student of international business asks in specific terms how *enterprises* (not merely individual entrepreneurs) moved across borders and contributed to economic progress in the home country and the host countries. He looks at market requirements, investments, and licensing arrangements. He studies international agreements. He explores managers' motivations and concerns himself with tariffs and patent laws. He attempts to monitor the strategies of *managers* as they evaluated investment outside their homeland. He is not content to count spindles, or to add up iron production, or to present totals on barrels of oil refined.   Rather, he wants to understand the dynamics — the strategies and structures of the firms that performed these tasks and the managers' plans as they crossed borders.   He is ready to deal with questions as disparate as the effect of enterprise on the balance of payments, on entrepreneurship, on capital accumulation.

The student of multinational business is in a position to ask and

---

[27] See IVAN T. BEREND, *Investment Strategy in East-Central Europe*, in « The Rise of Managerial Capitalism », p. 176; JOHN P. McKAY, *Pioneers for Profit* (Chicago: University of Chicago Press, 1970) and JOHN P. McKAY, *Foreign Enterprise in Russian and Soviet Industry*, in « Business History Review », XLVIII (Autumn, 1974), pp. 336-356. RICHARD L. RUDOLPH, in the *Journal of European Economic History*, Spring 1976, reviewing BEREND and G. RÁNKI, *Economic Development in East-Central Europe in the XIXth and XXth Centuries*, (New York: Columbia University Press, 1974), notes the book's weaknesses on the role of foreign capital; the weaknesses appear to be of the sort that research into multinational enterprise might rectify.   MIRA WILKINS, *Multinational Companies and the Diffusion of Technology to Africa: An Historical Perspective*, in D. BABATUNDE THOMAS, *Importing Technology into Africa* (New York: Praeger, 1976), pp. 25-43, explores one facet of the role of direct foreign investment in economic development in Africa. The multinational enterprise is seen as a conduit of technology.

[28] HANNAH, *Management Strategy*, p. 10.

often to help answer, why economic change occurred at a particular place and time.   In his consideration of enterprises moving over frontiers, he asks how individual men were linked, or not, with established national or international ventures; he is able to trace important facets of techonological transfer.[29]   Enterprise can be of a family nature or of a corporate nature (or both).   I would like to see far more discussion on the nineteenth and twentieth century international interrelationships (looking at investments and issues of control) of family firms in Europe and their impact on economic progress.

While most American multinational corporations expanded from U.S. headquarters, the single headquarters seems less distinct in the study of European multinational enterprise; at times there appears to be a complex pattern of headquarters that has to be traced. Thus, two of the most important twentieth-century European multinational enterprises (Royal Dutch Shell and Unilever) have more than single nation origins.   Each was instrumental in economic progress inside, and outside, Europe.   Perhaps, too, the British-German (Swedish) enterprise axis needs study (Liebig, Siemens, and Nobel enterprises).

In short, scrutiny of multinational enterprise stimulates us to reconsider both national and international economic history with an eye to seeing how goods, men, skills, technology, patents and trade marks, and management, along with capital (in the package called an enterprise) influenced economic devolopment.   There is no determinism or myopia in this approach.   We are far from implying that all facets of nineteenth and twentieth century natio-nal, or international, economic development were shaped by multinational enterprises.   Rather, we urge new attention be given to the role of these enterprises to enrich our understanding of national and international economic history.   The student of European economic development — using the research on multina-

---

[29] Technology transfer can go with or without multinational enterprise.   See exploratory essay, MIRA WILKINS, The Role of Private Business in the International Diffusion of Technology, « Journal of Economic History », XXXIV (March 1974), pp. 166-188.

tional corporations — asks, were there direct foreign investments involved in development? Were they part of a broader, extensive multinational business? How did direct foreign investment strategies of enterprises affect the pace and nature of economic development? What was the role of particular important companies and their managers? [30]

Two. Numerous historical studies on international capital flows exist.[31] This literature in the past often short-changed foreign *direct* investment.[32] There are certain problems of definition. Today, economists agree that portfolio and direct investments are different.[33] Students of international capital movements, in the past, frequently perceived such differences, but most either failed to emphasize them, or, and much more important, neglected to deal with them conceptually.

---

[30] In this section we have referred to economic development in *home* and *host* countries. Multinational direct investment has to be investigated from each vantage point. On the one hand, some writers see foreign investment as always to the benefit of the nation of the investor. See Hans Singer, *Distribution of Gains Between Investing and Borrowing Countries* (1950). Reprinted in Hans Singer, *International Development* (New York: McGraw-Hill, 1964), pp. 161-172, for example. Others see it as detrimental to that home country. John Maynard Keynes, *Foreign Investments and National Advantage*, [London] Nation, August 9, 1924, was very critical of foreign loans. Some of his comments could apply to direct foreign investment. The Liberal Industrial Inquiry, « Report on Britain's Industrial Future » (London 1928), Chap. IX, Sec. 1, to which Keynes contributed, praised Britain's "past" foreign investments in industry, agriculture, mining, and railways overseas, but was concerned that in 1928, investment *at home* should « be the first charge on the national savings ». Recently, I came across White's *French International Accounts,* Chaps. XII-XIV, which are extremely useful on the distribution of gains; these data need to be reinterpreted along with our new insights into multinational enterprise. See also the recent work of Robert Gilpin, *U.S. Power and the Multinational Corporation* (New York: Basic Books, 1975). The effects on the *host* country have likewise been seen in both positive *and* negative terms. Vernon, *Storm over the Multinationals,* has a good summary of the issues involved.

[31] See works cited in note 5 above and Arthur I. Bloomfield, *Patterns of Fluctuation in International Investment Before 1914,* Princeton: International Finance Series, 1968, for example.

[32] This has not been true of studies relating to the United States. Cleona Lewis, *America's Stake in International Investments* (Washington: Brookings, 1938) did not neglect direct foreingn investment.

[33] See Stephen Hymer, *The International Operations of National Firms* (Cambridge: MIT Press, 1976; this was Hymer's Ph. D. dissertation of 1960) and Charles Kindleberger, *American Business Abroad* (New Haven: Yale University Press, 1969), Chap. 1. The argument that direct and portfolio foreign investments have to be treated differently is now commonly accepted.

Modern European Economic History and the Multinationals

The U.S. Department of Commerce defines direct foreign investment as an investment that controls over 10 per cent of the equity interest in a business.   The potentials for management are there.   Investments in stocks and bonds that do not carry control (10 per cent or more) are called portfolio investments.[34]   Students of the history of European capital movements did not, in the past (before the mid-1960s), make such sharp distinctions, although often their materials can be used to sort out direct from portfolio investments.   Herbert Feis, studying European foreign investments, defined " direct investment " differently — as investment that did not leave traces in the securities markets.[35]   Multinational corporate investment may not leave traces in the securities market, since it can be done " directly ".   But, multinational corporate investment that carries control may also be made through securities markets.   It becomes important to look at European capital flows to ask, were they "pure" capital transfers, strictly for financial returns, or did they carry management and control as does the presentday multinational corporation?   The extensive literature on capital flows needs to be reconsidered to distinguish financial from business transactions.[36]   When I started to view the history of British foreign investments, through the eye glasses of studies of U.S. business abroad, it seemed to me that certain investments which historians of British capital exports (1870-1914) had been calling portfolio investments did carry management and control and

---

[34] Aarlier U.S. Department of Commerce definitions used a 25 per cent figure.

[35] FEIS, Europe: The World's Banker, p. 15 n.   It has long been recognized that the securities market was an inadequate source of information of foreign investment. Jacob Viner wrote about the difficulties in Canada's Balance of International Indebtedness 1900-1913 (Cambridge: Harvard University Press, 1924), pp. 120-126 in connection with measuring British investment in Canada. Y.S. PANDIT in India's Balance of Indebtedness 1898-1913 (London: George Allen & Unwin, 1937), p. 109, commented on Edgar Crammond figures on « British Investments Abroad », Quarterly Review, July 1907 and July 1911, that Crammond used the « value of Indian securities quoted in the Stock Exchange Official Intelligence... This method cannot be applied to estimate the amount of capital employed by British companies in carrying on their business in India. The capital of such concerns is therefore completely excluded by Crammond from his estimates ».   See PANDIT, India's Balance, 109-131, for intelligent discussion of the problems.   Yet, typically, securities markets were used to trace capital flows.

[36] Since the mid-1960s, studies of contemporary European capital movements have tended to look at both direct and portfolio investments.

Mira Wilkins

should be brought under the contemporary definition of direct investment.[37]   Independently, Professor John Stopford had begun to look at what he called a special category of portfolio investments — expatriate investments. He defined as an "expatriate invest- ment" a company that was incorporated in the United Kingdom, got financing in the United Kingdom, but got *no* managerial direction from there.   The managers were British expatriates. There was basically no London headquarters.   In time, however, many of these companies became part of British multinational enterprise, and a London headquarters did emerge.   It seemed what I was thinking of as a special category of direct investment, Professor Stopford was classifying as a special category of portfolio investment.[38]   In any case, both of us were looking more closely at the *nature* of British foreign investment and asking new questions derived from the study of American multinational enterprise.

Recently, Charles Wilson, using data from Herbert Feis' *Europe: the World's Banker* (1930), noted that by 1914, while one-third of British investment abroad was in lending to governmen- ts (portfolio investment), two-thirds were in industrial investments, including railroads.[39]   What percentage of these investments carried some form of management and control?   We need more inquiries.   Wilson points out that the management of capital and the railroad itself, " often built with British materials, equipment, and labor, remained frequently under British control.   Often two boards of directors existed, one in London mainly concerned with financial management, the other where the railway ran and concerned with its immediate management "[40]   He could have added that British investments in American railways (that did *not* carry management) were sometimes " tied investments ", tied to

---

37 WILKINS, *Multinational Enterprise*, p. 232 n. 9.
38 Stopford first presented these views in a paper given at the Harvard Business School in 1972. (I did not see this paper until 1973).   He delivered a paper on this at the Academy of International Business Meeting, December 1973.   His views were later refined and developed in his *Business History Review* article (see note 3 above). By that time, he felt « Most probably, there were thousands of "expatriate" British firms before 1914 » (see pp. 305-307).
39 WILSON, *The Multinational*, p. 268.
40 *Ibid.*, p. 269.

Modern European Economic History and the Multinationals

the export of British iron rails.[41]   How did this affect the nature of British capital flows?   Can an investment be purely portfolio, when there is direct business interest and control over a significant facet of the business?

The "double" board of directors needs to be looked at in terms of the management of capital exports.   Wilson tells us of similar arrangements for mining and plantation properties — gold and diamonds in Africa, copper in Africa and South America, tin in Malaya and Bolivia, and rubber plantations in Malaya.[42]   Robert Kindersley found there were in 1929 about 3,000 British companies "operating abroad" —that is, their main plant and equipment were in foreign countries.   This group excluded a "number of large companies" that did "extensive business both at home and abroad".   Kindersley discovered that "almost every British company operating abroad maintains an expensive London office or agency, which absorbs part of the company's capital". He also studied a large collection of other companies registered outside Great Britain in which British capital was invested.[43]

We need to go deeper into the nature and structure of British multinational management.[44]   Research on American multinational corporations suggests that we should look not only at the corporate structures devised, but the nature of decision-making that accompanied capital exports, as well as the relationship between the

---

[41] DOROTHY ADLER, *British Investments in American Railroads* (Charlottesville: University Press of Virginia, 1970), pp. XIII, 12, 14, 19 n., 20, 25, 41 ff. points out various types of control. E-Tu Zen Sun's study of Chinese railroads (*Chinese Railways and British Interests* [New York: Russell & Russell, 1954], p. 10) reveals that the "bond" was hardly a portfolio stake divorced from managerial control.   Rather, she writes, « The usual advantages that accompained the loans were the management of fiscal and general affairs of the railroad for the duration of the loan... ».   Yet, she found the British control through the loan proved « mild and inefficient » (that is, the British accomplished less railroad construction per amount invested) compared with the truly direct investments of the Russians in the Chinese Eastern Railroad, the Japanese in the South Manchurian Railway, and the Germans in lines in Shantung.

[42] WILSON, *The Multinational*, p. 269.

[43] ROBERT KINDERSLEY, *British Foreign Investments in 1929*, pp. 374, 376. Reprinted in WILKINS ed., *British Overseas Investments*.

[44] DEREK CHANNON, *The Strategy and Structure of British Enterprise* (Boston: Graduate School of Business Administration, Harvard University, 1973), does *not* deal with multinational management to any extent.

investment and the marketing of the output of the mine, plantation, and factory.   Inquiries into multinational enterprise push us far beyond the study of the international capital movements.   We look first at the business, then at its strategies, next at its expansion, then at its management (and its structure), and finally at the corporate organization that may or may not reflect administrative structures.   (Sometimes corporate structures reveal a great deal about management; sometimes they are established for tax, liability, local, or other requirements, and tell little about management).

There is evidence in the literature on British capital exports that multinational direct investment was far from insignificant. Gustav Cassel's *Foreign Investments* contains a table based on British Inland Revenue Department figures, entitled " Identifiable Income from Abroad ".   Group I includes " Government securities; dividends, interest, etc. on dominion and foreign stocks, shares, etc., payable in Great Britain; dividends of dominion and foreign railway companies payable in Great Britain; other foreign and dominion coupons and dividend warrants ".   Group II has " profits from certain concerns trading abroad and having assets abroad ".   " This entry covers (a) railways, tramways, etc. operating abroad; cables, telegraphs, and telephones situated abroad; (b) mines, oil wells, and nitrate fields situated abroad; (c) tea, coffee, rubber, sugar, etc. plantations abroad; (d) gas, water, harbor, mortgage, financial, manufacturing and trading operations abroad ". Group II seems to comprise many " direct investments ".   What is remarkable is that in 1913-1914, 1920-1921, and 1925-1926 (the years for which data are given), income from Group I was exceeded by that from Group II (1913-1914: £ 86.8 million v. £ 178.2 million; 1920-1921, £ 81.7 million v. £ 205.7 million; 1925-1926 £ 96.0 million v. £ 216.0 million).   Moreover, the Table omitted a Group III that included certain shipping, banking, insurance, manufacturing, and trading firms with " works or branches abroad" and more generally, British concerns doing business mainly at home " but partly abroad ".[45]   (These last

---

45 GUSTAV CASSEL, *Foreign Investments* (Chicago: University of Chicago Press, 1928), 140, 141, 126.

Modern European Economic History and the Multinationals

companies — which might well fit our U.S. definitions of multinational enterprise — also could not be traced by Kindersley).[46]   Of course, income does not measure size of investment; it does suggest, however, that there is an important topic to be pursued here.

Rondo Cameron, studying nineteenth-century French foreign investments, was surprised how often he discovered links between capital export and entrepreneurship.[47]   He found that French engineers, technicians, and skilled workers acted as personal carriers of science and technology abroad.   While some engineers went abroad on official missions (for the French government or at the request of a foreign government) and some went to work for foreign firms, many went abroad " in the service of French companies or French sponsored foreign companies operating abroad, and as entrepreneurs in their own right ".   Cameron made careful estimates of French foreign investments.   His tables show us approximate sums invested by the French in foreign government securities and in " private investments " 1816-1851 and French foreign investments in government securities, transport, and " industry and banking " 1852-1881.   While in his tables he does not use the words portfolio or direct, his text indicates that in the first half of the nineteenth century, French " foreign investments tended to take the form either of purchases of foreign government securities or direct investment abroad.   The latter ... if not in real estate was largely limited by the willingness of entrepreneurs to settle abroad at least temporarily ".   One could assume from this that most of the " private investments " were " direct " investments by American contemporary definition; but, this is too easy, for we learn that the French were purchasers of American railway securities (private investments, but investments that did not carry management — the management was American).   On the other hand, investments by the French in *European* railways often did employ French personnel and equipment (what about

---

[46] See note 43 above.
[47] CAMERON, *France and the Economic Development of Europe*, p. VII.

Mira Wilkins

French top management?)   Just as we need more careful scrutiny
of the extent to which British foreign investment carried
management, so too we need the same kind of careful scrutiny of
French investments.[48]   John McKay and Alice Teichova found
indications of French multinational behaviour in Russia and Czechoslovakia respectively.[49]   Larry Franko's new book on the continental European multinationals belies the notion that French foreign
capital went simply into portfolio investments.[50]

Research on American multinational corporations prompts us
to ask of capital exports, did they carry management and control?
What were the strategies and structures of multinational organization?   How much were individual foreign investments integrated
into an international pattern?

When we consider Belgian, Dutch, German, or Swiss capital
exports, the type of questions being asked about the history of
American business abroad seems extremely useful.   Each of these
countries had enterprises that made important multinational investments.[51]   Indeed, so important are the direct foreign investments
(defined in American terms) that they seem hopelessly neglected in
studies of capital flows.   More research is needed on these nation's
investments that carried management and control.

Research on multinational enterprise looks at the *business* (if
there are capital flows, it identifies their sources and rationale).[52]
Charles Wilson points out that in the case of mining companies operating in less developed countries, ownership was often shared between and among nationalities (with a blending of British, French,

48 *Ibid.,* pp. 54, 85, 86.   On French capital exports, see White, *The French International Accounts,* Chap. 5 and *passim.*

49 JOHN MCKAY, *Pioneers for Profit* and McKay, « Foreign Enterprise »; ALICE TEICHOVA, *An Economic Background to Munich: International Business and Czecho-slovakia 1918-1938* (London: Cambridge University Press, 1974).

50 FRANKO, *European Multinationals.*

51 *Ibid.*

52 It is altogether possible for there to be multinational enterprise without capital flows. For example, there are no international capital flows when profits earned abroad are reinvested abroad.   Likewise, if a multinational enterprise obtains an interest in a foreign firm in exchange for patents or other licensing arrangements, international busi-ness (with equity ownership) may exist without monetary capital flows.

Modern European Economic History and the Multinationals

Belgian, and American capital and personnel). Studies of multinational enterprise encourage us to ask why, to ask who initiates, what is the basis of the "sharing" (to share product to be sold, to share financial risks, to cope with political perils, to get under a colonial cloak)? Research on multinational corporations poses numerous questions on the ways of "international capital flows". There is a dissatisfaction *per se* with the explanations of capital "surpluses" or differences of interest rates; instead there is a new, close, in depth scrutiny into the nature, rationale, and character of the capital exports. Moreover, the course of the enterprise abroad is followed, not simply the capital flows.

Writing in 1968, Arthur Bloomfield stated « Portfolio investment was a far more important component of long-term capital movements before 1914 than direct investment . . . ". His exceptions were investments *in* China and U.S. investments abroad.[53] Are there other exceptions? Perhaps direct investment is more significant than has been generally recognized.

Three. Most research on American multinational corporations has been on industrial enterprises; the same methodology can, however, be used in relation to the expansion of international banks.[54] The ties between the Rothschilds and European multinational enterprise need careful exploration. Did the Rothschilds only furnish financial services, or more? What kinds of managerial roles did the Rothschilds have in their various European multinational ventures? Likewise, the story of the large German banks and their connections with multinational business would seem to warrant elaboration.[55] The large British banks, such as The Chartered Bank of India, Australia, and China need far more study as multi-

---

[53] BLOOMFIELD, *Patterns*, p. 3.

[54] Indeed, the Centre on Transnational Corporations of the United Nations has put as a top priority *contemporary* research on transnational banking. See « Policy Analysis Research Projects (1977-1979) » in *The CTC Reporter*, I (December 1976), p. 6. We have already suggested earlier in this paper that the term multinational enterprise should not be confined to manufacturing and should include trading companies, railroads, and so forth (the production of services).

[55] There is fascinating material on the international activities of German banks in J. RIESER, *The German Great Banks* (Reprinted: New York: Arno Press, 1977; first published 1911).

national enterprise.[56]   The new focus should be on the banks as multinational business — as furnishers of services and not merely as financial intermediaries.   Banking groups had substantial investments in Europe outside of their home country in the producing and marketing of oil before World War I, but this economic historian has not seen evidence on the exact nature of their role.   Was it merely financial, or did the banks furnish management?

Four.   There has been a large literature on European business from the vantage point of international cartelization.[57]   Research on multinational corporations profits from such studies and contributes to them.   It seems to me that when we talk about the growth of enterprises, we have to concern ourselves with cartelization.   In America, the rise of big business came after the pool and the agreement to restrain trade were ruled illegal.   I am not arguing that it would not have come anyway, but merely that a form of business behaviour common in Europe was barred in the United States. In dealing with the development of European multinational enterprise, it is useful to see the cartel structure as linked with the development of such enterprises, and also as an alternative possibility.   There are cases where multinational behaviour (direct foreign investment) did not occur because agreements between two, or more, otherwise independent enterprises precluded it.   The strategy of the multinational manager had division-of-territory agreements as alternatives or sometimes complements to direct foreign investment.   This became evident in studying American business abroad.[58]

---

56 COMPTON MACKENZIE, *Realms of Silver* (London: Routledge & Kegan Paul, 1954) is no substitute for a more detailed work.   A.S.J. BASTER, *The Imperial Banks* (Reprinted: New York: Arno Press, 1977; first published 1929) and A.S.J. BASTER, *The International Banks* (Reprinted: New York: Arno Press, 1977, first published 1935) are very useful.

57 For example, ALFRED PLUMMER, *International Combines in Modern Industry*, 3rd ed. (London: Pitman, 1951); ROBERT LIEFMANN, *Cartels, Concerns and Trusts* (London: Methuen & Co., 1932); ERVIN HEXNER, *International Cartels* (Chapel Hill, N.C.: University of North Carolina Press, 1945); GEORGE STOCKING and MYRON WATKINS, *Cartels in Action* (New York: Twentieth Century Fund, 1946).

58 WILKINS, *The Emergence*, Chap. 5, and WILKINS, *The Maturing*, passim. CHANDLER, *The Development*, p. 48 points out that different antitrust requirements had profound influence on structure variations between U.S. and British firms.

Modern European Economic History and the Multinationals

It needs systematic study in relation to British, German, French, Swiss multinational corporations.

Five. Studies of particular industries can be enriched by looking at the role of U.S. and European multinational corporations. For example, L.F. Haber's work on the chemical industry draws on company histories, has valuable material on direct investment, but fails to ask questions that historians of multinational corporations pose: what is the *specific interaction* (as carried out by managers) of the particular business activities in different countries? [59] Similarly, Ehrlich's splendid new book on the piano industry could profit from asking certain questions on direct investment experience.[60] I would suggest that the application of thinking about business investment across boundaries would greatly enrich the study of many industries.[61]

Six. Students of multinational corporations are, in general, convinced that a multinational enterprise goes abroad because it has an advantage. Some stress the technological advantage, others the marketing advantage, and still others have different emphases. This author believes that the concept of advantage is of great importance. When we find a European business going, and succeeding, abroad, we can look at its advantages and see why it was able to so perform. Studies of American multinational enterprises press us to ask new questions about advantages held by individual European multinational businesses.

Seven. European economic historians who write on imperialism will find much of value in the current research on multinational corporations. Multinational corporations make investments in industrial and non-industrial countries, in colonies and independent areas. If, instead of simply considering trade and investment in non-enterprise terms, attention is paid to the goals of multinational

---

59 L.F. HABER, *The Chemical Industry 1900-1930* (Oxford: Oxford University Press, 1971).

60 CYRIL EHRLICH, *The Piano* (London: J.M. Dent, 1976).

61 Already it has enriched the study of the rayon industry. See note 19 above. Markham's book, written before there was a large literature on multinational corporations, provides a splendid example of how useful thinking about such enterprises can be.

Mira Wilkins

corporate behaviour, the importance of a particular region in a multi-national investment, the role of industry (rather than finance), the development of vertically integrated enterprise, perhaps many ambiguities in the studies of imperialism may be clarified.   The work on multinational corporations suggests that the researcher should go into corporate archives to discover the extent to which enterprises needed (or did not need) colonial administrative protection.   European firms often invested outside their own colonies, even in raw materials.   Lever made palm oil investments in the Belgian Congo; the British steel companies had mines in Spain; Shell's first stake in oil production was in Dutch Borneo (before Shell merged with Royal Dutch), and so forth.[62]   Franko has argued in relation to Continental European investors that « the correspondence between colonial adventurers and business activities seems to be rather limited . . . The returns from colonies, if returns there were, were mainly non-industrial and psychic, for enterprise and state strategies were an imperfect match ».[63]   We require much more on direct foreign investment and the colonial experience.   The literature on imperialism seems to have neglected undertaking detailed studies of individual important investors, based on business records.   Studies of European multinational enterprises can augment our knowledge of the economic, and non-economic, dimensions of imperialism.

Eight.   Research on multinational corporations also contributes to the sub-field of economic history that looks at business-government relationhips.   Multinational corporations, because they move over frontiers, frequently deal with governments (home and host governments).   Studies of multinational corporation provide insights on the role of governments in economic development and on business and politics.[64]

---

62 WILKINS, *Multinational Enterprise*, p. 318; HANNAH, *Management Strategy*, p. 4.
63 FRANKO, *European Multinationals*, pp. 56-57.
64 IRVINE ANDERSON, *Standard-Vacuum Oil Company and United States East Asian Policy 1933-1941* (Princeton: Princeton University Press, 1975) and MIRA WILKINS, *Multinational Oil Companies in South America in the 1920s*, « Business History Review », XLVIII (Autumn 1974), pp. 414-446, touch on European as well as American companies in business-government relationships.   See also MARIAN KENT, *Oil and Empire: British Policy and Mesopotamian Oil 1900-1920* (London: Macmillan, 1976).

Modern European Economic History and the Multinationals

In summary, in this brief essay, I have argued that additional study of the history of multinational enterprises can contribute to many aspects of European economic history.[65] The scholar can ask new questions that deal with the nature of corporate strategies outside a domestsic setting. No longer is he simply talking about capital, individuals, skills, or technology, patents or trade marks as separate and distinct; the researcher becomes concerned with how a business enterprise seeking markets and supplies outside its home country comes to transfer to foreign countries (through direct investment, licensing, or agreements of various sorts) the advantages it can offer. The multinational corporation because it transfers a « package » has a distinct impact.

Franko's book on European multinationals provides a good start. He once and for all lays to rest the untenable but amazingly durable idea that multinational corporate behaviour is distinctive to American companies. But Franko is not an economic historian. Economic historians should be delving into business and government archives, business papers, and doing more studies of multinational behaviour when they write about (1) the economic development of Europe, particular countries in Europe, Europe's impact on world-wide economic development, (2) the nature of capital flows, (3) the role of European banks, (4) cartelization, (5) industrial organization, (6) economic advantage, (7), imperialism, and (8) business-government relationships. Each of these topics can profit from the ideas of and the questions asked by students of multinational enterprise.

---

[65] The eight topics are by no means all-encompassing. My colleague, Dr. Duane Kujawa, who has done studies on multinational corporations and contemporary industrial relations, suggests that research in this area might also provide ideas to the student of European economic history. Likewise, the research done on multinational corporations and national security might be useful to European economic historians.

[2]

The History of European Multinationals: A New Look *

Mira Wilkins
Florida International University
Miami, Florida

In the Winter of 1977, I published an article in the *Journal of European Economic History*, entitled "Modern European Economic History and the Multinationals", in which I suggested that more attention should be paid to the history of European multinational enterprise[1]. Since then, many economic historians have delved into this subject[2]; there was a conference in the fall of 1983 in Florence,

* The author wishes to thank the John Simon Guggenheim Foundation and the Florida International University Foundation for support of the research that has gone into this study.

[1] MIRA WILKINS, "Modern European Economic History and the Multinationals", *Journal of European Economic History*, VI (Winter 1977), 575-595.

[2] For example, on British multinationals, Geoffrey Jones of the London School of Economics has excellent articles on Dunlop in the *Economic History Review*, 2nd ser. XXXVII (Feb. 1984), 35-53 and on Cadbury in *Business History*, XXVI (Mar. 1984), 59-76 and on Gramophone Co., forthcoming in *Business History Review*. He has an article on the history of British multinationals in A. OKOCHI and T. INOUE, eds. *Overseas Business Activities* (Tokyo: University of Tokyo Press, 1984). T.A.B. CORLEY is doing research on British multinationals, including Beecham's (see his 1983 unpublished paper, "From National to Multinational Enterprise: The Beecham Business 1848-1945"). He has a new book, *A History of Burmah Oil* (London: William Heinemann Ltd., 1983). DONALD COLEMAN'S third volume of his history of Courtaulds (Oxford: Clarendon Press, 1980) has appeared. Theo C. BARKER, *The Glassmakers: Pilkington* (London: Weidenfeld & Nicolson, 1977), is subtitled "The Rise of an International Company". STEPHEN NICHOLAS has written, "British Multinational Investment before 1939", *Journal of European Economic History*, XI (Winter 1982), 605-630, and "Agency Contracts, Institutional Modes, and Transition to Foreign Direct Investment by British Manufacturing Multinationals before 1939", *Journal of Economic History*, XLIII (Sept. 1983),

Mira Wilkins

675-686. CHARLES WILSON has research in process on British direct investment in Australia. W.J. READER, *Bowater* (Cambridge: Cambridge University Press, 1981), deals with the history of an international business, as does RONALD W. FERRIER, *The History of British Petroleum Company* (Cambridge: Cambridge University Press, 1982). Another international enterprise is discussed in CHARLES E. HARVEY, *Rio Tinto Company 1873-1954* (Penzance, Cornwall: Alison Hodge, 1981) and still another, in DAVID K. FIELDHOUSE, *Unilever Overseas: The Anatomy of a Multinational 1958-1965* (London: Croom Helm, 1978). SHERMAN COCHRAN, *Big Business in China* (Cambridge: Harvard University Press, 1980) considers an American-owned multinational that became British. J.-F. HENNART is doing research on the history of the tin industry and using a multinational-enterprise framework in his consideration of British and other European firms. ALICE TEICHOVA has supervised a research project on multinational companies in inter-war Central-East Europe. One outcome was her "Versailles and the Expansion of the Bank of England into Central Europe," in NORBERT HORN and JURGEN KOCKA, *Law and the Formation of the Big Enterprises in the 19th and Early 20th Centuries* (Gottingen: Vandenhoeck and Ruprecht, 1979). GEOFFREY JONES, "Lombard Street on the Riviera," *Business History*, XXIV (July 1982), 186-210, provides new research on British banks abroad. He has a study in process on the history of the British Bank of the Middle East. At the London School of Economics, LESLIE HANNAH has stimulated substantial new work on British multinational enterprise. American historians of the frontier are interested in British investments in land and mortgages. Many of these stakes were multinational enterprise type investments. See, for example, LARRY A. McFARLANE, "British Investment and the Land: Nebraska 1877-1946, "*Business History Review*, LVII (Summer 1983), 258-272. D.C.M. PLATT, ed., *Business Imperialism, 1840-1930. An Inquiry Based on British Experience in Latin America* (Oxford: Clarendon Press, 1977) contains much of interest to the student of British multinational enterprise. On German multinationals, PETER HERTNER has published a number of articles; for example, see his "Fallstudien zu deutschen multinationalen Unternehmen vor dem Ersten Weltkrieg", in NORBERT HORN and JURGEN KOCKA, *Law and the Formation of the Big Enterprises*. His forthcoming, "German Multinational Enterprise before 1914, Some Case Studies", is most useful. ALICE TEICHOVA has a paper (1979) on "The Mannesmann Concern in Central-East Europe in the Interwar Period". THOMAS R. KABISCH, *Deutsches Kapital in den USA* (Stuttgart: Klett-Cotta, 1982), has much of interest. See also JURGEN SCHNEIDER, "German Investments in the US (1872-1914)", unpublished paper delivered at the 1982 Fuji Conference. On German business in Latin America, see GERHARD JACOB-WENDLER, *Deutsche Elekroindustrie in Lateinamerika: Siemens und AEG, 1890-1914* (Stuttgart: Klett-Cotta, 1982). The work on Swedish multinationals is extensive: See bibliography in and especially the contents of RAGNHILD LUNDSTRÖM, "Early Swedish Multinationals", forthcoming. Of particular interest are the four monographs on Swedish Match Co.: LARS HASSBRING, *The International Development of the Swedish Match Company*; HÅKAN LINDGREN, *Corporate Growth. The Swedish Match Industry in its Global Setting*; HANS MODIG, *Swedish Match Interests in British India during the Interwar Years*; ULLA WIKANDER, *Kreuger's Match Monopolies, 1925-1930. Case Studies in Market Control through Public Monopolies* all published Stockholm: LIBER FÖRLAG, 1979. A. STROBEL has done useful research on A.I.A.G., the

Italy, on "Multinationals: Theory and History[3]"; and for the International Economic History Association meetings in Bern in 1986, a session is scheduled on Multinational Enterprise and one of the reports on current international research projects will be on International

predecessor of Alusuisse. JOHN P. McKAY (who did earlier work on foreign business in Russia) is now engaged in a study of the Paris Rothschilds. On European multinationals in the United States, see FRANCESCA SANNA RANDACCIO, "European Direct Investments in U.S. Manufacturing", thesis, Wolfson College, Oxford University, 1980, and PETER J. BUCKLEY and BRIAN R. ROBERTS, *European Direct Investment in the USA before World War I* (London: Macmillan Press, 1982), which book is regrettably so filled with errors as to detract seriously from its value. JONATHAN LIEBENAU has in process research on patents, technology, and multinationals in the pharmaceutical business. On European business in Central Europe, see ALICE TEICHOVA and PHILIP L. COTTRELL, eds., *International Business and Central Europe 1919-1938* (Leicester: Leicester University Press, 1982). GEOFFREY JONES and GRIGORI GERENSTAIN have given us in English the 1922 work of P.V. Ol', *Foreign Capital in Russia* (New York: Garland Publishing, 1983). RONDO CAMERON, "Economic Relations of France with Central and Eastern Europe, 1800-1914", *Journal of European Economic History*, X (Fall 1981), 537-552, deals with important foreign direct investments. Likewise, see CLIVE TREBILCOCK and GEOFFREY JONES, "Russian Industry and British Business 1910-1930, Oil and Armaments", *Journal of European Economic History*, XI (Spring 1982), 61-103. More general, in MARK CASSON, ed., *The Growth of International Business* (London: George Allen and Unwin, 1983), 84-139, JOHN DUNNING writes on "Changes in the Level and Structure of International Production. The Last One Hundred Years". His discussion includes European multinational enterprise. Most of all, I have been greatly influenced by the work of ALFRED CHANDLER. See his "The Growth of the Transnational Industrial Firm in the United States and United Kingdom", *Economic History Review*, 2nd ser. XXXIII (Aug. 1980), 396-410; his "Global Enterprises: Economic and National Characteristics", unpublished paper (1982); his "Evolution of the Large Industrial Corporation: An Evaluation of the Transaction Cost Approach", unpublished paper (1982). Part of this paper was published in JEREMY ATACK, ed., *Business and Economic History*, 2nd ser., XI (1982). See also his latest articles, "The Emergence of Managerial Capitalism", Dec. 1983, American Historical Association address, publication forthcoming, and "The Evolution of Modern Global Competition" (1984). These titles represent only a sample of the proliferation of recent work related to European multinational enterprise.

[3] A book is forthcoming to be edited by GEOFFREY JONES and PETER HERTNER.

Mira Wilkins

Banking with a subtopic related to multinational corporations[4].

Recently, Raymond Vernon, who knows more about multinational enterprise than any single scholar, pointed out that "By the early 1980s... the multinationalizing trend was widely recognized as similar in nature irrespective of the nationality of the parent firm[5]". Much of the blossoming of research on the history of European multinationals has been based on this assumption. The research has reached the point where it seems appropriate to consider some of the new insights and some of the "unknowns"[6]. In this article I want to

---

[4] MAURICE LÉVY-LEBOYER is the convenor and ALICE TEICHOVA and OLGA NUSSBAUM the rapporteurs for the session on Multinational Enterprise. RONDO CAMERON is organizing the project on international banking. In addition, PETER HERTNER has sponsored meetings (one in December 1983 and one scheduled for October 1984) on the early history of French, German, and Italian multinational enterprise. Participants in Hertner's meetings have considered the history of the international business of such firms as Pirelli, SNIA Viscosa, La Société St. Gobain, I. G. Farben, La Société Schneider & Cie, and Fiat. Papers are available from Professor HERTNER.

[5] RAYMOND VERNON, TWO HUNGRY GIANTS (Cambridge: Harvard University Press, 1983). 12.

[6] The booming research has not only been among economic historians. The "Theory of Multinational Enterprise" has been greatly advanced in recent years. Since 1978 contributions include, MARK CASSON, *Alternatives to the Multinational Enterprise* (London: Macmillan, 1979); JOHN H. DUNNING, *International Production and the Multinational Enterprise* (London: George Allen and Unwin, 1981); JEAN-FRANCOIS HENNART, *A Theory of Multinational Enterprise* (Ann Arbor: The University of Michigan Press, 1982); OLIVER E. WILLIAMSON, "The Modern Corporation: Origins, Evolution, Attributes", *Journal of Economic Literature*, XIX (Dec. 1981), 1537-1568. Two particularly recommended summaries of the state of the art are NEIL HOOD and STEPHEN YOUNG, *The Economics of Multinational Enterprise* (London: Longmans, 1979) and RICHARD CAVES, *Multinational Enterprise and Economic Analysis* (Cambridge: Cambridge University Press, 1982). Caves' book contains a lengthy and invaluable bibliography as well as a bibliographical essay. Since the late 1970's a new vocabulary has been used by economists in considering the theory of multinational enterprise. There is concern with "internalization" and transaction costs. Discussions revolve around "transaction advantages" and when intrafirm transactions are more efficient than market ones. The "transactions" approach considers when firms carry on activities within the enterprise rather than with outsiders. It looks at the multinational enterprise's hard-to-value property rights (intangible assets such as technology and trademarks). SEE CAVES, *Multinational Enterprise and Economic Analysis*, for the most recent overview.

consider what is known of the history of American and European-headquartered multinational enterprise and ask, once again, was the pattern of development similar or different, and to the extent that there were differences, what were they? I am going to suggest herein that while the broad framework for analysis can be similar, more study is needed on some of the dissimilarities. The familiar model fits, but we ought not to apply it too rigidly[7].

A multinational enterprise is a business that has investments outside its home nation-investments that are managed and controlled (or where there is the potential for management and control)[8]. Capital transfer is embodied within the extended firm, not transferred to an independent entity abroad. A rudimentary multinational may have simply a sales branch abroad, a minor presence outside its home nation. We define the multinational activity as that of a firm extending over the national frontier. A full-fledged, modern multinational can have operations in over a hundred countries, some of which operations are themselves multiplant and multifunctional and which may have no trade connections whatsoever with the parent firm[9]. There is a process, a growth of business enterprise. In the early stages, stakes abroad were smaller, less extensive, less complex, than at a later time.

The modern multinational enterprise, as we know it today, began in embryo in the middle of the nineteenth century, but it seems more legitimate to date its origins from the last decades of the nineteenth

---

[7] I wrote this paper not long after reading LOUIS WELLS, *Third World Multinationals* (Cambridge: MIT Press, 1983). It argues on the "multinationalizing trend", but shows differences between less-developed country and industrial country head-quartered multinationals.

[8] I am not departing from the definition given in my 1977 *JEEH* article (p. 577).

[9] The size and importance of some of the contemporary multinationals is awesome. In 1980 General Motors had 746,000 employees. Philips Gloeilampen Fabrieken, 372,000; Siemens, 344,000; Fiat, 343,000; Unilever, 300,000; Peugeot, 245,000; B.A.T. Industries, 177,000. United Nations Centre on Transnational Corporations, *Transnational Corporations in World Development*. Third Survey (United Nations, N.Y., 1983), 357-358.

Mira Wilkins

century when communication and transportation facilities made it possible (for the first time in world history) to extend the span of managerial control over substantial distance. Cables and steamships, linked with the telegraph and railroads, created the modern world economy and, at the same time, the basis for the modern multinational enterprise[10].

When I studied the history of American multinationals, I found a pattern: a firm became national and, then, international in its search for new markets. It invested at home and then abroad. Likewise, the same firm (or others) looked for raw materials, domestically and, then, internationally; investment might follow the search. I found American business invested abroad more in some industries than in others. The expansion into certain countries was larger than into others. While in my 1964, 1970, and 1974 books on American business abroad[11], I was not as certain of the systematic pattern as I am now, nonetheless, my writings provided the basis for the generalizations that follow. Firms that were technologically-advanced, with trademarked products, with some "advantage" in the international arena, were the ones that went into selling and then manufacturing outside the United States[12]. Companies that required security of supply of their raw materials, had expertise in domestic mining and smelting, or oil production, went into such investments abroad. Foreign investment was influenced by experiences at home. The market-oriented foreign investments were first and foremost in the developed countries (where

[10] Professor ALFRED D. CHANDLER has made this point in a number of places, and I am convinced of its legitimacy. The earlier chartered companies bore many resemblances to modern multinational enterprise, *but* slow communication impeded administrative coordination. The volume of transactions per year was low compared with the modern multinational enterprise. SEE CHANDLER, "The Emergence of Managerial Capitalism".

[11] MIRA WILKINS, *American Business Abroad: Ford on Six Continents* (Detroit, Mich.: Wayne State University Press, 1964); MIRA WILKINS, *The Emergence of Multinational Enterprise: American Business Abroad from the Colonial Era to 1914* (Cambridge: Harvard University Press, 1970); and MIRA WILKINS, *The Maturing of Multinational Enterprise: American Business Abroad from 1914 to 1970* (Cambridge: Harvard University Press, 1974).

[12] I made this point in my 1977 *JEEH* article, p. 593.

there were high-income buyers of the goods to be sold). Firms went to familiar before unfamiliar nations. Supply-related investments went first to nearby locales and only subsequently farther afield. "Familiar" and "nearby" could be defined in terms of high-income level, geography, politics, or culture[13]. Managerial considerations appear to have dictated these choices.

As I have studied European multinationals (especially in the context of their interests in the United States)[14], it became clear that this "American" pattern was indeed a useful starting point. A number of differences, however, became evident. In this paper I want to discuss them as they appeared in the formative era of both American and European modern multinational enterprise, that is, the late nineteenth century, early twentieth century. The dissimiliarities help explain why the United States was, and is, so important vis-à-vis other nations as a headquarters for multinational enterprise[15].

Like U.S. multinationals, those of particular European countries emerged out of experiences at home. Lawrence Franko has argued (as others had before him) that American technology economized on labor; European technology economized on raw materials; therefore, the advantages of multinationals based in the United States and in Europe would be different. His explanations often seem too sweeping, but his fundamental argument is clearly valid. Enterprises founded in diverse milieus will have advantages that vary substantially[16]. In this regard, five aspects of the U.S. environment seemed worth added scrutiny.

First, the United States as a home for multinational enterprise

[13] I have learned from conversations with my colleague, J. - F. HENNART in making this definition.

[14] For more than a decade I have been doing research on the history of foreign investment in the United States.

[15] If we look at the leading multinational industrial enterprises today, seven of the top ten (measured by sales) are headquartered in the United States. U.N. Centre on Transnational Corporations, *Transnational Corporations*, 357.

[16] LAWRENCE G. FRANKO, *European Multinationals* (Stamford, Conn.: Greylock Publishers, 1976). SEE CAVES, *Multinational Enterprise and Economic Analysis*, 62, for some reasons for the differences.

Mira Wilkins

was very unique. By 1900, it was the world's "largest market". This did not mean that it had the most people; other countries had more. It did not have the largest geographical expanse; other nations fit that description. It probably did have the highest per capita income. What made it the "largest market" was the combination of the relatively high per capita income, sizable population, and a big geographical area that by 1900 was singular in that it was under one national sovereign and was well-connected by communication and transportation facilities. These characteristics — income level, population size, and the "compact" geographical expanse — put the country in a class by itself as a locale for multinational enterprise to develop[17].

European countries that in 1900 were homes to multinational enterprise — Britain, Germany, France, Holland, Sweden, Belgium, Switzerland, for example—shared the relatively high per capita income (by world standards), but not the domestic population size nor the geographical span that typified the United States. Some, to be sure, had command over vast area via Empire, yet this was not a "compact" home base[18]. American managers were educated in a very special classroom.

---

[17] RAYMOND VERNON has stressed the large market and high per capita income.

[18] Compare, for example, the U.S. *national* market in say 1914 with the British Empire market of that same year. 1. Income level: Britain's national market had a high per capita income; its Empire market did not. 2. Size of population: The British Empire had more people than the United States. 3. Geographical expanse. Here the difference is dramatic. The vast geographical reach of the British Empire bore no resemblance to the *compactness* of the American geographical phenomenon. Following H. G. WELLS' old but useful description of the state of affairs in 1914 (*The Outline of History*) (3rd ed. New York: Macmillan, 1922), 997-998), the British Empire had at its center the "crowned republic of the United British Kingdoms", England, Scotland, and Ireland. Then there were the "crowned republics" of Australia, Canada, Newfoundland, New Zealand, and South Africa, "all practically independent and self-governing states in alliance with Great Britain, but each with a representative of the Crown appointed by the Government in office". There was the Indian Empire, "with its dependent and 'protected' states". Wells included the "ambiguous possession of Egypt, still nominally part of the Turkish Empire and still retaining its own monarch", but virtually under British control. Still more "ambiguous" was the Anglo-Egyptian Sudan, administered by Britain and by the "British-controlled" Egyptian government. With

A second important distinguishing feature of the American market was the heterogeneity *within* this very compact geographical unity. America in the late nineteenth, early twentieth century was a land of immigrants. Part of American businessmen's training at home consisted not only of dealing with geographical grandness (wide variations in climate and terrain), but also with the absence of cultural uniformity. Likewise, the United States had a federal political system that meant that within the U. S. "common market", there was legal diversity from one state to the next. These heterogeneous conditions within a truly united nation were *sui generis*[19]

Third, in the early years of modern American multinational enterprise, the United States was a net importer of capital. So was Sweden. By contrast, the other major headquarters for multinational enterprise, Britain, France, Germany, Holland, were net exporters of capital.

Fourth, none of the United States' borders or inland seas touched on a nation that was a net capital exporter or a leader in technological development.

Fifth, U. S. public policies toward restraint of trade, toward monopoly power, were unlike those of any European nation. As F. M. Scherer has put it, "The *per se* prohibition of price-fixing and related agreements in the United States stands in contrast to the situation

segue nota 18

different governance were Malta, Jamaica, the Bahamas, and Bermuda. As Crown colonies, there were Ceylon, Trinidad, and Fiji. Then there were the tropical lands in Africa, nominally protectorates and administered by a High Commissioner (as in Basutoland) or a chartered company (as in Rhodesia). Compare this political complexity with the simple constitutionally-defined relationship of the American states to the federal government. Not only was there economic and political diversity within the Empire, but the transportation and communication revolution that united the American nation had not yet reached throughout the Empire. By 1915 San Francisco and New York were minutes from one another by telegraph or telephone and days apart by rail. Regions in the British Empire were still not connected by cable (much less telephone) and months apart by steamship and overland transport.

[19] Under the American constitution, no state could set up tariffs; this was confined to the U. S. Congress. Interstate activities were governed by federal law.

Mira Wilkins

overseas. While the *per se* rule was emerging in America during the early part of the 20th century, most European nations had no statutory antitrust laws at all, and cartels flourished''[20]. In the United States—with the Interstate Commerce Commission Act (1887), the Sherman Antitrust Act (1890), and subsequent acts and court decisions—American business grew in a manner separate from its counterparts in Europe. European businessmen had options not available to Americans.

The five considerations — "size of domestic market", "cultural and other heterogeneity at home", "capital importing status", "geographical location", and "public policy toward agreements in restraint of trade" — seem fundamental to understanding at least some of the variations in the evolution of American and European multinational enterprise. They seem to have been neglected, even while other distinctions between U. S. and European economic conditions have been pointed out[21].

Less clear in my mind is the overall impact of home government policies and general rules of the game. Other than antitrust matters, are there from one country to the next systematic differences in political influences that shaped multinational enterprise behavior? Laws on business organization varied from one country to the next, so legal forms available to enterprise were not identical. Did this shape their multinational expansion? My current, very tentative conclusion is that the particular "legal form" used for international expansion, as such, was unimportant, but as the text below will show, contemporaries often disagreed. The legal structure was, after all, associated with the maintenance of property rights.

Likewise, did home country laws that affected domestic business

[20] F. M. SCHERER, *Industrial Market Structure and Economic Performance* (2nd ed. Boston: Hougton Mifflin Co., 1980), 504.

[21] As noted, Franko, Caves, and others have emphasized factor cost differences. Caves gives a variety of differences, but he does not seem to cover the five points that I am emphasizing. While Caves, *Multinational Enterprise and Economic Analysis*, 67, does point to "different mixes of industries found in national economies", reasons for this variety seem traditional (i.e. factor cost explanations).

behavior create differences between nations in multinational enterprise operations? I think, for example, American banking laws did[22]. Larry Franko argued that German social insurance laws were important in encouraging the development of pharmaceutical companies[23]. What other rules and regulations had differential impact on the growth at home and subsequently, of the multinational operations of business in these formative years?[24]

Were there systematic variations in home country social, cultural, or economic life that influenced the development of multinational enterprise? When I listened to the presentations at the 1983 Florence Conference, it became evident to me that the experiences of French and German multinational enterprise were very different; the reasons were much less clear. Why were the Germans so superior in the electrical industry, and the French in rubber tires? This seems less easy to explain than the British international involvements in tea and the German ones in coffee-related products. Why did the Swedes develop multinational manufacturing enterprises so early, and the Norwegians and Danes did not? Was there something in the domestic economies that explains this? We need more comparisons of the early histories of multinational enterprise of various countries. What we include in "experience" must comprise taste, practice, chance, as well as level of development, resource base, and legal systems.

In 1977, in my *JEEH* article, I argued that there was asymmetry in the evolution of multinational enterprise, that European companies that invested in the United States and American ones that went to Europe did not do so with the same products[25]. Over the years, I

[22] Before 1913, American national banks were not allowed to branch abroad. The size of banks in America was curbed by rules that in effect prohibited interstate banking.

[23] FRANKO, *European Multinationals*, 26.

[24] European tax laws ought to be evaluated in this context.

[25] WILKINS, "Modern European History and the Multinationals", 580. See also my "Crosscurrents. American Investments in Europe, European Investments in the United States" in PAUL USELDING, ed. *Business and Economic History*, 2nd ser. VI (1977), 22-35. I felt a need to argue this since some of the earlier literature, for example, STEPHEN HYMER, *The International Operations of National Firms* (1960. first published, Cambridge: MIT Press, 1976), had assumed symmetry.

Mira Wilkins

have become more convinced of the asymmetrical character of multinational enterprise expansion. The five characteristics of the United States in the late nineteenth century, early twentieth century that I listed above assist us in clarifying some of the dissimiliarities that I and others have observed in the growth of American and European multinational enterprise[26]. I want to return to and to use these five points as a guide in exploring not only the differences between European and American multinational enterprise, but some of the dissimilarities among the multinationals of various European countries.

One. An important advantage American corporations held was their experience in the very special large U.S. market that lent itself to mass production and mass consumption. American managers learned at home how to manage multiregional operations[27]. No multinational enterprise manager from a European nation had comparable training in the domestic market.

Some of the new research on the history of British multinational enterprise suggests many failures[28]. My own studies indicate that in the late nineteenth and early twentieth century there was constant discussion in Britain on how to control and how to manage capital over distance[29]. The absence of a "large domestic market" similar to that in the United States meant there was no opportunity for a home "rehearsal" for international business. Perhaps, this accounts for some of the British difficulties. Management requires experience, reiteration.

British managers in parts of the Empire and distant parts of the

[26] As noted, I am not alone in commenting on these distinctions.

[27] ALFRED D. CHANDLER, *Visible Hand* (Cambridge: Harvard University Press, 1977). CHANDLER, "The Emergence of Managerial Capitalism", makes the point that "Because their domestic market was smaller... British industrialists had less incentives than their American counterparts to exploit scale economies..." and it was in these latter industries that modern managerial hierarchies developed.

[28] GEOFFREY JONES, "The Performance of British Multinational Enterprise 1890-1939", 1983 paper, forthcoming.

[29] This will be documented in my forthcoming history of foreign investment in the United States.

world learned, to be sure, from the trading companies about managing over great distances. Yet this was a different kind of instruction. Can it be that the extensive use in international direct investments by British mining, oil, and manufacturing operations of the managing agency, the consulting engineer, the service sector auxiliary to multinational enterprise, came from the very lack of knowledge at home of management over extended distance and the presence of that experience by the "service-related" trading firm?[30] Americans had trading firms; nonetheless, the domestic home market education by the late nineteenth century was far more influential in shaping multinational enterprise than what managers learned from the trading units. For British multinationals, the use of the managing agent, the manager separate from the operating firm, is an early phenomenon. (In the history of U.S. business abroad, the "service contract" is a late development).

When I studied American business abroad, I found that in countries overseas, U.S. manufacturers set up initially one producing facility and it was a long time before a foreign operation in a single nation became a multiplant establishment. By contrast, many European companies in the United States from the very start were mutiplant units: this was true of German silk mills in the United States; of British breweries in the country; of Swiss condensed milk plants; in 1900, Lever had three plants in the United States[31]. The reason for this difference lay in the size of market. National markets in Europe were smaller than the American one. Practically all of these European multiplant establishments in the United States created management problems for the parent firm: By 1914, Lever had only one plant in the United States; Anglo-Swiss sold out to Borden's (when it

---

[30] On the managing agent in India, see VERA ANSTEY, *The Economic Development of India* (1955. New York: Arno Press, 1977). FERRIER *The History of the British Petroleum Company*, has very useful data on the managing agent. On British use of mining engineers, see CLARK C. SPENCE, *Mining Engineers and the American West* (New Haven: Yale University Press, 1970), for example.

[31] The documentation will be in my forthcoming history of foreign investment in the United States.

Mira Wilkins

reentered, it was on a different basis); the British breweries were never satisfactory profit makers. The German silk mills, however, do seem to have been a success[32]. European managers produced and sold at home in relatively small markets. Nonetheless, the Germans seem to have able in many cases to transcend their background (we will see how later in this paper). The British obviously found their inexperience a serious constraint. So it seems did the French. The size of the domestic market also appears to have shaped the national advantages by industry[33].

My second point was that American society was heterogeneous in a manner unlike that of most other contemporary industrializing nations. American businessmen sold their products in the domestic market to people who came from different homelands, with diverse tastes, and varying needs. American goods, if sold nationally, had to be designed to function in different altitudes and under conditions of weather extremes. America was made up of many states and localities with separate laws. National businesses had to handle all these diversities at home. The challenge for the American manager was to meet such heterogeneity with mass produced and mass distributed goods[34]. Here again, the U.S. market served as an excellent, and unique, instructional arena for American managers, who would develop business abroad. Part of the American business achievement was to convince people who were very dissimilar that branded "uniform", mass produced products were indeed suitable. Colonial Empires contained this kind of heterogeneity, and in fact an even greater heterogeneity, but not the "high" income. When we look at the "domestic" market for the British, French, and Germans, for example, there is far more homogeneity. This very homogeneity, I would suggest, imposed impediments to managers of international

[32] See *ibid*.

[33] This is suggested in Chandler, "The Emergence of Managerial Capitalism", and see note 27 above.

[34] Chandler has made the point that certain technologies required large-volume output to bring down unit cost. Large-volume output required the development of marketing organizations.

business, enlarging for them as they invested abroad the realm of uncertainty, of the "unfamiliar".

In investing abroad, every enterprise had and has regardless of nationality three ways of coping with the unfamiliar, 1. seek out the most familiar within the unfamiliar; 2. create the familiar within the unfamiliar; and 3. adapt. Thus, American companies that invested to reach foreign markets went first to England and western Europe and Canada, "seeking the most familiar[35]". When the company dispatched its own managers and introduced replicaes of its plants and methods abroad, it was creating the familiar within the unfamiliar. And, when the enterprise hired abroad and changed its products (right-hand drive for British cars, for example), it was adapting. In less developed countries, American companies found it harder to locate the familiar (although marketing was often done to a small wealthy, high income elite). In seeking raw materials, enterprises set up their own towns; enclave economies were the creation of the familiar within the unfamiliar.

Every multinational enterprise takes all three paths, in varying degrees. Since American businesses started from a relatively heterogeneous cultural environment in which they had learned to impose a homogeneity (of production technique and through advertising), it seems likely that it would be relatively easier for the American enterprise to deal with the heterogeneity abroad[36]. How European businesses took these routes requires more study. The British seem to have been the least successful in adapting. Scots emigrated, so Scottish business abroad found the "familiar" when they hired emigrant Scots to manage their enterprise. The English and the Scots, but particularly the former, set up companies at home to operate

[35] WILKINS, *The Emergence*.
[36] One could perhaps argue the other side of the coin as well — that because the American labor force was heterogeneous, production methods related to this heterogeneity, and this made the transfer abroad easier. I only want to hint at this, since I have no documentation and in fact, the "production" response to the heterogeneity in the United States may often have been the substitution of capital for labor, which made American production techniques less applicable to smaller markets abroad and *less* transferable. This might warrant research.

in foreign lands. In this manner and in other ways, they tried to extend British law in an extraterritorial manner. They were successful in doing so within the Empire (and in China and parts of the middle east). It seems extraordinary to find a British manager asking his government to make arrangements in the 1880's to try to bypass American legislation (with a treaty). Of course, the U.S. government would have nothing to do with this[37]. Conceptually, however, this plea was very important, because it can be seen as path two — an attempt to create the familiar abroad. It was far easier for a British company to superimpose familiarity (through dispatching its men abroad, through U.K. incorporation, through sending its methods and products abroad, through requesting treaties that helped assure its property rights) than to adapt, because domestic experience with adaptation over distance was nil[38].

The French seem to have had much the same problem. The domestic market was homogeneous. Frenchmen seldom migrated. It was harder to find the familiar abroad. Creation of the known through French-incorporated companies and managers sent abroad did exist. In the Empire, there was the superimposition of language. It is not odd that early French foreign direct investment followed a Napoleonic route. France in Europe through Napoleon had created conditions less strange to French business; French enterprise then had a more understandable framework (infrastructure) for operations[39].

[37] In 1881, WILLIAM MACKENZIE, whose Dundee trust company had sizable U.S. investments, complained to the Foreign Office and urged a British treaty with the United States that would put British corporations "beyond the reach of prejudicial and hostile legislation" of American states. WM. MACKENZIE, Dundee, to EARL GRANVILLE, Jan. 7, 1881, FO 5/1763, Public Record Office, London. The British Government was not particularly sympathetic. The nineteenth century British commercial treaty structure, based on "Free trade, free competition, and equality of opportunity" — see D.C.M. PLATT, *Finance, Trade, and Politics in British Foreign Policy* (Oxford: Clarendon Press, 1968), 84-101 — can be interpreted as providing "familiar" conditions, rules of the game.

[38] Look, for example, at MICHAEL G. MULHALL, *The English in South America* (1878. New York: Arno Press, 1977). The English acted in South America exactly as they did at home.

[39] This was suggested to me by RONDO CAMERON, *France and the Economic Development of Europe 1800-1914* (Princeton: Princeton University Press, 1961).

When French businesses went to the United States, they attempted to create the familiar within the unfamiliar, using French personnel, French methods, and French products[40].

The Germans seem to have been much more successful in international business than the French. In the years 1880-1914 British, French, and other nationalities stood in awe of German trade and investment efforts. Contemporaries explained that German salesmen were willing to go with the product abroad, to advertise in other languages, to be aggressive[41]. What was there at home in Germany that made that difference? Part of the reason undoubtedly lay in the fact that what Germans produced at home was unique; to introduce the specialized products at home required salesmanship; the products also required salesmanship abroad[42]. Germans, to a far greater extent than the French, emigrated. When they did so, they adapted. Nonetheless, we should not stress too much the German ability to adapt. In the United States, German businesses often sought out and found the familiar. They used German immigrants as their agents and employes. Some even sold to the German language community in the United States, finding a specialized, familiar niche[43]. They transferred home methods and trademarks. In the United States and

[40] WILKINS, History of Foreign Investment in the United States, forthcoming.

[41] See, for example, data in HENRI HAUSER, Germany's Commercial Grip on the World (New York: Charles Scribner's Sons, 1918) and J.S. ROSS HOFFMAN, Great Britain and Germany Trade Rivalry 1875-1914 (Philadelphia: University of Pennsylvania Press, 1933). See also Alien Property Custodian, Report for 1918-1919.

[42] JURGEN KOCKA, "The Modern Industrial Enterprise in Germany", in ALFRED D. CHANDLER, Jr. and HERMAN DAEMS, Managerial Hierarchies (Cambridge: Harvard University Press, 1980), argues that German manufacturers' competitive strength lay in technical virtuosity, while that of U.S. firms lay in marketing skills. How does one reconcile this with the contemporary foreign trade literature that applauds German marketing skills? Professor CHANDLER writes me that he has substantial data on forward vertical integration of German firms.

[43] SEE HAROLD C. PASSER, The Electrical Manufacturers, 1875-1900 (Cambridge: Harvard University Press, 1953), which says that the main customers of the Siemens and Halske plant in Chicago were breweries and other firms operated by German-born businessmen, and Kabisch, Deutsches Kapital in den USA, 367, for a German-language advertisement of the U.S. affiliate of Heinr. Frank Söhne & Co.

Mira Wilkins

western Europe, when German business went abroad everyone knew they were German; they did not adapt so much that their origins (their advantages) were suppressed. Was there anything at home in Germany that gave that nation's businessmen an ability to cope with diversity abroad better than the French or the English? Did Germans perhaps have more "heterogeneity" at home than the latter? Was it important that Germany was a newer nation state? Coping with diversity within the nation may have given Germans more ability than the British or the French to carry forth business abroad. In France there appears to have been far less emphasis on marketing than in either the United States or Germany[44].

In many European countries, because of the smallness of the domestic market, the family dominated enterprise lasted longer and was relatively more important than in the United States. To create the familiar abroad, members of the family would be sent overseas. This lasted over a longer period in the history of European international enterprise than in U.S. business abroad. The reason, I would suggest, is related to both points one and two above. The smaller domestic market meant that at home the family rather than the managerial enterprise could suffice. When the firm embarked on business abroad, it took what it knew at home and extended it abroad. Trust within a family led to managerial coordination of the larger activity. Alfred Chandler has suggested that the persistence of "family" enterprise impeded the growth of modern multinational business[45].

Three. In my 1977 *JEEH* article, I urged European economic historians to look at multinational enterprises as conduits for foreign investment, to review the capital export literature, and to study international banks. My recent research has convinced me that in considering these issues, a nation's status as net capital exporter or net

---

[44] MAURICE LÉVY-LEBOYER, "The Large Corporation in Modern France", in CHANDLER and DAEMS, *Managerial Hierarchies*, 154, writes "In the United States, marketing was of cardinal importance from the start; in France it was neglected until after World War II".

[45] CHANDLER, "The Growth of the Transnational".

capital importer is important. As I have inquired into the history of European business in the United States, and more generally, in foreign lands I found something significant that I had not encountered to any great extent when I did similar research on American enterprise in foreign countries. The novelty was what I call the "free-standing company[46]". A free-standing company would be set up in a European nation to export capital. The capital was not to be sent abroad in a "disembodied" fashion. The investor wanted control. The company operated abroad. It supplied or hired management of the foreign activity. Where it differed from the typical multinational enterprise that we have all studied (based on the American model) was that it did not expand out of its operations at home. The advantage that the home country had was capital. Yet, the investors did not wish to export that capital without strings attached. Thus, a corporate entity was formed within the home country. It had a familiar legal structure, with a Board of Directors and a Secretary to monitor the use of the capital abroad. It was not at origin an affiliate or subsidiary of any existing enterprise, although the Board of Directors would frequently contain men who had knowledge and expertise related to the line of business and might even be involved fulltime at home in similar activities. "Free-standing companies" were ubiquitous. I have found many such British, French, and Dutch companies. I am less sure about how common they were in the German case. The form seems particularly important in relation to point 2 of my discussion. Business in large capital exporting countries — Britain in particular — sought to create the familiar abroad. The legal structure established at home served that function. Capital was not to be dispatched to independent foreign enterprises, but was to be managed through known channels by reputable men. "Free-standing" British com-

---

[46] JOHN STOPFORD, "The Origins of British-based Multinational Enterprise", *Business History Review*, XLVIII (Autumn, 1974), 303-345, was puzzled on how to handle what he called "expatriate" firms. I discuss the "free-standing firm" in my Florence Conference paper, "Defining a Firm: History and Theory", forthcoming. Most of the firms Stopford called "expatriate" ones were "free-standing" ones. I prefer the term free-standing. See footnote 70 below for the reasons.

panies, for example, built railroads in Argentina, ran breweries and cattle ranches in the United States, carried on banking activities in Canada, drilled for oil in Persia, mined gold in South Africa. Sometimes the home office hired people to go abroad; sometimes it carefully monitored foreign operations; sometimes it was merely a "brass plate on the door in the City[47]". Overtime, some home offices were transformed into impressive activities: thus, the history of the British Petroleum Company began with a free-standing company. After oil was found in Persia, the "home office", in time, developed a range of required functions from marketing to research[48]. Other free-standing companies had different histories[49].

In the most important European capital exporting countries, multinational enterprise, in a number of instances, emerged from free-standing, single country operations abroad. In these activities, originally, at home usually only capital markets (and sometimes human capital markets) were tapped. The new foreign enterprise did not draw on the expertise of an operating parent with know how about a product and process and their management. The free-standing company as a path to multinational behavior needs more careful study[50]. These were foreign direct investments, managed investment, but not the same pattern of multinational enterprise development as was characteristic in the American case. Often, Europeans lacked the advantage of (or experience with) "large-scale" management at home. Thus, when they wanted to manage capital over distance, they set up their own, "free-standing" legal, familiar structure. That the

[47] WILKINS, "Defining Firm".

[48] R. W. FERRIER, *The History of the British Petroleum Company*.

[49] We need to study their fate. Some never functioned at all, their promoters' having lost heart even before the first monies were raised.

[50] Many of the foreign direct investment considered by PETER SVEDBERG, "The Portfolio-Direct Composition of Private Foreign Investment in 1914 Revisited", *Economic Journal*, LXXX (Dec. 1978), 763-777, and I. STONE, "British Direct and Portfolio Investment in Latin America before 1914", *Journal of Economic History*, XXXVII (Sept. 1977), 690-722, fit into the category of "free-standing" investment. Likewise, JOHN P. McKAY, *Pioneers for Profit: Foreign Entrepreneurs and Russian Industrialization* (Chicago: University of Chicago Press, 1970), found that many of the foreign enterprises were of the "free-standing" variety.

enterprise was incorporated at home provided a known legal organization that they believed made a substantial difference[51].

A capital exporting country's legal structure could provide a suitable type of infrastructure for the business abroad. One of the most atypical British multinational enterprises, British American Tobacco Co. (now B.A.T. Industries), was apparently one of the most successful. It began as a consequence of American business abroad[52]. It had at origin no operations in Great Britain, (only a central office), yet it was a worldwide business. Initially, it was American-controlled. It came (in the 1920's) to be British-owned and controlled and the experience and continuity — the use of American management and the British "headquarters" — apparently offered the basis for a highly effective multinational, but one whose history bears no resemblance to that of most American multinationals[53].

Another aspect of European multinational enterprise that requires more investigation and that seems related to the position of European countries as capital exporters is the role of the banks. When American multinational enterprises began, they financed expansion abroad through the same channels as their domestic expansion. They moved outside the country with success, because of their advantage in technology, marketing ability, products, and so forth. They did not go abroad because of capital surpluses. In some European countries that were capital exporters, out-of-country opportunities looked superior to those at home. Capital availability was important. Europeans, no less than Americans, did not want their monies to go abroad without knowledge and information. Accordingly, banks played a different role. On this, more information on the relationship of banks to multinational enterprise — in capital exporting countries — would be of use. To what extent did a banking house go abroad

[51] SEE ELLIS T. POWELL, *The Mechanism of the City* (London: P.S. King and Son, 1910), 144-145.

[52] WILKINS, *Emergence*, 91-92.

[53] On B.A.T., see PHILIP L. SHEPHERD, "The Dynamics of the International Cigarette Oligopoly", Unpublished Discussion Paper, 1979, and Cochran, *Big Business in China*. There is no history of B.A.T.

Mira Wilkins

with its clients, or before its clients? Where exactly does the banking firm fit into the picture[54].

Most European countries that were homes to multinational enterprise in the decades before World War I were net capital exporting countries. Sweden seems the principal exception. It would be valuable to have research on what made Sweden, like the United States, so important as a home for multinational enterprise.

This brings me to my fourth point. Most Swedish business abroad was based on Swedish inventiveness; Swedish innovations gave a firm advantage abroad. Yet, a number of the Swedish companies that invested in foreign lands did so using German inventions[55]. At first blush, this seemed unique. It was not. Frenchmen complained when the Germans went overseas with French silk-making technology[56]. The French were innovators in rayon production, but not the first to develop multinational enterprise in this new industry. The Swiss-German aluminum company (the largest in the world in the late nineteenth century) was an early multinational; its technology was based on the Héroult process (a Frenchman's accomplishment). By contrast, when U.S. companies borrowed technology from abroad (and many did), the technology was employed at home and the companies did not normally use it as a basis for international enterprise[57]. In Europe, because of small domestic markets, along with the close geographical proximity of industrializing nations, companies borrowed a great deal from one another. I have noted the Swedes and the Germans borrowed and then used their acquisitions to develop international operations. Did the French? I know of only one French multinational enterprise investment in the United States in the pre-

---

[54] Hopefully, Rondo Cameron's research group (see footnote 4 above) will start to fill this gap.

[55] Lundström, "Early Swedish Multinationals".

[56] J. L. Duplan, *Lettres d'un vieil americain à un francais* (Paris: Payot, 1917).

[57] The *only* exceptions I can identify related to some U.S. companies that invested in Canada.

World War I years that used a foreign technology[58]. What about elsewhere? The Belgian, Solvay & Cie. sent Americans from its affiliate in the United States to the French Solvay works for training[59]. France was not behind in technology or inventiveness. Yet, unlike the Swedes and the Germans, tentatively any way, it seems that the French may have been too self-confident to use foreign technology in their international business. The jury is still out.

Five. In my *JEEH* article of 1977, I suggested that there should be more work on European multinationals and cartelization. Alice Teichova has embarked on such research[60]. Mark Casson is attempting theoretical modeling that is very exciting to economic historians[61]. The new literature on "internalization" suggests that in the expansion of a firm, that an enterprise internalizes certain activities and not others[62]. This pushes us to ask in a systematic fashion when and why does a firm invest abroad and when does it chose to make a licensing agreement (and an agreement to divide markets)? When is a firm ready to act on its own and when to join an arrangement to restrain trade? With American antitrust policies, American businesses often merged into a single firm rather than cooperated with domestic competitors (a path that was illegal). In Europe,

[58] Panhard and Levassor, which used German technology, apparently had a factory in the United States before 1914. On Panhard and Levassor's use of Daimer motors, ALLAN NEVINS, *Ford: The Times, the Man, and the Company* (New York: Charles Scribner's Son, 1954), 129-130. On its American factory, see Chambre Syndicale des Constructeurs d'Automobiles, *Annuaire* (Paris 1914). I am indebted to PATRICK FRIDENSON for this reference.

[59] See WILKINS, History of Foreign Investment in the United States, forthcoming. For more evidence on the borrowing versus the developing of technology and foreign investment by "free-standing" firms, see JOHN P. MCKAY *Tramways and Trolleys: The Rise of Urban Mass Transit in Europe* (Princeton: Princeton University Press, 1976).

[60] See her paper at the Florence Conference and her "West European Multinational Enterprise in Interwar Central-East Europe", paper delivered at the WILSON CENTER, Washington, D.C., 1981.

[61] "Multinational Monopolies and International Cartels", in Peter J. Buckley and Mark Casson, *The Economic Theory of Multinational Enterprise* (London: Macmillan, forthcoming).

[62] WILKINS, "Defining Firm".

Mira Wilkins

businesses had more choices. Some of the new research suggests we should look at cartels, and the question of management. There are clearly limits to efficient management[63]. The extension of the firm helps an enterprise to create stable, predictable conditions, and to reduce uncertainties, but it also raises the costs of internal management, as it extends the managerial span. In part because of antitrust rules, in part because of the size of the domestic market, and in part because of the nature of the technology that developed in the United States, American companies at home became far larger than their counterparts in European countries. Thus, as noted, American businessmen learned about managing multiregional operations. For the European that did not have that experience, cartels often served to lessen uncertainty[64]. Cooperation between firms was both a complement to and substitute for multinational enterprise[65]. The student of the history of European multinational enterprise has to ask many questions about the numerous agreements between otherwise independent firms that divided markets and acted to limit competition in global markets.

Alice Teichova, who has looked at cartels and multinational enterprise, sees the growth of international business as a process of concentration[66]. Research on the post World War II years[67] seems to show the opposite. Was there a tendency to concentration up to a certain point? In certain industries? Are there significant management limitations on the concentration process? Economic historians ought to look at cartels not simply in terms of their anticompetitive

[63] I have had useful discussions with J.-F. Hennart on this. See also Williamson, "The Modern Corporation".

[64] There is perhaps a "chicken-egg situation". Small markets meant inexperience. Absence of rules against cartels made them an easy route. Cartels, then, in turn created no need for learning about managing larger enterprises.

[65] CASSON, "Multinational Monopolies", makes this point.

[66] See, for example, her "West European Multinational Enterprise in Interwar Central-East Europe".

[67] See especially Raymond Vernon, *Storm over the Multinationals* (Cambridge: Harvard University Press, 1977) and, for example, United Nations Centre on Transnational Corporations, *Transnational Corporations in World Development*, 197.

consequences, but in terms of the inability of managers to extend effectively business organization. There is a learning process in business growth. Americans, because of the conditions at home, were in a position to learn faster about how to deal with organizational, with administrative, challenges[68]. Europeans frequently found the cartel the easier route[69].

In conclusion, while in many respects the "multinationalizing activities" of U.S. and European companies in the last decades of the nineteenth and the early twentieth century were similar, while in each case they were shaped by conditions at home, enterprises with "advantages" expanded internationally, and "nearby" countries (politically, economically, and culturally as well as geographically) were most interesting, conditions at home were very diverse and it is an error to confine considerations of the history of European multinational enterprise to similarities in pattern. Students of the history of European multinational enterprise should not be fettered by the American model. That the size of the U.S. market was larger than that of any European country, that American businessmen had a learning experience in a heterogeneous domestic environment, that the start of U.S. multinational enterprise came when America was a net capital importer, that the United States lacked close geographical proximity with other advanced industrial nations, and that America had unique rules against restraint of trade meant that American and European businesses developed with substantial differences. I would like to see more inquiries into variations between countries.

In my early studies of the history of American multinational enterprise, I was very impatient with international trade theory. I thought it offered little in the way of understanding for the student of multinational enterprise. I still retain some of that impatience; I still want

---

[68] This point comes from the work of CHANDLER and WILLIAMSON.

[69] In *international* business, American companies, at times, accepted divisions-of-markets. For many years, U.S. antitrust laws were far more stringently applied at home than in relation to multinational enterprise operations. See WILKINS, *The Emergence of Multinational Enterprise* and WILKINS, *The Maturing of Multinational Enterprise*.

Mira Wilkins

to concentrate on the firm rather than the traded product. Yet, as I go deeper into the study of European multinational enterprise, I am convinced that to understand multinational enterprise networks, we have to look at trade patterns, if not trade theory. What were the trading relationships, who were the trading partners, and how did these considerations reflect the spread of multinational enterprise?

Likewise, I think we should look at migration networks. Where did emigrants go? Since America was a country of immigrants, there was no need to study emigration. Yet, the movement of persons was closely related to the development of European multinational enterprise. What, for example, was the relationship between German emigration and German international business? Was German aggressiveness as traders and investors in part tied in with the spread of ethnic Germans? Did this compensate in part for the German lack of experience with large-scale markets at home. Information channels are associated with multinational enterprise, and emigration provided one such conduit[70].

[70] What I am suggesting here as applicable to foreign *direct* investment will be very familiar to students of foreign portfolio investments, who have long looked at trade and migration patterns. In considering migration, we must be careful to keep clear its relation to direct foreign investment. The emigrant who settles abroad and starts an enterprise there with money he has brought from his former home or money he has made or raised locally is *not* a foreign direct investor, since his old home is a former one and there is no international extension of the firm. More ambiguous is the man (Britisher, for example), who traveled abroad, settled, set up a business in the foreign country, made his money, and then returned ''home'': If he settled and then changed his mind and returned home, there is a change — no foreign direct investment initially and then a foreign direct investment if after his return home he retains control over the business. However, if his home (as he perceived it) was always Britain, if his ties remained, if the money for his new enterprise was raised there, and if the Britisher thinks of himself as British and eventually does, in fact, return there to manage the business from Britain, or arranges to send his successors to manage the business, we can call this an ''expatriate investment'' — a foreign direct investment. It would seem to have required a London ''address'' for it to quality as a foreign direct investment. The third category, ''the free-standing firm'', incorporated in Britain, headquartered in Britain, which often used British settlers or expatriates abroad to run it, was as noted above a clear ''foreign direct investment''. Often expatriates set up free-standing companies in their home countries in order to raise money there. I am making the distinction here between the ''emigrant or settler'' (who leaves home to settle abroad) and the ''expatriate'' (who leaves home temporarily and who thinks of ''home'' as the place he has left).

I would like to see more questions asked by European economic historians on why French and German multinational enterprise developed so differently. Why were there so few Italian multinational enterprises in the thirty-five years before World War I? As we look at the European rim, Italy, Austria-Hungary, for example, can we see their role in multinational enterprise behavior vis-à-vis the major European homes of multinational enterprise as comparable to Canada as a home vis-à-vis the United States?

More comparisons on Holland and Belgium as homes for multinational enterprise would be useful. We have little evidence on the small, prosperous home market and its impact on the history of multinational enterprise (Sweden and Switzerland as well as Holland and Belgium). How do conditions in such small markets shape the nature of multinational enterprise[71]? We need additional studies of the "international firm" in Europe where the very notion of "headquarters" is obscure: for example, with the Rothschild enterprise, it is hard to say that "home" in the late nineteenth, early twentieth century, was either Paris or London; the cousins kept in touch[72]. In discussing multinational enterprise our scope must be larger than industrial enterprises and must cover other international businesses as well.

Much has been said on the role of tariffs and European multinational industrial enterprise (often firms jumped tariff walls and invested behind them). Virtually nothing has been written by economic historians on tax. Did tax policies have any impact on the development

---

[71] CAVES, *Multinational Enterprise and Economic Analysis*, 59n., points out that "small countries tend to have more unbalanced industrial structures than do large ones—some industries proportionally large, others missing. This is a natural result of scale economies in production. Depending on its particular complement of industries we therefore expect that a small nation may have a very large foreign-investment stock (as do the Netherlands, Switzerland, and Sweden) or a very small one (Belgium, Denmark, and Norway)". This suggestion needs to be pursued by European economic historians, who need to ask why and how does the "particular complement of industries" emerge?

[72] How do the London-Paris centers in the Rothschild case compare to the British-Dutch "joint headquarters" in the Unilever and Royal Dutch-Shell cases? Are there parallels?

Mira Wilkins

of pre-1914 European multinational enterprises? We need more on how business-government relations affected the growth of European multinational enterprise?

What impact do the differences in domestic educational systems have on shaping management talent and, in turn, on the advantages held by multinational enterprise? Do variations in educational systems provide any helpful explanations of the differences in multinational behavior from one country to the next?

In this paper, I have confined my comments to the formative, pre-1914, years. Inquiries covering the twentieth century as a whole seem to indicate that World War I and World War II, in creating discontinuities in multinational enterprise operations, had quite separate influences on American and European business abroad. These impacts, especially as they affect managerial structures, require more study.

In short, numerous questions remain to be answered. While immensely valuable work is being pursued on the history of European multinational enterprise, there is more to be accomplished. I hope future research will aim at developing explanations not only for the similarities, but for the differences between multinational enterprises headquartered in various countries.

[3]

EUROPEAN AND NORTH AMERICAN MULTINATIONALS, 1870–1914: COMPARISONS AND CONTRASTS

By MIRA WILKINS

In the late nineteenth century and early twentieth centuries, the world shrank in its physical dimensions, as steamships, railroads, telegraph, and cables compressed distances. In Europe and North America, economic conditions changed. This was a time of substantial technological advance, with new products, processes, and forms of business organisation, challenging the older order. Because of improvements in transportation and communications, innovations spread rapidly throughout the industrialising world. One crucial conduit was business itself.

British businesses led in the process of multinational expansion. They were, however, not alone and companies headquartered in Continental Europe, the United States, and Canada also extended their activities over borders, making foreign direct investments, defined as those business investments that were or had the potential to be controlled or at least influenced in a significant manner from a headquarters in the United Kingdom, Germany, France, Belgium, Switzerland, Sweden, or other European countries or the United States or Canada.[1] Typically, the phrases 'multinational enterprise' and 'foreign direct investment' have been considered as synonymous, but it is more appropriate to see the relationship as follows: multinational enterprises make foreign direct investments – and carry on other tasks as well. The investments, the capital flows, are only part of the activities of a multinational enterprise. These companies must have a business association with the foreign operations.

British business historians can learn from looking at the experiences of British multinational enterprise, but they learn even more through comparisons. Thus, this article will cover British business overseas, but it will also deal with continental European and North American enterprise. In the conclusion, I will stress the insights that British business historians can obtain by virtue of such comparisons.

Some companies that did business across borders in the pre-1914 years did so in only a single foreign country; others by 1914 already had operations in several or even numerous lands and were truly multinational. The late nineteenth and the early twentieth century was the first period in world history when, owing to the transportation and communications innovations, it became possible to have meaningful business coordination, control, and influence over distance and for our purposes over country frontiers. The new products, processes, and forms of business organisation were integral to this development. Higher per capita income was also critical, placing more individuals in a market economy and providing disposable income for the purchase of a myriad of goods and services. For these reasons, 1870–1914 was the initial era of the modern multinational enterprise.

Because the late nineteenth and early twentieth centuries witnessed great economic change and growth, in considering modern multinational enterprise I am not merely concerned with the beginnings, but with the subsequent course of the institution. In the years prior to 1914, a firm with business abroad in only one foreign country might be starting in the direction of expanding into other countries as well. Yet, no determinism, no inevitability, existed – and the process might be truncated. The business might fail (domestically and internationally), or alternatively a business might succeed but shed its multinational character, becoming a national enterprise in a host country or in the home country, or as a fourth possibility, a purely bi-national relationship might persist over a long period, with no broad multinational spread. The paths in multinational enterprise growth might start from different origins and involve diverse strategies. No simple, single, neat model fits every case. It is important, however, in studying the evolving institution to look at both beginnings and growth.

My definition of multinational enterprise, for purposes of this article, is comprehensive. I include any company that has a headquarters in one country (a home) and that operates in at least one foreign country (the host). 'Foreign' is defined as synonymous with abroad, that is, not in the home country; it could be within or outside an overseas Empire. A company that crossed a border and made business (operating) investments in only one foreign country was by this definition a multinational enterprise; so, too, I will include a firm with operating investments in many foreign lands. 'Operations' could be in the production of goods or services: a trading company, a bank, a public utility, and an owned sales outlet that produced services are included under the rubric 'operations'. In short, I do not limit myself to manufacturing firms – either at home or abroad.

Multinational enterprise involves *cross-border* control, or potential for control, or, at least, influence. An enterprise run by expatriates or immigrants frequently did not represent an ongoing foreign investment, much less a foreign *direct* investment. If there was no headquarters at home, there was *no* multinational enterprise. This is very important. A Britisher or German who migrated to the United States (for example) and set up business in this nation, if he had no obligation to any investor in the home country, there was no ongoing foreign investment, or foreign direct investment. (To call Andrew Carnegie's steel business in America a British investment is bizarre). Likewise, Swedes and Germans resident in Russia or Britishers resident in Argentina, who retained no headquarters abroad, are not foreign direct investors.[2]

Mark Casson in his latest book has argued that 'the modern theory of the MNE [multinational enterprise] has the potential to become a general theory of the enterprise in space, and as such, to embrace theories of the multi-regional and multi-plant firm'.[3] How can the comparative study of the history of multinational enterprise contribute to the efforts of the theoretician? I believe that the way to do so is to present our findings as we inquire into the development of such companies.

The rise of multinational enterprise is receiving substantial attention. Scholars know a great deal about the history of American, British, German, and Swedish multinationals.[4] We know far less about the history of French, Belgian, and Swiss business abroad.[5] In this essay, I seek synthesis. What is known, what is absent? What can the British business historian learn from the comparisons? What appear to be the common features in the historical experiences? If not neat nor simple, is there none the less an 'ideal type' – a model? Does the evidence fit into the emerging theory of multinational enterprise? What is distinctive to multinationals of Great Britain and of other particular home countries; can the special features be ordered in any discernable pattern? How was the rise of multinational enterprise associated with the changing national and world economies, 1870–1914? Or, is generalisation impossible, and regional (or host country) differences so vast as to nullify attempts to find patterns?[6] What are the new frontiers for research? How will they help the British business historian in furthering his search for an understanding of British business overseas?

I am not considering the years after 1914, because of space constraints, but also because I am convinced that 1914–18 (the period of the First World War) forms a watershed[7] and that a post-First World War analysis requires a greatly expanded treatment. Yet, as indicated earlier, it is possible to study entries and growth, as well as retreats and frustration in the pre-1914 years. In short, what follows is a look at an institution, the multinational enterprise, that seeks private profit through managed business abroad (in 1870–1914 there were few government-owned multinational enterprises).[8]

Influences at Home on Multinational Enterprise

All companies with business investments abroad are and have been shaped by economic and other conditions in their homeland, and only subsequently, by economic and other conditions in the countries abroad in which they did business. In each home country circumstances differed from one another, and in addition there were regional differences *within* home countries (in a short article it is impossible to inquire whether there were systematic differences between London and Glasgow-headquartered companies as they operated abroad, or between New York and Chicago ones, or more obviously Vevey and

Basle ones – yet we accept the proposition that such differences existed).[9] In each headquarters nation unique national characteristics had an impact on the nature and extent of firms' foreign direct investments. The galaxy of influences include factor costs, level and pace of industrialisation, areas of technological expertise, size and nature of the domestic market, relationships between banking and industrial units at home, national endowments of and requirements for natural resources, the availability of professional education, national status as exporter or importer of capital, government policies, geographical position, trade patterns (exports and imports), emigration, and undoubtedly such vague imponderables as culture and taste.[10]

Factor costs are helpful in explaining what advantage a company might have *vis-à-vis* companies with head offices in other nations. For a company to venture abroad, it had to have some expected (anticipated) advantage – for otherwise there was no rationale for the expansion and no hope of persistence.[11] It has often been pointed out that American costs of labour were high; thus, Americans substituted machines for labour; American business tended to have advantages abroad in businesses that were capital intensive, in mass production industries.[12] An analysis of British multinationals in 1870–1914 in terms of factor costs would stress the relative cheapness of capital. A recent study suggests that British firms had a comparative disadvantage in goods that were intensive in the use of human capital.[13] Factor costs by themselves, however, seem inadequate as a complete explanation of differences between and among multinationals from different nations. Relatively high labour costs in Canada did not make Canadian development similar to that of the United States. Canadian business abroad varied in numerous ways from its south of the border counterpart. Likewise, I find it very difficult to explain the huge differences between German and French multinational enterprise solely or even fundamentally in terms of factor costs.

The more industrialised, the more economically advanced the country, *ceteris paribus*, the more likely for it to be a headquarters for business abroad. While the match is imperfect, we would predict more German enterprise abroad than Spanish headquartered business over borders and our prediction would in fact be fulfilled. So, too, the large number (in relative terms) of British multinationals fits well under this explanatory rubric. Britain was after all the 'first industrial nation'.

Often technological advantage has been behind specific business enterprise expansion into foreign lands. The explanation is especially helpful *vis-à-vis* many US and German multinationals, but it is by no means adequate as an all-encompassing rationale. Moreover, there have been identified a number of Swedish cases of business abroad based on technology obtained in Germany (a third country) and British cases of business overseas to obtain (to pull in) technology from abroad. Technological advantage is also often inadequate in explaining an enterprise's backward integration into resource development.

12   THE END OF INSULARITY

The size and nature of the domestic market (including the number of customers, disposable income, and geographical dispersion) shaped business at home and became a significant influence on the characteristics of both domestic business and business abroad.[14] It had impact on the shift from family firm to managerial enterprise.[15] Yet, the size-of- and nature-of-market impacts were not always consistent. Swedish and Swiss firms with geographically and demographically small domestic markets, but relatively high income ones, made substantial foreign direct investments, while Danish and Norwegian companies did not. The 'heterogeneous' American market (with consumers from different cultural backgrounds, with extremes in climate, and with other substantial regional variations) offered an excellent learning experience for American managers abroad; the more homogenous British domestic market had a limiting effect on operating companies' managerial training.[16] Business abroad required managing enterprises over distance. This was in no way a given. Coping with the problems of a long span of managerial control often made the difference between success and failure of the ventures.

In most European and North American countries, banks seem not to have been of major importance *vis-à-vis* the vast quantity of their nationals' foreign business operations,[17] but in Germany and Sweden, banks were highly instrumental.[18] And, the foreign direct investments made by British and to a lesser extent, Canadian banks were a significant type of pre-1914 multinational enterprise.[19]

Lack of natural resources at home – when there was a domestic demand for such resources – stimulated some businesses to extend their operations abroad, although the absence of (or alternatively high cost of) a particular raw material did not by definition mean a foreign direct investment in obtaining it (French business invested abroad in phosphate production; I have no evidence that Swiss companies did).

British professional education came later than that in America and Germany; educational systems seem to have had influence on the multinationals of the respective nations.

Operations in foreign countries were embarked on by companies in home countries that were net importers of capital (Russian insurance companies had multinational business) as well as by firms in countries such as Great Britain that were net capital exporters; creditor versus debtor nation status had an impact in shaping business abroad.

Home government policies had a complex collection of effects on business abroad, from those associated with imperial policies, antitrust policies, to tax policies, for instance. Empire created a familiar political infrastructure overseas that in general served to encourage nationals to invest in these countries, for uncertainty was reduced. Thus, British investment in Malaya and India exceeded that from continental Europe or the United States; Dutch companies had a relatively greater significance than any others in the Dutch East Indies. Antitrust policies (or their absence) altered the strategies of foreign investors: that restraint of trade agreements were illegal in the United States had substantial effects on American business abroad. Tax policies began to affect companies' investment tactics (if not strategies) by the early twentieth century; this is a subject about which we know very little; my own research, however, suggests that in the first decade of the twentieth century British taxes may well have influenced the path of British business abroad.[20] It has long been accepted that French taxes redirected French portfolio investment (much of which was done through Switzerland to avoid taxes); yet, whether taxation had a similar impact on French foreign *direct* investment is a subject that as far as I know has never been explored.

The geographical position of the home country seems crucial to an understanding of where a nation's companies invested abroad, when they went abroad, as well as important in understanding their relationships with firms in neighbouring lands. Yet, sometimes, being 'politically', 'culturally', or 'linguistically' nearby was more important that geographical proximity. Directions of trade gave enterprises greater familiarity with certain areas – and a clear connection exists between the extension of business investment abroad and a nation's commerce, albeit there was never a perfect correlation (and, at any particular time, thwarted trade – because of tariffs – might be an incentive to raise foreign direct investment). So, too, often (but not always) there existed a positive relationship between emigration and the locales for foreign direct investment. Once, again, migration served to provide information flows and lower uncertainty costs.

I included the impact of culture, with reluctance, since it seems an amorphous concept. I am not sure that there was one American or German 'culture' that has shaped foreign direct investments, although it is easy to note proto-typical national characteristics and attribute them to culture. The 'American frontier spirit' and 'German aggressiveness' are examples. As a Frenchman explained (in 1915), 'the German is industrious, a remarkably hard worker, who sets about his task with diligence and energy ... Germany is disciplined'.[21] 'Taste' must sometimes be resorted to as a sole explanatory factor. How else is it possible to understand the sizeable British foreign direct investments in tea and German multinationals' involvements in coffee. (Is perhaps taste a sub-set of culture?).

In sum, we can itemise crucial variables in a home country that have impact, but such a roster is merely a start. It is the combinations of these economic, demographic, political, social and cultural impacts that form the basis for our discussion and for the marked differences country-by-country in the development of European and North American multinationals.

British Business Abroad

Of all nations, the one with the greatest foreign direct investment and

14   THE END OF INSULARITY

the greatest number of overseas operations (1870–1914) was clearly Great Britain.[22] Vying for second place in this period were Germany and the United States, both of which nations headquartered numerous companies with business abroad.[23] After these three leaders, it is difficult to establish which country would rank fourth. Candidates include France and Sweden. Belgium is also a possibility for fourth place. Switzerland ranks high on the list, as does Holland.[24] Lower down on the tabulation are Canada, Austria-Hungary, Italy, Russia, and Bulgaria.

British business in 1870–1914 spanned the globe. Britain had in these years slower growth rates at home than did the United States and Germany. Its enterprises were, however (or as a consequence in some cases), very active abroad. The extent of British *business* overseas is just becoming known; many ventures were shortlived. For this article, I made a very rough count of British headquartered enterprises that I could document as having built or acquired manufacturing plants *in the United States* before 1914. The number of parent companies ran in excess of 100. Many had multiplant businesses in America. They owned roughly 255 manufacturing plants. But, approximately a third of these factories had shut down, or were no longer British-owned by 1914.[25]

British firms that operated overseas were of two basic varieties. First, and foremost, there were what I have called 'free-standing' companies.[26] Second, there were companies that did business in Britain and then expanded overseas, extending their existing operations.[27] There were many more free-standing companies than any other type of British foreign direct investment. The companies were registered in the United Kingdom and were established to do business typically in a single country abroad. Thus, there were Anglo-Argentine, Anglo-Australian, Anglo-Russian firms. Each usually operated in a single economic activity overseas, but together they covered the economic spectrum; they were in agriculture, manufacturing, and services (including public utilities, transportation, and banking services). The enterprises were both 'market-oriented' (to serve the host country markets) and 'supply-oriented' (to provide for British, or less often, third country needs). Their founders hoped to unite the abundant capital in Great Britain with the potentially or actually profitable opportunity abroad. Each had a board of directors in Britain, charged with managing the overseas business. The British headquarters was, however, at least at origin usually limited to the part-time board of directors and possibly one full-time secretary. In short, the head office did not amount to very much.

There were literally thousands of British free-standing companies. They attracted British capital, but also French, German, Belgian, and other foreign investors. The firms, however, were the investors abroad. The free-standing companies were frequently grouped in loose clusters – clusters that were often overlapping. A single firm might be classified in a handful of different clusters. The principals in the clusters provided a range of services to the free-standing companies.[28]

There were British free-standing companies in many different activities from rubber in Malaya to copper mining in Russia, from cattle ranches in the United States to nitrate mines in Chile, from railroads in Brazil to hotels in Egypt, from mortgage companies in Australia to meat-packing in Argentina. The variety was extraordinary.

In addition, there were in Britain many companies that first developed their business operations with the home market preeminent and then invested abroad to pursue added markets and to obtain sources of supply. Such businesses included 'industrials', but also numerous British producers of services (trade, shipping, insurance, accounting, engineering, and so forth). The British producers of goods that invested abroad in the years before 1914 appear to have been heavily concentrated in the consumer products sector (soap, thread, and patent medicines are excellent examples).[29] All were trademarked. If the companies made producer goods, the home industries were often related to textiles (Bradford Dyers, United Alkali, H & G Bullock). There seem to have been very little British overseas business based on advanced technology. The crucible steel makers – which had major technical advantages – appear to have had their advantage in long experience rather than especially new developments.[30] Four examples of British 'high-technology' companies that did invest abroad in this era are: (1) Courtaulds (rayon); (2) Burroughs & Wellcome (drugs); (3) Brunner, Mond (alkalies); and (4) Marconi (radio installations). The first case was in synthetic textiles (and the technology here was developed in part outside Britain or with the aid of foreign ideas); the second was of a company founded by Americans, which sold patent medicines as well as ethical drugs; the third was a firm that was part of a Belgian multinational enterprise (and it was the latter rather than the British one that was at the centre of the multinational business behaviour); and the fourth was a company founded by a man with an Italian father and a British mother (it was not a 'purely' British enterprise), and moreover, although radio was new, economic historian Hugh Aitken could write of the 'technological conservatism' of the Marconi organisation and that the technological leadership Marconi once held was already 'shaky' by 1914; 'confident in its technical supremacy, it [the Marconi organisation] had failed to mount a sustained research program'.[31]

It has often been assumed by American students of multinational enterprise that textile companies did not become multinationals. Yet, the largest British textile enterprises were engaged in overseas direct investments. By 1914 J. & P. Coats had mills in the United States, Canada, and Russia.[32] English Sewing Cotton Co. produced through affiliated companies in the United States, France, and Russia. Linen Thread Co., Ltd., had factories in the United States and France.[33] The Fine Cotton Spinners' & Doublers' Association acquired around the

16   THE END OF INSULARITY

turn of the century 'a dominant interest' in its most prominent French competitor, La Société Anonyme des Filatures Delebart Mallet Fils.[34] Bradford Dyers had a major plant in the United States and one in Germany. Nairn Linoleum (linoleum is made of jute or burlap – and thus can be classified as a textile) had factories in the United States, France, and Germany.[35] This is only a small sample of the British textile plants abroad. The host country list – the United States, Canada, France, Germany, Russia – is, however, worth noting.

British businesses also integrated backward to obtain needed raw materials, from cotton seed and palm oil (by Lever) to crude oil (by the 'Shell' Transport and Trading Co.), to iron ore (by Consett and Dowlais).[36] It was apparently even more common for British enterprises to use the free-standing firm for investments in basic inputs and other agricultural products.

Prominent among the 'service' sector multinationals were trading companies.[37] Often trading houses set up free-standing companies (combining the two forms). Likewise, men involved in overseas shipping frequently were associated with free-standing units.[38] So, too consulting and managing engineers had responsibility for managing free-standing mining companies.[39] As yet we know little about the role of the British overseas banks in assisting the expansion of British business abroad.[40] We do know that British banks abroad were a significant aspect of British business overseas.[41] We also know that many of the British international and imperial banks began as free-standing companies.[42]

In my *Economic History Review* article, I outline ten cluster sets that united British free-standing companies. These clusters and others need more attention. While most, as indicated, involved a very tenuous coupling of companies – joined by a functional service provided to the enterprise (promotion, engineering, accounting, services) – some cluster sets could be tighter and then we move to a description of the pivotal service firm as a multinational enterprise.[43] We need to think about the nature of influence and control, influence that is specific to particular functions (finance, construction, engineering, purchasing, marketing) and control (which determines or has the potential to establish overall administrative direction).[44] Faithful and effective performance in a single function might be simpler for a British business to achieve than full internalisation.

While the two basic forms of British overseas business before 1914 appear to have been the free-standing company and the enterprise that evolved from a home base, two other variants in origin have been identified. The first is what Geoffrey Jones has called the migrating multinational.[45] This is a company that began with a headquarters in one country, invested in Britain, and then became over time a British-headquartered multinational. The second variant is more difficult for me to incorporate in my frame of reference. This is a firm established abroad (with no UK registration) that attracted both British capital and

British management. It is not, by my definition, a free-standing firm, since it did not have a legal headquarters in Britain; it was not a *company* investing over borders. Yet, some have felt this type of activity should be included under the category of British business abroad.[46] Frequently, companies set up abroad became free-standing ones with British registration and then the free-standing company was dissolved, to be again replaced by a local firm. Sometimes, a free-standing company was set up anew and then the place of incorporation migrated abroad. My research suggests (tentatively) that when the last step occurred, the administrative control from Britain either weakened substantially, or terminated; what was once a direct investment became a portfolio one.[47] The 'British' management was by immigrants or expatriates – if it persisted. Some overseas-registered companies seem to have been established by British trading houses that provided their management and arranged their financing. Can it be said that such companies are part of a multinational enterprise in which the trading house provides the administrative guidance? The trading house, in turn, had the UK head office.

If we were able to identify a company *registered* abroad, with a concentrated ownership in the United Kingdom that provided a British 'head office' and assumed a 'managerial role' but had no 'operations' by the unincorporated head office – I would be prepared to call this a 'free-standing firm – variant I'.[48] More research needs to be done on the distinctions between British- and locally-registered firms and the management of the business institution.[49]

One significant British multinational captured aspects of three of the four categories, but, none the less, could be classified in one of them. Borax Consolidated, Ltd., by 1914 was a major British multinational – with a headquarters in London and operations in Britain, North and South America, and Europe. It was a vertically and horizontally integrated international enterprise with a legal and administrative headquarters in the United Kingdom.

Its genesis was when an American went to England – seeking markets and monies. He met a Britisher. What evolved was a merger of the British Redwood and Sons and the American's far more extensive operation. A headquarters was established in the United Kingdom, as was a British holding company. For Redwood this was backward vertical integration. I am prepared to call the new holding company, a *British* multinational enterprise. Yet, even though the legal and administrative head office was in Britain, the largest stockholding in the parent company was by the American. The parent was to integrate operations (uniting the British and American businesses), but also to raise capital in Britain for the entire business. While the new British enterprise was clearly not a free-standing one, it bore resemblances to many such companies. It had a prestigious chairman of the board – brought in to encourage Britishers to invest. And, when another British 'free-standing company' shifted its headquarters from London

18   THE END OF INSULARITY

to New York, the principal American stockholder in the borax company suggested that it follow suit. It did not. London remained the headquarters for not only the British and American, but the firm's newly-acquired worldwide business operations. Eventually, in 1913, the American was forced out of the business (and sold his shareholdings).[50] It could be argued (although I do not want to do so) that this was a migrating multinational; clearly, however, the insights and recognition of the existence of migrating multinationals helps us understand this British business abroad.

The idea of the migrating multinational provides even more insights into the activities of another giant British multinational enterprise (albeit I would argue that this firm did not become a *British* multinational until the 1920s). The British–American Tobacco Co. (BAT) came into being in 1902, as a part of a division of market agreement that followed American Tobacco's aggressive attempt to penetrate the British market. BAT at origin was owned two-thirds by American Tobacco and one-third by Imperial Tobacco, and had operations worldwide; it could not sell in the United States nor in the United Kingdom, but had export-related activities in both countries, and most important, it had a London headquarters. At the start, its top management seems to have been American. In 1902, it was an American business abroad. In time, the American stock ownership was reduced, the American management cut back, the home office well established in London, and this company became a British multinational (a migrating multinational enterprise).[51]

I am less sure that when a free-standing registered company shifted to foreign registration (as was often the case) that there was retained British direct investment characteristics. Thus, Otis Steel, an American company, was acquired by a British free-standing company. For years it was a British direct investment in the United States. In time, however, the British headquarters had seemed superfluous. The British-registered company was dissolved. A British accountant joined the US board of directors, presumably representing British investors. When the British registered company was dissolved, I would suggest that the *company* that had made the direct investment was also out-of-the-picture; now the individual British investors had portfolio rather than direct investment stakes (despite the accountant who represented their interests).[52]

In considering British business abroad, we must have a flexibility in evaluating what we find. We need to inquire why was the British free-standing company more common than the British enterprise that developed its operations abroad out of an existing business in Britain? What happened to the free-standing companies through time? How did they deal with the problems of managing business overseas? Why did consumer goods industries predominate in those British businesses that went abroad? Why was the textile industry so visible in British business abroad? To what extent was there foreign direct investment in

EUROPEAN AND NORTH AMERICAN MULTINATIONALS, 1870–1914   19

raw materials and foodstuff production? Why did the trading company take such a key role in diffusing British business abroad? What exactly was the role of banking institutions? What insights does the paradigm of the cluster set provide? What do the discoveries of migrating multinationals tell us about British business activities? Is the transfer of registration overseas an aspect of the migration of business head-quarters? What insights are cast on British managerial performance overseas?

The home country influences outlined earlier in this paper help us to start to answer some of these questions. Factor costs: British capital was abundant; the relative cheapness of capital meant that the British had the opportunity (the incentive) to invest it elsewhere around the world where the returns were higher than at home. Free-standing companies were the institutional device to maintain control. Britain was industrialised; it had been the first industrial nation. Britain used its technological advantage in textiles abroad – and on occasion British multinationals borrowed abroad to overcome technological deficien-cies. There was a high income domestic market in which consumer goods had been sold; the textile industry had grown first and foremost in that market. Many British investments abroad were designed to provide for the domestic market. But, the geographically small British domestic market was inadequate as a training ground for managers. The family firm without a well-developed managerial structure persisted in Britain. British companies had problems operating abroad. The free-standing firm was a compromise and may in many cases have substituted for British firms that apparently found the extension of management internationally a difficult proposition.[53]

Since Britain did not have 'universal' banks, it was often 'the investment group', with a trading company at the centre that assisted British business abroad.[54] Britain was a small island, dependent on international trade, which meant the emergence of well-developed and numerous trading companies with important roles in developing British business abroad.

Lack of certain basic natural resources (plus demand for them) encouraged not only trade, but also British business investment abroad. The investment, however, was highly selective and more needs to be done on the institutional structure and management of British mining and agricultural investments abroad and especially on the management of the marketing of the output.[55] Many British direct investments in railroads were associated with primary product procurement.

Scots abroad often ran British overseas investments from Burma to Canada to Chile. The overseas Scot provided the British company with a familiar dependable representative abroad. Culturally, Britain is frequently perceived as 'insular', and smug. A number of years ago, however, Charles Wilson pointed out that Unilever and Imperial Chemical Industries in the 1920s had involved a merging of multinational founders.[56] So did Royal Dutch-Shell much earlier. The more one deals with the British international business community, the more cosmopolitan it seems.[57] It is a paradox that contrasts with the stereotype – although it has long been recognised that British business innovation was promoted by 'outsiders' rather than by those in the mainstream of British life.[58] None the less, the insularity does appear to have created in many instances constraints on British management abroad,[59] constraints that the many Scots abroad could only partially rectify.

German and American Multinationals

The differences between British and German multinationals were vivid, yet, as we will see, there were similarities. There was not the same mix of the two (or four) varieties of German and British business abroad. There seem to have been few (or certainly far fewer than the British, in relative terms) German free-standing companies that operated in foreign countries – at least this is my present view – though the subject needs more investigation, especially as relates to public utilities, transportation, and raw material procurement (some of the German investments in US phosphate mining, for example, seem to have been by free-standing companies). Migrating multinationals do not appear to have been a particularly important feature in the origins of German multinationals (albeit could the Rheinische Stahlwerke AG be seen in these terms – it was established in 1869 by Frenchmen and Belgians and headquartered in Paris;[60] and what about Allgemeine Elektrizitäts Gesellschaft? could it be considered a migrating multi-national? its predecessor was part of an American business abroad).[61] I have not been able to identify *independent* German companies registered in the host country, with German capital *and* management direction *from* Germany (there were, however, numerous firms established by German immigrants and registered in the host country, but these either fit into the category of German multinational enterprise – where the immigrant represented a parent firm abroad – or were separate businesses of the immigrant and *not* part of a German business abroad, not a foreign direct investment). We need more study, however, of third-country registrations – London-registered companies that operated in Argentina (for example) – that were German-owned and probably (in the host country) German-managed. The London-registration seems to have been to aggregate capital, to have a convenient operating framework, but where was the real 'headquarters'? In a German city? I do not know, but that would be my hypothesis. If so, this might well be part of a German multinational enterprise expansion.

There were many German companies that began to do business in Germany and then based on their advantage at home, extended their business abroad, typically to reach foreign markets and to obtain raw materials.[62] Such investments included many in public utilities, designed to *sell* German electrical equipment. There were also numerous German trading companies – mercantile houses – that had outlets throughout Europe and in addition appear in locales from Guatemala to Turkey.[63] Especially important were the German metal traders.[64] And then there were the German banks active in Europe, North and South America, Asia, and Africa, encouraging and representing German business abroad.[65]

The extent of German-managed enterprise in foreign countries in the pre-First World War years is just being deciphered; there are studies of German foreign direct investment in the United States, in Great Britain, and elsewhere.[66] What seems evident is that unlike the British ones, German multinationals were particularly active abroad in 'high technology' products – especially in the chemical and in the electrical industries.[67] German companies also operated abroad in iron and steel manufactures.[68] They were involved in capital goods industries. German industrial enterprise took the initiative in world markets – exporting, setting up marketing organisations abroad, and establishing foreign manufacture, and foreign companies that would buy German output.

The British – as we have seen – excelled in trademarked consumer products. The Germans also used the trademark as an important property right in their business abroad. Yet, the use may have been different. In the United States Bayer, for example, sold aspirins, which it would claim was its trademarked product. The drug was sold through prescriptions; however, increasingly *before 1914*, consumers bought it over-the-counter and decided on 'self-medication'. Bayer advertised widely, *but* to physicians and to the trade, rather than to the final consumer. Ultimately (in 1921), Bayer would lose the trademark Aspirin in America; the reason the court gave was that before 1915, the company had let the retail druggist (or the manufacturing chemist, who bottled or transformed powder into tablets) sell to the consumer *without* the Bayer name on the product. Thus, in the trademark case, the court ruled that for the consumer the word had passed into the public domain.[69] Germans invested abroad in chocolates – a consumer product. Here again, the product was trademarked, but once again, Stollwerck in many instances sold not to the ultimate buyer, but as a cooking chocolate to other producers.[70]

Actually, there were a surprising number of trademarked German consumer products.[71] The A.W. Faber pencil was one. The German Faber firm by the 1870s was a multinational enterprise, with its main factory in Stein (near Nürnberg); a large slate facility at Geroldsgrun, Bavaria; branches in Paris and London; an agency in Vienna; and a pencil factory in Brooklyn, New York. In the early twentieth century, the American subsidiary, A.W. Faber, was advertising that the German company had manufactories in Germany, France, and the United States. The idea that there were no (or few) German

22   THE END OF INSULARITY

consumer goods manufactured by German multinationals abroad is false.[72]

Like the British, there were some important German textile investments in foreign countries – in woollens and silk (not the textiles most typically associated with British overseas business) – albeit some scholars have found that German textile producers were not active abroad.[73]

Certain German industrial firms integrated backward to obtain raw materials. This was true of German iron and steel manufacturers.[74] Trading companies also appear to have made investments in producing activities abroad. Metallgesellschaft is an excellent example.[75]

German banks were ubiquitous abroad, aiding industrial enterprises in numerous manners. They were active, for example, in relation to the German search abroad for oil – in Romania and in the Middle East.[76]

Like the German multinationals, US multinationals often invested abroad to sell and to make goods, based on new technology and typically trademarked products (whether sold to producer or consumer).[77] In some of the same industries, American and German business both expanded abroad, but, in the main, the industries were different. The US-registered free-standing company existed (in Cuban sugar, for example), although it was of little significance in American business abroad in the pre-1914 years. Again, while I can identify some migrating multinationals (W.R. Grace started in Peru, and then became a US-headquartered business), that pattern was atypical. In both the American and German cases, the prototype multinational was a firm that started at home and then expanded over borders – either to reach markets or to obtain sources of supply. Yet, in the German evolution of multinational enterprise, the role of the giant banks was key, whereas in the United States, to be sure private banks had London and Paris outlets (principally to encourage the flow of European monies to America), but US national banks could not branch abroad until after the passage of the Federal Reserve Act (1913). Thus, not only did the United States have virtually nothing comparable to the numerous British overseas banks (the International Banking Corporation established in 1902 is the one possible exception), it had nothing that was anywhere near equivalent to the Deutsche Bank or the other great German banks.[78]

Here again, home country characteristics help explain why the German and American multinational enterprise pattern differed from that of the British. Clearly, in each case, factor costs were different. German enterprise could draw on an abundance of skilled workers and professionals; in products that were skill- and research-intensive, German business excelled and expanded at home and abroad. This was especially relevant in the dyestuff sector of the German chemical industry, where literally thousands of products were produced in small batches by large companies, heavily manned with skilled and often university educated personnel. Americans found labour costs high

EUROPEAN AND NORTH AMERICAN MULTINATIONALS, 1870–1914   23

and substituted capital for labour. Mass production techniques used unskilled labour. American companies expanded abroad in sewing machines, harvesters, and mass produced automobiles. America had abundant oil; new refineries had large throughput; the country became a large exporter of refined oil, and Standard Oil became a major multinational enterprise.[79] Differences in factor costs in part accounted for the differing German and American advantages. In Alfred Chandler's terms, economies of scope and economies of scale created differences in cost advantages.[80] By 1914, Germany ranked second and the United States ranked first in world manufacturing (Britain was third). The growth of industrialisation spurred new enterprises that quickly expanded over national frontiers. It was often in the newest and most technologically advanced products that German and US businesses invested abroad. Technologically innovative enterprises abounded, and it was these companies that introduced the new processes and products abroad (through foreign direct investments).

German and US firms sold first at home and then abroad. In both Germany and the United States, administrative hierarchies in business organisation emerged more rapidly than in Britain. In Germany, however, the family firm seems to have lingered longer in sizeable enterprise (and in business abroad) than was the case in the United States. If family members went abroad, they often supported German business expansion (George Merck in America, for example). The Germans, like the British, and far more than Americans, found business over borders very difficult. The German electrical companies' problems in controlling their business investments in the United States are a case in point.[81] In the United States, where scale economies were key, the huge and heterogeneous US market offered a superb training arena for business managers who would move abroad. The ever-present German bank in domestic business reflected itself in the international scene.

US and American states' banking laws sharply restricted American banks in their expansion at home (and abroad). We need more information on German business abroad and natural resource procurement; there were many German foreign direct investments in production of primary products. The Germans had little oil – and German companies, accordingly, desired to fill domestic needs. By contrast, the US international oil industry began based on abundant oil and refined oil exports. The evolution of the German and US (and for that matter the British) international oil companies was entirely different. By 1914, one American tyre company (US Rubber) had begun to invest in rubber plantations in Sumatra; the British, Dunlop had invested in rubber estates in Malaya; did the leading German tyre company have similar investments? Many of the products required for the German economy – but not produced there – were obtained through German importing firms.

German professional education – the scientific training – had immense impact on German advantage in world markets. American education was more practical, more engineering-oriented. This seems to have had an influence on the firms in America that had advantages and that moved abroad. The connections in the German case are very specific; in the American one more general.

Germany was a net exporter of capital, but its growth at home absorbed substantial investment. None the less, that it was a net capital exporter may help explain the important role of banks in its international expansion. The United States before 1914 was a net importer of capital. Its portfolio investments abroad (1870–1914) were very small compared with its foreign direct investments. US companies moved abroad not to locate better financial returns, but to reach markets and to obtain sources of supply. When we compare American and British business abroad, this difference is vivid. In Britain, there was substantial surplus capital and rates of return were higher overseas. The evidence in the British case indicates that foreign portfolio investments were larger than foreign direct investments. The free-standing company served to direct and to monitor the use of passive investors' capital abroad. Since America was a net importer of capital, there was generally little need for the free-standing company form. Business abroad grew out of the requirements of business at home.

In Germany, because cartels were perfectly acceptable, there existed some foreign direct investments by cartel representatives to encourage exports.[82] Cartels may have also deterred some foreign direct investment. The restraint of trade rules in America encouraged mergers; domestic conditions required integration of operations; integrated business abroad was a natural extension.

German business crossed over into neighbouring countries; Austria–Hungary – especially the Austrian part, where the language was German – was especially attractive. In some ways, Austria–Hungary may have been to German enterprise rather like Canada to US business, with German business 'spilling over' the border. Likewise, there were sizeable German investments in other nearby countries; transportation and communication links within Europe had by 1870–1914 become very easy – and enterprising German businessmen often made their presence felt – from France to Switzerland, and in many other European countries. But German businesses made their greatest direct investments in United States (in part because that was where there was the major German immigration). American business abroad went first and foremost to nearby countries (geographically nearby such as Canada, Mexico, and the Caribbean) and culturally nearby (such as Canada and the United Kingdom). German emigrants were very significant in developing German business abroad. There were German settlers from China to Russia. (Odessa in 1910, for example, had a German community of 12,000).[83] There was nothing at all similar with American emigrants; the United States was a country of immigrants not emigrants. Germans abroad created familiar conditions for German business in foreign lands and helped overcome some of the difficulties of doing business in strange lands. (As noted earlier, American businessmen learned at home how to deal with 'foreigners' in the domestic markets, since American business was already selling at home to a nationally diverse population).

Clearly, 'the culture' of economic growth influenced German and American businesses in their expansion over borders. There was a vitality in the German and American people that reflected itself in the spread of business abroad. Whereas in Britain at least some of the business activities overseas (particularly those of the free-standing companies) involved a conscious reallocation of resources – at least capital resources – from domestic to international use; in the German and US cases, business abroad was more typically complementary to that at home.

French, Swedish, Belgian, Swiss, and Dutch Business Investments Abroad

French business abroad was extensive in the years 1870 to 1914; while substantial work has been done on French finance, we are slowly learning about the institutional mechanisms by which French industry extended itself over borders.[84] The St. Gobain glassworks as early as the 1850s had built a branch plant in Germany; by 1900 it was a multi-plant enterprise in that country.[85] Before the First World War, St. Gobain was also manufacturing in Italy, Belgium, Holland, Spain, and Austria–Hungary.[86] (How aggressive it seems compared with Pilkington; that British firm had manufacturing abroad in only one country – Canada).[87] The French family firm, Michelin, had by 1914 factories in the United States, Italy, and Great Britain (its rival, Dunlop, in 1914 manufactured in Germany, France, and Japan; no German nor US tyre company had three foreign manufacturing plants in 1914).[88] French car companies also had a collection of business investments abroad.[89]

Most extensive, however, were the international operations of Société Schneider et Cie. Claude Ph. Beaud has done remarkably well in deciphering its business abroad – from Italy to Chile to England (all disappointing ventures). Often the firm's participations were minority ones, but they were designed for business purposes – that is, to obtain orders for Schneider. In Morocco, Schneider set up a diversified group of companies, associated with Moroccan development – from mining companies to gas and electric ones. In Argentina, it made major investments, with the hope of obtaining orders from the newly-established firms. It invested in iron-mines in Lorraine and collieries in Belgium. In 1911 it participated in developing the Russian armaments industry.[90]

I have found a surprising number of French businesses that operated in the United States;[91] more operated in Russia; Spain was attractive to French businessmen (often operating through London-registered companies).[92] French free-standing companies seem to have existed, albeit the extent of them is unknown.[93] French trading companies need investigation,[94] as do French banks.[95] John McKay's 'The House of Rothschild (Paris) as a Multinational Industrial Enterprise, 1875–1914', breaks new ground in the study of French business abroad.[96] Where ever there was gold, French businessmen were interested; thus, students of British business in South Africa have encountered French (and German) involvements.

The French always complained that German business had grabbed, in international business, what was French technology (in silk, for example). The French were the innovators in rayon – but initially the prominent multinational in rayon was the British-headquartered Courtaulds. The Héroult process in aluminium was a French one – and yet, American, German-Swiss, and to a far lesser extent British companies took precedence over French business abroad in this new industry. In a number of different industries where the French excelled, we know little about why or how French business enterprises took, or failed to take, the initiative in business abroad. Often, in the French case we are talking about family firms, not publicly-owned companies. Yet, France was a large capital exporter in the years before 1914 (second only to Great Britain) and it does seem that some (and perhaps much) of this foreign investment was in the form of direct investment (business investment), probably more than is generally assumed.[97]

Ragnhild Lundström has documented the remarkable expansion of Swedish business abroad. Swedish companies (often based on German technology) spread internationally – seeking new markets, setting up plants abroad. Banks played a crucial role, in assisting Swedish international business and Swedish entrepreneurs who went abroad. Swedes established operations in Russia; they financed these ventures in European capital markets; often, the Swedes settled in Russia. Can this be called 'Swedish' business abroad, or Swedish direct investment? Once the migration took place, should this not be described as a Russian business, financed by European (portfolio) investment? Such activities bear resemblance to the Britisher, who went abroad, set up business in a country overseas, and then called on home capital for financing. It appears frequently that in neither case was there a real European head office administering operations. The investment from Europe seems to have been pure finance. Here, again, family associations must be traced.[98]

Lundström identified a hybrid-type operation. A man went abroad to do business, set up a manufacturing company, and got full equity financing from the Enskilda Bank. Is this a foreign direct investment by the Bank? The bank had control. Yet, the initiative came from the trusted entrepreneur, who was in a business abroad that had nothing to do with banking. How common was such a pattern?[99]

There were numerous Belgian businesses in foreign lands that are very well known – from Leopold's extensive activities in the Congo to

Solvay & Cie.'s international business.[100] Belgium had heavy industry. Société Générale de Belgique made direct investments in Spain, Italy, France, Austria, Russia, China, Mexico, Brazil, Argentina, and of course, the Congo, in railroad construction, to help secure markets for Belgian industry. The Société Générale also invested in an extensive chain of banks that did business outside of Belgium.[101] There were formidable Belgian foreign direct investments in tramways, especially those of the Empain group.[102] Individual Belgian entrepreneurs had many direct investments abroad.[103] The complex Belgian direct investments in the Russian iron and steel industry have been well documented by Ulrich Wengenroth.[104] More modest investments were those of Gevaert, an Antwerp maker of photographic paper. His production began in 1892 and by the eve of the First World War, Lieven Gevaert had opened branch distribution depots in Paris, Vienna, Berlin, Milan, Moscow, London, Buenos Aires, and Rio.[105] If Solvay & Cie.'s and Gevaert's business abroad seem comfortable in the conventional model of multinational enterprise, many of the other Belgian businesses outside the country do not conform as neatly. Robert Liefmann, many years ago, concluded that the big banks in Belgium 'have had a greater influence upon the initiation and financing of enterprises [at home and abroad] than in any other country'.[106] By all accounts, Belgian-managed business over borders was extensive. How and where did banks find managers that were appropriate to the task to be performed abroad? We need more studies on how the managerial structure emerged. Likewise, we require more evidence on where Belgian business went; from all appearances, Belgian enterprise was truly multinational; yet Solvay & Cie. excepted, it was conspicuously absent in the United States before the First World War.[107] Is the reason, that Belgian industrial advantages were not advantages in the United States?

Swiss multinational enterprise, likewise, requires far more attention. Many Swiss businesses invested abroad – in silk, cotton, wool and embroidery, canned goods, chocolates, pharmaceuticals, electrotechnical and electrochemical industries, machinery, and so forth.[108] By 1914, there were five Swiss hotel companies that ran hotels in Italy, France, and North Africa.[109] The common feature of all Swiss investments was always quality goods and services.[110] If Ernest Himmel's figures on 77 Swiss companies are to be trusted, in 1913 they had the most invested in France, followed by 'North America' (principally the United States), Germany, and then Italy.[111]

According to an obituary of Robert Schwarzenbach (1839–1904), this Swiss pioneer in silk power looms had by 1904 established silk manufacturing plants not only in Switzerland, but in the United States, Italy, France, and Germany.[112] When in 1900, Nestlé built its American factory in Fulton, New York, a local town directory announced that 'The milk received at the Fulton factory is subjected to the same high test as has been observed for 30 years and more at the Swiss factories of

Henri Nestlé at Vevey, Bercher and Payerne, as well as at the
Norwegian factory at Christiania, and those at Edlitz, Austria, and
Tutbury, England'.[113] Brown, Boveri & Co. – one of the largest
manufacturers in Switzerland – had by 1914 'branches' in Italy,
France, and Norway.[114] This is merely a small sample of Swiss multinational enterprises, in different industries. Where did the Swiss find
management for all these businesses abroad? How often were family
connections significant? How were these plants administered over
borders? What role did Swiss banks play? There are many unanswered
questions. Throughout the period Himmel studied (1898–1919), the
Swiss businesses he monitored had greater investments *outside*
Switzerland than at home.[115]

Whereas in the case of Switzerland, I identified very few 'free-
standing companies', by contrast, this form is prevalent in the case of
Dutch foreign direct investment.[116] Dutch finance has captured
substantial attention, as have certain Dutch businesses abroad (The
Royal Dutch Company and its successor, Royal Dutch-Shell, for
example). Yet, we require more information on the nature of Dutch
business abroad (1870–1914).[117] In Holland, private banks set up
administrative trusts to hold American railroad securities, which
securities were, in turn, owned by Dutch small investors. The effect was
concentrated ownership that gave the banks a say in the conduct of the
business abroad, at least *vis-à-vis* the financial function. Was this,
therefore, foreign direct investment? The railroads in the United
States were American-incorporated, American-administered, but the
Dutch bankers often had more influence (at least on financial matters)
than a typical 'portfolio' investor.[118] How does the student of multinational enterprise view such investments? This brings us to the matter
of influence and control, and 'functional' relationships to which I will
return in the conclusion.

In short, France exempted, all these contestants for fourth rank as
homes to foreign direct investors were geographically small, relatively
high income countries. In each case the nature of domestic business
operations shaped business abroad. There seem to have been identifiable business elites (sometimes cosmopolitan in nature) that can be
tracked in connection with the business abroad; some, but certainly not
by any means all, of these business elites had banking connections. All
of these countries except Holland and Switzerland appear to have
looked more east than west in their investments and had larger direct
investments in Russia than in the United States. Beyond this, it is
difficult to generalise about this very diverse group of home countries,
and I will leave that for future researchers. How many – aside from the
Swiss – had greater investments abroad than at home?

The Other Multinationals

Canadian business abroad went typically across the border into the

United States, albeit it did extend further into the Caribbean and Latin America. In public utilities particularly there was a marked expansion of Canadian business abroad.[119]

Austro-Hungarian businesses across Empire borders were few and isolated, but there were some important ones. The Austrian Hermann Schmidtmann, with his direct investments in Germany and the United States, provides a good case in point.[120] Often, multi-plant Austro-Hungarian enterprises became 'international', after the break-up of the Empire! Fiat was exceptional among the modern Italian businesses in this period to invest abroad; it had manufacturing branches in Austria, the United States, and Russia by 1913.[121] Russian and Bulgarian fire insurance companies were before 1914 multinational enterprises. 'Bulgaria', First Bulgarian Insurance Co. of Roustchouk, Bulgaria, in 1913 operated in England, Germany, Belgium, Bulgaria, France, Holland, Spain, Turkey, and the United States.[122]

In sum, such debtor countries and Empires as Canada, the Austro-Hungarian Empire, Italy, Russia, and Bulgaria were homes to multinational enterprise.[123] The business abroad that was headquartered in these places tended, in the case of Canada, to be very limited as to where it went abroad, and in all these 'homes' tended to be quite restricted in terms of the economic sectors represented.

The Host Countries

Of all the hosts to foreign direct investment, the United States was in 1914 by far the most important. It was a high income market, surrounded by a high tariff wall; it was rich in natural resources; and the opportunities for profit seemed immense. I will not give rankings beyond this, for I believe that any attempt to try to give the standing of host countries is at this stage premature.[124] Part of the problem in ranking hosts to foreign multinational enterprise is the lack of consensus on what is to be included as 'foreign direct investment'. In this article, I have tried to indicate what I believe should and should not be included. Until there is consensus in definition, however, country ranking will lead to nothing but frustration. This, however, is only part of the problem: each region or country has been studied separately, without comparative evaluations (scholars are trained as experts in European history, Chinese history, South African history, and so forth).

Without question, wherever a European or North American multinational enterprise invested, circumstances in the host country influenced its behaviour. It is, however, doubtful that each host country was so distinctive as to transform or to homogenise the foreign business, though over time, host country consumers might not be aware they were buying products of a foreign-owned firm.[125]

The evidence suggests that since a foreign direct investment by definition has a headquarters in the home country, the strategies of the

30   THE END OF INSULARITY

firm (at least initially) can be said to be more shaped by home rather
than host country considerations, albeit clearly both play an important
role and it goes almost without saying that the characteristics of the host
country – from size of market to resources available, to political
conditions (including tariff policies) – determine at the start whether a
company will invest, in what sectors it will invest, and the legal forms of
the investment. These matters also shaped the pace and the course of
the expansion (or contraction, in some cases) of the business. A
number of business investments of this era were 'joint-ventures' of one
type or another – and the joint-venture relationships varied substantially, based on host country considerations.

Such comments accepted as a given, none the less, it seems to me that
there are comparisons that can be made and that if one begins with the
firm and its investments, there are patterns that transcend host country
and regional impacts. One of the virgin territories for students of
multinational enterprise relates to how companies of different
nationalities performed differently in a host country.[126]

More is needed on the relationships between trade and emigration
patterns in considering why particular investors chose to invest in
particular host countries. As I study European-headquartered firms, I
find myself asking many questions about 'partial' relationships – how
these 'groupings', clusters, functional ties, reflected themselves in the
management of business abroad in different countries; this seems to
need more scrutiny.

Conclusions

While substantial research has been done on the history of multinational enterprise, much more is clearly required. The general,
comparative research is particularly important to the British business
historian, for it poses new questions and presses the historian toward a
recognition of what is and what is not distinctive about the British
experience. Research has made it evident that it is useful to look at the
behaviour of business over borders. Too often there have been two
constraints. The first is the assumption that the findings on the history
of American business abroad (the American model) can be rigidly
applied to business headquartered in Great Britain, Continental
Europe and Canada. The second is that multinational enterprise and
foreign direct investment are identical.

Let us look at each in turn. The application of the American model
has provoked exciting new research. British business historians have
been particularly active in this respect. Often, there is congruence in
the behaviour of multinationals from different countries. However,
the newer research shows considerable differences in the development
of multinational enterprise in the pre-1914 years from one country to
the next. The British experience is not exactly coincident with the
American one. The modes used (free-standing enterprise versus

EUROPEAN AND NORTH AMERICAN MULTINATIONALS, 1870–1914   **31**

operating base for example; involvement of banks, as another example) were different.[127] Whereas in the American case, by 1870–1914, it was the large-scale enterprises with administrative organisations that were the innovators in business abroad,[128] in the case of many British and continental European companies we are often describing family firms and kinship rather than corporate linkages over borders. Even in the German instance, where certain of the electrical and chemical companies had huge domestic employment and hier-archical managerial organisations,[129] at the same time, there were many family firms with business both at home and abroad.

These differences reflected themselves in motives. Because America was a net importer of capital, because profitable opportuni-ties were available at home, in 1870–1914, only in the rarest instance was the motive for foreign direct investment purely financial. In countries, particularly Great Britain, where there were 'free-standing' companies often the reason for a specific business investment abroad was purely and simply a higher return in the foreign country, albeit the investment was designed as a managed business abroad. Some free-standing companies were established by promoters that arranged the business investment abroad with the sole purpose of their own quick personal financial gain. Free-standing companies aside, the other rationales do not seem to vary. Thus, companies made foreign direct investment to obtain better representation abroad, to be closer to (and thus more responsive to) customers, to save on transportation costs, to get behind tariff walls (and on rare occasions other host government barriers to trade), to assure sales to an enterprise abroad, and to complement existing foreign direct investments. Some products do not travel well and must be made near the customer (for example, explosives, products that get stale, and beer in this period). Still other foreign direct investments were made to develop or to secure sources of supply. Some foreign direct investments were designed to obtain information. While these motives did not vary by home country, what varied was the relative importance of particular motives – and that needs further study.

One major difference between and among countries was the extent of the business abroad *vis-à-vis* domestic operations. American business at home was always larger than its firms' foreign direct investments. If Himmel is correct, by contrast, Swiss business invest-ments abroad were greater than those at home; are there other geographically small countries that fit this pattern? British business historians need to ask of companies engaged in business abroad, what percentage of their assets, sales, and employment were at home and what percentage abroad?

America was a country receiving immigrants. While there were individual Americans who went abroad to establish businesses, by 1870–1914 this was not the principal pattern and the 'American model' of multinational enterprise correctly excludes such activity. In the case of Great Britain (and some continental European countries), there was a dispersion – a worldwide spread – of business entrepreneurs. This has posed major problems for students of British multinational enterprise. British-born individuals spanned the globe; they went to the United States, Canada, Argentina, to Sicily, India, Hong Kong – and so forth. Some times they brought capital with them; sometimes, they established businesses using monies they had earned abroad. Sometimes they used locally available capital; sometimes they tapped British capital markets for their overseas businesses. I have argued in the introduction to this article (and elsewhere as well) that to fit the definition of multinational enterprise there must be *cross-border* control, or potential for control. The problem lies in defining 'home', in deciding, was there a *cross-border* activity? The Britisher who went to the United States and, in many instances, Canada settled in these countries. There was no ongoing foreign direct investment. Likewise, the Britisher who went to Argentina typically settled, but he often thought of Britain 'as home'. Since he actually settled, and if there was no British home office or British legal registration, I cannot (as indicated in the introduction to this article) refer to his managed business in Argentina as a British foreign direct investment. The matter gets far more difficult with the expatriate rather than the emigrant – with businesses in Sicily, India, and Hong Kong. Take the case of Benjamin Ingham, who spent most of his life in Sicily, but who kept his bank account in the United Kingdom and saw the United Kingdom 'as home'. In real terms, the United Kingdom was home for Ingham, even though his trading business was managed from his base in Sicily. What of British 'expatriates' in India and Hong Kong? They were conspicuously 'British' – white men in a non-white world. 'Home' was Britain: their children were educated there. Hong Kong was frequently a base for business elsewhere in the Far East, especially in China. How should the businesses of these expatriates (as distinct from emigrants) be treated by students of multinational enterprise? This question is important for several reasons: (1) how we define such business affects our statistics on 'British' capital abroad and particularly on British foreign direct investment; (2) in many cases, the expatriates in India and Hong Kong did seek capital in the United Kingdom. It seems to me that if there was no UK home office, the 'British' capital (the cross-border capital) invested in these expatriate ventures must be referred to as British portfolio investments; (3) even more important, from an institutional standpoint, what happened to these enterprises through time? When the individual entrepreneur died or went back 'home' to Great Britain, how were these ventures sustained? If there was some means of replenishing management through time in the United Kingdom, perhaps that can define a 'real' head office. The discussion of multinational enterprise pushes us to look not merely at the individual entrepreneur, but at the continuing managerial structure through time. The answers to these fundamental questions may help us in determining whether the business can legitimately be classified as a 'British' multinational enterprise. In any case, the operating characteristics and the administration of such expatriate businesses – as distinct from ones clearly headquartered in the United Kingdom – need further investigation.

An additional difference that emerges from the comparisons is associated with the 'partial' or functional relationships. Frequently, I found British and Continental European firms (or individuals joined with those companies) participated in business investments abroad, designed not to control the foreign enterprise, but nonetheless to capture a business opportunity. The business motive could be general, such as obtaining insider knowledge on how the foreign firm performed and whether there would be security of supply of a raw material, or it could be highly specific, such as an arrangement to handle the company's financing (the sale of a service) or a contract to sell goods or other particular services to the firm, or one to market the firm's output. Do such 'partial' relationships fit into the category of foreign direct investments? And if so in what manner? The investor often exercised influence (or even control) over a key function, yet in no way sought to run or even had the potential to manage or to control the entire foreign business. Such business investments usually have been dealt with in the literature as foreign direct investments and put in the context of joint-ventures, which seems reasonable.[130] And, what of the trading company – especially the British trading company – with an investment in a particular productive activity (beyond trade) abroad? Its earnings often came from the management contract (a sale of an important service), assured by the investment. It did have the potential to control the overseas enterprise, through the management contract. It seems to this author that the management contract may well be different from the purely functional relationships; in this case, the entire business of the 'joint-venture' is controlled, though the 'owners' of the business presumably had the power to void a management contract.[131]

The industries of key importance from one home country to the next were different. British business historians must ask why British business abroad was concentrated in particular industries *and* why certain companies in those same industries showed little interest in overseas business. So, too, the locales where investments were made differed by home country. The 'American model' would hypothesise that the firm goes first to the 'nearby' – defined not merely in geographical, but in cultural, linguistic, and political terms. Dr Geoffrey Jones has suggested to me that whereas American business went abroad initially to geographically nearby regions: Canada, Mexico, and the Caribbean (it also went to 'culturally nearby' ones: Canada and the United Kingdom), British business tended to favour the linguistically (the United States, but also Canada, Australia, and South Africa) and politically (imperial) 'nearby'. This needs more verification with added research on British business investments on the geographically nearby European continent.

The performance of management abroad also differed by home country, and in a way that may well be amenable to systematic treatment. Indeed, I believe that the distinctive British and other home country characteristics – an inquiry into the home environment – can be used to explain not only many of the differences in the way (including 'the why') firms moved abroad and how they behaved once there, which firms went abroad, but in addition how they performed in foreign lands.

On the second and related matter, multinational enterprise and foreign direct investments are not the same. To repeat what I wrote at the beginning of this article, multinational enterprises make foreign direct investments – and they also do other things as well *vis-à-vis* a business abroad. Management of such a business (just as at home) involved financial decisions; it also calls for operating ones: hiring workers, supervisors, and managers; making choices on technology; selecting appropriate machinery; finding suppliers and purchasing (as needed) raw materials, parts and components, and other supplies, as well as the capital goods; deciding what should be bought and what should be made; and developing relationships with suppliers.

None of these decisions on inputs is 'one-time': management consists (among other things) of training those who are hired, altering technology choices as appropriate and as the learning process goes forward, maintaining as well as buying machines, changing 'make-buy' decisions, and educating suppliers. It involves coordinating and administering the inputs once acquired, organising work, assigning tasks. There is, thus, not only management of the purchasing functions, but of the labour relations, the engineering, and the production activities.

And then there are output decisions. Some of these relate to how much of a process will be done by the firm: does a mining company own a concentrator, a smelter, and a refinery as well? does a plantation company do any further processing? All of these new activities must be managed. And, then if the output is not used or further processed within the firm, how is the product to be marketed? does the company integrate forward into the marketing activity? the management of the marketing function is again not a given. All of these (and many more) management requirements accompany the establishment and development of business abroad. Financing the operation, the foreign direct *investment*, is but one facet (a single function) of what a business does abroad. Thus, students of the history of multinational enterprise must consider and ask questions about how a business abroad is managed, how managers perform; it must separate overall management from the 'partial' functional relationships. British business historians have only begun their task when they identify foreign direct investments.

A study of the history of multinational enterprise needs to look at firms extending a specific business over borders. We must ask of the

EUROPEAN AND NORTH AMERICAN MULTINATIONALS, 1870–1914   **35**

origins, why, which, how, and where did a firm invest? What were its options? A firm grows over time, and I find myself fully in sympathy with Mark Casson and others who view the multinational enterprise in terms of the theory of the firm.[132] As the firm moves over borders, we must look not merely at the basis for the entry, but the subsequent choices and strategies pursued. The dynamics are critical. We have figures on numbers of British companies in particular regions (the materials are not as rich on other nationalities), but we have far less information on how the business abroad was pursued and managed over time. How and where was the output marketed? In the British case, the void is particularly evident in relation to the free-standing firm.[133]

A crucial subject is the relation between trade and foreign direct investment. British business historians need to ask the relationship between both British exports and imports and foreign direct investment. In many instances, foreign direct investment encouraged further exports of goods and services; in other instances it substituted for exports; and in still others it encouraged imports. The effects on trade need to be systematically studied by home country, through time; were there differences by home country?[134]

We need more discussion of performance and measures of success. Geoffrey Jones has suggested that British business abroad was often unsuccessful in its performance. Comparative studies help British business historians pinpoint some of the problems British enterprise had as it moved overseas.

We are by training comfortable in dealing with national behaviour and while it is now relatively easy to write about the international operations of national firms,[135] it is far harder to deal with some of the more complex multinational relationships. Regrettably, I do not have space here to discuss the cooperative ventures over borders that disclose the cosmopolitan nature of pre-1914 investment patterns – yet these must be analysed, particularly in relationship to the management of the cross-border participations.[136]

Comparative research on the pre-1914 years is probably simpler than for the post-1914 ones, because in the years 1880–1914 there was little fluctuation in foreign exchange values and also some of the greater complexities that developed later had not yet emerged. It ought to be possible to put together legitimate comparative figures, not significantly distorted by exchange variations. Before, however, the number game is played and the definitions are fixed in stone, the first step for British business historians is to establish the institutional dimensions of their nation's business over borders. This effort is greatly aided by the comparative approach that stimulates new questions. There seems no doubt that the business institution, controlling operations outside its home country, served as a key conduit of capital and also of production methods and new products, of personnel, technology, marketing arrangements, and managerial expertise. How it carried forth all these

36   THE END OF INSULARITY

functions within the firm – and using outside contractors – needs still to
be charted. How it succeeded in its own terms (profits to the business)
and in social terms (as an assister in economic growth and development
at home and abroad) requires additional investigation. The research –
while it explores home, and host country, circumstances – must
concentrate on the business enterprise per se. A good start has been
made, but the opportunities for further research are legion.

Florida International University

NOTES

I owe a great debt to Alfred D. Chandler and Geoffrey Jones in the development of the
ideas in this article. Likewise, I am grateful to Rondo Cameron for including me in his
'Bellagio group', which has broadened my horizons.

 1. For statistical purposes, the US Department of Commerce uses a ten per cent
    equity interest to qualify. A ten per cent interest is always adequate for 'influence';
    it may not, in fact – as this article will indicate – be enough for 'control'.
 2. Such settlers are often referred to as 'foreign' investors. I believe that it is
    inappropriate to refer to their activities as a foreign direct investment, if there was
    no financial obligation to a headquarters in Sweden, Germany, or Great Britain.
 3. Mark Casson, *The Firm and the Market* (Cambridge, MA, 1987), p.1.
 4. Much of the huge 1977–84 literature on the history of European multinationals is
    summarised in Mira Wilkins, 'The History of European Multinationals: A New
    Look', *The Journal of European Economic History*, Vol.15 (1986), pp.483–510.
    An immense amount has been published subsequent to 1984. While Geoffrey
    Jones (ed.), *British Multinationals: Origins, Management and Performance*
    (Aldershot, 1986) greatly advances our knowledge of the history of British
    multinationals, there is still no comprehensive history. Stephen Nicholas has one
    in process, albeit it will be confined to industrial enterprises. Charles A. Jones,
    International Business in the Nineteenth Century (Brighton, 1987), provides an
    excellent introduction to the network of trading companies that evolved in
    nineteenth-century Britain. Likewise, S.D. Chapman's 'British-Based Invest-
    ment Groups Before 1914', *Economic History Review*, 2nd series 38 (1985),
    pp.230–51, has stimulated new perspectives on British business abroad. While the
    work of Peter Hertner and others has greatly enlarged what we know of German
    multinational enterprise, there is once again no overall history. Likewise,
    although Ragnhild Lundström, 'Swedish Multinational Growth before 1930', in
    Peter Hertner and Geoffrey Jones (eds.), *Multinationals: Theory and History*
    (Aldershot, 1986), pp.135–56, covers the history of Swedish multinational enter-
    prise, there is no book-length synthesis. Alfred D. Chandler's forthcoming history
    of modern managerial enterprise will be immensely helpful on the rise of the major
    British and German multinationals.
 5. Harm Schröter is doing research on multinationals with headquarters in small
    European countries. There are also many firm-, industry-, and host-country-
    specific studies of French, Belgian and Swiss business abroad.
 6. Robert Vicat Turrell and Jean Jacques Van-Helten, 'The Investment Group: The
    Missing Link in British Overseas Expansion before 1914?' *Economic History
    Review*, 2nd series 40 (1987), p.269, scold Chapman for his generalisations and
    write 'In view of the historical specificity of economic developments in Africa and
    Asia ... it would have been more profitable to emphasise the different paths of

EUROPEAN AND NORTH AMERICAN MULTINATIONALS, 1870–1914   **37**

development of business enterprise'.

7. Because of (1) the breakdown of the international gold standard; (2) the loss of the clear primacy of Great Britain as the great creditor nation in the world; (3) the defeat of Germany and its effect on German business abroad; and (4) the shift of the United States from debtor to creditor country in international accounts.

8. Albeit there were some: For the Russian government's business investments in China, see C.F. Remer, *Foreign Investments in China* (1933; reprint, New York, 1968), pp.89, 558–9. The Russian bank in Persia was owned by the Russian state bank after 1894: Geoffrey Jones, *Banking and Empire in Iran* (Cambridge, 1986), p.56.

9. There is a large literature on Scottish overseas investments, as distinct from the broader literature on 'British' overseas investments, which usually includes both Scottish and English business abroad. However, the *Dictionary of Business Biography* – now the standard work on businessmen in 'Britain' – omitted business leaders based in Scotland, in deference to a project being carried out in Glasgow. The first volume of the *Dictionary of Scottish Business Biography*, edited by A. Slaven and S. Checkland, was published in 1987.

10. I began to identify crucial features of the home environment in Wilkins, 'The History of European Multinationals'. For some preliminary early testing, see Mira Wilkins, 'Japanese Multinational Enterprise before 1914', *Business History Review*, 60 (1986), pp.199–231.

11. Until recently this has been universally accepted among students of multinational enterprise (MNE). Casson, however, suggests that the high benefits of internalisation (integrating operations) offset the costs of such integration over borders and thus the theorist does not have to find an additional advantage. Casson, *The Firm and the Market*, pp.32, 34. He recognised, however, that the success (persistence) of MNEs does depend on some advantage, but stresses that this advantage may lie in internalisation, that is, in managing resources within the firm. Casson wants to separate choice (entry decisions) and performance. Ibid., pp.35–6. My problem with this analysis is that it does not explain which firms make the choice to go abroad; some do and some do not. The choice, it seems to me, must entail at least a perception of advantage.

12. This view is the accepted one. Professors Raymond Vernon, John Dunning, Lawrence Franko, and others have all made this point.

13. N.F.R. Crafts and Mark Thomas, 'Comparative Advantage in UK Manufacturing Trade 1910–1935', *Economic Journal* 96 (1986), pp.629–45.

14. I found this particularly true of American business abroad. Mira Wilkins, *The Emergence of Multinational Enterprise* (Cambridge, MA, 1970). See also Alfred D. Chandler, *The Visible Hand* (Cambridge, MA, 1977).

15. Professor Chandler has made this point in a number of places.

16. Wilkins, 'The History of European Multinationals'.

17. A forthcoming book edited by Rondo Cameron and V.I. Bovykin, *International Banking, Investment, and Industrial Finance, 1970–1914*, explores some of these relationships.

18. Ibid. See also J. Riesser, *The German Great Banks and Their Concentration* (1911; reprint, New York, 1977).

19. A.S.J. Baster, *The Imperial Banks* (1929; reprint, New York, 1977) and idem., *The International Banks* (1935; reprint, New York, 1977). Geoffrey Jones is in the process of preparing the basic work on British overseas banks since 1890. See also his two volumes on The British Bank of the Middle East: Jones, *Banking and Empire in Iran* and idem., *Banking and Oil* (Cambridge, 1987). F.H.H. King, *The History of the Hongkong and Shanghai Banking Corporation* (Cambridge, 1987), Vol.I, covers 1864–1902. (Volumes 2–4 are forthcoming, scheduled for 1988). For Canadian banks' extension into the United States, see Mira Wilkins, *The History of Foreign Investment in the United States to 1914*, forthcoming.

20. For example, because of new taxes imposed during the Boer War, Eastman Kodak, Ltd. changed from a legal British to an American headquarters. Carl W.

38   THE END OF INSULARITY

Ackerman, *George Eastman* (Boston, MA, 1930), pp.173–4. Other examples of tax motivated decisions are provided in Wilkins, *The History of Foreign Investment in the United States.*

21. Carl N. Degler's presidential address to the American Historical Association was entitled 'In Pursuit of an American History'. *American Historical Review,* 92 (1987), pp.1–12. Degler argues that there were significant national attributes, some of which he seems to define in terms of 'culture'. The quotation is from a chapter, entitled 'Qualities of the Germans', in Henri Hauser, *Germany's Commercial Grip on the World* (New York, 1918), p.9. This is a translation from the French. Hauser was a professor at Dijon University; the first edition of this work, in French, appeared in 1915.

22. I agree with Geoffrey Jones in this conclusion. Lawrence Franko, *The European Multinationals* (Stamford, CT, 1976), p.10, put the United States in first place as a home country, based on data collected by James Vaupel and Joan Curhan. These statistics – which are constantly reprinted – have been superseded by more recent research. They were, moreover, based on companies *still in existence* when the research was undertaken, which created a bias on the low side.

23. This is my own conclusion, based on my own research and my reading of the work of other students of the history of multinational enterprise. John H. Dunning, 'Changes in the Level and Structure of International Production: The Last One Hundred Years', in Mark Casson, *The Growth of International Business* (London, 1983), p.87, presents estimates on the level of foreign direct investment by country of origin in 1914. He ranked the United Kingdom first, and far out front, followed by the United States in clear second place, and then came France; he put Germany in fourth place. I think he has greatly underestimated the activities of German business abroad.

24. Franko, *European Multinationals,* the first book that dealt with the history of European multinationals – and one that holds up very well over time – never makes an attempt to rank continental European home countries.

25. Based on data provided in Wilkins, *The History of Foreign Investment in the United States.* Franko, in *The European Multinationals,* p.10, using the Vaupel and Curhan data, was able to identify only 60 UK 'manufacturing subsidiaries established or acquired' by UK parents before 1914 *worldwide*! Only nine were in the United States. See breakdown in Dunning, 'Changes in the Level and Structure', p.90. But, Dunning elsewhere in the same article did recognise that the UK was 'far and away' the largest source of foreign direct investment in 1914. See ibid., pp.86–7, and note 23 above.

26. Wilkins, 'The Free-Standing Company, 1870–1914: An Important Type of British Foreign Direct Investment', *Economic History Review,* 2nd series 41 (1988). I first used the term 'free-standing' firm at a conference in Florence in 1983. Wilkins, 'Defining a Firm', in Hertner and Jones (eds.), *Multinationals,* pp.84–7.

27. On these companies, see Jones (ed.), *British Multinationals, passim.*

28. I give more details on the clusters in 'The Free-Standing Company'. The theoretical literature on multinational enterprise has dealt with 'modes' of operations – direct investment, licensing, and market – or direct investment, contract, and market. The loosely-coupled groupings of the free-standing companies represent a mode of handling business abroad that the theoretical literature has failed to consider (because this institutional path is just coming to be understood). The British free-standing company could invest abroad directly or serve as a holding company, owning the securities of a locally-incorporated company. It made a difference.

29. On patent medicines, see the work of T.A.B. Corley, for example, 'Interactions between British and American Patent Medicine Industries', *Business and Economic History,* forthcoming.

30. The authority on crucible steel is Geoffrey Tweedale, *Sheffield Steel and America* (Cambridge, 1987).

31. Hugh G.J. Aitken, *The Continuous Wave* (Princeton, NJ, 1985), pp.317, 357–8.

32. Wilkins, *The History of Foreign Investment in the United States.*

EUROPEAN AND NORTH AMERICAN MULTINATIONALS, 1870–1914   **39**

33. US Federal Trade Commission, *Report on Cooperation in American Export Trade*, 2 vols. (Washington, 1916), I, pp.252, 254.
34. Ibid., I, p.250.
35. Wilkins, *The History of Foreign Investment in the United States*.
36. Consett and Dowlais were joint-venture partners with Krupp in Orconera Iron Ore Co., Ltd., that carried on mining in Spain. Ulrich Wengenroth, 'Iron and Steel', in Cameron and Bovykin (eds.), *International Banking*.
37. See Shin'ichi Yonekawa and Hideki Yoshihara (eds.), *Business History of General Trading Companies* (Tokyo, 1987), for fascinating material on British trading companies. See also Stephanie Jones, *Two Centuries of Overseas Trading. The Origins and Growth of the Inchape Group* (London, 1986); Charles Jones, *International Business*; and Chapman, 'British-Based Investment Groups'.
38. See, for example, Andrew Porter, *Victorian Shipping, Business and Imperial Policy: Donald Currie, the Castle Line and Southern Africa* (Woodbridge and New York, 1986).
39. John Taylor & Sons, for instance, were in 1907 managers of 45 companies around the world. Charles Harvey and Peter Taylor, 'Mineral Wealth and Economic Development: Foreign Direct Investment in Spain, 1851–1913', *Economic History Review*, 2nd series 40 (1987), p.189 n.22. See also Wilkins, *History of Foreign Investment in the United States*.
40. Geoffrey Jones's new research will rectify that.
41. Baster, *International Banks*, p.248, indicated that in 1910 24 British international banks had 308 foreign branches, while Baster, *Imperial Banks*, p.269, states that in 1915, 18 imperial banks had 1,169 branches and sub-branches overseas. According to Oliver Pastré and Anthony Rowley (in 'The Multinationalisation of British and American Banks', in Alice Teichova, *et al.*, *Multinational Enterprise in Historical Perspective* (Cambridge, 1986), p.233), who cite no source, in 1914, 36 banking companies in Britain had 2,091 branches 'in the world', and in addition, there were 3,538 colonial banks (surely, colonial bank branches and agencies?). It is hard to reconcile Pastré and Rowley's numbers with those of Baster.
42. The Imperial Bank of Persia, for example. See Jones, *Banking and Empire in Iran*.
43. Some of the trading companies at the centre of cluster sets were clearly multi-national enterprises.
44. Questions about control are, for example, posed in Turrell and Van-Helten, 'The Investment Group'.
45. Jones (ed.), *Multinationals*, p.7.
46. Discussions with Geoffrey Jones and Charles Jones.
47. In the case of British investment in America, this appears to have happened immediately. See text of this article. But take the case of the New Gellivara Co. Ltd. with mines in Sweden. In 1882, it was transformed into a Swedish Company (Gellivara Aktiebolog), which was 100 per cent owned by Sir Giles Loder, London. When the latter died, in 1889, his heirs lost all of their concessions. Wengenroth, 'Iron and Steel'. The suggestion was that control could no longer be maintained.
48. The description is theoretical. At present, I have no candidates that fit this model.
49. In this connection, host country policies were often crucial. In 1908, a Court in Alexandria ruled that a company formed to do business in Egypt, must be considered Egyptian, and a Khedivial decree was required before it could be legally constituted. The Court ruling, however, specifically stated that no restriction was placed on the operations in Egypt of a bona-fide branch of a foreign company with headquarters abroad. The Court's decision 'referred only to companies whose operations, headquarters and sole "raison d'être" were in Egypt'. A.E. Crouchley, *The Investment of Foreign Capital in Egyptian Companies and Public Debt* (Cairo, 1936), p.63.
50. The best history of Borax Consolidated is Norman J. Travis and E.J. Cocks, *The Tincal Trail* (London, 1984). See also Wilkins, *History of Foreign Investment in the United States*.

40   THE END OF INSULARITY

51. Wilkins, *The Emergence*, pp.91–3; Jones (ed.), *British Multinationals*, p.7.
52. Had the ownership been concentrated, perhaps control might have been main-
    tained.
53. I make this last point in 'The Free-Standing Company'.
54. On investment groups, see Chapman, 'British-Based Investment Groups'. On the
    absence of 'universal' banks, see P.L. Cottrell's forthcoming paper on British
    banking in Cameron and Bovykin (eds.), *International Banking*.
55. Harvey and Taylor, 'Mineral Wealth', provide rich information on British com-
    panies producing lead, iron ore and pyrites (sulphur and copper) in Spain. The
    article, however, tells us little about the extent to which these mining operations
    were part of integrated enterprises – in the United Kingdom, France, or Germany.
    Were the spectacular profits of the Orconera Co., for example, related to the intra-
    company pricing arrangements made by its three parent companies? On its
    parents, see note 36 above.
56. Charles Wilson, 'Multinationals, Management, and World Markets: A Historical
    View', in Harold F. Williamson (ed.), *Evolution of International Management
    Structures* (Newark, DE, 1975), p.193.
57. In this connection, see the fascinating Editor's Introduction (by Maryna Fraser) of
    Lionel Phillips, *Some Reminiscences* (Johannesburg, 1986), pp.11–30, on 'British'
    business in South Africa. See also D.C.M. Platt, *Britain's Investment Overseas on
    the Eve of the First World War* (New York, 1986), pp.31–6.
58. In this connection, see Everett E. Hagen, *On the Theory of Social Change*
    (Homewood, IL, 1962), pp.294–309.
59. Geoffrey Jones has found many cases where British management had severe
    difficulties in operating abroad.
60. Rondo Cameron, *France and the Economic Development of Europe* (Princeton,
    NJ, 1961), p.396; on the important Belgian role, see Wengenroth, 'Iron and Steel'.
61. Wilkins, *The Emergence*, pp.52–9.
62. Peter Hertner has written extensively on German business abroad. For a start, see
    his excellent 'German Multinational Enterprise before 1914: Some Case Studies',
    in Hertner and Jones (eds.), *Multinationals*, pp.113–34. See also W. Felden-
    kirchen, 'The Export Organisation of the German Economy', in Yonekawa and
    Yoshihara (ed.), *Business History*. Chandler's new book will consider the inter-
    national extension of German business.
63. The German trading house, Schuchardt and Schutte, for example, was probably
    'the most prestigious distributor of machine tools in Europe'; it had 'outlets' in
    Germany, Austria, Belgium, and Russia. Charles W. Cheape, *Family Firm to
    Modern Multinational: Norton Company, a New England Enterprise* (Cambridge,
    1985), p.50. See also, Feldenkirchen, 'The Export Organisation' on export
    houses. The firms in Guatemala and Turkey were more active in providing imports
    into Germany than in selling exports from Germany. Schuchardt and Schutte
    handled some American exports as well as German ones.
64. See Wilkins, *History of Foreign Investment in the United States*.
65. Richard Tilly, 'International Aspects of the Development of German Banking,
    1870–1914', in Cameron and Bovykin (eds.), *International Banking*.
66. My *History of Foreign Investments in the United States* has a sizeable amount on
    German business investments in the United States. Geoffrey Jones, 'Foreign
    Multinationals in Britain before 1945', *Economic History Review*, forthcoming,
    has much on German business in the United Kingdom. It has long been known that
    there were large German investments in Latin America – from railroads in
    Colombia to nitrate mines in Chile, but the nature of the management of such
    investments is still ambiguous. The reviews of Walther Kirchner, *Die Deutsch
    Industrie und die Industrialisierung Russlands 1815–1914* (St. Katharinen,
    F.R.G., 1986), indicate that it covers the activities of German multinationals in
    Russia.
67. Every basic history of the chemical industry, covering 1870–1914, deals with the
    German direct investments abroad (as well as at home). On the electrical industry,

EUROPEAN AND NORTH AMERICAN MULTINATIONALS, 1870–1914   **41**

see, for example, Peter Hertner, 'Financial Strategies and Adaptation to Foreign Markets: The German Electro-Technical Industry and Its Multinational Activities', Teichova, *et al., Multinational Enterprise*, pp.145–59, and Albert Broder, 'The Multinationalisation of the French Electrical Industry 1880–1914; Dependence and its Causes', in Hertner and Jones (eds.), *Multinationals*, pp.178–80, 184–5. According to Feldenkirchen, 'The Export Organisation', p.325 n.91, Siemens had in 1913, 17 plants in nine European countries.

68. On the foreign marketing organisation of the principal German iron and steel companies, see Feldenkirchen, 'The Export Organisation', pp.310–11. On Bochumer Verein, Mannesmann, and Rheinische Stahlwerke's major foreign investments, see ibid., pp.318–19, and Wengenroth, 'Iron and Steel', on the last two.

69. Bayer Co., Inc. v. United Drug Co., 272 Fed. 505 (SDNY, 1921).

70. Wilkins, *History of Foreign Investment in the United States*.

71. Here my conclusions depart from Franko, *European Multinationals*, p.22, who was struck by the fact that 'continental European' enterprises rarely had advantages in marketing and advertising.

72. Data on the Faber firm in the 1870s are based on an undated (probably 1872–73) newspaper article, provided to me by Eberhard Faber, Wilkes-Barre, Pennsylvania. See also A.W. Faber's US colour advertisement (in English), reprinted in L. Fritz Gruber, 'Das Bleistift Schloss', *Frankfurter Allgemeine Zeitung*, 13 Feb. 1987. My thanks go to Richard Tilly for directing my attention to this. The parent company became Faber-Castell in 1900. Peter Hertner describes Kathreiner's Malzkaffee-Fabriken, as having direct investments in manufacturing plants in Austria–Hungary, Sweden, Russia, and Spain by 1914. It marketed and advertised a consumer product, malt coffee. Hertner, 'German Multinational Enterprise', 118–19.

73. Compare Wilkins, *History of Foreign Investment in the United States*, with Feldenkirchen, 'The Export Organisation', p.317.

74. Franko, *European Multinationals*, p.50, and Wengenroth, 'Iron and Steel'.

75. On its interests in American Metal Company, see Wilkins, *The History of Foreign Investment in the United States*. Franko, *European Multinationals*, p.50, on other of its foreign direct investments.

76. For the involvements in Romania, see M. Pearton, *Oil and the Rumanian State* (Oxford, 1971) and Fritz Seidenzahl, *100 Jahre Deutsche Bank, 1870–1970* (Frankfurt, 1970), pp.205–24. For German oil activities in the middle east, see ibid., pp.224–7, and Marian Kent, *Oil & Empire* (London, 1976).

77. My *The Emergence of Multinational Enterprise*, published in 1970, provided a history of American business abroad in the years before 1914. Subsequently, there have been many studies of the history of US businesses abroad. Among the recent contributions are Fred V. Carstensen, *American Enterprise in Foreign Markets. Studies of Singer and International Harvester in Imperial Russia* (Chapel Hill, NC, 1984); Lawrence A. Clayton, *Grace. W.R. Grace & Co. The Formative Years 1850–1930* (Ottawa, IL, 1985); and Cheape, *Family Firm to Modern Multinational*.

78. On I.B.C., see Wilkins, *The Emergence*, p.107.

79. See Alfred D. Chandler, *The Visible Hand*; his 'Technological and Organisational Underpinnings of Modern Industrial Multinational Enterprise: The Dynamics of Competitive Advantage', in Teichova, *et. al., Multinational Enterprise*, pp.30–54; and his forthcoming book.

80. Ibid. Sometimes economies of scale and scope are viewed as part of an advantage – based on factor costs. More recently, new developments in trade theory have looked at economies of scale (and scope) as separate from traditionally-defined comparative advantages; trade (and, in turn, investments) arise directly from such economies. See Paul R. Krugman, 'Is Free Trade Passé?', *Economic Perspectives*, Vol.1 (1987), p.133. The distinction is between what is endogenous to the firm and exogenous. Yet, the achievements of economies of scope and scale (albeit

endogenous) were based, I firmly believe, on conditions in the home country.
81. Wilkins, *History of Foreign Investment in the United States*.
82. The Potash Cartel, for example, had a sales company in the United States. See ibid.
83. P. Chalmin, 'The Rise of International Commodity Trading Companies in Europe in the Nineteenth Century', in Yonekawa and Yoshihara (ed.), *Business History*, p.290.
84. Some of the best work on this subject remains that in Rondo Cameron's 1960 book, *France and the Economic Development*.
85. Ibid., pp.397–400. On St. Gobain's German factories, see Jean-Pierre Daviet, 'Un Processus de Multinationalisation de Longue Duree: L'Exemple de Saint-Gobain (1853–1939)', unpublished paper (1984). This paper has been published (in Italian) in Peter Hertner, *Per La Storia delli' impresa multinazionale in Europa* (Milan, 1987). Daviet completed a 1793-page doctoral dissertation at the Sorbonne in 1983.
86. Daviet, 'Un Processus'.
87. Theo Barker, 'Pilkington', in Jones (ed.), *Multinationals*, p.185.
88. Wilkins, *History of Foreign Investment in the United States*, on Michelin. On Dunlop, Geoffrey Jones, 'The Growth and Performance of British Multinational Firms before 1939: The Case of Dunlop', *Economic History Review*, 2nd series 37 (Feb. 1984), p.36. In addition, Dunlop had licensing agreements with companies in Canada, Australia, and Russia. Ibid., p.39.
89. Patrick Fridenson, 'The Growth of Multinational Activities in the French Motor Industry, 1890–1979', in Hertner and Jones (eds.), *Multinationals*, pp.157–9.
90. Claude Ph. Beaud, 'Investments and Profits of the Multinational Schneider Group: 1894–1943', in Teichova, *et al.*, *Multinational Enterprise*, pp.87–102. See also idem., 'La Schneider in Russia (1896–1914)', in Hertner, *Per La Storia*, pp.101–48.
91. Wilkins, *History of Foreign Investment in the United States*.
92. French investors often appear to have used British-registered companies for investments abroad – not only in Spain. I found this to be true of some French investments in the United States, principally in mining. Beaud found that Schneider (and other French investors) used the Bolivian Rubber and General Enterprise, Ltd., registered in London, for its investments in Bolivia. Beaud, 'Investments and Profits', p.90.
93. Robert L. Tignor, *State, Private Enterprise and Economic Change in Egypt, 1918–1952* (Princeton, NJ, 1984), pp.19–20, found that in the pre-First World War years 'French businessmen experienced great difficulty in maintaining managerial control over French firms in Egypt. French investment was widely dispersed, and small French shareholders took little interest in the management of companies so long as dividend payments continued to arrive. Hence, small groups of organised shareholders on the ground could gain control of companies, even though holding only a fraction of the shares.' This sounds like some of the problems faced by British free-standing companies. I suppose one could call the Suez company a free-standing firm. See Hubert Bonin, *Suez* (Paris, 1987).
94. On French trading companies (and French banks), see Chalmin, 'The Rise', especially pp.289–91. Chalmin argues that 'the first disease of French trade [was] the determination of the [French] industry to do its marketing itself' – and it was always a job badly done. The 'second disease' was that the French concentrated on quality and luxury products – perfumes, cognac, champagne, and fashion, which sold themselves. Thus there was no need to bother to have representatives abroad. He believes, however, that French trading houses were more efficient on the import than on the export side. On the large French West African chartered company, see Hubert Bonin, *La Compagnie Française d'Afrique Occidentale* (Paris, 1987).
95. Geoffrey Jones is planning a conference on 'banks as multinationals'. It will be extremely useful to compare the role of French banks with those of other

nationalities. For one recent contribution on French banking abroad, which despite its title does cover the pre-1914 years, see Yasuo Gonjo, 'La Banque de l'Indochine devant l'interventionisme (1917–1931)', *Le Mouvement Social*, 142 (Jan.–March, 1988), pp.45–7 ·.

96. John McKay, 'The House of Rothschild (Paris)', in Teichova, *et. al, Multinational Enterprise*, pp.74–86.
97. Cameron found this to be true. See *France and the Economic Development*. Maurice Lévy-Leboyer's work also suggests this.
98. The footnotes in Lundström, 'Swedish Multinational Growth', bear witness to the large literature on Swedish multinationals. Since her article was written, the synthesis volume on Swedish Match and its predecessors has been published, Karl-Gustaf Hildebrand, *Expansion Crisis Reconstruction, 1917–1939* (Stockholm, 1985). Lundström's contributions to Cameron and Bovykin's forthcoming book add further material on Swedish business abroad.
99. Data from Lundström on Empire Cream Separator Co. See also Wilkins, *History of Foreign Investment in the United States* on this company.
100. There is a history of Solvay & Cie. J. Bolle, *Solvay, L'Invention, L'homme, L'entreprise Industrielle* (Brussels, 1963).
101. This is all from Herman Van der Wee and Martine Goosen's splendid contribution, 'International Factors in the Formation of Banking Systems – Belgium', forthcoming in the Cameron and Bovykin volume.
102. Ibid. and John McKay, *Tramways and Trolleys* (Princeton, NJ, 1976), pp.149, 244 (on the Belgian role).
103. Van der Wee and Goosen, 'International Factors'.
104. Wengenroth, 'Iron and Steel'; see also John P. McKay, *Pioneers for Profit* (Chicago, 1970).
105. Lutz Alt, 'The Photochemical Industry' (Ph.D. dissertation MIT, 1986), pp.71–9.
106. Robert Liefmann, *Cartels, Concerns, and Trusts* (London, 1932), p.269.
107. Wilkins, *History of Foreign Investment in the United States*, and Van der Wee and Goosen, 'International Factors'.
108. For a list of Swiss companies engaged in international business, see Ernst Himmel, *Industrielle Kapitalanlagen der Schweiz im Auslande* (Langensalza, 1922), pp.116–37.
109. Ibid., pp.132–3.
110. Every Swiss company history – and they are numerous – attests to this.
111. Himmel, *Industrielle Kapitalanlagen*, Recapitulation, no page number. But see also Urs Rauber, *Schweizer Industrie in Russland* (Zurich, 1985). Rauber believes Himmel underestimated Swiss industrial investments in Russia. (Rauber's book sent me to Himmel, albeit I have had difficulty matching Rauber's numbers with Himmel's. The data in my text are from Himmel).
112. Silk Association of America, *Annual Report 1905*, pp.60–61.
113. *Fulton, New York 1901*, p.65.
114. Federal Trade Commission, *Cooperation*, I, p.145.
115. Himmel, *Industrielle Kapitalanlagen*, Recapitulation.
116. Based on my own research.
117. See F.C. Gerretson, *History of the Royal Dutch Company*, 4 vols. (Leiden: E.J. Brill, 1953–57). K.D. Bosch, *Nederlandse Beleggingen in De Verenigde Staten* (Amsterdam, 1948), is invaluable on Dutch investment in the United States.
118. See Wilkins, *History of Foreign Investment in the United States*, and Augustus J. Veenendaal, Jr. 'The Kansas City Southern Railway and the Dutch Connection', *Business History Review*, Vol.61 (1987), pp.291–316. Often, the Dutch delegated their authority to Americans; such delegation, however, would not by definition bar such stakes from the category of foreign direct investment.
119. Wilkins, *History of Foreign Investment in the United States*; Christopher Armstrong and H.V. Nelles, 'A Curious Capital Flow: Canadian Investment in Mexico, 1902–1910', *Business History Review*, Vol.58 (1984), pp.178–203.

120. Wilkins, *History of Foreign Investment in the United States*. Geoffrey Jones has
     directed my attention to the Hungarian Bank for Commerce and Industry of Pest's
     controlling interest in the Romanian oil company, Steaua Romana, from 1892–
     1902. See Pearton, *Oil and the Rumanian State*, pp.23–31. Three large Hungarian
     banks were owners of the Transatlantic Trust Co., New York, founded in 1912.
     Wilkins, *History of Foreign Investment in the United States*.
121. Fridenson, 'The Growth', p.157.
122. *Best's Insurance Report – Fire and Marine, 1914.*
123. There were, in addition, some non-European, non-North American head-
     quartered multinational enterprises. See, for example, Wilkins, 'Japanese Multi-
     national Enterprise before 1914'.
124. It is my own conclusion that the United States ranked first. For my forthcoming
     History of Foreign Investment in the United States, I prepared a ranking of debtor
     nations in 1914; this included, however, both foreign portfolio and direct invest-
     ments and does not offer a legitimate ranking for direct investment alone.
     Dunning, 'Changes in the Level and Structure', p.88, made estimates and pro-
     vided a 1914 ranking that is not broken down by country in Latin America (32
     per cent of the world's foreign direct investment), but which, excluding Latin
     America, suggests the following leading recipients: the United States (10.3 per
     cent), China (7.8 per cent), Russia (7.1 per cent), Canada (5.7 per cent). These
     were, as Dunning recognizes, 'estimates'. In Latin America, Argentina, Brazil,
     Mexico, Chile, Peru, and Cuba would figure as the most important recipients of
     foreign direct investment in 1914. All of Europe – excluding Russia, the UK (a
     mere 1.4 per cent), and 'Southern Europe' (2.8 per cent) – had by Dunning's
     reckoning, 9.2 per cent of the total.
125. This was true of aspirins in the United States (made by Bayer) and sewing
     machines in Germany (made by Singer) in this period.
126. For some thoughts on this matter, see Mira Wilkins, 'Efficiency and Management:
     A Comment on Gregory Clark's "Why Isn't the Whole World Developed?"'
     Journal of Economic History, Vol.47 (Dec. 1987), pp.981–3.
127. Since this article has space constraints, I have not discussed the pre-1914 licensing
     activities of multinationals as a separate 'mode'. However, the comparative
     evidence on the amount of licensing done by companies headquartered in
     different home countries seems too lean – at present – for anything but the most
     superficial conclusions. If joint-ventures are to be considered a 'mode', there were
     a large number of such by multinationals of all nationalities – although the exact
     nature of the shared relationships is still ill-defined and it would be impossible to
     choose say 1914 and to rank the prevalence of joint ventures by home country of
     the multinationals.
128. America had lots of small companies that had nothing but local business.
129. Professor Alfred D. Chandler has been important in pointing out to me how very
     large employers some of the pre-1914 German enterprises actually were, when
     compared with their American counterparts.
130. I found in my research on *American* business abroad a number of such 'partial'
     relationships, but they seem far more conspicuous in the European context –
     especially in connection with primary product production – agriculture, or mineral
     extraction.
131. Porter, *Victorian Shipping*, noted that the dividends paid by the Castle Line were
     not impressive; yet, Donald Currie, who had a management contract to run the
     line, emerged as a very wealthy man. He obviously obtained his returns from the
     management contract, *assured* by his equity holdings. Whenever management
     contracts exist, the scholar must check the account books carefully. Sometimes, a
     British agency house abroad could have a negligible (or even no) investment and
     still have a management contract that provided it good returns – whether there
     were or were not profits.
132. See Mira Wilkins, *The Maturing of Multinational Enterprise* (Cambridge, MA,
     1974), pp.414, 565 ns.8–9; Chandler, *The Visible Hand*; O.E. Williamson, 'The

Modern Corporation: Origins, Evolution, Attributes', *Journal of Economic Literature*, Vol.19 (1981), pp.1537–68; Wilkins, 'Defining a Firm', and most recently, Casson, *The Firm and the Market*, p.1. There has been some dispute as to who first applied the ideas of R.H. Coase to the theory of multinational enterprise. The first two published applications were in 1970 by Stephen Hymer, 'The Efficiency (Contradictions) of Multinational Corporations', *American Economic Review*, Vol.60 (1970), pp.441–8, and Robert Z. Aliber, 'A Theory of Direct Foreign Investment', in Charles Kindleberger (ed.), *The International Corporation* (Cambridge, MA, 1970), p.20. In 1974 I picked up on the idea (in a footnote which no one ever read). Wilkins, *The Maturing*, p.565 n.9.

133. I consider that my *Economic History Review* article poses more questions than it answers. For some of the applications, see Wilkins, 'Efficiency and Management'.
134. Kiyoshi Kojima has described US multinationals as trade-destroying, while Japanese ones were trade-creating. Kojima, *Japanese Direct Foreign Investment* (Tokyo, 1978) and idem., *Japan and a New World Economic Order* (Tokyo, 1977). I do not think that in 1870–1914, American multinationals were trade-destroying; in fact, I believe that all the multinationals of 1870–1914 were trade creating – albeit to different extents. It is very important to study exports and imports separately in this context.
135. Note that this was the title of Stephen Hymer's seminal Ph.D. dissertation (1960).
136. For example, when parent entrepreneurs have 'homes' in three countries and operate in a host nation, say South Africa, how does one decipher a 'home' or headquarters? I believe one must close one's eyes to 'nationality' and look at administrative and legal institutional relationships. Was Alusuisse, for instance, a German or a Swiss aluminium company – or a truly co-operative venture?

[4]

Excerpt from *The Growth of International Business*, Mark Casson (ed.)

5 Changes in the level and structure of international production: the last one hundred years

JOHN H. DUNNING

5.1 INTRODUCTION

Alongside advances in the theory of foreign direct investment and the multinational enterprise, the last two decades have seen the emergence of a wealth of new descriptive material about the activities of corporations outside their national boundaries in which they have a controlling equity stake.[1] This material ranges from macrostatistical data on the stock or flow of foreign direct investment in, or between nation states, through *ad hoc* country and sectoral case studies, to individual business histories and company profiles. Between them, these new sources of information enable us to piece together a much more comprehensive and reliable picture of the growth and pattern of international production than was thought possible even fifteen years ago. Certainly, it is difficult to think of any branch of economics or business studies which has generated so much interest, and caused so many books, articles, reports and papers to be written since 1960, as that of the MNE.

There is, however, one major snag with much of the published data. That is that they are rarely directly comparable with each other. Moreover, some of the historical facts a first-year student reading a course in international business may reasonably expect to be told are just not available. We still have only a rough idea of the number of MNEs operating in 1914 or the value of their foreign investments at that time; and even today, very few countries publish the kind of information which scholars need to evaluate properly either the causes or the effects of international production. Thus, to present a statistical portrait of the growth of MNE activity, which might enable us to test our new theories – or even the old ones – in any rigorous fashion, is not possible. Such testing must, at present, be largely confined to cross-sectional industry, firm or country data; and, certainly in the last twenty years, econometric studies of this kind have considerably enriched our understanding about the determinants of FDI.[2] But the most one can realistically expect from a broad overview of the kind presented in this chapter is an interpretation of major events, set within the framework, if not making use of the technical apparatus of recent theoretical advances. This is what the following pages seek to do.

The discussion proceeds in the following way. Section 5.2 reviews the main facts about the growth of international production over four periods in the last century, viz. from around 1870 to 1914, 1919 to 1939, 1945 to the mid-1960s, and the mid-1960s to the late 1970s. This section presents some new statistical estimates of the FDI stock in 1914, 1938, 1960, 1971 and 1978. Sections 5.3 to 5.5 attempt to explain and interpret these data, using the kind of conceptual framework favoured particularly by economists of the University of Reading; and a final section attempts to bring these strands of thought together.

5.2 THE FOREIGN ACTIVITIES OF FIRMS

(a) 1870–1914

Studies published in the last twenty or so years suggest that earlier scholars considerably underestimated the role of the MNE as an entrepreneur and as a transfer of intangible assets in the forty years prior to the First World War. By assembling widely disparate estimates of both the inward and the outward direct capital stake of countries, we can estimate that, by 1914, at least $14 billion had been invested in enterprises or branch plants in which either a single or a group of non-resident investors owned a majority or substantial minority equity interest, or which were owned or controlled by first generation expatriates who had earlier migrated.[3] This amount represented about 35 per cent of the estimated total long-term international debt at that time; a ratio considerably higher than was thought until fairly recently and, in relation to the national income of most capital-exporting countries, more significant than at any time before or since. There is also little doubt that, from the viewpoint of some home and host countries, FDI, both as a channel for the transfer of resources between countries, and as a means of controlling the use of these and complementary local inputs, played a no less important role than it has done since the mid-1950s, and a far greater one than it did

86   The Growth of International Business

in the inter-war period. There is also little doubt that several
economies, particularly developing countries, and some sectors, particularly capital-intensive primary product and technology-intensive
manufacturing sectors, were dominated either by affiliates of MNEs,
or by foreign entrepreneurs who both financed these activities and
organised the supply of technology and management for them.
Indeed, the territorial compass of FDI was probably wider than it has
been for most of the last thirty-five years; Eastern Europe and China,
for example, were both attractive to Western businessmen in the
years preceding the First World War, and there were few controls
exerted on investment flows, or on the scope of the activities of
foreign capitalists.

While for the first three-quarters of the nineteenth century, direct
capital exports[4] mainly comprised expatriate investment or finance
raised in the home country by corporations or individual entrepreneurs to purchase a controlling equity interest in a foreign company,[5] the subsequent forty years saw the infancy and adolescence of
the type of activity which mainly dominates today, viz. the setting up
of foreign branches by enterprises already operating in their home
countries. This latter thrust began around the middle of the
nineteenth century,[6] gathered pace after 1875, and, by 1914 had
become firmly established as a vehicle of international economic
involvement.

As revealed in Table 5.1, the UK was, by far and away, the largest
foreign capital stake holder in 1914, with the USA some way behind.
However, even at that time, US direct investments were more
directed to growth sectors, and a much larger proportion represented
the activities of affiliates of MNEs rather than absentee equity
investment by individuals or companies.[7] Such country-specific differences were reflected in the structure of resource endowments,
institutional mechanisms and existing international economic
involvement. Thus, while Europe had accumulated a pool of marketable venture capital, entrepreneurship and management expertise,
and was already a major portfolio capital exporter, the USA with
none of this background was building a strong comparative advantage
in corporate technology – management skills, which were often best
exploited within the enterprises generating them. Table 5.1 also
reveals that, in 1914, the German and French capital stakes were
about the same; and that there were some Russian, Canadian and
Japanese investments.

Table 5.2 shows that about three-fifths of the foreign capital stake
in 1914 was directed to today's developing countries; but taking a
contemporary definition of such countries to include all areas outside
Europe and the USA, the figure rises to more than four-fifths. The

Table 5.1 Estimated stock of accumulated foreign direct investment by country of origin 1914–78

	1914 $m	%	1938 $m	%	1960 $bn	%	1971 $bn	%	1978 $bn	%
Developed Countries	14302	100.0	26350	100.0	66.0	99.0	168.1	97.7	380.3	96.8
North America										
USA	2652	18.5	7300	27.7	32.8	49.2	82.8	48.1	162.7	41.4
Canada	150	1.0	700	2.7	2.5	3.8	6.5	3.8	13.6	3.5
Western Europe										
UK	6500	45.5	10500	39.8	10.8	16.2	23.7	13.8	50.7	12.9
Germany	1500	10.5	350	1.3	0.8	1.2	7.3	4.2	28.6	7.3
France	1750	12.2	2500	9.5	4.1	6.1	7.3	4.2	14.9	3.8
Belgium					1.3	1.9	2.4	1.4	5.4	1.4
Italy]					1.1	1.6	3.0	1.7	5.4	1.4
Netherlands	1250	8.7	3500	13.3	7.0	10.5	13.8	8.0	28.4	7.2
Sweden					0.4	0.6	2.4	1.4	6.0	1.5
Switzerland					2.0	3.0	9.5	5.5	27.8	7.1
Other Developed Countries										
Russia	300	2.1	450	1.7	—		—		—	
Japan	20	0.1	750	2.8	0.5	0.7	4.4	2.6	26.8	6.8
Australia ⎤ New Zealand ⎦	180	1.3	300	1.1	1.5	2.2	2.5	1.4	4.8	1.2
South Africa ⎤ Other ⎦	neg	neg	neg	neg	1.2	1.8	2.5	1.4	5.2	1.3
Developing Countries	neg	neg	neg	neg	0.7	1.0	4.0	2.3	12.5	3.2
TOTAL	14302	100.0	26350	100.0	66.7	100.0	172.1	100.0	392.8	100.0

Table 5.2 Estimated stock of accumulated foreign direct investment by recipient country or area

	1914		1938		1960		1971		1978	
	$m	%	$m	%	$bn	%	$bn	%	$bn	%
Developed Countries	5235	37.2	8346	34.3	36.7	67.3	108.4	65.2	251.7	69.6
North America										
USA	1450	10.3	1800	7.4	7.6	13.9	13.9	8.4	42.4	11.7
Canada	800	5.7	2296	9.4	12.9	23.7	27.9	16.8	43.2	11.9
Europe										
Western Europe:	1100	7.8	1800	7.4	12.5	22.9	47.4	28.5	136.2	37.7
of which UK:	(200)	(1.4)	(700)	(2.9)	(5.0)	(9.2)	(13.4)	(8.1)	(32.5)	(9.0)
Other European:	1400	9.9	400	1.6	neg	neg	neg	neg	neg	neg
of which Russia	(1000)	(7.1)	—	—	—	—	—	—	—	—
Australasia and South Africa	450	3.2	1950	8.0	3.6	6.6	16.7	10.0	23.9	6.6
Japan	35	0.2	100	0.4	0.1	0.2	2.5	1.5	6.0	1.7
Developing Countries	8850	62.8	15969	65.7	17.6	32.3	51.4	30.9	100.4	27.8
Latin America	4600	32.7	7481	30.8	8.5	15.6	29.6	17.8	52.5	14.5
Africa	900	6.4	1799	7.4	3.0	5.5	8.8	5.3	11.1	3.1
Asia	2950	20.9	6068	25.0	4.1	7.5	7.8	4.7	25.2	7.0
of which: China	(1100)	(7.8)	(1400)	(5.8)	(neg)	(neg)	(neg)	(neg)	(neg)	(neg)
India and Ceylon	(450)	(3.2)	(1359)	(5.6)	(1.1)	(2.0)	(1.5)	(0.9)	(2.5)	(0.7)
Southern Europe					0.5	0.9	1.7	1.0	3.4	0.9
Middle East	400	2.8	621	2.6	1.5	2.8	3.5	2.1	8.2	2.3
International and Unallocated	neg	neg	n.a.	n.a.	n.a.	n.a.	6.5	3.9	9.5	2.6
TOTAL	14085	100.0	24315	100.0	54.5	100.0	166.3	100.0	361.6	100.0

Changes in level structure of international production 89

Sources of Tables 5.1 and 5.2:

The data contained in these tables have been derived from a large number of sources but the main ones have been as follows:

1914   Allen and Donnithorne (China and Japan, 1954), Bagchi (India, 1972), Callis (South East Asia, 1942), Frankel, S. H. (Africa, 1938), Hou (China, 1965), Houston and Dunning (UK, 1976), Lewis (various 1938, 1945), McKay (Russia, 1970), Pamuk (Ottoman Empire, 1981), Paterson (Canada 1976), Rippy (Latin America, 1959), Svedberg (various, 1978).

1938   Allen and Donnithorne (China and Japan, 1954), Bagchi (India, 1972), Callis (South East Asia, 1942), Conan (Sterling Area, 1960), Hou (China, 1965), Lewis (various, 1938, 1945), Svedberg (various data collected by him, 1978), Teichova (East Europe, 1974), United Nations (1949).

1960   Various government publications are cited in United Nations (UNCTC) (1981) and especially those of the United States (Department of Commerce), United Kingdom (Department of Trade), and Canada (Dominion Bureau of Statistics). See also Conan (Sterling Area, 1960) and Kidron (India, 1965).

1971   OECD (various dates), United Nations (UNCTC) (1978), (1981) and various government publications as cited therein.

1978   OECD (various dates), United Nations (UNCTC) (1978), (1981).

distribution among recipient nations was quite diffused, with the combined Russian and Chinese share exceeding that of Western Europe and only slightly less than that of North America. About 55 per cent of the total capital stake was accounted for by the primary product sector, 20 per cent by railroads, 15 per cent by manufacturing activities, 10 per cent by trade and distribution and the balance by public utilities, banking and the like. The manufacturing investments, which were largely oriented towards local markets,[8] were mainly concentrated in Europe, the USA, the UK Dominions and Russia; while, apart from iron ore, coal and bauxite, almost all mineral investments were located in the British Empire or in developing countries.

Of especial significance in this era were the raw material and agricultural investments; this was the heyday of the plantations, e.g. rubber, tea, coffee and cocoa; of cattle raising and meat processing, e.g. in the USA and Argentina; and of the emergence of the vertically integrated MNE in tropical fruits, sugar and tobacco. Indeed apart, perhaps, from some transnational railroad activity in Europe and Latin America, it was in the agricultural sector, more than any other, where the international hierarchical organisation first made itself felt, particularly in economies whose prosperity rested mainly on a single cash crop, the production and marketing of which was controlled by a few (and sometimes only one) foreign companies, e.g. Cuba (sugar), Costa Rica (bananas), Ceylon (tea) and Liberia (rubber).[9]

Even in those early days, there were distinct geographical and

90   *The Growth of International Business*

industrial patterns of FDI which varied with the home country of the investor. Some details of the location of manufacturing subsidiaries of 187 and 226 non-US based MNEs which existed in 1968 or 1971 are given in Table 5.3.[10] Language, cultural, political and trading ties, as well as geographical distance, played a more important role than they do today. Thus, 72 per cent of US investment was in other parts of the American continent; while there was a strong colonial content in British, French and Belgian involvement in developing countries (Svedberg, 1981). For the most part, French and German manufac-

Table 5.3   *Percentage Breakdown of Number of Manufacturing Subsidiaries of MNEs by Country of Location*

(a)   Subsidiaries Established pre-1914

	US Based MNEs	UK Based MNEs	Continental European Based MNEs
Developed Countries	87.7	73.7	81.0
North America	27.0	15.3	6.6
of which: USA	—	3.3	5.4
Canada	27.0	15.0	1.2
Europe	57.5	41.7	73.2
of which:			
Western Europe	51.7	21.6	61.8
Northern Europe	5.8	11.7	5.4
Southern Europe	0.0	8.4	6.0
Australia and New Zealand	1.6	8.4	0.6
Japan	0.8	3.3	0.0
South Africa	0.8	5.0	0.6
Developing Countries	12.2	26.3	19.0
Latin America	8.1	16.2	1.2
of which: Mexico	0.0	1.7	0.0
Brazil	2.5	1.7	0.0
Middle East	4.1	3.3	15.4
Africa (other than South Africa)	0.0	3.4	0.6
Asia	0.0	3.4	1.8
of which: India	0.0	1.7	0.0
TOTAL	100.0	100.0	100.0
Number of Subsidiaries	122	60	167

Source: Compiled from data first published in Vaupel and Curhan (1974)

turing investments were sited elsewhere in Europe, while UK firms accounted for the great bulk of capital exports to the British empire outside Canada.

However, of the home countries, the UK was, perhaps, the most cosmopolitan foreign investor; *inter alia*, this reflected the diversity of her overseas possessions, her earlier technological lead and her established trading links. Her initial industrial investments were no less broadly based although, by 1914, UK MNE manufacturing activity was strongly oriented towards the production of consumer goods and heavy engineering equipment. The USA, by contrast, was developing a comparative investment advantage in the newer technology-intensive industries and in those supplying standardised products and/or consumer goods with a high income-elasticity of demand; while the Germans – as in trade – led the world in chemical investments.[11]

The pattern of involvement by the leading capital exporters in resource-based sectors was much the same, though in different territories. However, there were some exceptions, which reflected differences in consumer tastes and distance of markets; for example, whereas the US MNEs dominated tropical fruit production, UK MNEs owned most of the foreign tea plantations. While US MNEs probably pursued a more systematic policy of vertical integration, there was, nevertheless, some backward integration by UK manufacturing companies to secure supplies of raw materials, e.g. by Cadbury in cocoa, Lever in vegetable oils, Dunlop in rubber. Trade and service investments followed the main commercial arteries of the home countries.

(b) 1918–38

The First World War and the years which followed saw several changes in the level, form and structure of international production. The war itself caused several European belligerents to sell some of their pre-war investments, while subsequent political upheaval and boundary changes further reduced intra-Continental European corporate activity, and eliminated it altogether from Russia. Only the USA remained fairly unscathed by these events but she, along with other countries, subsequently suffered from the collapse of international capital markets in the late 1920s and early 1930s. Nevertheless, because her foreign investments largely took the form of branch plant activities by MNEs, and were directed to sectors supplying products with an above income-elasticity of demand, her share of the world capital stock rose from 18.5 per cent in 1914 to 27.7 per cent in 1938.

Overall, as Table 5.1 shows, the international capital stake rose quite substantially in the inter-war years.[12] There were also some changes in its geographical distribution; these are illustrated in Table 5.4, the data for which are derived from a similar source to those contained in Table 5.3.[13] In spite of some sizeable West European investments in Central Europe (Teichova, 1974),[14] the Americas, north and south of the USA, continued to attract more than

Table 5.4 *Percentage Breakdown of Number of Manufacturing Subsidiaries of MNEs by Country of Location*

(b) Subsidiaries Established 1920–38

	US Based MNEs	UK Based MNEs	Continental European Based MNEs
Developed Countries	78.0	71.5	74.4
North America	24.9	12.4	9.7
of which: USA	—	5.0	9.4
Canada	24.9	7.4	0.3
Europe	43.2	39.2	61.7
of which: Western Europe	38.4	29.5	47.6
Northern Europe	2.2	6.9	5.8
Southern Europe	2.6	2.8	8.3
Australia and New Zealand	6.2	15.7	1.9
Japan	0.8	—	1.1
South Africa	2.9	4.2	0.0
Developing Countries	22.0	28.5	25.7
Latin America	17.3	9.2	8.6
of which: Mexico	4.2	—	0.6
Brazil	2.6	1.8	2.8
Africa (other than South Africa)	—	5.1	1.9
Asia	3.2	11.0	3.0
of which: India	0.8	6.0	1.1
Middle East	1.5	3.2	11.3
TOTAL	100.0	100.0	100.0
Number of Subsidiaries	614	217	361

Source: Compiled from data first published in Vaupel and Curhan (1974)

two-thirds of the US direct investment stake; the role of intra-European and US participation in Europe fell in the 1920s and recovered somewhat in the 1930s, as did European investments in the USA. There was also some retrenchment of European economic involvement in Latin America – particularly in the railroad sector; this was partly compensated by a slight increase in the export of capital to the UK Dominions and, prior to the Sino–Japanese War, a sharp rise in Western business activity in China (Hou, 1965).

There was also quite a lot of new MNE participation in the developing world in the inter-war years; this included new oil investments in the Mexican gulf, the Dutch East Indies, and the Middle East; copper and iron ore in Africa; bauxite in Dutch and British Guyana; nitrate in Chile; precious metals in South Africa and, perhaps most noteworthy of all, non-ferrous metals in South America. Indeed, in 1929, two experts on mining observed that 'the bulk of productive mineral resources of South America are owned by American interests' (quoted by Wilkins, 1974a, p. 106). Outside the mineral sector, the growing industrial demand for rubber led both US and European manufacturers to invest in plantations in Liberia, Malaysia and Dutch East Indies; while rising real incomes at home prompted a further flurry of activity by MNEs in sugar, tropical fruit and tobacco. There was also a sizeable expansion of public utility investments in Latin America by US firms. Both US and UK MNEs extended their foreign sales and marketing ventures into production in these years.

Yet though the number of new subsidiaries set up by MNEs continued to rise throughout the period, it was only in the 1930s that the *value* of the direct capital stake exceeded its pre-war figure. During this period, investments by Continental European firms went mainly to other parts of Europe and the USA, while US firms were strongly oriented to South America, Canada and the larger European countries.[15] The first four Japanese manufacturing affiliates of the largest Japanese MNEs existing in 1970 were set up between 1920 and 1938 (Vaupel and Curhan, 1974).

(c) 1939–60

If the inter-war years witnessed a deceleration in the expansion of international business, the thirty-five years since the end of the Second World War have been ones of almost uninterrupted growth. The period may be conveniently divided into two phases. The first, up to around 1960, was one in which the USA dominated the international investment scene; of the increase in both the capital stake since 1938 and the number of new manufacturing subsidiaries (covered by the Vaupel and Curhan, 1974, study), the USA accounted for about two-thirds. The second, spanning the following two decades, witnessed the increasingly important role of first European, then Japanese and finally some Third World countries as international direct investors. Between 1960 and 1978, of the $318 billion increase in the world direct capital stake, the USA accounted for 48 per cent and West Germany and Japan for 18 per cent; between 1971 and 1978 the respective ratios were 46 per cent and 22 per cent.[16]

The effect of the Second World War was similar to that of its predecessor, in that each of the main European belligerents was forced to divest many of its foreign assets; however, unlike the first war, the second generated major technological advances, while its aftermath produced an international economic and political climate particularly favourable to foreign business activities. Also, it was not too long before the UK and the leading Continental European nations, apart from West Germany, began to renew their foreign investments. By 1960, for example, the French and Dutch capital involvement had more than matched its pre-war level.

As a percentage of both world output and trade, the international direct investment stake rose modestly between 1938 and 1960. During this period, there was a continuation of the pre-war trend for the MNEs to favour developed countries for new venture activity. In 1914, something like two-thirds of the capital stake was directed to developing countries; by 1938 this had fallen to 55 per cent, and by 1960 it was nearer 40 per cent. Partly, this reflected another major structural change, viz. the increased interest shown in market- *vis à vis* supply-oriented investments, which was designed to overcome trade barriers of one kind or another. In 1960, about 35 per cent of the US and UK accumulated investment was in manufacturing, compared with about 25 per cent in 1938 and 15 per cent in 1914. By contrast, interest in agricultural and public utility activities declined markedly, while – taken as a whole – mining investments recorded about average rates of growth. Yet, some of these latter, notably those made by UK and US MNEs in non-ferrous metals, e.g. copper in Chile and Peru, bauxite in the Caribbean etc. and oil in the Persian gulf, grew very rapidly.

Although this was a period which saw the start of enforced divestment or nationalisation of some primary product investments and the setting up of international producers' cartels, it was not until the 1960s that the thrust of these expressions of host country economic power was fully revealed.[17] Apart from state-owned oil MNEs, European firms were not very active in raw material exploration; the major capital exporters in the 1950s, viz. the Netherlands, France and Switzerland, preferred to invest in manufacturing, trade and service activities (including finance and insurance). As in the inter-war years, UK MNEs directed their attention mainly towards Commonwealth countries. Indeed, such countries increased their share of the total capital stake from around one-half in the 1930s to over 70 per cent in 1960. During the early post-war period, first South Africa and Australia and then Canada attracted the bulk of new UK direct investment; contrast this pattern with that of US MNEs where the focus of interest was strongly directed to Canada and Western Europe. Some details are set out in Table 5.5.[18]

Unfortunately for this, as for other periods, there are no comprehensive statistics on the entry or exit of MNEs; it is, therefore, not possible to estimate how much of the growth of the international capital stake was accounted for by firms existing at the beginning of the period and how much by new entrants. Even the Harvard data (Vaupel and Curhan, 1974) do not distinguish between subsidiaries

Table 5.5 *Percentage Breakdown of Number of Manufacturing Subsidiaries of MNEs by Country of Location*

(c) *Subsidiaries Established 1946–61*

	US Based MNEs		UK Based MNEs	Continental European Based MNEs	Japanese Based MNEs
Developed Countries	63.2		79.5	65.4	0.7
North America:	14.9		15.9	16.0	0.2
of which: USA	—	3.2		10.7	0.2
Canada	14.9	12.7		5.3	—
Europe	35.9		26.6	41.8	0.5
Japan	2.6		0.3	1.5	—
Australasia and South Africa	9.8		36.7	6.1	0.0
Developing Countries	36.8		20.5	34.6	99.3
Middle East	1.4		2.6	3.0	0.6
Africa	1.4		4.6	6.6	0.3
Asia	3.4		6.9	5.8	66.1
Latin America	30.6		6.4	19.2	32.3
TOTAL	100		100	100	100
Number of Subsidiaries	2009		684	609	65

Source: Compiled from data first published in Vaupel and Curhan (1974)

set up by established MNEs and new entrants; all that they tell us is how many affiliates the 413 MNEs studied had at different periods of time. However from these and related facts two things seem perfectly clear. First, over that part of the last century for which they had been operating as MNEs, something like 800 enterprises had set up affiliates in at least 10 countries. But second, of the total number of MNEs in 1973, nearly one-half operated only in one country and 70 per cent in three or less (Commission of the European Communities, 1976). These figures, coupled with other knowledge about the post-war entry of new Japanese MNEs[19] and of some high-technology MNEs from the USA and Europe, suggest that any explanation of international production must deal with the question 'Why is the number of MNEs growing?' as well as 'Why do MNEs grow?'

Two other points might be made about this era of international business expansion. First, the proportion of new subsidiaries of the MNEs surveyed by Vaupel and Curhan (1974), which were established by green field ventures (as compared with acquisition, merger, or reorganisation) fell from 55 per cent in 1946–52 to 48 per cent in 1959–61; the corresponding figures for the pre-1914 period and 1919–39 were 67 per cent and 58 per cent respectively. Second, in the case of both US and non-US based MNEs, the proportion of affiliates in which they had a 95 per cent or more equity stake fell from 60 per cent in 1946–52 to 54 per cent in 1959 –61.[20]

(d)   1960–78

The rate of growth of the international capital stake reached its peak in the late 1960s, decelerated in the early and mid-1970s, but picked up again in the last few years of the decade. But the continued fall in the UK and US share and the increase in that of the West German, Japanese and Swiss[21] is the most striking feature of Table 5.1. This is also confirmed by an examination of the growth of 483 of the world's largest industrial enterprises (Dunning and Pearce, 1981). Between 1962 and 1977 the number of those of US origin dwindled from 292 to 240; while that of Japanese companies rose from 29 to 64; and that of developing countries from 2 to 18. In terms of investments flows, the West German share in 1979 and 1980 was scarcely less than that of the UK; the Japanese contribution was about 60 per cent of the UK, but was (and is still) rising.

There have also been changes in the geographical distribution of the capital stake. Of an estimated $293 billion invested by the seven leading home countries in 1978, (United Nations – UNCTC – 1981), 26.5 per cent was in developing countries, a figure slightly higher than that in 1971, but below that recorded (at least by US and UK

Changes in level structure of international production   97

MNEs) in 1960. Most of the forced divestment in natural resources and public utilities occurred in the decade ending in 1975; these were mostly located in developing countries.[22] On the other hand, the 1970s saw a major surge in Japanese investment abroad which, more than its US and UK counterparts, is concentrated in developing countries. In 1978 such countries accounted for 56.5 per cent of all Japanese cumulative investment compared with 27.4 per cent of US and 19.8 per cent of UK investments (Kojima, 1980). Moreover, the decline in extractive investments has been largely counteracted by the growth in manufacturing and service industries; for example, the share of the total US capital stock in these two sectors located in developing countries rose from 21 per cent in 1971 to 26 per cent in 1978.

Within developed host countries, the last twenty years have seen a marked shift of interest by MNEs to Western Europe and the USA. In 1960 about 32 per cent of the foreign capital stock of developed market economies was located in Western Europe or the US; by 1970 this percentage had risen to 38, and by 1978 to 47. By contrast, the share of the British Commonwealth, which attracted so much investment in the early part of the post-war period, fell from 45 per cent in 1960 to 27 per cent in 1970 and to 17 per cent in 1978. This reallocation of activity has been particularly marked in the case of UK investors. In 1978 Western Europe accounted for 31 per cent of the UK direct capital stake (excluding oil), compared to 13 per cent in 1962; the share going to developing countries, however, fell from 37 per cent to 20 per cent. Japanese investment has also grown rather more rapidly in other industrialised countries, especially in the manufacturing and service sectors.

The industrial structure of the outward capital stake of the leading investing countries continues to reflect their factor endowments and market structures, though there is some suggestion of a convergence in patterns over the last two decades (Dunning, 1981a). However, US, West German and Swedish MNEs continue to dominate the high-technology and information-intensive industries, while those of UK and Japanese origin are more represented in consumer good sectors. In Japan's case, however, her investments up to the mid-1970s were in the traditional industries in which she once had a comparative trading advantage, e.g. textiles, or those in which she has always had a comparative trading disadvantage, e.g. primary metals; in the case of the UK, her strength appears to lie in branded goods, e.g. processed foods and cigarettes, where consistency of quality is an important competitive advantage, and in financial services.

Three other features of recent direct trends in MNE activity might also be mentioned. The first is the growth in two-way investment by countries. For example, not only has the USA's share of the outward capital stake fallen; her share of the inward capital stake has risen. In 1960, the USA's outward/inward capital stake ratio was 4.0, in 1970 it was 5.7, but by 1980 it had fallen to 3.3; by contrast, the West German ratio has risen from 0.40 in 1960 to 0.80 in 1970 and 1.09 in 1978, and the Canadian ratio from 0.19 to 0.23 and 0.31. Moreover, as has already been mentioned, in the later 1970s several developing countries, e.g. Hong Kong, Singapore, Brazil, Korea and India, also began to export capital on some scale (Kumar and MacLeod, 1981).

The second trend has been the shift away from traditional import-substituting and resource-based FDI to that designed to promote an integrated structure of production by MNEs and their affiliates. The rationale for this will be discussed later in this chapter, but the two fastest growing areas of MNE activity in the 1970s have been in export platform investments in the newly industrialising countries (NICs) and in horizontal intra-firm trade among affiliates, and between affiliates and parent companies with a regionally integrated area, e.g. EEC, LAFTA.[23]

Thirdly, the last twenty years has seen an increase not only in the importance of joint ventures and non-equity resource flows[24] but of liquidations and voluntary divestments by MNEs. According to Curhan, Davidson and Suri (1977) there were 3152 divestments by US MNEs between 1951 and 1975, while the ratio of divestments to new investments rose from 0.23 in 1968–9 to 0.56 in 1974–5. These divestments have been of two kinds, both underlining the dynamic character of MNE involvement. The first is in low or mature technology sectors in which entry barriers are falling; the second is in response to the move towards global or regional rationalisation, and, in the later 1970s, to domestic economic recession.

There were other developments of the late 1970s which space precludes us from discussing. These included the opening up of regions – notably parts of Eastern Europe and mainland China – previously closed to international business; the more ready acceptance by Japan of majority-owned foreign affiliates; the growth of MNE activity in several service sectors, notably banking, insurance, advertising and tourism; and the increasing use of cross-border arrangements not linked to equity investments.

Most of the data so far presented in this chapter relate to the aggregate FDI stake or to the numbers of the affiliates of large MNEs existing in 1970 (or thereabouts). Only *en passant* have this chapter touched on the growth of particular MNEs, or groups of MNEs as dealt with in the writings of Wilkins (1974a, 1974b), Wilson (n.d.), Franko (1976), Stopford (1974), Nicholas (1982a) and others. Nevertheless, if the statistical profile has been more macro- than micro-oriented, the analytical insights of these scholars will later be drawn upon very considerably. However, this part of the chapter concludes by illustrating, in Figure 5.1, some of the main historical landmarks in the genealogy of the contemporary MNE and indicating where some of today's international giants fit into this picture.

5.3 EXPLAINING CHANGES IN INTERNATIONAL PRODUCTION

Though several economists have been interested in explaining the phenomena of FDI *per se*,[25] most students of international business tend to view it as the vehicle by which resources are transferred and allocated across national boundaries without any change in their ownership. In Chapter 2 Peter Buckley summarised the state of our knowledge and areas of lacunae on theoretical issues. This section will just add our own particular gloss which will form the basis of the analysis which follows.

Changes in the level and pattern of international production may reflect both changes in the *number* of MNEs and/or their affiliates, and the growth or decline of established MNEs and/or their affiliates. Strictly speaking, the theory of the growth of the MNE, as a special case of the growth of the firm, is concerned with the second phenomena rather than the first; and, therefore, it cannot be expected to explain a lot of *de novo* foreign production, and particularly that which replaces domestic production.

Let us start with a few generally accepted propositions. A firm engages in two interrelated functions. First, it organises the production of individual goods and services. Second, it engages in transactions, i.e. it buys inputs and sells outputs. Some of these transactions will be with external buyers and sellers, e.g. households and other firms; others will be made within the same firm. A firm will then grow when it either increases the output of the products it is already producing (or replaces these by new and/or improved products), or internalises transactions which would otherwise have been undertaken via the market, i.e. by redistributing output from other producers to itself.[26]

While, in practice, the production and transaction functions of firms may not be easily separable, conceptually the distinction is a useful one, as is that between those transactions of a firm which are capable of being externalised and those which are not (Dunning, 1981a).

In performing these two activities, a firm may find it desirable to set up production units in more than one location, either in the country of its incorporation or elsewhere. How much output and how

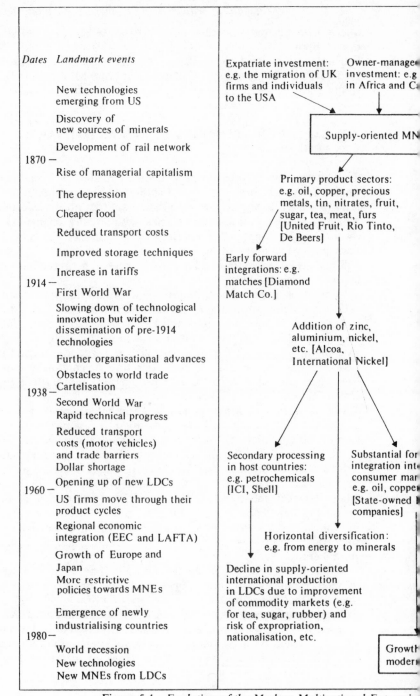

Dates   Landmark events

New technologies
emerging from US

Discovery of
new sources of minerals

Development of rail network
1870 —

Rise of managerial capitalism

The depression

Cheaper food

Reduced transport costs

Improved storage techniques

Increase in tariffs
1914 —

First World War

Slowing down of technological
innovation but wider
dissemination of pre-1914
technologies

Further organisational advances

Obstacles to world trade
Cartelisation
1938 —

Second World War
Rapid technical progress

Reduced transport
costs (motor vehicles)
and trade barriers
Dollar shortage

Opening up of new LDCs
1960 —

US firms move through their
product cycles

Regional economic
integration (EEC and LAFTA)

Growth of Europe and
Japan
More restrictive
policies towards MNEs

Emergence of newly
industrialising countries
1980 —

World recession
New technologies
New MNEs from LDCs

Expatriate investment:
e.g. the migration of UK
firms and individuals
to the USA

Owner-manage
investment: e.g
in Africa and C

Supply-oriented MN

Primary product sectors:
e.g. oil, copper, precious
metals, tin, nitrates, fruit,
sugar, tea, meat, furs
[United Fruit, Rio Tinto,
De Beers]

Early forward
integrations: e.g.
matches [Diamond
Match Co.]

Addition of zinc,
aluminium, nickel,
etc. [Alcoa,
International Nickel]

Secondary processing
in host countries:
e.g. petrochemicals
[ICI, Shell]

Substantial for
integration int
consumer mar
e.g. oil, coppe
[State-owned
companies]

Horizontal diversification:
e.g. from energy to minerals

Decline in supply-oriented
international production
in LDCs due to improvement
of commodity markets (e.g.
for tea, sugar, rubber) and
risk of expropriation,
nationalisation, etc.

Growth
moder

Figure 5.1   *Evolution of the Modern Multinational Enterpris*

ls of early-nineteenth-century FDI:

Finance capitalism:
e.g. European investment
in Russia

Trading investments:
[Hudson Bay Co., Royal
African Co.]

Market-oriented MNEs

y integrated
:turing MNEs:
:cco, oils, cocoa,

Bros, Cadbury
1ion Carbide]

Non-durable consumer
goods: e.g. branded,
packaged food products,
soaps, pharmaceuticals,
cigarettes
[Unilever, Nestlé]

Mass production metal-
using goods requiring
interchangeable parts: e.g.
sewing machines, type-
writers, cars [Singer Sewing
Machines]

Highly capital/technology-
intensive continuous
processing: e.g. chemicals,
synthetic fibres, plastics [Courtaulds]

Early forward
integration into
marketing: e.g.
sewing machines

of rubber,
graphite, etc.
Firestone,
:m Steel]

Additional branded
consumer products
[Burroughs Wellcome,
BAT]

Computers
[IBM]

Innovation of new multi-
component products: e.g.
consumer electronic products,
office machinery
[National Cash Register]

Geographical and
horizontal diversification

ns of vertical integration
advantage of cheap good
abour: e.g. electronics

Export-platform investment
Rationalisation of production
locations within free trade areas
[IBM, Ford, Honeywell]

Decline in MNE role in
standardised and mature
technology sectors

Micro-chip technology

many transactions are assigned to each location will normally be decided on the usual economic criteria, but in considering the growth of output of that part of a multilocational firm produced in *particular* regions or countries, the relative attractions of these regions or countries, as well as factors influencing the growth of the enterprise *as a whole* are relevant.

In seeking reasons for the growth of international production over the past hundred years, it is possible to suggest that an amalgam of three sets of forces has been at work. First, there has been an increase in the demand for the type of goods, services and rights which MNEs are particularly well equipped to supply, and/or an enhanced ability on their part to supply and market these relative to their competitors. Second, there has been a proliferation in the type of transactions, notably of intermediate products, which are best undertaken by hierarchies rather than by markets, and/or an improvement in the efficiency of hierarchies, particularly MNE hierarchies relative to other forms of governance, to organise these and other transactions. Third, the inducements to enterprises to produce goods and services from a foreign location have grown; and/or the demand for the type of output which is best supplied from a foreign location has increased.

This approach may also be used to explain the widening geographical origin of MNEs, shifts in the industrial and geographical pattern of FDI, changes in the size distribution and product diversification of MNEs, and the evolution of new kinds of ownership strategy. Thus the faster growth of Japanese relative to US MNE activity might be explained by the improved ability of the former *vis-à-vis* the latter to supply products the market wants; or by their greater propensity to internalise their competitive advantages (or create new advantages by internalising markets); or by their greater incentive to switch production from a domestic to a foreign location. Similarly, the expansion of MNEs in high-technology and information-intensive industries, relative to that in some resource-based sectors, might be explained by a growing failure in the international market for technology and information in the former case and/or by less market failure, or more government fiat in the latter. Finally, the increase of FDI in Hong Kong and Singapore relative to India over the last twenty years might be put down to the different types of foreign production attracted to the two groups of countries or to the very different locational attractions, e.g. attitudes of host governments, labour availability and efficiency, access to markets afforded by them.

Elsewhere (Dunning, 1981a) the kind of framework outlined above has been formalised by use of the ownership, location and internalisation (OLI) paradigm, which identifies and classifies par-

Changes in level structure of international production 103

ticular competitive advantages to enterprises and countries, which are hypothesised to influence the extent and character of a firm's international economic involvement. It has been suggested that the values of these variables will vary according to certain structural parameters, such as the characteristics of home and host countries,[27] the nature of productive and transaction activities of firms and other firm-specific attributes. Except perhaps for size, these latter attributes have been generally neglected by mainstream economists; however, in the last decade, with more attention being given to the economics of the MNE *per se*, and a welcome revival of interest in the firm as an organisational unit, these are now moving towards the forefront of discussion.

A great deal of work has been done on evaluating the determinants of particular types of international production. But it now seems generally accepted that, because of the very different motives for FDI, a single predictive theory of international production is just not possible, any more than it is realistic to expect that a general theory of international trade can explain all types of trade. But as in trade theory, there are some well established guiding principles, e.g. the importance of the distribution of factor endowments between countries and the nature of markets, which have stood the test of time, so it may be possible to identify similar principles which are fundamental to an understanding of international production. And if the OLI paradigm serves to do anything at all, it is to provide such an analytical framework. Clearly *which* OLI variables are the relevant ones will depend on the type of FDI and the kind of structural parameters earlier described. It would be unrealistic to suppose that the OLI advantages which explain investment by Standard Fruit in the banana industry of Costa Rica are the same (or have the same value) as that by NV Philips Gloeilampenfabrieken in the electrical appliances industry of Greece, or that of Trust House Forte in the hotel industry of the USA; but, in each instance the basic principles are the same. More than this: it may be possible to identify sets of key variables (as is done in trade theory where different types of labour and capital are grouped) which come close to providing the OLI paradigm with operational substance. In the present context, it should be possible to see how changes in the values of these might usefully explain changes in international production.

The following sections of this chapter focus on three such sets of interrelated factors. First, the state of knowledge (including information and organisational technology) is a key variable influencing the capacity of firms of different nationality of ownership to produce and market particular goods and services, independently from where, or by which means they are supplied. Second, market failure (as proxied by the costs of a market transaction and the externalities associated with it) is the key variable influencing the administrative mode of exploiting the capacity. Third, a group of locational variables such as transfer costs (including tariff barriers), size of markets and resource availability, affect the choice of firms of where to locate their activities.[28]

5.4 TECHNOLOGICAL CAPABILITY

(a) 1870–1914

From Schumpeter onwards, several economists have asserted that innovations and technological advances have been the major cause of economic growth of industrial societies.[29] According to this view, given the size and character of the market for a particular product, the share of that market enjoyed by any one firm rests primarily on its entrepreneurship, technological prowess and organisational strategy relative to that of its competitors. It may, then, be reasonably hypothesised that, in so far as international production is part of the total production of firms, its growth is likely to be positively rather than negatively related to world technological capacity; and for its geographical origin to be similarly related to the distribution of that capacity between countries. Moreover, in so far as it is possible to identify particular areas of activity in which MNEs are likely to participate, then the more technological advances stem from these activities, the more international production might be expected to grow.

Though innovations continued throughout the nineteenth century, they varied greatly in significance and character, by country of origin, sector and type of firm, and by their speed of international dissemination. Up to around the 1860s, most discoveries were based on the comparatively elementary technology of the industrial revolution, the results of which were fairly easily transferred across national boundaries and assimilated by their recipients. While these advances were accompanied by important organisational and institutional changes, e.g. the introduction of the factory system and the emergence of the joint stock company, for the most part in this era, firms remained small, were single product and owner-managed, and supplied local markets.

The last half-century before the First World War heralded a new wave of technological advances which, in many ways, were more profound and far reaching than their predecessors. These stemmed largely from the USA, and very much reflected both its particular factor endowments and its market characteristics. They were stimulated and supported by the creation of new transport and communications networks, which helped shift both the demand and the supply curves for goods to the right. Electricity and the internal combustion engine, the interchangeability of parts, and the introduction of continuous processing were the main technological lynchpins of the second industrial revolution.[30] They combined to make possible economies of scale in production which, however, required a regular flow of inputs and assured markets if they were to be profitably exploited.

Such technological, organisational and financial changes fundamentally affected the production functions of firms, their capacity for and strategy of growth, and the market environment in which they operated. They also introduced new kinds of competitive advantage, which affected both the ability of firms to exploit foreign markets and the form by which advantages were exploited. For unlike those which preceded them, these advantages created many more barriers to the entry of firms not possessing them, and to their transfer to other countries. These included the growing cost effectiveness of large plants, the economies of process, product or market integration, and the protection offered by the international patent system. They encouraged further technological and organisational changes, which eventually led to more concentration of industrial output and to the transformation of country-specific advantages into the proprietary rights of enterprises.

There are several statistical pointers to the acceleration of technological advances during this era. By the turn of the century the rate of major inventions and discoveries was twice that of the first quarter of the nineteenth century (Streit, 1949). More impressive, from a total annual application for new patents in the USA (from both US and non-US residents) of less than 1,000 in the 1840s and 5,000 in the late 1850s, the number rose substantially to more than 20,000 in the late 1860s, to 40,000 by the turn of the century and to nearly 70,000 by the outbreak of the First World War.

No less significant was the change in the geographical origin of such advances. As Table 5.6 shows, of some 322 major innovations recorded between 1750 and 1850, 37.9 per cent originated from Britain, 23.9 per cent from France, 11.8 per cent from Germany, 16.1 per cent from the USA and 10.3 per cent from other countries.[31] In the following 64 years, during which there were 453 innovations, the corresponding percentages were 15.9, 16.8, 20.5, 34.9 and 11.9. From a dominating position in the late eighteenth and nineteenth centuries, the UK's share fell, while that of her continental competitors and the USA rose: after 1870 the USA took the lead, although its hegemony did not reach its zenith until just after the Second World

106   The Growth of International Business

Table 5.6 Major Inventions, Discoveries and Innovations by Country, 1750–1950 (as a percentage of total)

| | | Inventions, discoveries and innovations | | | | |
	Total	Britain (%)	France (%)	Germany (%)	USA (%)	Others (%)
1750–1775	30	46.7	16.7	3.3	10.0	23.3
1776–1800	68	42.6	32.4	5.9	13.2	5.9
1801–1825	95	44.2	22.1	10.5	12.6	10.5
1826–1850	129	28.7	22.5	17.8	22.5	8.5
1851–1875	163	17.8	20.9	23.9	25.2	12.3
1876–1900	204	14.2	17.2	19.1	37.7	11.8
1901–1914	87	16.1	8.0	17.2	46.0	12.7
1915–1939	146	13.0	4.1	13.0	58.6	11.3
1940–1950	34	2.9	0.0	6.7	82.4	8.8

Source: Calculated from Streit (1949); see also Pavitt and Soete (1981)

War. Allowing for the time lag between innovation and foreign production, this pattern of technological advance mirrors fairly well the distribution of the stock of foreign investment set out in Table 5.1. Data on non-resident patents registered in the USA suggest a similar decline in the proportion originating from the UK. They also show that, in the period between 1883 and 1914, Germany was a more important patentor than France; and, as one might expect from its geographical proximity, Canada.[32] In the mid-nineteenth century, the proportion of the population which had some kind of tertiary education was highest in the UK and Germany. By 1914, the USA had overtaken both countries, with the UK second, Germany third and France fourth.

Changes in the character of the new technologies were no less important. Those coming from Europe tended to reflect the region's earlier pre-eminence in the basic industries, e.g. iron and steel, shipbuilding, heavy engineering and chemicals. Moreover, both in the UK and on the Continent, where most businesses were family owned, there was comparatively little vertical integration. By contrast, in the USA innovations were more directed towards light engineering, electrical goods, motor vehicles and consumer durables.[33] US firms also tended to pioneer labour-saving and/or capital-intensive production processes, while European companies scored relatively well in materials-saving innovations.

The innovations of the later nineteenth century were different in another sense. Although the earlier discoveries in metallurgy, power generation and transport were interrelated and mutually reinforcing,

Changes in level structure of international production 107

such interdependence rarely extended across national boundaries. The later advances were truly trans-continental; by drastically reducing transport costs and preserving quality, the railroad, the iron-steamship and the introduction of refrigeration and temperature controlling techniques opened up new sources of food and raw materials from distant countries. *Inter alia* these developments led to an increase in the size of the foreign trade sector in most European economies and of inter-regional US trade. But whereas the UK's comparative advantage was most clearly seen in the products which it had pioneered a half-century earlier, that of Germany, France and the USA was in the products first produced in the later nineteenth century, e.g. motor vehicles, electrical equipment and light chemicals. Indeed some economists assert that changes in the structure of a country's trade is a better indicator of its competitiveness than its share of world trade. Viewed in this perspective, and measured in terms of the rate of growth in world exports in the twentieth century, the USA, Germany and, to a lesser extent, France, consistently outperformed the UK.

Two other features about the sectors embracing the newer technologies should be mentioned. First, they demanded a higher and more consistent quality of inputs, e.g. technology, management, skilled labour, than their predecessors; at the same time, the materials they used were more widely found. Often the possession of these inputs generated advantages to firms which were not only exclusive (at least for a period of time) but which were transferable across national boundaries via FDI or licensing. Second, they tended to be more complex, in that their products needed a larger number of divisible production processes, both lateral – in the case of fabricating industries – and vertical – in the case of continuous processing industries. Yet to be fully effective, these separate processes needed to be coordinated within the same firm. Hence economies of scale and specialisation went hand in hand with economies of joint production. This integration extended beyond production to the purchasing of inputs and the marketing of outputs (Chandler, 1977). Teece (1981b) has argued that those economies which encouraged, by one means or another, the vertical integration of their industries in the nineteenth and early twentieth century, were those which exhibited the greatest technological advances and improved competitive position in world markets. Kindleberger (1964) has suggested the same thing, particularly in the context of the reluctance of UK firms to integrate production and selling operations. He compares the case of the UK woollen industry, which moved to direct trading in the nineteenth century and maintained its rate of technical change, with that of the cotton industry which preferred to separate selling and production activities[34] and fared less well. Frankel (1955) asserts that it was the inability of the organisational and ownership structure in the UK to adapt to the needs of new technologies which caused the UK to slip behind in the competitive race; Teece (1981b) cites the UK iron and steel industry as a case in point, although a number of the large manufacturers, e.g. Consett, expanded overseas to secure ore supplies after 1870.

An examination of the two hundred largest firms in the USA, UK, Germany and Japan at the time of, or shortly after, the First World War, as set out in Table 5.7, reveals that in the newer and/or faster growing industrial sectors of chemical, petroleum, machinery, transport equipment and measuring instruments, there were 99 US firms, 56 UK, 91 German and 53 Japanese. By contrast, in the traditional

Table 5.7   *Percentage Distribution of Two Hundred Largest Manufacturing Firms in Selected Countries by Industry at the Time of the First World War*

	US (1917) %	UK (1919) %	Germany (1913) %	Japan (1913) %
Newer or Mainly Producer Good Industries	49.5	28.0	45.5	25.0
Chemical	10.0	5.5	13.0	11.5
Petroleum	11.0	1.5	2.5	3.0
Rubber	2.5	1.5	0.5	—
Machinery	10.0	4.0	10.5	2.0
Electrical Machinery	2.5	5.5	9.0	3.5
Transport and Equipment	13.0	10.0	9.5	4.5
Measuring Instruments	0.5	—	0.5	0.5
Older or Mainly Consumer Good Industries	50.0	70.5	54.1	74.5
Food and Tobacco	18.0	33.0	12.0	16.0
Textiles and Apparel	4.0	13.5	6.6	28.0
Lumber and Furniture	1.5	—	0.5	1.5
Paper and Printing	3.5	4.5	0.5	6.5
Leather	2.0	—	1.0	2.0
Stone, Clay and Glass	2.5	1.0	5.0	8.0
Primary Metal	14.5	17.5	24.5	10.5
Fabricated Metal	4.0	1.0	4.0	2.0
Miscellaneous	0.5	1.5	0.5	0.5
TOTAL	100.0	100.0	100.0	100.0

Source: Derived from data in Chandler (1981)

Changes in level structure of international production 109

sectors which led the industrial revolution a century earlier, viz. textiles and apparel, primary metals and fabricated metals, the respective figures were 45, 64, 70 and 81 (Chandler, 1981). Partly, of course, these statistics reflect comparative resource endowments of the countries in question; but, in retrospect, in the UK's case at least, they also suggest a failure of the economy to adapt its resource allocation to market needs and/or an inability of UK firms in the new sectors to organise themselves efficiently.

(b) 1919–38

During the inter-war years, the pace of technological advance slowed down, and what progress there was strongly favoured the US economy. For example, while patent applications in the USA doubled in the twenty years before 1914, between 1919 and 1939 they fell slightly. Major inventions, discoveries and innovations held up rather better; there were 148 in the former period and 127 in the latter. But of these later advances, the USA accounted for 60 per cent – while those originating from the UK fell to 12.5 per cent, those from France to 8.5 per cent and those from Germany to 13.0 per cent. Of the patents registered in the USA, those of UK residents rose from 1,288 in 1919 to 1,347 in 1939; the corresponding figures for Germany were 131 and 2,480; for France 363 and 634; and for Japan 56 and 57. The impressive growth in non-resident patenting in the USA at a time when the number of major innovations was falling may be explained by the growing interest of foreign firms in the US market, and the fact that many post-1918 patents were based on pre-war discoveries.

In spite of some notable inventions of the inter-war period – television, radar, the jet engine, colour photography, several manmade fibres and some antibiotic drugs, for example – these were mainly years of the development, adaptation and dissemination of the technological and organisational breakthroughs of the late nineteenth and early twentieth centuries. In consequence, one sees the most substantial increase in the share of the largest firms concentrated in these sectors; at the same time, the events of the 1920s and 1930s not only forced traditional industries to rationalise their structures and diversify into new lines of activity, but also prompted the growth industries to reorganise themselves around the new process innovations such as semi-automated production. For example, the number of vehicle and other transport equipment firms in the top 200 companies of the USA, UK, Germany and Japan fell from 74 in 1914–19 to 62 in 1930. This obviously reflected a more pronounced growth in the output of some firms than in that of the industry as a whole. Many

110   *The Growth of International Business*

companies in this era were moving through the later stages of their
product cycles initiated several years earlier, and were paying more
attention to reducing production costs, standardising product quality
and promoting new sales, particularly at the lower end of the market
where price sensitivity tends to increase as the product becomes
available to a larger number of consumers (the introduction of the
Model T by the Ford Motor Company in the UK is an example). The
growing threat from European MNEs to US technological hegemony
in some newer industrial sectors also led to more international cartel
arrangements than in pre-war days, e.g. in aluminium, electrical
equipment, and chemicals, which – in part at least – reduced the
incentive for FDI.

On the purely technological front then, the inter-war years saw
some restructuring of European industry but, for the most part, the
US continued to retain its advantage in the newer sectors. Throughout this period the proportion of investment in non-manufacturing
personnel and facilities by manufacturing firms grew as increases in
hierarchical efficiency and/or market failure enabled the boundaries
of the firm to be pushed further out. The need to gain control of
materials to service an industrial machine increasingly vulnerable to
disruptions in production flows, and the growing role of oil-based
products substituting for natural materials, also combined to prompt
further backward integration.

(c)   1945–60

The Second World War proved an important watershed for technological advances; indeed, it also speeded up the exploitation of
certain discoveries in the 1930s, which later provided the mainspring
of commercial expansion. Between 1945 and 1965 the number of
patents granted in the USA trebled, with the proportion awarded to
foreigners rising from 8.2 per cent to 19.9 per cent. However the
increase in patenting by foreigners occurred mainly in the latter half
of the 1950s; in the years immediately following the war the proportion hovered around the 10–12 per cent level. After a dramatic fall in
its share of non-resident patenting, West Germany made a no less
impressive recovery, and by 1960 had replaced the UK as the leading
grantee. By this time France had also regained her pre-war position,
while Japan was just emerging as a technological force. Most other
European nations had also recovered or surpassed their pre-war
shares.

No comparative data on R & D expenditure (as an alternative proxy
for technological capability) are available until the mid-1960s. In
1967 the USA still accounted for 68.7 per cent of the R & D under-

Changes in level structure of international production   111

taken by OECD countries, with the UK (7.3 per cent), West Germany (6.3 per cent), France (6.0 per cent) and Japan (4.7 per cent) a long way behind. One imagines that in 1960 the percentages for the first three countries would have been higher and that of Japan lower. The proportion of R & D expenditure to GNP was also higher in the USA than in other OECD countries in that year, as was the percentage of the population receiving tertiary education.

(d) 1960–78

The last two decades have seen the rate of innovation falling back again. The number of new patents granted in the USA remained more or less constant in the later 1960s, moved up in the early 1970s, slackened off in the mid-1970s and recovered at the end of the decade. In most industrial countries – Japan and West Germany being two exceptions – the share of GNP allocated to R & D fell in the late 1960s and 1970s; at the same time the US share of R & D in OECD countries dropped substantially, so that by 1977 it accounted for 49.5 per cent. By contrast, all European countries increased their shares – especially West Germany from 6.3 per cent to 11.9 per cent – but the most spectacular gain was that of Japan, from 4.7 per cent in 1967 to 13.6 per cent in 1977. Germany and Japan were then the leading foreign patent grantees in the USA with shares of 23.9 per cent and 27.7 per cent of all non-resident recipients; by contrast, the UK's share had fallen to its lowest point of 10.1 per cent. Most other European countries also lost out in the 1970s to Japan. However, as a whole, non-US sources accounted for two-fifths of all patents granted in the USA in 1979 – a three-fold increase since 1960 compared with only a 9 per cent increase in US patenting. The late 1970s also saw a sharp increase in patenting by some NICs, e.g. Brazil, Mexico, Hong Kong and Korea.

More recently, some researchers have attempted to compare the trade and innovatory performance of OECD countries. One of the most interesting findings is that not only is there an apparently close correlation between those manufacturing sectors in which there is a revealed comparative trading advantage (RCA) and those in which there is a revealed innovatory advantage – the latter being proxied by number of patents granted in the USA – but also that, in those industries in which both indices are greater than one, the propensity to engage in FDI is above average (Pavitt and Soete, 1981). Further, the patterns of the two sets of RCA differ between the leading industrialised countries in a way that is consistent with variations in their revealed comparative advantage of foreign direct assets, as has been demonstrated elsewhere (Dunning, 1981a).

Other data confirm that since the early 1960s the share of the leading US industrial enterprises in world output has fallen relative to that of other countries (Dunning and Pearce, 1981; Franko, 1978). Only in computers, measuring instruments and aerospace have US firms retained their dominance; elsewhere, the erosion of the USA's position has been generally greater in the technology-intensive sectors. It is also worth recalling that it is these industries which have increased their non-manufacturing personnel the most – both absolutely and relative to manufacturing personnel – and where the average size of firm has risen the most. On the other hand, product diversification has been no less pronounced in some of the non-research-intensive sectors.

Finally, statistics on the technological balance of payments of countries tell a similar story.[35] They point to a relative decline in the USA's position as measured by its rate of growth of payments for technology to foreigners (in the form of royalties, fees, etc.) exceeding that of its receipts, while in the case of Japan and Germany the reverse phenomenon has taken place. It should be observed, however, that these data are subject to many errors, and, in part at least, reflect the propensity of companies to invest overseas.

In summary, the last hundred years have seen an ebb and flow of technological advance with major changes in the distribution of technological capacity between countries. It would seem that the main thrusts of such advances have generally preceded those of FDI and that, although the time lag between many kinds of invention and their commercialisation is probably increasing, that between their embodiment in domestic and foreign production is falling (Mansfield, Teece and Romeo, 1979). The evidence also suggests that the changing geographical origin of the foreign direct capital stake mirrors fairly well changes in the distribution of technological capabilities. Innovations in information, and in organisational, transport and communications technologies have sometimes followed and sometimes preceded changes in product, process and materials technologies, but these too have been discontinuous. Here there have been three main breakthroughs: the first was necessitated by the new manufacturing technologies of the third quarter of the nineteenth century, including those of the railroad and the telegraph; the second was brought about by the advent of the jet aircraft and the computer immediately after the end of the Second World War; and the third by the advances in satellite communication, micro-chip technology and bio-engineering of the mid-1970s, the results of which are only just being felt. These initially benefited the economies which introduced them, but via FDI and other modalities of transfer quickly spread to impinge on firms of other nationalities. On the whole, however, large firms – and large MNEs in particular – seem to have been both the main instigators and the main beneficiaries of such advances.

5.5 MARKET FAILURE AND ORGANISATIONAL FORM

However much advances in technology may be a primary cause of the growth in world production over the last century, except in a most indirect sense they cannot satisfactorily explain the changes in the distribution of that output. In particular, they cannot explain, first, the increase in the average size of firms and the extent of product or process diversification and, second, the greater propensity of some firms to produce their output from a foreign rather than a domestic location. It is now generally recognised that the answer to the first question lies in the extent to which the market or administrative fiat is the preferred mechanism of resource (or property right) allocation. In the absence of any kind of market failure (in the sense that transaction costs in the intermediate goods market are zero and there are no externalities), the function of any firm would be limited to the production of a single and indivisible product, service or right. On the other hand, if market failure was complete, then only one firm (or a government agency) would produce all products, services and rights: apart from buying factor inputs from, and selling its final output to, households, all other transactions would be internalised.

In practice of course, both markets and hierarchies coexist, and most transactions are neither pure spot or pure administered. Richardson (1972) has emphasised that many activities between firms are cooperative rather than competitive; this is borne out by the growth of a wide variety of non-equity contractual arrangements concluded between firms of different nationality. For the purpose of this chapter, however, we shall consider these intermediate organisational forms as market transactions, even though *de facto* they have many of the characteristics of internalised cooperative agreements (Nicholas (1982b)).

In applying these concepts to explaining the growth of international production, it may be argued that, in the absence of inter-country transaction costs, all firms would conduct their buying and selling with firms producing in another country via the market; i.e. there would be no incentive for FDI. Therefore, *pari passu*, the growth of international production must be associated with increased market failure of the type of output and inputs in which firms wish to trade.

The literature surveyed in Chapter 1 suggests that firms may wish to internalise transactions for two reasons. First, they may believe that this is the best way to appropriate the economic rent in whatever property right is being bought or sold. Thus a firm might internalise the transfer of technology rather than license it, because it believes this organisational route will yield a greater net benefit (or the same benefit at less risk); or it may engage in international vertical integration in a resource-based sector so as to capture the full benefits of resource exploitation for itself – rather than share them with its seller. Second, the internalisation of a particular transaction may confer benefits to the internalising company external to that transaction. Most economies of joint production and lateral diversification arise in this way. In both cases, a firm will embrace new transactions as long as the marginal cost of so doing is covered by the marginal revenue derived from the two advantages of internalisation just outlined.

In the pages which follow, the analysis will be confined to the factors influencing the choice of organisation for engaging in transactions in or between a *given location*. The next section will discuss the appropriate location of production, given the organisational form. In other words, unlike some writers, e.g. Rugman (1981), I prefer not to consider the choice between exports and FDI as one primarily involving matters of governance.[36]

The proposition following from these observations is that the growth in international production is likely to be positively rather than negatively associated with market failure and the growing incentive of firms to internalise transactions for one or two of the reasons stated above. As in the case of ownership advantages arising from the possession of a superior intangible asset, so internalisation advantages will vary according to country-, sector- and firm-specific characteristics.

(a) 1870–1914

The period up to 1870 was one in which, for most international transactions undertaken by firms, and given the environment in which they were undertaken, markets operated reasonably well, while the costs of internalising such transactions were generally prohibitive. The former situation reflected the relative simplicity, homogeneity and easy transferability of most kinds of knowledge and technology, and the comparative ease at which most raw materials and foodstuffs could be obtained; the latter manifested the diseconomies of operating distant branch plants, as well as the technical and organisational limitations on the growth of hierarchies. During this period the ratio of the number of external transactions to gross output produced by a firm was generally high. Where market prospects abroad were favourable and exports were uneconomic, then, rather than set up branch plants, enterprises found it preferable to

Changes in level structure of international production 115

migrate, lock, stock and barrel. Examples assembled by Coram (1967) and Buckley and Roberts (1982) include the migration of Dundee capitalists and mill superintendents to Paterson, New Jersey in 1844, that of the Clark family from Lancashire to set up the machine-making of cotton thread in Newark, New Jersey in 1850, and that of Irish hosiery manufacturers establishing knitting mills in Needham, Massachusetts in the 1850s. Later, as a direct result of rising US tariffs and difficult trading conditions in the UK, there was a substantial exodus of the tin-plate industry from South Wales, the silk industry from Macclesfield, the lace industry from Nottingham and the cutlery industry from Sheffield.[37]

In the period after 1870 several events occurred which dramatically affected the organisation of business. These included the evolution of managerial capitalism, the opening up of the US and European Continents by the railroad, improvements in intercontinental sea transport and advances in communication techniques. These events made possible the translation of single-unit into multi-unit enterprises, which in turn caused the number of transactions undertaken within firms to increase, and those between firms to decrease. At the same time, partly as a consequence of these developments, partly as a result of the increasing cost and complexity of new technology and the widening disparity of the technological capabilities between countries, and partly because of their growing need to protect themselves against the risk of disruptions to supplies of inputs affecting efficient scheduling and distributor efficiency,[38] firms found the market a less attractive mode of exchange. The latter years of the nineteenth century saw an increasing ability of firms to cope with, and a greater need to initiate, hierarchical methods of organising transactions.

From the perspective of the foreign activities of firms, it may be expected that companies which find it economic to internalise transactions in their home country would also do so abroad, i.e. those producing high technology or branded consumer goods where quality control is important. But in some cases, especially with supply-oriented direct investments in primary products, there was little experience of domestic production, e.g. investment in tropical fruits by companies located in temperate climates, and in minerals by manufacturing companies in the consuming countries. In such cases the choice between licensing (or sub-contracting) a foreign supplier or backward integration rests on the ability of the supplier to supply the product at the right price and quality at the right time, the risk of being dependent on an external source of supply, and the competitive strategy of the purchasing company. In these and other respects, primary product markets in the nineteenth and early twentieth centuries were becoming increasingly imperfect; hence the growth of FDI in mines and plantations.[39]

But country-specific factors are no less important in influencing the modality of international resource transfer (Dunning, 1982). As a general rule, market failure is likely to be greatest when one of the parties to the exchange is located in a poorer country. Partly because of this, and partly because most MNE activity in developing countries was directed to the primary product sector, non-resident resource transfer tended, even in the late nineteenth century, to be more internalised than in developed countries. The only exception was where host government policy was directed against inward investment, and this was unusual at the time. It has been shown that, in some cases, metropolitan governments deliberately tried to limit the ability of their own foreign colonies to develop markets for certain goods; in other words, imperialism fostered its own form of internalisation.

Unfortunately, data limitations do not enable us to test these ideas systematically. We do know, however, from the work of Svedberg (1978) that the proportion of the total investment accounted for by direct investment was higher in developing than in developed countries in 1914. It would seem also, from business histories, as well as case studies of particular sectors and countries, that externalised technology and managerial transfers were more common within Western Europe or between Europe and the USA than between the USA and Europe and the USA and the rest of the world. One other relevant fact is that almost all the cartels and cooperative agreements concluded prior to 1914 (i.e. where ownership advantages were traded between independent firms) were concluded between European firms – although sometimes these had very similar characteristics to internalised resource transference.

There is also some suggestion that the motives for internalisation differed between home countries. The UK manufacturing MNEs, for example, which were strongly oriented towards the supply of consumer goods (Stopford, 1974), were prompted more by the advantages of vertical selling than the US MNEs whose particular internalising needs were less to do with the protection of the quality of branded products and the assurance of adequate distributive outlets, than with the problems of international technology markets. According to Nicholas (1982a), of 119 UK MNEs giving reasons for their direct investment abroad between 1879 and 1939, 21 per cent stated 'to sell vertically', only 3 per cent less than those who put 'technology' as a factor.[40] Backward integration was mentioned by 15 per cent of UK firms, and the tariff factor, or market protection, by 23 per cent of firms. A cursory examination of the list of 50 large US MNEs established before 1914, contained in Wilkins' classic work (1970), would suggest that the internalisation of technology and the economies of synergy already gained through domestic multiplant operations were a more important consideration.[41]

(ii) 1919–38

Comparatively little change in the conditions affecting the form of international involvements occurred in the inter-war years. What data we have suggest that direct investment weathered the economic vicissitudes of the period much better than portfolio investment. We also know that the growth of foreign production by established MNEs increasingly took the form of product, process or market diversification. As a result, the typical foreign affiliate was translated from a monocentric to a polycentric entity (Wilkins, 1974a). During these years foreign affiliates began to assume an identity of their own. Sometimes this was largely autonomous of the parent company, but in other cases it was a direct consequence of further internalisation of markets by the parent company. At the same time, a lot of new MNE entrants appeared on the scene. Continual improvements in the organisation and management of firms[42] and in transport and communications technology also aided hierarchical transactions, as did the growth of markets for the kind of goods which MNEs, as a result of their integrated network of international activities, were best able to supply. This was a period in which both the average size and the number of internal transactions of firms increased sharply. It was also one which saw the growth of international cartels in the secondary sector. Although some of these associations were of pre-war origin, they flourished in the less robust economic climate of the inter-war years. The outcome was that to prevent destructive competition between oligopolists – particularly the inter-penetration of markets via international production – some kind of market sharing mechanism was thought desirable. These were also years in which governments, on the whole, chose not to exercise strong anti-trust or anti-monopoly policies.

It is worth observing that the propensity of firms to choose one form of involvement rather than another again varied by sector, country and enterprise. There were, for example, few cartels among motor vehicle producers; this was a rapid growth industry in which the technological and marketing advantages of US MNEs were particularly strong. Each firm produced a limited range of products, there were substantial economies of scale, and the need to closely schedule the flow of inputs and outputs were especially noticeable.

By contrast, in the electrical equipment industry and some branches of the chemical and heavy engineering industries, where cartels were more common, these conditions were less in evidence. Moreover, contractual technological exchanges were favoured by the recovering large companies of Western Europe – particularly those of German origin – as a way of penetrating USA markets without a substantial capital investment (which also explains why joint ventures were more common among European firms investing in the USA than *vice versa*). During this time there was also a reduction in some kinds of vertical direct investment as new international commodity markets were set up. On the other hand, in those primary sectors in which large indivisible costs and high barriers to entry kept the number of firms small, and the need to protect against variations in output was especially marked (e.g. oil, tropical fruit, rubber and several non-ferrous metals), MNEs tightened their hierarchical control.

(c)   1945–60

The conditions in the third period covered by our study were dramatically different. First, as we have seen, the USA dominated the supply of new technology for much of the period. Second, it was a period of substantial economic expansion – or recovery in the case of Europe and Japan. Third, these were years when a lot of new idiosyncratic and non-codifiable technology was produced, the market for which was extremely imperfect (see Chapter 4). Fourth, antitrust policy – particularly in the USA – made both domestic and international mergers or agreements much more difficult to conclude than in pre-war days. Fifth, the advent of the jet plane and the computer initiated a new generation of organisational advances which reduced hierarchical transaction costs. Sixth, while for the early part of the period at least international markets of almost all kinds were in disarray, the underlying environment for direct investment and trade, created at Bretton Woods and Havana, was both more congenial and stable than that which guided policy makers in the inter-war years. Add to these factors the type of sectors in which world output was expanding the fastest, the countries which were most eager to attract foreign entrepreneurship, technology and capital, and/or offered the best prospects to MNEs, and the relative unattractiveness of alternative routes of resource transfer, and it is not surprising that international production rose so markedly in these years.

This period also saw a continuation of the pre-war trend to a more integrated product and market structure on the part of established MNEs. At the same time, a reading of many country studies of FDI, published in the late 1950s and early 1960s suggests that rationalised production as we know it today was still the exception rather than the rule within the manufacturing sector. Certainly intra-firm manufacturing imports and exports by MNEs were a small fraction of what they are today and, for the most part, there was little specialisation between parent and subsidiary. Indeed the early field studies of Dunning (1958), Safarian (1966) and Brash (1966) all suggest that, in the main, US manufacturing subsidiaries were truncated replicas of their parent organisations, and, after a learning period, tended to operate with the minimum of parental interference. In other words, the benefits of foreign production to the investing company were perceived in terms of the economic rent earned on the assets transferred rather than in any synergistic gains to the parent system. Because of the very rapid growth of new affiliates – often set up to overcome tariff barriers or other import controls – monocentric foreign production flourished. Even in 1973, 62 per cent of over 9,400 MNEs surveyed by the European Commission had only one foreign affiliate, compared with less than 3 per cent which had more than 20 affiliates (Commission of the European Communities, 1976).

This leads us to a general observation. While the setting up of a foreign affiliate may be likened to that of a branch plant of the parent company in the home country, it has also some of the characteristics of a *de novo* firm. This being so, a purely Chandlerian explanation (e.g. Chandler, 1977) of the growth of a large enterprise within a country may not be wholly pertinent to the decision to undertake foreign production. This is not only because many MNEs are quite small firms,[43] but because a foreign investment decision, unlike its domestic counterpart, is often prompted by the need to protect an *existing* market, i.e. to relocate rather than to expand output. If, then, we include all kinds of barriers to trade associated with traversing space between two countries, quite a lot of manufacturing investment over the last hundred years – but especially in the inter-war and early post-war periods – originated in this way. For example, some 75 per cent of the UK and US MNEs operating in the mid-1970s first set up outside their home countries in the post-1945 period. The proportion is probably nearer 85 per cent in the case of German firms and 95 per cent in the case of Japanese firms.

Both in the capital-intensive resource-based and technology-intensive manufacturing sectors there is some evidence of the bunching of new activities by rival MNE oligopolists in this period (Knickerbocker, 1973). Vernon (1981) argues that this behaviour reflects a form of risk-minimising strategy, which in a wider context helps to explain much of the integrating imperative among MNEs. At the same time, capital investment entails a risk of its own, which, when it outweighs the risk-reducing aspects of internalisation, may lead firms to prefer a cooperative or contractual route of exploiting foreign markets.

(d)   1960–78

The last two decades have seen a further considerable change in the organisation of international resource transfer, the net result of which has been to decrease the role of multinational hierarchies in some sectors and in some countries, and increase it in others. Supporting the former tendency has been a marked improvement in some international markets for transacting resources. Reinforcing this fait has been the voluntary divestment by MNEs or enforced use of the market route by host governments in many primary industries and some key secondary and tertiary industries. So international production, initially designed to exploit a unique technological advantage which has eroded over time, has tended to fall, except in countries where user capacity is still inadequate. By contrast, in fast innovating sectors, where technology is idiosyncratic, complex and not easily codified, the MNE continues to flourish. However, both these phenomena are parts of the same story and fit in well with the ideas contained in the product or industry technology cycles. Where MNEs act primarily as a transferor of assets and a tutor in the use of these and other inputs, their role in supplying any particular asset is likely to be a temporary one. In such cases, their permanent presence can only be explained by the continual innovation of new ownership advantages. Hence, as was said earlier, one would expect the outward direct investment of a country to be related to its rate of innovation, both absolutely and compared with that of its competitors. It is also likely to be allied to the technological capacity of the countries which it services. Thus it is quite consistent for US MNEs to reduce their stake in the French pharmaceutical sector, while Hong Kong investors increase theirs in the Sri Lankan textiles industry.

At the same time, changes in environmental risks have influenced the propensity of firms to internalise their international markets. On the one hand, the threat of interruption to oil and other raw material supplies has encouraged supplying MNEs to cut off the unintegrated processors they previously supplied. On the other, the added uncertainty of a loss of sunk capital (through nationalisation) has prompted partial or full divestment of 100 per cent affiliates (Vernon, 1981).

But quite apart from the ebb and flow of these kinds of international production, the most marked development of the last fifteen years has been the growth of the multi-divisional form of affiliates of MNEs. This is what Wilkins (1974) calls the third phase in MNE development: the motive for foreign production is not to gain the economic rent which marketable advantages can earn, but to capture the economies of integration and diversification arising from such production. Such ownership advantages are different in kind from the first type, partly because they accrue to the parent system rather than any one of its affiliates and partly because they are not transferable outside the MNE, i.e. there is no market for them.[44] This multi-divisional form may result in rationalised production between a group of affiliates within a region, or between parent companies and a number of affiliates.

Such rationalisation tends to take two main forms. The first is a reorganisation of a group of largely import-substituting activities in a number of countries which were initially designed to meet domestic needs. If and when the markets are large enough and/or become integrated, then the MNE may find it economic to pursue a different strategy, based upon the economies of product specialisation and intra-group trading; e.g. instead of each affiliate replicating the other's products, it specialises in only one product with which it supplies the markets of all countries. Secondly, corporate integration may take the form of export platform manufacturing investment or downstream processing of primary products, where the division of labour tends to be between stages of production and between parent and subsidiaries, and is based on international cost differences.

The expansion of these and similar forms of MNE activity has been made possible both by a reduction in trade barriers between particular countries and by the continued improvements in hierarchical efficiency. However, in some cases (particularly within the EEC) what, in fact, has happened is that the MNE has transferred a system of organisation to the group of affiliates located in a particular region. It is less the prospective gains from internalised transactions between parent and subsidiary which has led to new foreign production and more the gains from internalised transactions between the individual subsidiaries and their regional headquarters. In this case, synergistic advantages gained in the multi-divisional form in the parent company may be usefully replicated at a regional level; examples include the benefits of centralised purchasing, the use of sophisticated accounting systems, the reduction of exchange risks, and the ability to move top personnel between affiliates.[45]

Again, one notices differences in the forms of international economic involvement both between home countries and between home and host countries. Very often these reflect industry- or firm-specific characteristics. Reference has already been made to the interdependent behaviour of MNE oligopolists. In the latter 1960s and early 1970s this was noticeable in the way in which technology was diffused in the semi-conductor industry and the drug industry

122   *The Growth of International Business*

(Lake, 1979). Davidson and McFetridge (1979) have suggested that international transfers of technology are more likely to be internalised if the transferor already operates an affiliate in the recipient country, and if previous transfers have been internalised. *Inter alia*, this might explain the greater propensity of Japanese firms to conclude licensing agreements with foreign motor vehicle firms, rather than establish their own manufacturing affiliates. On the other hand, the preference of US manufacturing firms for 100 per cent ownership of their affiliates may be due to their much greater degree of international product and process integration. This, in turn, may be a function of the extent of MNE manufacturing activity; Japan is still mainly at the monocentric stage of its international production. Moveover, as Mason (1980) has suggested, the main synergistic advantages between Japanese parent and affiliate companies are captured via the 100 per cent stake of the major trading companies in their foreign subsidiaries which, in turn, often have close financial and operating ties with foreign manufacturing companies.

It would seem, then, that in the last twenty years or so, US and some European MNEs have come of age; and that, at least in some areas of the world, their foreign operations have increasingly come to resemble their domestic operations and their growth patterns to follow broadly similar paths. The convergence of international consumer and producer tastes is accelerating this trend.

It is noteworthy that, although since around the mid-1960s the share of US direct investment has been steadily falling, it is the established US MNEs that have most pursued a Chandlerian strategy towards international production. And in the 1970s there was some evidence that European firms, particularly with respect to their activities in the US, were undertaking growth for similar reasons, although here the associations sought were often of a conglomerate rather than a horizontal or vertical kind. In a study of the growth of US FDI between 1962 and 1968 based on Internal Revenue data, Kopits (1979) estimated that the share of conglomerate diversification rose from 14.1 per cent to 22.3 per cent. It is possible, of course, that such diversification may be undertaken to exploit imperfections in the capital and foreign exchange markets. However, such opportunities, which do not normally occur within a country, may also open up new channels for investment, and thus be viable organisational avenues of growth. At the same time, the new MNEs which accounted for an increasing share of international production in the 1970s did not, in general, integrate their foreign and their domestic operations (although at a macro level there is reason to suppose Japanese foreign and domestic investments are more interrelated than, for example, their US counterparts (Kojima, 1980). Finally, with innovations in trans-border information flows, some of the obstacles to hierarchical growth are being further reduced. Such innovations of course, do not only benefit MNEs. For example, the introduction of international reservation systems for hotels has meant that this particular advantage may be sold on a contractual basis rather than within a multinational hotel system, thereby reducing the need for MNE systems (Dunning and McQueen, 1981). This is an example of where a particular ownership advantage has become widely codified and specialist companies established to sell it; some management consultancy firms operate in the same way.

The previous paragraphs suggest that changes in the advantages of alternative organisational forms for transferring ownership advantages across national boundaries have played a significant role in affecting the level and patterns of international production over the last hundred years. In particular, the internalisation model explains why in those sectors where the market for transacting either inputs or the outputs (including intermediate outputs) has improved the contribution of the MNE *qua* MNE,[46] has fallen. But in other sectors, where ownership advantages have become more idiosyncratic or dependent on the integration of interrelated activities, it has become even more important.[47] We have also argued that, while Chandlerian-type theories may not always be the most useful explanation of the initial foreign investment decision by firms, the growth of established subsidiaries of MNEs, and particularly those located in large integrated markets, is increasingly following the pattern of large domestic firms. Indeed, the generally faster rate of growth of international production *vis-à-vis* domestic production may be reasonably attributed to the additional incentive to integration which is consequential upon the diversification of production facilities outside national boundaries.[48]

5.6 LOCATIONAL DETERMINANTS

Even accepting the superior ownership advantages of firms of one nationality over those of another and the incentive to internalise these advantages, it is a prerequisite for international production that it must be more profitable (or otherwise in their best interests) for firms to undertake at least some of their productive activities outside their home countries. Similarly, a growth in international production might (though not necessarily will) reflect a shift of the locational advantages in favour of foreign countries *vis-à-vis* the home country, or an increase in the type of production which favours a foreign rather than a domestic location.

The determinants of the siting of international production have been well set out in the literature (e.g. Vernon, 1974). They include all those variables likely to influence the location of activities within a country, and others which specifically arise as a result of producing in different sovereign territories and/or currency areas. Considering, then, a particular siting decision in isolation from the rest of its activities, a firm contemplating foreign production may behave differently from one considering setting up a new plant within its home country, either because the values of the first group of variables (e.g. transport, labour, material, etc. costs, market characteristics, behaviour of competitors, etc.) are different in the two cases, or because the second group (e.g. tariffs, tax rates) are more significant.

This much is fairly straightforward. Where it is possible to supply a market from alternative sites, the entry of firms into foreign production may be solely explained by a shift in the relative attractions of these sites.

In the context of the OLI paradigm, changes in the value of locational variables have other effects. For example, international diversification of activities may itself offer its own ownership advantage. For example, an MNE, by its presence in different countries may be better able to monitor inputs and outputs or to engage in international specialisation and risk spreading (Rugman, 1979). On the other hand, differences in the efficiency of markets, e.g. for technology and primary products, and the uncertainty attached to market failure and changes in government fiat, may lead a firm to internalise activities in a foreign country that it may not feel it necessary to do at home. But it should be noted that the interaction between O, L and I variables is not involved in all locational decisions – particularly those involving *de novo* international production. Neither is it helpful to think of transfer costs as a kind of market failure associated with distance which firms internalise by switching from exports to local production.

The contention of this chapter is that the growth of the MNE has seen a gradual shift in locational determinants from those associated with the production and transfer costs of a single activity to those to do with economising transaction costs or maximising benefits external to that activity, but internal to the MNE, through the appropriate deployment over space of a group of interrelated activities. In such cases, the variables likely to influence MNEs in their selection of international sites will depend less on the effect which they have on the profitability of the affiliates, and more on that of the enterprise as a whole.

While investment incentives, tariffs, differences in labour costs, economies of plant size, etc. may effect *de novo* FDI, as the degree of

Changes in level structure of international production   125

multinationalisation intensifies, so the role of other locational variables becomes more decisive (Dunning, 1972). These include the
general climate for international investment and trade (e.g. the extent
of regional integration), the efficiency of markets for intermediate
products transferred across national boundaries, the international
market structure in which MNEs compete, and the presence, or
otherwise, of economies of plant scale. One result of such a shift is
seen in the growth of both intra-firm and intra-industry trade and
FDI (Dunning, 1981b; Krugman, 1979, 1981). Let us now review
some of these changes in an historical context.

(a)   1870–1914

Earlier in this chapter it was shown that before the First World War
FDI was mainly directed either to natural resource exploitation (particularly so in the non-industrialised countries) or import-substitution
(mainly in Europe, the USA, China and Japan). Obviously a necessary condition for the former kind of investment is the presence of the
resources, but other variables (e.g. exploration and extraction costs,
the extent to which it is economic to engage in secondary processing,
marketing – including internal and external transport costs – host
government policy towards the foreign ownership of natural
resources, and the demand for the products incorporating the
resources) might be no less important, particularly in the case of
ubiquitous primary products. Most of the early expansion in MNE
activity in mines, oil wells and plantations was prompted by the prospects of market growth in home countries,[49] together with a gradual
reduction in the production and marketing costs of the primary product. And, as stated in the previous sections, the fact that the ownership of these facilities in the host country was in foreign hands
reflected both the superior access to technical knowledge, capital and
marketing facilities possessed by the foreign firms and their belief
that by internalising the use of their knowledge they could best capture the economic rents on these assets. The early vertical integration
of the banana industry (see Chapter 7) is an excellent example of how
MNEs dominated the development of this sector. But it is also worth
observing that for a variety of reasons, including the colonial domination of many host countries, there were few restrictions placed on the
ownership of natural resources by foreigners. The conditions for the
growth of such investment, the end products of which were usually
free of tariffs or import controls by recipient countries, were then
exceptionally favourable in the years leading up to the First World
War.

The literature suggests that import-substituting investment is determined by such variables as the size of the local market, the relevant stage of the product cycle, comparative input costs, transport costs, government policy, plant economies of scale, and the extent to which the firm needs to be close to its input or finished goods markets (e.g. because of differences in the availability of raw materials, customer tastes, local laws, etc.) *Ceteris paribus*, because of additional communication costs between parent and subsidiary (Hirsch, 1976), firms may have a natural preference for exporting rather than for foreign production; this is enhanced when there are additional political and economic risks in producing abroad. However, some of these costs are incurred mainly at the time of entry, and the marginal costs of expansion may be small. Moreover, as we have seen, there may be compensating risk-spreading benefits from foreign investment. Further, it cannot be assumed that a foreign environment is always less uncertain (or the behaviour of affiliates more constrained) than that of domestic affiliates; this, for example, is the case of some investment by Third World MNEs today.

The history of foreign manufacturing production before the First World War strongly suggests that artificial barriers to exports, in the form of tariffs and other import controls, were perceived at the time to be the most important locational determinant for the initial foreign investment by MNEs; but that, with the benefit of hindsight, many firms would accept that these affected the timing of foreign participation rather than its form, as, even in the absence of trade barriers, this could be justified on other grounds. It is quite clear that there was a perceived threshold for FDI in the nineteenth century, which was probably higher than was justified due to lack of information on the part of firms of the economics of producing outside their home environment; also that the fear of losing an existing or prospective market, rather than any aggressive marketing strategy, was the main stimulus for such investment.

Contrary to popular belief, the forty years prior to the First World War were not ones of undiluted free trade; indeed, both in Continental Europe and in the USA the infant industry argument dominated international economic policy. At the same time, many world markets were expanding rapidly and offered attractive prospects to firms possessing the ability to supply them. Often too, for reasons described earlier, the newer industries of the era soon became the growth sectors dominated by international oligopolists, whose defensive strategy undoubtedly accelerated the switch from exports to foreign production (Knickerbocker, 1973; Graham, 1978). In due course the innovations of the last quarter of the nineteenth century were disseminated and the products arising from them became more standardised and price elastic. Differences in production costs, and transfer costs between home and host countries then became a more important determinant of corporate strategy.

The product cycle theory of international production is an excellent explanation of this kind of investment and why its extent and pattern varies between countries. *Ceteris paribus*, such production is likely to originate from wealthy industrialised countries and be initially directed to well populated economies following one or two steps behind in the development process. The pattern reflects the comparative innovating advantages of the home countries, their psychic distance from other main markets, the size of the domestic relative to the export market, and the strategy and organisational approach adopted by firms to their foreign activities and international production in particular. Thus, even before 1914, the overseas production/export ratio was considerably higher for US firms than for European firms, and varied considerably between industrial sectors.

We conclude that locational factors were important in explaining the growth in international production relative to exports in the forty years before the First World War, in spite of the reduction in transport costs and the economies of centralised production made possible by new technologies.

(b) 1914–38

In the inter-war years locational advantages continued to shift in favour of international production; indeed, in the case of import substituting investment they were probably *the* main factor leading to what growth there was in FDI. Between 1914 and 1939 the ratio of the stock of FDI to the value of world trade rose substantially. Although part of this rise was accounted for by foreign subsidiaries existing in 1914, there were a large number of new ventures set up, particularly in the 1930s.

During these years, too, an increasing proportion of MNE activity was accounted for by US firms; in the manufacturing sector this more than quadrupled in the years 1914–43, and more than four-fifths of US MNE activity was located in Canada and Europe. There was also some syndicate direct investment in Europe – especially in the 1920s (Teichova, 1974; Franko, 1976). Contemporary empirical studies, e.g. by Southard (1931), Marshall, Southard and Taylor (1936) and the Royal Institute of International Affairs (1937), suggest that most market-oriented investment in developed countries was defensive in character; in Canada, Marshall, Southard and Taylor regard tariffs as 'of overwhelming importance in the branch plant movement' (p.

201). By contrast, the same writers estimate that only between 15 per cent and 20 per cent of Canadian–American branch factories owed their existence 'in any measurable extent to transportation savings' while the factory costs of US companies in Canada were 'in most cases definitely higher than those in the parent company' (p. 207).

In Europe, Southard (1931) concluded that US firms were prompted to establish branch plants mainly by the need to customise goods (particularly consumer goods) to local tastes, by savings on transatlantic transport costs, especially for bulky or fragile articles, and by non-tariff barriers, e.g. local government purchasing policies and 'buy at home' sales pitches. They also sought to forestall the entry of European firms into US markets through the takeover of European companies. These, and other reasons were to figure in the motives influencing post-Second World War investors, as recorded by Brash (1966 – Australia), Safarian (1966 – Canada), Stubenitsky (1970 – Netherlands), Deane (1970 – New Zealand) and Forsyth (1972 – Scotland) and summarised by Dunning (1973).[50]

It is perhaps worth repeating that, rather more than its national branch plant counterpart, the foreign plant may simply replace part of the domestic production by the parent firm.[51] However, beyond a certain point, foreign production may lead to additional growth, particularly where MNEs already ensconced in foreign countries are instrumental in persuading their hosts to introduce or increase import controls. Research also reveals that once abroad – and indeed in the act of going overseas – US MNEs may have substantially different policy objectives to American exporters (e.g. *vis-à-vis* their domestic operations). In other words, foreign production may bring with it internalising economies which exporting does not. Other studies reveal instances when exports and foreign production are directly complementary to each other (Horst, 1974).

Supply-based investments (in mining and plantations) recorded a mixed performance in the inter-war period. Due to the rapidly increasing demand for oil, both US and European MNEs expanded their investments in crude oil production. Due also to the growing popularity of tropical fruits, US investment in banana and pineapple plantations rose sharply, but in the recession of the 1930s these were cut back sharply. Mining investments rose only slightly, however, except in some of the newer metals, nitrates, etc. As mentioned earlier, the inter-war years saw the establishment of several mineral cartels, although the non-members of these cartels tried to develop alternative materials (e.g. French and German producers switched to aluminium and developed their own bauxite interests in France, Italy and Eastern Europe). There was also some mineral investment in European colonies, while investments in rubber plantations in

Changes in level structure of international production 129

Malaysia and Liberia also expanded. Generally speaking, there was little secondary processing activity by MNEs in the developing countries in this period and few attempts by governments to disinternalise investments in resources. But in the later 1930s new commodity and futures markets began to emerge, which were later to erode the advantages of vertical integration, e.g. in rubber and tea. Reddaway, Potter and Taylor (1968) observe that by the late 1950s there was very little backward integration by UK firms in the raw materials sectors which they had dominated half a century earlier.

(c) 1945–60

The early post-war period favoured the expansion of all kinds of international commerce, and international production in particular. The reasons were both 'defensive' and 'aggressive', and market- and supply-oriented investments were similarly affected. By 1960 it was estimated that the value of international production was approaching that of world trade; and in the case of some countries, e.g. the USA, UK, Switzerland and the Netherlands, it was considerably higher. In the following decade the growth in the FDI stake outpaced that of trade by half as much again. During the 1950s the USA reached the peak of her economic hegemony, but, because of a world shortage of dollars, US firms were obliged to produce overseas to sell their products. There were also push factors at work – such as the growing differential in labour costs between the USA and other industrialised countries, and a revival of American antitrust policy which checked one avenue of domestic growth. Anxious to be the leaders in exploiting their new ownership advantages in foreign markets, US oligopolists in the pharmaceutical, electrical goods, computer, industrial instrument and other industries were quick to establish branch plants in Europe, Canada, Australia and some wealthier Latin American economies. Again, investing firms initially perceived these ventures less as an expansion of their domestic activities as a replacement for part of them.

Much post-war UK direct investment in Canada and Australia was of this kind and there was a certain pattern to it. First a sales and service facility was set up to promote exports; then came local production using imported materials and components, and this was followed by production with some local components, and so on. This process was frequently observed in the 1960s in both UK and US manufacturing investments. Again, rising markets, often protected by import controls, were the main inducements, together with the fear of losing markets to competitors. The abandonment of interna-

130 The Growth of International Business

tional cartel arrangements led several UK firms to set up in the USA, while others saw such investment as the best way to obtain access to American technology.[52]

The recovery of Western Europe, the move towards economic integration there and in Latin America, and the introduction of export processing zones heralded a new era for manufacturing MNEs and fundamentally affected their production and locational strategies. In the later 1960s and 1970s rationalised investment was the fastest growing sector of MNE activity, and the one which caused host countries almost as much concern as resource-based investment had done previously.

The rapid growth in industrial output following the end of the Second World War led to an unprecedented demand for raw materials to sustain that output, and increasingly the main industrial countries were forced to seek new outlets of supply. For reasons exactly parallel to those prompting backward integration in the nineteenth century, large firms purchasing primary products for processing and fabrication sought to internalise their outlets. So the surge outwards to supply-oriented investment was in direct proportion to the growth in manufacturing output and domestic incomes in the industrialised North. At the same time, there was growing concern among the supplying countries, on both political and economic grounds, about the increasing presence of foreign firms in key natural resource sectors. This was not just a matter of the ability of such firms to extract monopoly rents; much more important was their control over the way in which local resources were used, their rate of exploitation and to whom, on what terms, and by what means they were sold. There was also disquiet about the ways some MNEs earned (or were thought to earn) their economic rent, e.g. by manipulation of transfer pricing, which were not always possible to detect or control. Many of these costs of FDI were attributed to the internalising of transactions between MNEs and their affiliates.

The story about the reactions of host countries to these events is well known. In the present context, the main effect was to encourage or enforce divestments by MNEs in many resource-based sectors, and to change the terms in which others – particularly new investors – were allowed to be involved. Public fiat replaced firm fiat, while at the same time, due to the increasing competition among MNEs and the growth of indigenous firms, markets for many products became less imperfect. The consequence was a decline in the relative importance of supply-based foreign investments in the 1960s and 1970s, except in certain resource-rich developed countries, e.g. Canada, Australia and the UK (for North Sea Oil), and in countries in the Far East which appeared to have the same political persuasion as the main investors. It was in this region that Japanese investors made their first major thrust in the 1960s, and even today they have a much larger stake in resource-based investment than either their US or European counterparts. These investments are closely controlled, either directly or indirectly, by Japanese industrial or trading companies.

(d) 1960–78

Let us now turn to the major locational development of the past two decades. Partly as a result of the enlargement of markets, occasioned *inter alia* by rising living standards and regional economic integration, and partly as a consequence of changes in production and marketing strategies on the part of MNEs, the factors influencing the spatial distribution of MNE activity in manufacturing and associated activities has dramatically changed. It now rests less on the kind of determinants associated with either a single import-substitution or supply-oriented investment and more on the appropriate locations for a group of interrelated activities. In this respect there are considerable similarities between inter-regional specialisation within a large market area and international specialisation of activity. There are also parallels with the explanation of the location of similar activities across national boundaries but under separate ownership which give rise to intra-industry trade.

The best illustration of this form of FDI is that of US MNEs in the EEC since around 1960. To capture the economies of scale and centralisation of production, but to take advantage of a free trade area, firms which previously were truncated replicas of their parent companies, each producing similar products for individual markets without trade, have found it economic to specialise in particular products and processes for all markets in the region, and to trade these products across national boundaries. The choice of location and the effect of the rationalisation on the totality and distribution of the capital stake is partly determined by the disposition of existing capacity, partly by production and transaction costs, and partly by country-specific variables, e.g. the availability of skilled labour and materials, transport and communication costs, consumer tastes, government regulations, and so on (Dunning, 1972; Hood and Young, 1980). The result is a balance of activities which is based as much on the comparative resource endowments of a country as on the absolute advantages offered by particular locations. In this respect, companies may behave as countries. The allocation of the activities of companies like N. V. Philips, Honeywell, Ford and International Harvester, in the EEC is based upon this type of strategy. It helps create substantial economies of integration, and can usually only be successfully achieved through internalisation of resource transfers. This, in turn, is only viable if there are no restrictions on trade in goods, and policies towards international direct investment are reasonably harmonised.

In Europe, and to a lesser extent in Latin America, the kind of trade associated with this kind of rationalised investment is not obviously based upon differences in the distribution of factor endowments in the classical or neoclassical sense. But in other parts of the world, another type of rationalised investment – the export platform type – is of this kind. Perhaps the most rapidly growing activity of manufacturing MNEs in East Asia, Mexico and some parts of Southern Europe is to take advantage of cheap, plentiful and well motivated labour to produce those products or processes which require such a resource. The main locational impetus giving rise to this has been the growth of manufacturing capacity in a number of NICs, and the generally liberal attitude of these countries to export oriented FDI. It is here where fiscal incentives have been the most generous and most significant in influencing locational choice.

It is worth observing that much of the first and some of the second kind of rationalised production reflect a form of *growth* of foreign participation rather than an *initial* means of entry. Essentially they embrace 'specialisation within diversification', and the benefits realised are entirely those of scale and integration. Some of these economies may be specific to geographical diversification, i.e. those to do with intra-firm trade, and those arising from imperfections in exchange and capital markets and differences in the tax treatment of corporations. These strongly suggest that the common ownership of spatially separated production units *does* influence the way in which resources are allocated.[53]

The way that economic integration affects the structure of ownership of firms in a common market as well as their location has not been fully explored in the literature. Like other influences on a firm's growth to which we have given scant attention in this chapter, it underlines the interdependence between the different elements of growth. Neither a purely technological nor an organisational approach to growth is sufficient in itself, and the significance of each varies very greatly according to structural factors. And while in some cases locational theory may be used to explain why a firm chooses to internalise its ownership specific advantages across rather than within national boundaries, in many cases – and especially with rationalised production – there are additional integrative gains which affect the extent and pattern of its activities.

There is one other point which should be made. The 1970s have seen a gradual liberalisation of the attitudes of many governments toward both outward and inward direct investment. At the same time, as a result of the learning process of the previous two decades, policies with respect to entry, performance and exit conditions of foreign firms have become more enlightened. Partly too, the world recession has made countries more aware of the potential gains of inward investment; but it has also caused MNEs to cut back on some of their foreign operations to protect their domestic interests. This has been particularly noticeable in the case of US MNEs and, in part, is a reflection of the devaluation of the dollar. By contrast, the expansion of European direct investment in the USA illustrates the increasing profitability of producing in rather than exporting to the USA. Again, this shift in the pattern of international production is a location-substituting kind rather than growth-oriented. To make things more complicated, part of the investment classified as FDI in official statistics may not really be that at all but rather portfolio investment, as there is no *de facto* supervision exercised over the capital exported.

It may be concluded then, that for most of the past one hundred years, foreign production has been of an import-substituting or resource-exploitative kind. As far as the initial entry decision is concerned, quite a lot of the former was a response to changes in the profitability of supplying a foreign market from a foreign rather than a domestic base, and quite a lot of the latter a response to the inability of markets to guarantee a regular flow of inputs of the required quality and at the right price. Once established, however, the growth of affiliates of MNEs became influenced by other factors to do with exploiting the economies of geographical diversification. In the last fifteen or twenty years, the integrated manufacturing and service MNE has come of age, and the strategy of international location now includes the optimisation of integrative gains and production opportunities. These changes have been due to factors both endogenous and exogenous to MNEs; the resulting economies in transaction costs suggest that, as an organisational unit, the MNE may well claim to be 'first and foremost an efficiency instrument' (Williamson, 1981). *Inter alia* they are demonstrated by the growing quantity of intra-group and intra-industry trade among MNE affiliates and between affiliates and their parent companies (Dunning, 1981b).

5.7 SUMMARY AND IMPLICATIONS FOR FUTURE RESEARCH

This chapter began by describing some of the changes in the FDI stake of countries since the 1870s. While recognising that the most

widely published data are often a poor proxy for the foreign operations of MNEs, they nevertheless give a fairly clear cut picture of how
the major investing and recipient countries have fared over the years.

What however, such macro data – even at sectoral level – do not
show is the extent and pattern of the growth of individual MNEs.
Instead one has to turn to the growth in the size of firms in general,
and see how far this is related to their propensity to engage in foreign
production. And here the data strongly suggest that, when one has
isolated other variables, such as industry, size, country of origin, etc.,
the firms which are the most multinational are also the largest and
fastest growing.

This chapter has attempted to explain the growth of international
production using the framework of the OLI paradigm (also referred
to as the 'eclectic theory'). First, it has examined the role of technological advances backed by appropriate institutional change in creating
proprietary production, marketing and transactional advantages for
firms of particular nationalities; second, it has examined the organisational framework by which these advances are disseminated across
national boundaries; and third, it has looked at some of the reasons
why, given their technological capacity, firms of a particular country
of origin should choose to locate their production activities outside
rather than within their boundaries.

While this chapter has sought to identify the main factors, it has not
attempted to quantify their individual significance. But what can be
said is this. The growth of international production reflects a composite of interrelated forces at work. Viewed from a macroeconomic
standpoint it is impossible to predict which of the OLI variables is
likely to be the most important in motivating such production, in the
first place, and in expanding it, in the second. Basically, it is possible
to contend that at least one of each of the OLI variables must be
present before foreign production takes place, though it is true that a
discriminatory policy in favour of foreign compared to domestic firms
may be the only ownership advantage which the former may have
over the latter.[54] In some cases the technological superiority of the
investing firm may be the primary force, in others the need to internalise, and in others locational forces.

Once in existence, however, it may be that only one of the components of the OLI paradigm may be necessary to explain the further
growth of a foreign affiliate. It is very likely that the concentration of
international production in the hands of a relatively few MNEs[55] is
witness to the growing significance of hierarchical advantages which
themselves follow from the growth of foreign production prompted
by market forces. In some years over the past century, expansion has
mainly occurred through *new* MNE entrants; such was the period

immediately before and after the First World War, when technological progress was particularly rapid and locational forces encouraged a re-siting of plants outside home countries. In other periods, the pressures of existing firms to grow through integration have been particularly strong; this has always been the case in some resource-based industries, and over the last two decades has become especially pronounced in some branches of manufacturing and service industry. In the inter-war years, there was less technological advance and less powerful reasons for firms to internalise markets; but the pursuance of import-substitution policies on the part of many governments led many exporting firms to react by setting up plants in the countries in question.

It may be that this kind of analytical framework explains much the greater part of FDI over the last hundred years. Obviously, according to home and host countries, sectors and firms – not to mention time *per se* – the configuration of the OLI variables will alter a great deal. But with a little ingenuity and imagination, it should be possible to construct a matrix of OLI values and structural determinants, and then apply a time period to each to produce a reasonably comprehensive and persuasive explanation of the major changes in international production over the last century. But only when a lot more data are available will it be possible to do this.

NOTES

1 This chapter adopts the 'threshold' definition of the MNE as an enterprise which engages in production financed by foreign direct investment. According to *Who Owns Whom*, the number of such enterprises was over 12,000 in 1978.
2 A selection of these is listed in Dunning (1981a) pp. 42–5, 70–1 and 103–108.
3 I recognise that the foreign direct capital stake (a partial input measure) may not always mirror accurately foreign production (an output measure). But until fairly recently, apart from some details of numbers of the leading MNEs and their affiliates, these were the only data available. Note, too, that part of the foreign capital stake, particularly of European countries, took the form of expatriate, entrepreneurial or syndicate investment rather than branch plant activity of firms.
4 The definition of FDI – in so far as nineteenth-century investment is concerned – is still a matter of dispute among economists. But current thinking, as articulated especially by Svedberg (1978, 1981), Stone (1977) and authors of industry and country studies, suggests that quite a large part of investment originally classified as portfolio by the statisticians of the day was, in fact, managed or controlled by non-residents; while contemporary estimates of direct investment often excluded reinvested profits.
5 This was the modality chosen by many European mining companies – e.g. Rio Tinto, originated by a group of UK entrepreneurs purchasing a mine of that name in Spain in 1873 – and also for some railroad investment. In such cases, there were often two boards of directors – one in London mainly concerned with the invest-

136 *The Growth of International Business*

ment management, and the other in the host country which dealt with immediate organisational and operational matters (Wilson, n.d.).

6 For some examples of British and Continental European investment in the US see Coram (1967). For a more general account of the early activities of MNEs see Wilson (n.d.) and Wilkins (1974b).

7 According to Vaupel and Curhan (1974), some 122 manufacturing subsidiaries of 187 large US-based MNEs in existence in 1968 were set up prior to 1914; the corresponding number of subsidiaries for 48 UK MNEs (including Unilever) was 60; and that of 88 Continental European MNEs (including Royal Dutch Shell) was 167. There were no subsidiaries of 67 Japanese large MNEs in 1971 which were set up prior to 1914.

8 Included among these were a whole range of new consumer industries supplying branded goods, e.g. cigarettes, soap, margarine, chocolate, glass, preserved milk, etc., which companies like Nestlé, Levers (the Dutch margarine makers) and Cadbury, were able to take advantage of: Wilson (n.d.) links the origin of this kind of MNE to the fall in living costs (and hence rise in real incomes) which occurred as a result of the Great Depression between 1873 and 1896.

9 Although there were also instances of such dependence in the mining industry, e.g. copper in the Congo, gold in the Gold Coast, etc.

10 As derived from data presented in Vaupel and Curhan (1974).

11 Using data derived from business histories and company archives, Nicholas (1982a) has set out details on the industrial structure of 119 UK MNEs which made a foreign direct investment between 1870 and 1930, and has compared this with that of a sample of pre-1914 US MNEs and of the largest 50 UK firms in 1919 and 1930. His findings about the structure of large UK and US firms at that time correspond to those of earlier writers, e.g. Chandler (1977); but perhaps of greater interest in the present context is the considerable similarity revealed between those sectors which 'dominated' the UK corporate economy and those which dominated UK direct investment.

12 Deflating the data set out in Table 5.1 by the British price indices, the real value of the foreign direct investment stake rose by at least 50 per cent between 1914 and 1938.

13 See Vaupel and Curhan (1974).

14 It is difficult to disentangle how much of these were branch plant investments. But, as in the case of the pre-war investment in Russia, one suspects that the majority were undertaken by foreign capitalists acquiring a majority equity shareholding in indigenous companies; and by foreign entrepreneurs mobilising and allocating capital and technology from their home countries.

15 For further details see Table 5.4.

16 Data on the number of new manufacturing affiliates of MNEs collected by the Harvard researchers are not available for non-US enterprises after 1970, but by that date the number of new US affiliates was falling below its peak in the mid-1960s while that of parent companies of other nationalities was rising.

17 For example of 1369 instances of nationalisation recorded by United Nations (UNCTC) (1978) between 1960 and 1976, 67 per cent were recorded in the final six years. Of some 19 producers' associations existing in 1976, only one (OPEC) was operating in 1960.

18 This table is also extracted from data compiled by Vaupel and Curhan (1974).

19 For example Sekiguchi (1979) estimates that of 1271 Japanese companies with foreign direct investments in March 1975, 482 had a paid up capital of less than 100 million yen (about $0.5 million). The great majority of these were first set up after 1960. See also Tsurumi (1976).

20 The corresponding figures for pre-1914 and 1919–39 were 62 per cent and 63 per

Changes in level structure of international production   137

cent respectively. Throughout these years, the propensity of US MNEs to operate wholly-owned subsidiaries was greater than that of non-US MNEs.

21 In the case of Switzerland, one suspects a large proportion of this increase is accounted for by an outward re-channelling of investment by foreign MNEs in Switzerland, prompted by tax and/or exchange rate advantages. In several other countries, however, foreign affiliates themselves engage in outward direct investment. Examples include Australia, Canada, Bermuda, Hong Kong and the UK. Sometimes this is for administrative or tax convenience, e.g. where the responsibility for running a group of affiliates is allocated to a regional office; in others, an affiliate may be better able to serve and/or produce in some foreign markets than its parent company.

22 By contrast, most US *voluntary* divestments or liquidations of manufacturing affiliates occurred in Europe (see Boddewyn, 1979).

23 In 1975 some 59 per cent of total sales by majority owned affiliates of US MNEs were intra-company.

24 We shall not be concerned with these latter flows in this chapter.

25 For a review, and suggested integration of these approaches see Casson (1982).

26 Imagine, for example, an economy which produces a given quantity of 10 separate products, the production of each of which involves 6 different inter-firm intermediate transactions. The maximum mumber of different kinds of firm which might produce these goods is then 60, but by internalising the transactions the number could be reduced even to one firm producing the entire output.

27 These comprise the economic environment, system and policies of government – the so-called ESP combination.

28 These factors are not necessarily sequential in the decision-taking process. Moreover other writers express them rather differently. For example, David Teece in Chapter 3 of this book suggests that an understanding of the MNE involves an answer to two sets of questions, first 'what determines the location of productive activities across the globe', and second 'what determines the governance of these activities'. One may, however, reverse the order of these questions by asking 'what determines whether companies headquartered in one country are able to supply markets independently of where they are located', and 'what determines where they locate their productive activities to supply these markets'. I prefer this latter format, believing the organisational mode of MNE activity is more likely to be influenced by the extent and nature of that activity, than by its spatial distribution. But see Section 5.6, p. XXff.

29 For a recent review of the literature see Kamien and Schwartz (1982).

30 By the 1880s, continuous processing machinery and plants had been developed in the production of such products as cigarettes, matches, breakfast cereals, flour, soap and a wide variety of canned goods (Chandler and Daems, 1974). See also Wilson (n.d.). However, a working paper by James (1981) suggests that in the USA over the period 1850–90, technological arguments do not explain firm size. See also Wilkins (1976), (1977a), (1977b).

31 Mostly other European countries and Russia.

32 Between these years the UK was responsible for 31.3 per cent of all foreign patents granted in the USA, Germany for 26.2 per cent, France for 10.1 per cent and Canada for 15.3 per cent.

33 It is noteworthy that there were several inventions in Europe that were later adapted and commercialised with greater success in the USA, e.g. the internal combustion engine, the fluorescent lamp, photo-lithography.

34 And in so doing imposed barriers of communication between the ultimate customer and the producer (Kindleberger, 1964, p 148).

35 As set out, for example, in United Nations (UNCTC) (1978).

138   *The Growth of International Business*

36   But see Section 5.6, p. XXff.
37   For a discussion of such exports of technology from the perspective of the product cycle theory of international investment, see Dunning (1971).
38   This was one of the key motives for the internalisation by the Singer Sewing Machine Company of its selling outlets. For a fascinating discussion of the move from agency to direct selling organisations by UK firms in the 1870–1939 period, see Nicholas (1982a).
39   In some cases, e.g. in the early non-ferrous and precious metal ventures by UK firms, the original thrust outwards was essentially an entrepreneurial one, in which it was intended to sell the mined product on the open market, or by contract. Out of this kind of investment, many of todays mining giants, e.g. Rio Tinto Zinc, emerged.
40   It should be noted that some of these motives are interdependent. In most cases, vertical selling implies a technological advantage on the part of the integrating company, while most kinds of technology exploited via FDI imply forward integration.
41   In an extremely perceptive article, Chandler (1981) has pointed out that in the UK the invisible hand of the market worked more effectively than in the USA. He puts this down to the early dominance of the family firms in Britain which were reluctant to surrender their autonomy, and to a tightly organised distributional network. By contrast, the growth of US firms coincided with the development of managerial capitalism and the railroad; and from the start hierarchies became a more attractive way of organising production and selling activities.
42   Such as the Dupont/GM financial control system and the organisational innovations made within the Bell system which helped free businesses from the diseconomies of scale inherent in the military form of organisation; see Quirin (1980).
43   For an analysis of the factors influencing the investment of smaller MNEs, see Newbould, Buckley and Thurwell (1978).
44   In other words, at a price at which the MNE could recoup the gains of internalisation.
45   Put in another way, the common ownership of productive facilities generates particular advantages to the owner quite apart from those which might have arisen through the rationalisation of these activities by independent entities. This proposition negates the prediction of the so-called separation theorem; see Caves (1980), and the next section of this paper.
46   In some cases, host government policy towards inward direct investment has been the crucial factor determining the organisational form by which foreign resources are imported. The two examples which come most readily to mind are Japan and India, but, throughout the developing world, there has been a general preference of governments for joint ventures and/or contractual resource flows relative to a 100 per cent foreign equity stake.
47   There is a good deal of evidence about the ownership strategies of MNEs and other firms with non-equity foreign interests to back this up (see e.g. Stopford and Haberich, 1976).
48   For an analysis of the differential risks involved, see e.g. Rugman (1979).
49   This was especially notable in the case of agricultural products at the time of the Great Depression (1870–95), when both raw material and transport costs fell sharply. This, together with improved methods of quality control, raised consumer demand and encouraged further investment in both food products and in several types of raw materials which were ingredients of processed goods which had a high income elasticity of demand, e.g. cocoa (for chocolate), tobacco, sugar, palm oil (for soap) and many canned foods.

Changes in level structure of international production 139

50 Some authors, e.g. Forsyth (1972), distinguish between factors prompting out-ward investment by US firms in general and those which favour one host country rather than another. It is in this latter group that investment and labour availabil-ity are shown to be of some relevance.
51 But of course a foreign affiliate may act as a sales agent for the export of goods not produced by itself.
52 For a survey of research on FDI in the US see Arpan, Flowers and Ricks (1981).
53 This suggestion counters the proposition that administrative links between multi-production units, and particularly among affiliates of MNEs and between them and their parent companies, do not affect the allocation of resources. In a study of US direct investment in Canada, Caves (1980) finds 'appreciable although incomplete support' *against* this proposition.
54 In other words, I agree with those who argue that monopoly advantage on the part of a particular firm is a necessary condition for FDI. For a view of international trade which preserves the role for the traditional sources of comparative advan-tage, yet also takes account of economies of scale and imperfect competition see Krugman (1979), (1981).
55 Even though in particular sectors concentration ratios may be falling (Dunning and Pearce, 1981).

Part II
The Pioneers

[5]

Mira Wilkins, 'The American Model'

Excerpt from Mira Wilkins *The Maturing of Multinational Enterprise: American Business Abroad from 1914 to 1970*, Cambridge, Mass.: Harvard University Press, 1974, pp.414–422.

414

Epilogue

The present author's research brings her squarely in agreement with those theorists who look at the dynamics of direct foreign investments and view such investments as part of a process—a process developing over time out of the requirements of the innovative business enterprise. Students of direct foreign investment, she believes, have to consider both the growth of the firm and the many diverse external factors (political, economic, and military) that influence its growth. The complexity of today's U.S.-headquartered multinational corporation seems, in general, to mirror the rise of complexity of the U.S. enterprise at home. As this author has pointed out many times herein the expansion abroad cannot be isolated from the growth pattern at home.[9] Alfred D. Chandler, Jr. has documented the evolution in the United States from the single-plant, single-product enterprise to the multidivisional corporation. The expansion outside the United States seems part of the same process.[10] The present author's analysis insists on the evolutionary, cumulative, nature of direct foreign investment.

For some American enterprises the emergence of the multinational corporation began in the 1850s and for others in the 1960s. While there were direct foreign investments by American traders in the colonial period and thereafter, while in the early years of our history as a nation, U.S. investors established businesses abroad in manufacturing, mining, agriculture, banking, transportation, and other public utilities, the evolution of what is today known as the American multinational corporation owes its origins to the decade before the American Civil War.[11] The outline below seems to apply to U.S. international business, whether the company started to develop its foreign activities in the 1850s *or* in the

International Business in Perspective

1960s. The timing in moving through this configuration, the size of each
foreign investment, and the specific reasons why a corporation moved
from one stage to the next varied greatly *among* U.S. companies—
depending on such factors as (1) the company's technological, product,
managerial, or marketing advantage; (2) its concern with national versus
local or regional markets in the United States; (3) the actions of its customers and competitors; (4) the extent to which its resource requirements
could be met at low cost through domestic investment or domestic or foreign purchases. Likewise, there failed to be uniformity in direct foreign
investment activities *within* a single company, since the course of the investment depended on a multiplicity of factors, including (1) where the
foreign investment was made, (2) the type of investment, (3) when the decisions were made, and (4) who made the decision.* Thus, we are in no
way minimizing the vast variety in experience. Yet, we will nonetheless
venture to present an overall outline.

But first one more caveat: no inevitability is implied by the growth
pattern that the author is about to describe. Companies did fall by the
wayside. Some started on the route to becoming multinational, but never
arrived, having met with political and commercial losses, expropriation,
and even bankruptcy of units abroad. Colt, the first American manufacturer that this author can verify as having had a foreign "branch" factory,† [12] in the late 1960s had no business abroad. Many corporations
have not expanded outside the United States. Certain ones have retreated
from investment abroad for years, only to reenter such activities under
new circumstances and with new fervor. Some retreats have been partial,
some quite comprehensive. Yet for every retreat in the history of American international business, there have been compensating advances, if not

---

* Some examples of the variations within a single company may add clarity: (1) A
foreign investment by a U.S. manufacturing company in an industrial country *tended*
to grow faster than one is a less developed country, because the market in the first
country was larger. (2) A foreign investment in manufacturing would generally not be
followed by social overhead expenditures, while one in mining would be, since in an
urban area (where most manufacturing gravitated) social overhead facilities generally
existed; elsewhere they would have to be newly installed. (3) A foreign investment
made by a U.S. manufacturing company in Brazil in the first decade of the twentieth
century would be apt to be in a sales outlet; one made in the late 1950s would be
more apt to be in a manufacturing plant. Brazilian government policies had changed
in the interim. (4) A manager with good experiences with foreign investments would
be more likely to take risks than one with poor experience.
† In England in the 1850s.

416

Epilogue

by one company then another, if not in one sector then another. The following is the way the emergence and maturing of multinational enterprise seems to this author to have occurred.*

In the beginning of the growth of the American multinational enterprise, a U.S. company invested abroad with little complexity. In what we will call stage one, its approach was monocentric. The American parent company reached out to sell or to obtain and in doing so felt the necessity or saw the opportunity to cross over domestic boundaries. It might be a trader, making investments in houses in principal foreign centers. The American parent might be a manufacturer that had first exported (with no foreign investments) and then made a negligible investment in sales branches overseas—in direct marketing. It might license a manufacturer abroad and obtain a small interest in the licensee; it might buy the stock or assets of one or several foreign manufacturers to penetrate that alien market. The U.S. parent might be an oil company seeking outlets abroad for U.S. refined oil and investing overseas to market that oil, or, alternatively, it might obtain oil producing properties in another land. The American company might invest in a foreign mining property. It might establish a foreign outpost to buy bananas. Direct foreign investments, in general, began as spokes on a wheel, with the parent company at the hub. At the very start, chief executives in the parent company were generally directly involved in the establishment of the foreign units, the financing of them, and the staffing of them.

Then, in the *growth of each* branch, subsidiary, or affiliate *outside the United States*, its functions might broaden. What triggered each expansion varied, but the growth occurred.† A foreign trading establishment might integrate backward and invest in a sugar plantation. A foreign sales branch might reinvest its profits and build an assembly plant. A foreign unit that had been bottling drugs imported from the United States might start to synthesize the drugs abroad. A subsidiary that had marketed refined oil might construct its own refinery and process imported

---

* Having studied the history of literally hundreds of U.S. companies with foreign operations, this author finds there are probably fewer than a dozen that do not fit this pattern. Such an exceptional firm would typically start abroad, set up international business *including* American operations, and then transfer its headquarters to the United States; from that point, taking advantage of an established international enterprise the company would grow into multinational business.

† Sometimes, the growth was triggered by enterprise efficiencies, sometimes by host government pressure, sometimes by accidental events (for example, loan defaults), sometimes by a combination of factors.

crude oil. An affiliate that produced oil might erect a plant to refine that oil for its host nation market and possibly for export. A factory abroad for packing might integrate backward into making its own packing materials rather than purchasing them. A subsidiary manufacturing lead piping might buy a lead mine. A copper mining company abroad might integrate forward into refining abroad. A foreign factory acquired to serve one national market might start to sell in several countries. And all the while, as these changes were occurring *abroad,* the American parent company would probably be expanding at home and in the process establishing and acquiring abroad new and distinct units—each one of which would in time have its own history. The added functions taken on by the branches and companies abroad as well as the development of new units radiating from the United States would generally be approved or initiated by parent company executives. By this time, what exists is a growing international business. Within the parent company there would generally emerge an administrative organization to handle foreign operations.*

We now enter stage two. In effect, the initial monocentric relationship has been shattered. To be sure, new and distinct foreign units established, or acquired, by the parent company may and generally will be inaugurated as in stage one, radiating from the parent company. But what characterizes stage two is the presence of foreign units that have developed their own separate histories and their own satellite activities. In stage two, each major foreign unit of the U.S. parent continues to take on larger functions, integrating its operations and introducing new products. It might acquire other firms; it might recruit its own product planning staff; in time, it might come to do its own research; it might make its own *foreign* (third-country) investments. In its growth, the foreign unit might expand out of reinvested profits; it might borrow abroad. Within a single international enterprise, some foreign units developed at one speed, others at a different rate, while others failed and disappeared.†

* Such a structure might be the appointment of an export manager and his staff; it might involve an export company or an international company or division; it might mean the appointment of a man in charge of foreign mining and one in charge of foreign refining. The structure introduced varied by company. My research has indicated that in practically every case where an international division or international company was formed, the parent company *already* had foreign investments of some sort, although there are cases where the formation of the international division was coincident with the program of only expanding exports or of making initial foreign investments.

† By disappeared, we mean was separated from the parent enterprise, that is, went bankrupt, was sold to others, or was expropriated.

418

Epilogue

Each of those that remains takes on over time a certain autonomy and assumes its own distinct role within a foreign industry. Each operates in an economic and political environment different from its parent corporation. The management of each makes certain decisions on its own, independent of parent company direction. Other decisions, however, must have parent company approval. Still others are made exclusively in the United States. To a certain extent, the expansion abroad is analogous to domestic growth—with the relations between headquarters and field being replicated. Yet, there are profound differences. The first is geographical distance: usually, the foreign operation is farther from the home office than the domestic field office. This distance gives the foreign unit more independence. The second, and more important, is political distance: because the foreign unit is in another country, because of both the structure of and restrictions on international trade and payments, because foreign governments have different laws and regulations, because foreign nations have different languages, customs, and practices, because foreign countries have diverse industrial structures, a subsidiary abroad far more than the field office has to formulate its own unique responses. More rapidly than a domestic field office, as noted, the unit outside the United States integrates vertically and horizontally, and also diversifies.

As each foreign entity comes to possess its separate history, what evolves in stage two to replace the initial monocentric structure is a polycentric industrial relationship,[13] with heterogeneous foreign centers having varied trading, administrative, and corporate relationships with the American parent. At this point, however, the complexity has not yet reached culmination. The planets (so to speak), some with their own moons, still revolve around the parent company sun. A large chart showing lines of trade (for supply and sales), as well as lines for managerial and financial control is still possible.

Meanwhile, at home as the parent company expands geographically (deciding on new entries into foreign markets with existing products) or by diversification (increasing its line of products for the domestic, and subsequently the foreign, market),[14] if efficient, as Alfred D. Chandler, Jr. has shown, it will generally create a new administrative structure. It will frequently come to establish a central office and a multidivisional organization.[15] We have noted that between stages one and two of our model, the company that goes abroad usually develops some kind of an administrative structure to deal with foreign business. In fact, often the interna-

tional company (becoming in time the international division) is among
the earliest divisions established in a multidivisional company.

The third stage in the evolution of the multinational corporation may
come rapidly after stage two or may be long delayed. It garbles any
chart's attempt to delineate international trade and control lines. The
parent company comes to have a number of foreign multifunctional centers, serving overlapping geographical areas with various products. Supply and market lines cross international boundaries in such seemingly
chaotic confusion as to defy even colored pencils. Similarly, lines describing financing, personnel placement, and administrative control represent
no simple configuration. The complexity of the third stage in the creation of multinational enterprise evolves from two sets of happenings, involving (1) the parent company, and (2) the existing foreign branches,
subsidiaries, and affiliates.

First, as the parent company grows, it continues—as in stage one and
stage two of our model—to expand abroad, starting new foreign units radiating from the parent company in its traditional products but now
often further afield. Since at home it has introduced new products, these
can be presented abroad and as foreign demand for them arises new foreign investments often seem wise. Likewise, the parent may require different raw materials from outside the United States. Thus, in stage three, as
the parent company has new products and new needs, it accordingly continues its move abroad. The parent grows not only internally, but it may
grow through foreign and domestic acquisitions. The by-now large. U.S.
enterprise is in a position to buy substantial foreign firms, which may already have their own international business. Likewise, such a U.S. corporation in acquiring other *domestic* enterprises may discover that these,
too, have foreign operations. Thus, in the cases of both the foreign and
domestic mergers, a new monocentric or polycentric *foreign* business
structure is introduced. The implications become clear in the question:
What is to be the relationship between (1) the established parent company's units abroad (with their ramifications developed through time);
(2) the new units initiated abroad, generally covering an ever broader
geographical range; (3) the new foreign units, representing new products
and new raw material needs of the expanding parent; (4) companies acquired abroad through takeovers and *their* foreign subsidiaries; and (5)
the existing foreign subsidiaries and affiliates obtained as a consequence
of domestic mergers? In sum, there emerges abroad as an outcome of the

420

Epilogue

U.S. company's growth at home a new collection of distinct foreign units to be merged or not merged (grouped or not grouped) abroad according to corporate policy. Here, too, of course, there are analogous domestic problems: should each new field unit report back to headquarters, or should established field units assume regional authority to take in new ventures? Should established divisions or field units introduce new products, or should new divisions or field organizations be created? Should a merged company be kept separated or integrated into existing operations? If integrated, how and to what extent? The solutions of international business are not necessarily identical to those in domestic operations. In the United States, with its mass market, after a domestic merger it might make sense to retain separate organizational structures. In India, by contrast, there might be no justification for two administrators to remain totally independent of one another and to report back to different divisions within the parent company.

If the added complexity brought about through domestic growth and diversification is not sufficient, *abroad* in stage three, all the *established* foreign affiliates and subsidiaries through their own continued development contribute a further element of intricacy. For many diverse reasons —among them, increasing profits (by more efficiently using resources), U.S. tariffs or import quotas (obstacles to imports may cause a foreign subsidiary to seek third-country markets), U.S. antitrust policy (forbidding territorial divisions that affect U.S. commerce), competition from a third country (that demands new responses), foreign dollar shortages (for a U.S. company to maintain a market abroad under such circumstances may mean it will have a foreign subsidiary serve the third-country market that it can no longer handle), foreign dollar surpluses (that provide funds for expansion programs), foreign government attitudes (that encourage import substitution and export expansion), regional group policies (a plant in Germany can better serve a sales subsidiary within the common market than the U.S. company), location (it often will be more economical to supply eastern Europe from a British factory than from U.S. exports), and even the aggressiveness of management of the foreign unit— the old polycentric industrial structure (with the parent company as a sun and the subsidiaries as planets with satellite moons) breaks down. Systematically delineated market territories exist no longer. What is substituted is a formidable labyrinth. Over time, certain foreign subsidiaries and affiliates have become full-fledged, fully integrated, multiprocess,

multiproduct enterprises, with engineering, product planning, and research staffs, with a continuity of employee, supplier, dealer, consumer,
and banking relationships, with their own prominent role in foreign industries, with their own dealings with foreign governments, and with
their own third-country investments. Such subsidiaries or affiliates become centers not of limited but of truly international trade. They can
and do sell in many countries and purchase from many suppliers, not
necessarily in the nation of operations or in the United States; they recruit their unskilled, skilled, and managerial personnel not only in the
lands where they do business or in the United States, but in various nations. They raise money for their operations where available, irrespective
of sovereignty. Some have foreign stockholders. Often, they manufacture
products not made in the United States. Some specialize in particular
components that will complement the components manufactured by
other foreign subsidiaries or affiliates of the American parent. Some specialize in one facet of production and others in another facet. They engage in trade with other affiliates of the parent firm, often in third countries, as well as with outsiders. The American parent may be to a large
extent or even completely excluded from the trading relationship. Moreover, *their* satellite operations also begin to follow the same evolution as
they have followed vis-à-vis the American parent. The relatively simple
polycentric industrial structure is shattered. Thus is created the conglomerate entangled structure in the present or near future of large American
companies that participate in multinational business. Business abroad is
no longer confined to several foreign countries, a few products, or one or
two major processes but exists in numerous foreign nations and in a
range of different products and production processes. Complicated,
many-faceted relationships have replaced simple bilateral connections. In
the process of moving from stage two to stage three the control of the operations abroad by the parent company may loosen and then retighten as
managements change at home and abroad. At home, faced with the problems in stage three, U.S. businesses may again radically revise their administration to cope with and control the new complexity. Such
reorganization may mean the U.S. parent will reject the old "isolated" international division and restructure its corporate administration on a
worldwide basis related to product, geographical area, a combination of
both, or an overlapping "grid" structure.

Most important, into the new situation in stage three is introduced an

422

Epilogue

element of choice. As Peter Odell has written, multinational companies can decide "where the productive potential shall be worked to capacity or even extended, or, on the other hand, left partially unused." There is in the multinational corporation a unique element of flexibility.[16] Resources are dispersed. Patterns of production and trade can be altered. Financing and personnel recruitment need not be confined to one or two nations. The complete multinational corporation would probably have to have dividend payments as multinational as resources, trade, financing, and employment. In the sense that an American parent enterprise aspires to have its assets grow worldwide, it is multinational, but in that it wishes to return to the United States as high dividends and royalties as possible, it remains national. On the other hand, certain American parent companies (General Motors in the lead) have tried to sell the parent company's stock on a global basis.[17] The achievement of this on a large scale would end one significant vestige of the national enterprise (the insistence on dividends being returned to one country). But this is still for the future.

565

9. In this we find relevant the work of Edith Penrose, *The Theory of the Growth of the Firm,* New York 1959, and more specifically, her "Foreign Investment and the Growth of the Firm," *Economic Journal* 66:220–235 (June 1956). Likewise, Aliber, "A Theory," 20, has directed our attention to the work of R. H. Coase, "The Nature of the Firm," *Economica,* n.s. 4(1937):386–405, from which Aliber indicates an explanation of business abroad involving enterprise efficiencies "realised by coordinating activities that occur in several different countries." Coordination within the firm results in cost reductions—as in the multinational integrated oil company. Business abroad is seen under such an explanation as an aspect of the growth of the firm. This would mesh well with our own interpretation.

10. Alfred D. Chandler, Jr., *Strategy and Structure,* Cambridge, Mass. 1962.

11. Mira Wilkins, *The Emergence of Multinational Enterprise, American Business Abroad from the Colonial Era to 1914,* Cambridge, Mass. 1970, 30, 37ff.

12. *Ibid.,* 30.

13. The use of the words "monocentric" and "polycentric" were first suggested to the present author by an address by Hans Thorelli at the International Business Association meeting, Dec. 30, 1965. Professor Thorelli, however, used the terms to apply to *organizational* structure and not as I am using them to apply to industrial structure.

14. Chandler, 299–300.

15. *Ibid.,* 299–326.

16. Peter R. Odell, *An Economic Geography of Oil,* London 1963, 33. The present author has generalized his idea to apply to more than the multinational oil company.

17. See Frederick G. Donner, *The World-Wide Industrial Enterprise,* New York 1967, for General Motors' ideas on this. Such companies as du Pont, Eastman Kodak, Ford Motor, G.E., G.M., and Goodyear had by the late 1960s their U.S. company's stock listed on Belgian, French, Dutch, and West German stock exchanges. Sidney Rolfe, *The International Corporation,* Paris 1969, 202.

[6]

By John M. Stopford

PROFESSOR OF INTERNATIONAL BUSINESS
LONDON GRADUATE SCHOOL OF BUSINESS STUDIES

The Origins of British-Based Multinational Manufacturing Enterprises*

❡ *Professor Stopford explores the patterns of British direct investment in overseas manufacturing in the nineteenth and twentieth centuries, paying special attention to the quality of Victorian entrepreneurship and the opportunities and problems presented by the Empire and then the Commonwealth.*

During the second half of the 1960s, most of the largest United Kingdom manufacturing firms established or acquired production units in continental Europe.[1] This surge of investment provoked much comment in the press and elsewhere. Many observers considered that, at last, British firms were relaxing from their previous undue concentration on Commonwealth markets in favour of a closer involvement with an enlarged EEC. Some observers commented that British firms were beginning to resemble American multinational enterprises after years of somehow being a different kind of multinational. Others must have considered such comments irrelevant, since they took the position that Britain did not possess more than a handful of multinationals.[2]

That there was an upsurge of investment by British firms is indisputable: the book value of direct investments in the EEC of over £800,000,000 at the end of 1970 was double the level of five years earlier.[3] The commentaries provoked by the upsurge, however, were too sweeping, especially when British foreign direct investments are viewed in an historical perspective. The evidence indicates that most of the very early manufacturing investments were in

Business History Review, Vol. XLVIII, No. 3 (Autumn, 1974). Copyright © The President and Fellows of Harvard College.

* The author gratefully acknowledges the partial financial support of the Ford Foundation through its grant to the Harvard Business School's Multinational Enterprise Research Project, and the many helpful comments of Raymond Vernon and Mira Wilkins on an early draft.

[1] Company annual reports and press releases.

[2] See, for example, J. J. Servan-Schreiber, *Le Défi Américain* (Paris, 1967), and Jack Behrman, *Some Patterns in the Rise of Multinational Enterprises* (Chapel Hill, N.C., 1969).

[3] *Business Monitor*, Miscellaneous Series, M4, Overseas Transactions (various issues); excludes banking, insurance, and oil industries.

TABLE 1

THE 100 LARGEST U.K. MANUFACTURING FIRMS, CLASSIFIED BY INDUSTRY AND EXTENT OF FOREIGN PRODUCTION, END OF 1970

SIC No.	Industry	Total No. of Firms	No. of Firms with 25% or more of total manufactured output originating outside UK
20	Food and Drink	25	8
21	Tobacco	3	1
22	Textiles	4	2
24–27	Wood, Paper, Printing	6	4
28	Chemicals	5	5
283	Drugs	3	2
29	Oil	3	3
30	Rubber	1	1
31	Leather and Footwear	2	1
32	Stone, Clay, Glass	6	4
33	Primary Metals	5	4
34	Fabricated Metals	9	2
35	Non-electrical Machinery	7	1
36	Electrical Machinery	9	5
37	Transportation	6	1
	Other (including highly diverse companies)	6	4
	TOTAL	100	48

Sources: Size and industry classification from *The Times 1000,* 1972/1973. Non-manufacturing firms and foreign-owned firms have been excluded from the list; foreign production data from company publications.

Europe and the United States. Only during the 1920s and 1930s did an Empire, or later on a Commonwealth, preference in investment become a predominant influence on location decisions. As for the existence of British-based multinationals, the data in Table 1 show that a large number of manufacturing firms were well advanced in 1970 along the road to spreading a production network around the world.[4] Indeed, at least fourteen firms had become multinational before World War I.

The purpose of this paper is to explore the factors that conditioned the early expansion of British firms into manufacturing abroad. The conclusions drawn are tentative and subject to further research. Nevertheless, the data strongly suggest that the long-established high propensity of the British to export capital in

[4] There are many competing definitions of what constitutes a multinational enterprise in the manufacturing sector. For the purposes of this article, one of the simplest definitions — if it can really be called a definition — is used: a firm that has more than 25 per cent of its manufacturing output abroad.

various forms had a direct influence on the investment behaviour of individual firms. One particular class, foreign direct investments, sowed the seeds of today's multinational enterprises. Initially of trivial importance compared to portfolio investments, direct investments later became the predominant mode of exporting capital. Although most of the British-based multinationals are a product of the upsurge of capital exports that started in the 1950s, the origins of the stimuli that led to the upsurge can be traced back to Victorian days.

CLASSES OF INVESTMENT DISTINGUISHED

For the purposes of this article, three classes of capital exports — portfolio, direct, and "expatriate" — need to be distinguished. Not only are different types of investors involved in each class, but also the relative importance of each class has changed considerably over time.

The first class, portfolio, was by far the most important in Victorian Britain. These investments were principally in the form of bonds, preference shares, or small percentages of a foreign firm's ordinary shares. Portfolio capital exports are not concerned with the management of the foreign enterprise and are the foreign equivalent of normal domestic dealings on the London Stock Exchange.

Both direct and "expatriate" exports are directly concerned with management. Foreign direct investments are frequently defined as the ownership of 25 per cent or more of the ordinary shares of a foreign enterprise, the assumption being that the degree of ownership gives a measure of, if not complete, control. In most instances, direct investments are made by firms in one country investing in firms with similar products or services in another. The ties of ownership and strategic control across national boundaries are central to the notion of a multinational enterprise. There are, however, foreign investments that involve a sense of management, but that do not at the same time involve strategic control exercised from Britain. For example, an entrepreneur who emigrates, starts a firm in his new homeland, and finances the venture with money raised in his old homeland creates what can be labelled an "expatriate" investment.

Very little is known about the numbers of such firms or their financial importance. Most probably, there were thousands of "expatriate" British firms before 1914. Their importance is two-fold:

they provided a convenient means of entry by acquisition for the British manufacturing firms that were later to extend their reach abroad; and some later created UK operations and developed into multinationals. They are distinguished from direct investments in that they had at best a financial "shell" located in Britain. The Rangoon Oil Company, which was established in 1871 and later became Burmah Oil, is a classic example of British (in this case Scottish) interests promoting a company that initially traded exclusively in the Far East. For the financiers who responded to the sales talk of the promoters, these "expatriate" investments were portfolio investments of a special kind. They represented investments in skills that had been transferred abroad, not with linkages to a strong home base as for direct investments, but by the emigration of skilled people.

Some of these "expatriate" investments withered away leaving no trace; some disappeared on being acquired by others; and still others survived and gradually severed all financial ties with Britain to become local companies. The few that made the transition to manufacturing multinational status did so when they acquired or established factories in the UK that either made products similar to those first produced abroad or used the raw materials imported from the firm's foreign sites. In some cases, the precise point at which the "expatriate" becomes a British-based multinational is fuzzy. For example, Glaxo started in 1904 by making dried-milk products in New Zealand, mainly for sale in the UK, and did not manufacture these products in the UK until 1937. But Glaxo transferred its management centre to England in 1914, and started research in England soon after. Manufacture of pharmaceuticals started in England in 1924, and elsewhere by the early 1930s. The transition to multinational status with a British base was therefore during the period 1914–1937.

Examples of the activities of these "expatriate" firms are scattered through the growing literature on economic and social development in many countries. Many were active in extractive industries — mining in the USA, Russia, and Latin America, and agriculture in India are examples — using new techniques and aiming to supply the world commodity markets. Some established utilities to supply the needs of growing urban areas. Manufacturing activities were of small financial importance compared to the other activities and were mostly limited to supplying local market needs with such products as beer, refined sugar, tanned leather, and soap.

These were small-scale enterprises that did not depend for survival upon ties to technological developments or upon access to world markets. Further research is needed to establish the full extent of all these "expatriate" activities, but the available evidence strongly suggests that, in manufacturing at least, the business horizons of the expatriates were bounded by the needs of the local market and the particular skills they happened to possess when they emigrated from Britain.[5]

Distinguishing among these three classes of capital exports before 1914 is a formidable task. Most of the existing analytical work concentrates on portfolio investment. The data used for such analyses are drawn from capital flows through the securities market. Such data inevitably do not include direct investments financed by the internal cash flows of the investing firm. But they do include most, perhaps all, of the "expatriate" investment. "Expatriate" investment, it should be noted, has typically been labelled hitherto as portfolio.

A further difficulty of definition exists when tracing the origins of manufacturing multinationals. Some of these enterprises started their corporate existence in extractive industries and only later began to manufacture. Some, like Anglo-Persian, the forerunner of British Petroleum, and Burmah Oil, were both "expatriate" and extractive. The boundary lines are not clear and can only be established with the aid of hindsight for those firms that at some point successfully made the transition to manufacturing multinationals.

Much additional work needs to be done to disentangle the various strands of evidence and to clarify the differences among the classes of investment and the motivations of the investors. In the sections that follow, only the crudest estimates of the distinctions are attempted.

BRITISH CAPITAL EXPORTS BEFORE 1939

Britain first began exporting capital of all forms after Waterloo in order to finance reconstruction in Europe. The British govern-

[5] Country and regional studies provide a rich source of data that can be explored further than has been attempted here. See, for example, J. Fred Rippy, *British Investments in Latin America, 1822-1949* (Hamden, Conn., 1966); Amiya K. Bagchi, *Private Investment in India, 1900-1939* (Cambridge, 1972); John P. MacKay, *Pioneers for Profit, Foreign Entrepreneurship and Russian Industrialisation 1885-1913* (Chicago, 1970). Also useful are industry studies such as Charlotte Erickson, *British Industrialists: Steel and Hosiery 1850-1950* (Cambridge, 1959). Also, firms, such as Bowring, which started when Benjamin Bowring moved his clock and watch making business to Newfoundland in 1811, are increasingly beginning to publicise their origins. Finally, works such as Leland H. Jenks, *The Migration of British Capital to 1875* (London, 1963) are invaluable.

ment initially used capital exports as an instrument of policy, but after about 1830 treated them with a laissez-faire attitude. Friendly diplomatic relations and the use of "gun-boat" diplomacy had, of course, an influence on the investment choices made in the London market.[6]

The remarkable rise of foreign investments during the remainder of the nineteenth century is a story of waves of speculative fever followed by bad debts. One wave promoted investment in one country, or region, the following one another. Latin America was the recipient of a series of such waves, beginning in the late 1820s, and continuing for fifty years. By 1890, British investments there had a nominal value of £426,000,000.[7] This was the era when "young Benjamin Disraeli was employed to write prospectuses for bubble companies, when Robert Stephenson went to Buenos Aires to construct mine tramways, when Scottish miners were shipped to the Andes to improve mining techniques, and Scottish milkmaids to the Pampas to teach the gauchos to make butter."[8] Speculative money poured into other areas, such as the USA in the mid-1830s, often with disastrous results.

Over the period from 1820 to the end of the century, the direction of British capital exports changed slowly to favour the developing areas of the world, most particularly the "white" dominions: Australia, Canada, New Zealand, and South Africa. In the early years, Europe and the USA were the preferred areas, and as late as 1850, they still accounted for more than half of the capital exports. Between 1860 and 1900, the proportion of investments going to Europe declined rapidly from nearly 30 per cent to little over 5 per cent, while those in the USA slowly dropped until there was a sharp fall during World War I.[9] India accounted for around 20 per cent of total investments in the 1850s,[10] but thereafter fell in relative importance. The persistently underdeveloped world received, as one might expect, very little British capital. It was the developing world that received a growing proportion of the capital. The "white" dominions accounted for only 12 per cent of the total in the 1860s, but almost 30 per cent by the 1880s, and a steadily increasing proportion thereafter. In Latin America, countries such as Argentina — dubbed "honorary dominions" by one observer be-

6 For a fascinating account of government attitudes, see D. C. M. Platt, *Finance, Trade and Politics in British Foreign Policy, 1815-1914* (Oxford, 1968).
7 Rippy, *British Investments*, 37.
8 C. E. Carrington, *The British Overseas* (Cambridge, 1968), 474.
9 £600,000,000 of railway bonds alone were sold to help finance the war effort.
10 Due mainly to a spate of government-guaranteed railway issues, and its special im-

cause of their similar economies [11] — experienced similar growth.[12]

After World War I, the share of the dominions became even larger. By 1929, they accounted for over 40 per cent of the total. Indeed, the Empire as a whole accounted for approximately 75 per cent of all exported British capital on the eve of World War II.[13] Latin America's share of the total remained at about 20 per cent during the inter-war years. Thus the broad geographical spread of earlier decades had largely given way to regional specialization. The basic reasons are not hard to find: war, inflation, and political upheaval discouraged the investor. As the direction of capital exports changed, so did their composition. Up to 1914, the bulk of investment was portfolio. For example, Table 2 shows that 46 per cent of British investments in Latin America in 1890

TABLE 2
BRITISH INVESTMENTS IN LATIN AMERICA, END OF 1890

	Nominal Capital (£ million)
Government Securities	194.4
Railways	166.8
Other Utilities	25.3
Mining	18.0
Banks, Finance, Land	17.6
Manufacturing	3.6
TOTAL	425.7

Source: J. Fred Rippy, *British Investments in Latin America, 1822–1949* (Hamden, Conn., 1966), Tables 7, 8, 9, 10, 12.

were in government securities. Most of the investments in railways, utilities, and mines were also portfolio, even though many of the companies were under British management. Typically, entrepreneurs promoted a new railway, obtained capital by public subscription in Britain, and then either managed the construction and operation of the line themselves or put in a management team to do the job. Such companies can be classified as either "expatriate" or portfolio, depending on the precise nature of the financing

---

portance in the Empire, India was one major exception to the general "laissez-faire" policies towards capital exports.

[11] Eric J. Hobsbawm, *Industry and Empire* (London, 1968), 148.

[12] For more detailed figures, see Herbert Feis, *Europe: The World's Banker 1870–1914* (New Haven, Conn., 1930).

[13] This figure excludes investments in oil, and is an estimate based on data from A. R. Conan, *Capital Imports into Sterling Countries* (London, 1960), 85. Data for Canada from Dominion Bureau of Statistics, *Canada's International Investment Position 1926–1954* (Ottawa, 1956). See also A. R. Conan, *The Problem of Sterling* (London, 1966), 68.

(bonds, ordinary or preference shares), and the nationality of the promoters and managers. Much of the available evidence suggests that portfolio investments were by far the larger category.[14] Major "expatriate" investments developed later on as the activities of such men as Cowdray in Mexico bore fruit. Direct investments, concentrated in manufacturing, finance, and land, accounted for only a very small proportion of the total.

Only a rough guess as to the composition in 1913 of the stock of British foreign investments can be made from available statistics. Based on capital flows through the securities market, Herbert Feis adjusted Paish's estimates to arrive at a total of £3,763,000,000. To that total Feis estimated that a further £300,000,000 should be added to take account of direct investments that had by-passed the market.[15] By allocating part of the so-called portfolio investments to both direct and "expatriate" investments, the composition among the three types in 1913 can be estimated as:

Portfolio	68 per cent
"Expatriate"	22 per cent
Direct	10 per cent

These figures should be treated with caution, because they are no more than order of magnitude estimates.[16]

After the First World War, the British preference for portfolio investments began to decline. As for the earlier period, imperfections in the available data, together with the troublesome problem of changing definitions as to what constitutes a direct investment, make estimates no more than crude guesses. Nevertheless, by combining the statistics available for 1927 with what is known about the foreign investment record of the major British firms, the direct component can be estimated to have risen to about 20 per cent, or double its share of the total fourteen years earlier. The direct component had most probably doubled again to over 40 per cent in 1939.[17]

---

[14] Rippy, *British Investments*, provides much information that can be interpreted to support this point.

[15] For details, see Feis, *Europe: World's Banker*.

[16] The estimates were derived as follows: manufacturing investments (£209,000,000) were allocated half to direct, one quarter to "expatriate," and one quarter to portfolio; investments (£891,000,000) in utilities, extractive industries, banks, finance, and land, were allocated equally between portfolio and "expatriate;" railways (£1,531,000,000) were allocated as three-fourths portfolio and one-fourth "expatriate;" government and municipal securities (£1,125,000,000) were portfolio.

[17] Sources for the estimates are: for 1927 data, Sir Robert Kindersley, "A New Study of British Foreign Investments," *The Economic Journal*, XXXIX (March, 1929); for the firms, the London Business School Multinational Data Bank, some components of which are included in James W. Vaupel and Joan P. Curhan, *The World's Multinational Enterprises*

While direct investment gained in popularity, "expatriate" investments declined. Migration from the British Isles was reduced; many of the companies were liquidated, or in the case of the Latin American utilities, sold to United States interests; and many "expatriates" sold out to British interests as British firms began aggressively to expand abroad. The vulnerability of small local enterprise to foreign takeover became pronounced as new technologies developed, economies of scale became important, and communications improved.

These aggregate data raise a number of important questions. Why was the preference for portfolio investments so marked for so long? What determined the changes in geographical composition? How were these changes linked, if at all, to changes in exports? Given the general pattern, why did some firms break out of the common mould early on? No complete answers are available, but some shreds of evidence can be assembled to suggest partial answers. Many of these concern developments in Britain with respect to technology and management, as well as political and economic developments elsewhere.

INDUSTRIAL RETARDATION IN BRITAIN

After 1880, Britain began to fall behind other nations, particularly Germany and the USA, in the development of new industries and the modernisation of old ones.[18] The reasons for this relative decline are the subject of much controversy. Nevertheless, an examination of the arguments can suggest some of the forces that shaped the British propensity to develop multinational enterprises.

Two major events in the world economy had a bearing on the story. First, the relatively free trade economy of the 1860s was replaced after 1880 by a situation of increasing protectionism, especially in Germany, France, and the USA. Some historians have called the period 1873–1896 the Great Depression in Britain, because of the dampening effects on growth of increasing protectionism. Although there was substantial growth in most sectors during this so-called Depression, the long-term growth rates — measured

(Harvard Business School, Division of Research, 1974). During the 1930s, Britain's foreign investments fell in nominal value by over £100,000,000. Though direct investments continued to be made, albeit at a low level, repayments of portfolio investments were made on a massive scale. For details, see Kindersley's series of articles in *The Economic Journal*, up to 1959. Note that Kindersley's figures apply only to capital flows through the securities markets and must be supplemented by internal transactions of the multinationals.

[18] The title of this section and much of the analysis is taken from A. L. Levine's excellent study, *Industrial Retardation in Britain 1880–1914* (London, 1967).

by such indices as industrial production, productivity, and per capita income – were lower than those in Germany, the USA, and, in some cases, below those in France.[19] The second major event was a period of unprecedented advance in the application of mass-production methods and the development of large-scale enterprises – labelled by some a Second Industrial Revolution.[20]

"However strongly the winds of change blew elsewhere," wrote Eric Hobsbawm, "as soon as they crossed the Channel to Britain, they grew sluggish." [21] Judged relative to other countries, economies of scale were not exploited, mass production techniques were not introduced, the new industries were not developed, and income elasticities of demand were not exploited in Britain. Where new methods of production were introduced, as in the use of machine tools or in the adoption of automatic machinery for producing glass bottles, American technology had to be imported. The new industries, such as sewing machines, cars, and electrical machinery, which were heavily dependent on income elasticities of demand, were also based on foreign technology, and often foreign firms dominated the British market.[22]

This backsliding of the economy has been attributed to many causes, not many of which hold up under critical evaluation.[23] It seems clear, however, that there were a number of interrelated symptoms of the malaise. The lag in mechanisation was undoubtedly influenced by relative factor costs and supply. The availability of an abundant, low-paid work-force made the potential returns from investment in machinery unattractive to many firms. The handicap of an early start in industrialisation and the unwillingness to treat investments in obsolete machinery as sunk costs were also important. Early investments in the LeBlanc process for making soda inhibited the rapid adoption of the new Solvay process.[24] The im-

---

[19] The severe limitations of the data make comparisons difficult. For a critical review of this period, see A. E. Musson, "The Great Depression in Britain, 1873-1896: A Reappraisal," *Journal of Economic History* (June, 1959). For an interpretation of the available indices, see Derek H. Aldcroft's introduction to Aldcroft, ed., *The Development of British Industry and Foreign Competition, 1875-1914* (London, 1968), 11-36.

[20] See, for example, J. A. Hobson, *The Evolution of Modern Capitalism* (London, 1949), 146, and David S. Landes, *The Unbound Prometheus* (Cambridge, 1969).

[21] Hobsbawm, *Industry and Empire*, 178.

[22] For detailed examinations of the role of foreign technology, and of foreign firms in many industries, see the series of excellent papers in Aldcroft, ed., *Development of British Industry*.

[23] See Levine, *Industrial Retardation*, for a careful evaluation and dismissal of such familiar arguments as the handicap of an inadequate resource base, the small size of the home market, the heavy exports of capital, non-competitive behaviour of firms due to sociological causes, and so on.

[24] For a discussion of the relative merits of these processes and the reasons why the Solvay process became the basic process of the modern chemical industry, see L. F. Haber, *The Chemical Industry 1900-1930* (London, 1971).

portant British invention of the Gilchrist-Thomas process for making steel from locally available phosphoric ores was neglected by British steelmakers (but not those in Germany and France), despite its advantage in reducing costs.[25] Examples of such responses to change and risk abound. Adherence to the status quo allowed only a very slow diffusion of innovation throughout British industry.[26] Other related symptoms were an unwillingness on the part of many entrepreneurs to invest in research and development, a lack of standardisation of products, and a general lack of social interest in education.

The incidence and severity of these symptoms varied enormously from industry to industry. Not all British industries declined relatively after 1880. In building ships, for example, Britain outdistanced her rivals technically and did not lose her lead until after World War II.[27] Nevertheless, the fact remains that many British industries were overtaken by rivals in Germany, the USA, or other European countries.

For some years now it has become fashionable for writers to criticise Victorian entrepreneurs for the sins listed above. Only recently has there been any serious reappraisal of their impact on the economy.[28] Actions that, with hindsight, appear sinful were often perfectly rational within the contemporary context. With respect to investing in research, for example, Britain had no strong incentive to develop materials-saving technology comparable to that existing for its continental rivals; privileged access to Empire sources of cheap raw materials was the critical difference.

In general terms, one can argue that Britain responded to the Great Depression by exploiting the untapped potential of the Empire and the nation's traditional trading position. British industry was in effect following the path of least resistance. It was relatively easier to develop exports to previously undeveloped regions than it was to compete directly with the technically and competitively more energetic firms in the developed world.

As tariff barriers went up to protect local fledgling industries from

---

[25] For details, see Duncan Burn, *The Economic History of Steelmaking 1867–1939* (Cambridge, 1961), 172–182.

[26] For a useful summary, see Charles Wilson, "Technology and Industrial Organisation," in C. Singer *et al.*, eds., *History of Technology: Volume 5* (Oxford, 1958), 807, 808.

[27] Hobsbawn, *Industry and Empire*, 178–179, however, argues convincingly that ship building was one of the few industries where economics of scale were not important, and where the complex subdivisions of the construction process both multiplied the opportunities and minimised the risks of technical advance and specialisation.

[28] For a summary of recent reappraisals, see Donald N. McCloskey, ed., *Essays on a Mature Economy: Britain after 1840* (London, 1971). See also D. N. McCloskey, *Economic Maturity and Entrepreneurial Decline: British Iron and Steel, 1870–1913* (Cambridge, Mass., 1973).

BRITISH-BASED MULTINATIONALS   313

the might of British exporters, the exporters frequently abandoned those markets altogether and concentrated their efforts elsewhere. This tendency to flee from developing, resistantly competitive markets to undeveloped ones was most marked in cotton. In 1820, Europe and the USA took 60 per cent of total exports of cotton piece goods, but in ,1900 those areas received only 7 per cent.[29] Similar, though less dramatic, shifts occurred in other industries. Latin America and China became crucial new markets for many products, as did the dominions and other parts of the Empire. But even the discriminating protection in the Empire was often not sufficient to restrict the entry of non-British goods once the previously fledgling industries of Europe and the United States had developed in the forge of the Second Industrial Revolution to the point where they became internationally competitive. By 1914, many Empire markets were no longer the *chasse gardée* of the British. Britain could not continue indefinitely to find easy outlets.

Loss of export markets frequently provokes one of two reactions in a firm. Either the firm jumps the tariff barrier and produces locally (a direct investment), or it adjusts its prices and products to retain its competitive edge in exporting. Because less risky alternatives were available elsewhere, the stimuli for technical development or foreign investment were frequently ignored. The events of the inter-war period, particularly the growing protection of local industries in the dominions, were to change this situation, at least to the point where foreign investments became imperative.

It is curious that many Victorian manufacturers who would not readily make foreign direct investments for their firms would readily make portfolio investments.[30] The nation as a whole seemed predisposed to risk capital abroad just as much as at home. Indeed, Britain's annual investments abroad began to exceed her net capital formation at home after 1870 and continued to do so until 1914. Quite why this was so has not satisfactorily been explained. Was it merely a slackening of entrepreneurial drive and a growing predisposition to live on the fruits of accumulated capital? Was it an acceptance that higher yields could be obtained from investments in, say, South African gold than from investments in the Lancashire mills? If it was the latter, why did investors continue to ignore the appalling risks that accompanied each wave of speculation? Perhaps there was a perverse streak of romanticism in even the toughest

[29] Hobsbawm, *Industry and Empire*, 146.
[30] One telling example of this behaviour was provided by the Pilkington family. See T. C. Barker, *Pilkington Brothers and the Glass Industry* (London, 1960), 197.

mill owner's breast. Many, like Mr. Dombey, must have considered that to break one's heart on account of an adverse speculation in Peruvian mines was "a very respectable way of doing it."

Undoubtedly, there were many such social as well as economic factors at work to produce the observed result. From the perspective of the would-be foreign direct investor, there was an important additional factor: in many industries there was a lack of skills with which to compete once located abroad. If the thesis that most British industries had become competitively retarded at home is right, then the handicap of exporting obsolete skills was almost insuperable. Given that handicap, then the added discouragement of managing at a distance and grappling with unfamiliar problems of communication and organisation must have been immense.[31] Unlike their American competitors, who were learning how to manage on a continental scale, British managers had no such domestic experience.

There were, nevertheless, firms that managed even before 1914 to surmount these handicaps. As the next section shows, they were distinctive from the general run of British firms on a number of critical variables. They blazed a trail that many others began to follow after the shock of World War I.

THE PIONEERS

A search of materials on the largest 100 manufacturing firms in Britain in 1970 produced a list of fourteen that had invested abroad on a significant scale before 1914. In some cases, the search concerned firms that had been absorbed into larger groups in the intervening years. Their foreign investments were principally in factories (see Table 3 for locations), though some had major investments in plantations and other extractive activities. Most of them, of course, had also established elaborate overseas networks of agencies, branch houses, and sales subsidiaries. Apart from having been more internationally expansionist than other British firms of the period, they were also distinctive in that they had all established strong oligopolistic — in some cases almost monopolistic — positions in their home industries. Leadership in an oligopoly was perhaps

[31] There are well documented instances of firms, even those with unrivalled skills, that refused to make foreign investments when approached by local interests primarily because they would require too much effort. See, for example, Lorna Houseman, *The House that Thomas Built: The Story of De La Rue* (London, 1968), 99, for a refusal to invest in Italy in 1864; see also T. A. B. Corley, *Quaker Enterprise in Biscuits* (London, 1972), 218 for a refusal in the U.S.A. on the grounds of undue management difficulties.

TABLE 3

LOCATION OF MAJOR FOREIGN MANUFACTURING INVESTMENTS OF U.K. FIRMS BEFORE 1914

Firm	Industry	Dominions	Rest of British Empire	Europe	U.S.A.	Other
British American Tobacco	Tobacco	Australia Canada°	India° Trinidad	Germany, Denmark	–	Japan, Korea, Puerto Rico, China
Bryant & May (later British Match)	Matches	Australia, S. Africa, N. Zealand°	–	–	–	Brazil°
J & P Coats (later Coats Patons)	Cotton thread	Canada	–	Belgium, Italy, Portugal, Spain	+	Brazil, Mexico, Russia, Japan
Courtaulds	Synthetic textiles	–	–	Belgium	+	–
Dunlop	Rubber	S. Africa Canada	–	Germany	–	Argentina, Japan
English Sewing Cotton (later Tootal)	Cotton thread	Canada	–	Spain, France	+	–
The Gramophone Company (later EMI)	Records	–	India	Denmark	–	Brazil
Lever Brothers (later Unilever)	Soaps	S. Africa Australia Canada	–	Germany, Austria, Belgium, France	+	Japan

Liebig Extract of Meat (later Brooke Bond Liebig)	Food	—	—	Belgium	—	Argentina,° Uruguay°
Nobel Explosives (later part of ICI)	Explosives	Australia Canada	—	—	—	—
Pilkington	Glass	Canada	—	France, Germany	—	—
Reckitts (later Reckitt and Colman)	Starch	Australia	—	Germany	+	Argentina
Royal Dutch Shell	Oil	S. Africa	—	Germany	+°	Russia,° Indonesia,° Mexico,° Borneo,° Romania,° Egypt°
Vickers	Armaments	Canada	—	Italy, Spain, Turkey	—	Japan, Russia

Note: ° indicates a manufacturing investment closely tied to local sources of raw materials.

Sources: Company publications and company histories, among which the following were of major importance: Mira Wilkins, *The Emergence of Multinational Enterprise* (Cambridge, Mass., 1970), 91–93; Sir Duncan Oppenheim, *The Growth and Organisation of British American Tobacco Company Limited* (private paper for the London School of Economics, May, 1961); P. A. Wright, *The Development of the Organisation of Patons and Baldwins Limited* (private paper given at the London School of Economics, February, 1959); D. C. Coleman, *Courtaulds: An Economic and Social History*, 2 vols. (Oxford, 1969); R. Geddes, *The Development and Organisation of the Dunlop Rubber Company Limited* (private paper given at the London School of Economics, January, 1965); Dunlop Information Service, *Dunlop — A Brief History* (London, 1971); J. E. Wall, *The Development and Organisation of Electrical and Musical Industries Limited* (private paper given at the London School of Economics, May, 1964); E.M.I. Ltd., *World Record Markets* (London, 1971); C. Wilson, *The History of Unilever*, 3 vols. (London, 1970); "Liebig's Extract of Meat Co. Ltd," in G. A. Smith, C. R. Christensen, and N. A. Berg, *Policy Formulation and Administration* (Homewood, Ill., 1968); W. J. Reader, *Imperial Chemical Industries: A History, Volume I: The Forerunners, 1870–1926* (London, 1970); T. C. Barker, *Pilkington Brothers and the Glass Industry* (London, 1960); B. N. Reckitt, *The History of Reckitt and Sons* (London, 1965); Kendall Beaton, *Enterprise in Oil (History of Shell in the United States)* (New York, 1957); F. C. Gerretson, *The History of Royal Dutch* (Leiden, 1953); H. Deterding, *An International Oil Man* (New York, 1934); J. D. Scott, *Vickers, A History* (London, 1926); Henry W. Macrosty, *The Trust Movement in British Industry* (London, 1970); and Alfred Plummer, *International Combines in Modern Industry* (London, 1937).

BRITISH-BASED MULTINATIONALS   317

a necessary though by no means a sufficient condition for international expansion; other leaders in oligopolies had remained at home. The fourteen pioneers were all led by men who shared a global vision.

British-American Tobacco was unusual in that it had been established specifically to operate outside the UK. The company was the product of intensive bargaining between James B. Duke's American Tobacco Company and Imperial Tobacco, the British group hastily merged in 1901 to fight off American Tobacco's entry to Britain. In 1902, American Tobacco ceded to Imperial all its UK interests, and Imperial agreed not to sell in the United States, its dependent territories, and Cuba. All interests in the rest of the world were pooled in BAT, thus cementing the boundaries of the cartel. American Tobacco received two-thirds of the stock of BAT and transferred to the new company all its existing subsidiaries in Australia, Canada, Germany, Japan, and Puerto Rico, while Imperial Tobacco received the remaining one-third of the stock. Thus BAT was, initially, an American multinational. With such immense backing, BAT could move very quickly to continue the expansion started by American Tobacco. The factory in China set up soon after 1902 was one of the very few Western-owned enterprises tolerated by the Chinese authorities.[32] As was the case earlier on, high discriminating tariffs on manufactured tobacco continued to be the motive force behind new investments. The American Supreme Court in 1911, however, had ordered American Tobacco to abrogate all its foreign restrictive covenants. Full ownership of BAT eventually ended in British hands early in the 1920s.

The Gramophone Company, Courtaulds, Dunlop, Nobel, and Vickers were all possessors of new technology, and all were engaged by 1914 in entering high-income markets. Their behaviour was primarily influenced by the need to jump tariff barriers and to compete in rapidly changing economies.[33] Special circumstances, however, shaped the particular mode of expansion of each of these firms.

For Courtaulds, the critical development was the purchase in 1904 of the British rights to the Stearn patents for viscose silk. The

[32] The constraints against factory production in China were great, as was governmental resistance to foreign incursions. See George C. Allen and Audrey G. Donnithorne, *Western Enterprise in Far Eastern Economic Development* (London, 1954).

[33] For expositions of the theory of how both oligopoly and new technology influence investment behaviour, see Richard Caves, "International Corporations: The Industrial Economics of Foreign Investment," *Economica* (February, 1971); F. T. Knickerbocker, *Oligopolistic Reaction and Multinational Enterprises* (Boston, 1973), Louis T. Wells, Jr., *The Product Life Cycle and International Trade* (Boston, 1972).

unusual event of a traditional, family-controlled silk company launching out into new technology was largely due to the persistence of H. G. Tetley, an outsider to the family.[34] The development of the patents and the subsequent rivalry with the European Syndicate led to the purchase of the United States rights and the establishment of the American Viscose Company in 1909 shortly after the imposition of a high tariff on imported artificial silk. Courtaulds' other major investment, in Belgium, was largely a portfolio investment to provide a listening post inside the protective European ring. Once the need for that post had been eliminated by other developments, the investment was sold in 1924. Cartels, disputes over patent rights, and high tariff barriers shaped Courtauld's early expansion policies. Once in train, however, these policies quickly led Courtaulds to a dominant position in the world rayon industry, a position which was maintained for many years.[35]

Dunlop's developments in rubber technology soon established the company as the dominant force in the UK and one of the few important international competitors in this new industry. Principally a tyre company, Dunlop had, like such major American competitors as Firestone, added golf balls and other rubber products to its line. Unlike the American firms, which had expanded only into Canada by 1914, Dunlop early on set up a number of tyre factories behind the rising tariff barriers. Their Japanese factory, built in 1899, can be interpreted more as a pre-emptive move against the Americans and less as a defence against the prospect of local competitors sheltered by a newly created tariff.[36] By contrast, the Gramophone Company's early investments apparently were based on the need to record local music in the easiest possible fashion. In India, for example, almost all records made were, and still are, of Indian rather than of Western music. In 1931, the Gramophone Company merged with the Columbian Gramophone Company to end the long-protracted negotiation over patent rights on either side of the Atlantic. The resulting company, EMI, emerged with manufacturing facilities in nineteen countries and a position of pre-eminence in the world record market.

Nobel's Explosive Company was originally the British Dynamite Company, established in 1865 to exploit Nobel's dynamite patents

[34] See D. C. Coleman, *Courtaulds: An Economic and Social History* (Oxford, 1969), II, Chapters 2–5 for details of Tetley's long struggle to overcome the scepticism of the Courtaulds family.
[35] A major factor that helped Courtaulds achieve its position of dominance was that it was the only one of the patent holders to have a well-developed textile business; the others were not initially as experienced in the weaving of fabric.
[36] Allen and Donnithorne, *Western Enterprise in Far Eastern Development*, 231.

BRITISH-BASED MULTINATIONALS   319

in Britain. British Dynamite was, in fact, Scottish and "owed nothing whatever, either financially or technically, to England. It was neither a private partnership nor a family business, and in both respects, in its day, it was unusual."[37] It was a limited liability company in which Alfred Nobel held three-eighths of the shares. Later on, in 1877, when the company was recapitalized and re-named, Nobel exchanged his shares for a royalty agreement. There-after, until World War I, the expansion of Nobel's Explosives was constrained geographically to the Empire by the presence of the Dynamite Trust. In the absence of the Trust, the pattern of ex-pansion would undoubtedly have been different.

Vickers, as one of Britain's leading armament manufacturers, had the strong and continuous spur of government contracts to develop new technology. From the vantage point of the 1970s, it seems odd that governments would wish to have foreigners in residence to make their crucial weapons. Yet that was precisely the wish that led the Italian, Spanish, Turkish, Japanese, and Russian govern-ments to request Vickers' presence, sometimes in partnerships with local interests, sometimes with Armstrong's (Vickers' main British rival), sometimes alone. If the managers at Vickers did not exactly welcome these invitations, at least they accepted them.[38]

The history of Lever Brothers and the development of Sunlight Soap is one of the great stories of marketing innovation.[39] Soap was highly income elastic and, after the 1880s, highly protected by tariffs in the advanced countries. Leverhulme was one of the few British industrialists to exploit income elasticities of demand, not simply in Britain but all over the world. Although widely scat-tered, the large majority of Lever's interests in 1914 were in the dominions,[40] while their United States operations were still con-fined to a toehold on the East Coast. One possible explanation is that the expansion, based principally on the acquisition of existing businesses, was facilitated by the "expatriate" firms in the do-minions that once acquired (often after stiff resistance) were rela-tively easier to manage than firms elsewhere.

Reckitt's and Bryant & May's pre-war expansions resemble that of Lever Brothers in miniature. "The early development of Reckitts," wrote B. N. Reckitt, "shows a gradual, not an immediate, realization

[37] W. J. Reader, *Imperial Chemical Industries: A History* (London, 1970), I.
[38] For fascinating glimpses of the negotiations, both with governments and with other armaments manufacturers, see J. P. Scott, *Vickers, A History* (London, 1962).
[39] The saga is told in authoritative detail by Charles Wilson, *The History of Unilever* (London, 1970), I.
[40] *Ibid.*, 196.

of the vital importance of standard quality, distinctive brand and advertising, in that order."[41] Their trade in starch prospered, as did Lever's, with rising incomes. Their first foreign factory was established in Australia in 1901, in order to take advantage of the abolition of inter-state tariffs behind a common external tariff at the formation of the Commonwealth. Other investments followed in rapid succession for similar reasons. Bryant & May also capitalised on a strong brand position at home by extending into the dominions and Brazil. This expansion was cut short, however, during the 1920s by financial and competitive problems in the UK, which led to Kreuger's powerful Swedish Match Syndicate taking partial control.

By 1900, J & P Coats and English Sewing Cotton, both in cotton thread, and Pilkington in glass, had built up dominant positions in their home markets by means of specialisation of product and by continuously introducing new lower-cost methods of production. They may be considered as true pioneers of the Second Industrial Revolution. Pilkington, for example, was one of the very early firms to use electricity as a source of power.[42] Pilkington did not, however, aggressively expand abroad before 1914, partly because of their continuing (though somewhat reduced) ability to export. Even so, they invested in France in 1898, and thereby established what proved to be an important pawn in numerous arguments with the continental Convention Internationale des Glaceries. But they cooperated with the Convention, even to the extent of contributing in 1913 to a new German factory set up as a reprisal against an unruly local firm.[43] As part of a general settlement with the continental producers, both subsidiaries were eventually sold in the mid-1930s. J & P Coats, by contrast, were faced with ever-increasing tariff barriers abroad, but did not shy away from investments. Together with English Sewing Cotton, Coats controlled the lion's share of the world market for cotton thread. The architect of their foreign expansion, D. E. Philippi, the German-born chief salesman of this Scottish company, was as distinctive among his peers in the cotton trade as were Coats' policies.[44]

Liebig's Extract of Meat Company (LEM Co.) was originally an "expatriate" company of mixed Belgian and English parentage. In 1863, a Belgian engineer, Gilbert, established a factory at Fray

[41] B. N. Reckitt, *The History of Reckitt & Sons* (London, 1965), 43.
[42] T. C. Barker, *Pilkington*, 165.
[43] *Ibid.*
[44] For details of these policies, and of the series of amalgamations that shaped the industry, see Henry W. Macrosty, *The Trust Movement in British Industry* (London, 1907), 126-147.

Bentos on the river Uruguay to produce a beef extract by means
of a new German technology. Gilbert ran out of money and had
to form a new company in London in 1865. LEM Co., established
with a capital of £500,000, can thereafter be considered to have had
a British base. The success of the company was due originally to
the difficulty of providing enough meat in Europe in the days before refrigerated ships; Liebig's extract was an excellent substitute
that could readily be transported. By 1913, the firm owned vast
estancias in Argentina and Uruguay on which cattle to be processed
were raised. Even the advent of refrigeration did not seriously
impair the growth of the firm, since by then it had established a
strong brand name in Britain and Europe. Over the years, LEM
Co. transferred much of the overall direction of the operations and
development work to Britain. In 1914, a factory for secondary
processing of the extract was built in England, at which point
LEM Co. effectively ceased to be an "expatriate" company and
joined the ranks of British-based multinationals.[45]

Shell Transport and Trading was a trading company turned oil
processor. The story of Marcus Samuel's early investments and his
merger with Deterding's Royal Dutch Company in 1907 has been
told many times.[46] Initially the location of oil determined where
the refineries were situated. Royal Dutch Shell's expansion from
its original Far Eastern base was principally one of buying new
oilfields, as in Russia and Romania, and of developing a distribution and marketing network. The fierce struggle with Standard Oil
shaped many of Royal Dutch Shell's moves, particularly the entry
into the United States. The purchase of Californian oilfields was
a direct riposte to Standard's incursions in the Far East, as well as
an entry to the world's largest market for oil. Royal Dutch Shell,
though only 40 per cent British-owned, was the classic example of
British capital at work to exploit natural resources on a world-wide
scale.

All these companies pioneering the development of international
manufacturing had the energy and ability to take advantage of their
special skills. These skills were either technological, or marketing,
or, in the case of Shell, logistical. Many other companies might
have done the same but chose not to. In the cotton trade, for example, very few manufacturers entered into foreign trade directly

---

[45] For some details of the early investments, see "Liebig's Extract of Meat Co.," in G. A.
Smith, C. R. Christensen, and N. A. Berg, *Policy Formulation and Administration* (Homewood, Ill., 1968).
[46] See, for example, F. C. Gerretson, *The History of Royal Dutch* (Leiden, 1953).

— at least three-quarters of the exports were handled by foreign merchants resident in Manchester [47] — and were not therefore intimately exposed to the pressures to invest abroad. This attitude, amounting in some instances almost to a casual disdain of foreign markets and foreigners, was to be observed in many other industries. The fourteen pioneers did not suffer from this lethargy. That they did not is attributable, at least in part, to the influence of foreigners within the firms or, in five of them, the influence of foreign capital.

Table 3 shows that these firms chose to establish factories abroad on the basis of economic advantage or cartel considerations, not Empire loyalty. With few exceptions, the investments were in the high-income countries with the greatest demand for the products in question. Investments in the Empire were almost exclusively restricted to the "white" dominions, where the burgeoning populations had income levels comparable to or higher than those in Europe.[48]

Many other British companies had, to be sure, established manufacturing bases abroad by 1914. And some "expatriate" companies such as Anglo-Persian Oil were on the threshold of a period of growth that led to their transformation into manufacturing multinationals. A diligent search of many records did not reveal, however, any British manufacturers that had become as deeply committed overseas as had the fourteen pioneers.[49] Where they had invested in production, the factories were often extremely small and represented little more than "outposts" in a network of selling agencies. Some, such as Ruston's, were repair workshops providing a local after-sales service that did a little assembly work on the side. Table 4 shows a list of typical "outpost" factories, which were generally located in the high-income countries.

If the early manufacturing investments were made without regard to the existence of the Empire, investments by British manufacturers to control sources of raw materials for their own factories were distinctly biassed towards Empire sources. Table 5 shows the raw materials investments of the pioneers, together with those of a few other typical investors. In general, such investments by manufacturers were rare. The existence of well developed London

[47] R. E. Tyson, "The Cotton Industry," in Aldcroft, ed., *Development of British Industry*, 125.

[48] For some detailed estimates and comparisons of income per capita in 1914, see Staff of the National Bureau of Economic Research, *Income of the United States: Its Amount and Distribution 1909-1919* (New York, 1921), I.

[49] Many of the important empire trading companies, such as Dalgety, had small manufacturing units attached to their import/export activities. They represent a special category of investment that is not considered here.

BRITISH-BASED MULTINATIONALS 323

commodity markets removed much of the fear of supply difficulties that typically pushes a manufacturer into backwards integration.

Quite why there should have been such a pronounced Empire preference is unclear. Perhaps, like Leverhulme, the investors were

Table 4
Location of "Outpost" Foreign Manufacturing Investment of Selected UK Firms, Pre-1914

Firm	Industry	Empire	Other Locations
Albright and Wilson	Chemicals	Canada	U.S.A.[a]
Armstrong Whitworth (acquired by Vickers)	Armaments	–	Italy Japan
Clayton and Shuttleworth	Agricultural machinery	–	Austria Russia
Consolidated Diesel Engine Manufacturers	Diesel engines	–	Belgium [b]
Crosfield (acquired by Unilever)	Soaps	S. Africa	China [c] France [c]
J. Dickinson (later Dickinson Robinson)	Paper	S. Africa	–
Dubs	Locomotives	Canada	–
Greens of Wakefield	Engineering	–	Germany, U.S.A.
Howard & Bullock (acquired by Stone-Platt Industries)	Textile machinery	–	U.S.A.
Mackintosh (later Rowntree Mackintosh)	Food	–	U.S.A.
New Premier Company	Bicycles	–	Austria Germany
Renold Chain	Engineering	–	France
Ruston	Agricultural machinery	–	China Russia
Schweppes (later Cadbury Schweppes)	Drinks	Australia	–
United Alkali (later part of ICI)	Chemicals	–	U.S.A.

Notes: [a] Sold in 1920.
[b] Failed in 1914.
[c] These two factories were planned or under construction in 1914, but did not begin production until 1917.

Sources: Company publications, including B. Newman, *One Hundred Years of Good Company: Study of Ruston & Hornsby* (Ruston & Hornsby, 1957); Basil H. Tripp, *Renold Chains: A History of the Company and the Rise of the Precision Chain Industry* (London, 1956); A. E. Musson, *Enterprise in Soap and Chemicals: John Crosfield & Sons Ltd. 1815–1965* (Manchester, 1965); also L. F. Haber, *The Chemical Industry 1900–1930* (Oxford, 1971); and D. H. Aldcroft, ed., *The Development of British Industry and Foreign Competition 1875–1914* (London, 1968).

TABLE 5
LOCATION OF FOREIGN INVESTMENTS BY SELECTED MAJOR UK
MANUFACTURING FIRMS TO SECURE SOURCES
OF RAW MATERIALS, BEFORE 1914
(EXCLUDES OIL INDUSTRY)

Firm	Commodity	Empire	Others
Brunner Mond (later part of ICI)	Vegetable Oils	British W. Africa	—
British-American Tobacco	Tobacco	India	—
Cadbury Bros. (later part of Cadbury Schweppes)	Cocoa	Gold Coast [a] Trinidad	--
Crosfield (acquired by Unilever)	Vegetable Oils	British W. Africa	—
Dunlop	Rubber	Malaya	Liberia [b]
Fitch Lovell	Meat	—	Argentina
Lever Bros. (later Unilever)	Vegetable Oils	Australia British W. Africa British Pacific Is.	U.S.A.[c] Congo
Pilkington	Silver Sand	—	Belgium [d]
Reckitt (later Reckitt & Coleman)	Graphite	Ceylon	Germany
Turner Bros. (later part of Turner and Newall)	Asbestos	Rhodesia	—
United Alkali (later part of ICI)	Copper	—	Spain

Notes: [a] Sold in 1912.
[b] Sold in 1918.
[c] This investment was made in 1894, and sold within a year.
[d] Sold in 1930s.

Sources: See Tables 3 and 4, together with I. A. Williams, *The Firm of Cadbury 1831-1931* (London, 1931); *Cadbury Brothers Industrial Record 1919–1939* (Cadbury, 1945); *Turner and Newall Limited: The First Fifty Years, 1920–1970* (London, 1970).

looking for some form of government preference or protection.[50] If so, they would have been disappointed. Leverhulme, a great believer in controlling his sources of supply (despite the commodity markets), bought a number of incompetently managed trading companies in the Gold Coast (now Ghana), in the expectation of being able to gain permission to develop plantations on specific lines. The British Colonial office was deaf to his proposals, thus forcing him to continue trading in the traditional local manner and to look elsewhere. The Belgian government was more receptive,

[50] Wilson, *Unilever*, I, 165ff.

and an enormous plantation in the Belgian Congo was created. Ignoring his early rebuff, Leverhulme persevered in looking for Empire sites, going as far afield as the Solomon Islands and eventually back to West Africa in 1920, when he bought the remnants of the Royal Niger Company, and the African and Eastern Company, both "expatriate" companies.

In sum, when war broke out in 1914, most British manufacturing firms were viewing the world at a distance. Ostrich-like, they had not taken the trouble to keep closely in touch with developments in markets and technology abroad. The few exceptions to this tendency had, by one means or another, been stimulated to go abroad and find out for themselves. Direct investments in the aggregate stood at roughly £400,000,000 (10 per cent of the total), and of this amount, probably no more than £250,000,000 was in manufacturing. In comparison, United States firms controlled £530,000,000 of foreign direct investment (75 per cent of the total), and manufacturing accounted for the lion's share.[51] Very few British firms in 1914 emulated the early international performance of such technology-based giants as Ford and Westinghouse Electric.[52]

THE FOLLOWERS AND THE INTER-WAR YEARS

The aftermath of World War I provided a set of conditions that changed the foreign investment picture dramatically. During the 1920s and 1930s, more and more firms were forced to wake up to the fact that to continue to play a role in world markets required far reaching changes in policy. Their response was, often reluctantly, to establish foreign factories, primarily in the dominions. Many, to be sure, did not invest abroad at all. Nevertheless, by 1939 almost all the leading firms in every industry had at least a toe-hold abroad.

The inter-war period was the beginning of an era when British firms investing abroad preferred Empire locations above all others and continued to do so until the 1960s. The incentive to invest elsewhere was blunted by a combination of factors. Relatively cheap materials and labour together with a conservative home market continued, as in Victorian Britain, to blunt the incentive to

[51] Estimates from W. S. Woytinsky and E. S. Woytinsky, *World Commerce and Development* (New York, 1955), 191.

[52] For a detailed and fascinating account of the early foreign investments of American firms, see Mira Wilkins, *The Emergence of Multinational Enterprise* (Cambridge, Mass., 1970).

innovate new processes and new products. The cartels, which started at the turn of the century and remained in force until 1945, frequently left the British Empire to British firms in return for no competition elsewhere, and thus contributed further to that blunting.[53] Europe, quite apart from the dominant presence of many highly innovative local firms buttressed by cartels and government policy, was plagued by inflation and unrest. Latin America was at best an uncomfortable location for foreigners (*pace* the *Yanquis*). To British eyes, the Empire must have seemed a haven of sanity and security. Given the traditional ties of trade, it is small wonder that the dominions, with their high income levels, so frequently became first choice for new investors, and that less developed parts of the Empire became second choice.

The followers listed in Table 6 were, with few exceptions, oriented to the Empire. They are representative of investment behaviour of the period. Together with the pioneers, they accounted for a substantial proportion of all British foreign direct investment in manufacturing. All the followers that did not slavishly follow the well-beaten path to the Empire had links with foreign sources of a stimulus to be different. Baker Perkins, for example, had its origins in an American and a Canadian who both emigrated to England, and in a German company. Between 1919 (when Baker Perkins was formed by merger) and 1939, the company operated a triangular alliance with a German and a French company to exploit the world market for food and chemical machinery.[54] Metal Box was dependent on technology from Continental Can in the United States. Babcock and Wilcox, in boilers, was partially owned by the American firm of the same name until the 1930s. Turner and Newall went outside the Empire simply because the Canadian asbestos mine they wished to purchase in 1934 happened to be owned by a United States company; Keasbey and Mattison would not sell the mine and had to be purchased outright.[55]

Many firms needed a considerable shock before they would reconsider their previous policies on investing abroad, even in the relatively secure Empire. Loss of export markets and the lack of alternatives were the principal shocks, but often they had to be dramatic before action resulted. For Cadbury, wartime rationing had prevented exports of chocolate and had led to the appearance

---

[53] George W. Stocking and Myron Watkins, *Cartels in Action* (New York, 1946); and Ervin Hexner, *International Cartels* (London, 1946), provide many examples in chemicals, steel, rubber, and other industries.
[54] Baker Perkins Limited, *An Introduction to Baker Perkins* (Peterborough, 1957), 8.
[55] *Turner and Newall Limited: The First Fifty Years, 1920–1970* (London, 1970), 22.

BRITISH-BASED MULTINATIONALS   327

of local manufacturers in the dominions. These new firms were later protected by their governments. By 1921, after the post-war boom, Cadbury's exports were down to half the 1914 levels. Local production was the only possible answer, and Cadbury's first (Canadian) venture started up that year.[56] The Cadbury story was repeated many times over.

Some firms, as one might expect, stumbled into overseas manufacturing by accident. Lewis Berger and Sons, for example, started manufacturing paint in South Africa in 1918 because of a clerical error. A clerk had inadvertently added two noughts to a purchase order, and enough paint to supply five years' demand was shipped. Rather than waste so much paint, which at that time solidified if kept too long, an old paint mill had to be secured to process the surplus.[57] In general, however, the evidence suggests that decisions to manufacture abroad were carefully planned, last-ditch defensive moves.

Many of the firms that followed the pioneers into foreign manufacturing were also followers in their industries, in the sense that they were establishing important domestic positions in industries created by foreign firms. In electrical machinery, for example, by means of merger and wrangling over patent rights, English Electric, Associated Electrical Industries, and others were attempting to catch up on the lead of the U.S. General Electric, Westinghouse, and others. With respect to foreign investments, their competitive position was different from that of the pioneers, who had been part of the creation of new international industries. The followers had to face competition from firms already well established abroad. In these circumstances, Empire territories often provided investment sites with the least competitive disadvantage. There are many instances of follower firms (such as William Morris in France) attempting to manufacture first in Europe, quickly recoiling and trying again more successfully in the Empire. Those followers with strong international ties were not subject to quite the same pressures and could afford to look outside the Empire.

The inter-war years also saw the expansion of many mining and other natural resource companies outside their countries of initial development. British Petroleum was beginning to extend its reach outside the Middle East, though the development of its international

---

[56] *Cadbury Brothers: Industrial Record 1919–1939* (Cadbury, 1945), 77.

[57] The story is told by A. P. Cartwright, *The Dynamite Company* (London, 1964), 234. Note that Lewis Berger was wholly owned by Sherwin Williams of Canada Limited, which in turn was closely affiliated with the U.S. Sherwin Williams Company. Such "accidents" happen, of course, to companies of any nationality.

network had to wait until after its Abadan refinery had been seized and later returned in the early 1950s. Burmah Oil, originally the "expatriate" Rangoon Oil Company, had thrown out a distribution net in the Far East, centered on its Rangoon oil fields and refinery, and had built a refinery in India in the 1920s.[58] Consolidated Gold Fields, another "expatriate" company in origin, had developed mines outside its South African interests before 1914 and continued to do so on a massive scale.[59] Unlike manufacturing companies seeking selectively to secure sources of supply, such companies were not greatly influenced by any preference for the Empire; they went where the best resources happened to be.

While the followers were coming to grips with their new Empire possessions, the fourteen pioneers were on a different tack. Their major preoccupation was filling in the gaps. Lever Brothers, merged with the Dutch consortium Margarine Unie in 1929 to form Unilever, was clearly the leader in the development of a global network. Table 6 shows the overall pattern of development. Nearly half of the manufacturing investments made between the wars by these fourteen companies were in Europe, whereas the Empire accounted for less than 30 per cent of the total.

Why was there this marked difference in behaviour? In part, the answer may be that these firms had already crossed the threshold of international experience beyond which a sense of Empire security was not needed. In addition, these firms were much better equipped than most to compete head-on with the most progressive firms abroad; their propensity to innovate survived the war unimpaired. They maintained their leading positions in international oligopolies that they had helped to create, and they were able, by and large, to continue investing abroad according to the economic dictates of their industries.

One exception was Imperial Chemical Industries (ICI), or rather its four constituent companies before the merger in 1926. The merger was a defensive move against major inroads by foreign firms, such as I. G. Farbenindustrie, in all sectors of the UK chemical industry. Once created, ICI moved only slowly to take advantage of scale economies, and for many years it resembled a collection of very small companies. Consequently, research and development was inhibited, and no strong central office was formed.

---

[58] Burmah also owned, and still does, approximately 23 per cent of British Petroleum, due to its involvement in the early development of Anglo-Persian.

[59] Consolidated Gold Fields was one of the few major British investors in Tsarist Russia, and also owned mines in many parts of Africa, Colombia, Mexico, and the United States.

BRITISH-BASED MULTINATIONALS   329

TABLE 6

FOREIGN MANUFACTURING INVESTMENTS OF SELECTED UK FIRMS, PRE-1939 [a]

Firm (and Industry)	Dominions				Empire		U.S.A.	Europe							Central & S. America			Far East		Other Countries
	Canada	Australia	S. Africa	New Zealand	India	Rhodesia		Belgium	France	Germany	Italy	Netherlands	Denmark	Spain	Argentina	Brazil	Mexico	Japan	Indonesia	
Pioneers																				
British-American Tobacco (Tobacco)	(+)[*]	(+)	+	+	(+)[*]		+[*]			(+)		+	(+)	(+)	(+)	+	+	(+)	+	Numerous
Bryant & May (Matches)	+	(+)	(+)	(+)[*]												(+)[*]				
J & P Coats (Cotton Thread)	(+)						(+)	(+)	+	+	(+)			(+)		(+)	(+)	(+)		Numerous
Courtaulds (Synthetic Textiles)	+				+[b]		(+)[c]	(+)[c]	+	+	+		+[a]	+[a]						
Dunlop (Rubber)	(+)	+	(+)	+	+		+			(+)					(+)		,	(+)		
English Sewing Cotton (Cotton thread)	(+)	+	+				(+)	+	(+)[b]	+				(+)[d]						
E.M.I. (Records)	(+)	+	(+)	+	(+)	+	+	+	+	+	+	+	(+)	+	+	(+)		+		Numerous
Unilever (Soaps)	(+)	(+)	(+)	+	+		(+)	(+)	(+)	(+)	+	+	+	+	+	+		(+)	+	Numerous
Liebig's Extract of Meat (Food)	+					+[*]	+	(+)	+	+					(+)[*]					Switzerland, (Uruguay[a]) Paraguay[a]
I.C.I. (Chemicals)	(+)	(+)	(+)		+		(+)[b]		+	+						+				Numerous
Pilkington (Glass)	(+)	+	+						(+)[a]	(+)[b]					+					
Reckitt & Colman (Household Products)	+	(+)	(+)		+		(+)	+	+	(+)		+		+	(+)	+				Numerous

										Numerous
Royal Dutch Shell (Oil)	+	+	(+)*	+	(+)	+	+°	(+°)ᵇ +	(+)°	
Vickers (Armaments)	(+)	+	+			(+)ᵇ	+°	(+)ᵇ		Yugoslavia,ᵃ Romaniaᵇ (Turkey)ᶜ
Followers										
Babcock & Wilcox (Engineering)	+		+	+	+	+				
Baker Perkins (Machinery)	+	+	+	(+)	+					
British Oxygen (Gases)	+	+	+							Norway*
British Petroleum (Oil)	+	+		+						Persia,* Egypt,* Israel
Cadbury (Food)	+	+	(+)	+						
Distillers (Drink)	+	+	(+)	+						
Glaxo (Foods and Drugs)	+	(+)*	(+)*	+	+	+				Greece
G.K.N. (Engineering)	+	+	+		+	+				Turkey
Metal Box (Metal Cans)	+	+	+		+	+				
Rowntree (Foods)	+	+	(+)ᶠ	+						
Turner & Newall (Asbestos)	+*	+	(+)*	+						

* Indicates manufacturing closely tied to local sources of raw materials.

( ) Indicates investments made before 1914.

Notes:

ᵃ Includes only those firms with factories in four or more foreign countries before 1939.

ᵇ Sold, liquidated or expropriated between the mid-1930s and 1940.

ᶜ Sold by UK Government fiat in 1942.

ᵈ Control passed to J & P Coats in 1910.

ᵉ Liquidated in 1929.

ᶠ Liquidated in 1915.

Sources: As for Tables 3, 4, and 5, together with: *An Introduction to Baker Perkins* (Peterborough, 1957); J. S. Hutchinson, *The Development and Organization of the British Oxygen Company Ltd.* (private paper given at the London School of Economics, January, 1963); H. Longhurst, *Adventure in Oil: The Story of B.P.* (London, 1959); *A Short Guide to D.C.L.* (London, 1971); R. P. Brooks, *The Development and Organisation of G.K.N. Ltd.* (private paper given at the London Graduate School of Business Studies, December, 1969); D. Ducat, *The Development and Organisation of Metal Box Limited* (private paper given at the London School of Economics, February, 1964); Rowntree Mackintosh Limited, *Some Basic Dates in the History of Rowntree Mackintosh Limited* (London, 1972).

Comparing ICI with I. G. Farben during the 1930s, one observer concluded that ICI "depends for success on making comparatively few products extremely well and selling them at prices usually fixed by international agreement," unlike I. G. Farben which "relies on making a variety of substances constantly changing in range as new products appear in a laboratory and are taken up for large scale manufacture because they seem to have profit-making capacity." [60] Not until the 1950s did ICI make any determined effort to reshape itself into a more cohesive group. Until that time, only those overseas ventures in the dominions were of significance; ICI's pre-war international behaviour was in many respects that of a follower rather than a pioneer. [61] The complex of alliances with DuPont and others in a series of cartels did not, of course, encourage expansion into new territories.

Some of the pioneers, it must be noted, faced considerable competitive difficulties outside the Empire territories during the interwar years. As Table 6 indicates, Vickers lost all their European and Japanese armaments subsidiaries, and only subsidiaries (mainly in steel and ships) in the dominions survived. Pilkington abandoned Europe to the cartel. Courtaulds lost millions in their European ventures during the 1930s. In addition to selling some of their subsidiaries, they had, by 1939, reduced to purely nominal levels their initially enormous holdings in such companies as Snia Viscosa. The European cartel allied with economic nationalism proved too strong to tolerate British incursions for long. If one adds to this tale of woe the forced sale of the American Viscose Company in 1942 on the orders of the British government, one sees Courtaulds' international strategy in ruins.

Despite such disasters, the continuing stimulus of competing (and often cooperating) with the world's most innovative firms had a beneficial influence on the way the British companies were managed. This stimulus greatly strengthened each firm's development — Courtaulds, for example, gained considerably by its technical exchange agreements — and provided a strong base from which to build larger foreign empires in the more favourable international climate after World War II. Even so, it was clearly more difficult to enter markets in Europe or the United States than to develop an Empire base. Faced with the shocks of changed trading con-

[60] Herbert Levenstein, "From Within the Dyestuffs Industry," *Journal of the Society of Chemical Industries*, vol. 50 (1931).

[61] For example, the investments in France and Germany were in small zip-fastener factories managed by the metals side of Nobel Industries. See Reader, *Imperial Chemical Industries*, 405–407.

ditions, a modified version of the Victorian policies of following the path of least resistance made sense for all but the very strongest and most internationally experienced firms.

POSTSCRIPT

Immediately after World War II, the same general preferences for what had by then become the Commonwealth influenced new entrants to the arena of international manufacturing. This time, however, the Commonwealth preference was neither so pervasive among the newcomers nor so long-lived as before.

Table 7 provides a very crude measure of a shift in preference back towards that prevailing in the pre-1914 era. Each of the eighty firms in the table is classified by the decade when it first entered into manufacturing abroad on a significant scale. Judgment of what constitutes significance is inevitably subjective. For example, a firm that set up overseas factories in, say 1908, 1952, 1953, and 1958 would normally be classified as entering international manufacture in the 1950s, especially if the first venture was known to be small relative to the others. If, however, the first venture rapidly grew to be large relative to its parent company, as was

TABLE 7
80 U.K. FIRMS' PREFERENCE FOR COMMONWEALTH LOCATIONS, CLASSIFIED BY DECADE OF ENTRY TO INTERNATIONAL MANUFACTURING, END OF 1970 ᵃ

Decade of Entry ᵇ	No. of Firms	Percentage of Foreign Manufacturing Output in 1970 Located in the Commonwealth		
		Zero	Less than 50%	More than 50%
Before 1914	11	—	7	4
1920s	12	—	1	11
1930s	11	—	2	9
1940s	3	—	1	2
1950s	28	1	13	14
1960s	15	7	4	4
TOTAL	80	8	28	44

Source: London Business School Multinational Data Bank.
Notes: ᵃ Includes all of the largest 100 UK-owned manufacturing firms on the *Times 1000* index (1972/73) that had more than 3 foreign manufacturing subsidiaries; except Unilever, mining and oil companies.
ᵇ See text for definition.

the case for the American Viscose Company and Courtaulds, the firm would be classified as entering before 1914. Commonwealth preference is measured on a cross-sectional basis by the location of each firm's overseas output in 1970.

Forty-four of the firms in Table 7 produced more than half of their foreign output in Commonwealth locations during 1970. All but seven of these firms went abroad between 1920 and 1959. The data suggest that, once started on an Empire or Commonwealth track, firms find it difficult to branch out. The rigidity of attitude might be called the "dead hand" of history; [62] attitudes and procedures of management appropriate for Commonwealth subsidiaries can become so institutionalized that managers at many levels in the organization neither recognize the need for change nor welcome efforts to impose new thinking.

The pioneers, by going abroad before Empire preferences became so prevalent, had a body of prior experience that protected them from such a rigid approach. Despite all the commercial disasters in prewar Europe, none of them retrenched wholly within the Commonwealth. The most recent entrants were also protected from the "dead hand." By the time they began to feel pressure to invest abroad, the EEC was a much more immediate problem than the Commonwealth.

Among four of the newest entrants, however, the old attitudes still lingered. All four were in engineering industries, which have been the most loyal of Empire supporters. Nearly 70 per cent of the thirty-one engineering firms included in Table 1 had over half of their foreign output located in the Commonwealth in 1970. The major engineering industries, such as cars, were slow to develop their own British-based and British-owned multinationals. In many sectors of the engineering industry, the same process of catching up with foreign-based leaders that occurred in some sectors during the inter-war years is still going on, and the same rationale for an Empire preference remains.

Those firms with no Commonwealth manufacturing were the most recent entrants in the food and building products industries. The English brewers especially made major investments in Europe in the late 1960s and early 1970s. Had they first expanded abroad in the 1920s, they would almost certainly have gone first to the dominions rather than across the Channel. Even the more internationally experienced food companies, with long histories of man-

[62] This expressive phrase was used during an interview by one manager of a large firm suffering from this disease.

aging Empire plantations, had by 1973 begun to change their policies away from further expansion in the Commonwealth and into Europe. Similar stirrings are occurring in other industries, as the figures cited at the beginning of this article indicate.

The wheel appears to have come almost full cycle between the late 1800s and 1970. The lure of Empire markets waxed and began to wane in a forty-year span, not only for British exports of goods, but also for British direct foreign investments. Whether the newly multinational British manufacturers will be able to withstand the cold competitive winds both in Europe and the United States remains to be seen, but that is another story.

[7]

By Lawrence G. Franko

CENTRE D'ETUDES INDUSTRIELLES,
GENEVA

The Origins of Multinational Manufacturing by Continental European Firms*

❧ *European multinationals followed a different path of development from that pursued by United States firms, but European multinational manufacturing began even earlier than did American, and its story is no less significant. Dr. Franko offers a range of relevant data and analysis about the evolution of direct foreign investment by Western European manufacturers.*

Unlike its European counterpart, the origins of the spread of U.S. multinational manufacturing enterprise are reasonably well understood. It seems generally agreed that American firms started down the road to multinational manufacturing because they had a penchant for introducing new, labor-saving, highly income elastic products; they specialized in what has come to be termed "product pioneering." As innovators, they had proprietary knowledge of the production of these goods, which were clearly differentiable from other articles because of their novelty.[1] Rising per capita incomes in Europe and elsewhere first pulled such new products into those nations as exports.[2] When income distributions in Europe shifted toward the U.S. pattern, as they did in post-World War II Britain, Sweden, and Holland, the pull was probably all the

Business History Review, Vol. XLVIII, No. 3 (Autumn, 1974). Copyright © The President and Fellows of Harvard College.

* The research on which this article is based was made possible by the financial support of the Ford Foundation, the Centre d'Etudes Industrielles, and the Harvard Business School. It was done as part of the Harvard-CEI comparative multinational enterprise study of the foreign operations of the world's largest manufacturing enterprises.

[1] In this paper, "innovation" refers to first commercial introduction, rather than first invention of a product.

The relationship between differentiability of products and the spread of foreign manufacture "horizontally," i.e., in the same product lines, by U.S. firms, has been particularly emphasized by Caves. See R. Caves, "International Corporations: The Industrial Economics of Foreign Investment," *Economica* (February, 1971).

[2] Empirical evidence for this view of the causes of U.S. foreign investment is accumulating at a rapid rate. For example, A. E. Scaperlanda and L. J. Maurer have shown that changes in EEC market size, not trade barriers nor differential U.S.-EEC growth rates were most closely correlated with the massive influx of American direct investment in Europe between 1952 and 1966. See Scaperlanda and Maurer, "The Determinants of U.S. Direct Investment in the EEC," *American Economic Review* (September 1969). See also the evidence summarized in Raymond Vernon, *Sovereignty at Bay* (New York, 1971), Chapter III.

harder.[3] The American Challenge thus met the European attraction, most often in the form of foreign customers' requests.[4]

For American firms, the transition from exporting to foreign manufacturing often came as non-American markets for new products became large enough and certain enough to warrant investments in additional plant capacity. Foreign production seemed in order when scale economies in U.S. production were about to be exhausted, when foreign production began to look as if it could be undertaken for an average cost less than U.S. marginal cost plus transport and tariffs, and when customer needs and production techniques were standardized so that such costs could be calculated. All these events inevitably occurred as new products went from birth to maturity over their life cycles.[5] They were hastened by the fact that wage rates were almost invariably lower outside, as opposed to inside the U.S. In such circumstances, even profit maximizing firms with world-wide product monopolies had reason to put up foreign plants. Conceptually, their decision was identical to that of a domestic manufacturer considering expansion into a less developed region of his home market. The evidence suggests, however, that managers of few U.S. firms reasoned in quite such a comfortable manner. The threat of losing established markets, rather than opportunities offered by new ones, was the most frequent trigger of foreign manufacturing investment.[6] Even in the early days of their international export expansion, most U.S. firms were threatened by competition, either from local entrepreneurs awakening to newly feasible production opportunities,[7] or (more importantly) from either potential or actual threatening moves by American oligopolistic competitors.[8]

Much less is known about the evolution of European-based multinationals. Indeed, even the magnitude of those "other multinationals" has often remained obscure. During the 1960s it was

[3] This hypothesis has been subjected to a very preliminary (although positive) test in J. Neill Fortune, "Income Distribution as a Determinant of Imports of Manufactured Consumer Commodities," *Canadian Journal of Economics*, V (May, 1972).

[4] The importance of foreign customers' requests as a factor pulling U.S. firms into foreign markets has been repeatedly emphasized in surveys of motivations both for exporting and for foreign manufacturing investments. H. J. Robinson, in *The Motivation and Flow of Foreign Private Investment* (Stanford Research Institute, 1961), 37, notes that over 90 per cent of external triggers for investment mentioned by U.S. firms in his survey involved proposals by foreign industrialists.

[5] A further description of this process is given in Raymond Vernon, "International Trade and International Investment in the Product Cycle," Chapter II of *Sovereignty at Bay*.

[6] See *Ibid.*, Chapter 3 for evidence on this point.

[7] *Ibid.*

[8] See Frederick T. Knickerbocker, *Oligopolistic Reaction and Multinational Enterprise* (Boston, 1973), for statistical evidence. See also Mira Wilkins, *The Maturing of Multinational Enterprise* (Cambridge, Mass., 1974) for historical material on specific firms.

sometimes said that virtually all multinational enterprises were American in origin.[9] However, the historical record shows that multinationality of manufacturing operations is no American monopoly.[10] During the century and a half that has elapsed since Cockerill of Belgium put up its first foreign plant in Prussia in 1815, the majority of today's large Western European companies have come first to sell and then to produce outside their home countries.

In 1970, seventy-eight of the eighty-one continental European companies on the *Fortune* "200" list were manufacturing outside their home countries. Even "domestic" coal and steel producers such as Buderus'che, Salzgitter, Vallourec, and Charbonnages de France, owned at least 25 per cent of one or more foreign manufacturing ventures in that year. Moreover, some sixty of the seventy-one firms for which information is available derived 25 per cent or more of their total sales from exports and foreign production in 1970.[11]

Already in 1960, thirty-four of the eighty-one large continental firms owned manufacturing operations in seven or more countries.[12] On the eves of World Wars 1 and II, the number of such firms, or of their direct predecessors with a corresponding degree of multinationality, had been seven and fourteen respectively. By 1970, no fewer than sixty-two of the eighty-one European companies on the *Fortune* "200" list had attained such a multinational spread. The distribution of the continental companies by industry and by degree of multinationality in 1970 is given in Table 1.

[9] Such at least was the implication most readers carried away from a reading of J. J. Servan-Schreiber's famous statement that, after the U.S. and the U.S.S.R., the third largest producing unit in the world would soon consist of American subsidiaries abroad. The impression was made all the stronger by chapter titles such as "Europe Without a Strategy" and by sentences such as: "L'Europe n'a presque rien sur le plan industriel, de comparable aux entreprises à grande aire d'activité qui caractérisent les sociétés américaines s'implantant sur son sol. Une exception intéressante: L'Imperial Chemical Industries (Angleterre), seule compagnie européenne qui ait organisé un état-major à l'échelon du continent pour prendre en main l'administration de ses cinquante filiales. Les efforts déployés par quelques autres sociétés européennes apparaissent timides." Servan-Schreiber, *Le Défi Américain* (Paris, 1967), 20, emphasis added.

In 1969, Jack Behrman also appeared to underestimate the importance of European companies' international operations: "If one postulates that the awakening point (of transition to multinational enterprise) occurs when foreign operations become something over 25 percent of total activity of the enterprise, there are close to 200 U.S.-based enterprises which are candidates for becoming multinational – if they are not already in that category. But, there are few European-based companies meeting the criterion." Behrman, *Some Patterns in the Rise of Multinational Enterprise* (Chapel Hill, N.C., 1969).

[10] The word "multinational" as used here only denotes the existence of manufacturing operations, owned to significant extent by the parent firm, in numerous countries.

[11] Company annual reports and documents.

[12] Manufacturing operations were counted as belonging to a particular European company if they were 25 per cent or more owned by it. Source: Tabulation done by the author from company reports and partly reported in L. G. Franko, "Multinational Corporations in the 1970's: Will They Matter?" in P. Uri, ed., *Trade and Investment Policies for the 1970's* (New York, 1971).

TABLE 1

MULTINATIONALITY OF EUROPEAN ENTERPRISE, 1970
(DISTRIBUTION OF THE 81 LARGEST CONTINENTAL EUROPEAN
MANUFACTURING ENTERPRISES BY MAIN INDUSTRY OF PRODUCTION
AND BY EXTENT OR FOREIGN MANUFACTURE, 1970)

SIC No.	Main Industry of Firm (°)	Number of Firms In Sample	Number of Firms with Manufacturing Operations in 7 or more Countries at End of 1970 (°°)
20	Food and Beverages	2	2
24–27	Wood, Paper and Printing products	3	2
28	Chemicals and Pharmaceuticals	14	14
284	Soaps and Toiletries	1	1
29	Petroleum	6	6
299	Coal products	1	0
30	Rubber	3	3
32	Glass	2	2
331	Primary Ferrous Metals	15	6
333	Primary non-Ferrous Metals	7	5
35	Non-Electrical Machinery	7	5
361–2	Industrial Electrical Machinery	6	6
363–9	Consumer Electrical and Electronic products	4	4
37	Transportation equipment	10	6
	Total	81	62

(°) Defined as the indicated Standard Industrial Classifications (SIC) industry in which firms had the largest portion of their sales.
(°°) Firms were counted as having manufacturing operations in a given country only if they owned 25 per cent or more of a manufacturing subsidiary in it.

Many continental European companies have been active in international manufacturing for a very long time. A significant number of today's major European chemical, pharmaceutical, electrical equipment, and food companies had some manufacturing outside their home countries by World War I.[13]

The earliest pioneers are cited in Table 2. Out of a total of seventeen, nine were German. By and large, when they undertook foreign manufacturing, they did so in other European countries. Eight were based in the chemical industry, and four produced elec-

[13] Information in the Comparative Multinational Enterprise Data Bank, Harvard Business School; see also sources for Table 2.

trical equipment. European multinational enterprise was beginning to emerge at least as early as the American variety.[14]

During the inter-war period, these international enterprises were in turn joined by others. Dutch, Swiss, and Swedish newcomers such as Philips, Margarine Uni, Alusuisse, and Swedish Match were perhaps the most prominent additions in those years. A number of inveterate German internationalizers (I. G. Farben, Bosch, Siemens, and AEG) were stubbornly reconstituting the foreign outposts lost in World War I. They were to do so once again after their foreign manufacturing subsidiaries had again been confiscated during World War II.

The major expansion in the number of European companies with significant multinational operations, to be sure, occurred in the post-World War II era. Despite early efforts such as Renault's establishment of two assembly plants in Russia in 1914, Europe's automobile companies were to have significant international manufacturing activities only after 1946.[15] Anglo-Dutch Shell excepted, continental European petroleum companies with important international operations emerged only during the 1950s. In sectors such as electrical and non-electrical machinery, the few firms with lengthy international experience, such as Siemens, AEG, and Bosch of Germany were joined by a host of newcomers, including Thomson-Brandt of France and Olivetti of Italy. Nevertheless, neither the state nor the process of multinationality are unusual for European enterprise.

PROLIFERATION OF FOREIGN MANUFACTURING SUBSIDIARIES

The spread of foreign manufacturing by the large firms of continental Europe has, however, been anything but gradual. If a look at the numbers of parent firms with international operations could convey an impression of a smooth European expansion into multinationality, a quite different picture is painted by the record of foreign subsidiaries set up or acquired. Table 3 suggests that the numbers of entries into subsidiaries by continental parents have alternately expanded very rapidly or stagnated. The number of foreign manufacturing outposts of continental firms proliferated just before and just after World War I. The next great spurt did

[14] On the pre-World War I U.S. multinational company expansion, see Mira Wilkins, *The Emergence of Multinational Enterprise* (Cambridge, Mass., 1970), especially 212 and 213.

[15] Patrick Fridenson, *Histoire des Usines Renault* (Paris, 1972), 66. One of Renault's factories was located in Petrograd (later Leningrad).

TABLE 2
LOCATION OF FOREIGN MANUFACTURING OF SELECTED CONTINENTAL EUROPEAN COMPANIES, ABOUT 1914

Parent Firm and Country	Main Industry	Location of Foreign Manufacturing Operations									
		Russia	France	Germany	U.S.	U.K.	Spain	Austria	Italy	Holland	Elsewhere
Switzerland:											
Ciba	Chemicals	X	X	X	X	X					
Geigy	Chemicals	X	X	X	X	X					
Brown–Boveri	Electrical		X	X				X	X		Norway
Nestlé	Food			X	X	X	X			X	Norway, Australia
Germany:											
Siemens	Electrical	X	Xf		Xf	X		X			Belgium f
AEG	Electrical	X					X	X	X		Belgium
Degussa	Chemicals						X				
Bosch	Electrical	X	X		X		X				Japan
BASF	Chemicals	X	X		X	X					Norway
Hoechst	Chemicals	X	X			X					
Bayer	Chemicals	X	X		X	X					
Agfa	Chemicals		X								
Metallgesell-schaft	Non-ferrous metals		Xf		X	X		X		X	Belgium, Mexico

								Host country
France: Cie. de St. Gobain	Glass			X		X	X	X	Belgium
Netherlands: Margarine Uni (later Unilever)	Food	X	Xw	X			X		Belgium, Denmark
Belgium: Solvay	Chemicals	X	X	X	X		X	X	
Sweden: SKF	Machinery	Xw	X	Xw	X		X		

Notes: f = failed or abandoned prior to World War I.
W = entered between the years 1914 and 1918.

Sources: L. F. Haber, *The Chemical Industry during the Nineteenth Century* (London, 1958), and *The Chemical Industry, 1900–1930* (London, 1971); Brown-Boveri, *75 Years Brown-Boveri* (Baden, 1966); Jean Heer, *Reflets du Monde: Présence de Nestlé* (Rivaz, 1966); Georg Siemens, *History of the House of Siemens* (Freiburg/Munich, 1957); AEG, *50 Jahre AEG* (Berlin, 1956); Degussa, *Aller Anfang ist Schwer, Bilder sur hundertjähriger Geschichte der Degussa* (Frankfurt, 1973); Robert Bosch GmbH, *75 Jahre Bosch* (Stuttgart, 1961); W. Dabritz, *Fünfzig Jahre Metallgesellschaft, 1881–1931* (Frankfurt, 1931); J. Choffel, *St. Gobain, du miroir à l'atome* (Paris, 1960); Charles Wilson, *The History of Unilever* (London, 1954); Jacques Bolle, *Solvay: l'invention, l'homme, l'entreprise industrielle, 1863–1963* (Brussels, 1963); SKF, *SKF, 1907–1957: A History in Pictures* (Stären, 1957).

EUROPEAN MULTINATIONALS   283

not occur until the late 1960s, as is shown in Table 3. This was quite a different evolution from the continually increasing expansion of U.S. company subsidiaries documented in the same table.

TABLE 3
ENTRY INTO FOREIGN MANUFACTURING: COMPARATIVE HISTORIES OF U.S., BRITISH, CONTINENTAL EUROPEAN AND JAPANESE ENTERPRISE

| Period | Numbers of Foreign Manufacturing Subsidiaries Entered by Parents from: | | | |
	U.S.A.	U.K.	Continental Europe	Japan
Pre–1914	122	60	167	0
1914–1919	71	27	51	0
1920–1929	299	118	249	1
1930–1938	315	99	112	3
1939–1945	172	34	44	40
1946–1952	386	202	129	2
1953–1955	283	55	117	5
1956–1958	439	94	131	14
1959–1961	901	333	232	44
1962–1964	959	319	229	90
1965–1967	889	459	532	113
1968–1970	n.a.	729	1,030	209

Notes: Data on subsidiaries of U.K., continental European, and Japanese-based firms were collected for all 200 parent firms on the 1971 *Fortune* "200" list of non-U.S. industrial enterprises, as well as for a few financial holding companies and family groups that had more than $400,000,000 of sales in 1970 coming from manufacturing operations. Data on subsidiaries of U.S.-based parents were collected for 187 U.S. firms on the 1968 *Fortune* "500" list with an equity interest of at least 25 per cent in manufacturing subsidiaries in at least six foreign countries as of January 1, 1968. Some fifty of these U.S. firms were smaller than the non-U.S. companies surveyed. A similar number of non-U.S. firms do *not* manufacture in six or more foreign countries. Data incomparabilities thus exist. They do not, however, seem critically to alter the order of magnitude indicated by the above comparisons. For a fuller explanation of the data in the Comparative Multinational Enterprise Data Bank, see the Vaupel and Curhan book.

Source: James W. Vaupel and Joan P. Curhan, *The Making of Multinational Enterprise* (Harvard Business School, Boston, 1973, and C. E. I., Geneva, 1974), Tables 1.17.2, 1.17.3, 1.17.4, and 1.17.5, pages 72–103.

TECHNOLOGICAL INNOVATIONS AND EXPORTS

If the spread of European multinational company activity was unique in its timing, most of it nonetheless had origins that appeared to resemble those of U.S. multinational expansion in one critical respect. Like their U.S. counterparts, continental European manufacturing firms almost always seem to have begun the process of becoming multinational by exporting on the basis of oligopolistic advantages in technological innovation.[16] Yet, the

[16] As indicated above, the word innovation as used here signifies first commercial introduction, *not* invention. European inventors often preceded American innovation, as Table

kinds of oligopolistic innovations developed by Europe's nascent multinationals tended to be quite unlike those first commercialized in the U.S. market.

As in the case of U.S. exports that later led to multinational production, it was innovation, or first commercial introduction, that mattered, not first invention. European invention, that is to say, discovery, often led neither to home nor export sales. On the contrary, European inventions were often transferred to the U.S. and first applied there.[17] The examples of penicillin, the computer, and the integrated circuit are cases in point. Even within the European context, the same phenomenon could be observed, for example in the invention of margarine in France followed by first commercial introduction in Holland.[18]

Examples of the connection between continental European innovation, exports, and subsequent foreign production are numerous and convincing, despite the fact that the link has not been rigorously demonstrated. The history of synthetic dyestuffs is another case in point. Table 2 above indicated that numerous foreign manufacturing operations had been begun before 1914 by dyestuffs firms such as Ciba, Geigy, BASF, Hoechst, Bayer, and Agfa. L. F. Haber, H. Friedlander, and others have chronicled how, prior to this multinational spread, the invention of synthetic dyestuffs in England and France was followed not by English and French exports, but rather by large-scale commercialization and process and product development in Germany and Switzerland. Massive exports, and then industrial implantation back into the countries of invention later emanated from the innovating German and Swiss enterprises.[19] Something of the export phase of this sequence

4 points out. It was typically this innovative step that led to the rise of multinational enterprise. The role of oligopolistic competitive advantage and market imperfection in explaining the rise of multinational enterprise was first examined systematically in S. Hymer, "The International Operations of National Firms: A Study of Direct Investment," (Doctoral dissertation, Massachusetts Institute of Technology, 1960). The importance of oligopolistic imperfections based on technology in explaining the international spread of U.S. enterprise has been the subject of a vast and growing literature. See *inter alia*: R. Vernon, "International Investment and International Trade in the Product Cycle," *Quarterly Journal of Economics* (May, 1966), and the studies included and cited in L. T. Wells, Jr., ed., *The Product Life Cycle and International Trade* (Boston, 1972). See also: A. Harmann, *The International Computer Industry* (Cambridge, Mass., 1970); and Harvard Business School, "The U.S. Automobile Industry in the World Market," Note ICR 530, 1971.

[17] No systematic study of the frequency or causes of the international transplant of inventions appears to have been made. But examples of European inventions followed by U.S. application are abundant enough. See David Landes, *The Unbound Prometheus* (Cambridge, 1969); OECD, *Gaps in Technology*, Vols. I–V (Paris, 1971); J. Jewkes, *et al.*, *The Sources of Invention* (London, 1969).

[18] Charles Wilson, *The History of Unilever* (London, 1954) II, 25 and 26.

[19] L. F. Haber, *The Chemical Industry in the Nineteenth Century* (London, 1958); H. Friedlander and J. Oser, *Economic History of Modern Europe* (New York, 1953), especially 243.

prior to World War I can be glimpsed from Table 4 below. The impression of a connection between innovation and exports becomes still stronger upon noting that synthetic dyestuffs exports from firms in countries other than Germany and Switzerland were virtually nil.[20]

TABLE 4

GROWTH OF THE SYNTHETIC DYESTUFF INDUSTRY

Quinquennia Ending:	Dyestuff Patents Granted in England to: German Inventors	British Inventors	Number of Employees of the "Badische Anilin und Sodafabrik"	Exports in Metric Tons: Germany	Switzerland
1860	8	20			
1880	47	13	1,534	8,294	
1900	427	52	6,711	46,858	3,116
1910	561	30	7,610	84,110	6,975

Source: Encyclopaedia of the Social Sciences, V, 302.

Innovative advantages also appeared intimately linked with the extraordinary export successes of Germany's Siemens and AEG. Some of their innovative advantages were indigenous, others originated with exclusive European licenses from U.S. companies for the production of electric lights, automatic telephone exchange, and the like. On the eve of World War I, Germany accounted for over 48 per cent of total world electrical exports.[21] Indeed, Germany remained the largest single exporting country for electrical equipment until the outbreak of World War II.[22] Exports of unique goods, or goods produced with unique processes, preceded essentially all the pre-World War II expansion by Siemens and AEG into foreign manufacturing (noted in Table 2). Only one important exception appeared: Siemens quite unusually began the production of telegraph cables and water meters in England in the 1850s — products the firm did not then manufacture at home.[23]

A link between innovation and export can be found in the histories of virtually all the other parent firms prominent in the expansion of European multinationals before World War II. The formation of Ivar Kreuger's Swedish Match empire in the 1920s

[20] Haber, *Chemical Industry in the Nineteenth Century*, 243.
[21] Friedlander and Oser, *Economic History*, 247.
[22] Georg Siemens, *History of the House of Siemens* (Freiburg and Munich, 1957), II.
[23] *Ibid.*, I, 32ff.; AEG, *50 Jahre AEG* (Berlin, 1956).

followed a half century of Swedish exports based on innovations in safety matches.[24] Alusuisse had been the first firm formed to exploit the Herault process for producing aluminum. It exported aluminum for many years prior to entering significant foreign production.[25] I. G. Farben earned much foreign exchange for Weimar and then for Nazi Germany by first spending up to 12.7 per cent of its sales revenue (in 1927) on research and development in order to secure innovative advantages.[26] By 1908, Philips of Holland had ceased simply imitating carbon filament electric lamps and exporting only on the basis of a price advantage secured through relatively low cost labor. Development efforts underlay increasing product and process singularity that in turn preceded Philips' major moves into foreign manufacturing in the 1930s.[27]

After World War II much the same sort of sequence seemed again in motion. The distinctive post-1945 European innovations in autos, pharmaceuticals, plastics, and metalworking processes, cited in Table 5, led first to exports, and only then to production abroad. There were, however, some exceptions to the rule, and perhaps the most notable were the petroleum companies started and owned by governments in France and Italy.

Western Europe, as it again abruptly came to realize in the 1970s, has never had the indigenous resources of petroleum that allowed U.S. firms to develop innovative advantages in refining — let alone exploration — comparatively quickly. Of the continental countries, only Holland had oil-producing colonies during the first half of the twentieth century. After the Russian Revolution eliminated foreign-owned firms from the Caucasus, Western European governments felt dependent on either Anglo-Saxon companies (and on the partly British Royal Dutch Shell) or the Soviet government for their oil supply. Some were content with neither choice. One result was what the historian of the Compagnie Française des Pétroles refers to, in jest, as the "immaculate conception" of that firm out of the debris of World War I.[28] The company was formed at the initiative of the French government to administer that part of the Turkish Petroleum Company (later the Iraq Petroleum Company)

[24] Friedlander and Oser, *Economic History*, 417.
[25] D. H. Wallace, *Market Control in the Aluminum Industry* (Cambridge, Mass., 1937), 6, 33, 34.
[26] H. Gross, *Further Facts and Figures on I. G. Farben* (Kiel, 1950), 12.
[27] N. V. Philips, *Facts About Philips* (Eindhoven, 1970), 3–8; P. J. Bouman, *Anton Philips of Eindhoven* (London, 1958), 48, mentions Philips' original low wage competitive advantage. The book subsequently describes its move toward its own proprietary technology.
[28] Jean Rondot, *La Compagnie Française des Pétroles* (Paris, 1962), 5.

TABLE 5
SOME EUROPEAN INNOVATIONS LEADING TO THE RISE OF MULTINATIONAL ENTERPRISE

Product or Process	Year	Firm	Apparent Market Stimulus
Ammonia-Soda Process	1864	Solvay (Belgium)	Desire to reduce fuel needs, eliminate sulphuric acid inputs and recover nitrogen-rich ammonia.
Alizarin	1870	BASF (Germany)	Desire to substitute for imports of natural dyes for military uniforms previously obtained from France.
Ammonia Synthesis for Fertilizer	1913	BASF (Germany)	Scarcity of arable land; intolerable strategic dependence on Chilean nitrates.
Margarine	1872	Jurgens/Unilever (NL)	Low-income, mass demand. High price of butter.
Anti-Syphilitic Drugs (Salvarsin)	1910	Hoechst (Germany)	Low-income, mass demand guaranteed by government health insurance.
Synthetic Rubber	1930's	Bayer/I. G. Farben (Germany)	Military fear of cutoff from natural rubber supplies.
Low Power Utilization for Aluminum Electrolysis	1930's to 1960's	Pechiney (France)	High cost of French electricity.
Volkswagen Beetle	1951	VW (Germany)	Low-income, mass demand.
Polypropylene	1957	Montecatini (Italy)	Desire to use waste products.

Sources: As listed for Table 6.

awarded to France at the San Remo Diplomatic Conference as part of the spoils of World War I.[29] After oil was discovered, CFP's British and American partners in IPC built a refinery in Iraq to process the crude. Thus, politics (and a cash contribution) first put the now multinationally active CFP into the business of both foreign manufacturing (i.e., oil refining) and exporting refined petroleum products. With the experience thus gained, and later with a protected home market as well, such a government-instrument firm could subsequently apply lessons learned in its hothouse environment to foreign countries in the manner of a more "spontaneously generated" multinational. Indeed, even if it never developed marked oligopolistic *technological* advantages by this process, such a firm could, and often did, offer a differentiated, non-Anglo-Saxon "political" product.[30]

THE ROLE OF HOME MARKET CONDITIONING

More than "immaculate conceptions" have, however, set the story of the spread of continental European multinational enterprise apart. Early home market conditioning seems to have played a considerable role. It is clear that the economic characteristics of home markets in continental Europe were different from those facing innovators in the U.S. Distinctive home markets appear to have left their mark on Europe's nascent multinationals primarily in terms of the kinds of product and process innovations they developed. The frequency distribution of European innovations eventually put into foreign production appears to have long been biased toward material-saving processes, *ersatz* material substitutes, and goods oriented toward low-income consumers. This tendency is illustrated in Table 5. By way of contrast, the examples presented in Table 6 indicate that U.S. innovations were typically skewed towards goods and processes that had an appeal to the unique high-income, labor short American market.

CONDITIONING BY DIFFERENT INCOME LEVELS

Part of the explanation for differences between European and American patterns of innovation doubtless lies in differences in

---

[29] *Ibid.*, 11ff.

[30] ENI, the Italian state oil company in particular appears to have gained entry into refining in various countries in Africa largely as a result of such political product differentiation. See M. Tiger and L. G. Franko, *E.N.I.* (Geneva, 1973); P. Frankel, *Mattei: Oil and Power Politics* (New York, 1966); Elena Chiado-Fiorio, *Il Caso ENI* (Torino, 1973).

TABLE 6
SOME AMERICAN INNOVATIONS LEADING TO THE RISE OF MULTINATIONAL ENTERPRISE

Product or Process	Year	Firm	Apparent Market Stimulus
Sewing Machine	1851	Singer	Shortage of seamstresses.
Telephone	1878	Bell Telephone (Later Western Electric & ITT)	Desire to save travel time.
Strowger Bar Telephone Switch	1892	Strowger (Later Western Electric & ITT)	Shortage of telephone operators leading to unreliable service.
Moving Assembly Line for Automobile Production (*)	1914	Ford	Skilled labor shortages; middle-income market.
Automatic Transmission	1939	General Motors	Relatively high-income, convenience demand.
Vat Fermentation for Penicillin (*)	1945	Pfizer, Lederle	Shortage of skilled labor.
The Computer (*)	1951	Sperry-Rand	Military demand; shortage of clerical labor.
Planar Process for Integrated Circuit Production (*)	1961	Fairchild	Shortage of labor to assemble transistor circuits; military demand.

(*) Indicates that product associated with this commercialized innovation was invented in Europe.

Sources: Various, including Haber, Chemical Industry in the Nineteenth Century and Chemical Industry, 1900–1930; OECD, Gaps in Technology: Electronic Components, and Gaps in Technology: Computers (Paris, 1971); J. Jewkes et al., The Sources of Invention (London, 1969); E. Bäumler, Etappen des Fortschritts (Hoechst, A. G., 1966); U. Eco and G. B. Zorzoli, Histoire Illustrée des Inventions (Paris, 1961).

absolute levels of income per capita. Average national income per capita data for ten countries in 1914 are presented in Graph 1. Graph 2 presents similar data for twenty-four of the world's 186 nations for 1959 and 1969. These tables show that the U.S. was highest on the list for both 1914 and 1969. Moreover, the relative rankings of income levels for the U.S., France, Germany, and Italy did not change over this fifty-five-year span. Even changes in proportional differences have not been great. U.S. per capita income throughout the first half of the twentieth century was nearly twice that of France and Germany, and roughly three times that of Italy. Some nations have changed their relative positions for the better (Japan) or worse (the U.K.), but the relationship between the U.S. and the largest continental countries has remained relatively stable.

International differences in income levels are important for innovative activity because consumers appear to behave as if they have a hierarchy of needs varying with their income levels. Evidence suggests that the order in which consumers acquire house-

GRAPH I

INCOME PER CAPITA OF VARIOUS COUNTRIES IN 1914

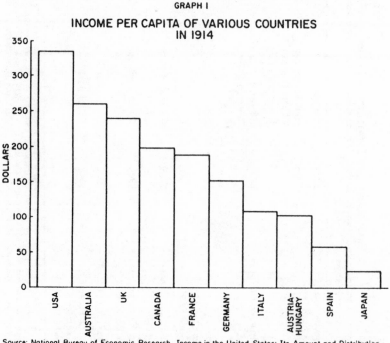

Source: National Bureau of Economic Research, Income in the United States: Its Amount and Distribution, 1909-1919 (New York, 1921), I.

GRAPH 2
INCOME PER CAPITA OF VARIOUS COUNTRIES IN 1959 AND 1969

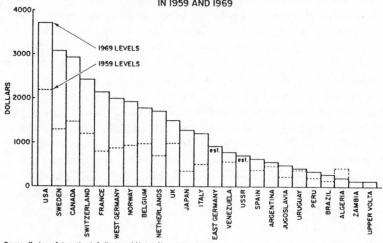

Source: Business International, *Indicators of Market Size*, various issues.

hold appliances is primarily a function of income, rather than of broad cultural factors.[31] Setting aside obvious differences due to resource endowments, it also appears that there is an order of acquisition of industrial goods that is followed fairly predictably as a result of economic growth.[32] By extension, one expects new needs to emerge as incomes grow to previously unreached levels. If scientific and technical skills are available, would-be innovators will presumably respond to such new needs. Moreover, would-be innovators located in a "first market" seem to have an enormous advantage over those located outside it. It is they who will be most conscious of the emergent market opportunity; it is they who can most rapidly respond to customer wants and define concretely a product that at first may be only a hazy, uncertain idea.[33]

Given the historical constants shown in Graphs 1 and 2, it is understandable that the U.S. market long acted as midwife to the development by U.S. companies of the time-saving, convenience products that substituted for high-income, high-cost labor.[34] The

[31] See, for example, Y. Parush, "The Order of Acquisition of Durable Goods," *Bank of Israel Bulletin* (February, 1964).

[32] Such appears to be the implication of findings like those of Pong S. Lee, in "Structural Change in Rumanian Industry," *Soviet Studies* (October, 1968). Lee, following on work of Chenery, shows that industrial structure varies much more with per capita income and population size than with ideological systems.

[33] S. Hirsch, *Location of Industry and International Competitiveness* (London, 1967). Vernon, "International Investment," 191–192.

[34] Vernon, "International Investment," 193; and Vernon, *Sovereignty at Bay*, Chapter 3.

link between such product innovations and exporting is also rather
clear. Such products tended to be demanded in ever-increasing
quantities in Europe, as income levels continually moved up toward
the level prevailing previously in the U.S. What, however, would
be the case in continental European countries, where potential innovators have long had a level of scientific and technical ability
similar to that found in the highest income, U.S. market? [35]

A certain amount of product innovation designed to tap rising
consumer incomes appears to have occurred in the European continent in spite of the tendency of the U.S. to lead. Nestlé's mothers'
milk substitute that allowed women to begin breaking away from
their traditional ties to *Kinder, Kirche, Küche*, was just the sort of
product one might have expected to be a U.S. innovation in the
1890s but was Swiss instead.[36] And in at least one case, that of
the Compagnie de Saint Gobain, a European firm obtained an innovative lead in income-elastic mirrors and glass in the early 1700s,
well before the U.S. existed as a nation.[37]

Still other European innovators seem to have directed their activity toward applying new processes to American-type, high income products. A number of observers have commented on the
seeming tendency of American companies to innovate new products, whereas European firms tended to introduce new manufacturing processes.[38] The available data are too fragmentary to show
whether such a clear dichotomy between U.S. and European innovation existed. Nevertheless, examples suggest that process innovation was a major European theme. Philips of Holland and
AEG of Germany even began life as independent entities in the
1890s by innovating processes for the production of Edison's product, the electric lamp.[39]

Nevertheless, most innovative activity undertaken on the Continent appears to have been oriented to ends other than time-
saving products or processes for producing them. Distinctive patterns of distribution of income around the average per capita levels
presented in Graphs 1 and 2 gave European innovators one set of
unique stimuli. Patterns of relative factor costs that long diverged

---

[35] It is generally agreed that there is little or no scientific gap among the countries under
consideration here. The supply of technical ability does not seem to have been a significant
constraint on innovation. See OECD, *Gaps in Technology*, various reports (Paris, 1971).

[36] J. Heer, *Reflets du monde, présence de Nestlé* (Rivaz, 1966).

[37] J. Choffel, *St. Gobain, du miroir à l'atome* (Paris, 1960).

[38] This finding has been documented for the steel industry in Roger Emile Miller, *Innovation, Organization and Environment: A Study of Sixteen American and West European Steel Firms* (Université Catholique de Louvain, Belgique, Nouvelles Series, No. 86),
152.

[39] Philips, *Facts About Philips*, 4-8.

from those prevailing in the U.S. provided another. In the history of European innovation, these factors more than others appear to underlie the recurring emphasis on material-saving processes and substitutes and products designed for consumers with lower incomes than those prevailing in the U.S.

INCOME DISTRIBUTION AND COMPARATIVE INNOVATION

Over long periods of time, the pattern of distribution of personal income in most European countries has been notably unlike that prevailing in the U.S. Sociologists, historians, and business writers have often referred to the U.S. as a middle-class society.[40] European countries, particularly the large continental countries, have often been described as societies composed of aristocratic and semi-aristocratic elites on the one hand and peasants and workers on the other — without terribly many people in between.[41] Table 7 suggests that such generalizations must be made with considerable care, and with attention to variations among European countries and among historical periods. In 1936, the middle classes in Nazi Germany were receiving a somewhat higher percentage of total personal income than the middle classes in the U.S., although contrasts were still in evidence at the high and low income levels. In the 1960s, Sweden, the Netherlands, the U.S., and also the U.K., came to have broadly similar income distribution patterns: in these countries similar percentages of total income went to the lowest 40, the upper-middle 40 and the top 20 per cent of their populations. Nevertheless, clear contrasts between the U.S. and the largest European countries emerge from Table 7.[42] Moreover, one is struck

[40] See J. Fayerweather, *International Marketing* (Englewood Cliffs, N.J., 1965), 32. D. Krech, *et al.*, *Individual in Society: A Textbook of Social Psychology* (New York, 1962), 304–316.

[41] See Landes, *Unbound Prometheus* 48, 129, and 131 for such characterizations concerning the eighteenth and nineteenth centuries. See Ralf Dahrendorf, *Society and Democracy in Germany* (London, 1968), especially Chapter 6 for a recent characterization of this sort.

[42] The data presented in Table 7 are clearly imperfect. Different natural propensities in tax evasion and income declaration are but two of the many sources of potential error mentioned in the sources for that table. These data do not adjust for the effect on market demand of direct or indirect, progressive or regressive tax systems, nor do they account for government social security, insurance, and transfer payments. It is worth noting, however, that the United Nations Economic Commission for Europe, the source for many of the figures cited in Table 7, argues that after-tax and transfer payment adjustments do not have a major effect on the distribution patterns derived from before-tax data in the three countries for which estimates can be made: the U.K., Germany, and Norway. (Economic Commission for Europe, *Incomes in Postwar Europe*, Chapter 6.) The likely effect of such adjustments, could they but be made, would, of course, very likely accentuate the already favorable position of the lowest 10 per cent of European populations relative to that of the U.S. As tax evasion and underreporting of income tends to be a privilege of the rich, one might expect either a neutral effect across countries, or, if it is true that such

TABLE 7

DISTRIBUTION OF FAMILY PERSONAL INCOME IN EUROPE AND THE U.S.
(PERCENTAGE OF TOTAL INCOME BEFORE
TAX RECEIVED BY INDICATED FRACTION OF FAMILIES)

Country & Year	Lowest Tenth	Lowest Two Fifths	Fortieth to Eightieth Percentile	Highest Fifth	Highest Tenth
ABOUT THE TIME OF WORLD WAR I					
US 1918	2 %	18 %	36 %	46 %	34 %
Germany 1913	3.5	18	27	55	41
DURING THE INTER-WAR PERIOD					
US 1935–6	n.a.	12.7	34.1	53.2	36
UK 1929	3	18	31	51	41
Germany 1936	1	11	36	53	39
Sweden 1935	n.a.	n.a.	n.a.	58.1	39.5
Netherlands 1938	n.a.	n.a.	n.a.	52.5	38.7
AROUND 1950					
US 1950		15.8	38.5	45.7	30.3
UK 1949	n.a.	17	35.5	47.5	33
Germany 1950	1	12.5	39.5	48	34
Sweden 1948	n.a.	12.8	40.6	46.6	30.3
Netherlands 1950	1.3	13.8	37.2	49	35
DURING THE 1960s					
US 1969	1	15	40	45	27
UK 1964	2	15.3	40.5	44.2	29.3
Germany 1964	2.1	15.4	31.7	52.9	41.4
France 1962	0.5	9.5	36.8	53.7	36.8
Sweden 1963	1.6	14	42	44	27.9
Netherlands 1962	1.3	14	37.6	48.4	33.8

Note: The percentages for the fortieth to eightieth percentiles are highlighted to call attention to the fraction of incomes received by what most observers might be inclined to refer to as the "middle-class."

Sources: For the U.S. in 1918: Wesley C. Mitchell and others, *Income in the United States: Its Amount and Distribution, 1909–1919* (1921), I, 141. For Germany in 1913, the U.K. in 1929, and the U.S. in 1935–1936: W. S. and E. S. Woytinsky, *World Population and Production* (New York, 1953), 409, 407. For Germany, Sweden, and the Netherlands in the 1930s, and for the U.K., Germany, Sweden, and the Netherlands in the 1940s and in 1950: United Nations, Economic Commission for Europe, *Economic Survey of Europe in 1956* (Geneva, 1957), chapter IX, 6. For the U.S. in 1950 and 1969: U.S., Department of Commerce, *Statistical Abstract of the United States 1971* (Washington, 1972), Table 504, p. 317. For European countries in the 1960s: United Nations, *Economic Survey of Europe in 1965, Part 2: Incomes in Postwar Europe — A Study of Policies, Growth and Distribution* (Geneva, 1967), chapter 6, p. 15.

activities are rather more European than American hobbies, they would once again merely emphasize the contrasts to which Table 7 points.

by the persistence of the basic patterns. The resemblance between the German and U.S. distributions of 1964 and those of 1913 is a case in point.[43]

These contrasts in income distribution made the home environments in which European multinationals were born clearly different from that which nurtured U.S. multinational enterprise. Where markets diverged, innovations were introduced accordingly, and distinctive oligopolistic strengths were developed. As the history of the auto industry was to show, European companies tended to introduce either luxury products or near-necessities for the masses. U.S. firms were pulled toward satisfying middle and upper-middle income needs.[44]

Daimler and Benz first marketed workable automobiles in Germany in 1888 and 1886. Conditioned then and later by their home market demand, "the German manufacturers concentrated on luxury cars, since the German middle class was not large enough to support the scale needed for the innovation and manufacture of an inexpensive automobile."[45] For French auto manufacturers before World War I, the market demand was much the same. One examination of the market for automobiles between 1899 and 1928 in the French *Département* of Indre-et-Loire led to the conclusion that "the demand for private automobiles comes principally from the group comprising people of independent means, noblemen and large land-owners."[46] A government report in 1917 went even further. It argued that past successes meant that the orientation of the French industry to luxury demands ought to be elevated to the level of doctrine: "It is the luxury article that has given birth to our worldwide reputation. . . . we must defend this patrimony . . . it is this that has led to the development of our automobile industry. . . . purity and harmony of form, even more than luxury

[43] Dr. Emilio Fontela and others of the Batelle Institute in Geneva, Switzerland have published a number of discussions of income distribution in Europe in which cogent arguments are presented for the existence of a relationship between increases in average per capita incomes and moves toward the U.S. type of income distribution. Their hypothesis is that as economic growth proceeds, markets of masses-plus-aristocrats will be replaced by markets in which a middle class, itself having a wide range of incomes, will constitute the dominant market segment. The long-term data presented in Table 7 provide little evidence in favor of such a hypothesis. See H. L. Dotti and Emilio Fontela, "Distribution des revenues et intégration de l'Europe," *Revue du Marché Commun* (Janvier, 1970).

[44] For brief but comprehensive summaries of the history of the auto industry, see B. McKern, "The U.S. Automobile Industry in the World Market," in R. Vernon, *Manager in the International Economy* (Englewood Cliffs, N.J., 1972); L. T. Wells, Jr., "National Policies in International Industry: The Europeans and the Automobile," forthcoming in R. Vernon, ed., *Big Business and Governments in Europe* (Cambridge, Mass., 1974).

[45] Wells, "National Policies," 4.

[46] Fridenson, *Histoire des Usines Renault,* 21.

manufacture, must be one of the primordial elements of the maintenance of our supremacy." [47]

It was not until the automobile was uprooted from Europe, in
the manner of the jet engine, the computer, penicillin, the aerosol
can, the continuous strip mill, and other inventions, that it was introduced into the huge U.S. market. By accident rather than design,
the low price (then) middle class U.S. market was discovered
when one of the factories of Ransom Olds burned down. The only
car he could produce was the least expensive of his line. The demand turned out to be enormous. When Olds was unable to finance the expansion of the Oldsmobile, Ford stepped in with the
mass-produced Model T in 1908 and the moving assembly line in
1914.[48] It was during these years that U.S. production and exports outstripped those of Germany and France.[49] But France and
Germany were exceeded in products that had little else but the name
"automobile" in common.

Much later, in 1970, continental European auto production was
once again to equal that of the Americans.[50] In addition, Europe's
auto exports in the 1950s, 1960s, and 1970s were to be vastly greater
than those of America.[51] The oligopolistic advantages that underlay
these developments, however, had much to do with mass markets
consisting largely of customers with incomes still lower than those
that had tempted American producers. In 1946, following nationalization, Renault introduced its low price R-4.[52] Then came
Citroën's 2-CV.[53] Shortly thereafter came the market introduction
of Germany's Volkswagen.[54] Automobiles all, but of a very different sort than those which set U.S. manufacturers on the path to
multinationality. Indeed, it was not until the late 1960s that the
introduction of Citroën's GX and Volkswagen's Audi gave hints
that perhaps broad middle-class markets were beginning to become
significant on the Continent.

Developments in other industries, it appears, often paralleled
European-U.S. contrasts in automobiles. The comparatively favorable income position of the lowest classes plus the introduction
of social insurance legislation as early as the 1880s meant that
European (and particularly German) companies were to lead in

[47] *Ibid.*, 37.
[48] McKern, "U.S. Automobile Industry," 433.
[49] *Ibid.*, 435.
[50] U.N., *Statistical Yearbook, 1971* (New York, 1972).
[51] McKern, "U.S. Automobile Industry," 443.
[52] Wells, "National Policies," 13.
[53] *Ibid.*
[54] *Ibid.*, 10.

EUROPEAN MULTINATIONALS   297

basic pharmaceuticals.[55] As a recent study noted, "Germany was not alone in having the technology to translate a laboratory synthesis into a full-scale operating production operations. Both England and France had strong chemical industries, capable of producing what was discovered in Germany. The missing ingredient [in these former countries] was demand."[56] Important U.S. pharmaceutical companies emerged only after World War II. They then made their distinctive contribution in antibiotics and psychopharmaceuticals. These U.S. innovations apparently reduced hospitalization time, but they were probably less important than aspirin, novocaine, and entero-vioform for stomach upsets — all introduced in Europe by Bayer, Hoechst, and Ciba before World War I.[57]

The phenomenon of European, and especially Italian, specialization in small household appliances and American company dominance in large models also seems related to differences in income distribution, as well as to those in income levels.[58] Although the companies that produce timepieces are too small to be among those systematically included in this study, the split in the world watch industry between Swiss producers of luxury goods and U.S. middle class, mass merchandisers, seems another variation on the auto industry theme.[59]

RELATIVE FACTOR COSTS AND INNOVATION

Perhaps, however, the distinctive histories of European and American commercial innovation have been most conditioned by persistent international differences in the relationship between labor costs and the costs of other production inputs. The most obvious transatlantic contrast has been in comparative ratios of labor to raw-material costs. Quantitative and impressionistic historical sources are in accord. Save for partial exceptions such as resource-endowed

[55] L. Wortzel, "The Pharmaceutical Industry Study: An Overview," unpublished ms., presented at a conference sponsored by the Agnelli Foundation in Turin, Italy on the Comparative Multinational Enterprise Project, June, 1971.
[56] *Ibid.*, 11.
[57] Haber, *Chemical Industry In the Nineteenth Century.*
[58] L. T. Wells, Jr., "Test of a Product Cycle Model of International Trade: U.S. Exports of Consumer Durables," *Quarterly Journal of Economics* (February, 1969).
[59] Harvard Business School, "Note on the Watch Industries in Switzerland, Japan and the United States," 1972. Dotti and Fontela, "Distribution," point out that income level and distribution differences among nations will lead to differences in market demand structure across industries as well as within industries. These factors may explain, for example, why there have been so few innovations, large firms, or multinational firms in food processing arising on the European continent. As yet, the hypothesis has not been systematically tested.

Sweden and colonial Belgium, European entrepreneurs have faced the cost consequences of a relative scarcity of land and raw materials. U.S. entrepreneurs have been, and remain, faced with an environment in which labor commands a relative premium because of its scarcity.

Table 8 presents quantitative estimates of these differences in relative costs for the years 1913, 1929, 1950, 1963, and 1971. The estimates are crude, but the orders of magnitude shown are in broad accord with what qualitative sources tell us of differences among countries and in different periods of time.

TABLE 8

INTERNATIONAL COMPARISONS OF RATIOS OF
RAW MATERIAL TO LABOR COSTS, 1914–1971

(APPROXIMATE RELATIVE COST OF ONE ARBITRARY UNIT OF RAW MATERIAL TO THE COST OF ONE HOUR OF LABOR WITH THE U.S. RATIO OF MATERIAL TO LABOR COSTS TAKEN AS 100.)

	1913	1929	1950	1963	1971
U.S.A.	100	100	100	100	100
Belgium		136	176	330	263
France	194	180	448	460	364
Germany	294	356	290	290	190
Italy		524	502	460	345
Netherlands		224	420	370	251
Sweden	158	144	113	180	139
Switzerland		144	181	210	182

Method of Calculation:

Historical information concerning prices paid for raw materials by entrepreneurs within national markets is difficult or impossible to obtain. Price series, such as they are, tend to be based on public quotations on international markets, like the London Metal Exchange. Thus, they were not useful for our purposes. National indices of raw materials prices, however, were readily available, as were indices and values for wage rates. If one assumed that in any given year, a relatively open, one-price international market in raw materials prevailed, it then became possible to derive indicators of earlier or subsequent divergences in relative factor cost ratios based on domestic price indices. In this table, it is assumed that 1963 was such a year, and that raw materials' prices were identical in all markets. Wage and price series were first put on a comparable 1963 = 100 basis. Wage indices were then adjusted to reflect differences in wage levels among countries in 1963, i.e., since the Swedish average wage rate was equal to 57 per cent of that in the U.S. in that year, the whole Swedish series was adjusted in proportion to this difference. This meant that the Swedish index was shifted 43 per cent lower to reflect absolute U.S.–Swedish differences. It did *not* mean that the margin between Swedish and U.S. revised indices was ever at 100:57 in any year other than 1963. Once this adjustment was made, wage and raw materials' price indices could be treated as if they were money-price series. One arbitrary unit of raw materials could be said to cost whatever one average hour of labor cost in the U.S. in 1963. National materials "cost series" were divided by the adjusted labor cost series and the resulting ratios proportioned to the base of U.S. = 100 shown in the table.

Sources: U.N., *Statistical Yearbook*, various issues, for 1929–1971 data on hourly earnings and raw material costs. International Labor Organization, *Year Book of Labor Statistics*, various issues.

Throughout the twentieth century, indeed from its earliest days as a nation, the U.S. had comparatively little labor relative to its abundant land and material resources.[60] Prior to World War I, neither the slave trade nor successive waves of immigration seemed to make much of a dent in this fact of life facing the U.S. entrepreneur.[61] With the passage of restrictive immigration laws in 1917, 1921, and 1924, the relative scarcity of labor was aggravated even further.[62]

In Europe, and particularly on the Continent, labor was long in substantial surplus.[63] From the mid-1800s to the 1960s, most of Europe worried about what to do with its reserve army of the unemployed. The scarce resources in Europe were neither hands nor brains — they were raw materials. This scarcity was sometimes relieved by trade or colonial expansion, but the fundamental, autarkic reflexes first nurtured by Colbert under Louiş XIV in the seventeenth century continually re-asserted themselves as successive European governments declared their dependence on foreign supply to be politically and militarily intolerable. The result was a concern for substitution, and saving, of raw materials that recurred again and again in European history. Innovation of synthetic nitrogenous fertilizers, dyestuffs, rubber, and artificial silk, or rayon, constituted one sort of response to the stimuli provided in such markets. Products and processes that saved fuel were another. European firms, for example, pioneered in high efficiency auto engines, electric furnaces, and fuel injection apparatus, as well as in industrial processes such as that of Solvay for soda-ash, and of Pechiney for producing aluminum with high-cost electricity. Similar examples abound in the history of relative factor costs conditions in Europe and their relation to innovations.[64]

CONCLUSIONS

Much remains to be done in the study of European multinational manufacturing before a complete picture can emerge. One area that needs to be explored, for example, concerns the contrasts between American and European firms' motivations for switching

[60] H. J. Habakkuk, *American and British Technology in the Nineteenth Century* (London, 1962), especially chapter 3.
[61] "Immigration Law," *Encyclopaedia Britannica* (New York, 1973), 1106ff.
[62] *Ibid.*, 126–131.
[63] See, for example, A. V. Desai, *Real Wages in Germany 1871–1913* (London, 1968), 43.
[64] For more details, see Chapter II of the author's forthcoming book, *The Other Multinationals: The International Firms of Continental Europe, 1870–1970.*

from exporting to foreign manufacturing. This is all the more so since tariffs and other trade restrictions like exchange controls, quantitative quotas, patent–working regulations, and subsidies appear to have been the primary influence on the decisions of European firms to manufacture in, rather than export to, foreign markets. Such government–imposed restrictions often triggered foreign production of the material-saving innovations emphasized above. Government measures appear to have been much less important in the spread of foreign manufacturing of the income-elastic products carried forth by American multinational enterprise. The lenient attitude long held in Europe toward cartels, mergers, and other private agreements also seems to have affected the amount and form of foreign activity by continental firms. Points of similarity between the American and European multinational spread, may, however, exist in the history of the internationalization of production of Europe's low-income mass products, such as autos and pharmaceuticals, into the less developed world. These and other factors require examination before we can arrive at a comprehensive treatment of the multinational firms of continental Europe, but they cannot be considered in detail here.[65]

The present paper has sought to contribute to an understanding of the origins of the multinational manufacturing enterprises based on the European continent. Those enterprises followed a different path of development from that pursued by United States firms, but European multinational manufacturing began even earlier than did American, and its story is no less significant. Beginning with Cockerill's 1815 plant in Prussia, European companies engaged in important manufacturing activity, mostly in other European nations. Rather than the relatively even pattern of the spread of United States enterprises abroad, European firms tended to expand in spurts and then to undergo periods of stagnation. They were especially active in the years just before and after World War I, and in the post-World War II period.

Throughout a century and a half of multinational production, European companies followed several basic patterns. In most cases, a firm would innovate a product or process (usually the latter), thereby securing an oligopolistic advantage which it would initially exploit by marketing in other countries and would finally end up manufacturing inside those countries. The particular *kinds* of products and processes innovated by European multinationals tend-

---

[65] More analysis and data will be contained in the author's forthcoming book, *The Other Multinationals*.

ed to be influenced by the distinctive nature of income levels and income distribution in their home markets, and by the relative factor costs. Europe's evolution of a luxury market side-by-side with a large lower class market, and its historical lack of a large middle class market like the United States, was of major significance. Similarly, the abundance of labor and the shortage of raw materials in the western part of the European continent played a large role in shaping patterns of product and process development. The result of such factors was an evolutionary pattern distinct from the United States experience in many ways but rich in its own lessons about the history of multinational enterprise in the modern world.

[8]

Japanese Multinational Enterprise before 1914

MIRA WILKINS

¶ *The current scholarly interest in contemporary Japanese businesses has somewhat obscured their equally fascinating early historical development. In this article, Professor Wilkins emphasizes both the extent and the variety of Japanese multinational enterprise before the First World War, and offers a basis for comparing its differences and similarities with the conventional American model.*

Just as American and European multinational enterprises have a history preceding recent times, so Japanese multinational enterprises have existed since well before the Second World War—indeed, since the late nineteenth century.[1] Yet, although a substantial literature has grown up on the current remarkable expansion of Japanese business abroad, considerably less attention has been paid to the historical developments.[2] This article explores some of the early (pre–1914) activities of Japanese multinationals.

MIRA WILKINS is professor of economics at Florida International University.

This many-times revised paper had its genesis in a lecture delivered in Japan in the summer of 1984. I am deeply indebted to Professor Tetsuo Abo of the Institute of Social Science, University of Tokyo, and to that university for the invitation to Japan; Professor Abo was immensely helpful in the development of the ideas presented herein. I have also benefited from comments on earlier versions made by Professors Alfred D. Chandler, Jr., Richard Tedlow, Nobuo Kawabe, Hiroaki Yamazaki, Ken-ichi Yasumuro, Tetsuya Kuwahara, Frank H. H. King, Hafiz Mirza, William D. Wray, Simon Pak, Amitava Dutt, Ali M. Parhizgari, Panos Liossatos, and Maria Willumsen, as well as two anonymous critics. My thanks go to the John Simon Guggenheim Foundation, which provided funding for a year's sabbatical, as well as to the Florida International University Foundation.

[1] Mira Wilkins, *The Emergence of Multinational Enterprise: American Business Abroad from the Colonial Era to 1914* (Cambridge, Mass., 1970), and Wilkins, *The Maturing of Multinational Enterprise: American Business Abroad from 1914 to 1970* (Cambridge, Mass., 1974); John M. Stopford, "The Origins of British-Based Multinational Manufacturing Enterprise," *Business History Review* 48 (Autumn 1974): 303–56; Lawrence G. Franko, *The European Multinationals* (Stamford, Conn., 1976); Mira Wilkins, "Modern European Economic History and the Multinationals," *Journal of European Economic History* 6 (Winter 1977): 575–95. Raymond Vernon's Harvard project on foreign multinationals paid special attention to the history of European business abroad. Recently, there has been a proliferation of interest in the history of European multinational enterprise. Much of the newer work has been surveyed in Mira Wilkins, "The History of European Multinationals—A New Look," *Journal of European Economic History*, forthcoming. Alfred D. Chandler, Jr., has in process a major work that will encompass the history of both American and European multinational enterprise.

[2] Included among the best works on post–Second World War Japanese multinationals are M. Y. Yoshino, *Japan's Multinational Enterprises* (Cambridge, Mass., 1976); Yoshi Tsurumi, *The Japanese Are Coming* (Cambridge, England, 1976); Kiyoshi Kojima, *Japanese Direct Foreign Investment* (Tokyo, 1978); and Terutomo Ozawa, *Multinationalism, Japanese Style* (Princeton, N. J., 1979). Nobuo Kawabe's work on the history of Japanese multinationals was unique. His Ph.D. dissertation at Ohio State (1980) was on Mitsubishi Shoji Kaisha's pre–Second World War history in the United States; he has published a revision in Japanese. He continues to pursue research on the history of Japanese multinationals. More recently, there have been the innovative articles in *Overseas Business Activities*, ed. Akio Okochi and Tadakatsu Inoue (Tokyo, 1984). See also Mira Wilkins, "American-Japanese Direct Foreign Investment Relation-

VIEWS OF MULTINATIONAL ENTERPRISE

The ensuing discussion adopts the now-common practice of including not only those multinationals that manufacture, but also all business enterprises that extend over borders and have regular employees overseas. This definition is broad enough to include trading companies and other "service-sector" investments, such as banking and shipping. Alfred D. Chandler, Jr., has questioned whether the seventeenth-century English, Dutch, and other East India companies—trading companies—should be termed multinational enterprises.[3] These firms did possess many attributes of contemporary multinationals: they operated over borders, they coordinated operations within a single enterprise, and they participated in activities beyond trade, since they had representatives stationed outside their homelands. Chandler argued that they were nonetheless substantially different from modern multinational corporations in one fundamental respect—the quantity of their transactions. In the seventeenth century, when these giant Western trading firms came of age, months were required to send messages and receive replies. The slowness and uncertainty of communications precluded development of the coordination and control of large numbers of transactions—the administrative organizations—that are the characteristics of the modern multinational enterprise. The literature has therefore come to reflect the view that the modern multinational firm developed only in the late nineteenth century when steamships, cables, railroads, and telegraphs united distant areas.

This discussion needs refinement in the Japanese context. Much of the early international business of the Japanese trading companies clearly was constrained by distance and delays in the transmission of messages. Yet, a very important distinction exists between the East India companies of the seventeenth century and the Japanese trading firms: the Japanese enterprises have survived into the twentieth century as viable and important economic units, taking advantage of the modern innovations in transportation and communication. Because

---

ships, 1930–1952," *Business History Review* 56 (Winter 1982): 497–518. Unquestionably, however, the most outstanding contribution in recent years relevant to the history of early Japanese multinational enterprise is William D. Wray, *Mitsubishi and the N.Y.K., 1870–1914: Business Strategy in the Japanese Shipping Industry* (Cambridge, Mass., 1984). At the University of Bradford in England, Hafiz Mirza is preparing a Ph.D. dissertation on pre–Second World War Japanese overseas investments.

[3] Most current discussions of multinational enterprise include more than manufacturing. Thus, for example, *The Growth of International Business*, ed. Mark Casson (London, 1983) has a chapter on the growth of transnational banking. The issue of the status of early European trading companies first arose, I believe, at a conference held in Delaware in May 1972 on the evolution of international management structures. Wilkins, *The Emergence of Multinational Enterprise*, 3, begins with a discussion of early trading companies. Some of the first textbooks on multinational enterprise began with brief historical reviews, including materials on these European enterprises. See, for example, Richard D. Robinson, *International Business Policy* (New York, 1964).

these businesses bridge the gap between historical and contemporary study, no treatment of Japanese multinational enterprise should exclude them.

One of the most fascinating topics in the history of Japanese multinationals is the "layering" of the Japanese trading company and the Japanese manufacturing enterprise, as the two types of firms both expanded overseas. The large Japanese trading companies with general experience in international trade could not develop specialized knowledge of the varied products that constituted parts of their business; on the other hand, an individual manufacturing company knew its particular goods thoroughly, but did not have international business experience. As a response to this difficulty, the producer came to replace the trader in some international investments, while in others joint ventures between trading company and manufacturer were organized. These relationships need systematic analysis, for which the historical record provides fruitful data. The timing and nature of the shifts relate to the volume and importance of the activity; the extent to which they were also a function of the type of product requires further investigation.[4]

Much of the research on multinational enterprise has been based on an American model, which views the company (usually an industrial one) as expanding abroad out of domestic growth and particularly out of experiences in its own domestic market. Students of multinational enterprise have been impressed by the general applicability, in both contemporary and historical terms, of that paradigm, in which the advantages of manufacturing firms at home (in their home activities) become advantages in foreign countries. Firms internalized—that is, handled within the single enterprise—added operations abroad. Sometimes the American model has been carried further; scholars have argued that certain industries in which American business excelled worldwide were by their very nature amenable to multinational-type behavior.[5]

---

[4] Ozawa, *Multinationalism,* 31, noted that in 1976, the first five of Japan's top fifty overseas investors were trading companies: Mitsui, Mitsubishi, Marubeni, C. Itoh, and Sumitomo. I have borrowed the concept of layering from Fernand Braudel, *Afterthoughts on Material Civilization and Capitalism* (Baltimore, 1977). Lest one think in a parochial manner that the Japanese trading company is *sui generis* in the modern world, the reader should consult Philippe Chalmin, *Negociants et Chargeurs,* 2d ed. (Paris, 1985).

[5] Beginning with Stephen Hymer's 1960 MIT dissertation, published as *The International Operations of National Firms* (Cambridge, Mass., 1976), many economists have studied the theory of multinational enterprise in the context of industrial organization theory and oligopolistic behavior. Since most of the industries in which American multinational enterprises were active seemed characterized by a market structure that involved relatively few large firms, it came to be assumed that this was true of multinational enterprises in general. The very influential "product cycle" theory of multinationals, developed by Raymond Vernon and Louis Wells, in its early renditions began with advantages (principally technological advantages) held by American manufacturing firms. For the current state of multinational enterprise theory, see, for example, Richard Caves, *Multinational Enterprise and Economic Analysis* (New York,

Students of contemporary multinational enterprise have not been content to look only at investment, but have also examined the institutional nature of corporate expansion. The path American companies took internationally seemed to represent a universal one. Studies of contemporary European, and, to a large extent, Japanese, multinational enterprises therefore followed the same pattern of analysis. The outstanding work of Raymond Vernon, John Dunning, Charles Kindleberger, Richard Caves, and Mark Casson—to mention a few leading scholars— makes the assumption that a general model of multinational enterprise is broadly applicable.[6]

Just as contemporary studies of multinational enterprise multiplied when American business was triumphant around the world, so historical scholarship on multinational enterprise blossomed then. The history of American companies abroad accordingly formed the basis for the initial research on the history of multinational enterprise. In the 1970s and early 1980s new and substantial attention turned to the growth of European multinational enterprise, and many students of this development assumed that the historical course of European business abroad was fundamentally the same as that of its American counterpart. Systematic variations were usually explained by reference to differences in comparative advantage in the home countries, while the similarities seemed remarkable. Reflecting this view, a leading student of multinational enterprise who has dealt with both the contemporary and historical aspects of the subject, Raymond Vernon, has written, "By the early 1980s . . . the multinationalizing trend was widely recognized as similar in nature irrespective of the nationality of the parent firm."[7]

While striking similarities unquestionably exist, some scholars have had doubts. Kiyoshi Kojima described Japanese multinational enter-

---

1983) and the charming essay by Charles Kindleberger, "Plus ça change—A Look at the New Literature," in his *Multinational Excursions* (Cambridge, Mass., 1984), 180-88. Even the British scholars; including John Dunning, assumed the applicability of an "American model." I have barely touched on the exciting work that is being done on the theory of multinational enterprise.

[6] Raymond Vernon's large-scale study of multinational enterprise began at Harvard in the 1960s with American business abroad; by the 1970s he was asking identical questions of European and Japanese enterprises, and then his students were discussing the same issues in terms of the Third World multinationals.

[7] For example, on the history of American international business, see Mira Wilkins and Frank Ernest Hill, *American Business Abroad: Ford on Six Continents* (Detroit, 1964); Wilkins, *Emergence of Multinational Enterprise*; Wilkins, *Maturing of Multinational Enterprise*; Alfred D. Chandler, Jr., *The Visible Hand: The Managerial Revolution in American Business* (Cambridge, Mass., 1977). On European international business, see Stopford's and Franko's work, cited in note 1 above. The influence of the American experience was evident at a conference on "European Multinational Enterprise: Theory and History," held in Florence in 1983; some of the papers given there have been published as *Multinational Enterprise: Theory and History*, ed. Peter Hertner and Geoffrey Jones (Aldershot, 1986). See Franko, *European Multinationals*, on variations; other variations have been suggested—for example, that European investors were more prone to joint ventures—but systematic historical analysis of the differences does not exist. Raymond Vernon, *Two Hungry Giants* (Cambridge, Mass., 1983), 12 (the quotation).

prises as trade-creating, American ones as trade-destroying. Keiichiro Nakagawa stated at a business history conference in 1982, "I do not think Japanese and Western firms developed their overseas activities in the same way."[8] This article looks at the early history of Japanese business overseas, and asks whether it resembled or differed from the pattern familiar to students of either contemporary multinationals or multinationals in historical perspective. A critic of a preliminary draft of this article asked, rhetorically, "Why wouldn't one assume that cultural and situational factors led to different business practices [by Japanese enterprises] prior to 1914, especially when it is evident that they still do today?" Obviously, this historian is correct, yet this assumption has frequently not been made, because of the acceptance of the more general model by students of multinational enterprise.[9] It is inadequate, moreover, to allude to vague cultural differences or to special historical traditions. Patterns might exist in the similarities and differences, patterns that this essay seeks to decipher.

The present article is not meant to be definitive. Its uniqueness lies in its attempt to understand the course of pre-1914 Japanese multinational enterprise based on available statistics and evidence, and to suggest some of the reasons for the similarities and, more important, for the differences, between the beginnings of modern Japanese and modern American multinational enterprise. This article applies general insights developed through research on the history of multinational enterprise specifically to the history of Japanese developments. It demonstrates the extent of Japanese multinational enterprise before the First World War (which may surprise some readers) and endeavors to explain the breadth of the involvement. Hopefully, it will stimulate additional inquiries.[10]

[8] Kojima, *Japanese Direct Foreign Investment*, and his *Japan and a New World Economic Order* (Tokyo, 1977). From a historical standpoint, I do not see evidence to substantiate Kojima's differentiation; early U.S. multinationals were clearly trade-creating. Nakagawa's statement is in Okochi and Inoue, *Overseas Business Activities*, 62. In a forthcoming article in the *Journal of European Economic History*, I question whether an identical model—without modifications—can be used to study the history of American multinational enterprises and those headquartered in various different Western European countries. That article seeks to delineate some of the differences (other than those based on comparative advantage) in the evolution of American and European multinational enterprise and to clarify what seemed distinctive about the American environment that in a special manner had shaped U.S. multinational enterprise growth. Wilkins, "History of European Multinationals."

[9] Anonymous critic. Almost a decade ago, I gave a paper at a business history conference on asymmetry in foreign direct investment. Wilkins, "Crosscurrents: American Investments in Europe, European Investments in the United States," in Paul Uselding, ed., *Business and Economic History*, 2d ser. 6 (1977): 22–35. Historians there made the same comment: why should one assume symmetry? But the literature on multinational enterprise, beginning with Hymer, *International Operations of National Firms*, has assumed just that; the theory of the oligopolistic behavior of multinationals assumes that, irrespective of home countries, firms in particular industries will be prone to make foreign investments.

[10] I was surprised at the extent of Japanese business abroad before 1914 when I started to write this, but became less surprised as I delved deeper. Students of Japanese business history will be less surprised than students of the history of multinational enterprise.

BASES FOR COMPARISON

In the late nineteenth and early twentieth century, when American and Japanese modern multinational enterprises first took form, Japan was far behind the United States in the industrialization process. As noted, others have pointed out that multinationals in various home countries develop differently based on different comparative advantages. America was a nation where labor costs were high; land was available and raw material costs were relatively cheap. Thus, American technology emphasized labor-saving devices (substituting capital for labor) and was wasteful of raw materials. In terms of inputs for a modern industrial economy, Japan's development was characterized by the need for imported raw materials and for the exports to pay for those imports. To be sure, in the late nineteenth century Japan was an exporter of raw materials—of coal and raw silk; and while silk exports retained their importance, Japan became aware of its requirements for basic raw material imports far faster than the United States did. The United States after all had cotton, iron, and coal—all the key items of the early Industrial Revolution. Japan soon became an importer of raw cotton and of iron, and even its coal eventually became inadequate for its needs.

Other significant features of the American and Japanese home environments can be compared: 1) the size of the home market; 2) heterogeneity or homogeneity at home; 3) national status as importer or exporter of capital; 4) geographical position vis-à-vis other economic leaders; and 5) antitrust attitudes. Why select these particular aspects through which to study Japanese multinationals? I have already used these items to define differences between American and European firms; it is valuable, for comparative purposes, to employ the same framework in considering American and Japanese business. Moreover, using these aspects as a handle for discussion brings out key elements in the history of Japanese multinationals.[11] The five points utilized in this inquiry (which are by no means all-inclusive) provide help in understanding some significant similarities in the evolution of U.S. and

[11] Wilkins, "History of European Multinationals." I could have chosen to discuss in isolation the role of government (more in the Japanese case than in the American) or the role of educational systems (important in both countries). To add these separate categories seemed unnecessary, since they would not alter the basic analysis that follows. Professor Frank H. H. King (historian of the HongKong and Shanghai Banking Corporation), on reading the penultimate draft of this article, presented the stimulating notion that specific Japanese government-inspired national goals should be considered with "special reference to the replication of foreign-type institutions as an end in itself." (Letter to the author, 4 Oct. 1985.) To incorporate (or to refute) this contention would involve a major revision of this paper. Ultimately, I believe that the Japanese (through imitation and innovation) developed appropriate institutions and that the development of multinationals per se was not in its essence a government-inspired replication of foreign behavior, albeit in some instances—for example, the Yokohama Specie Bank compared with the HongKong and Shanghai Banking Corporation—this may have been a relevant consideration.

Japanese multinationals, important differences, and in addition the nature and extent of pre–1914 Japanese multinational enterprise.

THE HOME MARKET

By the beginning of the twentieth century the United States constituted the world's largest market, while Japan did not yet rank as an important market, based on international comparisons. Put simply, Japan was a far less developed country than the United States. In 1913 the United States had the world's greatest manufacturing output, representing some 35.8 percent of world production; Japan's represented a mere 1.2 percent. By every criteria, Japan's national market was smaller than that of the United States: in geographical size, per capita income, and population size. (Japan's average annual population [1905–9] was 47.5 million, compared to the U.S. population at the time of 87.1 million.) These differences in the size of the home market would almost by definition lead one to anticipate a separate pattern of multinational enterprise development.[12]

When one views Japanese industrialization in the late nineteenth and early twentieth century, what stands out? Not the mass production, not the beginnings of mass consumption that were characteristic of the American economy and that presented the managerial challenges in the United States. Rather, in Japan the important circumstances were the rapid coming of age of the Japanese domestic textile industry; economic growth and military triumphs (in the Sino-Japanese War and the Russo-Japanese War); and a recognition that because of its resource limitations and the smallness of the country—as defined earlier—Japan would by its very nature be highly dependent on trade, on imports of raw materials. Exports were required, in turn, to pay for these imports, creating a fundamental need for an infrastructure in support of trade—banking facilities, shipping companies, shipbuilding, insurance, and, most of all, enterprises familiar with the complexities of doing business abroad—that is, trading companies. Without such activities, Japanese economic development could not occur.[13]

All of these functions, however, could be carried on by foreigners. Indeed, in many countries around the world, foreign-headquartered multinational enterprise did control international trade. Why was Ja-

[12] League of Nations, *Industrialization and Foreign Trade* (Geneva, 1945), 13; W. W. Lockwood, *The Economic Development of Japan* (Princeton, N. J., 1954), 89 (1905–9 Japanese figures). U.S. figures (1905–9 average) from U.S. Bureau of the Census, *Historical Statistics of the United States* (Washington, D. C., 1960), 7.

[13] In studying the history of Japanese business, I have found extremely useful Johannes Hirschmeier and Tsunehiko Yui, *The Development of Japanese Business 1600–1973* (Cambridge, Mass., 1975).

pan different? Why did its nationals come to handle and to control all these important functions? Perhaps Japanese companies undertook these activities, on a broad scale, because foreign business was not prepared to do so, and because the trade was more important to Japan than to her trading partners.[14] The relatively limited Japanese home market, resulting in small domestic firms incapable of handling extensive international trade by themselves, was an even more significant influence on the development of a Japanese-run infrastructure for overseas trade: specialized companies were required to carry forth operations abroad. The Japanese management challenge was, accordingly, different from that facing U.S. business.

Interestingly, in late nineteenth- and early twentieth-century Britain, also a small country by geographical size, constant problems of management over distance also existed, and the response to them was often the establishment of specialized institutions: trading companies, managing agencies, consulting engineers and, of course, shipping companies—in short, a service apparatus. The Japanese use of trading companies and development of service-sector companies in general seem closer to the British than to the American experience.[15] Also, like the British, the Japanese made some large foreign direct investments in railroads, specifically designed to meet Japanese domestic requirements.

HETEROGENEITY AND HOMOGENEITY

If one assumes that multinational enterprises arise out of domestic conditions, one must look to other specific circumstances as well. Japan, unlike the United States, was not a country of immigrants. The American market was characterized by domestic diversity. In contrast, a visitor to Japan is impressed by the homogeneous nature of the population. Years of isolation produced a separate development, a distinctive ethic, that must be taken into account in any discussion of the evolution of Japanese multinational enterprise. Two pertinent consequences were inexperience at home in working closely with outsiders

[14] As Angus Maddison, *Economic Growth in Japan and the USSR* (New York, 1969), 28, points out, as late as 1887, nine-tenths of Japan's external trade was handled by foreigners—mainly British houses. Yet, the Japanese replaced them and as trade expanded, Japanese firms handled the bulk of it. Wray, *Mitsubishi and N.Y.K.*, 20, suggests that foreign shipping companies in the early 1870s were a threat to Japan's economic security because they exacerbated Japan's balance of payments difficulties by carrying all its foreign trade; but this was true of many countries that failed to make the transition from foreign to domestic control.

[15] The British problems with management over distance will be discussed in my forthcoming history of foreign investment in the United States. Large British trading companies of the late nineteenth and early twentieth century included firms such as Jardine, Matheson & Company, Butterfield & Swire, and Balfour, Williamson. Some American companies of this sort, such as the American Trading Company, existed in this era, but they seemed dwarfed by their British counterparts.

(creating a larger sphere of what was alien and unfamiliar) and a less varied demand for goods (resulting in a rigidity in taste). Here again, the parallels between the Japanese and British situations seem far closer than those between the Japanese and American experiences.

Comparison of American and European multinationals suggests that business enterprises investing abroad use three methods in coping with the unfamiliar: they seek out the most familiar within the unfamiliar; they try to create the familiar within the unfamiliar; and they adapt. It is easier to adapt in relatively familiar circumstances than in unfamiliar ones. In the American case, early foreign investment went disproportionately to geographically nearby areas—Canada, Mexico, and the Caribbean—and to culturally nearby ones—Great Britain.[16] The earliest Japanese foreign investments were, likewise, in geographically close and relatively familiar regions.

JAPANESE INVESTMENT IN CHINA

In 1931, the Bank of Japan prepared statistics on Japanese foreign investments in 1914 at the special request of American economist Harold Moulton (see Table 1). Moulton added estimates for other investments not covered and concluded that the total for 1913–14 amounted to 600 million yen (or $295.5 million at 100 yen = $49.25). A recent Japanese source provides similar figures (see Table 2), based on estimates of Japanese investment in China prepared for C. F. Remer for his 1933 study and the Moulton 1931 figures from the Bank of Japan on the United States and Hawaii. All of the Moulton–Bank of Japan "elsewhere" figures are attributed in this rendition to the Philippines and the South Sea Islands. The estimates indicate Japanese investments abroad in 1914 of between $227 and $296 million.[17] To provide a sense of the dimension of such foreign investments, they can be calculated as a percentage of 1914 Japanese gross national product, amounting to 9.9 percent and 12.8 percent, respectively—surprisingly high percentages; the figures include both portfolio and direct investments.[18]

[16] Wilkins, "History of European Multinationals"; Wilkins, *The Emergence of Multinational Enterprise*.
[17] See Harold Moulton, *Japan* (Washington, D. C., 1931), 391–92; on my Japanese trip in July 1984, I tried to obtain the originals of the Moulton figures. Professor Hiroaki Yamazaki of the Institute of Social Science, University of Tokyo, discovered that the Bank of Japan had prepared these figures at Moulton's special request and hand-delivered them to him in the United States. The figures in Ken-ichi Yasumuro, "The Contribution of Sogo Shosha to the Multinationalization of Japanese Industrial Enterprises in Historical Perspective," in Okochi and Inoue, *Overseas Business Activities*, 84, should be compared with C. F. Remer, *Foreign Investments in China* (New York, 1933), 446 (a different rate of exchange altered these numbers slightly), and Moulton, *Japan*, 391.
[18] I used the gross national product figure in current prices (4,665 million yen) as given in Kazushi Ohkawa and Henry Rosovsky, *Japanese Economic Growth* (Stanford, 1973), 278. At the rate of exchange

The estimates show that Japanese foreign investments in 1914 were largest in China (including Manchuria), and consisted overwhelmingly of foreign direct investments that carried management and control. All the foreign direct investments seem to be closely related to Japanese development, including the Japanese government's sizable investment in the South Manchurian Railway (1906). They need to be studied within the framework provided by current knowledge on the nature of multinational enterprise.[19]

The Shimonoseki Treaty between Japan and China was signed in 1895, for the first time permitting foreigners to manufacture in Chinese treaty ports. Almost at once a British trading firm, Jardine, Matheson & Company, established the Ewo Cotton Spinning and Weaving Company in Shanghai, and three other foreign textile firms quickly followed (another British, one American, and one German).[20]

Japanese spinners saw their export markets in China threatened by these foreign-owned manufacturing facilities. Accordingly, two Japanese spinners established plants in Shanghai, but, as Tetsuya Kuwahara found, these initial ventures failed because of inadequate evaluation of the market and ineffective management. The Japanese retreated to a more familiar activity—exporting from Japan.[21]

Then, in 1902, Jōtarō Yamamoto, the Shanghai branch manager of Mitsui & Co., purchased a Chinese cotton mill and reestablished it under the name Shanghai Cotton Spinning Company, Ltd. Four years

used in the tables, that equals about $2.3 billion. By way of comparison, U.S. investment abroad (direct *and* portfolio investment) in 1914 was $3.5 billion; as a percentage of the American GNP of $36.4 billion in 1914, it equaled 9.6 percent. Based on data in Wilkins, *Emergence of Multinational Enterprise*, 201. Thus, in 1914, even using the lowest Japanese figure, the Japanese foreign investment was relatively larger than that of the United States. Japanese GNP was smaller in 1914 than in 1913. In 1913 it was 5,212 million yen (or about $2.57 billion). Ibid. When I calculated the Japanese foreign investment estimates as a percentage of the higher 1913 GNP, the figures still came out surprisingly big: 8.8 to 11.5 percent of the GNP.

[19] Remer, *Foreign Investments in China*, and Chi-ming Hou, *Foreign Investment and Economic Development in China 1840–1937* (Cambridge, Mass., 1965) are the basic works on foreign investment in China. See also Tien-yi Yang, "Foreign Business Activities and the Chinese Response, 1842–1937," in Okochi and Inoue, *Overseas Business Activities*, 215–25. On Japanese investments in China everyone has to start with Remer, *Foreign Investments in China*, 414–46, 474–92, and passim. Hou, *Foreign Investment*, 19, calculated that 36 percent of the total Japanese direct investment in China in 1914 was in transportation, chiefly in the South Manchurian Railway. Remer did not differentiate between investments made by Japanese firms headquartered in Japan and by Japanese residents in China; a student of multinational enterprise would do so.

[20] Kang Chao, *The Development of Cotton Textile Production in China* (Cambridge, Mass., 1977), 115–16, notes that the second British-owned mill was called Laou Kung Mow Cotton Spinning Company; the American one was that of the International Cotton Manufacturing Company; and the German-owned one was built by Soy Chee Spinning Company. See an interesting article on the cotton-spinning industry in Shanghai, in *The Times* (London), 11 Feb. 1896.

[21] Tetsuya Kuwahara, "The Business Strategy of Japanese Cotton Spinners: Overseas Operations 1890 to 1931," in Akio Okochi and Shin-ichi Yonekawa, *The Textile Industry and its Business Climate* (Tokyo, 1982), 140; interestingly, S. D. Chapman, "British-Based Investment Groups before 1914," *Economic History Review*, 2d ser. 38 (May 1985): 234, writes that Jardine, Matheson had built its cotton spinning mill in Shanghai "to meet incipient Japanese competition." The article in the London *Times*, 11 Feb. 1896, evaluates the Japanese entry plans and suggests an added reason why a Japanese firm in China might *not* succeed: inland taxes on raw cotton.

TABLE 1

Japanese Foreign Investment, July 1914
(based on unpublished Bank of Japan figures)

	VALUE IN MILLIONS OF	
LOCATION AND TYPE	YEN	DOLLARS
China:		
Loans to	54.70	26.9
Foreign securities purchased	6.45	3.2
Business enterprises:	400.00	197.0
In China	(310.00)	(152.7)
In the United States and Hawaii	(50.00)	(24.6)
Elsewhere	(40.00)	(19.7)
Totals	461.15	227.1

Source: Harold Moulton, Japan (Washington, D.C., 1931), 391–92. Rate of exchange used: 100 yen = $49.25.

TABLE 2

Japanese Foreign Investment in 1914
(Ippei Yamazawa and Yuzou Yamamoto estimates)

	VALUE IN MILLIONS OF	
LOCATION AND TYPE	YEN	DOLLARS
China	439	216.2
comprising		
Loans to government	(19)	(9.4)
Loans to private enterprise	(35)	(17.2)
Direct investments	(385)	(189.6)
The United States and Hawaii	50	24.6
The Philippines and the South Seas	40	19.7
Totals	529	260.5

Source: Ken-ichi Yasumuro, "The Contribution of the Sogo Shosha to the Multinationalization of Japanese Industrial Enterprise," in Overseas Business Activities, ed. Akio Okochi and Tadakatsu Inoue (Tokyo, 1984), 84. Professor Yasumuro's source was a 1979 Japanese volume on foreign trade and the balance of payments by Ippei Yamazawa and Yuzou Yamamoto. Rate of exchange used: 100 yen = $49.25.

later, Mitsui & Co. acquired the Santai Cotton Spinning Company, Ltd., another Chinese cotton mill, extended its capacity, and placed Yamamoto in charge. On 5 December 1908, Mitsui organized a new local subsidiary, Shanghai Cotton Manufacturing Company, which owned the two spinning mills. Yamamoto managed this affiliate separately from Mitsui & Co., because Takashi Masuda, the risk-averse head of Mitsui, did not want the trading company itself to become directly involved. Ken-ichi Yasumuro noted that Masuda "preferred to earn commissions by acting as an intermediary between buyers and sellers"; should the Chinese mills fail, Yamamoto would take the blame. In fact, Shanghai Cotton proved very profitable. By 1914, the firm had also installed 886 looms, and thus participated in weaving as well as spinning.[22]

The Japan Cotton Trading Company, a major firm in the raw cotton trade, had a cotton spinning mill in Shanghai by that time. In 1909 the Naigaiwata Company, a Japanese spinner, built what has been described by Yasumuro as "a new and powerful spinning mill in Shanghai." Equipped with the most advanced machinery and managed by a Japanese staff sent from the parent company, its labor-management relations replicated Japanese practice—for example, by providing dormitories for Chinese girls working at the mill. It was extremely successful. The Naigaiwata Company had been a trading firm, but it had bought out two Japanese spinners and established itself as a spinner in Japan before entering China.[23] Naigaiwata was the first Japanese spinner (as distinct from trading company) to be a success in manufacturing in China. Whereas the Japanese trading companies had bought existing Chinese mills, it constructed its own mill, following its own designs. While the Naigaiwata Company was not one of the largest spinning establishments in Japan, it gained experience from its Japanese mills before it began to manufacture abroad; by 1914, based on its Japanese and Chinese assets, it ranked nineteenth among the one hundred largest Japanese mining and manufacturing companies.[24]

By 1913, the Shanghai mill of the Naigaiwata Company was far more efficient than any Chinese-owned mill. Kuwahara explains that when

---

[22] Yasumuro, "The Contribution," 67, and Albert Feuerwerker, *China's Early Industrialization* (Cambridge, Mass., 1958), 224. Chao, *Development of Cotton Textile Production*, 116, appears to mix up Mitsui and Mitsubishi. Data from Professor Kuwahara, 16 Jan. 1986, and from Professor Yasumuro, Osaka, 24 July 1984; Chao, *Development of Cotton Textile Production*, 138, shows Shanghai Cotton's profitable performance.

[23] Kuwahara, "The Business Strategy," 140; the Japan Cotton Trading Company had established its first branch in China in Shanghai in 1903; Mitsui & Co., *The 100 Year History of Mitsui & Co., Ltd. 1876–1976* (Tokyo, 1977), 64. Yasumuro, "The Contribution," 68; Tetsuya Kuwahara, "The Formation of Oligopolistic Structures of the Cotton Spinning Industry in Japan and the Growth Strategies of the Latecomers: Case of Naigaiwata Company," *Japan Business History Review* 18 (Jan. 1984): iii–iv; Kuwahara, "The Business Strategy," 158; and data from Professors Yasumuro and Kuwahara, Osaka, 24 July 1984, on the Naigaiwata Company.

[24] Mitsui & Co., of course, had close connections with the Osaka Spinning Mills. Takashi Masuda of Mitsui & Co. in 1879 had prompted the plans for this modern establishment; Masuda became a chief shareholder of the Osaka Spinning Mills; and Mitsui & Co. had the responsibility for importing spinning machines. See Mitsui & Co., *100 Year History*, 44–47. Mitsui & Co.'s relations with other spinners appear to have related to raw cotton sales. Nonetheless, Mitsui & Co. cannot be called "a spinning company" in the same manner as the Naigaiwata Company. For the ten largest cotton spinners in Japan in 1913 see S. Yonekawa, "The Growth of Cotton Spinning Firms," in Okochi and Yonekawa, *The Textile Industry*, 8. The Naigaiwata Company is not included. I am indebted to Professor Yamazaki (22 July 1984) for finding the Naigaiwata ranking for me. Ranked by total assets, only three other Japanese cotton spinners were larger. None of the latter, in 1914, had investments in Chinese spinning.

the other, larger Japanese spinners made plans for mills in China, one important factor encouraging their subsequent entry was their recognition of the capability of Naigaiwata's Shanghai mill to compete in the Chinese market, a competitiveness that Kuwahara attributes to management knowledge. The Japanese mill owners also had the advantage of experience in buying raw cotton. Hiroaki Yamazaki suggests that a third advantage lay in their practice of blending raw cotton from different sources to obtain low-cost raw materials.[25]

Recently Stephen C. Thomas has argued that "the initiation of the Chinese-owned cotton industry was one of the most promising achievements of the pre–1897 period." He maintains that the foreign investments in China were a consequence of the profits being made by Chinese-owned mills. Then, severe competition from foreign-owned mills reduced profits. "By the early 1900s, three of [Chinese entrepreneur] Sheng [Hsuan-huai]'s mills had to be sold to Japanese interests. . . ."[26] What does Thomas mean by "had to be sold"? It seems likely that they were not competitive with imports and the European-owned mills.

All the Japanese textile investments in manufacturing in China served the Chinese market. They appear to have been established in response to the presence of both Western and Chinese investments in Chinese spinning mills, as well as to the sale in China of cheap Indian yarn. They all grew out of existing business operations. The Japan Cotton Trading Company and the Naigaiwata Company's initial interest in China seems to have been in the export of raw cotton from China to Japan. As the Japanese cotton textile industry developed, interest in export markets grew, and Japanese businessmen, whether trader or spinner, needed to know conditions in China.[27] The early twentieth-century Japanese investments in Chinese manufacturing may initially have been made to discover Chinese costs, test out Chinese raw cotton, and keep close to the Chinese textile market. Tariffs were not a consideration in these early investments.

Thomas maintains that "unlike sovereign countries . . . China could not control ownership of this [cotton textile] technology after 1895,

[25] Kuwahara, "The Business Strategy," 158, 165; M. Miyamoto, "Comments," in Okochi and Inoue, *Overseas Business Activities*, 172; Yamazaki in conversation with the author, Tokyo, 19 July 1984.
[26] Stephen C. Thomas, *Foreign Intervention and China's Industrial Development, 1870–1911* (Boulder, Colo., 1984), 150–51.
[27] Mitsui & Co., *100 Year History*, 47. China had been an importer of raw cotton, but from roughly 1888 to the time of the First World War it was a net exporter of raw cotton; coincidentally, it was an importer of cotton yarn and cotton cloth. Bruce L. Reynolds, "The East Asian 'Textile Cluster' Trade, 1868–1973: A Comparative Advantage Interpretation," in *America's China Trade in Historical Perspective*, ed. Ernest R. May and John K. Fairbank (Cambridge, Mass., 1986), 137. The Japanese trade in cotton manufactures came to be very important. In 1913 exports of cotton manufactured goods and yarn totaled 33.9 percent of Japanese exports to China and 11.7 percent of total Japanese exports. Remer, *Foreign Investments in China*, 462.

regulate imports with a protective tariff, or tax foreign-owned mills in China."[28] None of Thomas's commentary, however, explains Japanese competitiveness. The technology was not proprietary; and China's inability to regulate the import of products is irrelevant to foreign investment in manufacturing. The influx of Indian yarn, for example, may have stimulated Japanese investment, but Chinese businessmen could have responded in a comparable manner. Presumably tax policy could have been framed to void any advantages of the Japanese mills. Japanese superiority was not a consequence of suppression of Chinese sovereignty, but of experience and entrepreneurial ability. A Chinese-American historian, Kang Chao, writes:

> . . . the cotton textile industry in Japan . . . [by the early twentieth century] had developed some excellent management systems, marketing organizations, and raw material procurement organizations. It did not take long for the Japanese to apply these organization principles to their plants in China. Furthermore, managers of Japanese mills in China quickly learned to adapt to local conditions, probably because of the high degree of cultural and linguistic similarities between the two countries. All these factors contributed to the quick establishment of an overall superiority of Japanese mills over both Chinese and British mills.[29]

The Japanese investments were overwhelmingly in spinning, although, as noted, the Shanghai Cotton Manufacturing Company owned looms. In 1913, Japanese spinning mills in China had 111,900 spindles (compared to British-owned mills in China with 138,000 spindles); that year in China there were 886 Japanese-owned power looms (and 800 British-owned ones). Whereas 63 percent of the spindles in China in 1897 were Chinese-owned and 37 percent Western-owned (with no Japanese ownership), by 1913 the ratios were 60 percent Chinese, 27 percent Western, and 13 percent Japanese. For power looms, in 1897 the ratios were 70 percent Chinese-owned and 30 percent Western-owned (none Japanese-owned); in 1913, 56 percent were Chinese-owned, 25 percent Western-owned, and 19 percent Japanese-owned.[30]

[28] Thomas, *Foreign Intervention*, 151.
[29] Chao, *Development of Cotton Textile Production*, 140; Chao, p. 157, presents production cost data for Chinese and Japanese mills in China for 1935. Japanese management had obtained remarkably lower costs than the Chinese. Regrettably, similar comparative data are not available for 1913–14, but see Kuwahara, "The Business Strategy," 165, which indicates that in 1913 Naigaiwata's Shanghai mills produced 1.24–1.32 pounds of 16-count yarn per spindle each 24-hour day, while the Chinese mills produced 0.87–1.00 pound.
[30] Hou, *Foreign Investment*, 88; Chao, *Development of Cotton Textile Production*, 117, 301, 305. Hou's breakdowns are by spindles and looms rather than by company. Chao (p. 301) shows the rapid rise of Japanese-owned spindles, 1902–13. He notes that the looms were "power looms" (p. 305), but not whether they were of Western or Japanese design. Ibid. ("Western" includes British, German, and American). Kuwahara—using Minejiro Yoshida, *Zaishi Hojin Boseki no Shōrai ni tsuite* (1927) as a source—has established that the 886 Japanese-owned looms in Shanghai Cotton Manufacturing Company's mill no. 1 and mill no. 2 were of British manufacture—by Platt Bros.

The pre–First World War Japanese investments in Chinese spinning and weaving were harbingers of far larger and more important ones to follow. They are, however, of particular interest in that they offer a preview of some of the dilemmas of trading (as opposed to manufacturing) companies as manufacturers abroad. The management of Mitsui & Co. in Tokyo was prepared to delegate decision making and management at the Shanghai spinning mills to its branch manager on the scene; the home company had little interest in the venture. The Naigaiwata Company, which used its direct experiences with its Japanese spinning operations as a basis for its Chinese mill, was the most successful of these early Japanese investors in China.[31] This was a case of creating the familiar abroad—creating the familiar within the unfamiliar. It was their transfer of familiar experience to China that contributed to the Japanese success. And, as Chao points out, the Japanese were also prepared to adapt to Chinese conditions; it was easier for them than for westerners to do so.

What else do we know of the pioneer Japanese businesses in China? Albert Feuerwerker, using materials published in Peking in 1957, found that of the 136 foreign and Sino-foreign manufacturing and mining firms established in China, 1895–1913, forty-nine of them, or 36 percent of the total, were Japanese. The Japanese were the largest investors in terms of number of firms, followed by the British with thirty-seven firms and 27 percent of the total. In value, however, based on initial capitalization, the British investments represented 48 percent, the Japanese 25 percent. While Remer's 1933 book and Hou's 1965 study give details, we need to know much more about these ventures. They included the manufacture of bean oil in Manchuria (Nisshin founded a mill in Dairen in 1907 with a capital of 3.75 million yen), and the making of flour in Shanghai and Manchuria (Mitsui & Co., for example, had a flour mill in Shanghai).[32]

---

[31] All the sources stress that these early Japanese investments in manufacturing were small compared with what followed. For the first time, in 1919 Japanese-owned cotton spindles in China exceeded those in *all* Western-owned mills. By 1936, roughly 44 percent of the cotton spindles in China were in Japanese-owned mills. See Chao, *Development of Cotton Textile Production*, 125–29, 301–2. On looms, ibid., 125–29, 305–7. Remer, *Foreign Investments in China*, 497, gives slightly different figures for 1909–31 but documents the same formidable expansion in Japanese involvement in spinning. See also Kuwahara, "The Business Strategy," 141–60. Profit figures provided in Chao, *Development of Cotton Textile Production*, 138, seem to show larger profits for Shanghai Cotton than for Naigaiwata, but none of the years monitored coincide and the 1908 results for Naigaiwata were *before* its mill was built.

[32] Albert Feuerwerker, "The Chinese Economy, ca. 1870–1911," Papers in Chinese Studies (Ann Arbor, Mich., 1969), 34. These figures should be compared with data in Remer, *Foreign Investments in China*, 431. Remer identified 63 "Japanese" manufacturing "plants or firms" in China in 1914, all of which appear to have been inaugurated after 1900; see ibid., 419. It is not clear how Feuerwerker defined "foreign." Does he include resident Japanese investors in China? As noted, Remer did. Economists would predict that British enterprises in China would employ relatively more capital than the Japanese ones; after all, Britain was in these years a capital-rich economy, relative to Japan. Remer, *Foreign Investments in China*, 431, is a good starting point for further study, even though he did not differentiate nonresident and resident foreign investment. See Hou, *Foreign Investment*, 11, for a good discussion of Remer's

The Japanese exported matches in large quantities in the early twentieth century. In 1900–1914, the Chinese match market "was entirely in Japanese hands," and the Japanese were also making inroads into India and the Dutch East Indies. According to Remer, Japanese investors had five match manufacturing "plants or firms" in Manchuria and in north, central, and south China in 1914, though the sums invested were not large. The Japanese—with their highly competitive "cottage" match industry at home, using Japanese wood and chemicals imported from Europe—could compete through exports.[33]

The Hanyehping Coal and Iron Company, located just south of Hankow, represented one of the most important Japanese investments in China. From this firm's mines came the bulk of iron ore needed for the Japanese government-owned Yawata iron and steel works in Kyushu. The Japanese investments appear to have been in the form of loans, although by agreements the Japanese were given a "considerable degree of control, which was exercised through the Yokohama Specie Bank." The Japanese-controlled South Manchurian Railway (SMR) took part in developing the Fushin coal mines—the richest ones in Manchuria. In 1907 sales of Fushin coal were a mere 202,320 long tons; by 1913–14, they were 2.5 million long tons, roughly half of which was consumed in Manchuria (mainly meeting the SMR's re-

---

methodology; ibid., 89, 246, and Remer, *Foreign Investments in China*, 500, on the flour mills. Remer wrote that the oldest flour mill in China was probably the Mitsui mill at Shanghai. He does not give a date of origin, but obviously it preceded the Japanese-owned South Manchuria Milling Company at Tiehlin in Manchuria, which was founded in 1906; ibid.

[33] Håkan Lindgren, *Corporate Growth: The Swedish Match Industry in Its Global Setting* (Stockholm, 1979), 53–54 and Hans Modig, *Swedish Match Interests in British India during the Interwar Years* (Stockholm, 1979), 41–45. Remer, *Foreign Investments in China*, 431. Since Remer did not differentiate between nonresident and resident foreign investments, these may have been small plants run by Japanese businessmen who lived in China. It was not all "cottage" industry in Japan. Modig, *Swedish Match Interests*, 41–42, cites an "eye-witness" report of 1910 on the Japanese match industry, which indicated that the Japanese had to a large degree adopted the German system of match making; the Japanese built machinery

> which imitate the German but with some small alterations, in order that the patent law is not infringed. The appearance of the machines and the manufactures does not completely come up to the German standard but they only cost from a third to a quarter as much as the German machines. As far as possible wood is used in the Japanese machines instead of iron. . . . A Japanese factory works as far as possible without expensive and continuous machines but uses instead homemade machines often constructed by the factory manager.

Japanese matches before the First World War were "a good third cheaper wholesale than the Swedish"; ibid., 43. One wonders whether Mitsui had match factories in China. Mitsui Bussan made volume purchases from domestic producers and well before 1914 had established a trademarked Japanese match export business. Wray, *Mitsubishi and the N.Y.K.*, 450. In the mid-1920s Mitsui Bussan controlled the greater part of Japanese match exports. Lindgren, *Corporate Growth*, 338. By 1922, in response to Indian tariffs, unspecified "Japanese interests" in partnership with Indian wholesalers had started to manufacture matches in India; the splints and boxes were imported. See Modig, *Swedish Match Interests*, 76, 66. On the expansion of Japanese-owned match factories in the Bombay area in 1923, see ibid., 79.

quirements and those of the Chinese Eastern Railway) and half of which was exported to Japan.[34]

The government-supported Yokohama Specie Bank, founded in 1880, was international from its origin. It developed an extensive network of branches, facilitating trade through its participation in foreign exchange activities, trade financing, and even long-term financing of the raw material procurement needs of Japanese industry, as in its loans to the Hanyehping Coal and Iron Company in China. The Yokohama Specie Bank set up its first representative office in Shanghai in 1893, associated with the growing triangular cotton trade among Japan, India, and China. It did so at the request of Japanese businessmen, who—when India ended free coinage of silver that year—had major difficulties with foreign exchange transactions.[35]

The Industrial Bank of Japan, organized in 1900, and in operation by 1902, was used by the Japanese government to attract foreign capital and to help finance government-sponsored ventures. It provided early loans, for example, to the Tayeh mines that became part of the Hanyehping Company complex, and it raised monies for the South Manchurian Railway and for other investments in China. Hugh Patrick

[34] Wray, *Mitsubishi and the N.Y.K.*, 395; Remer, *Foreign Investments in China*, 104, 507–8. Particularly useful on Japanese interests in the Hanyehping Company is William D. Wray, "Japan's Big Three in China: International Business and Changing Industrial Structure," unpub. paper (Feb. 1986), 23–26. See Kungtu C. Sun, *The Economic Development of Manchuria* (Cambridge, Mass., 1969), 65, on the Fushun coal mines.

[35] Yang, "Foreign Business," 222–23. Hirschmeier and Yui, *Development of Japanese Business*, 183, call the Yokohama Specie Bank a "special bank established under government auspices." G.C. Allen, *A Short Economic History of Modern Japan* (London, 1962), 53, describes the Yokohama Specie Bank's operations as "from the beginning closely supervised by the government. The state provided one-third of its initial capital and the appointment of its President and Vice-President required the authorization of the Ministry of Finance. The Yokohama Specie Bank was entrusted with funds from the Treasury Reserve Fund to enable it to deal in foreign bills of exchange. . . ." As of June 1913, the "Imperial Household" owned 121,000 shares of the 480,000 shares issued. *Stock Exchange Official Intelligence, 1914* (London), 419. Hugh Patrick, "Japan 1868–1914," in *Banking in the Early Stages of Industrialization*, ed. Rondo Cameron (New York, 1967), 267–68, writes that while the Yokohama Specie Bank was at the start of private origin, within a decade it became in effect a government bank. "The government initially provided one-third of the capital and up to three-quarters of the deposits. The bank suffered major losses in its early operations, and in the process of repeatedly bailing it out the government assumed complete control." He writes that in the late 1880s the Ministry of Finance arranged that the Bank of Japan would "not engage in foreign exchange business, would provide cheap deposits to the Yokohama Specie Bank, and would rediscount its foreign exchange bills at preferentially low interest rates." Thus, the specialized bank not only came to dominate foreign trade financing, but could subsidize export industries by making them low interest-rate loans. See also Phra Sarasas, *Money and Banking in Japan* (London, 1940), 158–61. There are several histories of the Yokohama Specie Bank in Japanese: one was published by the bank, in Tokyo, in 1920; another is a recent multivolume work by Shinji Arai, *History of the Yokohama Specie Bank* (this is partly a documentary collection, mixed with historical summaries; Shinji Arai was the project editor; Japanese scholars cite it as *YSG zenshi*). Very useful is Japan, Ministry of Finance, *Business Report of Banking and Trust Business* (Tokyo, 1916). The bank's *Annual Reports* are located at the University of Tokyo. I am indebted to Professor Yamazaki for his gracious and splendid help with the Japanese-language literature. His insights were invaluable. On YSB's first branch office in Shanghai, see Wray, "Japan's Big Three in China," 17, and Wray to Wilkins, 25 June 1986.

calculated that "of the 294.4 million yen in foreign portfolio capital underwritten by the Industrial Bank [1902–13] 46 percent was exported as semigovernmental direct investment," primarily to China and Korea. By 1902 a private bank, the Yasuda Bank, apparently also had important Chinese interests.[36]

Japanese companies assumed importance in Chinese shipping, as well as in other international shipping routes. Japan's first overseas shipping line was a weekly service from Yokohama to Shanghai, started by Mitsubishi as early as February 1875. Less than nine months later, in October, Mitsubishi acquired four ships from the Pacific Mail Steamship Company, an American firm, which relinquished its Yokohama-Shanghai service to its new Japanese rival.[37]

Mitsui & Co.'s first shipments to China (of coal) were on Mitsubishi ships. In 1880, Mitsui started its own Tokyo Fūhansen Kaisha (sailing ship company) for freight between domestic ports and China and Korea; it also continued to use Mitsubishi vessels. In 1885, Nippon Yūsen Kaisha (NYK) was established, replacing the old Mitsubishi shipping lines. Mitsubishi retained an interest in NYK; the latter became a "national policy company," with a large government interest. NYK, at origin, was in domestic, coastal shipping, but it had three overseas lines to nearby areas: to Shanghai, Vladivostok, and Inch'on. Of the foreign routes, only the Shanghai line was of any significance. Later in the nineteenth century and in the early twentieth century, NYK developed close ties with the Japanese cotton spinners, which added to its cargo in the China trade. Its Chinese shipping activities expanded.[38]

The Osaka Shōsen Kaisha (OSK), organized in 1884, also played a significant role in Chinese shipping. OSK was the first major Japanese shipping company to operate on the Yangtze River. With a subsidy from the Japanese government, it opened a Shanghai-Hankow line in

[36] Sarasas, *Money and Banking in Japan*, 258; Wray, *Mitsubishi and the N.Y.K.*, 395 (loans to the Tayeh mines); Patrick, "Japan," 271; Allen, *Short Economic History*, 51, writes that the Industrial Bank of Japan raised monies in London, guaranteeing and selling several issues of South Manchurian Railway sterling debentures between 1907 and 1911. The South Manchurian Railway Company, Ltd., registered in Tokyo, 7 Dec. 1906, was listed in the *Stock Exchange Official Intelligence, 1914* (London), 379, but with no mention of the Industrial Bank of Japan. Employees of the Yokohama Specie Bank, Ltd., 7 Bishopsgate, London, were "The London Agents for the Sterling Bonds" of this railway. Principal and interest on the sterling bonds were guaranteed by the Japanese government and payable at the Yokohama Specie Bank office in London. I think Allen is wrong, and that the Industrial Bank raised money on its *own* debentures in London and then (as Hugh Patrick suggests) channeled it through Japan to the South Manchurian Railway and other ventures. According to Sarasas, the Industrial Bank's first overseas investments were in 1906 in public utilities and loans to private enterprises in Korea. *Money and Banking in Japan*, 258. Sarasas seems to have neglected the earlier loan to the Tayeh mines in China in 1903 that preceded the Korean loans. Wray, *Mitsubishi and the N.Y.K.*, 349 (on the Yasuda Bank).
[37] Ibid., 60, 85–86.
[38] Ibid., 2, 61, 133–36, 219ff., 342, 355–56. At first Mitsubishi was the largest single stockholder in NYK, but by the mid-1890s, the Imperial Household was in first place; ibid., 239, 258. By the early 1880s, the connections between Yokohama and Shanghai had become very easy with almost daily steamers plying the route. See J. Whitie, London, to E. M. Sang, Brussels, 6 March 1883, acq. 2, box 7, Singer Manuscripts, State Historical Society of Wisconsin.

January 1898, penetrating deep into the Chinese interior. NYK soon followed, further augmenting its Chinese routes. In 1906, Nisshin Kisen Kaisha (NKK) was formed for Yangtze river shipping (the dominating influences in NKK were OSK and NYK); by 1911, NKK carried almost 47 percent of the traffic of the main carriers on the Yangtze. By 1913 almost 32 percent—measured by tonnage—of the foreign ships calling at Chinese ports were Japanese.[39] The shipping interests involved branch offices, wharves, and warehouse facilities.

Trading companies, especially Mitsui & Co., developed a sizable business in China. Mitsui & Co. opened it first overseas branch in Shanghai in 1877—just a year after its founding—for the purpose of selling Japanese coal in China. Its principal customers were the British trading companies, Jardine, Matheson & Company and Butterfield & Swire. By 1886 this branch of Mitsui was being used to buy Chinese raw cotton for the Osaka Spinning Mills, which was closely associated with Mitsui, and then to sell Japanese cotton yarn and fabrics in China. As noted above, Mitsui's Shanghai branch manager was responsible for an early Japanese investment in Chinese spinning, and the company also had a flour mill in Shanghai. Indeed, Mitsui & Co. opened branches throughout China, and as an adjunct to its Chinese business had a branch in Hong Kong. By 1910, its Shanghai office had forty-eight employees, its Hong Kong office forty-one.[40] China was without doubt the major locale for pre–1914 Japanese foreign investment.

Japanese business did invest elsewhere in Asia, however. Well before Korea became a Japanese colony in 1910, business involvements had developed.[41] Japanese banking, shipping, and trading companies also established branches in India. Yokohama Specie Bank opened a branch in Bombay in November 1894; Nippon Yūsen Kaisha had begun regular shipping service to India the year before. About the same time, Mitsui & Co. opened a Bombay office for direct purchase of Indian cotton. The Naigaiwata Company and Japan Cotton Trading Company also had agents in Bombay to buy cotton. The Gosho Company

    [39] Wray, Mitsubishi and the N.Y.K., 186, 342, 346, 348ff., 388–89, 391; Hou, Foreign Investment, 61. The British, with 52 percent, were in first place among the shipping companies calling at Chinese ports.
    [40] Mitsui & Co., Ltd., 100 Year History, 27, 31, 44–46. For its early activity importing raw cotton into Japan, see Kazuo Sugiyama, "Trade Credit and the Development of the Cotton Spinning Industry," in Marketing and Finance in the Course of Development (Proceedings of the Third Fuji Conference), ed. Keiichiro Nakagawa (Tokyo, 1978), 69. Mitsui & Co., 100 Year History, 63; data on employment from unpublished material in the Japanese Business History Institute, Tokyo.
    [41] Note that neither Table 1 nor 2 includes Korea, undoubtedly because Korea was annexed to Japan in 1910 and thus in 1914 was a Japanese colony. Before 1910, Korea had attracted sizable Japanese investments in banking, trade, and shipping facilities, as well as in railroads and certain agricultural ventures; investments grew after colonization. The Japanese interests were not nearly as large as those in China, but their precise extent is not clear. See the extremely useful article by Peter Duus, "Economic Dimensions of Meiji Imperialism: The Case of Korea, 1895–1910," in The Japanese Colonial Empire 1895–1945, ed. Raymond H. Myers and Mark R. Peattie (Princeton, N.J., 1984), 128–63.

sent procurement agents into the Indian interior to deal with cotton farmers and local cotton merchants.[42]

JAPANESE INVESTMENT IN THE UNITED STATES

Though Japanese business interests in Asia outside China were not insignificant, second place (in monetary value) for Japanese foreign investments in 1914 was held by the United States. The sums invested were small relative to those placed in China, but not minuscule or unimportant. By 1914, according to Bank of Japan figures (see Table 1), they constituted a little over 10 percent of Japanese overseas investment.

How can one explain the extent of Japanese investment in the United States in terms of the categories of "familiar" and "unfamiliar"? Clearly, the United States was not familiar. A tentative hypothesis is that Japan found the United States to be an important trading partner. The trade was lopsided, however, with Japan relatively more dependent on it than the United States. The pursuit of trade in this unfamiliar land required a familiar infrastructure. Thus, the Japanese faced the management challenge of recreating in the United States institutions for conducting business that were familiar to them.[43]

As early as 1881, fourteen Japanese trading companies had branches in New York, and thirty-one Japanese employees lived in the city as representatives of these firms.[44] They used the Yokohama Specie Bank for trade financing, foreign exchange transactions, and as a source of general information. The bank was an active member of the Silk Association of America in the early twentieth century. It established its New York office in 1880, the same year that it was incorporated in Japan; its San Francisco "branch" opened in 1899, and a sub-branch was established in Los Angeles in 1913. It also inaugurated a branch in Hawaii in 1899. Other Japanese banks operated in San Francisco and Los Angeles in the early twentieth century, but these may have

---

[42] Data on India are also missing in Tables 1 and 2. Wray, *Mitsubishi and the N.Y.K.*, 229, 289, 293–302, and 400–408 (on the Bombay and Calcutta lines of NYK, 1896–1914). Mitsui & Co. began importing Indian raw cotton into Japan in 1892–93, buying it from Ralli Brothers, a British trading house. Soon, Mitsui & Co. bypassed Ralli Brothers and purchased cotton directly at the cotton exchange in Bombay. By 1897, the Bombay office of Mitsui & Co. was purchasing all its cotton directly, independently of the Bombay cotton exchange. Mitsui & Co., *100 Year History*, 48. On Ralli Brothers, see Chalmin, *Negociants et Chargeurs*, 25–26; Ralli Brothers had established itself in Calcutta in 1850 and then in Bombay. On Naigaiwata, see Mitsui & Co., *100 Year History*, 48–49; on Gosho, Chao, *Development of Cotton Textile Production*, 99, though this information may refer to a period after 1911 (Chao is not explicit).

[43] In 1913, the share of Japan's trade with China (22.9 percent) roughly equaled its share with the United States (22.5 percent). In subsequent years, the United States became far more important than China in Japan's foreign trade. Remer, *Foreign Investments in China*, 460.

[44] Mitsui & Co., *100 Year History*, 27.

been banks set up by Japanese emigrants to the United States rather than foreign direct investments.[45]

Japanese shipping companies were well established in the trans-Pacific trade by 1914. As early as 1876, Yatarō Iwasaki had contemplated a trans-Pacific line for the Mitsubishi Company, which did not materialize at that point; but when the Japanese government approved emigration of its citizens to Hawaii in 1884, a new demand for passenger shipping was established. In the next decade (1885–94) Nippon Yūsen Kaisha ships made twenty-four trips, delivering twenty-seven thousand immigrants to Hawaii. In May 1886, NYK entered into a through-freight agreement with the Pacific Mail Steamship Company and the Occidental & Oriental Steamship Company (based on an earlier contract between Mitsubishi and the two shipping firms); NYK covered Shanghai–Yokohama, while the two American firms handled the Yokohama–San Francisco route. This agreement was canceled a decade later, in 1896, when NYK initiated its own American line. It originated with a July 1896 contract between NYK and the Great Northern Railroad; the combined transportation network allowed NYK to quote through-freight rates for trade between Asia and the U.S. Midwest to the American east coast. In 1899, Shanghai was made the departure port for that line, and Seattle became the terminus. In 1898, Tōyō Kisen Kaisha (established in 1896 by Sōichirō Asano) opened a route to San Francisco. In 1909, the Osaka Shōsen Kaisha started a line to Tacoma.[46] Thus by 1914 Japanese shipping was providing regular service to Seattle, San Francisco, and Tacoma. By 1913, 51 percent of the ships entering Japanese ports were Japanese, 52 percent of Japanese exports were carried on Japanese ships, and 47 percent of Japanese

[45] Silk Association of America, *Annual Reports*; Shinji Arai, *History of the Yokohama Specie Bank* (Tokyo, 1981), 2: 36, 38 (in Japanese; I am indebted to William Johnston for the translation), and U.S. Alien Property Custodian, *Annual Report 1943–1944*, 87–88. Actually, as early as 1880, the Japanese Finance Ministry gave permission to the Yokohama Specie Bank to set up "branches, agencies or representative offices in London, Paris, New York, San Francisco, and Shanghai." Arai, *History of the Yokohama Specie Bank*, 2: 38. As noted, the bank did not open a Shanghai office until 1893. But a small representative office (or "agency") appears to have opened in San Francisco in 1886, supplementing the one opened in New York in 1880. See Yokohama Specie Bank, *The History of the Yokohama Specie Bank* (Tokyo, 1920), in Japanese (Professor Yamazaki referred me to the 1886 date in this reference). Arai, *History of the Yokohama Specie Bank*, 2: 91, notes that in 1899, according to a decision of the bank's directors, the offices in Tokyo, Nagasaki, Lyons, San Francisco, Hawaii, Bombay, Hong Kong, Shanghai, and Tientsin were made branches, but because of U.S. law (actually because of New York state law), the New York "agency" remained as it was, as an agency. See Ira Cross, *Financing an Empire: History of Banking in California* (Chicago, 1927), 2: 641, on the San Francisco branch of the Yokohama Specie Bank from 1899 onward, ibid., 3: 517, on the branch in Los Angeles. The Yokohama Specie Bank appears to have had some kind of representation in Hawaii in 1892 (before U.S. annexation). See Japan, Ministry of Finance, *Business Report*, 66. On the Hawaiian "branch," Arai, *History of the Yokohama Specie Bank*, 2: 91. Undoubtedly, the latter was a facility to cope with the needs of Japanese emigrants to Hawaii. See Wilkins, *History of Foreign Investment in the United States*, forthcoming. Cross, *Financing an Empire*, is very good on the "Japanese" banks in California, but says nothing on the place of the owners' residence.
[46] Wray, *Mitsubishi and the N.Y.K.*, 91 (initial plans), 264 (Hawaii), 264–66, 277, 344, 400, 408–9, 421.

imports arrived on Japanese ships; the presence of Japanese shipping lines in the trans-Pacific trade is therefore not surprising. On 15 August 1914, the Panama Canal opened, providing new possibilities for Japanese shipping.[47]

The trading companies, again led by Mitsui & Co., were also active in the United States. Mitsui had opened a branch in New York as early as 1879 and then closed it at the start of the 1880s, when the Japanese government changed its policy of direct export subsidies. Then, in 1895, Kenzo Iwahara of Mitsui & Co. left Tokyo to reopen the New York office. Mitsui & Co., New York, handled imports into the United States of Japanese raw silk and exports of U.S. railroad equipment, machinery, and most important, raw cotton.[48]

Japan's raw cotton requirements were met, in the main, by imports from India, the United States, and China. In 1911, Mitsui & Co. founded the wholly owned Southern Products Company in Houston, Texas, to facilitate its American raw cotton export trade. Mitsui came to handle more than 30 percent of the raw cotton imported into Japan from the United States, and by 1914 was also responsible for 33.6 percent of all Japanese silk imports into the United States. Mitsui & Co. had its own fleet and, in addition, chartered ships from Nippon Yūsen Kaisha.[49]

The number of Japanese trading firms present in the United States in 1914 is uncertain. The fourteen in New York in 1881 did not survive the change in Japanese government policy. A one- to three-person office was easy to close, and when the Japanese government stopped direct subsidies of exports in the early 1880s, many shut down. A sample of the annual reports and directories of the Silk Association of America reveals a changing pattern of Japanese involvement. The 1882 directory, for example, listed Oria Kai (a Japanese weaving association) as "agent" for the Yamato Trading Company, which advertised that its home office was in Tokyo and that it had branches in Yokohama, London, and Vladivostock, as well as a corresponding house in Lyons,

---

[47] U.S. House of Representatives, Committee on Merchant Marine and Fisheries, *Steamship Agreements and Affiliations in the American Foreign and Domestic Trade,* 63d Cong. (1914), 131; Allen, *Short Economic History,* 92; before the opening, NYK was already making plans to take advantage of the canal; Wray, *Mitsubishi and the N.Y.K.,* 400, 409.

[48] Mitsui & Co., *100 Year History,* 32, 34, 69; *Report of Business Conditions of Mitsui Bussan,* Nov. 1913–April 1914, in Mitsui & Co., Ltd., Archives, Tokyo. Professor Yamazaki was most helpful with the translation of this Japanese-language report.

[49] *Report of Business Conditions.* Prior to 1911, Chinese raw cotton imports into Japan had exceeded American raw cotton imports. After 1912, U.S. raw cotton imports grew rapidly. In first place, throughout, were imports into Japan of Indian raw cotton. See *A Yearbook of the Cotton Industry of the World and Japan* (1935), pt. 2, p. 7 (in Japanese). My thanks go to Professor Yamazaki for this reference. As noted earlier in this paper, the Japanese trading companies were buying cotton directly in India; Mitsui & Co., *100 Year History,* 50, and Kazuo Yamaguchi, et al., "100 Year History of Mitsui & Co.," unpub. MS (1978), 1: 357 (in Japanese); Mitsui & Co., *100 Year History,* 50, 71–72; 77–78.

France. The same directory included R. Arai as "New York General Representative of the Doshin Silk Company (Doshin Kaisha), Yokohama." Doshin Kaisha, an export company made up of Japanese silk manufacturers, was also reported to have a branch office in Lyons. By the early twentieth century, the Yokohama Silk Trading Company was important in silk imports into the United States.[50]

Nobuo Kawabe found that the Japan Cotton Trading Company had established a subsidiary in Fort Worth in 1910 for the export of raw cotton, and that the Gosho Company had opened an office in San Antonio in 1913. Thus, all three of the major Japanese trading firms participating in the raw cotton trade—Mitsui & Co., Japan Cotton Trading Company, and the Gosho Company—had Texas-based offices before the First World War. A historian of the American chemical industry recorded that Mitsui, Suzuki, Iwai, Miura Shozo, and Kuhara—all Japanese trading firms—brought camphor, menthol, pyrethrum (a flower used in making insect repellant), rhubarb root, and other medicinal and aromatic products into New York from Japan and China. Yamanaka and Company, Osaka, in about 1900 established a New York Fifth Avenue retail showroom, selling antique Chinese paintings, furniture, brocades, and porcelain to wealthy Americans.[51] The more one looks, the more evidence of Japanese business activity in the United States one finds.

At least one Japanese insurance company invested in the United States. Tokio Marine Insurance Company, Ltd. was included in the American publication *Best's Insurance Reports;* its Japanese parent had a worldwide business. In the United States in 1913, Tokio Marine collected $135,000 in net premiums—not much compared with other insurers in America; and its so-called admitted assets were a modest $347,000. Nonetheless, Tokio Marine operated in the United States and formed part of the network of investments associated with Japanese-American trade.[52]

---

[50] Details are in Wilkins, *History of Foreign Investment in the United States,* forthcoming. I am grateful to Professor Kawabe for the identification of "Oria Kai." On the Yokohama Silk Trading Company, Mitsui & Co., *100 Year History,* 70. "R. Arai" was Rioichiro Arai, the grandfather of Haru Matsukata Reischauer. He came to the United States in 1876 and at once began to handle Japanese silk imports into America. Haru Reischauer's new book documents this Japanese immigrant's experiences—as representative of Japanese silk exporters. *Samurai and Silk* (Cambridge, Mass., 1986), 190–257, 223 (Doshin Kaisha).

[51] Nobuo Kawabe, "Japanese Business in the United States before World War II: the Case of Mitsubishi Shoji Kaisha, the San Francisco and Seattle Branches," (Ph.D. diss., Ohio State University, 1980), 18. In addition, Rioichiro Arai in 1903 established a separate cotton department in his silk trading company. Reischauer, *Samurai and Silk,* 237. Williams Haynes, *American Chemical Industry* (New York, 1954), 2: 274; Wilkins, "American-Japanese Direct Foreign Investment," 510.

[52] *Best's Insurance Report, 1914,* 360, which describes the firm as operating all over the world. Professor Tsunehiko Yui has been very helpful in discussing with me the international character of this particular Japanese insurance firm.

Yosuke Kinugasa has written about Kikkoman's 1892 direct investment in Denver, Colorado, in a factory to make soy sauce for Japanese emigrants—a perfect example of creating the familiar in the unfamiliar (from the standpoint of the plant) and finding the familiar in the unfamiliar (from the standpoint of the market).[53]

A picture emerges from all these activities of an investment infrastructure tailored to Japanese requirements that had arisen in the United States before 1914. Because Japan was a highly homogeneous society, both its citizens and its emigrants had difficulty adapting to conditions outside the country; thus Japanese businessmen before the First World War—and later as well—established abroad their own familiar environment, where Japanese could be spoken and communication breakdowns avoided. Ease of communication resulted in substantial savings of time and energy.[54] In terms of transaction cost economics, the results were lower information, bargaining, and negotiating costs. If the Japanese were to enlarge their trade, they had to create their own international infrastructure to do so.

Thus, it was not solely in Asia that Japanese business expanded. The network of interconnections, not only in China, the rest of Asia, and the United States, but also in London, Hamburg, Paris, and particularly Lyons (the center of the French silk industry), remains a fruitful area for research. The Yokohama Specie Bank had an important London office. In shipping, William Wray found that NYK's European line was more significant than its American one. In 1899, NYK received special annual government subsidies of 2,673,894 yen for its European line, compared to a mere 654,030 yen for its American route. In 1903, NYK had twelve ships on its European line and only six on the American one. By contrast, if number of employees is a guide, Mitsui & Co.'s New York office with twenty-eight employees was more significant than its London one, which had eighteen employees in 1910.[55]

As one studies the early Japanese businesses abroad, several questions—based on other nationalities' experiences—arise: How often were Japanese businesses abroad "transplanted enterprises," that is, set up by Japanese entrepreneurs without any Japanese company as

---

[53] Yosuke Kinugasa, "Japanese Firms' Foreign Direct Investment in the United States—The Case of Matsushita and Others," in Okochi and Inoue, *Overseas Business Activities*, 57. W. Mark Fruin, *Kikkoman: Company, Clan, and Community* (Cambridge, Mass., 1983), regrettably does not mention this early foreign direct investment.

[54] As Ozawa, *Multinationalism*, 83, points out, the Japanese "in general are notoriously poor linguists."

[55] I can document the pre–1914 presence of Japanese business in all these places and other cities as well; Wray, *Mitsubishi and the N.Y.K.*, 14–15, 306, 414 (on NYK). NYK also had an Australian line, which had three ships in 1903; ibid., 414; data on Mitsui employment from Japanese Business History Institute, Tokyo. In 1908, Japanese immigrants began arriving in Brazil as wage workers. In time, a thriving Japanese community developed and Japanese multinational enterprise invested. Ozawa, *Multinationalism*, 127; I have found no evidence, however, of multinational enterprise involvements before 1914.

parent? These would not be considered foreign direct investments by students of multinational enterprise. What different types of joint ventures grew up, and what factors influenced the choice? Most important, how was foreign investment joined with trade, and when was a company (as distinct from an arm's-length relationship or a contract) required to organize transactions?

CAPITAL IMPORTER VERSUS EXPORTER

When American business abroad began, the United States was a net importer of capital; when Japanese multinational enterprise started, the same was true of Japan. This circumstance was extremely relevant to the nature of the investments: it is clearly inappropriate to explain Japanese business abroad before 1914 in terms of capital surpluses: they did not exist. There was also no need for "flight capital"—capital that escapes from insecurity; the Japanese had ample opportunities to invest at home. So, like U.S. investments abroad before the First World War (and for the same reasons), Japanese foreign investments were predominantly business investments (direct investments), those carrying management and control and related specifically to Japanese business growth.[56] The 1914 figures (see Tables 1 and 2) show clearly that there was far more Japanese direct than portfolio investment abroad.

Even though the Japanese were net importers of capital when multinational enterprise began, one Japanese bank—the Yokohama Specie Bank—appears to have played a far more strategic role in extending Japanese foreign direct investment than any single U.S. bank played in American foreign enterprise. America's largest banks, its national banks, were not permitted to establish overseas branches until the Federal Reserve System was established in 1914. Some U.S. trust companies had one or two branches abroad, private banks had houses in London and Paris, and America's national banks had foreign correspondents, but no real American counterpart to the Japanese international banking story exists.

The history of the Yokohama Specie Bank was intimately associated with the rise of Japanese worldwide business. Historians of Mitsui & Co. wrote that "the relationship between the company" and that bank became so close that "almost every time Mitsui & Co. opened a new branch overseas a new Yokohama Specie Bank branch opened in the same city." In 1893, Kōkichi Sonoda, president of the Yokohama Specie Bank, joined the board of directors of Japan's largest shipping enter-

---

[56] For U.S. figures, see Wilkins, *Emergence of Multinational Enterprise*, 201.

prise, Nippon Yūsen Kaisha.[57] The Yokohama Specie Bank was ubiquitous in Japanese multinational business activities in a manner totally unlike the role of any single American bank. Can it be that Americans could rely on London for trade financing in a manner that the Japanese could not? Anglo-American financial connections were long-standing, and a whole coterie of London facilities were available to Americans. By contrast, Japan was a new entry into the international trading arena. London as a source for trade financing was probably not as accessible to the Japanese as to Americans. Accordingly, the Japanese may well have had more need to develop their own specialized institution for that purpose, whereas Americans could be more reliant on existing intermediaries.[58] The Yokohama Specie Bank in London and New York also served to pay interest on the Japanese debt. Its presence and reliability made it possible for the Japanese government to raise monies abroad.

The role of other Japanese banks in early international business requires further research. The Industrial Bank of Japan (Nippon Kogyo Ginko) was, as noted, a conduit for foreign investment into Japan. It sold its own debentures abroad to obtain monies for other Japanese domestic and foreign undertakings. Though it was listed in the London *Stock Exchange Official Intelligence, 1914*, it had no London office. The principal and interest on its sterling bonds were "unconditionally guaranteed by the Japanese government"; payments of interest were made at the London office of the Yokohama Specie Bank. The Industrial Bank recycled monies it raised abroad into enterprises outside Japan.[59]

The first Japanese bank to branch abroad had been the Dai Ichi Ginko—the First National Bank in Japan—which opened a branch in Korea in 1878, before the Yokohama Specie Bank was formed, and long before Korea was annexed to Japan. After Formosa (Taiwan) became a Japanese possession in 1895, an Osaka bank opened a branch there and, in 1896, so did the Bank of Japan. Three years later, the Bank of Taiwan came into being; one-fifth of its five million yen capital was subscribed by the Japanese government; the rest appears to have been Japanese private capital. It issued notes and became the government's fiscal agency. It also functioned as an ordinary commercial bank. Ac-

---

[57] Mitsui & Co., *100 Year History*, 55; Wray, *Mitsubishi and the N.Y.K.*, 270.

[58] The Japanese did use British and Continental banks. See the fascinating table in *Report of Business Conditions of Mitsui Bussan*, Nov. 1913–April 1914, on the lines of credit from foreign (principally British) financial houses. Clearly, however, the Japanese could not expect the same kind of regular steady financing from Britain as Americans could; the difference in degree is crucial. There was also the "Mitsui Bank," founded in 1876, but in these years Mitsui & Co. appears to have used it at home and the specialized Yokohama Specie Bank for its international business transactions.

[59] Allen, *Short Economic History*, 54; Patrick, "Japan," 271; *Stock Exchange Official Intelligence, 1914*, 404.

cording to *Palgrave's Banking Almanac, 1914,* the Bank of Taiwan by
that year had branches in San Francisco, Manila, Singapore, Calcutta,
Bombay, seven points in China, and about fourteen in Japan and its
dependencies.[60]

Meanwhile, in Korea after 1905 the Dai Ichi Ginko served as a note-
issuing central bank. It was replaced in this function by the Bank of
Korea in 1909, which in turn was transformed into the Bank of Chosen
after the Japanese colonization of Korea was completed. Like the Bank
of Taiwan, the Bank of Chosen was a note-issuing bank, engaged in
financing development, and it was in part Japanese government-
owned. In time, it too developed foreign branches, but probably not
before 1914.[61]

In short, because Japan was before 1914 a net debtor nation (and
there was no reason for flight capital), multinational enterprise investment was a far larger component of total foreign investment than portfolio investment, as in the case of the United States in the pre–First
World War years. But while in the United States banks were relatively
unimportant vis-à-vis U.S. business abroad, in Japan banks—in particular the government-sponsored Yokohama Specie Bank—engaged in
banking abroad and played a major role in aiding the expansion of Japanese international business and intermediating the flow of foreign
capital into Japan for use there and for recycling for Japanese use
abroad. Before 1914 British banks to a great extent performed these
functions for Americans; the Japanese, in large part, provided at least
a bridge for their requirements.

GEOGRAPHICAL POSITION

Although America was a net importer of capital in the formative
years of U.S. multinationals, it was still the key economic power within
its region. This was equally true of Japan, for by the end of the first
decade of the twentieth century, no Asian nation was as economically
advanced as Japan. Like the United States, Japan solved many problems itself because of its geographical isolation. Note, however, how
asymmetrical a discussion of the isolation of the two countries must be.
America was not isolated in terms of trade financing, but Japan was;

---

[60] Sarasas, *Money and Banking in Japan,* 271, and Duus, "Economic Dimensions," 154–55. Also on
the Dai Ichi Ginko, see Patrick, "Japan," which says nothing about its role in Korea. On Taiwan banking,
see Sarasas, *Money and Banking in Japan,* 269–371 and *Palgrave's* as cited in U.S. Federal Trade Commission, *Report on Cooperation in American Export Trade* (Washington, D.C., 1916), 1: 64.

[61] The Bank of Korea had an original paid up capital of ten million yen, of which three million came
from the Japanese government. By 1940 the Bank of Chosen had branches in Korea, Japan, China (especially in Manchuria), and a "branch" in New York. Sarasas, *Money and Banking in Japan,* 271, 274–
76. See also Allen, *Short Economic History,* 55.

America was more isolated than Japan in terms of some technological transfers, because of the special characteristics of the huge U.S. market and the relatively high cost of American labor that required major modifications in imported technology. Japanese industry, for example, apparently could more readily adopt British textile technology than the United States.[62]

British technicians, technology, and machinery played a crucial role in the development of Japan's textile industry, and when the Japanese invested in spinning mills in China, they entered using the same British technology and equipment. Likewise, the looms installed in Chinese mills by the Japanese were made by Platt Brothers in Britain. This technology was also available to Chinese-owned mills. The Japanese, however, came to have the advantage over *both* Chinese and British mills, and the question is, why? Experts on the Japanese spinning companies in China have asserted that the advantages Japanese business had in China—which increased over time—were not related to production technology, but to other factors: management (Japanese *spinners* proved to be better managers of foreign spinning mills than the British *trading* companies); raw cotton procurement techniques (the Japanese developed means of buying raw cotton direct from the growers that resulted in cheaper supplies than the British could procure); and the blending of raw cotton from different locales (that improved input quality and lowered cost). Geographical proximity reduced the costs of management over distance. Alfred Chandler suggests that the Japanese may also have had a marketing advantage, based on their earlier trading company experiences.[63]

ANTITRUST ATTITUDES

In a study of Japanese business abroad, it is more essential than in the American case to look at cooperative efforts. In Japan the whole issue of antitrust was irrelevant. The industrial structure of Japanese

[62] I am arguing here that Americans *altered* British textile technology to meet U.S. conditions, while the Japanese appear to have adopted the technology—at least in spinning—in a more exact manner. On this see Gary Saxonhouse, "A Tale of Japanese Technological Diffusion in the Meiji Period," *Journal of Economic History* 34 (March 1974): 150–55. In weaving, the Toyoda Automatic Loom was an important Japanese innovation. Mitsui & Co., *100 Year History*, 74–77. Yet, it was not until after our period that it was widely adopted in Japan and in Japanese mills abroad. Data from Professor Kuwahara, 16 Jan. 1986.

[63] These conclusions have been developed out of lengthy discussions I had in Japan in July 1984 with Professors Yamazaki, Yasumuro, and Kuwahara. As noted in my introduction, students of multinational enterprise emphasize that for a company to succeed abroad it must have some kind of advantage. Substantial attention had been paid specifically to "technological advantages." Thus, in attempting to explain the Japanese success in China, my first search was for a technological advantage. Obviously, I found none, since Chinese firms as well as Japanese ones could adopt the British technology. Then I asked, why did the Japanese do better than the British with the same British technology? I found Japanese advantages, but not in production technology. These advantages contributed to Japan's economic superiority in the region.

foreign investment in these early years appears unified and holistic, with a cooperative effort among the manufacturer, the trading company, and the shipping enterprise. In the more general coterie of trade-related investments, community of interest typified activities among the banks and shipping, insurance, and trading companies in pursuing trade and investment. William Wray has correctly identified the "big four" in Japanese international business before 1914 as the Yokohama Specie Bank, Nippon Yūsen Kaisha, Tokio Marine Insurance, and Mitsui Bussan.[64] The quartet were joined in numerous transactions. The absence of antitrust obstacles gave the Japanese more options in their international expansion. As influential, an antitrust policy reflects an adversarial relationship between government and business, which never developed in Japan. Cooperation existed not only among companies, but also between the government and companies. The Japanese government had sizable investments in two of the largest international businesses—NYK and Yokohama Specie Bank. It also had major stakes in the important South Manchurian Railway. What stands out in Japanese history is not business-government conflict (that occasionally arose), but rather the typically supportive role the Japanese government played for its business enterprises.

CONCLUSIONS

Some of the more significant pre–1914 Japanese foreign direct investments have now been surveyed. Five basic points—1) size of domestic market; 2) heterogeneity or homogeneity at home; 3) national status as exporter or importer of capital; 4) geographical position in the region; and 5) antitrust attitudes—have been used as a basis of analysis and have served to bring out key characteristics of the pioneer Japanese multinational enterprises. First, because domestic markets were limited and because crucial natural resources to provide for home markets were not available, foreign trade became very important to Japan. American companies learned about business management at home, and then used that knowledge in their expansion abroad. Most Japanese manufacturers were too small to do that effectively. To develop international trade, the Japanese needed an international business in-

---

[64] Wray, *Mitsubishi and the N.Y.K.*, passim, makes it very clear how tied shipping was to the textile industry. In this context, Wray writes, "If we take, for example, the 1893 Bombay line alliance of the cotton spinners, the Japanese government, the Yokohama Specie Bank, Tata's Indian raw cotton-exporting firm, Japanese importers like Mitsui Bussan, and N.Y.K., it is hard to imagine this organized entrepreneurial system working for several decades with a foreign shipping company in place of N.Y.K." Ibid., 453. The only alien element in this cooperative scheme was the Tata group, which eventually withdrew from the coalition; ibid., 509. Mitsui Bussan and Mitsui & Co. were the same firm. Ibid., 6 (on the big four).

frastructure, with personnel stationed abroad; the service network came to be separately managed from the producing companies in Japan. An exception was in textiles, where Naigaiwata—which had spinning mills at home—developed its own cotton spinning in China.[65] Also, because of raw material shortages, large investments were made in the South Manchurian Railway (for access to raw materials).

Second, because of the homogeneity of the population within Japan, Japanese businessmen had little experience with different customs, languages, or cultural norms. Like American and European companies they went initially to nearby, relatively familiar areas. In order to do business in alien lands—nearby and afar—Japanese businessmen very often replicated familiar infrastructures, providing channels where the Japanese language could be spoken, and where they could deal with men of their own nationality in the foreign land. The process created a core of businessmen with experience in international transactions. Third, because Japan was a net importer of capital and because it had political stability at home, its foreign investments were made overwhelmingly with operating purpose, rather than with purely financial goals. There was no surplus capital. Here it is the similarity with the United States, rather than the difference, that stands out. The difference lies, however, in the role of banks (especially the Yokohama Specie Bank), which was important in Japan's international business and not significant in American business abroad before 1914.

Fourth, just as the United States was the leader in its region, so too Japan was by 1914 far more developed than other countries in Asia. The sizable Japanese investments in nearby China reflect that leadership. Both America and Japan had advantages over other foreign investors in nearby regions. Each fended for itself to assert its own prominence. Fifth, because of an absence of antitrust policy, in creating an international business infrastructure Japanese businesses could cooperate with one another in a manner very dissimilar from that of American enterprises. Moreover, Japanese international business was at crucial times supported by the government to a significant extent, much more so than American international investment. Japanese managers were highly entrepreneurial; nonetheless, a supportive government certainly assisted multinational expansion.

This survey of some of the more important pre–1914 Japanese overseas direct investments makes it evident that Japanese multinational enterprise did not begin in the 1950s, or even in the 1920s or 1930s, as has often been assumed.[66] There were many Japanese foreign direct

[65] Kikkoman's soy sauce plant in Denver was another exception.

[66] Most authors on Japanese multinational enterprise have assumed that the phenomenon is new. Kojima, *Japanese Direct Foreign Investment*, 7, for example, writes that "the activities of multinational

investments in service activities. Large ones existed in the South Manchurian Railway. Trading, banking, and industrial companies also made some overseas direct investments in manufacturing and mining before the First World War. Japanese gross overseas investments in 1914 (the bulk of which were direct investments) represented between 9.9 and 12.8 percent of the nation's 1914 gross national product.

A number of the special characteristics of contemporary Japanese multinational enterprise had already surfaced before 1914. The first emerging pattern was the important role of textiles in Japanese foreign investment. Even today, Japan has, relative to other home nations involved in international business, a disproportionate amount of its multinational investments in textiles. A second feature was the significant role of service-sector companies, especially the trading company. A 1983 *Annual Report* of Mitsui & Co. described how crucial Japan's general trading companies were, "with their unmatched combination of capabilities in collecting and analyzing information, providing and arranging for finance for trade and projects, and their extensive knowhow in organizing major projects."[67] The scale has obviously altered, but clearly the skill that the Japanese now display in raw material procurement is not newly acquired.[68]

A third feature, already apparent before the First World War, was what I have called the layering effect of foreign investments by trading companies and those by manufacturers. In later years, trading companies often acted for Japanese manufacturers abroad, setting up small plants, or they went into joint ventures abroad with Japanese producers and with nationals in the host countries. Then, in time, Japanese manufacturers acted on their own—bypassing the trading company.

---

corporations are new dynamic elements in the international economy" (my italics); Ozawa, *Multinationalism*, 3, notes that before the Second World War, Japanese companies set up production facilities abroad, but only in Japanese colonies—Manchukuo, Korea, and Formosa. Tsurumi, *The Japanese Are Coming*, 2, gives a chronology of Japanese foreign direct investments with the first one in the 1920s. He lists nothing during or before the First World War, and only four manufacturing subsidiaries worldwide before the Second World War. He looked at manufacturing subsidiaries of trading as well as manufacturing companies. Until very recently historians of Japan have neglected the history of Japanese multinational enterprise. When they have dealt with corporate histories, they have not taken into account the extensive literature on multinational enterprise. Wray, *Mitsubishi and the N.Y.K.*, who does look at business managers' international strategies, found a dearth of comparable studies (see his comments on Japanese business historiography on p. 11). A partial exception is the research on Mitsui & Co.

[67] In 1975, 22.2 percent of Japanese worldwide investments were in textiles—the largest single sector for its foreign direct investment. Ozawa, *Multinationalism*, 29. More recent figures show a lesser role for textiles, but still one of importance. United Nations Centre on Transnational Corporations, *Transnational Corporations in World Development, Third Survey* (New York, 1983), 296. In its *Annual Report 1983*, 13, Mitsui & Co. pointed out that it had the highest level of overseas investment of any Japanese company. "In recent years, Mitsui & Co. has had more than U.S. $1 billion investments and loans committed to more than 280 ventures, located in diverse parts of the globe." Together, these ventures and Mitsui & Co. itself employed 129,900 persons; ibid., 16.

[68] Ozawa, *Multinationalism*, 166, recounts how the Japanese responded to the aftermath of the 1973–74 oil crisis, by buying oil directly from nationalized companies and saving costs in the process. The student of Japanese direct raw cotton purchasing techniques has a sense of *déjà vu*.

This pattern too was present between Japanese textile manufacturers and trading companies before 1914.

When one compares the history of Japanese and American business abroad, there were, to be sure, similarities. In each case, conditions in the home country influenced the evolution of international business. In each case it was the new, dynamic industries that led the move into foreign direct investment (textiles in Japan, mass production industries in the United States). In each case, specialists have found that an advantage of the U.S. and Japanese companies abroad lay in managerial abilities. In each case, the U.S. and Japanese foreign direct investors went initially, to a disproportionate extent, to areas either geographically or culturally "nearby." Before the First World War, when in each nation the evolution of modern multinational enterprise began, both the United States and Japan were net debtors in world accounts. Both countries, however, had investments in foreign lands, and each had a far higher proportion of its gross investments abroad in direct than in portfolio stakes. In its own region, by 1914, the United States and Japan each held economic leadership that provided a setting for the expansion of entrepreneurial enterprise abroad. Both the United States and Japan in 1914 had firms that engaged—relative to the domestic economy of each—in substantial foreign direct investments.

These shared attributes notwithstanding, when compared with American business abroad before 1914, Japanese practices show significant differences. Japanese multinational enterprise had a far greater role in providing services—in trade, banking, shipping, and marine insurance. The textile industry was important in early Japanese overseas development, while there were no early American multinational enterprises in this industry. The cooperation of separate Japanese firms in international business operations was commonplace, while similar cooperative behavior among American enterprises was uncharacteristic. And, the Japanese government role seems different from that of the U.S. government; the former was more directly supportive of international business activities.[69]

---

[69] The U.S.-owned textile mill in China, noted earlier in this paper, was *not* owned by an American textile manufacturer. While clearly there was more Japanese government ownership participation in its nationals' pre-1914 international business—in shipping and banking—than in the U.S. case (U.S. government ownership of pre-1914 multinational enterprises was nonexistent), I do not see how this served to change—or to determine—Japanese entrepreneurial strategy in a significant manner. My finding in this regard seems to coincide with that of other researchers, including Kozo Yamamura, *A Study of Samurai Income and Entrepreneurship* (Cambridge, Mass., 1974), 187. Duus, "Economic Dimensions," 147, writes of Japanese businessmen in the early twentieth century that, while they "supported political expansion [in Korea], they did not regard the acquisition of new territory as necessary for the expansion of private business interests abroad. The prevailing view among business leaders [at this time] was that the most promising business opportunities in East Asia lay not in Korea but in China, where there was no possibility of extending political control." The large Japanese government direct investments in the South Manchurian Railway suggest, however, a highly supportive role.

Although Japanese business overseas expanded far more dramatically during the First World War and in the 1920s than in the period with which this article deals, nonetheless the very early Japanese foreign direct investments are important and require further attention.[70] They set the stage for much of what followed. They need to be studied in the context of the growth of the Japanese firm, using the work that has been done on the history of multinationals as a guide. What has been presented here is merely an initial, exploratory effort, meant to be suggestive rather than conclusive. A model based on the evolution of U.S. multinational enterprise is useful in asking questions about Japanese multinational business, but one must bear in mind that departures from the model are at least as significant as the congruencies.

---

[70] On subsequent expansion, for a start see data in Kuwahara, "The Business Strategy," and Remer, *Foreign Investments in China*, 446–50, 469–553. Lockwood, *Economic Development in Japan*, asserts that the war years, 1914–18, brought a "sudden reversal" in Japan's debtor nation position, and that Japan in the post–First World War years became a creditor nation. In any study of early Japanese multinationals, it is important that students deal with the companies' worldwide investments, not simply those in East Asia.

[9]

Excerpt from Geoffrey Jones, *British Multinationals: Origins, Management and Performance*, Aldershot: Gower, 1986.

1   Origins, management and performance

Geoffrey Jones

The Multinational and the Historian

Multinationals, with their connotations of international mystery and power, have long been an object of fascination to politicians, journalists and economists. It is only in recent years, however, that historians have turned their attention to the phenomenon, as it became clear that many of today's multinationals have existed since the nineteenth century. This book presents some fruits of this new research on the historical growth of British-based manufacturing multinationals.

The aims of this work are modest. It is not the definitive history of British multinationals, on the lines of Mira Wilkins' magisterial survey of American business abroad.[1] Nevertheless, this book does add a new dimension to our understanding of international business, by examining in detail the multinational growth of selected British companies. There is a large literature devoted to the analysis of aggregate data about contemporary multinationals.[2] By its very nature this approach is highly abstract, and usually depends on American concepts and experience. The multinationals in this book are not numbers in a table or corporate bogeymen, but individual companies run by real people facing real-life business situations.

This approach is only possible because this is a historical work. Since companies are understandably reluctant to divulge information about their activities, writers on contemporary multinationals have to resort to questionnaires and interviews to extract information. There are valuable studies using such methods,[3] but there is a limit to which such an approach can penetrate such matters as motives and performance. Because the authors of the essays in this book do not extend their analysis of companies beyond the 1960s, and in some cases no later than the 1940s, they were able to use the internal confidential records of the companies themselves. The distinction of this book rests in its reliance on these confidential records to elucidate how and why firms became multinational, and how they subsequently organised themselves. The mystique of the multinational should never be quite the same again.

The companies selected for study cover a wide spectrum of British industry. There is Dunlop, the rubber goods manufacturer; Vickers, the armaments and engineering company; a group of six Sheffield high-grade steel firms; Cadbury, Fry and Rowntree, chocolate and confectionery manufacturers; Courtaulds, manufacturer of rayon; Glaxo, the food products and pharmaceuticals manufacturer; GKN, the steel and engineering group; and Pilkington, the glass manufacturer. Some of these companies have long since fallen by the wayside. Most are still, in 1986, among Britain's leading multinationals. A listing of Britain's 50 largest foreign producers in 1983 included Dunlop, Cadbury Schweppes, Rowntree Mackintosh, Courtaulds, Glaxo, GKN and Pilkington,[4] although Dunlop was subsequently dismembered and the residual absorbed by BTR, the diversified conglomorate, in 1985.

History, because it is concerned with the real world, is an inexact science, and this book reflects this inexactness. Many well-known companies are missing. In some cases, such as ICI and Unilever, this is because they have excellent business histories. For the same reason the chapter on Courtaulds confines itself to only one aspect of that company's international growth.[5] The archives of other companies have not survived the ravages of time, or are closed to historians. Britain's great extractive multinationals, such as the oil companies, are also excluded. They deserve a book of their own. Of the companies that are in this study, it must be admitted at the outset that they are not 'representative' in the sense used by economists. They are not a random sample of companies in each industry, or of British multinationals as a whole. They were selected because they had accessible records and they seemed, in a variety of ways, interesting and significant. The companies do represent a wide range of industries, size and historical periods, but it is recognised that generalisations from such a sample are hazardous. Nevertheless, later in this chapter such generalisations are attempted, if only in the hope of provoking further research in this field.

History is also inexact because of the inadequacy of much surviving historical evidence. The authors of these essays asked similar questions of their historical data: Why were multinational investments made? Why were alternatives such as licensing sometimes chosen? What structures were devised to manage overseas companies? How did overseas subsidiaries perform? Yet often the information to answer these questions no longer existed. Nor is it an easy matter to make inter-company comparisons of such things as 'profit'. Business history resembles the market it studies: it is imperfect.

The next section presents a historical overview of British multinational development. The following three sections look at aspects of that development: origins, management and performance. An attempt is made to highlight general themes from the experience of the case studies. However, as the individuality of multinational companies is one of the most striking things which emerge from the essays in this book, it is vital that the company studies should be read as well as the general survey.

British Multinationals in Historical Perspective

Although multinationals have existed for decades, the word itself only came into general use in the 1960s. Since then it has acquired a variety of meanings. In popular usage it often carries unfavourable connotations of largeness and foreignness. This book, however, follows the practice of most economists in defining multinationals in a more prosaic fashion as companies which own (in whole or in part), control and manage income-generating assets in more than one country.[6] This excludes enterprises which merely export, but otherwise it is an inclusive rather than an exclusive definition. It should be noted that some writers

2

have laid down stricter criteria for membership of the multinational club. Richard E. Caves, for example, would only classify a firm as multinational if it had *production* units, rather than marketing or sales companies, in at least *two* foreign countries. Raymond Vernon has suggested the qualifying number of countries should be six.[7]

Until 1939 Britain was the world's largest multinational investor, and since the Second World War it has been second in importance only to the United States as a source of multinational investment. The roots of this investment go back to the nineteenth century, when Britain was the world's largest capital-exporting economy. It used to be maintained that the bulk of this lending was portfolio investment, involving the acquisition of foreign securities without any control over the foreign institutions or companies concerned. However it now seems that as much as 40 per cent may have taken the form of foreign direct investment, involving the ownership and management of a foreign operation.[8]

Very little of this foreign direct investment was made by entities which resemble the modern multinational enterprise. In many cases these investments were made by what Mira Wilkins has termed 'free-standing' firms.[9] A typical free-standing company would comprise a venture with a board of directors, perhaps supported by a small secretariat, in Britain, which owned an Argentine railway, an American mine or an Iranian oilfield. These companies would have no mining, rail or oil interests within Britain itself, and typically their business would be concerned with one foreign country only.

The 'free-standing' firm was often a fragile and transient phenomenon, although some of these companies cannot be so easily dismissed. One example of a vigorous 'free-standing' venture was the Imperial Continental Gas Association, which was formed in 1824, and is the predecessor of today's IC Gas.[10] By the middle of the 1820s most important towns in Britain had gas lighting, but the commercial application of gas had made little progress in Continental Europe. It was to fill this gap that the Association was formed by a syndicate largely composed of British financiers and political dignitaries. There was at first no connection with any domestic British gas company.

Over the following decades the Imperial Continental Gas Asociation established gas manufacturing plants on the Continent. By 1900 it operated 1775 miles of gas main in ten major European towns (including Berlin) and 29 smaller towns, and manufactured over 7403 cubic feet of gas per year. This business was controlled from the firm's London offices. Two executive committees, for Works and Finance, met weekly, and there were also weekly board meetings, which decided all aspects of policy, including such matters as staffing and salary increases at the gas works. The London office staff was small, with the Secretary comprising the only responsible official. The control of the board over the local gasworks was reinforced by periodic visits by directors to the plants. When, during the late nineteenth century, the Association's monopolistic contracts with large cities came under increasing criticism on the grounds that such public utilities should be under municipal control rather than that of a foreign company, it began to operate in various cities and countries through local companies which, however, it continued to control.

By 1914, therefore, the Imperial Continental Gas Association had many features of a modern multinational. It is unknown how many other British 'free-standing' companies evolved in such a fashion, but even a cursory survey of the secondary literature suggests that the Association's experience was not unique. The engineering contractors S. Pearson & Son and the trading house of Balfour, Williamson, for example, owned and managed

3

diversified international businesses before 1914, which included manufacturing and oil production and marketing activities in a number of countries.[11]

In the 1880s and 1890s the modern manufacturing multinational began to appear, with
the United States, Germany and Britain being the leading home economies. Firms with
manufacturing operations in their own countries began to establish factories in foreign countries. By 1914 over 40 American companies had two or more factories abroad, including
such familiar names as Ford, Eastman Kodak, Quaker Oats and Coca Cola.[12]

British firms were active in this process. By the eve of the First World War many of
Britain's largest companies had established foreign factories. Sixteen of the 30 largest British
companies in 1919 (by estimated market value) had at least one foreign factory before the
First World War.[13] The pioneer companies in the late nineteenth century included Dunlop,
whose international career is examined in Chapter 2 of this book, Lever Brothers (soap),
J. and P. Coats (cotton thread), Nobel Explosives (dynamite). By 1914 many of these firms
had widespread foreign manufacturing networks. J. & P. Coats and Lever Brothers, for
example, owned and managed factories in the United States, Canada, South Africa, Australia,
Russia, Switzerland, France and Germany.[14] Subsidiaries of British firms monopolised the
American artificial silk industry and the American and Russian cotton thread industry before
1914.

Nor was multinational activity confined to Britain's largest manufacturing companies.
In Britain, as in Sweden but unlike the United States, small and medium-sized enterprises
made foreign direct investments. The Sheffield steelmakers, examined in Chapter 4, are
one example, but there are many others. The Gramophone Company (which in 1931 merged with another firm to form EMI), makers of records and gramophones, had factories
in India, Russia, France, Spain and Austria by 1914. Albright and Wilson, a small phosphorus
company from the West Midlands with a total staff of just over 550 in 1920, established
factories in the United States and Canada before the First World War. Edward Lloyd Ltd,
a publishing house which diversified into paper manufacture, established pulp mills in
Norway.[15]

It is difficult to quantify the extent of British and multinational investment by 1914. John
H. Dunning has estimated the stock of accumulated foreign direct investment in 1914 at
US \$14,302 million. According to Dunning, Britain was responsible for 45.5 per cent of
this investment, the United States for 18.5 per cent, France for 12.2 per cent and Germany
for 10.5 per cent.[16] However such statistics provide at best orders of magnitude, and it is
impossible to know how much of this investment was of the 'free-standing' variety, and
how it was distributed between the manufacturing, extractive, banking and service sectors.

Nevertheless, one is struck by the extent of British multinational manufacturing by 1914.
In geographical terms, market-oriented investments were naturally located in the high per
capita income countries of the period – North America, Western Europe and Australia.
While American and German companies tended to invest in neighbouring countries, British
companies were active in investing in the full range of high per capita income markets.
The British companies making foreign direct investments also came from a wide spread
of industrial sectors – in contrast, for example, to most American multinationals which
were located in the food and machinery sectors. In Britain, the most extensive foreign investors seem to have been the manufacturers of branded consumer durables, but shipbuilding,
engineering, steel and chemical firms were also active foreign investors. Even some

4

companies in the traditional staple industry of textiles had made their first foreign direct investments by the time of the First World War. The Fine Spinners and Doublers, formed in 1898 to take over various companies engaged in spinning fine (Sea Island) cotton, purchased a controlling interest in one of its most important French competitors, while Bradford Dyers acquired a factory in Rhode Island in the United States in 1912.

The First World War interrupted the growth of British multinational enterprise, and demonstrated the risks of international investment. British companies with investments in Germany were stripped of their assets, and although some of these recovered after the Armistice, in other cases valuable properties and trademarks were lost permanently.[17] On the other hand, companies with investments in the United States, such as Courtaulds and Lever Brothers, prospered during the war.[18] The experience of the war does not seem to have discouraged British companies from foreign direct investment, although it may have encouraged a shift of activity from Western Europe to the Dominions. The Second World War had a similar effect.

Multinational investment increased in the interwar years. According to Dunning, the stock of accumulated foreign direct investment had risen to US $26,350 by 1938, of which 39.8 per cent was British and 27.7 per cent American.[19] Some companies which already had multinational investments, such as Dunlop and Courtaulds, made further investments. Chapter 6 examines Courtaulds' expansion in Continental Europe in this period. A new generation of companies made their first foreign direct investments, such as the chocolate manufacturers (Chapter 5) and GKN (Chapter 8). This growth was matched and even exceeded by the expansion of multinationals from other countries, especially the United States, and a new wave of Dutch, Swiss and Swedish multinationals also appeared.

In the 1930s the growth of multinational enterprise seems to have slackened. Although some British firms continued to make new investments, the depressed market conditions, exchange controls and Fascist governments in Europe did not provide a promising investment climate. There was a preference instead for international cartels designed to allocate market shares, fix prices and exchange technology. ICI's division of the world between its American and German rivals, DuPont and I G Farben, was a classic example of a widely prevalent type of agreement in this era.[20] There were very similar arrangements in the plate glass industry, where in the 1930s Pilkington and Continental and American producers were allied in agreements sharing out world markets. By 1935 products covered by such international agreements amounted to about 16 per cent of the output of British industry.[21]

After the Second World War multinational enterprise expanded on an unprecedented scale. The economic and technological background which allowed this expansion is well known. Important factors included the steady growth of world trade and living standards until the 1970s; a revolution in communications which allowed companies to monitor their foreign investments more satisfactorily; and the General Agreement on Trade and Tariffs which opened the way to the establishment of interrelated plants in different countries. During the 1950s it was American companies, benefiting from the strength of their domestic economy, which dominated new multinational investment. By 1960, according to Dunning, the stock of accumulated world foreign direct investment stood at $66 billion, of which the United States held 49.2 per cent and the United Kingdom 16.2 per cent. After 1960 the era of American predominance declined, as European, and later Japanese, firms began

5

making extensive foreign direct investments. In 1978 total world foreign direct investment stood at $380.3 billion, of which $162.7 billion (41.4 per cent) originated in the United States, $50.7 billion in Britain (12.9 per cent), $28.6 billion (7.3 per cent) in Germany, $28.4 billion (7.2 per cent) in the Netherlands and $27.8 billion (7.1 per cent) in Switzerland.[22]

Despite the large American lead in foreign direct investment after the Second World War, Britain's continued vitality as a multinational investor is striking. British direct investment grew at an average rate of 8 per cent per annum (at current prices) between 1962 and 1971, and 16 per cent between 1971 and 1978. At the end of 1981 1509 British firms, excluding oil companies, banks and insurance companies, were engaged in overseas direct investment.[23] The extent of this foreign investment has led some critics to suggest a correlation between it and Britain's poor relative economic performance, especially since 1973. A range of possible linkages have been explored, including the impact of foreign direct investment in Britain's balance of payments and employment levels, and on the overall structure of the British economy.[24] Perhaps the most significant result of such work has been the inconclusiveness of its conclusions.[25] The whole field has been bedevilled by the problem of the alternative position: what would have happened if the overseas manufacture had not occurred? The upshot is that no satisfactory answer has emerged to the very important question of the impact of British multinational investment in the British economy in the twentieth century.

The Origins of British Multinational Enterprise

Why did British manufacturing firms establish foreign factories? This is not the place to review the formidable theoretical literature by economists such as S. Hymer, Richard E. Caves, Raymond Vernon, John H. Dunning and Mark Casson.[26] Instead, this section highlights the conclusions of the case studies on this subject, drawing when appropriate on theoretical insights.

It is logical to begin with what have been termed the 'preconditions' of multinational growth. It is generally agreed that a company undertakes an investment in a foreign country if it has an 'advantage' of some nature over that country's domestic companies. Such 'ownership-specific' advantages can take a number of forms. They may include access to cheap capital, technology and market skills, or superior entrepreneurial and management ability. Considerable attention has also been given to the view that companies will be in an oligopolistic market structure at home before venturing to foreign markets. It is often assumed that such companies are large-scale, or at least that there is a critical size below which a company does not envisage overseas expansion.

The evidence presented here suggests that size was not a necesary precondition of multinational growth. Some companies in this book were large (for their time) and oligopolistic before they ventured abroad. Vickers, together with Armstrong, Whitworth, dominated the British armaments market before the company expanded abroad in the 1900s. Pilkington was the sole British plate glass producer by the 1900s. However, Dunlop's international growth began soon after the company was founded, and when its key patents were under attack both in Britain and elsewhere. The Sheffield steel manufacturers which established manufacturing units in the United States were among the larger firms in their particular specialist sectors, but represented very small enterprises in the context of the British economy as a whole. As suggested in the previous section, it was by no means unusual for small British companies to make multinational investments, at least before 1914. In the chocolate and confectionery industry it was the small, specialist toffee manufacturer, Mackintosh, which established factories in the United States and Germany before 1914, while the market leaders Cadbury, Fry and Rowntree confined their international involvement at that time to exporting.[27]

There were also a number of routes to multinational enterprise. Glaxo provides the most peculiar example in this volume. Its dual New Zealand/British parentage was far removed from the conventional picture of a multinational growing through a company in one country establishing a factory in another. Glaxo did not become fully British in ownership and management until 1947. The company was additionally peculiar in its complete product switch from baby foods to pharmaceuticals. There were other examples beyond the case studies in this book of what may be termed 'migrating' multinationals. British American Tobacco Co. (now BAT Industries) began as an American company which in the 1920s became British-owned and controlled.[28] The importance of the City of London and the value of British diplomatic support were among the factors which may have encouraged companies in the past to 'migrate' to Britain.

Despite doubts about whether companies needed to be a particular size or possess an oligopolistic market situation before undertaking foreign investments, the concept of 'advantage' is a helpful one. Most of the companies in this book had an 'advantage' of one kind or another, even if it was not always a secure one. The specialist Sheffield steel firms, for example, were ahead of their American competitors in technological terms. Sometimes the technology was acquired under patents. Glaxo's international growth before the 1960s was based on patented products licensed from American competitors. The successful international marketing of imported (usually American) technology was by no means unusual for British multinationals. Before the 1950s, for example, both ICI and Metal Box benefited considerably in this way.[29] Indeed, contrary to the stereotyped image of British business as being good at invention but poor at marketing, it would seem that many British companies have been indifferent inventors but skilled at applying technology acquired under licence.

Entrepreneurship was often a vital asset for British companies expanding abroad, but one sometimes overlooked by those schooled in neoclassical economics who see the entrepreneur solely as an economic agent. Individual entrepreneurs affected the timing, direction and success of foreign investment ventures. In Vickers a select group of senior directors were the driving forces behind overseas expansion. Conversely, during the First World War the machinations of a financier nearly wrecked Dunlop's investment in the United States, and indeed brought the whole company to the verge of collapse.

The possession of an 'advantage' explains why a company should be interested in selling its products abroad. It does not explain why it should prefer to manufacture overseas rather than simply export its products. In fact most companies which make multinational investments begin their international careers as exporters. One estimate is that 94 per cent of British multinationals in the period 1870–1939 exported before they undertook foreign direct investment.[30] The companies examined in this volume fall into this category. Companies which did not have an export trade, such as British breweries, did not undertake foreign manufacture.

Why, then, did exporting companies establish factories? Table 1.1 lists the 'primary' motive behind each of the decisions to undertake foreign manufacturing by the fifteen companies covered in this book. The frailty of this table should be emphasised. There was usually a mix of factors behind each investment decision, and in some cases motives can only be inferred from the surviving evidence.

Table 1.1   Factors behind foreign direct investment decisions of selected British multinationals before 1966

	% No. of Cases		
Factor	Pre–1914	1914–44	1945–66
Tariffs and/or host government pressure	29%	38%	7%
Patent protection	17%	—	—
Competition behaviour	4%	18%	7%
Market attraction/size	42%	35%	46%
Unsatisfactory licensing agreement	—	6%	7%
Acquisition of another company	4%	3%	33%
Other[a]	4%	—	—
Total number of investment decisions	24	34	15

Note: [a] This represents the Glaxo factory in New Zealand, where the company was in part based.

The first point which emerges from Table 1.1 was that for all chronological periods market attraction was a minority motive behind foreign investment decisions. While it would be an exaggeration to suggest, as Alfred D. Chandler has for the interwar years, that all British multinational investment was primarily caused by tariffs,[31] it would appear that many company strategies were defensive rather than aggressive. There were conspicuous exceptions. Before 1914 Vickers had an aggressive strategy to secure foreign orders by establishing arsenals and dockyards abroad. In contrast the chocolate firms in the interwar years were convinced exporters who were more or less forced to establish foreign factories. The nature of the market, and of a company's product, seem to have been major influences behind whether aggressive or defensive strategies were followed.

8

A number of factors, sometimes termed 'location-specific', prompted exporters to turn to manufacture. Tariffs and host government policies were among the most significant of these for the companies considered here. The United States and most of Western Europe abandoned free trade in the second half of the nineteenth century, and the importance of tariffs as a stimulus for the growth of multinational enterprise in this period cannot be overemphasised. As tariff barriers in the United States and Europe, combined with the growth of native industries, squeezed out imports of traditional British exports such as textiles, these products were increasingly sent to the less sophisticated markets of the world, especially India and the Far East. However, for the British makers of consumer goods such as cycle tyres and soap, of industrial raw materials and armaments, the strategy of merely switching from developed markets to less developed markets was not an attractive one. Their products found their markets in high per capita income countries and industrialising countries. The real choice was either to pull out of these markets, or devise a means of supplying them other than by exports. Manufacture behind the tariff barrier was an obvious option.

The importance of tariffs prompting the Sheffield steelmakers to invest in the United States comes out clearly in Chapter 4, and there is much supporting evidence from other sources on the importance of tariffs in prompting multinational growth. Tariffs were the major factor behind the establishment of all the Lever soap factories in foreign countries before 1914, and they also prompted Courtaulds to establish its first – and highly successful – overseas factory in the United States in 1911.[32]

In the interwar years tariffs remained an important factor in prompting multinational investments. Despite the 'preference' Commonwealth countries afforded British exports, their trade barriers were sufficiently high to oblige British exporters to those markets to consider local manufacture. It was tariffs, or else the fear of them, which forced the British chocolate companies into foreign manufacture. In addition, other forms of host government pressure were exercised on companies. Dunlop, GKN and Cadbury experienced direct pressure from governments to establish factories and expand plants.

The post-1945 period is conventionally seen as a period of free trade compared to the interwar years, and Table 1.1. does suggest a sharp decline in governmental factors prompting foreign direct investment. However, trade barriers persisted in the world economy.[33] Host government policies remained an important influence on corporate strategies. Almost all of Glaxo's investments in this period were influenced by such considerations, and the company was frequently pressured by governments to manufacture certain products. The Australian government, for example, encouraged Glaxo to start the local manufacture of penicillin in Australia in the mid-1950s. Pilkington and GKN both came under sustained South African government pressure after 1945 to manufacture in that country.

Despite their importance, tariffs and government pressure were only one of several 'location-specific' factors encouraging British multinational manufacture. The desire to protect patents by local working of them stimulated several investments before 1914, notably those of Dunlop, although none thereafter for the companies considered here.

The behaviour of competitors was also a major consideration behind some multinational investments. As in the case of government pressure, even when this was not the primary influence behind an investment decision it was often a background consideration. The companies considered in this volume had in some cases domestic, and in all cases foreign,

9

competitors, and international strategies were often formulated with an eye to these competitors. Before 1914 Pilkington established a small plant in France so as to be able to influence the policies of its Continental rivals. In the interwar years this kind of behaviour seems more common. Dunlop's French subsidiary, for example, was supported so it could be used as a threat should the firm's French rival invade the British market.

Sometimes the acquisition of a competitor was a route into multinational enterprise. GKN's overseas expansion was particularly influenced by takeovers and mergers. Its merger with Lysaghts in 1920 took the company to Australia, while its acquisition of the Birfield Group in 1966 brought with it a minority shareholding in a German company.

A number of other 'location-specific' factors have been suggested to explain why firms undertake foreign direct investment, but they find only slight echoes in the case studies in this book. There is, for example, no evidence that companies were searching for lower labour costs, although labour was sometimes a consideration. The Sheffield steelmakers seem to have been attracted by the higher productivity and adaptability of the American workforce, even though labour costs in Sheffield were lower than in the United States. The British companies which invested in South Africa after the First World War were motivated by the attraction of the market and government pressure rather than any search for lower labour costs. This seems to be the general experience of British companies, with some minor exceptions.[34]

The decision to invest having been made, how was it implemented? Table 1.2 shows that companies surveyed in this book often preferred to invest abroad in joint ventures rather than wholly-owned subsidiaries.

Table 1.2 Wholly-owned and joint venture manufacturing subsidiaries of selected British multinationals before 1966

	% No. of Cases		
	Pre-1914	*1914–44*	*1945–66*
Wholly-owned	29%	47%	67%
Joint venture	71%	53%	33%
Total number of subsidiaries	24	34	15

The frequency of joint venture arrangements, especially in the pre-1944 period, is noteworthy. British, host country and third country partners were all taken. With the exception of small and unsuccessful Spanish and Canadian subsidiaries, all of Vickers foreign direct investments before 1945 were joint ventures. The Sheffield steel firms also preferred joint ventures, as did the chocolate companies in the interwar years. Only Glaxo and Pilkington seem to have preferred wholly-owned subsidiaries.

The popularity of joint ventures for early British multinationals can be readily explained. The managements of these companies had only a narrow range of options in international manufacturing. Joint ventures, by providing some measure of outside capital, plant and labour, widened this range, and they had a strong attraction for small producers such as the Sheffield steel firms. The taking of partners was an obvious means of spreading risks, an important consideration for companies such as the British chocolate manufacturers which preferred export to overseas manufacture in any case. The wish to meet nationalistic criticism about foreign companies provided a further stimulus to joint ventures. Finally, some joint ventures were formed as part of international alliances, designed to cement relationships between companies. Courtaulds' establishment of a joint venture in Germany in 1925 was one instance of such a strategy.

Table 1.2 suggests a decline in the willingness of British companies to form joint ventures over time. Perhaps British firms had gained sufficient confidence of international markets to attempt more wholly-owned ventures. There may also have been some disillusionment with joint ventures, for several of the case studies here point to the managerial and business problems which can arise between partners. However political factors, such as pressure from host governments, continued to encourage joint venture arrangements among many British multinationals in the post-Second World War period.[35] About 20 per cent of British foreign direct investment in the early 1980s was in the joint venture form.[36]

The policy options of British companies, however, were not limited to the establishment of wholly-owned and joint venture subsidiaries. It emerges clearly from the case studies that textbook divisions between foreign direct investment, portfolio investment and licensing rapidly break down in the real business world. Companies had international business strategies, and within those strategies a spectrum of contractual relationships was possible. Some companies took equity shareholdings, with no management control, in foreign enterprise. The chapter on Vickers illustrates the extensive use in the interwar years of such a strategy. Such investments could be made for a variety of reasons. They were used as a means of strengthening licensing arrangements. Small shareholdings were also sometimes acquired as part of a longer-term policy of forming a joint venture or wholly-owned subsidiary. Cadbury took shares in a German company in the interwar years for such a reason, but subsequently decided to remain at arm's length from the German company.

Licensing played an important role in the international business strategies of many British multinationals. A considerable body of literature has been built up over the last decade which seeks, among other things, to explain why companies seek to establish foreign direct investments rather than license its products.[37] This work focuses on transaction costs and, to put the arguments baldly, it is argued that multinationals appear where it is less costly to allocate international resources internally than to use the market. 'Such has been the popularity of the argument', one recent book has observed, 'that the transactions model has become established as *'the* explanation of international firms'.[38] A reaction is probably now under way among economists, partly because transactions costs have proved very hard to verify empirically. Shepherd, Silberston and Strange (1985) have suggested that the choice between licensing and overseas production may be more satisfactorily explained by a number of other factors. For example, a management may gain satisfaction from being part of a large international organisation. Company policies will also be determined by the nature

11

of the competition it faces, and in turn by management's attitude to risk.

The historical evidence assembled in this book lends support to both the transactions and alternative approaches to licensing. Dunlop's unhappy experiences before 1914 with licensing and minority shareholding agreements demonstrated the high transaction costs which could arise with this kind of arrangement. It was a similar story with Glaxo's first venture in Australia before 1914, when a short-dated licence only served to create a long-term competitor. But it was often a company's market situation which exercised a decisive influence on the strategy chosen. In the chocolate industry in the interwar years, it was the smaller company Rowntree which showed a much greater willingness to license than its larger competitor Cadbury.

A final aspect of multinational strategy worth examining is whether foreign direct investments were 'greenfield' or acquired through takeover or merger. Table 1.3 assembles the evidence from the case studies.

Table 1.3   Method of entry of affiliates of selected British multinationals before 1966

	% No. of Cases		
Methods of entry	*pre-1914*	*1914–44*	*1945–66*
Newly formed	75%	68%	47%
Acquired	25%	32%	53%
	—	—	—
Total number of investment decisions	24	34	15

The table shows that greenfield investments predominated before 1944, but subsidiaries acquired through takeover or merger steadily grew over time. The wish to avoid the prohibitive costs of 'learning by doing' often led companies to acquire a going concern, or else a local partner. It was also far from uncommon, as the case studies make clear, for a British company to be approached by a foreign company seeking, for example, access to greater capital supplies or better technology so as to expand. American steel interests on several occasions approached the Sheffield companies, and the British chocolate companies were approached by local companies in South Africa and New Zealand. Expansion abroad through acquisition rather than greenfield investment remained, in the 1980s, the preferred strategy of British multinationals.[39]

The Management of British Multinational Enterprise

The willingness of British companies to invest abroad from the late nineteenth century through to the 1980s was striking. However, it was less clear that the results were always as striking. A study in 1985 by Stopford and Turner castigated contemporary British multinationals for their inadequate response to the challenges of global competition, accusing them of lack of vision, inadequate management structures and over-confidence in their technological prowess.[40] This section suggests that some of these problems had a long historical origins. The discussion focuses on the organisation of the multinationals, and the geographical destination of their investments.

It is now generally accepted among business historians that modern management structures and hierarchies were slower to develop in Britain than the United States. By 1914 the level of industrial concentration in the United Kingdom was well below that of the United States. Moreover, the separation of ownership and managerial control remained much rarer in Britain than in America. At least until the interwar years industry consisted primarily of family firms and loose holding companies. Large corporations were less common in almost all industries than in the United States. During the 1920s a merger wave created larger companies in the United Kingdom, and some of these larger companies, such as ICI, which was created in 1926, developed extensive managerial hierarchies that operated through centrally administered functional departments. However, it was not until the 1950s and 1960s that the multidivisional organisation structure was adopted on a widespread scale in British industry. British subsidiaries of American multinationals were often pioneers in adapting this form of organisation.[41]

It is within this context that the management structures of British multinationals have to be examined. At the risk of gross oversimplification, it would seem that British multinationals passed through a number of organisational stages in their evolution. The first stage was characterised by a lack of systematic control by the parent company and, often, a high degree of operational autonomy by the foreign subsidiary. Until the 1930s many British companies paid only spasmodic attention to their foreign subsidiaries, and coherent overseas business strategies were rare. As the parent company was also the main operating company, the affairs of overseas subsidiaries rarely had a high place on board agendas. Before 1914 the foreign subsidiaries of Dunlop and Vickers simply reported their affairs, in irregular and haphazard fashion, to their parent company. The same situation existed at Courtaulds until 1928.

The usual form of parent control over foreign subsidiaries came when a director or official from Britain was despatched on an investigation or special mission. This was regular practice at Vickers and Courtaulds, and also with the Sheffield steel firms, which would often despatch members of the owner families to survey developments in the American subsidiaries. This system had a high capacity for disruptive and inconsistent management, even if it did offer peripatetic directors an escape route from British winters. Nevertheless it was a system which survived in some firms beyond the Second World War. It was still alive and well in Glaxo in the 1950s, where vital executive decisions would be heavily influenced by the chairman's frequent visits to overseas subsidiaries. Nor was Glaxo an isolated case. The chairman of Bowater in the 1950s travelled to and fro across the Atlantic. 'Where Eric Bowater went', that company's historian has observed, 'the direction of Bowaters'

13

affairs went with him, acting on one side of the Atlantic as chairman of Bowaters' parent company in the United Kingdom and on the other as President of the appropriate North American company.[42]

Except when a representative of the British parent company was in town, the foreign subsidiaries during the first stage had a high degree of operational autonomy. Vickers, Dunlop, Courtaulds and Glaxo all seem to have run their early subsidiaries on a loose rein, and to have suffered in a variety of respects as a result. The large number of joint ventures entered into by British companies hampered any attempt at tight control by parent companies. Moreover, many companies, such as Courtaulds, held a firm view that the 'man on the spot' knew best.[43]

On the whole this first stage of multinational organisation was not very successful. The case studies in this book suggest a story of management difficulties in the period before the Second World War, with many companies proving unable to find a correct balance between the parent and the subsidiaries. Research on British oil companies in the early twentieth century has also revealed acute management problems.[44] It would seem fair to conclude that although British companies were prolific in establishing foreign subsidiaries before the Second World War, they lagged in developing appropriate multinational management structures. Companies remained 'national', rather than 'multinational', in their outlooks.

A number of explanations can be put forward to account for these apparent problems. A preliminary point is that research on contemporary United States multinationals has shown that the parent–subsidiary organiation is often loose during a company's first bout of overseas expansion. It takes time for performance targets to be established and appropriate management hierarchies established.[45] Historical conditions before the First World War years encouraged such looseness. Regular and tight monitoring of subsidiaries in distant countries was near impossible before the era of telephones and jet aircraft. However, there were also other considerations apart from these underlying technical difficulties. Mira Wilkins has drawn attention to the importance of the different British and American home markets. The managers of American corporations learned within the United States how to manage businesses operating on a geographically large, prosperous and heterogeneous domestic market. British managers, lacking such a home market, had to learn by experience how to control and manage capital over distance and in alien conditions.[46]

The persistence of family firms and loose holding companies in the United Kingdom helps to explain why this learning process was often a slow one. Multinational business is typically more difficult to conduct than domestic business, as it requires a considerable extension of managerial control. If domestic management structures were defective, it was not surprising that their foreign activities were inadequately managed. The willingness of British managers to join international restraint of trade agreements may have been a recognition of their difficulties of managing business operations abroad.

A further factor which needs to be taken into consideration when explaining managerial failure is that overseas ventures were often afforded a low priority compared to mainstream British business. Cadbury in the interwar years was preoccupied by the modernisation of its domestic manufacturing units, and with solving the management problems caused by the merger with Fry in 1919. It could afford to take a long-term view about its overseas investments, in which only a small percentage of its assets were employed. Companies may be forgiven for allocating only a limited amount of attention to very marginal activities, although failed multinational ventures could and did loom large if a disaster occurred.

A final factor worth noting is that some British firms operating in the Dominions were slow to devise appropriate multinational structures because they did not believe they were doing business in *foreign* countries. It was quite usual for managers to talk of Australia, New Zealand and even Canada almost as extensions of the British market, although to be fair the problems of managing over a distance were widely recognised. British managers may have had several categories of risk, with the Empire in an intermediate level between the domestic market and 'proper' foreign countries, such as Continental Europe. In fact, as will be argued below, both Canada and Australia offered difficult market conditions, and were far from being extensions of the domestic British market.

During the interwar years some firms began to adopt a second, more centralised, form of multinational organisation. Board committees were sometimes established to oversee foreign manufacturing operations. Courtaulds set up a Foreign Relations Committee for this purpose in 1928, and this was followed by Cadbury's Overseas Factory Committee in 1929. In Dunlop improved management accounting led to closer financial monitoring of subsidiaries and the calculation of rates of return. However, the movement in this direction of other companies was slower. Rowntrees did not establish an Overseas Committee until the 1950s. Unilever maintained a highly decentralised, if sophisticated, international management structure until the 1960s.[47] At Glaxo, too, it was not until the 1950s that there were steps towards the greater coordination and integration of subsidiaries with the parent firm. Centralisation sometimes stifled initiative at subsidiary level. Glaxo's determined concentration of its research and development effort on its British base in the post-1945 period probably had this consequence. Nevertheless, the general effect of closer coordination and rationalisation was that by the 1960s most British multinationals seem to have been better equipped to compete on international markets than they had been in their early years.

Over the last two decades, a period which none of the essays in this book covers in depth, some British multinationals have entered a third stage of their multinational evolution. Foreign subsidiaries of British multinationals have sometimes developed their own subsidiaries. Production decisions have begun to be taken on a world basis, with factories in individual countries making parts of the whole product. Manufacturing companies such as ICI and the oil companies Shell and BP have been in the forefront of these developments. Yet, as Stopford and Turner have suggested, the number of British multinationals with 'global' vision, and appropriate global management structures remain limited. Shepherd, Silberston and Strange found that the majority of companies they studied still seemed to be in the second, centralised, stage of their evolution. Most of the subsidiaries carried out activities similar to those of the British parent, and their autonomy was very largely restricted to day-to-day trading operations. Most remained dependent on central research facilities.[48] The management of large-scale operations in foreign countries still seems to present problems to many British companies, as the series of unfortunate experiences of British banks with American subsidiaries acquired in the late 1970s and early 1980s demonstrated. Smaller companies, who have not faced the problems of large-scale management at a distance, have been amongst the most dynamic British multinationals.[49]

Paradoxically, the alleged lack of global vision of many British multinationals may have redeeming features. The managements of some companies that have become 'global' now regard their businesses as 'international' rather than British, and as the United Kingdom

15

assumes a declining importance in their turnover figures one might anticipate the 'migration' of some company headquarters to more prosperous markets. The decisions of some British multinationals to raise funds on American capital markets may prefigure such a trend.[50]

In some aspects of overseas business British multinationals have proved skilled. Historically British companies seem more adept, or at least more adept than their American counterparts, at adapting to local political conditions. Non-American multinationals in the contemporary world have often been seen as more willing to take local partners or admit local equity participation than American companies, thus defusing nationalistic criticism of their presence.[51] Several of the case studies in this book – such as Dunlop in the interwar years and Glaxo after 1945 – do show companies concerned to make their foreign subsidiaries more acceptable in host countries. Almost certainly British enterprises were more willing to accommodate themselves to local sentiment in the developed than the less developed world. Recent research on a major British overseas bank operating in the Middle East has revealed an appalling failure to accommodate itself to changing local political conditions in the interwar years, but with a much improved performance on this score after 1945.[52]

The direction of British foreign direct investment has been the subject of much debate in the context of the alleged weaknesses of British multinational enterprise. Between 1945 and the mid-1960s British companies concentrated on the Empire and Commonwealth. One recent estimate is that about 80 per cent of British direct investment overseas between 1946 and 1960 was in Commonwealth countries, mostly Australia, Canada and South Africa. In the late 1960s there was a renewed interest by British firms in investing in Western Europe, and after 1970 there was a surge of new investment in the United States. By the end of 1981 over a third of stock of British investment overseas was located in North America, and 23 per cent on the Continent.[53] The pre-Second World War destination of British direct investment is much less clear. While some writers have detected a strong Empire bias before 1914, others have seen this as an interwar phenomenon.[54]

Table 1.4 shows the destination of the investments of the British companies examined in this book.

Before 1914 the activities of the companies were widely dispersed among high per capita income markets, with the Continent attracting the lion's share. Dunlop made its first foreign investments in France and Germany in the 1890s, and Vickers focused its international activities in Europe. In the interwar years there was a realignment towards the Commonwealth. Despite small ventures in Germany and Sweden respectively, the British chocolate manufacturers and GKN concentrated their multinational investments on the Commonwealth. Dunlop also centred its new overseas ventures in the 1930s on the Commonwealth. After the Second World War this pattern was maintained, and combined with investments in the newly independent Commonwealth states of India and Pakistan.

The declining interest in the United States market shown in Table 1.4 is interesting. In important respects the result reflects the frail data base. The inclusion of the small American investments by the six Sheffield steel firms accounts for the high percentage shown in the table before 1914. On the other hand the table does not take into account the large American subsidiary, the American Viscose Corporation, owned by Courtaulds between 1911 and 1942. Nevertheless, the fact remains that apart from Courtaulds, only Dunlop of the large British manufacturing companies studied here made a sustained assault on the United States before the 1960s and 1970s. Cadbury, Rowntree, Vickers, Glaxo, Pilkington and GKN all steered clear of the world's largest market, or at best entered licensing agreements with American corporations.

Table 1.4 Geographical destination of selected British multinationals before 1966

Region/country	% No. of cases		
	Pre-1914	1914–44	1945–66
'Old Commonwealth'[a]	13%	53%	67%
Other Commonwealth	—	9%	13%
USA	25%	6%	—
Continental Europe	54%	26%	7%
Other	8%	6%	13%
Total number of investment decisions	24	34	15

Note:[a] Australia, New Zealand, Canada, South Africa, Eire. Eire was part of the United Kingdom until 1921, and left the Commonwealth in 1949. South Africa left the Commonwealth in 1961.

The preference for the Commonwealth has often been taken as evidence of a lack of international competitiveness by British companies. British companies, it has been suggested, took 'the path of the least resistance' in the 'safe haven' of the Empire.[55] This view is not helpful for the interwar years. The Commonwealth was not a safe haven. Several of the British firms in this study suffered from extremely strong competition in the interwar years from both indigenous and foreign companies in Australia and Canada, although more tranquil conditions often prevailed in South Africa and New Zealand. There were also rational reasons for investing in the Commonwealth. Many Continental economies offered falling and depressed markets for products during the 1930s. In the United States certain products, such as tyres, suffered from massive surplus capacity. In contrast, the South African GNP grew by 70 per cent between 1930 and 1937. British managements understood the Dominions. The risks of operating there were reduced by the many established commercial links, ties of culture and language, and the stable political situations. British companies on the Continent were faced not only by different languages and legal systems, but by political instability, Fascism and exchange controls in many countries.[56]

However the continued focus of British multinational investment on the Commonwealth

17

after 1945 had more worrying features. As Continental markets recovered in the 1950s and the United States market boomed, a clearer case can be made for British companies hugging the safe haven of the smaller, less dynamic Commonwealth markets. Glaxo's post-1945 investments in the Commonwealth seem to have been substantially based on its chairman's preference for the English-speaking world rather than a rational analysis of the merits of alternative markets. Commonwealth markets were still not easy – Courtaulds, for example, tried and failed to sustain a manufacturing operation in Australia in the 1950s and 1960s[57] – but it would seem that many British companies were a decade too late in recognising that the United States and Europe in the 1950s and 1960s offered opportunities which needed to be taken.

It was not until the 1960s, and even more the 1970s, that British multinationals finally attacked Continental and American markets.[58] Appreciating the market possibilities created by the rise in oil prices, and in particular the emphasis on economical front-wheel drive vehicles, GKN established the first of their constant velocity joint factories in North Carolina in 1980. Glaxo ended its licensing agreements with an American company in the mid-1970s, and purchased an American drugs company in 1978. Pilkingtons, after relying on licensing to exploit the revolutionary float glass process in many markets, turned to foreign direct investment in the Continent and the United States from the late 1970s.

The Performance of British Multinational Enterprise

Few of the companies examined in this volume seem to have found multinational expansion a guaranteed route to enormous profitability. Those who equate multinationals with wealth and power should study the various sagas of multinational failure revealed in this book. The evidence presented here supports earlier suggestions that, historically, the performance of British multinational enterprise has been very mixed, with a considerable number of investments performing below expectations.[59] Within individual companies there was also considerable diversity in performance of different subsidiaries, a feature which has also been noted in the case of Unilever.[60]

It is, unfortunately, a complex task to measure 'success' or 'failure'. A calculation of the internal rate of return would be ideal, but such data rarely exist. By the 1930s Dunlop was calculating rates of return of foreign subsidiaries, but this was a pioneering development seen in few other British firms until after 1945. The Dunlop calculations in the mid-1930s suggested that the company earned higher returns on its capital employed in the United Kingdom than elsewhere, and that overall the firm's overseas subsidiaries had a negative impact on overall profitability. This kind of financial information is not available for the other companies in this study. We do have profit figures for some at least of the subsidiaries, but concepts of profit varied widely and inter-company comparisons can be misleading.

Yet using qualitative evidence there is no doubt that many parents were dissatisfied with their foreign subsidiaries. Neither Dunlop's nor Vickers' pre-1914 foreign subsidiaries appear to have been great commercial successes. Only one of the Sheffield steel firms sustained a successful position in the United States. In the interwar years both Dunlop and the chocolate companies had very troubled experiences abroad. Courtaulds' investments in

18

Continental Europe were also very slow to yield a profit. Glaxo's foreign subsidiaries in the 1950s seem also to have yielded patchy returns: the group's phenomenal growth in international markets was a product of the 1970s and 1980s.

However 'success' or 'failure' is not completely captured by profit figures, or the pessimistic assessments of boards. The study of the Sheffield steel producers suggests that in technical terms they were very successful, serving as a means by which best-practice British technology was diffused to the American industry. The German and Italian subsidiaries of Courtaulds made important technological advances which were transferred back to the parent company. These represented clear gains to the British parent, even if they did not appear in the profit figures. A further complication is the difficulty of establishing the 'alternative position', to which reference has already been made. As we have seen, many although not all foreign investments were made because tariffs, government pressure or patent legislation made a strategy of exporting impractical. A full assessment of, say, Dunlop's multinational investment would need to take a view of what would have happened if the firm had not made the investment and attempted to maintain an export strategy. It would seem likely that a thorough examination of the 'alternative position' would lead to a more favourable view of the performance of the multinational investments.

The factors influencing the performance of British multinationals have been discussed already in this chapter in other contexts, and have also been examined elsewhere in more. detail.[61] It needs to be borne in mind that as multinational investment is acknowledged as a more risky strategy than domestic investment, a high failure rate could be anticipated. It would also be reasonable to expect there to be a time-lag before subsidiaries became profitable, although some of the long-term loss-making subsidiaries shown in this study are surprising.

Exogenous factors often had a decisive impact on corporate performance. The First and Second World Wars wiped out many British investments in Continental Europe. One estimate is that 40 per cent of total overseas business assets were lost through destruction, expropriation, nationalisation or sale during 1939–56.[62] The Depression ruined markets for many products on the Continent and in the United States in the 1930s. The only course for a prudent company was to insure against risk through, say, diversification into safer markets. The investments in the Commonwealth might be judged in this context.

Despite such considerations, it is clear that endogenous factors need to be taken into account when exploring poor performance. As argued elsewhere, British multinationals seem to have required a large 'advantage' for their products over local competitors to survive and prosper.[63] The unsatisfactory management structures of many of the firms help to explain this, but British companies also seem to have demonstrated a lack of competitive vigour. Many firms seem to have had a preference for the negotiated business environment rather than high competition, and they seem to have prospered where market-sharing agreements were in existence and had difficulties when they had not. The permissive attitude of the British legal system towards trade associations and agreements was an important factor here. In the late 1940s and 1950s it was often action by the Department of Justice in the United States which ended long-standing restraint of trade agreements between British and American companies.[64]

Conclusions

At first glance British multinational enterprise, like the City of London, would appear as one of the success stories of twentieth-century Britain. From the late nineteenth century, British companies were active in establishing manufacturing subsidiaries in foreign countries. Even by 1914 some of these investments had reached a substantial size. There was further growth in the interwar years. After 1945 Britain lost its place as the world's largest multinational investor to the United States, but the country remained in second place. British companies, more than those of any other European country, were household names in much of the world.

It is only when moving from this general picture to consider the detailed evidence from the case studies in this book that some blemishes begin to appear. Many British companies made their early overseas investments for defensive rather than aggressive reasons, rather like Japanese companies in the 1980s. Tariffs and host government pressures were important factors in obliging companies to abandon their preferred strategy of exporting. Decisions to invest were also made in response to moves by competitors.

If the motivation of British multinational investment was often far from dynamic, aspects of the subsequent performance also seem open to criticism. Appropriate managerial hierarchies were slow to develop. British companies manifested a liking for cartels. There was a tendency, perhaps of particular concern between 1945 and the 1970s, to go for smaller, safer markets rather than larger, faster-growing ones. There is evidence that the financial performance of the overseas investments of British companies was below expectations.

Many of the historical problems of British multinationals remain problems in the 1980s. Anxious and willing to invest abroad, British companies often lack the dynamism to capture the full rewards from their foreign endeavours. It is hoped that this book will not only elucidate an important area of Britain's business history, but contribute to the debate about the nature and effectiveness of contemporary British multinationals.

Notes

1. Mira Wilkins, *The Emergence of Multinational Enterprise* (Cambridge, Mass., 1970); and *The Maturing of Multinational Enterprise* (Cambridge, Mass., 1974).
2. There are excellent surveys in N. Hood and S. Young, *The Economics of Multinational Enterprise* (London, 1979); and R.E. Caves, *Multinational Enterprise and Economic Analysis* (Cambridge, 1982).
3. D. Shepherd, A. Silberston and R. Strange, *British Manufacturing Investment Overseas* (London, 1985).
4. John M. Stopford and Louis Turner, *Britain and the Multinationals* (Chichester, 1985), pp. 14-15.
5. C. Wilson, *The History of Unilever*, 2 vols (Oxford, 1954); and *Unilever 1945–1965* (Oxford, 1968); D.K. Fieldhouse, *Unilever Overseas* (London, 1978); W.J. Reader, *Imperial Chemical Industries, A History*, 2 vols (London, 1970 and 1975); and D.C. Coleman, *Courtaulds, An Economic and Social History*, 3 vols (Oxford, 1969 and 1980).

6. Hood and Young, *Economics*, p.3.
7. Caves, *Multinational Enterprise*, p. 1; R. Vernon, *Sovereignty at Bay* (London, 1973 edn), p. 17.
8. P. Svedberg, 'The Portfolio-Direct Composition of Private Foreign Investment in 1914 Revisited', *Economic Journal* (1978).
9. Mira Wilkins, 'Defining a Firm: History and Theory', in Peter Hertner and Geoffrey Jones (eds), *Multinationals: Theory and History* (Aldershot, 1986).
10. *Imperial Continental Gas Association, 1824–1974* (London, 1974), pp. 1-28.
11. The foreign activities of S. Pearson & Son can be followed in J.A. Spender, *Weetman Pearson, First Viscount Cowdray 1856–1927* (London, 1930); K. Middlemas, *The Master Builders* (London, 1963); and Geoffrey Jones, *The State and the Emergence of the British Oil Industry* (London, 1981). Balfour, Williamson's international growth is surveyed in Wallis Hunt, *Heirs of Great Adventure*, 2 vols (London, 1951–60).
12. Wilkins, *Emergence*. For the early growth of German multinationals see Peter Hertner, 'German Multinational Enterprise before 1914: Some Case Studies', in Hertner and Jones (eds), *Multinationals: Theory and History*.
13. I have used the ranking of companies given by L. Hannah, *The Rise of the Corporate Economy* (2nd edn, London, 1983), pp. 189-90. The sixteen firms (in order of ranking) were J. & P. Coats (cotton thread), Lever Brothers (soap), Vickers (ship-building and armaments), Nobel Industries (chemicals), Courtaulds (rayon), Metropolitan Carriage Wagon and Finance (vehicles), Armstrong Whitworth (ship-building and armaments), Fine Spinners and Doublers (textiles), Dunlop (rubber), Reckitt and Sons (chemicals), John Brown (shipbuilding), Conset Iron (metals), Babcock and Wilcox (engineering), Maypole Dairy (food), Bradford Dyers (textiles) and Mond Nickel (metals). In addition, the third largest company, Imperial Tobacco, was a minority shareholder in British-American Tobacco Company, which had widespread foreign manufacturing activities.
14. A fuller survey of British multinational enterprise before 1939 is given in Geoffrey Jones, 'The Expansion of British Multinational Manufacturing, 1890–1939', in A. Okochi and T. Inoue (eds), *Overseas Business Activities* (Tokyo, 1984). As this volume is not readily available in many western libraries, some of the material in that essay is duplicated in this one.
15. Geoffrey Jones, 'The Gramophone Company: An Anglo-American Multinational, 1898-1931', *Business History Review* (1985); L. Haber, *The Chemical Industry 1900–1930* (Oxford, 1971), p. 144; W.J. Reader, *Bowater, A History* (Cambridge, 1981), p. 12.
16. John H. Dunning, 'Changes in the level and structure of international production: the last one hundred years', in Mark Casson (ed.), *The Growth of International Business* (London, 1983), p.87.
17. This happened, for example, to the Gramophone Company. See Jones, 'The Gramophone Company', *Business History Review*, pp. 89-93.
18. Coleman, *Courtaulds*, vol. 2, pp. 137-47; Wilson, *Unilever*, vol. 1, pp. 224-5. On the general issue of British multinational investment in the United States, there is a book by Peter J. Buckley and Brian R. Roberts, *European Direct Investment in the USA before World War 1* (London, 1982). This will be superseded, however, by

21

Mira Wilkins' forthcoming historical study of European investment in the United States.

19. Dunning, 'Changes in the Level and Structure', in Casson, (ed.), *Growth*, p. 87.
20 Reader, *ICI*, vol. 2 deals extensively with this subject, and on pp. 506-11 reprints in full an agreement with du Pont signed in 1929.
21. J.D. Gribbin (ed.), *Survey of International Cartels*, (London, 1975), p. 8.
22. Dunning, 'Changes in the Level and Structure', in Casson (ed.), *Growth*, p. 87.
23. Shepherd, Silberston and Strange, *British Manufacturing Investment Overseas*, p. 7.
24. W.B. Reddaway, *Effects of U.K. Direct Investment Overseas* (Interim and Final Reports, Cambridge, 1968); M. Panic, 'International Direct Investments in Conditions of Structural Disequalibrium: U.K. Experience since the 1960s'; J. Black and J.H. Dunning (eds), *International Capital Movements* (London, 1982).
25. Shepherd, Silberston and Strange, *British Manufacturing Investment Overseas*, pp. 156-62; Stopford and Turner, *Britain and the Multinationals*, Chapter 7, is a useful survey, which suggests an overall beneficial effect of British foreign direct investment.
26. For critical literature surveys see Hood and Young, *Economics*; and Caves, *Multinational Enterprise*.
27. David J. Jeremy, 'John Mackintosh', in David J. Jeremy and C. Shaw (eds), *Dictionary of Business Biography*, vol. 4 (London, 1985), p. 55.
28. There is no business history of BAT, but see T.C. Cochran, *Big Business in China* (Cambridge, 1980).
29. Reader, *ICI*, vol. 2, passim; W.J. Reader, *Metal Box: A History* (London, 1976), pp. 54-5.
30. S.J. Nicholas, 'British Multinational Investment before 1939', *Journal of European Economic History* (1982), p. 620.
31. A.D. Chandler, 'The Growth of the Transnational Industrial Firm in the United States and the United Kingdom: A Comparative Analysis', *Economic History Review* (1980), p. 401.
32. Wilson, *Unilever*, vol. 1, p. 99; Coleman, *Courtaulds*, vol. 2, p. 107.
33. Shepherd, Silberston and Strange, *British Manufacturing Investment Overseas*, p.50.
34. Labour costs do seem to have been a factor in the decision of Metropolitan Carriage Wagon and Finance to establish a factory in Belgium before 1914. See Richard Davenport-Hines, *Dudley Docker* (Cambridge, 1984), pp. 41-2.
35. Hood and Young, *Economics*, pp. 30-1.
36. Stopford and Turner, *Britain and the Multinationals*, p. 111. Research on aggregate data has suggested a long-run historical trend towards the *greater* use of joint ventures by British firms since 1918. See J.H. Dunning and J.A. Cantwell, 'Joint Ventures and Non-Equity Foreign Involvement by British Firms', University of Reading Discussion Papers in International Investment Studies No. 68 (1982), pp. 3-4.
37. See, for example, Mark Casson, *Alternatives to the Multinational Enterprise* (London, 1979); Caves, *Multinational Enterprise* has the most recent overview of this approach.
38. Shepherd, Silberston and Strange, *British Manufacturing Investment Overseas*, p. 35.
39. Stopford and Turner, *Britain and the Multinationals*, p. 132.
40. Ibid., passim.

22

41. The classic book on the growth of the modern corporation in the United States is A.D. Chandler, *The Visible Hand* (Cambridge, Mass., 1977); for developments in Britain, see Hannah, *Rise.*

42. Reader, *Bowater,* p. 173.

43. Coleman, *Courtaulds,* vol. 2, pp. 232-3.

44. See Geoffrey Jones, *The State and the Emergence of the British Oil Industry* (London, 1981), pp. 246-7; and R.W. Ferrier, *The History of the British Petroleum Company* (Cambridge, 1982), passim.

45. J.M. Stopford and L.T. Wells, *Managing the Multinational Enterprise* (New York, 1972), Chapter 2.

46. Mira Wilkins, 'The History of European Multinationals – A New Look', *Journal of European Economic History* (forthcoming). This is an outstanding article, full of challenging ideas, and it has coloured much of my argument in this chapter.

47. Fieldhouse, *Unilever Overseas,* pp. 564-5; W.J. Reader, *Fifty Years of Unilever 1930–1980* (London, 1980), pp. 104-5.

48. Shepherd, Silberston and Strange, *British Manufacturing Investment Overseas,* pp. 92-7.

49. Stopford and Turner, *Britain and the Multinationals,* pp. 109-10.

50. Ibid., pp. 130-1.

51. Hood and Young, *Economics,* p. 260.

52. Geoffrey Jones, *Banking and Empire in Iran* and *Banking and Oil* (forthcoming, Cambridge, 1986).

53. Shepherd, Silberston and Strange, *British Manufacturing Investment Overseas,* p.11.

54. J. Stopford, 'The Origins of British-Based Multinational Manufacturing Enterprises', *Business History Review* (1974), p. 313; Nicholas, 'British Multinational Investment before 1939', pp. 624-7.

55. Stopford, 'Origins', p. 333; Stopford and Turner, *Britain and the Multinationals,* p. 62.

56. Jones, 'The Expansion of British Multinational Manufacturing', p. 146.

57. Coleman, *Courtaulds,* vol. 3, pp. 120-1, 265-6.

58. Stopford and Turner, *Britain and the Multinationals,* Chapter 4.

59. Geoffrey Jones, 'The Performance of British Multinational Enterprise, 1890–1945', in Hertner and Jones (eds), *Multinationals: Theory and History.*

60. Fieldhouse, *Unilever Overseas,* p. 566.

61. Jones, 'Performance', in Hertner and Jones (eds), *Multinationals: Theory and History.*

62. Cited in Shepherd, Silberston and Strange, *British Manufacturing Investment Overseas,* p.13.

63. Jones, 'Performance', in Hertner and Jones (eds), *Multinationals: Theory and History.*

64. Reader, *ICI,* vol. 2, Chapter 24.

Part III
New Perspectives

[10]

The Nature of the Firm

By R. H. Coase

ECONOMIC theory has suffered in the past from a failure to state clearly its assumptions. Economists in building up a theory have often omitted to examine the foundations on which it was erected. This examination is, however, essential not only to prevent the misunderstanding and needless controversy which arise from a lack of knowledge of the assumptions on which a theory is based, but also because of the extreme importance for economics of good judgment in choosing between rival sets of assumptions. For instance, it is suggested that the use of the word " firm " in economics may be different from the use of the term by the " plain man."[1] Since there is apparently a trend in economic theory towards starting analysis with the individual firm and not with the industry,[2] it is all the more necessary not only that a clear definition of the word " firm " should be given but that its difference from a firm in the " real world," if it exists, should be made clear. Mrs. Robinson has said that " the two questions to be asked of a set of assumptions in economics are : Are they tractable ? and : Do they correspond with the real world ? "[3] Though, as Mrs. Robinson points out, " more often one set will be manageable and the other realistic," yet there may well be branches of theory where assumptions may be both manageable and realistic. It is hoped to show in the following paper that a definition of a firm may be obtained which is not only realistic in that it corresponds to what is meant by a firm in the real world, but is tractable by two of the most powerful instruments of economic analysis developed by Marshall, the idea of the margin and that of substitution, together giving the idea of substitution at

---

[1] Joan Robinson, *Economics is a Serious Subject*, p. 12.
[2] See N. Kaldor, " The Equilibrium of the Firm," *Economic Journal*, March, 1934.
[3] Op. cit., p. 6.

the margin.[1] Our definition must, of course, " relate to formal relations which are capable of being *conceived exactly.*"[2]

I

It is convenient if, in searching for a definition of a firm, we first consider the economic system as it is normally treated by the economist. Let us consider the description of the economic system given by Sir Arthur Salter.[3] " The normal economic system works itself. For its current operation it is under no central control, it needs no central survey. Over the whole range of human activity and human need, supply is adjusted to demand, and production to consumption, by a process that is automatic, elastic and responsive." An economist thinks of the economic system as being co-ordinated by the price mechanism and society becomes not an organisation but an organism.[4] The economic system " works itself." This does not mean that there is no planning by individuals. These exercise foresight and choose between alternatives. This is necessarily so if there is to be order in the system. But this theory assumes that the direction of resources is dependent directly on the price mechanism. Indeed, it is often considered to be an objection to economic planning that it merely tries to do what is already done by the price mechanism.[5] Sir Arthur Salter's description, however, gives a very incomplete picture of our economic system. Within a firm, the description does not fit at all. For instance, in economic theory we find that the allocation of factors of production between different uses is determined by the price mechanism. The price of factor A becomes higher in X than in Y. As a result, A moves from Y to X until the difference between the prices in X and Y, except in so far as it compensates for other differential advantages, disappears. Yet in the real world, we find that there are many areas where this does not apply. If a workman moves from department Y to department X, he does not go because of a change in relative prices, but because he is ordered to do so. Those who

[1] J. M. Keynes, *Essays in Biography*, pp. 223-4.
[2] L. Robbins, *Nature and Significance of Economic Science*, p. 63.
[3] This description is quoted with approval by D. H. Robertson, *Control of Industry*, p. 85, and by Professor Arnold Plant, " Trends in Business Administration," ECONOMICA, February, 1932. It appears in *Allied Shipping Control*, pp. 16-17.
[4] See F. A. Hayek, " The Trend of Economic Thinking," ECONOMICA, May, 1933.
[5] See F. A. Hayek, op. cit.

object to economic planning on the grounds that the problem is solved by price movements can be answered by pointing out that there is planning within our economic system which is quite different from the individual planning mentioned above and which is akin to what is normally called economic planning. The example given above is typical of a large sphere in our modern economic system. Of course, this fact has not been ignored by economists. Marshall introduces organisation as a fourth factor of production; J. B. Clark gives the co-ordinating function to the entrepreneur; Professor Knight introduces managers who co-ordinate. As D. H. Robertson points out, we find " islands of conscious power in this ocean of unconscious co-operation like lumps of butter coagulating in a pail of buttermilk."[1] But in view of the fact that it is usually argued that co-ordination will be done by the price mechanism, why is such organisation necessary ? Why are there these " islands of conscious power " ? Outside the firm, price movements direct production, which is co-ordinated through a series of exchange transactions on the market. Within a firm, these market transactions are eliminated and in place of the complicated market structure with exchange transactions is substituted the entrepreneur-co-ordinator, who directs production.[2] It is clear that these are alternative methods of co-ordinating production. Yet, having regard to the fact that if production is regulated by price movements, production could be carried on without any organisation at all, well might we ask, why is there any organisation ?

Of course, the degree to which the price mechanism is superseded varies greatly. In a department store, the allocation of the different sections to the various locations in the building may be done by the controlling authority or it may be the result of competitive price bidding for space. In the Lancashire cotton industry, a weaver can rent power and shop-room and can obtain looms and yarn on credit.[3] This co-ordination of the various factors of production is, however, normally carried out without the intervention of the price mechanism. As is evident, the amount of " vertical " integration, involving as it does

---

[1] Op. cit., p. 85.

[2] In the rest of this paper I shall use the term entrepreneur to refer to the person or persons who, in a competitive system, take the place of the price mechanism in the direction of resources.

[3] *Survey of Textile Industries.* p. 26.

the supersession of the price mechanism, varies greatly from industry to industry and from firm to firm.

It can, I think, be assumed that the distinguishing mark of the firm is the supersession of the price mechanism. It is, of course, as Professor Robbins points out, " related to an outside network of relative prices and costs,"[1] but it is important to discover the exact nature of this relationship. This distinction between the allocation of resources in a firm and the allocation in the economic system has been very vividly described by Mr. Maurice Dobb when discussing Adam Smith's conception of the capitalist : " It began to be seen that there was something more important than the relations inside each factory or unit captained by an undertaker ; there were the relations of the undertaker with the rest of the economic world outside his immediate sphere . . . . the undertaker busies himself with the division of labour inside each firm and he plans and organises consciously," but " he is related to the much larger economic specialisation, of which he himself is merely one specialised unit. Here, he plays his part as a single cell in a larger organism, mainly unconscious of the wider rôle he fills."[2]

In view of the fact that while economists treat the price mechanism as a co-ordinating instrument, they also admit the co-ordinating function of the " entrepreneur," it is surely important to enquire why co-ordination is the work of the price mechanism in one case and of the entrepreneur in another. The purpose of this paper is to bridge what appears to be a gap in economic theory between the assumption (made for some purposes) that resources are allocated by means of the price mechanism and the assumption (made for other purposes) that this allocation is dependent on the entrepreneur-co-ordinator. We have to explain the basis on which, in practice, this choice between alternatives is effected.[3]

[1] Op. cit., p. 71.

[2] *Capitalist Enterprise and Social Progress*, p. 20. Cf., also, Henderson, *Supply and Demand*, pp. 3–5.

[3] It is easy to see when the State takes over the direction of an industry that, in planning it, it is doing something which was previously done by the price mechanism. What is usually not realised is that any business man in organising the relations between his departments is also doing something which could be organised through the price mechanism. There is therefore point in Mr. Durbin's answer to those who emphasise the problems involved in economic planning that the same problems have to be solved by business men in the competitive system. (See " Economic Calculus in a Planned Economy," *Economic Journal*, December, 1936.) The important difference between these two cases is that economic planning is imposed on industry while firms arise voluntarily because they represent a more efficient method of organising production. In a competitive system, there is an " optimum " amount of planning !

II

Our task is to attempt to discover why a firm emerges at all in a specialised exchange economy. The price mechanism (considered purely from the side of the direction of resources) might be superseded if the relationship which replaced it was desired for its own sake. This would be the case, for example, if some people preferred to work under the direction of some other person. Such individuals would accept less in order to work under someone, and firms would arise naturally from this. But it would appear that this cannot be a very important reason, for it would rather seem that the opposite tendency is operating if one judges from the stress normally laid on the advantage of " being one's own master."[1] Of course, if the desire was not to be controlled but to control, to exercise power over others, then people might be willing to give up something in order to direct others ; that is, they would be willing to pay others more than they could get under the price mechanism in order to be able to direct them. But this implies that those who direct pay in order to be able to do this and are not paid to direct, which is clearly not true in the majority of cases.[2] Firms might also exist if purchasers preferred commodities which are produced by firms to those not so produced ; but even in spheres where one would expect such preferences (if they exist) to be of negligible importance, firms are to be found in the real world.[3] Therefore there must be other elements involved.

The main reason why it is profitable to establish a firm would seem to be that there is a cost of using the price mechanism. The most obvious cost of " organising " production through the price mechanism is that of discovering what the relevant prices are.[4] This cost may be reduced but it will not be eliminated by the emergence of specialists who will sell this information. The costs of negotiating and

[1] Cf. Harry Dawes, " Labour Mobility in the Steel Industry," *Economic Journal*, March, 1934, who instances " the trek to retail shopkeeping and insurance work by the better paid of skilled men due to the desire (often the main aim in life of a worker) to be independent " (p. 86).

[2] None the less, this is not altogether fanciful. Some small shopkeepers are said to earn less than their assistants.

[3] G. F. Shove, " The Imperfection of the Market : a Further Note," *Economic Journal*, March, 1933, p. 116. note 1, points out that such preferences may exist, although the example he gives is almost the reverse of the instance given in the text.

[4] According to N. Kaldor, " A Classificatory Note of the Determinateness of Equilibrium," *Review of Economic Studies*, February, 1934, it is one of the assumptions of static theory that " All the relevant prices are known to all individuals." But this is clearly not true of the real world.

concluding a separate contract for each exchange transaction which takes place on a market must also be taken into account.[1] Again, in certain markets, e.g., produce exchanges, a technique is devised for minimising these contract costs ; but they are not eliminated. It is true that contracts are not eliminated when there is a firm but they are greatly reduced. A factor of production (or the owner thereof) does not have to make a series of contracts with the factors with whom he is co-operating within the firm, as would be necessary, of course, if this co-operation were as a direct result of the working of the price mechanism. For this series of contracts is substituted one. At this stage, it is important to note the character of the contract into which a factor enters that is employed within a firm. The contract is one whereby the factor, for a certain remuneration (which may be fixed or fluctuating), agrees to obey the directions of an entrepreneur *within certain limits*.[2] The essence of the contract is that it should only state the limits to the powers of the entrepreneur. Within these limits, he can therefore direct the other factors of production.

There are, however, other disadvantages—or costs—of using the price mechanism. It may be desired to make a long-term contract for the supply of some article or service. This may be due to the fact that if one contract is made for a longer period, instead of several shorter ones, then certain costs of making each contract will be avoided. Or, owing to the risk attitude of the people concerned, they may prefer to make a long rather than a short-term contract. Now, owing to the difficulty of forecasting, the longer the period of the contract is for the supply of the commodity or service, the less possible, and indeed, the less desirable it is for the person purchasing to specify what the other contracting party is expected to do. It may well be a matter of indifference to the person supplying the service or commodity which of several courses of action is taken, but not to the purchaser of that service or commodity. But the purchaser will not know which of these several courses he will want the supplier to take. Therefore,

---

[1] This influence was noted by Professor Usher when discussing the development of capitalism. He says : "The successive buying and selling of partly finished products were sheer waste of energy." (*Introduction to the Industrial History of England*, p. 13). But he does not develop the idea nor consider why it is that buying and selling operations still exist.

[2] It would be possible for no limits to the powers of the entrepreneur to be fixed. This would be voluntary slavery. According to Professor Batt, *The Law of Master and Servant*, p. 18, such a contract would be void and unenforceable.

the service which is being provided is expressed in general terms, the exact details being left until a later date. All that is stated in the contract is the limits to what the persons supplying the commodity or service is expected to do. The details of what the supplier is expected to do is not stated in the contract but is decided later by the purchaser. When the direction of resources (within the limits of the contract) becomes dependent on the buyer in this way, that relationship which I term a " firm " may be obtained.[1] A firm is likely therefore to emerge in those cases where a very short term contract would be unsatisfactory. It is obviously of more importance in the case of services— labour—than it is in the case of the buying of commodities. In the case of commodities, the main items can be stated in advance and the details which will be decided later will be of minor significance.

We may sum up this section of the argument by saying that the operation of a market costs something and by forming an organisation and allowing some authority (an " entrepreneur ") to direct the resources, certain marketing costs are saved. The entrepreneur has to carry out his function at less cost, taking into account the fact that he may get factors of production at a lower price than the market transactions which he supersedes, because it is always possible to revert to the open market if he fails to do this.

The question of uncertainty is one which is often considered to be very relevant to the study of the equilibrium of the firm. It seems improbable that a firm would emerge without the existence of uncertainty. But those, for instance, Professor Knight, who make the *mode of payment* the distinguishing mark of the firm—fixed incomes being guaranteed to some of those engaged in production by a person who takes the residual, and fluctuating, income— would appear to be introducing a point which is irrelevant to the problem we are considering. One entrepreneur may sell his services to another for a certain sum of money, while the payment to his employees may be mainly or wholly a share in profits.[2] The significant question would

[1] Of course, it is not possible to draw a hard and fast line which determines whether there is a firm or not. There may be more or less direction. It is similar to the legal question of whether there is the relationship of master and servant or principal and agent. See the discussion of this problem below.

[2] The views of Professor Knight are examined below in more detail.

appear to be why the allocation of resources is not done directly by the price mechanism.

Another factor that should be noted is that exchange transactions on a market and the same transactions organised within a firm are often treated differently by Governments or other bodies with regulatory powers. If we consider the operation of a sales tax, it is clear that it is a tax on market transactions and not on the same transactions organised within the firm. Now since these are alternative methods of " organisation "—by the price mechanism or by the entrepreneur—such a regulation would bring into existence firms which otherwise would have no *raison d'être*. It would furnish a reason for the emergence of a firm in a specialised exchange economy. Of course, to the extent that firms already exist, such a measure as a sales tax would merely tend to make them larger than they would otherwise be. Similarly, quota schemes, and methods of price control which imply that there is rationing, and which do not apply to firms producing such products for themselves, by allowing advantages to those who organise within the firm and not through the market, necessarily encourage the growth of firms. But it is difficult to believe that it is measures such as have been mentioned in this paragraph which have brought firms into existence. Such measures would, however, tend to have this result if they did not exist for other reasons.

These, then, are the reasons why organisations such as firms exist in a specialised exchange economy in which it is generally assumed that the distribution of resources is " organised " by the price mechanism. A firm, therefore, consists of the system of relationships which comes into existence when the direction of resources is dependent on an entrepreneur.

The approach which has just been sketched would appear to offer an advantage in that it is possible to give a scientific meaning to what is meant by saying that a firm gets larger or smaller. A firm becomes larger as additional transactions (which could be exchange transactions co-ordinated through the price mechanism) are organised by the entrepreneur and becomes smaller as he abandons the organisation of such transactions. The question which arises is whether it is possible to study the forces which determine the size of the firm. Why does the entrepreneur not organise one less transaction or one more ? It is interesting to note that Professor Knight considers that :

"the relation between efficiency and size is one of the most serious problems of theory, being, in contrast with the relation for a plant, largely a matter of personality and historical accident rather than of intelligible general principles. But the question is peculiarly vital because the possibility of monopoly gain offers a powerful incentive to *continuous and unlimited* expansion of the firm, which force must be offset by some equally powerful one making for decreased efficiency (in the production of money income) with growth in size, if even boundary competition is to exist."[1]

Professor Knight would appear to consider that it is impossible to treat scientifically the determinants of the size of the firm. On the basis of the concept of the firm developed above, this task will now be attempted.

It was suggested that the introduction of the firm was due primarily to the existence of marketing costs. A pertinent question to ask would appear to be (quite apart from the monopoly considerations raised by Professor Knight), why, if by organising one can eliminate certain costs and in fact reduce the cost of production, are there any market transactions at all ?[2] Why is not all production carried on by one big firm ? There would appear to be certain possible explanations.

First, as a firm gets larger, there may be decreasing returns to the entrepreneur function, that is, the costs of organising additional transactions within the firm may rise.[3] Naturally, a point must be reached where the costs of organising an extra transaction within the firm are equal to the costs involved in carrying out the transaction in the open market, or, to the costs of organising by another entrepreneur. Secondly, it may be that as the transactions which are organised increase, the entrepreneur fails to place the factors of production in the uses where their value

---

[1] *Risk, Uncertainty and Profit*, Preface to the Re-issue. London School of Economics Series of Reprints, No. 16, 1933.

[2] There are certain marketing costs which could only be eliminated by the abolition of "consumers' choice" and these are the costs of retailing. It is conceivable that these costs might be so high that people would be willing to accept rations because the extra product obtained was worth the loss of their choice.

[3] This argument assumes that exchange transactions on a market can be considered as homogeneous : which is clearly untrue in fact. This complication is taken into account below.

is greatest, that is, fails to make the best use of the factors of production. Again, a point must be reached where the loss through the waste of resources is equal to the marketing costs of the exchange transaction in the open market or to the loss if the transaction was organised by another entrepreneur. Finally, the supply price of one or more of the factors of production may rise, because the " other advantages " of a small firm are greater than those of a large firm.[1] Of course, the actual point where the expansion of the firm ceases might be determined by a combination of the factors mentioned above. The first two reasons given most probably correspond to the economists' phrase of " diminishing returns to management."[2]

The point has been made in the previous paragraph that a firm will tend to expand until the costs of organising an extra transaction within the firm become equal to the costs of carrying out the same transaction by means of an exchange on the open market or the costs of organising in another firm. But if the firm stops its expansion at a point below the costs of marketing in the open market and at a point equal to the costs of organising in another firm, in most cases (excluding the case of " combination "[3]), this will imply that there is a market transaction between these two producers, each of whom could organise it at less than the actual marketing costs. How is the paradox to be resolved ? If we consider an example the reason for this will become clear. Suppose *A* is buying a product from *B* and that both *A* and *B* could organise this marketing transaction at less than its present cost. *B*, we can assume, is not organising one process or stage of production, but several. If *A* therefore wishes to avoid a market transaction, he will have to take over all the processes of production controlled by *B*. Unless *A* takes over all the processes of

---

[1] For a discussion of the variation of the supply price of factors of production to firms of varying size, see E. A. G. Robinson, *The Structure of Competitive Industry*. It is sometimes said that the supply price of organising ability increases as the size of the firm increases because men prefer to be the heads of small independent businesses rather than the heads of departments in a large business. See Jones, *The Trust Problem*, p. 531, and Macgregor, *Industrial Combination*, p. 63. This is a common argument of those who advocate Rationalisation. It is said that larger units would be more efficient, but owing to the individualistic spirit of the smaller entrepreneurs, they prefer to remain independent, apparently in spite of the higher income which their increased efficiency under Rationalisation makes possible.

[2] This discussion is, of course, brief and incomplete. For a more thorough discussion of this particular problem, see N. Kaldor, " The Equilibrium of the Firm," *Economic Journal*, March, 1934, and E. A. G. Robinson, " The Problem of Management and the Size of the Firm," *Economic Journal*, June, 1934.

[3] A definition of this term is given below.

production, a market transaction will still remain, although it is a different product that is bought. But we have previously assumed that as each producer expands he becomes less efficient ; the additional costs of organising extra transactions increase. It is probable that A's cost of organising the transactions previously organised by B will be greater than B's cost of doing the same thing. A therefore will take over the whole of B's organisation only if his cost of organising B's work is not greater than B's cost by an amount equal to the costs of carrying out an exchange transaction on the open market. But once it becomes economical to have a market transaction, it also pays to divide production in such a way that the cost of organising an extra transaction in each firm is the same.

Up to now it has been assumed that the exchange transactions which take place through the price mechanism are homogeneous. In fact, nothing could be more diverse than the actual transactions which take place in our modern world. This would seem to imply that the costs of carrying out exchange transactions through the price mechanism will vary considerably as will also the costs of organising these transactions within the firm. It seems therefore possible that quite apart from the question of diminishing returns the costs of organising certain transactions within the firm may be greater than the costs of carrying out the exchange transactions in the open market. This would necessarily imply that there were exchange transactions carried out through the price mechanism, but would it mean that there would have to be more than one firm ? Clearly not, for all those areas in the economic system where the direction of resources was not dependent directly on the price mechanism could be organised within one firm. The factors which were discussed earlier would seem to be the important ones, though it is difficult to say whether " diminishing returns to management " or the rising supply price of factors is likely to be the more important.

Other things being equal, therefore, a firm will tend to be larger :

(*a*) the less the costs of organising and the slower these costs rise with an increase in the transactions organised.

(*b*) the less likely the entrepreneur is to make mistakes and the smaller the increase in mistakes with an increase in the transactions organised.

(c) the greater the lowering (or the less the rise) in the supply price of factors of production to firms of larger size.

Apart from variations in the supply price of factors of production to firms of different sizes, it would appear that the costs of organising and the losses through mistakes will increase with an increase in the spatial distribution of the transactions organised, in the dissimilarity of the transactions, and in the probability of changes in the relevant prices.[1] As more transactions are organised by an entrepreneur, it would appear that the transactions would tend to be either different in kind or in different places. This furnishes an additional reason why efficiency will tend to decrease as the firm gets larger. Inventions which tend to bring factors of production nearer together, by lessening spatial distribution, tend to increase the size of the firm.[2] Changes like the telephone and the telegraph which tend to reduce the cost of organising spatially will tend to increase the size of the firm. All changes which improve managerial technique will tend to increase the size of the firm.[3-4]

It should be noted that the definition of a firm which was given above can be used to give more precise meanings to the terms "combination" and "integration."[5] There is a combination when transactions which were previously

---

[1] This aspect of the problem is emphasised by N. Kaldor. op. cit. Its importance in this connection had been previously noted by E. A. G. Robinson, *The Structure of Competitive Industry*, pp. 83–106. This assumes that an increase in the probability of price movements increases the costs of organising within a firm more than it increases the cost of carrying out an exchange transaction on the market—which is probable.

[2] This would appear to be the importance of the treatment of the technical unit by E. A. G. Robinson, op. cit., pp. 27–33. The larger the technical unit, the greater the concentration of factors and therefore the firm is likely to be larger.

[3] It should be noted that most inventions will change both the costs of organising and the costs of using the price mechanism. In such cases, whether the invention tends to make firms larger or smaller will depend on the relative effect on these two sets of costs. For instance, if the telephone reduces the costs of using the price mechanism more than it reduces the costs of organising, then it will have the effect of reducing the size of the firm.

[4] An illustration of these dynamic forces is furnished by Maurice Dobb, *Russian Economic Development*, p. 68. " With the passing of bonded labour the factory, as an establishment where work was organised under the whip of the overseer, lost its *raison d'être* until this was restored to it with the introduction of power machinery after 1846." It seems important to realise that the passage from the domestic system to the factory system is not a mere historical accident, but is conditioned by economic forces. This is shown by the fact that it is possible to move from the factory system to the domestic system, as in the Russian example, as well as *vice versa*. It is the essence of serfdom that the price mechanism is not allowed to operate. Therefore, there has to be direction from some organiser. When, however, serfdom passed, the price mechanism was allowed to operate. It was not until machinery drew workers into one locality that it paid to supersede the price mechanism and the firm again emerged.

[5] This is often called " vertical integration," combination being termed " lateral integration."

organised by two or more entrepreneurs become organised
by one. This becomes integration when it involves the
organisation of transactions which were previously carried
out between the entrepreneurs on a market. A firm can
expand in either or both of these two ways. The whole
of the " structure of competitive industry " becomes tractable by the ordinary technique of economic analysis.

III

The problem which has been investigated in the previous
section has not been entirely neglected by economists and
it is now necessary to consider why the reasons given above
for the emergence of a firm in a specialised exchange economy
are to be preferred to the other explanations which have
been offered.

It is sometimes said that the reason for the existence
of a firm is to be found in the division of labour. This is
the view of Professor Usher, a view which has been adopted
and expanded by Mr. Maurice Dobb. The firm becomes
" the result of an increasing complexity of the division of
labour . . . . The growth of this economic differentiation
creates the need for some integrating force without which
differentiation would collapse into chaos ; and it is as the
integrating force in a differentiated economy that industrial
forms are chiefly significant."[1] The answer to this argument
is an obvious one. The " integrating force in a differentiated
economy " already exists in the form of the price mechanism.
It is perhaps the main achievement of economic science
that it has shown that there is no reason to suppose that
specialisation must lead to chaos.[2] The reason given by
Mr. Maurice Dobb is therefore inadmissible. What has
to be explained is why one integrating force (the entrepreneur)
should be substituted for another integrating force (the
price mechanism).

The most interesting reasons (and probably the most
widely accepted) which have been given to explain this
fact are those to be found in Professor Knight's *Risk,
Uncertainty and Profit*. His views will be examined in
some detail.

[1] Op. cit., p. 10. Professor Usher's views are to be found in his *Introduction to the
Industrial History of England*, pp. 1-18.
[2] Cf. J. B. Clark, *Distribution of Wealth*, p. 19, who speaks of the theory of exchange as
being the " theory of the organisation of industrial society."

Professor Knight starts with a system in which there is no uncertainty :

" acting as individuals under absolute freedom but without collusion men are supposed to have organised economic life with the primary and secondary division of labour, the use of capital, etc., developed to the point familiar in present-day America. The principal fact which calls for the exercise of the imagination is the internal organisation of the productive groups or establishments. With uncertainty entirely absent, every individual being in possession of perfect knowledge of the situation, there would be no occasion for anything of the nature of responsible management or control of productive activity. Even marketing transactions in any realistic sense would not be found. The flow of raw materials and productive services to the consumer would be entirely automatic."[1]

Professor Knight says that we can imagine this adjustment as being " the result of a long process of experimentation worked out by trial-and-error methods alone," while it is not necessary " to imagine every worker doing exactly the right thing at the right time in a sort of ' pre-established harmony ' with the work of others. There might be managers, superintendents, etc., for the purpose of co-ordinating the activities of individuals," though these managers would be performing a purely routine function, " without responsibility of any sort."[2]

Professor Knight then continues :

" With the introduction of uncertainty—the fact of ignorance and the necessity of acting upon opinion rather than knowledge—into this Eden-like situation, its character is entirely changed . . . . With uncertainty present doing things, the actual execution of activity, becomes in a real sense a secondary part of life ; the primary problem or function is deciding what to do and how to do it."[3]

This fact of uncertainty brings about the two most important characteristics of social organisation.

" In the first place, goods are produced for a market, on the basis of entirely impersonal prediction of wants, not for the satisfaction of the wants of the producers themselves. The producer takes the responsibility of

---

[1] *Risk, Uncertainty and Profit*, p. 267.
[2] Op. cit., pp. 267–8.   [3] Op. cit., p. 268.

forecasting the consumers' wants. In the second place, the work of forecasting and at the same time a large part of the technological direction and control of production are still further concentrated upon a very narrow class of the producers, and we meet with a new economic functionary, the entrepreneur. . . . . When uncertainty is present and the task of deciding what to do and how to do it takes the ascendancy over that of execution the internal organisation of the productive groups is no longer a matter of indifference or a mechanical detail. Centralisation of this deciding and controlling function is imperative, a process of ' cephalisation ' is inevitable."[1] The most fundamental change is :

" the system under which the confident and venturesome assume the risk or insure the doubtful and timid by guaranteeing to the latter a specified income in return for an assignment of the actual results. . . . With human nature as we know it it would be impracticable or very unusual for one man to guarantee to another a definite result of the latter's actions without being given power to direct his work. And on the other hand the second party would not place himself under the direction of the first without such a guarantee. . . . The result of this manifold specialisation of function is the enterprise and wage system of industry. Its existence in the world is the direct result of the fact of uncertainty."[2]

These quotations give the essence of Professor Knight's theory. The fact of uncertainty means that people have to forecast future wants. Therefore, you get a special class springing up who direct the activities of others to whom they give guaranteed wages. It acts because good judgment is generally associated with confidence in one's judgment.[3]

Professor Knight would appear to leave himself open to criticism on several grounds. First of all, as he himself points out, the fact that certain people have better judgment or better knowledge does not mean that they can only get an income from it by themselves actively taking part in production. They can sell advice or knowledge. Every business buys the services of a host of advisers. We can imagine a system where all advice or knowledge was bought

[1] Op. cit., pp. 268–95.   [2] Op. cit., pp. 269–70.
[3] Op. cit., p. 270.

as required. Again, it is possible to get a reward from better knowledge or judgment not by actively taking part in production but by making contracts with people who are producing. A merchant buying for future delivery represents an example of this. But this merely illustrates the point that it is quite possible to give a guaranteed reward providing that certain acts are performed without directing the performance of those acts. Professor Knight says that "with human nature as we know it it would be impracticable or very unusual for one man to guarantee to another a definite result of the latter's actions without being given power to direct his work." This is surely incorrect. A large proportion of jobs are done to contract, that is, the contractor is guaranteed a certain sum providing he performs certain acts. But this does not involve any direction. It does mean, however, that the system of relative prices has been changed and that there will be a new arrangement of the factors of production.[1] The fact that Professor Knight mentions that the "second party would not place himself under the direction of the first without such a guarantee" is irrelevant to the problem we are considering. Finally, it seems important to notice that even in the case of an economic system where there is no uncertainty Professor Knight considers that there would be co-ordinators, though they would perform only a routine function. He immediately adds that they would be "without responsibility of any sort," which raises the question by whom are they paid and why? It seems that nowhere does Professor Knight give a reason why the price mechanism should be superseded.

IV

It would seem important to examine one further point and that is to consider the relevance of this discussion to the general question of the "cost-curve of the firm."

It has sometimes been assumed that a firm is limited in size under perfect competition if its cost curve slopes upward,[2] while under imperfect competition, it is limited

---

[1] This shows that it is possible to have a private enterprise system without the existence of firms. Though, in practice, the two functions of enterprise, which actually influences the system of relative prices by forecasting wants and acting in accordance with such forecasts, and management, which accepts the system of relative prices as being given, are normally carried out by the same persons, yet it seems important to keep them separate in theory. This point is further discussed below.

[2] See Kaldor, op. cit., and Robinson, *The Problem of Management and the Size of the Firm.*

in size because it will not pay to produce more than the
output at which marginal cost is equal to marginal revenue.[1]
But it is clear that a firm may produce more than one product
and, therefore, there appears to be no *prima facie* reason
why this upward slope of the cost curve in the case of perfect
competition or the fact that marginal cost will not always
be below marginal revenue in the case of imperfect competition should limit the size of the firm.[2]   Mrs. Robinson[3]
makes the simplifying assumption that only one product
is being produced. But it is clearly important to investigate
how the number of products produced by a firm is determined,
while no theory which assumes that only one product is
in fact produced can have very great practical significance.

It might be replied that under perfect competition, since
everything that is produced can be sold at the prevailing
price, then there is no need for any other product to be
produced. But this argument ignores the fact that there
may be a point where it is less costly to organise the exchange
transactions of a new product than to organise further
exchange transactions of the old product. This point can
be illustrated in the following way. Imagine, following
von Thunen, that there is a town, the consuming centre,
and that industries are located around this central point
in rings. These conditions are illustrated in the following
diagram in which *A*, *B* and *C* represent different industries.

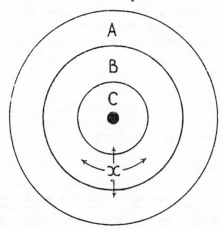

---

[1] Mr. Robinson calls this the Imperfect Competition solution for the survival of the small firm.
[2] Mr. Robinson's conclusion, op. cit., p. 249, note 1, would appear to be definitely wrong.
He is followed by Horace J. White, Jr., " Monopolistic and Perfect Competition," *American
Economic Review*, December, 1936, p. 645, note 27. Mr. White states " It is obvious that
the size of the firm is limited in conditions of monopolistic competition."
[3] *Economics of Imperfect Competition*.

Imagine an entrepreneur who starts controlling exchange transactions from x. Now as he extends his activities in the same product (B), the cost of organising increases until at some point it becomes equal to that of a dissimilar product which is nearer. As the firm expands, it will therefore from this point include more than one product (A and C). This treatment of the problem is obviously incomplete,[1] but it is necessary to show that merely proving that the cost curve turns upwards does not give a limitation to the size of the firm. So far we have only considered the case of perfect competition ; the case of imperfect competition would appear to be obvious.

To determine the size of the firm, we have to consider the marketing costs (that is, the costs of using the price mechanism), and the costs of organising of different entrepreneurs and then we can determine how many products will be produced by each firm and how much of each it will produce. It would, therefore, appear that Mr. Shove[2] in his article on " Imperfect Competition " was asking questions which Mrs. Robinson's cost curve apparatus cannot answer. The factors mentioned above would seem to be the relevant ones.

V

Only one task now remains ; and that is, to see whether the concept of a firm which has been developed fits in with that existing in the real world. We can best approach the question of what constitutes a firm in practice by considering the legal relationship normally called that of " master and servant " or " employer and employee."[3] The essentials of this relationship have been given as follows :

" (1) the servant must be under the duty of rendering personal services to the master or to others on behalf

---

[1] As has been shown above, location is only one of the factors influencing the cost of organising.

[2] G. F. Shove, " The Imperfection of the Market." *Economic Journal*, March. 1933. p. 115. In connection with an increase in demand in the suburbs and the effect on the price charged by suppliers, Mr. Shove asks " . . . . why do not the old firms open branches in the suburbs ? " If the argument in the text is correct. this is a question which Mrs. Robinson's apparatus cannot answer.

[3] The legal concept of " employer and employee " and the economic concept of a firm are not identical, in that the firm may imply control over another person's property as well as over their labour. But the identity of these two concepts is sufficiently close for an examination of the legal concept to be of value in appraising the worth of the economic concept.

of the master, otherwise the contract is a contract for sale of goods or the like.

(2) The master must have the right to control the servant's work, either personally or by another servant or agent. It is this right of control or interference, of being entitled to tell the servant when to work (within the hours of service) and when not to work, and what work to do and how to do it (within the terms of such service) which is the dominant characteristic in this relation and marks off the servant from an independent contractor, or from one employed merely to give to his employer the fruits of his labour. In the latter case, the contractor or performer is not under the employer's control in doing the work or effecting the service ; he has to shape and manage his work so as to give the result he has contracted to effect."[1]

We thus see that it is the fact of direction which is the essence of the legal concept of " employer and employee," just as it was in the economic concept which was developed above. It is interesting to note that Professor Batt says further :

" That which distinguishes an agent from a servant is not the absence or presence of a fixed wage or the payment only of commission on business done, but rather the freedom with which an agent may carry out his employ- ment."[2]

We can therefore conclude that the definition we have given is one which approximates closely to the firm as it is considered in the real world.

Our definition is, therefore, realistic. Is it manageable ? This ought to be clear. When we are considering how large a firm will be the principle of marginalism works smoothly. The question always is, will it pay to bring an extra exchange transaction under the organising authority ? At the margin, the costs of organising within the firm will be equal either to the costs of organising in another firm or .to the costs involved in leaving the transaction to be " organised " by the price mechanism. Business men will be constantly experimenting, controlling more or less, and in this way, equilibrium will be maintained. This gives the position of equilibrium for static analysis. But

[1] Batt, *The Law of Master and Servant*, p. 6.
[2] Op. cit., p. 7.

it is clear that the dynamic factors are also of considerable importance, and an investigation of the effect changes have on the cost of organising within the firm and on marketing costs generally will enable one to explain why firms get larger and smaller. We thus have a theory of moving equilibrium. The above analysis would also appear to have clarified the relationship between initiative or enterprise and management. Initiative means forecasting and operates through the price mechanism by the making of new contracts. Management proper merely reacts to price changes, rearranging the factors of production under its control. That the business man normally combines both functions is an obvious result of the marketing costs which were discussed above. Finally, this analysis enables us to state more exactly what is meant by the " marginal product " of the entrepreneur. But an elaboration of this point would take us far from our comparatively simple task of definition and clarification.

[11]

FOREIGN INVESTMENT AND THE GROWTH
OF THE FIRM [1]

I

Such is the desire for an accelerated rate of capital formation in most of the less-industrialised countries to-day, that fears about the ultimate problem of servicing foreign capital invested in the country are often pushed, rather uneasily, into the background, while inducements are held out to attract such capital, in particular to attract private direct investment. In Australia, however, a recent event has emphasised once again the controversial aspect of foreign investment when the investment takes the form of the successful establishment of a foreign subsidiary enterprise in which the ordinary capital, or common stock, is largely held abroad. Most successful firms grow, and if a firm grows by virtue of its own earnings, that is to say, if the rate of new investment in the firm does not exceed the rate of earnings on its past investment, then the foreign equity in the firm grows without any net import of new foreign exchange—i.e., foreign investment in the firm is increasing while there may be a net outflow of foreign funds.

Thus, a relatively small initial dollar investment, for example, may establish a firm whose earnings are sufficient to permit extensive expansion through ploughed-back profits, each increment of expansion increasing the foreign liabilities of the country. It is therefore likely that dividend remittances, when they become an important proportion of profits, will be enormously high in relation to the original dollar investment, although not necessarily high in relation to the total foreign investment in the firm. This paper is concerned with the economic implications of this form of foreign investment for the economic policies of some of the less-industrialised countries to-day.

We shall consider first the particular case of General Motors–Holden's Ltd. in Australia, secondly, the general question whether it makes any difference if foreign investment takes place through the expansion of existing foreign-controlled firms rather than in some other form, and finally what solutions, if any, there are to the problems raised.

General Motors–Holden's in Australia

With the publication of its Annual Report for 1954, General Motors–Holden's Ltd., the Australian wholly-owned subsidiary of General Motors Corporation in the United States, raised a hornet's nest of controversy about its corporate ears, and became more firmly than ever committed to the

[1] I want to acknowledge here the criticism of the staff of the Economics Department of the Australian National University, and in particular that of Professor T. W. Swan, who saved me from some serious errors in the latter part of the paper. I am also indebted to Professor Fritz Machlup and to Professor E. F. Penrose for much helpful criticism, and to the John Simon Guggenheim Memorial Foundation for granting me a Fellowship for research in Australia.

necessity of convincing the Australian public that "What's good for General Motors is good for the country." The storm arose over the revelation that: (a) GMH made a profit A£9,830,000 after taxes in 1953–54, which is variously portrayed as 560% on ordinary capital (the ordinary capital representing in this case the original dollar investment of GMH), 39% on shareholders' funds (net worth), 24% on funds employed or 14% on sales, depending on how the speaker feels about the size of the profit; and (b) that a dividend was declared to the parent company of A£4,550,000, which again is 260% on ordinary capital, 18% on shareholders' funds or 11% on funds employed.[1] The dividend declared is about 8% of the dollar export receipts in the Australian balance of payments for 1954–55.[2]

Newspaper stories and editorials critical of the profit (the highest ever declared by a firm in Australia) and of the dividend payment were followed by an attack by Dr. H. V. Evatt, Leader of the Labor Party (the Government Opposition) on the GMH "Colossus," and letters pro and con appeared in the correspondence columns of the Sydney and Melbourne Press.   Economists immediately began debating the issues raised for the Australian economy, and H. W. Arndt, Professor of Economics of Canberra University College, stated on the air "As far as policy towards future overseas investment in this country is concerned, the Holden case may induce some caution in giving indiscriminate encouragement." He suggested that Australia might do well to " concentrate less on attracting American capital and more on hiring American technical and managerial know-how."

The background of the General Motors situation is as follows: The firm began in Australia in 1926 with chassis-assembly plants in various States, and in 1931 bought out the Australian-owned Holden's Motor Body Builders Ltd. with an issue of Preference Shares.   Until 1945 the combined firm was engaged in building bodies and assembling imported chassis units, but in that year began planning the manufacture in Australia of the Holden car.   This car appeared in 1948, and has steadily gained a larger and larger share of the automobile market in Australia.[3]   All Australian produced, it is the cheapest and most popular car in its class (medium weight—by Australian standards— and in the middle price range).   GMH has been unable to produce enough cars to meet demand at existing prices, and the waiting list was announced as being equal to twelve months production.   In 1953–54 the retail price of the car was reduced by A£84, or 7%.   Further reductions in price would only intensify the shortage and put profits in the hands of " grey-market " dealers. (It is alleged that at present prices many people buy new Holdens and immediately resell them at A£100 profit.)

Along with the release of the Annual Report, expansion plans were

---

[1] The par value of the ordinary shares is A£1,750,000; there are in addition A£561,600 of Preference Shares owned by Australians.   The net worth of the company (or shareholders' funds) is A£25 million; total funds employed are A£41 million.

[2] There is a 15% tax on dividends, and hence the actual dollar remittance was less by this amount.

[3] From 1953 to 1954, however, the Holden share of the market actually declined from 36·5 to 35·1% as a result of the inability of the company to keep up with the demand in an expanding market.

announced involving a 50% increase in production of the Holden (from the present 65,000 a year to 100,000), expansion of the household and commercial refrigeration business and entry into the production of central-heating units and other household appliances.   The planned expansion is estimated to cost A£21,622,000, bringing the Company's post-war expenditure on new plants and facilities to A£47,750,000 and the funds employed in the business to more than A£61 million.   (The total assets of the largest firm in Australia, a firm which comprehends the entire steel industry, were A£76·4 million in 1954.)

GMH has successfully established a completely Australian automobile,[1] thus reducing import requirements for automobiles and promoting efficient industrialisation.   In other words, it has done "just what the doctor ordered "; for the promotion of industrial development by " import replacement " through efficient home production is established national policy. But if the post-war rate of expansion continues for long GMH will not only be far more important in the automobile market than all other producers combined,[2] but will also be reaching out into more and more industries.   This continued expansion will not involve any further import of dollars; on the contrary, it will be accompanied by an ever-increasing stream of dollar dividends paid out as the equity increases on which the dividends are paid. Taking the ten-year period 1945–54, total profit of GMH was about 10% on sales and 27% on the average capital over the period, but 72·4% of the profit was retained in the business.[3]   And there is little reason for believing that either smaller increments of expansion or lower earning rates are going to mark the reasonably foreseeable future.

At first sight it might seem that the problem is basically one of monopolistic profits; the task, accordingly, being to increase the amount of effective competition in the automobile industry.   In general, and in spite of the periodic pronouncements of the Labor Party against " monopolies," neither the Australian Government nor the Australian public tend to be much concerned about monopoly as such.   There is a very high degree of " concentration " in the economy—the largest seventy-five firms owning nearly 45% of the total fixed assets in manufacturing.[4]   The steel industry

[1] As the saying goes, " Australian except for the key "—which is made in Wisconsin.

[2] The three largest producers are GMH, Ford and British Motors Corporation.   Since 1949 the GMH share of the market has risen from 23 to 35½%, that of Ford from 14 to 21%, while that of BMC has fallen from 31 to 20%.   Thus the " Big Three " have 76% of the market, and Ford and GMH together have risen from 37 to 54%.   Of these only GMH publishes a balance sheet in Australia; nothing is known about the profits of the other two.

[3] Consequently, the actual dividends paid out have not until this year been appreciable, only some 7·4% on the average capital employed in the ten years.   But this, of course, means that the equity upon which profits are expected to be earned and eventually realised in significant amounts is so much the greater.   From now on it may be expected that the GMH dividend will remain high.

[4] This figure is subject to a fair margin of error because some of the largest companies in Australia are subsidiaries of foreign firms and do not publish balance sheets.   Hence we have no information about their fixed assets.   The figure was obtained by taking the largest manufacturing firms listed on the stock exchanges and comparing their fixed assets net of depreciation (because the gross figure is not usually available) with the net fixed assets in manufacturing as given by the Commonwealth Statistician.

and the glass industry are each in the hands of a single firm, 70% of the paper industry in the hands of another, 50% of the rubber industry is in the hands of still another and so on for many important industries.   For one firm to gain a dominant position in the automobile industry would not be contrary to the general development of the structure of industry in Australia, and would not be expected to raise many eyebrows, especially since the industry is already highly concentrated.   In addition, efficiency in meeting market demand seems to be the chief reason for the predominance of GMH—it is hard to trace the failure of competition to reduce its profits to any significant monopolistic practices on the part of GMH itself.   Other companies have not produced a car as popular as the Holden (Ford is the only company significantly close to GMH in the market).   The tariff on cars not wholly manufactured in Australia is of some importance, but not so much as is generally assumed.   To encourage manufacturing in Australia there is a duty on automobile parts of around A£87 on a car equivalent to the Holden when imported from Britain already assembled, and A£38 on a vehicle to be assembled in Australia.   Since automobiles other than the Holden are assembled in Australia partly from imported and partly from domestically manufactured parts, the duty naturally raises their cost, depending on the extent to which parts are imported.[1]   Import restrictions imposed for balance-of-payments purposes are much more important and at present are very severe.

One simple and obvious step to take would seem to be a reduction in the tariff and of import restrictions.   But this might have two unwanted effects.   First, it is very probable that it would hurt other local manufacturers of component parts more than it would GMH.   There is a large scope for the reduction of the price of the Holden in the face of competition, and there is strong reason to believe that while GMH would stand up well to increased competition, especially after the new expansion program is well under way, the others would not.   In view of the Government's attitude towards the motor-car industry up to the present, it seems unlikely that it would be prepared at this point to risk a discouragement of further local manufacture.   Second, and even more compelling from the Government's point of view, is the possible effect on the balance of payments.   Any increase in imports is considered highly undesirable under present circumstances. Because of a current deterioration in the balance of payments, import restrictions have recently been severely increased.   Since it is not at all certain that increased competition from imports would in fact go far to reduce GMH profits but might involve a partial destruction of the rest of the automobile manufacturing industry, a reduction of the tariff, or of restrictions, might have little effect on GMH and merely cause a further deterioration in the balance of payments.

Nevertheless, the tariff is one of the factors in the situation, and a full-scale inquiry into the state of the automobile industry, which has been scheduled by the Tariff Board for some time, is now in process.   It is possible

---

[1] However, several companies are well forward with plans to produce in Australia.

that tariff revision may to some extent increase competition and reduce the monopolistic element in the GMH profit rate. But competition in this sense will not eliminate the fundamental difficulty—the continued profitable expansion of the firm—unless it eliminates the differentials in expected profit rates which are the very basis for international direct investment.[1]

Various other approaches to the GMH problem have been offered. A favorite of some of the financial commentators is the suggestion that GMH should forthwith accept Australian equity capital. Even apart from the fact that this implies a repatriation of capital for which special permission is required from the Government, the proposal is highly impractical if it is expected to be on more than a token scale designed primarily for its psychological effect. To reduce significantly the foreign-exchange payments if profits and dividends near the present scale are continued, the Australian-held proportion of the total equity in the company would have to be substantial. Let us assume that the parent company would have no objection to 49% of the equity being transferred to Australian hands. Given the present net worth of the company, this might involve a diversion of Australian investable funds to GMH of something like A£90 million. The total investment funds raised in Australia on the capital market by Australian companies and semi-government authorities was not over A£200 million in 1954. Clearly it would take many years before a transfer of funds, including the repatriation of the capital, on this scale could be absorbed by the Australian economy without serious complications.

Finally, it is possible for the Government to limit the remittance of dividends either by direct limitation of the amount that can be exported or by very heavy progressive taxation. Some of the problems raised by this are discussed below; it is sufficient at this point to note that in order to attract foreign capital the Government has made it more or less clear that this type of action would not be taken; hence it would inevitably be viewed as a repudiation of previously incurred obligations and would create bad feeling all around. As is suggested below, once a foreign firm is established, it is not, from an economic point of view, desirable to limit its growth or to buy it out at its market value, in whole or in part, although from a political point of view a case can be made for acquiring it.

II

Let us now examine the problem in more general terms. It will be argued that the growth of foreign investment through the reinvestment of retained earnings by firms is subject to different influences from those determining the inflow of foreign investment from other sources. Once a foreign firm is established its continued growth is an increase in foreign investment, but an increase which is more appropriately analysed in the light of a theory of the growth of firms rather than a theory of foreign investment. The issues raised for the receiving economy will then be discussed.

[1] See Section II below for discussion of this point.

The Growth of the Firm

In the absence of markedly unfavorable environmental conditions, there is a strong tendency for a business enterprise possessing extensive and versatile internal managerial resources continually to expand, not only in its existing fields but also into new products and new markets as opportunity offers.   The expansion is not usually a continuous straight-line process; rather it fluctuates with external conditions, and may be retarded by internal difficulties. But for the successful firms over the long haul—and there always are such firms—there seems to be no reason to assume that the process cannot continue indefinitely, or at least for any relevant future.   The " productive opportunity " which invites expansion is not exclusively an external one. It is largely determined by the internal resources of the firm: the products the firm can successfully produce, the new areas in which it can successfully set up plants, the innovations it can successfully launch, the very ideas of its executives and the opportunities they see, depend as much on the kind of experience, managerial ability and technological know-how already existing within the firm as they do upon external opportunities open to all.[1]

Direct foreign investment—and by this I mean the ownership and operation of business organisations in a foreign country [2]—can, in its origin, be of several types.   Here we are interested only in direct investment in manufacturing activity which takes the form of the establishment of branches or subsidiaries in foreign countries.   In the realm of manufacturing this kind of investment is probably more effective in expanding productivity and promoting industrial efficiency than any other kind of foreign investment.[3]   Its advantages derive largely from the fact that behind the new foreign firm are the resources and experience of the parent concern, including not only managerial and technical personnel but also that indefinable advantage in its internal operations which an efficient going concern usually has over a new one.   Consequently the receiving country, in addition to foreign capital, foreign technicians and management, also obtains an unlimited drawing account, as it were, on the intangible resources of the investing company.   The establishment of foreign subsidiaries or branches is, for the parent company, not essentially different from the establishment of subsidiaries or branches in its own country.   To be sure, greater allowance for risk must be made, and greater profits are expected if the venture succeeds according to plan.   But the new expansion is still part of the process of growth of the parent company.

Once established, however, a new subsidiary has a life of its own, and its growth will continue in response to the development of its own internal

---

[1] For a fuller, though still incomplete, discussion of the theory of the growth of the firm upon which part of the argument in this paper is based see my " Limits to the Growth and Size of Firms," *American Economic Review*, XLV, No. 2 (May 1955), Papers and Proceedings, pp. 531–43.

[2] This begs the question of what constitutes ownership or, more precisely, a controlling interest. For the purposes of this paper we need not worry about the kind of precise definition necessary for statistical analyses.

[3] By the emphasis on manufacturing I want to exclude from consideration the development of public utilities, railroads and similar industries basic to manufacturing through inter-governmental loans or through international financial intermediaries.   Obviously such investment may be equally effective in promoting development.

resources and the opportunities presented in its new environment. This means, in the first instance, expansion in the production of the products contemplated when the subsidiary was originally established, an expansion which may well continue for a considerable period if, as is usually the case, the firm is introducing a new product or was established in an industry with the prospect of rapid growth. In time, however, the possibilities of expanding in other fields will appear attractive, either because expansion in the original lines at the same rates as before is no longer profitable, because new market opportunities have appeared, or because the firm has itself developed, or can draw on the parent company for productive services suitable for other types of products (*e.g.*, by-products, innovations related in production or consumption to the original product, a market standing facilitating the sale of other products, etc.). One of the notable characteristics of the growth of large modern corporations is the extent to which they change the range and nature of the product they produce as they grow. They introduce entirely new products, they improve and alter existing products, they enter into a wide range of industries, continually adding to their product lines. In other words, firms are not limited to their original fields; they tend to branch out in many directions. The extent to which this process of diversification can continue depends upon the flexibility of management and upon the resources of the firm—no clear limit is as yet discernible, even in the largest United States corporations. GMH in Australia illustrates the principle: even if the profitability of automobile production declines as competition develops, GMH can in principle, and very likely will in practice, continue to expand by going into other activities where a higher rate of return is still available. As noted above, the firm is already making provision for expanding production into a wide range of fields. In short, so long as there are openings in industry in which the firm expects a rate of return on investment sufficient to justify entering it, there is nothing in principle to limit its continued expansion. And if foreign firms have any advantage in management, technology, capital or other resources, foreign firms may be expected to grow somewhat faster than domestic firms, even in the absence of any exorbitant degree of monopoly power. This conclusion is reinforced by the fact that foreign firms tend to enter the newer, and therefore faster-growing and more profitable, industries.

On the whole, foreign subsidiaries have, for a variety of reasons, a greater degree of independence of the parent than have domestic subsidiaries. Where they are in a distant country the distance itself tends to restrict the mobility of personnel; where the subsidiaries operate in a radically different political, economic and social environment more weight is often given to the judgment of their executives, who are likely to possess an understanding of conditions that is not easily available to the parent company; where foreign subsidiaries are concerned, the area over which a close co-ordination of policy is considered necessary is often smaller than it is with respect to domestic subsidiaries operating in a more closely connected national market. For these and similar reasons, a foreign subsidiary, once it is established, is, with important exceptions, more appropriately treated in many ways as a separate firm. The most important of these exceptions relates to finance.

Foreign subsidiaries can obtain additional capital from their parent companies or, like local firms, from the local capital market. If funds for expansion are obtained from local equity sources the firm will represent foreign investment to a progressively smaller degree as it grows, and the problems discussed in this paper will not arise.[1] But a preference for expansion through retained earnings is becoming increasingly characteristic of the modern corporation, and of particular interest from the point of view of foreign investment is the situation, especially favored by American firms, in which the parent company holds all, or nearly all, of the equity and permits the subsidiary to expand with its own earnings.

Internally Financed Foreign Investment

The preference of American firms for nearly complete ownership of their foreign subsidiaries contrasts sharply with British practice.[2] Several reasons for the contrast have been put forward by business-men and economists—on the part of the Americans, a desire for freedom from interference from minority stockholders, a desire to avoid shareholder criticism of a ruthless dividend limitation in the early stages of growth even when profits are high, a desire to avoid precise inter-company book-keeping (such as charging part of the overhead of the parent concern to the subsidiary, charging it for managerial and technical advice, service and " know-how "), a desire for secrecy;[3] and on the part of the British, an appreciation of the political importance of a shared ownership. Whatever the reasons may be, the preference is clear. The result is that virtually the entire growth of most American-owned subsidiaries is properly classed as a growth in foreign investment. And a very large proportion of the total increment in United States investment abroad in recent years has taken the form of re-investment of retained earnings of such subsidiaries.[4]

[1] There are a variety of ways in which foreign concerns can co-operate with local firms and financial interests in establishing and developing manufacturing activity and without creating the kind of problem typified by the GMH case. See, for example, the methods discussed in *Processes and Problems of Industrialization in Under-developed Countries* (New York: United Nations, Department of Economic and Social Affairs, 1955), pp. 85–6.

[2] It has been estimated that on the average American companies hold 85% and British companies 40% of the Ordinary Shares of their subsidiaries in Australia.

[3] Foreign subsidiaries in Australia, for example, do not have to publish balance sheets unless they are " public companies " (some shares being publicly held); GMH issued Preference Shares in order to acquire the Holden company, and for this reason has to publish a balance sheet.

[4] " Between 1946 and 1951, for example, no less than three-quarters of all United States new direct foreign investment in manufacturing industry was the result of the ploughing back of profits earned in foreign branches and subsidiaries." United Nations, *op. cit.*, p. 84. According to a very interesting paper on the contribution of overseas companies to Australian post-war industrial development presented to the 1955 meeting of the Australian and New Zealand Association for the Advancement of Science by D. M. Hocking, which was based upon figures developed by the Australian Department of National Development, direct investment in secondary industry in Australia from the United States increased by A£80·1 million between 1945 and 1953. The United States Department of Commerce (*Survey of Current Business*, December 1954) estimates that the undistributed profits of Australian subsidiaries of United States firms amounted to A£65·2 million in the period from January 1946 to December 1953.

Because of the potentialities for expansion inherent in the modern corporation with its extensive techniques of decentralised management, its emphasis on developing new markets, on innovations and on research, and its power to generate internal funds for expansion, there are several reasons for believing that the flow of direct foreign investment when it is the result of the growth of foreign firms through retained earnings will proceed at a faster rate, in larger amounts and for a longer period than was characteristic of direct investment of the past. Furthermore, a decision by the parent firm to embark on a new foreign venture is taken under substantially different circumstances from those surrounding a decision to permit an already existing (and profitable) venture to expand.

Although it is true that foreign investment is undertaken because a rate of return on capital that is higher than alternative rates obtainable elsewhere is expected (although not necessarily in the short run), it should not be forgotten that a very considerable input of the managerial and technical resources of the investing firm may be required to ascertain what foreign opportunities exist and how they may best be taken advantage of. Indeed, the original investment of many a foreign firm has been little more than an exploratory venture which can be classed essentially as part of the cost of discovering whether or not investment is desirable. The cost of investigation, together with the cost of planning, organising and actually establishing the new firm must, other things being equal, obviously limit the number and extent of such ventures undertaken. When, however, a profitable foreign subsidiary presents a request that it be permitted to retain some or all of its profits for further investment, the case is different. The parent firm is presented with a program for expansion which has already been evaluated by the management of the subsidiary. It has to consider this program, to be sure, and it may modify it, but the exploratory work has already been done, and been done by men who know local conditions and (presumably) are trusted and responsible officials of the firm. In other words, an interested group in the firm itself presents a case and makes a plea. The degree of uncertainty surrounding such investment, and the cost of making it, is surely much lower than that associated with a new venture, and the investment, therefore, much easier to make.

Secondly, the very operations of the subsidiary in the foreign country, its knowledge of the market and of the conditions of production, the experience gained by its officials and the position it may have established for itself with its own customers and in the country generally all tend to create new opportunities for further investment, opportunities that did not exist at the time the firm was established. These, since they are new opportunities for the growth of the foreign firm, are by definition, new opportunities for the growth of foreign investment.

Finally, there is the fact that it is often easier not to go into an activity than it is to abandon it once it has been firmly established. In the modern corporate world, maintaining an established position often requires net new investment to keep up with the innovation of products, production techniques and marketing methods of competitors.   Thus new investment may be required indefinitely to enable the foreign subsidiary even to maintain its position in the foreign market.   And here enters, in a sense, a non-economic factor.   More is involved in a going concern than an investment of funds. An organisation has been created, men and women have vested interests in the concern, a publicly recognised entity exists.   It seems highly probable, and the suggestion has been confirmed in various conversations with business-men, that there will be a strong tendency for the parent company to take its " cut " of the profits and to permit the subsidiary to retain a part long after a comparison of rates of return on capital would attract new investments in the absence of the existing subsidiaries.[1]   In other words, even if increasing investment reduces, or even eliminates, the original differential between foreign and domestic rates of return on capital, foreign investment will still increase because foreign-owned firms will continue to grow through their own earnings.   There is very little information available to enable us to evaluate the importance of this aspect of the matter.   But from what we do know of the general processes of growth of business firms, there seems no good reason for expecting that the growth of the successful foreign firms will cease at any time, and the only important question relating to the growth of foreign investment is whether finance will be obtained from retained earnings or whether the parent company will gradually permit a dilution of the equity with domestically raised capital.

In effect, the profitable operation of foreign companies means, in the first place, that there are likely to be more funds available for foreign invest-ment than there would otherwise have been, and in the second place, that the opportunities for foreign investment are enlarged.   More funds are likely to be available because of the general bias in favor of permitting a successful subsidiary to retain some of its earnings for expansion, and because of the reduction in uncertainty and risk associated with foreign investment of this kind in comparison with the launching of entirely new ventures.   New opportunities are created in the same way in which any growing and aggres-sive firm creates its own opportunities; it just happens that opportunities for expansion created by foreign firms are at the same time new opportunities for foreign investment.

Such are the reasons for expecting that the flow of foreign investment will increase at a more rapid rate and continue longer when it depends on the expansion of existing firms than it would if it depended on fresh imports of capital for new firms.   And I suggest that the increasing importance of direct foreign investment in manufacturing in recent years is partly explained by these factors—some investment that would not otherwise have been made is being made for the reasons outlined above.   It is direct investment, but of a much less speculative and risky kind than is usually assumed.

[1] This is particularly true if capital repatriation is not permitted and the foreign firm has no alternative but to continue to invest to protect its existing investment.

The Balance-of-payments Problem

Such investment, though ardently desired by the less-industrialised countries, is not accepted without misgivings. The misgivings relate to two potential difficulties: the political implication of foreign control and the economic problem of paying for the investment. Both are greatest in the case of direct investment; here we are concerned only with the economic problem. There can be little doubt that in order to provide the means of paying for foreign investment, an economy may, in the absence of expanding exports, be faced with the difficult task of inducing an unpalatable reduction in domestic consumption and investment.

This task may be especially difficult when incomes are expanding rapidly in response to a high rate of investment pursuant to government industrial-development and full-employment policies. Under such circumstances, with consumption and investment at high levels, import demand is likely to be very high, not only for consumers' goods, but especially for capital goods. The problem of maintaining economic stability—sustained full employment without inflation—becomes crucial, and is particularly difficult in countries whose export proceeds are subject to wide and unpredictable fluctuations from season to season. The goal of governments is to keep inflationary pressures under some sort of control without precipitating deflation, or if deflation threatens, to counteract the recession quickly and thus prevent depression. In pursuance of this goal there is often little hesitation in applying direct exchange and import restrictions or in using Central Bank credit to maintain financial liquidity in order to ensure that unfavorable movements of the foreign balance do not interfere with domestic policy. Yet the foreign balance is likely to be a continual source of trouble because of an excessive demand for imports consequent upon the difficulty of controlling " excess demand " within the economy without creating unacceptable unemployment. At the same time depreciation as a remedy is looked on with great suspicion, to be used only rarely and *in extremis*.

Such policies have several effects on the problem under discussion. High levels of activity mean high business profits, which not only attract foreign firms but also furnish an easy source of funds for the expansion of already established firms. In a raw-material-exporting economy, where industrial development does not contribute substantially to exports, large amounts of foreign lending may well be necessary to sustain the development program unless demand for the country's raw-material exports is also expanding rapidly. The high levels of activity attract the foreign investment required in the form of direct private investment, and particularly, after foreign firms have become well established, in the form of the growth of foreign firms through retained earnings. We have already shown that direct private investment will tend to grow rapidly and without practical limits as foreign firms grow. So long as these firms retain the greater part of their earnings for re-investment the effect on the balance of payments of servicing the investment is masked, for the re-investment of profits is equivalent to an import of foreign funds. In not exercising their right to export their profits, the firms leave foreign exchange available to the country that would otherwise have gone into dividend remittances.[1] The effect is similar to the familiar process by which old loans are serviced partly out of the proceeds of new ones. No problem is apparent until the new lending stops. When profits are not paid out it is as if new loans were being made, but when this new " lending " slows down and dividends are paid on the existing investment the country may find that some difficult readjustments in the economy are required. It has been traditionally held that loans with fixed interest payments are likely to be more of a burden on the economy than equity investment, because in the former case the payments have to be made at the same rate in periods of depressed economic activity, while in the latter dividend payments fall when profits are low. This appraisal of the two forms of investment must be revised if, as seems likely, the more severe depressions can be prevented by appropriate internal government policy.

When the readjustments in the economy required to service foreign investment are difficult to make they create what is called a " balance-of-payments problem." And they will be the more difficult to make the greater the pressure of domestic demand on imports and the larger the foreign payments required. Rapidly developing economies attempting to maintain consistently high levels of employment will have continually to struggle to control excess domestic demand. Under the circumstances assumed in this paper dividend remittances from direct private investment will tend to involve larger transfers of foreign funds than would have been the case if only loans had been received. Consequently, a real " balance-of-payments problem " in this sense may arise. But it is, in essence, a " technical " problem, a problem of how best to reduce domestic consumption and investment—whether to use import restrictions, tariffs, exchange rates, taxation, monetary policy or some combination of these, and how to mitigate, if desired, the effects on the distribution of income and on the direction of domestic investment. However, in so far as foreign investment goes into industries producing for the domestic market, total dividend payments are likely to move slowly upward without much fluctuation. If export proceeds fluctuate widely from season to season the dividend payments may cause severe strains on the country's reserves from time to time. In so far as foreign investment takes place in export industries, the profits, and hence the dividends, of foreign firms are more likely to fluctuate with export proceeds and less likely to cause temporary strains. Economic authorities have an understandable reluctance to force far-reaching economic adjustment because of temporary difficulties. In the absence of sufficient flexibility in exchange rates the only alternative lies in the creation of adequate inter-

---

[1] We are not, of course, taking into account here the effect on the demand for imports (or supply of exports) of the investment which is itself the alternative to the building up of cash balances for the purpose of paying dividends. This is part of the whole question of how industrialisation in a primarily raw-material-exporting country affects the demand for imported goods—a question we cannot explore in this paper.

national reserves to maintain service on investment in periods when export proceeds are low.

Australia is an excellent illustration. Exports are only a little influenced by its industrial development.[1] Import demand is continually straining the country's foreign resources. Foreign investment, in particular direct dollar investment through the growth of American firms, is increasing rapidly. The balance-of-payments problem that this investment may create is masked so long as substantial proportions of the profits of foreign firms are retained. But as the total profits of foreign firms grow and the firms become more solidly established, the tendency to pay out a goodly portion of their profits to the parent companies will increase, particularly if foreign firms become nervous about the balance-of-payments position. It is highly probable that in time this portion paid out of a growing total will become large enough to make an appreciable contribution to the already existing difficulties of keeping the demand for foreign exchange within bounds, for the profit of the foreign firms, and the firms themselves, will continue to grow so long as the efforts of the Government to maintain domestic incomes at a full-employment level are successful. The adjustments required, together with the foreign payments made, are indeed a " cost " to the economy, and the basic question is whether the foreign investment is worth the cost. Is there anything in the nature of the type of foreign investment considered here—the growth of foreign firms—that makes the high cost of this investment " too high "?

Cost vs. Benefits

In principle, the growth of foreign indebtedness, like the growth of domestic indebtedness, need not be of particular concern in a growing economy, providing that the net income out of which the indebtedness can be serviced also grows correspondingly. If the increments of investment involved in the growth of foreign firms are of such high productivity that domestic real income is raised to an extent equal to, or greater than, the return on the investment to the owners of the capital it will pay the economy to accept them. There may be " technical " problems associated with the remittance of dividends, but in principle if the increase in the economy's productivity is not less than the cost, it will pay the economy to make the required adjustments, provided that the same increase in productivity could not have been obtained at a cheaper price.

There are two types of benefits realised from foreign investment: additional supplies of capital, on the one hand, and, on the other, new techniques of production and management, entrepreneurial skill, new products, new ideas. We have suggested that loan capital is in general cheaper than equity capital, but that probably less foreign investment would take place if loans alone were relied on. But it is primarily in the second category of benefits that the special advantages of direct investment lie. The benefits

---

[1] However, we should not overlook the fact that industrialisation may have *reduced* exports by diverting exportable products to domestic consumption and by attracting factors of production away from the export industries.

of direct foreign investment, when it takes the form of the establishment of new foreign firms, the introduction of new technology and the provision of experienced managerial and technical services can hardly be exaggerated.[1] In addition, the development of subsidiary industries and the improved productivity of other resources which the entry of a progressive foreign firm into a major industry may stimulate is of great importance in increasing the total productivity of the economy. The importance of the opportunities afforded for training not only the domestic labor supply but also domestic managerial and technical personnel is attested to by the lengths to which many countries go in insisting that foreign firms make special efforts in these directions. If the benefits of direct investment can be obtained in some cheaper way it will, of course, pay to do so. The intrinsic difficulties of controlling direct private investment once it gets established, the problem of paying for it, together with the political fear of foreign " exploitation " and domination, have led many countries to explore ways of hiring foreign management and technical personnel and purchasing access to foreign technology.[2] Such efforts have met with considerable success in some of the Latin American countries, but from an economic point of view it seems doubtful that they would obtain for the country the full set of advantages which are brought in by new foreign firms, although this will vary appreciably between industries. Nevertheless, a great deal can be gained in these ways which benefits the economy. Furthermore, it must be conceded that from a political point of view there is much to be said for this approach.

Even if a great many of the advantages of foreign investment can be obtained by these cheaper methods, it is still true that so long as still more capital and still further " intangible " benefits can be acquired by permitting the establishment of foreign firms whose contribution to the domestic product is greater than the cost of the investment, it will pay the economy to accept them. And so long as this condition holds true for further increments of expansion of foreign firms, it will pay the economy to permit the indefinite expansion of these firms.[3] If a point is reached where it does not hold true, *i.e.*, where the profits of the foreign firms contain a strong element of private monopoly gain, the situation is changed and the increase in foreign liabilities may be, to the extent of this gain, a net loss to the economy. This brings us up against the moot question whether the monopoly elements almost inevitably associated with the position of the very large firms are almost necessary conditions for further research, innovation and progress, as has been powerfully argued by many, Schumpeter in particular. In some cases

---

[1] For a survey of the enormous contributions made to the Australian economy by foreign firms see D. M. Hocking, " New Products, New Skills Follow Overseas Capital," *The Australian Financial Review*, September 29, 1955, p. 2. John H. Dunning has discussed a significant aspect of the importance of the contribution of American firms to the British economy in an article " United States Manufacturing Subsidiaries and Britain's Trade Balance," *District Bank Review*, September 1955, pp. 20–30.

[2] See United Nations, *op. cit.*, pp. 85–7.

[3] This is, of course, apart from the political question of whether large and powerful firms— foreign or domestic—should be countenanced.

this may be true; in others it plainly is not true. In any event, this is the element in the growth of foreign firms that will cause the increments of foreign investment it represents to take place at " too high " a cost to the economy, and it is this element, consequently, that receiving countries should pay especial attention to. It is obvious that this particular type of foreign investment is more likely than most others to contain an appreciable amount of unproductive monopoly profit.

Now all of this bears on the proposition, so often put forward, that there is some gain to the economy if arrangements are made after a point to buy out the foreign investor. It is probably true that the contributions of direct foreign investment are of greatest importance in the early stages of the growth of the foreign firms and of industrial development. It seems very likely that as the firm grows the point is reached where the specifically foreign contribution to the operation of the firm becomes less important in relation to the contribution of the locally recruited staff who have grown up with and have been trained in the firm. But if the firm is still paying its way—if the contribution to the productivity of the economy is greater than the return to the owners—it will not be to the domestic economy's advantage to divert scarce domestic capital to replace the foreign capital so long as there are opportunities for the profitable use of domestic capital. On the other hand, if the firm is making monopoly profits it would even less pay the economy to buy the firm at its market value, which would inevitably include the capitalisation of prospective monopoly profits. If there is no other way of eliminating the monopoly profit, then the purchase of the firm at a price which did not reflect prospective monopoly profits may be the only economic solution to the problem—this is usually referred to as " expropriation."

Thus it is clear that if it is economic to accept direct private foreign investment at all and to permit the establishment of foreign firms, that is to say, if the benefits of foreign investment cannot be obtained in cheaper ways (perhaps over a longer period of time), then it is desirable to permit the continued growth of foreign firms so long as they pay their way.[1] Furthermore, once they are established, under no circumstances does it pay to buy them out at their market value if domestic capital can be more profitably used elsewhere.

The fact still remains, however, that if extensive amounts of direct foreign investment are obtained, the balance-of-payments problem of the type discussed earlier may require adjustments which create awkward difficulties for many established government policies. If, therefore, there is not a reasonably large gain to be had from direct foreign investment, the country may well consider that the investment is not worth the cost of the adjustments required to pay for it. Furthermore, the political repercussions of policies designed to

---

[1] It has been implicitly assumed in this entire argument, of course, that industrialisation itself is, in the long run, a profitable use of the country's resources, or rather that the rate of industrial development implied in the investment program is not excessive. If this is not true and if real income would be increased if more resources were devoted to the raw-material-exporting industries and less to domestic industry, then further foreign investment, just as further domestic investment, in industry will be unprofitable to the economy as a whole.

restrict domestic expenditure when it is realised that the restrictions are partly for the sake of paying foreign " capitalists," may make such adjustments virtually impossible. By calling the balance-of-payments problem a " technical " one I do not mean to minimise its difficulties. Policies designed to force the rate of industrialisation, coupled with the potentialities for almost indefinite growth inherent in the modern corporation, the modern trend for increasing reliance on internal financing of expansion and the preference, particularly of United States firms, for nearly complete ownership of foreign subsidiaries, raises the possibility that much larger amounts of direct foreign investment may take place in a much shorter period of time when political conditions are favorable than was generally the case in the past. When and if the foreign payments become significant, the countries accepting the investment must also be willing to accept the adjustments in domestic consumption and investment required to service it. One suspects that for some countries there may be a basic incompatibility between the economic objectives of fostering very rapid industrial development and at the same time promoting domestic full employment at all times regardless of the state of the foreign balance, and the acceptance of an unlimited, unknown and uncontrollable foreign liability.

Edith Tilton Penrose

The Johns Hopkins University.

[12]

Journal of Economic Literature
Vol. XIX (December 1981), pp. 1537–1568

The Modern Corporation: Origins, Evolution, Attributes

By OLIVER E. WILLIAMSON

University of Pennsylvania

This paper has benefitted from the very helpful comments of Moses Abramovitz, Alfred Chandler, Sanford Grossman, Paul Joskow, Scott Masten, Richard Nelson, and Douglass North. Parts of it were given at Rice University as a 1981 Peterkin Lecture, and comments of the faculty and students in attendance were also helpful. For related recent assessments of the modern corporation which, however, emphasize somewhat different aspects, see Richard Caves (1980), Robin Marris and Dennis Mueller (1980), and Richard Cyert and Charles Hedrick (1972).

THERE IS VIRTUAL UNANIMITY with the proposition that the modern corporation is a complex and important economic institution. There is much less agreement on what its attributes are and on how and why it has successively evolved to take on its current configuration. While I recognize that there have been numerous contributing factors, I submit that the modern corporation is mainly to be understood as the product of a series of organizational innovations that have had the purpose and effect of economizing on transaction costs.

Note that I do not argue that the modern corporation is to be understood exclusively in these terms. Other important factors include the quest for monopoly gains and the imperatives of technology. These mainly have a bearing on market shares and on the absolute size of specific technological units; but decisions to make or buy, which determine the distribution of economic activity, as between firms and markets, and the internal organization (including both the shape and the aggregate size) of the firm are not explained, except perhaps in trivial ways, in these terms. Inasmuch as these are core issues, a theory of the modern corporation that does not address them is, at best, seriously incomplete.

Specifically, the study of the modern corporation should actively concern itself with and provide consistent explanations for the following features of the organization of economic activity: What are the factors that determine the degree to which firms integrate—in backward, forward, and lateral respects? What economic purposes are served by the widespread adoption of divisionalization? What ramifications, if any, does internal organization have for the long-standing dilemma posed by the separation of ownership from control? Can the "puzzle" of the conglomerate be unravelled? Do similar considerations apply in assessing multinational enterprise? Can an underlying rationale be provided for the reported association between innovation and direct foreign investment?

It is my contention that transaction cost economizing figures prominently in explaining these (as well as related) major features of the business environment. Since transaction-cost economizing is socially valued, it follows that the modern corporation serves affirmative economic purposes. But complex institutions often serve a variety of purposes—and the corporation can and sometimes is used to pursue antisocial objectives. I submit, however, that (1) objectionable purposes can normally be recognized and dealt with separately and (2) failure to understand the main purposes of the corporation has been the source of much confusion and ill-conceived public policy.[1] Specifically, antisocial purposes have often been attributed where none existed.

Inasmuch as a sensitivity to transactions and transaction-cost economizing can be traced to the 1930s (John Commons, 1934; Ronald Coase, 1937), it is somewhat surprising that the importance of the modern corporation as a means of reducing transaction costs has been so long neglected. The main reason is that the origins of transaction costs must often be sought in influences and motives that lie outside the normal domain of economics. Accordingly, a large gap separated an identification of transaction costs, as the main factor to which the study of the organization of economic activity must repair, and efforts to give operational content to that insight.

This paper is organized in two parts. Sections 1 and 2 sketch the background and set forth the arguments that are subsequently employed to interpret a series of organizational innovations that have successively yielded the modern corporation. Sections 3 and 4 deal with these changes. My discussion of organizational innovation begins with the latter half of the nineteenth century. In this regard, I follow Alfred Chandler who traces the origins of complex hierarchical forms of business organization to this period (1977). To be sure, others have identified interesting organizational developments in both Japanese[2] and English[3] business history that predate, if not prefigure, those in the U.S. But these earlier developments were not widely adopted by other firms—and in any event represent very primitive forms of divisionalization.[4] As a consequence, these earlier developments were of isolated economic importance and are properly distinguished from the general transformation of American industry that began in the nineteenth century and has continued since.

Key legal features of the corporation—limited liability and the transferability of ownership—are taken as given. Failure to discuss these does not reflect a judgment that these are either irrelevant or uninteresting. The main focus of this essay, however, is on the internal organization of the corporation. Since any of a number of internal structures is consistent with these legal features, an explanation for the spe-

---

[1] This argument is elaborated in Williamson (1981). It is briefly discussed below in conjunction with what is referred to as the "inhospitality tradition" within antitrust. See Section 1.

[2] Sadao Takatera and Nobaru Nishikawa, in an unpublished manuscript (undated), discuss the "Genesis of Divisional Management and Accounting Systems in the House of Mitsui, 1710–1730."

[3] Gary Anderson, Robert E. McCormick, and Robert D. Tollison, in an unpublished manuscript (May 1981), describe the "East India Company as a Multidivisional Enterprise" early in the 18th century.

[4] Primitive divisionalization is often confused with but needs to be distinguished from multidivisionalization. See Alfred Sloan (1965) and Chandler (1962) for a discussion of the origins of the M–form structure in the twentieth century.

cific organizational innovations that were actually adopted evidently resides elsewhere. Among the more significant of these innovations, and the ones addressed here, are: the development of line-and-staff organization by the railroads; selective forward integration by manufacturers into distribution; the development of the multidivisional corporate form; the evolution of the conglomerate; and the appearance of the multinational enterprise. The first three of these changes have been studied by business historians, the contributions of Chandler (1962; 1977) being the most ambitious and notable.

1. *Some Background*

1.1 *General*

Assessing the organization of economic activity in an advanced society requires that a bewildering variety of market, hierarchical, and mixed modes be evaluated. Economists, organization theorists, public policy specialists, and historians all have an interest and each have offered interpretations of successive organizational innovations. A coherent view, however, has not emerged.

Partly this is because the principal hierarchical structure to be assessed—the modern corporation—is formidably complex in its great size, diversity, and internal organization. The natural difficulties which thereby resulted would have been overcome sooner, however, had it not been for a number of conceptual barriers to an understanding of this institution. Chief among these are the following: (1) the neoclassical theory of the firm, which is the main referent to which economists appeal, is devoid of interesting hierarchical features; (2) organization theorists, who are specialists in the study of internal organization and unencumbered by an intellectual commitment to neoclassical economic models, have been preoccupied with hierarchy to the neglect of market

modes of organization and the healthy tension that exists between markets and hierarchies; (3) public policy analysts have maintained a deeply suspicious attitude toward nonstandard or unfamiliar forms of economic organization; and (4) organizational innovation has been relatively neglected by business and economic historians.

To be sure, this indictment sweeps too broadly. As discussed in 1.2 below, there have been important exceptions. The main features, however, are as I have described. Thus neoclassical theory treats the firm as a production function to which a profit maximization objective has been ascribed. Albeit useful for many purposes, such a construction is unhelpful in attempting to assess the purposes served by hierarchical modes of organization. The firm as production function needs to make way for the view of the *firm as governance structure* if the ramifications of internal organization are to be accurately assessed. Only recently has this latter orientation begun to make headway—and is still in a primitive state of development.

The preoccupation of organization theory specialists with internal organization is a potentially useful corrective. An understanding of the purposes served by internal organization has remained elusive, however, for at least two reasons. First, efficiency analysis plays a relatively minor role in the studies of most organization theory specialists—many of whom are more inclined to emphasize power. The economizing factors that are crucial to an understanding of the modern corporation are thus effectively suppressed. Second, and related, firms and markets are treated separately rather than in active juxtaposition with one another. The propositions that (1) firms and markets are properly regarded as alternative governance structures to which (2) transactions are to be assigned in discriminating (mainly transaction cost economizing) ways are unfa-

1540   *Journal of Economic Literature, Vol. XIX (December 1981)*

miliar to most organization theory specialists and alien to some.

Public policy analysts with an interest in the modern corporation might also have been expected to entertain a broader view. In fact, however, many of these likewise adopted a production function orientation—whereby markets were regarded as the "natural, hence efficient" way by which to mediate transactions between technologically separable entities. This was joined by a pervasive sense that the purposes of competition are invariably served by maintaining many autonomous traders. Even sensitive observers were trapped by this combined technological/atomistic logic. Thus Donald Turner, at a time when he headed the Antitrust Division, expressed skepticism over nonstandard business practices by observing that "I approach territorial and customer restrictions not hospitably in the common law tradition, but inhospitably in the tradition of antitrust law."[5] The possibility that efficiency might be served by imposing restraints on autonomous market trading was evidently thought to be slight. This inhospitality tradition also explains ingrained public policy animosity towards vertical integration and conglomerate organization; more generally, industrial organization specialists were encouraged to discover what were often fanciful "distortions" at the expense of a more basic understanding of the modern corporation in economizing terms.

The neglect of organizational innovations by business and economic historians has been general but by no means complete and shows recent signs of being corrected.[6] Mainly, however, interpreta-

tion has played a secondary role to description in most historial studies of organizational change—which, while understandable, contributes to the continuing confusion over the purposes served by the changing organizational features of the corporation.

This essay attempts to provide a coherent view of the modern corporation by (1) augmenting the model of the firm as production function to include the concept of the firm as governance structure, (2) studying firms and markets as alternative governance structures in a comparative institutional way, (3) supplanting the presumption that organizational innovations have anticompetitive purposes by the rebuttable presumption that organizational innovations are designed to economize on transaction costs, and (4) interpreting business history from a transaction cost perspective. Such an approach to the study of the modern corporation (and, more generally, to the study of organizational innovation) owes its origins to antecedent contributions of four kinds.

1.2 *Antecendents*

(a)   Theory of Firms and Markets

The unsatisfactory state of the theory of the firm was recognized by Ronald Coase in his classic 1937 article on "The Nature of the Firm." As he observed:

> Outside the firm, price movements direct production, which is co-ordinated through a series of exchange transactions on the market. Within a firm, these market transactions are eliminated and in place of the complicated market structure with exchange transactions is substituted the entrepreneur–co-ordinator, who directs production. It is clear that these are *alternative means of co-ordinating production* [1952, p. 333; emphasis added].

Coase went on to observe that firms arose because there were costs of using the price system (1952, pp. 336–38). But internal organization was no cost panacea, since it experienced distinctive costs of its own

---

[5] The quotation is attributed to Turner by Stanley Robinson, 1968, N.Y. State Bar Association, Antitrust Symposium, p. 29.

[6] For an interesting commentary and contribution, see Douglass North (1978). The earlier Lance Davis and North book, however, gave relatively little attention to institutional changes that occurred within firms (1971, p. 143).

(1952, pp. 340–42). A balance is struck when the firm has expanded to the point where "the costs of organizing an extra transaction within the firm become equal to the costs of carrying out the same transaction by means of an exchange in the open market or the costs of organizing in another firm" (1952, p. 341).

Related insight on the study of firms and markets was offered by Friedrich A. Hayek, who dismissed equilibrium economics with the observation that "the economic problem of society is mainly one of adaptation to changes in particular circumstances of time and place" (1945, p. 524), and who held that the "marvel" of the price system was that it could accomplish this without "conscious direction" (1945, p. 527). Setting aside the possibility that Hayek did not make adequate allowance for the limitations of the price system, three things are notable about these observations. First is his emphasis on change and the need to devise adaptive institutional forms. Second, his reference to particular circumstances, as distinguished from statistical aggregates, reflects a sense that economic institutions must be sensitive to dispersed knowledge of a microanalytic kind. And third was his insistence that attention to the details of social processes and economic institutions was made necessary by the "unavoidable imperfection of man's knowledge" (1945, p. 530).

The organization of firms and markets has been a subject to which Kenneth Arrow has made repeated contributions. He has addressed himself not only to the economics of the internal organization (Arrow, 1964) but also to an assessment of the powers and limits of markets (Arrow, 1969). Like Coase, he expressly recognizes that firms and markets are alternative modes of organizing economic activity (Arrow, 1974). Moreover, whereas the limits of markets were glossed over by Hayek, Arrow specifically traces these to transac-

tion cost origins: "market failure is not absolute; it is better to consider a broader category, that of transaction costs, which in general impede and in particular cases block the formation of markets" (1969, p. 48)—where by transaction costs Arrow has reference to the "costs of running the economic system" (1969, p. 48).

(b) Organization Theory

Although organization theorists have not in general regarded efficiency as their central concern, there have been notable exceptions. The early works of Chester Barnard (1938) and Herbert Simon (1947) both qualify.

Barnard was a businessman rather than a social scientist and he addressed internal organizational issues that many would regard as outside the scope of economics. Economizing was nevertheless strongly featured in his approach to the study of organizations. Understanding the employment relation was among the issues that intrigued him. Matters that concerned him in this connection included: the need to align incentives, including noneconomic inducements, to achieve enterprise viability; the importance of assent to authority; a description of the authority relation within which hierarchical organizations operate; and the role of "informal organization" in supporting the working rules upon which formal organization relies. The rationality of internal organization, making due allowance for the attributes of human actors, was a matter of continuous concern to Barnard.

Simon expressly relies on Barnard and carries rationality analysis forward. A more precise vocabulary than Barnard's is developed in the process. Simon traces the problem of organization to the joining of rational purposes with the cognitive limits of human actors: "it is precisely in the realm where human behavior is *intendedly* rational, but only *limitedly* so, that there is room for a genuine theory

1542   Journal of Economic Literature, Vol. XIX (December 1981)

of organization and administration" (1957, p. xxiv). Intended rationality supplies purpose, but meaningful economic and organizational choices arise only in a limited (or bounded) rationality context.

Simon makes repeated reference to the criterion of efficiency (1957, pp. 14, 39–41, 172–97), but he also cautions that organizational design should be informed by "a knowledge of those aspects of the social sciences which are relevant to the broader purposes of the organization" (1957, p. 246). A sensitivity to subgoal pursuit, wherein individuals identify with and pursue local goals at the possible expense of global goals[7] (Simon, 1957, p. 13), and the "outguessing" or gaming aspects of human behavior (Simon, 1957, p. 252) are among these.

Although Simon examines the merits of centralized versus decentralized modes of organization (1947, pp. 234–40), it is not until his later writing that he expressly addresses the matter of factoring problems according to rational hierarchical principles (Simon, 1962). The issues here are developed more fully in Section 2.

(c) Nonstrategic Purposes

The "inhospitality tradition" referred to above maintained a presumption of illegality when nonstandard or unfamiliar business practices were brought under review. These same practices, when viewed "through the lens of price theory"[8] by

Aaron Director (and his students and colleagues at Chicago), were regarded rather differently. Whereas Turner and others held that anticompetitive purposes were being served, Director and his associates reported instead that tie-ins, resale price maintenance, and the like were promoting more efficient resource allocation.

In fact, nonstandard business practices (such as tie-ins) are anomalies when regarded in the full information terms associated with static price theory. Implicitly, however, Chicago was also relying on the existence of transaction costs—which, after all, were the reason why comprehensive price discrimination could not be effected through simple contracts unsupported by restrictive practices from the outset.[9] Be that as it may, Chicago's insistence that economic behavior be assessed with respect to its economizing properties was a healthly antidote and encouraged further scrutiny of these same matters—with the eventual result that an economizing orientation is now much more widely held. Indirectly, these views have spilled over and influenced thinking about the modern corporation as an economizing, rather than mainly a monopolizing, entity.[10]

(d) Business History

The study of organizational innovation has been relatively neglected by business and economic historians. Aside from the Research Center in Entrepreneurial History at Harvard, which was established in 1948 and closed its doors a decade later, there has not been a concerted effort to work through and establish the impor-

---

[7] The term "local goals" subsumes both the functional goals of a subunit of the enterprise and the individual goals of the functional managers. In a perfectly harmonized system, private goals are consonant with functional goals, the realization of which in turn promotes global goals. Frequently, however, managers become advocates for parochial interests that conflict with global goal attainment. If, for example, R&D claims a disproportionate share of resources—because of effective but distorted partisan representations from the management and staff of this group—profits (global goals) will suffer. Aggressive subgoal (or local goal) pursuit of this kind is a manifestation of opportunism (see 2.2, below).

[8] The phrase is Richard Posner's (1979, p. 928).

[9] For a discussion of this point, see Williamson (1975, pp. 11–13, 109–10).

[10] Although the nonstrategic tradition inspired by Aaron Director makes insufficient allowance for anticompetitive behavior, it was a useful counterweight to the inhospitality tradition to which it was paired. For a critique of the more extreme versions of this nonstrategic—or, as Posner (1979, p. 932) puts it, the "diehard Chicago"—tradition, see Williamson (1981).

tance of organizational innovation. Probably the most important reason for this neglect is that business history has not had "the support of an established system of theory" (Henrietta Larson, 1948, p. 135).

Despite this general neglect, notable contributions have nevertheless been made. The works of Lance Davis and Douglass North (1971) and of Alfred Chandler (1962; 1977) have been especially important. The first of these takes a sweeping view of institutional change and employs a market failure theory for assessing successive changes. It pays only limited attention, however, to the corporation as a unit whose attributes need to be assessed.[11]

Chandler, by contrast, is expressly and deeply concerned with the organization form changes which, over the past 150 years, have brought us the modern corporation as we know it. The story is told in two parts, the first being the evolution of the large, multifunctional enterprise (Chandler, 1977), the second being the subsequent divisionalization of these firms (Chandler, 1962). Both of these transformations are described and interpreted in Sections 3 and 4 below. Suffice it to observe here that (1) Chandler's is the first treatment of business history that de-

scribes organizational changes in sufficient detail to permit a transaction cost interpretation to be applied, (2) Chandler's 1962 book was significant not only for its business history contributions but because it clearly established that organization form had an important impact on business performance—which neither economics nor organization theory had done (nor, for the most part, even attempted) previously, and (3) although Chandler is more concerned with the description than with the interpretation of organizational change, his careful descriptions are nevertheless suggestive of the economic factors that are responsible for the changes observed.

2. Transaction Cost Economics

Each of the antecedent literatures just described has a bearing on the transaction-cost approach to the study of economic institutions in general and the modern corporation in particular. Following Commons (1934), the transaction is made the basic unit of analysis. Specifically, attention is focused on the transaction costs of running the economic system (Coase, 1937; Arrow, 1969), with emphasis on adaptation to unforeseen, and often unforeseeable, circumstances (Hayek, 1945). The issues of special interest are connected with the changing structure of the corporation over the past 150 years (Chandler, 1962; 1977). Rather than regard these inhospitably, the new approach maintains the rebuttable presumption that the evolving corporate structure has the purpose and effect of economizing on transaction costs. These transaction-cost and business history literatures are linked by appeal to selective parts of the (mainly older) organization theory literature.

As Barnard (1938) emphasized, differences in internal organization often had significant performance consequences and could and should be assessed from a rationality viewpoint. Simon (1947) ex-

---

[11] Davis and North make repeated reference to the limited liability and unlimited life features of the corporate form and explicitly discuss the importance of organizational changes made by the railroads (1971, pp. 143–44). Their treatment of organization form changes in manufacturing, however, emphasizes economies of scale, monopolization (cartelization), protection against foreign competition, and resistence to regulation (1971, pp. 167–90). A sense that the corporation is progressively refining structures that economize on transaction costs—in labor, capital, and intermediate product markets— is nowhere suggested.

Although this is partly rectified in North's recent survey paper, where he observes that recent organizational changes have had transaction cost origins, he defines transaction costs narrowly in terms of the "measurement of the separable dimensions of a good or services" (1978, p. 971). As developed below, measurement is only one aspect—and not, in my judgment, the most important one—for understanding the modern corporation.

tended and refined the argument that internal organization mattered and that the study of internal organization needed to make appropriate allowance for the attributes of human actors—for what Frank Knight has felicitously referred to as "human nature as we know it" (1965, p. 270). Then, and only then, does the comparative institutional assessment of alternative organizational forms take on its full economic significance.

2.1 Comparative Institutional Analysis

The costs of running the economic system to which Arrow refers can be usefully thought of in contractual terms. Each feasible mode of conducting relations between technologically separable entities can be examined with respect to the ex ante costs of negotiating and writing, as well as the ex post costs of executing, policing, and, when disputes arise, remedying the (explicit or implicit) contract that joins them.

A transaction may thus be said to occur when a good or service is transferred across a technologically separable interface. One stage of processing or assembly activity terminates and another begins. A mechanical analogy, while imperfect, may nevertheless be useful. A well-working interface, like a well-working machine, can be thought of as one where these transfers occur smoothly.

In neither case, however, is smoothness desired for its own sake: the benefits must be judged in relation to the cost. Both investment and operating features require attention. Thus extensive prior investment in finely tuned equipment and repeated lubrication and adjustment during operation are both ways of attenuating friction, slippage, or other loss of mechanical energy. Similarly, extensive pre-contract negotiation that covers all relevant contingencies may avoid the need for periodic intervention to realign the interface during execution so that a contract may

be brought successfully to completion. Simultaneous attention to both investment (pre-contract costs) and operating expenses (harmonizing costs) is needed if mechanical (contractual) systems are to be designed effectively. The usual study of economizing · in a production function framework is thus extended to include an examination of the *comparative costs of planning, adapting, and monitoring task completion under alternative governance structures*—where by governance structure I have reference to the explicit or implicit contractual framework within which a transaction is located (markets, firms, and mixed modes—e.g., franchising—included).

The study of transaction-cost economizing is thus a comparative institutional undertaking which recognizes that there are a variety of distinguishably different transactions on the one hand and a variety of alternative governance structures on the other. The object is to match governance structures to the attributes of transactions in a discriminating way. Microanalytic attention to differences among governance structures and microanalytic definition of transactions are both needed in order for this to be accomplished.

Although more descriptive detail than is associated with neoclassical analysis is needed for this purpose, a relatively crude assessment will often suffice. As Simon has observed, comparative institutional analysis commonly involves an examination of discrete structural alternatives for which marginal analysis is not required: "In general, much cruder and simpler arguments will suffice to demonstrate an inequality between two quantities than are required to show the conditions under which these quantities are equated at the margin" (1978, p. 6).

2.2 Behavioral Assumptions

Human nature as we know it is marvelously rich and needs to be reduced to manageable proportions. The two behavioral assumptions on which transaction-cost analysis relies—and without which the study of economic organization is pointless—are bounded rationality and opportunism. As a consequence of these two assumptions, the human agents that populate the firms and markets with which I am concerned differ from economic man (or at least the common caricature thereof) in that they are less competent in calculation and less trustworthy and reliable in action. A condition of bounded rationality is responsible for the computational limits of organization man. A proclivity for (at least some) economic agents to behave opportunistically is responsible for their unreliability.

The term bounded rationality was coined by Simon to reflect the fact that economic actors, who may be presumed to be "intendedly rational," are not hyperrational. Rather, they experience limits in formulating and solving complex problems and in processing (receiving, storing, retrieving, transmitting) information (Simon, 1957, p. 198). Opportunism is related to but is a somewhat more general term that the condition of "moral hazard" to which Knight referred in his classic statement of economic organization (1965, pp. 251–56).[12] Opportunism effectively extends the usual assumption of self-interest seeking to make allowance for self-interest seeking with guile.

But for the *simultaneous* existence of both bounded rationality and opportun-

ism,[13] all economic contracting problems are trivial and the study of economic institutions is unimportant. Thus, but for bounded rationality, all economic exchange could be effectively organized by contract. Indeed, the economic theory of comprehensive contracting has been fully worked out.[14] Given bounded rationality, however, it is impossible to deal with complexity in all contractually relevant respects (Radner, 1968). As a consequence, incomplete contracting is the best that can be achieved.

Ubiquitous, albeit incomplete, contracting would nevertheless be feasible if economic agents were completely trustworthy. Principals would simply extract promises from agents that they will behave in a stewardship fashion, while agents would reciprocally ask principals to behave in good faith. Such devices will not work, however, if some economic actors (either principals or agents) are dishonest (or, more generally, disguise attributes or preferences, distort data, obfuscate issues, and otherwise confuse transactions) and it is very costly to distinguish opportunistic from nonopportunistic types ex ante.

Although the dual assumptions of bounded rationality and opportunism complicate the study of economic behavior and may be inessential for some purposes, the study of alternative modes of organization does not qualify as an excep-

---

[12] Moral hazard is a technical term with a well defined meaning in the insurance literature. It refers to an ex post insurance condition and is clearly distinguished from adverse selection, which is responsible for a troublesome ex ante insurance screening problem. Opportunism is a less technical but more general term that applies to a wide set of economic behavior—of which adverse selection and moral hazard are specific kinds. Unless, therefore, moral hazard is given a broader meaning, the substitution of moral hazard for opportunism focuses attention on a subset of the full range of human and economic conditions of concern.

[13] The co-existence of cunning and bounded rationality is troublesome to some. How can economic agents simultaneously be more clever and less competent than the hyperrational man that populates neoclassical models? Is he a maximizer or is he not? This is not a useful dichotomy. Maximizing is an analytical convenience the use of which is often justified by the fact that human agents are "*intendedly* rational" (Simon, 1957b, p. xxiv). As discussed in the text, however, comprehensive contracting, which is an ambitious form of maximizing, is infeasible. Opportunism has important economic ramifications for this reason.

[14] I have reference, of course, to the Arrow–Debreu contracting model.

1546   *Journal of Economic Literature, Vol. XIX (December 1981)*

tion. To the contrary, failure to recognize and make allowance for both is virtually to invite mistaken assessments of alternative modes.[15] Taking these two behavioral assumptions into account, the following compact statement of the problem of economic organization is suggested: assess alternative governance structures in terms of their capacities to economize on bounded rationality while simultaneously safeguarding transactions against opportunism. This is not inconsistent with the imperative "maximize profits!," but it focuses attention somewhat differently.

2.3 *Dimensionalizing*

As Coase observed in 1972, his 1937 paper was "much cited but little used" (1972, p. 63). The reasons for this are many, including a preoccupation by economists with other matters during the intervening 35 years. The main reason, however, is that transaction costs had not been operationalized and it was not obvious how this could be accomplished.

The postwar market failure literature, especially Arrow's insight (1969) that market failures had transaction costs origins, served to focus attention on the troublesome issues. A recognition that market (and internal) failures of all kinds could be ultimately traced to the human factors described above was a second step. The remaining step was to identify the critical dimensions with respect to which transactions differ.

The attributes of transactions that are of special interest to the economics of organization are: (1) the frequency with which transactions recur, (2) the uncertainty to which transactions are subject,[16] and (3) the degree to which transactions are supported by durable, transaction-specific investments (Williamson, 1979). A considerable amount of explanatory power turns on the last.[17]

Asset specificity can arise in any of three ways: site specificity, as when successive stations are located in cheek-by-jowl relation to each other so as to economize on inventory and transportation expenses; physical asset specificity, as where specialized dies are required to produce a component; and human asset specificity that arises in a learning-by-doing fashion. The reason why asset specificity is critical is that, once the investment has been made, buyer and seller are effectively operating in a bilateral (or at least quasi-bilateral) exchange relation for a considerable period thereafter. Inasmuch as the value of highly specific capital in other uses is, by definition, much smaller than the specialized use for which it has been intended, the supplier is effectively "locked into" the transaction to a significant degree. This is symmetrical, moreover, in that the buyer cannot turn to alternative sources of supply and obtain the item on favorable terms, since the cost of supply from unspecialized capital is presumably great. The buyer is thus committed to the transaction as well. Accordingly, where asset specificity is great, buyer and seller will make special efforts to design an exchange relation that has good continuity properties. Autonomous contracting gives way to

---

[15] The argument that effective ex ante competition for the right to supply service (franchise bidding) vitiates the need to regulate decreasing cost industries sometimes goes through but not always. Incomplete contracting (bounded rationality) coupled with the hazards of ex post opportunism place great strain on the franchise bidding mode if assets are durable and specific. For a critique of what I believe was a mistaken assessment of the feasibility of using franchise bidding for CATV, see Williamson (1976).

[16] As Knight observes: "With uncertainty entirely absent, every individual being in possession of perfect knowledge of the situation, there would be no occasion for anything of the nature of responsible management or control of productive activity" (1965, p. 267).

[17] Williamson (1979). Also see Benjamin Klein, Robert Crawford, and Armen Alchian (1978) for an illuminating discussion of transaction specific investments in the context of what they refer to as "appropriable quasi-rents."

more complex forms of market contracting and sometimes to internal organization for this reason.

2.4 Three Principles of Organizational Design

The criterion for organizing commercial transactions is assumed to be the
strictly instrumental one of cost economizing. Essentially this takes two parts:
economizing on production expense and
economizing of transaction costs. In fact,
these are not independent and need to
be addressed simultaneously. The study
of the latter, however, is much less well
developed and is emphasized here.

The three principles of organizational
design employed here are neither exhaus-
tive nor refined. They nevertheless offer
considerable explanatory power in dealing with the main changes in corporate
organization reported by Chandler and
addressed here. Transaction cost reasoning supports all three, although only
the first, the asset-specificity principle,
is tightly linked to dimensionalizing.
Bounded rationality and opportunism,
however, operate with respect to all three.

The asset-specificity principle turns on
the above described transformation of an
exchange relation from a large-numbers
to a small-numbers condition during the
course of contract execution. The second,
the externality principle, is often discussed under the heading of "free rider"
effects. The more general phenomenon,
however, is that of subgoal pursuit, that
is, in the course of executing contracts,
agents also pursue private goals which
may be in some degree inconsistent with
the contract's intended purpose. These
two principles influence the choice of contracting form (mainly firm or market). In
fact, however, the efficacy of internal organization depends on whether sound
principles of internal organizational design are respected, which is to say that
the details of internal organization matter.

The hierarchical decomposition principle
deals with this last.

It will be convenient to assume that
transactions will be organized by markets
unless market exchange gives rise to serious transaction costs. In the beginning, so
to speak, there were markets. Both bureaucratic and production cost considerations favor this presumption. The bureaucratic argument is simply this: market
exchange serves to attenuate the bureaucratic distortions to which internal exchange is subject. (Although the reasons
for this have been set out elsewhere—
James Thompson, 1967, pp. 152–54; Williamson, 1975, Chapter 7—the study of
firm and market organization is greatly
in need of a more adequate theory of bu-
reaucracy.) The production cost advantages of market procurement are three:
static scale economies can be more fully
exhausted by buying rather than making
if the firm's needs are small in relation
to the market; markets can aggregate un-
correlated demands, to thereby realize
risk pooling benefits; and markets may enjoy economies of scope[18] in supplying a
related set of activities of which the firm's
requirements are only one. Accordingly,
transactions will be organized in markets
unless transaction cost disabilities appear.[19]

---

[18] Whereas scale economies refer to declining average costs associated with increasing output of a
single line of commerce, scope economies are realized "where it is less costly to combine two or more
product lines in one firm rather than to produce
them separately" (John Panzar and Robert Willig,
1981, p. 268). Retail outlets that carry many products
and brands (drug stores, department stores) presumably enjoy significant economies of scope in the retailing function.

[19] Bureaucratic disabilities aside, any given firm
could realize all of these production benefits for itself
by an appropriate increase in the scale and scope
of its activities. Pursuit of this logic, however, leads
to the following anomaly: all firms, of which there
will be few, will be comprehensively integrated and
diversified in sufficient degree to obviate the need
for market exchange. The fact that we do not observe
comprehensive integration—as Coase puts it, "Why
is not all production carried on by one big firm?"

(a) Asset Specificity Principle (All Transactions)

Recall that transactions are described in terms of three attributes: frequency, uncertainty, and asset specificity. Although interesting organizational issues are posed when transactions are of only an occasional kind (Williamson, 1979, pp. 245–54), this paper deals entirely with the governance of recurring transactions. Also, it will facilitate the analysis to hold uncertainty constant in intermediate degree—which is to say that we are dealing neither with steady state nor highly uncertain events. Accordingly, asset specificity is the transactional dimension of special interest. The first principle of efficient organizational design is this: *the normal presumption that recurring transactions for technologically separable goods and services will be efficiently mediated by autonomous market contracting is progressively weakened as asset specificity increases.*

The production cost advantages of markets decrease and the (comparative) governance costs of markets increase as assets become progressively more specific. Thus as assets become more fully specialized to a single use or user, hence are less transferable to other uses and users, economies of scale can be as fully realized when a firm operates the asset under its own internal direction as when its services are obtained externally by contract. And the market's advantage in pooling risks likewise shrinks. Simultaneously, the transactions in question take on a stronger bilateral character, and the governance costs of markets increase relatively.

The distinction between ex ante and ex post competition is essential to an understanding of this condition. What may have been (and commonly is) an effective large-numbers-bidding situation at the outset is sometimes *transformed* into a bilateral trading relation thereafter. This obtains if, despite the fact that large numbers of qualified bidders were prepared to enter competitive bids for the initial contract, the winning bidder realizes advantages over nonwinners at contract renewal intervals because nontrivial investments in durable specific assets are put in place (or otherwise accrue, say in a learning-by-doing fashion) during contract execution. As set out elsewhere (Williamson, 1979), the efficient governance of recurring transactions will vary as follows: classical market contracting will be efficacious wherever assets are nonspecific to the trading parties; bilateral or obligational market contracting will appear as assets become semi-specific; and internal organization will displace markets as assets take on a highly specific character.[20]

Internal organization enjoys advantages over market contracting for transactions that are supported by highly specific assets at both contract-writing and contract-execution stages. Since highly specific assets cannot be redeployed without sacrificing productivity, both suppliers and purchasers will insist upon contractual safeguards before undertaking such projects. Writing and negotiating such contracts is costly. Additionally, implementation problems

---

(1952, p. 340)—suggests that the bureaucratic disabilities of internal organization are very serious. But since we do observe that some transactions are organized within firms, this poses the question of which and why. The answer resides in the transaction cost disabilities of markets that arise when asset specificity and demand externalities appear.

[20] Note that the nature of the asset specificity matters. If the assets in question are mobile and the specificity is due to physical but not human asset features, market procurement may still be feasible. This can be accomplished by having the buyer own the specific assets (e.g., dies). He puts the business up for bid and awards it to the low bidder, to whom he ships the dies. Should contractual difficulties arise, however, he is not locked into a bilateral exchange. He reclaims the dies and reopens the bidding. This option is not available if the specific assets are of a human asset kind or if they are nonmobile. See David Teece (1980) for a related discussion.

need to be faced. The internal direction of firms confers execution advantages over bilateral trading in three respects. First, common ownership reduces the incentives of the trading units to pursue local goals. Second, and related, internal organization is able to invoke fiat to resolve differences whereas costly adjudication is needed when an impasse develops between autonomous traders. Third, internal organization has easier and more complete access to the relevant information when disputes must be settled. The incentive to shift bilateral transactions from markets to firms also increases as uncertainty increases, since the costs of harmonizing a relation among parties vary directly with the need to adjust to changing circumstances.

(b) Externality Principle (Forward Integration)

Whereas the asset specificity principle refers to transactions that are transformed from large- to small-numbers bidding situations—as buyers, who initially obtained assets or their services in a competitive market, subsequently face suppliers with some degree of monopoly power—the externality principle involves no such market transformation. Also, the asset-specificity principle applies to backward, forward, and lateral integration; by contrast, the externality principle mainly applies to distribution stages.

The externalities of concern are those that arise in conjunction with the unintended debasement of quality for a branded good or service. As discussed below, such debasement is explained by costly metering. The externality is thus a manifestation of the measurement problems to which North refers in his discussion of transaction costs (1978, p. 972). It appears mainly at the interface between production and distribution. The differential ease of inspecting, and thereby controlling, the quality of components and materials that are purchased from earlier-stage and lateral suppliers as compared with the cost of exercising quality controls over distributors is responsible for this condition.[21]

End-games and fly-by-night distributors aside, the unintended debasement of quality by distributors poses a problem only where the activities of individual distributors affect one another, as when one retailer's poor service in installation or repair injures a product's reputation for performance and limits the sales of other retailers. More generally, if the quality enhancement (debasement) efforts of distributors give rise to positive (negative) externalities, the benefits (costs) of which can be incompletely appropriated by (assigned to) the originators, failure to extend quality controls over distribution will result in suboptimization. Autonomous contracting thus gives way to obligational market contracting (e.g., franchising) if not forward integration into distribution[22] as demand interaction effects become more important. More generally, the second principle of efficient organizational design is this: *the normal presumption that exchange between producers of differentiated goods and distribution stages will be efficiently mediated by autonomous contracting is progressively weakened as demand externalities increase.*

Product differentiation is a necessary but not a sufficient condition for troublesome demand externalities to appear. Manufacturers can sometimes insulate a product against deterioration by special packaging (say by selling the item in hermetic containers with an inert atmosphere and providing replacement guar-

[21] Manufacturers may, of course, decide to integrate into components if work-in-process inspections are much cheaper than final inspections.

[22] Franchising will be more prevalent if aggregation economies are present at the distribution stage. It will be inefficient in these circumstances for a single product firm to integrate forward into distribution.

1550   *Journal of Economic Literature, Vol. XIX (December 1981)*

antees). If, however, such safeguards are very costly, and if follow-on checks and penalties to discourage distributors from debasing the quality image of a product are likewise expensive, autonomous trading will give way to forms of distribution that have superior quality control properties.

(c) Hierarchical Decomposition Principle (Internal Organization)[23]

Merely to transfer a transaction out of the market into the firm does not, by itself, assure that the activity will be effectively organized thereafter. Not only are bounded rationality and opportunism ubiquitous, but the problems presented by both vary with changes in internal organization. Accordingly, a complete theory of value will recognize that firm structure as well as market structure matters.

Simon makes provision for bounded rationality effects in arguing that the organizational division of decision making labor is quite as important as the neoclassical division of production labor, where, from "the information processing point of view, division of labor means factoring the total system of decisions that need to be made into relatively independent subsystems, each one of which can be designed with only minimal concern for its interactions with the others" (Simon, 1973, p. 270). This applies to both vertical and horizontal aspects of the organization. In both respects the object is to recognize and give effect to conditions of near decomposability. The vertical slice entails grouping the operating parts into separable entities, the interactions within which are strong and between which are weak. The horizontal

slice has temporal ramifications of a strategic versus operating kind. Problems are thus factored in such a way that the higher frequency (or short run dynamics) are associated with the operating parts while the lower frequency (or long run dynamics) are associated with the strategic system (Simon, 1962, p. 477). These operating and strategic distinctions correspond with the lower and higher levels in the organizational hierarchy, respectively. Internal incentives and information flows need, of course, to be aligned, lest distortions be deliberately or inadvertently introduced into the internal information summary and transmittal processes.

The hierarchical decomposition principle can thus be stated as follows: *internal organization should be designed in such a way as to effect quasi-independence between the parts, the high frequency dynamics (operating activities) and low frequency dynamics (strategic planning) should be clearly distinguished, and incentives should be aligned within and between components* so as to promote both local and global effectiveness.

Each of these three principles of organizational design is responsive to considerations of both bounded rationality and opportunism. Thus asset specificity would pose no problems if comprehensive contracting were feasible (which is tantamount to unbounded rationality) or if winning bidders could be relied upon to behave in an utterly reliable and trustworthy fashion (absence of opportunism). The externality principle is mainly a reflection of opportunism (autonomous distributors permit their suppliers' reputations to be degraded because they bear only part of the costs), but, of course, quality control checks would be unneeded if all relevant information could be costlessly displayed and assessed. The hierarchical decomposition principle recognizes the need to divide problems into manageable units and at the same time prevent agents from en-

---

[23] The hierarchical decomposition principle is due to Simon (1962; 1973). As he observes, the anatomy of an organization can be viewed either in terms of the groupings of human beings or the flows and transformations of symbols (1973, p. 270). He emphasizes the latter, which is in the spirit of transaction cost analysis.

gaging in dysfunctional pursuit of local goals, which reflect bounded rationality and opportunism concerns, respectively.

A more comprehensive analysis would embed these principles of organization within a larger optimizing framework where demand as well as cost consequences are recognized and where production versus transaction costs tradeoffs are made explicit.[24] For the purposes at hand, however, which take product design as given and focus on distinguishably different rather than close cases, such refinements do not appear to be necessary.

3. The Nineteenth Century Corporation

The 1840s mark the beginning of a great wave of organizational change that has evolved into the modern corporation (Chandler, 1977). According to Stuart Bruchey, the fifteenth century merchant of Venice would have understood the form of organization and methods of managing men, records, and investment used by Baltimore merchants in 1790 (1956, pp.

---

[24] Thus, whereas I argue that the object is to minimize the sum of production and transaction costs, taking output and design as given, the more general problem is to maximize profits, treating output and design as decision variables. A rudimentary statement of the optimizing problem, for a given organization form (f), is to choose output (Q) and design (D) so as to maximize:

$$\pi(Q,D;f) = P(Q,D) \cdot Q - C_f(Q,D;S) - G_f(Q,D),$$

where π denotes profit, $P(Q,D)$ is the demand curve, S denotes combinatorial economies of scope, and C_f and G_f are the production costs and governance (transaction) costs of mode f. Transaction costs become relatively more important to this calculus as the assets needed to support specialized designs become progressively more specific—which they normally will as designs become more idiosyncratic.

Plainly the tradeoffs that run through this optimizing relation are more extensive than my earlier discussion discloses, but a detailed assessment of these is not needed for the types of purposes to which the asset specificity principle is herein applied. Both the externality and hierarchical decomposition principles should likewise be qualified to recognize tradeoffs. Again, however, second order refinements are not needed for the comparative institutional purposes to which these are applied below.

370–71). These practices evidently remained quite serviceable until after the 1840s. The two most significant developments were the appearance of the railroads and, in response to this, forward integration by manufacturers into distribution.

3.1 The Railroads

Although a number of technological developments—including the telegraph (Chandler, 1977, p. 189), the development of continuous process machinery (Chandler, pp. 252–53), the refinement of interchangeable parts manufacture (Chandler, 1977, pp. 75–77), and related mass manufacturing techniques (Chandler, Chap. 8)—contributed to organizational changes in the second half of the nineteenth century, none was more important than the railroads (Glenn Porter and Harold Livesay, 1971, p. 55). Not only did the railroads pose distinctive organizational problems of their own, but the incentive to integrate forward from manufacturing into distribution would have been much less without the low cost, reliable, all-weather transportation afforded by the railroads. Forward integration is discussed in 3.2 below; the railroads are treated here.

The appearance and purported importance of the railroads have been matters of great interest to economic historians. But with very few exceptions, the organizational—as opposed to the technological—significance of the railroads has been neglected. Thus Robert Fogel (1964) and Albert Fishlow (1965) "investigated the railroad as a construction activity and as a means of transport, but not as an organizational form. As with most economists, the internal workings of the railroad organizations were ignored. This appears to be the result of an implicit assumption that the organization form used to accomplish an objective does not matter" (Peter Temin, 1980, p. 3).

The economic success of the railroads

entailed more, however, than the substitution of one technology (rails) for another (canals). Rather, organizational aspects also required attention. As Chandler puts it:

> [the] safe, regular, reliable movement of goods and passengers, as well as the continuing maintenance and repair of locomotives, rolling stock, and track, roadbed, stations, roundhouses, and other equipment, required the creation of a sizeable administrative organization. It meant the employment of a set of managers to supervise these functional activities over an extensive geographical area; and the appointment of an administrative command of middle and top executives to monitor, evaluate, and coordinate the work of managers responsible for the day-to-day operations. It meant, too, the formulation of brand new types of internal administrative procedures and accounting and statistical controls. Hence, the operational requirements of the railroads demanded the creation of the first administrative hierarchies in American business [1977, p. 87].

The "natural" railroad units, as these first evolved, were lines of about fifty miles in length. These roads employed about fifty workers and were administered by a superintendent and several managers of functional activities (Chandler, 1977, p. 96). This was adequate as long as traffic flows were uncomplicated and short hauls prevailed. The full promise of the railroads could be realized, however, only if traffic densities were increased and longer hauls introduced. How was this to be effected?

In principle, successive end-to-end systems could be joined by contract. The resulting contracts would be tightly bilateral in negotiation, interpretation and execution, however, since investments in site-specific assets by each party were considerable. Severe contractual difficulties would, therefore, predictably arise.[25] Un-

less supporting governance structure were simultaneously created,[26] the potential of the railroads for long-haul and high-density traffic would evidently go unrealized. One possibility was for heavily traveled end-to-end links to be joined under common ownership.

But while the consolidation of ownership reduced the restraints on long-haul operations, it did not guarantee that the end-to-end systems would work smoothly. Indeed, early operation of the Western and Albany road, which was just over 150 miles in length and was built in three sections each operated as a separate division with its own set of functional managers, quickly proved otherwise (Chandler, 1977, pp. 96–97). As a consequence, a new organizational structure was fashioned whereby the first "formal administrative structure manned by full-time salaried managers" in the U.S. appeared (Chandler, 1977, pp. 97–98).

This structure was progressively perfected, and the organizational innovation that the railroads eventually evolved is characterized by Chandler as the "decentralized line-and-staff concept of organization." This provided that "the managers on the line of authority were responsible for ordering men involved with the basic function of the enterprise, and other functional managers (the staff executives) were responsible for setting standards" (Chandler, 1977, p. 106). Geographic divisions were defined and the superintendents in charge were held responsible for the "day-to-day movement of trains and traffic by

---

[25] Problems of two kinds would need to be faced. Not only would the railroads need to reach agreement on how to deal with a series of complex operating matters—equipment utilization, costing, and maintenance; adapting cooperatively to unantici-

pated disturbances; assigning responsibility for customer complaints, breakdown, etc.—but problems of customers contracting with a set of autonomous end-to-end suppliers would need to be worked out. Plainly, complex contracting issues proliferate.

[26] Railroad regulation can be interpreted, in part, as an effort to deal with these contractual difficulties by inventing specialized governance structures. Pursuit of these matters is beyond the scope of this paper. Aspects of the general problem are dealt with in Williamson (1976) and Victor Goldberg (1976).

an express delegation of authority" (Chandler, 1977, p. 102). These division superintendents were on the "direct line of authority from the president through the general superintendent" (Chandler, 1977, p. 106), and the functional managers within the geographic divisions—who dealt with transportation, motive power, maintenance of way, passenger, freight, and accounting—reported to them rather than to their functional superiors at the central office (Chandler, 1977, pp. 106–07).

Confronted, as they were, by the contractual dilemmas that arise when highly specific assets are in place and by complexities that exceeded, perhaps by several orders of magnitude, those that had been faced by earlier business enterprise, the managements of the railroads supplanted markets by hierarchies of a carefully crafted kind. Although military organizations had earlier devised similar structures, the railroad innovators brought engineering rather than military backgrounds to the task (Chandler, 1977, Chapter 3). The hierarchical structure that they evolved was consistent, at least broadly, with the hierarchical principles stated by Simon. Thus support activities (lower frequency dynamics) were split off from operations (higher frequency dynamics), and the linkages within each of these classes of activity were stronger than the linkages between. This organizational innovation, in Chandler's judgment, paved the way for modern business enterprise. As with most significant organizational developments, it evolved in a piecemeal rather than a full-blown way (Richard Nelson and Sidney Winter, 1981). Failure to recognize the opportunities for decomposition of functions and to perfect the hierarchical governance structures by which these could be realized would have arrested the development of the modern corporation at a very primitive stage.

3.2 Forward Integration

Forward integration by manufacturers into distribution was one of the significant consequences of the appearance of the railroads. Low cost transportation combined with telegraph and telephone communication permitted manufacturers efficiently to service a larger market and, as a consequence, realize greater economies of scale in production. The points of connection between manufacturing, wholesaling, and retailing, however, also required attention. Forward integration was a common but by no means uniform response. To the contrary, it was highly selective rather than comprehensive, and it is this selectivity that is the matter of special interest to this paper.

At least four degrees of forward integration can be recognized. From least to most, these are:

A: none—in which event traditional wholesale and retail distribution was continued (many grocery, drug, hardware, jewelry, liquor, and dry goods items were of this kind) [Porter and Livesay, 1971, p. 214].

B: minor—efforts to presell product and to monitor wholesale inventories, but not to include the ownership and operation of wholesale plants, are examples. Certain branded nondurables (soups, soaps), especially those for which staling was a problem (cigarettes, cereals), are included.

C: wholesale—this was undertaken for perishable, branded items that required special handling;[27] often specialized investments in refrigeration were involved (meat and beer are examples). [Chandler, 1977, p. 299].

---

[27] The Whitman candy case involved the use of two different merchandising methods. Wholesalers were bypassed in the sale of high-grade, packaged candies. Small, inexpensive, bar and packaged candies, by contrast, were sold through the usual jobber and wholesale grocer network. Control of the wholesaling function for the former was arguably more important for quality control purposes. These high-grade items were "sold directly to retailers so that the company could regulate the flow of the perishable items and avoid alienating customers," (Porter and Livesy, 1971, p. 220)—who were presumably prepared to pay a premium to avoid stale candy.

D: retail–integration into retail was rare and was reserved for "new, complex, high priced machines that required specialized marketing services—demonstration, installation, consumer credit, after-sales service and repair" (Chandler, 1977, p. 288). Certain consumer durables (sewing machines, automobiles) and producer durables (some electrical machinery and office machines) were of this kind.

Actually, there is a variant of this fourth category that I will designate "mistaken" retail integration. Such integration involved none of the transaction specific investments in sales and service referred to above but had the purpose of foreclosing rivals. The ill-fated efforts of American Tobacco to integrate forward into the wholesaling and retailing of cigars (Porter and Livesay, 1971, p. 210) and of American Sugar Refining to "drive its competitor John Arbuckle out of business by buying into wholesale and retail houses" (Porter and Livesay, 1971, p. 211, p. 52) are examples.[28]

The question is how to interpret these developments. Although the data that would be needed for a quantitative analysis have yet to be worked up, a systematic qualitative interpretation along the lines of the discussion in Sections 2.2 and 2.3 above is nevertheless feasible. The attributes of the five integration classes are set out in Table 1, where ++ denotes considerable, + denotes some, ~ is uncertain, and 0 is negligible.

Markets remain the main mode for effecting distribution for classes A and B. Markets enjoy substantial economies of scope for these products while asset specificity is negligible and externalities are

dealt with by monitoring inventory. Integration into wholesale occurs for products that involve some asset specificity (refrigeration) and the reputation of branded products needs protection. Integration into retail does not occur, however, until asset specificity at the retail level is great (and these are products for which separate sales and service entails negligible loss of scope economies).[29] Finally, mistaken retail integration involves the sacrifice of scope economies without offsetting governance cost benefits (externalities and asset specificity are negligible). This pattern of integration is broadly consistent with transaction cost reasoning and explains why forward integration occurred selectively rather than comprehensively in response to the transportation and communication infrastructure.[30]

TABLE 1			
Integration Class	Economies of Scope	Externalities	Asset Specificity
A: none	++	0	0
B: minor	+	+	0
C: wholesale	~	+	+
D_1: retail/viable	0	+	++
D_2: retail/mistaken	+	0	0

4. The 20th Century Corporation

Three developments are particularly noteworthy in the evolution of the modern corporation in the 20th century. The first of these was the appearance of the

---

[28] This is not to say that foreclosure will never be successful unless accompanied by transaction specific investments. But it should not entail sacrifice of scale economies. Forward integration by the motion picture producers into theatres may have been a viable means of foreclosing entry into the production stage because theatre ownership by major producers entailed little or no sacrifice of scale economies.

[29] Concessions in department stores are devices for effecting retail sales for products that are efficiently marketed in conjunction with others but which nevertheless require transaction specific investments. Chandler does not discuss such products, but a more comprehensive microanalytic analysis would, I conjecture, disclose the existence of some where mixed modes arise because aggregation economies and asset specificity are simultaneously present.

[30] For a more complete assessment, on which the above is based, see Williamson (1980).

multidivisional (or M–form) organization. Later developments are the conglomerate and the multinational corporation.

4.1 *The Multidivisional Structure*

The most significant organizational innovation of the 20th century was the development in the 1920s of the multidivisional structure. Surprisingly, this development was little noted or widely appreciated as late as 1960. Leading management texts extolled the virtues of "basic departmentation" and "line and staff authority relationships," but the special importance of multidivisionalization went unremarked.[31]

Chandler's pathbreaking study of business history, *Strategy and Structure,* simply bypassed this management literature. He advanced the thesis that "changing developments in business organization presented a challenging area for comparative analysis" and observed that "the study of [organizational] innovation seemed to furnish the proper focus for such an investigation" (1966, p. 2). Having identified the multidivisional structure as one of the more important of such innovations, he proceeded to trace its origins, identify the factors that gave rise to its appearance, and describe the subsequent diffusion of this organizational form. It was uninformed and untenable to argue that organization form was of no account after the appearance of Chandler's book.

The leading figures in the creation of the multidivisional (or M–form) structure were Pierre S. du Pont and Alfred P. Sloan; the period was the early 1920s; the firms were Du Pont and General Motors; and the organizational strain of trying to cope with economic adversity under the old structure was the occasion to innovate in both. The structures of the two companies, however, were different.

[31] The treatment of these matters by Harold Koontz and Cyril O'Donnell (1955) is representative.

Du Pont was operating under the centralized, functionally departmentalized or unitary (U–form) structure. General Motors, by contrast, had been operated more like a holding company by William Durant—whose genius in perceiving market opportunities in the automobile industry (Livesay, 1979, pp. 232–34) evidently did not extend to organization. Chandler summarizes the defects of the large U–form enterprise in the following way:

> The inherent weakness in the centralized, functionally departmentalized operating company . . . became critical only when the administrative load on the senior executives increased to such an extent that they were unable to handle their entrepreneurial responsibilities efficiently. This situation arose when the operations of the enterprise became too complex and the problems of coordination, appraisal, and policy formulation too intricate for a small number of top officers to handle both long-run, enterpreneurial, and short-run, operational administrative activities [1966, pp. 382–83].

The ability of the management to handle the volume and complexity of the demands placed upon it became strained and even collapsed. Unable meaningfully to identify with or contribute to the realization of global goals, managers in each of the functional parts attended to what they perceived to be operational subgoals instead (Chandler, 1966, p. 156). In the language of transaction cost economics, bounds on rationality were reached as the U–form structure labored under a communication overload while the pursuit of subgoals by the functional parts (sales, engineering, production) was partly a manifestation of opportunism.

The M–form structure fashioned by du Pont and Sloan involved the creation of semi-autonomous operating divisions (mainly profit centers) organized along product, brand, or geographic lines. The operating affairs of each were managed separately. More than a change in decomposition rules were needed, however, for the M–form to be fully effective. Du Pont and Sloan also created a general office "consisting of a number of powerful general executives and large advisory and financial staffs" (Chandler, 1977, p. 460) to monitor divisional performance, allocate resources among divisions, and engage in strategic planning. The reasons for the success of the M–form innovation are summarized by Chandler as follows:

> The basic reason for its success was simply that it clearly removed the executives responsible for the destiny of the entire enterprise from the more routine operational activities, and so gave them the time, information, and even psychological commitment for long-term planning and appraisal. . . .
> [The] new structure left the broad strategic decisions as to the allocation of existing resources and the acquisition of new ones in the hands of a top team of generalists. Relieved of operating duties and tactical decisions, a general executive was less likely to reflect the position of just one part of the whole [1966, pp. 382–83].

In contrast with the holding company—which is also a divisionalized form but has little general office capability and hence is little more than a corporate shell—the M–form organization adds (1) a strategic planning and resource allocation capability and (2) monitoring and control apparatus. As a consequence, cash flows are reallocated among divisions to favor high yield uses, and internal incentive and control instruments are exercised in a discriminating way. In short, the M–form corporation takes on many of the properties of (and is usefully regarded as) a miniature capital market,[32] which is a much more ambitious concept of the corporation than the term holding company contemplates.

Although the structure was imitated very slowly at first, adoption by U.S. firms proceeded rapidly during the period 1945 to 1960. Acceptance of this structure by European firms came later. Lawrence

[32] Others who reported that the modern corporation was assuming capital market resource allocation and control functions include Richard Heflebower (1960) and Armen Alchian (1969).

Franko (1972) reports that most large European companies administered their domestic operations through U–form or holding company structures until late in the 1960s, but that rapid reorganization along M–form lines has occurred since. The advent of zero tariffs within the European Economic Community and the postwar penetration of European markets by American multinationals were, in his judgment, important contributing factors.

As W. Ross Ashby has observed, it is not sufficient to determine the behavior of a whole machine to know the behavior of its parts: "only when the details of coupling are added does the whole's behavior become determinate" (1956, p. 53). The M–form structure represented a different solution to the coupling problem than the earlier unitary form structure. It effected decomposability along product or brand lines to which profit center standing could be assigned and it more clearly separated operating from strategic decision making. It carried Simon's hierarchical decomposition principles to a higher degree of refinement.[33]

As compared with the U–form organization of the same activities, the M–form organization of the large, complex corporation served both to economize on bounded rationality and attenuate opportunism. Specifically:

> Operating decisions were no longer forced to the top but were resolved at the divisional level, which relieved the communication load. Strategic decisions were reserved for the general office, which reduced partisan political input into the resource allocation process. And the internal auditing and control techniques which the general office had access to served to overcome information impactedness conditions and permit fine timing controls to be exercised over the operating parts [Williamson, 1975, pp. 137–38].

[33] Moreover, whereas the line-and-staff structure that the railroads adopted in the 1850s could be said to have been prefigured by the military, there is no such military precedent for the M–form. Rather, the reorganization of the military after World War II has certain M–form attributes.

4.2 The Conglomerate

Chandler's studies of organizational innovation do not include the conglomerate and multinational form of corporate enterprise. These are more recent developments, the appearance of which would not have been feasible but for the prior development of the M–form structure. Inasmuch as transaction cost economizing is socially valued and has been relatively neglected by prior treatments, my discussion of both of these emphasizes affirmative aspects. But this is intended to redress an imbalance and should not be construed to suggest either that a transaction cost interpretation is fully adequate or that conglomerates and multinationals pose no troublesome public policy issues.[34] Unrelieved hostility to these two forms of organization, however, is clearly inappropriate. Specifically, conglomerates that have the capacity to allocate resources to high valued uses and multinationals that use the M–form to facilitate technology transfer warrant more sympathetic assessments.

Although diversification as a corporate strategy certainly predates the 1960s, when general awareness of the conglomerate began to appear, the conglomerate is essentially a post World War II phenomenon. To be sure, General Electric's profit centers number in the hundreds and GE has been referred to as the world's most diversified firm. Until recently, however, General Electric's emphasis has been the manufacture and distribution of electrical appliances and machinery. Similarly, although General Motors was more than an automobile company, it took care to limit its portfolio. Thus Sloan remarked that "tetraethyl lead was clearly a misfit for GM. It was a chemical product, rather

[34] For a discussion of the public policy issues posed by conglomerates, see Williamson (1975, pp. 163–71).

than a mechanical one. And it had to go to market as part of the gasoline and thus required a gasoline distribution system" (Burton and Kuhn, 1979, p. 6). Accordingly, although GM retained an investment position, the Ethyl Corporation became a free-standing entity rather than an operating division (Sloan, 1965, p. 224). Similarly, although Durant had acquired Frigidaire, and Frigidaire's market share of refrigerators exceeded 50 percent in the 1920s, the position was allowed to deteriorate as rivals developed market positions in other major appliances (radios, ranges, washers, etc.) while Frigidaire concentrated on refrigerators. The suggestion that GM get into air conditioners "did not register on us, and the proposal was not . . . adopted" (Sloan, 1965, p. 361). As Richard Burton and Arthur Kuhn conclude, GM's "deep and myopic involvement in the automobile sector of the economy, [prevented] product diversification opportunities in other market areas—even in product lines where GM had already achieved substantial penetration—[from being] recognized" (1979, pp. 10–11).

The conglomerate form of organization, whereby the corporation consciously took on a diversified character and nurtured its various parts, evidently required a conceptual break in the mind-set of Sloan and other prewar business leaders. This occurred gradually, more by evolution than by grand design (Robert Sobel, 1974, p. 377); and it involved a new group of organizational innovators—of which Royal Little was one (Sobel, 1974). The natural growth of conglomerates, which would occur as the techniques for managing diverse assets were refined, was accelerated as antitrust enforcement against horizontal and vertical mergers became progressively more severe. Conglomerate acquisitions—in terms of numbers, assets acquired, and as a proportion of total acquisitions—grew rapidly with the result

1558   *Journal of Economic Literature, Vol. XIX (December 1981)*

that "pure" conglomerate mergers, which in the period 1948–1953 constituted only 3 percent of the assets acquired by merger, had grown to 49 percent by 1973–1977 (Frederic Scherer, 1980, p. 124).

Morris Adelman's (1961) explanation for the conglomerate is that this form of organization has attractive portfolio diversification properties. But why should the conglomerate appear in the 1960s rather than much earlier? After all, holding companies, which long predated the conglomerate, can accomplish portfolio diversification. And individual stockholders, through mutual funds and otherwise, are able to diversify their own portfolios. At best the portfolio diversification thesis is a very incomplete explanation for the postwar wave of conglomerate mergers.[35]

The Federal Trade Commission also ventured an early assessment of the conglomerate in which organization form features were ignored. The conglomerate was a natural target for the inhospitality tradition. Thus the FTC Staff held that the conglomerate had the following properties:

> With the economic power which it secures through its operations in many diverse fields, the giant conglomerate corporation may attain an almost impregnable economic position. Threatened with competition in any one of its various activities, it may sell below cost in that field, offsetting its losses through profits made in its other lines—a practice which is frequently explained as one of meeting competition. The conglomerate corporation is thus in a position to strike out with great force against smaller business in a variety of different industries [1948, p. 59].

[35] The diversification of personal portfolios is not a perfect substitute for conglomerate diversification because bankruptcy has real costs that the firm, but not individuals, can reduce by portfolio diversification. Bankruptcy costs have not sharply increased in the past 30 years, however, hence these differences do not explain the appearance of the conglomerate during this interval.

I submit that some phenomena, of which changing internal organization is one, need to be addressed on their own terms. Adopting this view, the conglomerate is best understood as a logical outgrowth of the M–form mode for organizing complex economic affairs. Thus once the merits of the M–form structure for managing separable, albeit related, lines of business (e.g., a series of automobile or a series of chemical divisions) were recognized and digested, its extension to manage less closely related activities was natural. This is not to say that the management of product variety is without problems of its own. But the basic M–form logic, whereby strategic and operating decisions are distinguished and responsibilities are separated, carried over. The conglomerates in which M–form principles of organization are respected are usefully thought of as internal capital markets whereby cash flows from diverse sources are concentrated and directed to high yield uses.

The conglomerate is noteworthy, however, not merely because it permitted the M–form structure to take this diversification step. Equally interesting are the unanticipated systems consequences which developed as a byproduct. Thus once it was clear that the corporation could manage diverse assets in an effective way, the possibility of takeover by tender offer suggested itself. In principle, incumbent managements could always be displaced by waging a proxy contest. In fact, this is a very expensive and relatively ineffective way to achieve management change (Williamson, 1970, Chapter 6). Moreover, even if the dissident shareholders should succeed, there was still a problem of finding a successor management.

Viewed in contractual terms, the M–form conglomerate can be thought of as substituting an administrative interface between an operating division and the stockholders where a market interface had existed previously. Subject to the condition that the conglomerate does not diversify to excess, in the sense that it cannot competently evaluate and allocate funds among the diverse activities in which it is engaged, the substitution of internal organization can have beneficial effects in goal pursuit, monitoring, staffing, and resource allocation respects. The goal-pursuit advantage is that which accrues to M–form organizations in general: since the general management of an M–form conglomerate is disengaged from operating matters, a presumption that the general office favors profits over functional goals is warranted. Relatedly, the general office can be regarded as an agent of the stockholders whose purpose is to monitor the operations of the constituent parts. Monitoring benefits are realized in the degree to which internal monitors enjoy advantages over external monitors in access to information—which they arguably do (Williamson, 1975, pp. 145–48). The differential ease with which the general office can change managers and reassign duties where performance failures or distortions are detected is responsible for the staffing advantage. Resource-allocation benefits are realized because cash flows no longer return automatically to their origins but instead revert to the center, thereafter to be allocated among competing uses in accordance with prospective yields.[36]

This has a bearing on the problem of separation of ownership from control, noted by Adolph Berle and Gardiner C.

[36] To be sure, this substitution of internal organization for the capital market is subject to tradeoffs and diminishing returns. Breadth—that is, access to the widest range of alternatives—is traded off for depth—that is, more intimate knowledge of a narrower range of possible investment outlets—(Alchian and Harold Demsetz, 1972, p. 29), where the general office may be presumed to have the advantage in the latter respect. The diminishing returns feature suggests that the net benefits of increased diversity eventually become negative. Were further diversification thereafter to be attempted, effective control would pass back into the hands of the operating divisions with problematic performance consequences.

Means in 1932. Thus they inquired, "have we any justification for assuming that those in control of a modern corporation will also choose to operate it in the interests of the stockholders" (1932, p. 121). The answer, then as now, is almost certainly no. Indeed, the evident disparity of interest between managers and stockholders gave rise in the 1960s to what has become known as the managerial discretion literature (William Baumol, 1959; Robin Marris, 1964; Williamson, 1964).

There are important differences, however, between the U–form structure, which was the prevailing organization form at the time Berle and Means were writing, and the M–form structure, which in the U.S. was substantially in place by the 1960s. For one thing, as argued above, U–form managers identified more strongly with functional interests and hence were more given to subgoal pursuit. Secondly, and related, there was a confusion between strategic and operating goals in the U–form structure which the M–form served to rectify—with the result that the general office was more fully concerned with enterprise goals, of which profits is the leading element. Third, the market for corporate control, which remained ineffectual so long as the proxy contest was the only way to challenge incumbent managements, was activated as conglomerates recognized that tender offers could be used to effect corporate takeovers. As a consequence, managements that were otherwise secure and would have permitted managerial preferences to prevail were brought under scrutiny and induced to self-correct against egregious managerial distortions.

To be sure, managerial preferences (for salary and perquisites) and stockholder preferences for profits do not become perfectly consonant as a result of conglomerate organization and the associated activation of the capital market. The continuing tension between management and stockholder interests is evident in the numerous efforts that incumbent managements have taken to protect target firms against takeover (William Cary, 1969; Williamson, 1979; George Benston, 1980). Changes in internal organization have nevertheless relieved these concerns. A study of capitalist enterprises which makes no allowance for organization form changes and their capital market ramifications will naturally overlook the possibility that the corporate control dilemma posed by Berle and Means has since been alleviated more by *internal* than it has by regulatory or external organizational reforms.

Not all conglomerates respected M–form principles when they were first organized. The above argument applies only to those where rational decomposition principles were observed and leads to the following testable proposition: conglomerates that were organized along holding company rather than M–form lines (as many were initially) would be less able to cope when adversity appeared, at which time they would be reorganized as M–form firms. Voluntary divestiture is also an interesting conglomerate phenomenon. Such a rationalization of assets is commonly accompanied by internal organizational reforms. Growth maximization theories are mainly at a loss to explain such behavior.

4.3 Multinational Enterprise

The discussion of the multinational enterprise (MNE) that follows deals mainly with recent developments and, among these, emphasizes organizational aspects—particularly those associated with technology transfer in manufacturing industries. As Mira Wilkins has reported, direct foreign investment by American firms has a long history: the book value of cumulative U.S. direct foreign investment, expressed as a percentage of GNP, was in the range of 7 to 8 percent in 1914, 1929, and 1970 (Wilkins, 1974, p. 437).

Both the character of this investment and, relatedly, the organization structure within which this investment takes place have been changing, however. It is not accidental that the term MNE was coined neither in 1914 or 1929 but is of much more recent origin.

Thus whereas the ratio of the book value of U.S. foreign investments in manufacturing as compared with all other (petroleum; trade; mining; public utilities) was 0.47 in 1950, this had increased to 0.71 in 1970 (Wilkins, 1974, p. 329). Also, "what impressed Europeans about American plants in Europe and the United States [in 1929] was mass production, standardization, and scientific management; in the 1960s, Europeans were remarking that America's superiority was based on technological and managerial advantage . . . [and] that this expertise was being exported via direct investment" (Wilkins, 1974, p. 436).

The spread of the multinational corporation in the post World War II period has given rise to considerable scrutiny, some puzzlement, and even some alarm (Yoshihiro Tsurumi, 1977, p. 74). One of the reasons for this unsettled state of affairs is that transaction-cost economizing and organization form issues have been relatively neglected in efforts to assess MNE activity. An important exception is the work of Peter Buckley and Mark Casson (1976).

Organization form is relevant in two related respects. First is the matter of U.S.–based as compared with foreign-based investment rates. Tsurumi reports in this connection that the rate of foreign direct investments by U.S. firms increased rapidly after 1953, peaked in the mid-1960s, and has leveled off and declined since (Tsurumi, 1977, p. 97). The pattern of foreign direct investments by foreign firms, by contrast, has lagged that of the U.S. by about a decade (Tsurumi, 1977, pp. 91–92).

Recall that the conglomerate uses the

M–form structure to extend asset management from specialized to diversified lines of commerce. The MNE counterpart is the use of the M–form structure to extend asset management from a domestic base to include foreign operations. Thus the domestic M–form strategy for decomposing complex business structures into semi-autonomous operating units was subsequently applied to the management of foreign subsidiaries. As noted in 4.1 above, the transformation of the corporation along M–form lines came earlier in the U.S. than in Europe and elsewhere. U.S. corporations were for this reason better qualified to engage in foreign direct investments at an earlier date than were foreign-based firms. Only as the latter took on the M–form structure did this multinational management capability appear. The pattern of foreign direct investments recorded by Tsurumi and reported above is consistent with the temporal differences of U.S. and foreign firms in adopting the M–form structure.

That U.S. corporations possessed an M–form capability earlier than their foreign counterparts does not, however, establish that they used it to organize foreign investment. John Stopford and Louis Wells have studied this issue. They report that while initial foreign investments were usually organized as autonomous subsidiaries, divisional status within an M–form structure invariably appeared as the size and complexity of foreign operations increased (Stopford and Wells, 1972, p. 21). This transformation usually followed the organization of domestic operations along M–form lines (Stopford and Wells, 1972, p. 24). The adoption of a "global" strategy or "worldwide perspective"—whereby "strategic planning and major policy decisions" are made in the central office of the enterprise—could only be accomplished within a multidivisional framework (Stopford and Wells, 1972, p. 25).

Even more interesting than these organization form issues is the fact that foreign direct investments by U.S. firms have been concentrated in a few industries. Manufacturing industries that have made substantial foreign direct investments include chemicals, drugs, automobiles, food processing, electronics, electrical and non-electrical machinery, nonferous metals, and rubber. Tobacco, textiles and apparel, furniture, printing, glass, steel, and aircraft have, by comparison, done little foreign direct investment (Tsurumi, 1977, p. 87).

Stephen Hymer's "dual" explanation for the multinational enterprise is of interest in this connection. Thus Hymer observes that direct foreign investment "allows business firms to transfer capital, technology, and organizational skill from one country to another. It is also an instrument for restraining competition between firms of different nations" (1970, p. 443).

Hymer is surely correct that the MNE can service both of these purposes and examples of both kinds can doubtlessly be found. It is nevertheless useful to ask whether the overall character of MNE investment, in terms of its distribution among industries, is more consistent with the efficiency purposes to which Hymer refers (transfer of capital, technology, and organizational skill) or with the oligopolistic restraint hypothesis. Adopting a transaction cost orientation discloses that the observed pattern of investment is more consistent with the efficiency part of Hymer's dual explanation.

For one thing, oligopolistic purposes can presumably be realized by portfolio investment coupled with a limited degree of management involvement to segregate markets. Put differently, direct foreign investment and the organization of foreign subsidiaries within an M–form structure are not needed to effect competitive restraints. Furthermore, if competitive restraints were mainly responsible for these investments, then presumably all concen-

1562   Journal of Economic Literature, Vol. XIX (December 1981)

trated industries—which would include tobacco, glass, and steel—rather than those associated with rapid technical progress would be active in MNE creation. Finally, although many of the leading U.S. firms that engaged in foreign direct investment enjoyed "market power," this was by no means true for all.

By contrast, the pattern of foreign direct investments reported by Tsurumi appears to be consistent with a transaction cost economizing interpretation. Raymond Vernon's 1970 study of the *Fortune* 500 corporations disclosed that 187 of these firms had a substantial multinational presence. R&D expenditures as a percentage of sales were higher among these 187 than among the remaining firms in the *Fortune* 500 group. Furthermore, according to Vernon, firms that went multinational tended to be technological innovators at the time of making their initial foreign direct investments.

This raises the question of the attributes of firms and markets for accomplishing technology transfer. The difficulties with transferring technology across market interface are of three kinds: recognition, disclosure, and team organization (Arrow, 1962; Williamson, 1975, pp. 31–33, 203–07; Teece, 1977).[37] Of these three, recognition is probably the least severe. To be sure, foreign firms may sometimes fail to perceive the opportunities to apply technological developments originated elsewhere. But enterprising domestic firms that have made the advance can be expected to identify at least some of the potential applications abroad.

Suppose, therefore, that recognition problems are set aside and consider disclosure. Technology transfer by contract can break down if convincing disclosure to buyers effectively destroys the basis for

exchange. A very severe information asymmetry problem exists, on which account the less informed party (in this instance the buyer) must be wary of opportunistic representations by the seller.[38] Although sometimes this asymmetry can be overcome by sufficient ex ante disclosure (and veracity checks thereon), this may shift rather than solve the difficulty. The "fundamental paradox" of information is that "its value for the purchaser is not known until he has the information, but then he has in effect acquired it without costs" (Arrow, 1971, p. 152).

Suppose, *arguendo*, that buyers concede value and are prepared to pay for information in the seller's possession. The incentive to trade is then clear and for some items this will suffice. The formula for a chemical compound or the blueprints for a special device may be all that is needed to effect the transfer. Frequently, however, and probably often, new knowledge is diffusely distributed and is poorly defined (Nelson, 1981). Where the requisite information is distributed among a number of individuals all of whom understand their speciality in only a tacit, intuitive way, a simple contract to transfer the technology cannot be devised. See Michael Polanyi (1962).

Transfer need not cease, however, because simple contracts are not feasible. If the benefits of technology transfer are sufficiently great, exchange may be accomplished either by devising a complex trade or through direct foreign investment.

---

[37] The material that follows is based on Williamson and Teece (1979). Our argument is similar to that advanced by Buckley and Casson (1976).

[38] Markets for information are apt to be especially costly and/or hazardous when transmission across a national boundary is attempted. Language differences naturally complicate the communication problem, and differences in the technological base compound these difficulties. If, moreover, as is commonly the case, cultural differences foster suspicion, the trust that is needed to support informational exchange may be lacking. Not only will contract negotiations be more complex and costly on this account, but execution will be subject to more formal and costly procedures than would obtain under a regime of greater trust.

Which will be employed depends on the circumstances. If only a one-time (or very occasional) transfer of technology is contemplated, direct foreign investment is a somewhat extreme response.[39] The complex contractual alternative is to negotiate a tie-in sale whereby the technology and associated know-how are transferred as a package. Since the know-how is concentrated in the human assets who are already familiar with the technology, this entails the creation of a "consulting team" by the seller to accompany the physical technology transfer—the object being to overcome start up difficulties and to familiarize the employees of the foreign firm, through teaching and demonstration, with the idiosyncracies of the operation.[40]

Inasmuch as many of the contingencies that arise in the execution of such contracts will be unforeseen and as it will be too costly to work out appropriate ex ante responses for others, such consulting contracts are subject to considerable strain. Where a succession of transfers is contemplated, which is to say, when the frequency shifts from occasional to recurring, complex contracting is apt to give way to direct foreign investment. A more harmonious and efficient exchange relation— better disclosure, easier reconciliation of differences, more complete cross-cultural adaptation, more effective team organization and reconfiguration—all predictably result from the substitution of an internal governance relation for bilateral trading under these recurrent trading circumstances for assets, of which complex technology transfer is an example, that have a highly specific character.[41]

The upshot is that while puzzlement with and concerns over MNEs will surely continue, a transaction cost interpretation of this phenomenon sheds insight on the following conspicuous features of multinational investment: (1) the reported concentration of foreign direct investment in manufacturing industries where technology transfer is of special importance; (2) the organization of these investments within M–form structures; and (3) the differential timing of foreign direct investment between U.S. and foreign manufacturing enterprises (which difference also has organization form origins). I furthermore conjecture that the application of transaction cost reasoning will lead to a deeper understanding of other specific features of MNE activity as these are discovered and/or become subject to public policy scrutiny.

5. Concluding Remarks

There is widespread agreement, among economists and noneconomists alike, with the proposition that the modern corporation is an important and complex economic institution. Such agreement is mainly explained by the obtrusive size of the largest firms—running to tens of billions of dollars of assets and sales, with employment numbering in the hundreds of thousands. The economic factors that lie behind the size, shape, and performance of the modern corporation, however, are poorly understood.

This puzzlement is not of recent origin. Edward Mason complained over twenty years ago that "the functioning of the corporate system has not to date been ade-

---

[39] This is an implication of transaction cost reasoning in which the frequency dimension has explanatory power (Williamson, 1979, pp. 245–54).

[40] On the importance of on-site observation and of teaching-by-doing, see Polanyi (1962), Peter Doeringer and Michael Piore (1971, pp. 15–16), and Williamson, Michael Wachter, and Jeffrey Harris (1975).

[41] The argument can be extended to deal with such observations as those of Edwin Mansfield, Anthony

---

Romeo and Samuel Wagner (1979), who report that firms use subsidiaries to transfer their newest technology overseas but rely on licensing or joint ventures for older technology. The transaction cost argument is that the latter are more well defined, hence are more easily reduced to contract, and require less firm specific know-how to effect successful transfer.

quately explained. . . . The man of action may be content with a system that works. But one who reflects on the properties or characteristics of this system cannot help asking why it works and whether it will continue to work" (1960, p. 4). The predicament to which Mason refers is, I submit, largely the product of two different (but not unrelated) intellectual traditions. The first of these holds that the structural features of the corporation are irrelevant. This is the neoclassical theory of the firm that populates intermediate theory textbooks. Structural differences are suppressed as the firm is described as a production function to which a profit maximization objective has been assigned. The second has public policy roots; this is the inhospitality tradition that I referred to earlier. In this tradition, distinctive structural features of the corporation are believed to be the result of unwanted (anti-competitive) intrusions into market processes.

The transaction-cost approach differs from both. Unlike neoclassical analysis, internal organization is specifically held to be important. Unlike the inhospitality tradition, structural differences are assumed to arise primarily in order to promote economy in transaction costs. The assignment of transactions between firms and markets and the economic ramifications of internal structure both come under scrutiny in these terms. The application of these ideas to the study of transactions in general and of the modern corporation in particular requires that (1) the transaction be made the principal unit of analysis, (2) an elementary appreciation for "human nature as we know it" supplant the fiction of economic man, (3) transactions be dimensionalized, (4) rudimentary principles of market and hierarchical organization be recognized, and (5) a guiding principle of comparative institutional study be the hypothesis that transactions are assigned to and organized within governance structures in a discriminating (transaction-cost economizing) way.

The view that the corporation is first and foremost an efficiency instrument does not deny that firms also seek to monopolize markets, sometimes by engaging in strategic behavior, or that managers sometimes pursue their own goals to the detriment of system goals. But specific structural preconditions need to be satisfied if strategic behavior is to be feasible[42]—and most firms do not qualify, which is to say that strategic behavior is the exception rather than the rule. Furthermore, most firms will be penalized if efficiency norms are seriously violated for extended periods of time—which serves to curb managerial discretion. The strongest argument favoring transaction cost economizing, however, is that this is the only hypothesis that is able to provide a discriminating rationale for the succession of organizational innovations that have occurred over the past 150 years and out of which the modern corporation has emerged.

To recapitulate, although railroad mergers between parallel roads can have monopolizing purposes, the joining of end-to-end systems under common management is explained by transaction cost economics. The hierarchical structures evolved by the railroads were the outcome of internal efforts to effect coordination across interfaces to which common operating responsibilities had been assigned. Older and simpler structures were unable to manage such complex networks, while coordination by end-to-end contracts between successive stations was prohibitively costly.

Forward integration out of manufacturing into distribution was widespread at the turn of the century. More interesting,

---

[42] For a discussion of these preconditions—mainly high concentration coupled with high barriers to entry—see Joskow and Klevorick (1979), and Williamson (1981).

however, than this general movement is the fact that forward integration was selective—being extensive in some industries (e.g., sewing machines), negligible in others (e.g., dry goods), and mistaken in still others (e.g., sugar). This selective pattern is predicted by and consistent with transaction-cost reasoning—whereas no other hypothesis makes comparably detailed predictions.

The efficiency incentive to shift from the earlier U–form to the M–form structure is partly explained in managerial discretion terms: the older structure was more subject to distortions of a managerial discretion kind–which is to say that opportunism had become a serious problem in the large U–form firm. Equally and probably more important, however, is that the managerial hierarchy is the U–form enterprise was simply overburdened as the firm became large and complex. The M–form structure represented a more rational decomposition of the affairs of the firm and thereby served to economize on bounded rationality.[43] The subsequent diffusion of this structure was hastened by a combination of product market (pressure on rivals)and capital market (takeover) competition.

The M–form structure, which was originally adopted by firms in relatively specialized lines of commerce was subsequently extended to manage diversified assets (the conglomerate) and foreign direct investments (MNE). A breadth-for-depth tradeoff is involved in the former case, as the firm selectively internalizes functions ordinarily associated with the capital market. MNE activity has also been selective—being concentrated in the more technologically progressive industries where higher rates of R&D are reported and technology transfer arguably

poses greater difficulties than is true of technologically less progressive industries. This pattern of foreign direct investment cannot be explained as the pursuit of monopoly but is consistent with transaction-cost reasoning.

The upshot is that a transaction-cost approach to the study of the modern corporation permits a wide variety of significant organizational events to be interpreted in a coherent way.[44] It links up comfortably with the type of business history studies that have been pioneered by Chandler. It has ramifications for the study of regulation (Williamson, 1976; Goldberg, 1976) and for antitrust enforcement. Applications to aspects of labor economics and comparative systems have been made, and others would appear to be fruitful. More generally, while there is room for and need for refinement, a comparative approach to the study of economic institutions in which the economy of transaction costs is the focus of analysis, appears to have considerable promise.

REFERENCES

ADELMAN, M. A. "The Antimerger Act, 1950–1960," *Amer. Econ. Rev.*, May 1961, 51, pp. 236–44.

ALCHIAN, A. A. "Corporate Management and Prop-

---

[43] Had "normal" managerial preferences prevailed, the U–form, which favored the exercise of those preferences, would presumably have been retained.

[44] Recent contributions to the theory of the firm that are held to have a bearing on the study of the modern corporation are Alchian and Demsetz (1972) and Michael Jensen and William Meckling (1976). Both, however, deal with a microcosm much smaller than the modern corporation. Thus Alchian and Demsetz focus on the reasons why technological nonseparabilities give rise to team organization. Although small groups may be explained in this way (manual freight loading, whereby two men are required to lift coordinately, is the standard example), the existence of complex hierarchies cannot be explained in terms of the imperatives of such nonseparabilities. (The largest work group which, to my knowledge, qualifies is the symphony orchestra.)

Similarly, while the Jensen and Meckling paper is an important contribution to the principal-agent literature, it does not generalize to the modern corporation—as they expressly acknowledge (1976, p. 356). Although they conjecture that their analysis can be applied to the large, diffusely owned corporation whose managers own little or no equity (1976, p. 356), I have serious doubts.

erty Rights," in _Economic policy and regulation of corporate securities._ Edited by H. G. MANNE. Washington: American Enterprise Institute for Public Policy Research, 1969, pp. 337–60.

_____ AND DEMSETZ, H. "Production, Information Costs, and Economic Organization," _Amer. Econ. Rev._, Dec. 1972, 62(5), pp. 777–95.

ARROW, KENNETH J. "Economic Welfare and the Allocation of Resources of Invention," in _The rate and direction of inventive activity: Economic and social factors._ Edited by NATIONAL BUREAU OF ECONOMIC RESEARCH. Princeton: Princeton University Press, 1962, pp. 609–25.

_____ "Control in Large Organizations," _Mange. Science_, April 1964, 10(3), pp. 397–408.

_____ "The Organization of Economic Activity: Issues Pertinent to the Choice of Market Versus Nonmarket Allocation," in _The analysis and evaluation of public expenditure: The PPB system_, Vol. 1. U.S. Joint Economic Committee, 91st Congress, 1st Session, U.S. Government Printing Office, 1969, pp. 59–73.

_____ _Essay in the theory of risk-bearing._ Chicago: Markham Pub. Co., 1971.

_____ _The limits of organization._ First edition. New York: W. W. Norton & Co., 1974.

ASHBY, W. R. _An introduction to cybernetics._ New York: John Wiley and Sons, 1956.

BARNARD, C. I. _The functions of the executive._ Cambridge, Mass.: Harvard University Press, 1938.

BAUMOL, W. J. _Business behavior, value and growth._ New York: Macmillan, 1959; Harcourt, Brace and World, 1967.

BENSTON, GEORGE J. _Conglomerate mergers: Causes, consequences and remedies._ Washington, D.C.: American Enterprise Institute for Public Policy Research, 1980.

BERLE, A. A. AND MEANS, G. C. _The modern corporation and private property._ New York: Macmillan, 1932.

BRUCHEY, STUART W. _Robert Oliver, merchant of Baltimore, 1783–1819._ Baltimore: Johns Hopkins University Press, 1956.

BUCKLEY, P. J. AND CASSON, M. _The future of multinational enterprise._ New York: Holmes and Meier, 1976.

BURTON, R. H. AND KUHN, A. J. "Strategy Follows Structure: The Missing Link of Their Intertwined Relation," Working Paper No. 260, Fuqua School of Business, Duke University, May 1979.

CARY, W. "Corporate Devices Used to Insulate Management from Attack," _Antitrust Law Journal_, 1969–70, 39(1), pp. 318–24.

CAVES, R. E. "Corporate Strategy and Structure," _J. Econ. Lit._, March 1980, 18(1), pp. 64–92.

CHANDLER, A. D., JR. _Strategy and structure: Chapters in the history of the industrial enterprise._ Cambridge, Mass.: MIT Press, 1962; Garden City, N.J.: Doubleday & Co., 1966.

_____ _The visible hand: The managerial revolution in American business._ Cambridge, Mass.: Belknap Press, 1977.

COASE, R. H. "The Nature of the Firm," _Economica N.S._, 1937, 4, pp. 386–405; and in _Readings in_

price theory. Edited by G. J. STIGLER AND K. E. BOULDING. Chicago: Richard D. Irwin for the American Economic Association, 1952.

_____ "Industrial Organization: A Proposal for Research," in _Policy issues and research opportunities in industrial organization: Economic research: Retrospect and prospect._ Edited by VICTOR R. FUCHS. New York: NBER; distributed by Columbia University Press, New York and London, 1972, pp. 59–73.

COMMONS, JOHN R. _Institutional economics; its place in political economy._ New York: Macmillan, [1934] 1951.

CYERT, RICHARD M. AND HEDRICK, CHARLES L., "Theory of the Firm: Past, Present, and Future; An Interpretation," _J. Econ. Lit._, June 1972, 10(2), pp. 398–412.

DAVIS, LANCE E. AND NORTH, DOUGLASS C. _Institutional change and American economic growth._ Cambridge, England: Cambridge University Press, 1971.

DOERINGER, P. AND PIORI, M. _Internal labor markets and manpower analysis._ Boston: D.C. Heath and Co., 1971.

DRUCKER, P. _Management: Tasks, responsibilities, practices._ New York: Harper & Row, 1974.

FISHLOW, ALBERT. _American railroads and the transformation of the antebellum economy._ Cambridge, Mass.: Harvard University Press, 1965.

FOGEL, WILLIAM R. _Railroads and American economic growth: Essays in econometric history._ Baltimore: Johns Hopkins University Press, 1964.

FRANKO, LAWRENCE G. "The Growth, Organizational Efficiency of European Multinational Firms: Some Emerging Hypotheses," _Colloques internationaux aux C.N.R.S._, 1972, pp. 335–66.

GOLDBERG, V. P. "Regulation and Administered Contracts," _Bell J. Econ._, Autumn 1976, 7(2), pp. 426–52.

HAYEK, F. "The Use of Knowledge in Society," _Amer. Econ. Rev._, Sept. 1945, 35, pp. 519–30.

HEFLEBOWER, R. B. "Observation on Decentralization in Large Enterprises," _J. Ind. Econ._, Nov. 1960, 9, pp. 7–22.

HYMER, S. "The Efficiency (Contradictions) of Multinational Corporations," _Amer. Econ. Rev._, May 1970, 60(2), pp. 441–48.

JENSEN, M. C. AND MECKLING, W. H. "Theory of the Firm: Managerial Behavior, Agency Costs and Ownership Structure," _J. Finan. Econ._, Oct. 1976, 3(4), pp. 305–60.

JOSKOW, PAUL L. AND KLEVORICK, ALVIN K. "A Framework for Analyzing Predatory Pricing Policy," _Yale Law J._, Dec. 1979, 89, pp. 213–70.

KLEIN, B.; CRAWFORD, R. A. AND ALCHIAN, A. A. "Vertical Integration, Appropriable Rents, and the Competitive Contracting Process," _J. Law Econ._, Oct. 1978, 21(2), pp. 297–326.

KNIGHT, FRANK H. _Risk, uncertainty and profit._ New York: Harper & Row, [1921] 1965.

KOONTZ, H. AND O'DONNELL, C. _Principles of management; an analysis of managerial functions._ New York: McGraw-Hill, 1955.

LARSON, HENRIETTA M. _Guide to business history;_

materials for the study of American business history and suggestions for their use. Cambridge, Mass.: Harvard University Press, 1948.

LIVESAY, H. C. American made: Men who shaped the American economy. First edition. Boston: Little, Brown, 1979.

MANSFIELD, E.; ROMEO, A. AND WAGNER, S. "Foreign Trade and U.S. Research and Development," Rev. Econ. Statist., Feb. 1979, 61(1), pp. 49–57.

MARRIS, R. The economic theory of managerial capitalism. New York: Free Press, 1964.

_____ AND MUELLER, D. C. "The Corporation, Competition, and the Invisible Hand," J. Econ. Lit., March 1980, 18(1), pp. 32–63.

MARSCHAK, J. AND RADNER, R. Economic theory of teams. New Haven: Yale University Press, 1972.

MASON, E. S. "Introduction," in The corporation in modern society. Edited by E. S. MASON. Cambridge, Mass.: Harvard University Press, 1960, pp. 1–24.

NELSON, R. R. "Assessing Private Enterprise: An Exegesis of Tangled Doctrine," Bell J. Econ., Spring 1981, 12(1), pp. 93–111.

_____ AND WINTER, S. G. An evolutionary theory of economic behavior and capabilities. Cambridge, Mass.: Harvard University Press, 1981.

NORTH, D. C. "Structure and Performance: The Task of Economic History," J. Econ. Lit., Sept. 1978, 16(3), pp. 963–78.

PANZAR, JOHN C. AND WILLIG, ROBERT D. "Economies of Scope," Amer. Econ. Rev., Papers and Proceedings, May 1981, 71(2), pp. 268–72.

POLANYI, M. Personal knowledge: Towards a postcritical philosophy. New York: Harper & Row, 1962.

PORTER, G. AND LIVESAY, H. C. Merchants and manufacturers: Studies in the changing structure of nineteenth century marketing. Baltimore: Johns Hopkins University Press, 1971.

POSNER, R. A. "The Chicago School of Antitrust Analysis," Univ. Pennsylvania Law Rev., April 1979, 127(4), pp. 925–48.

RADNER, ROY. "Competitive Equilibrium Under Uncertainty," Econometrica, Jan. 1968, 36(1), pp. 31–58.

SCHERER, F. M. Industrial market structure and economic performance. Second edition. Chicago: Rand McNally College Pub. Co., 1980.

SIMON, H. A. Models of man: Social and rational mathematical essays on rational human behavior in a social setting. New York: John Wiley and Sons, 1957a.

_____ Administrative behavior; a study of decision-making processes in administrative organization. Second edition. New York: Macmillan, [1947] 1957b.

_____ "The Architecture of Complexity," Proceedings of the American Philosophical Society, Dec. 1962, 106(6), pp. 467–82.

_____ "Applying Information Technology to Organization Design," Pub. Admin. Rev., May–June 1973, 33(3), pp. 268–78.

_____ "Rationality as Process and as Product of Thought," Amer. Econ. Rev., May 1978, 68(2), pp. 1–16.

SLOAN, A. P., JR. My years with General Motors. New York: MacFadden-Bartell, [1963] 1965.

SOBEL, R. The entrepreneurs: Explorations within the American business tradition. New York: Weybright and Talley, 1974.

STOPFORD, JOHN M. AND WELLS, LOUIS T., JR. Managing the multinational enterprise; organization of the firm and ownership of the subsidiaries. New York: Basic Books, 1972.

TEECE, D. J. "Technology Transfer by Multinational Firms," Econ. J., June 1977, 87, pp. 242–61.

_____ "Economies of Scope and the Scope of the Enterprise," J. Econ. Behavior Org., Sept. 1980, 1(3), pp. 223–45.

TEMIN, P. "The Future of the New Economic History," J. of Interdisciplinary Hist., Autumn 1981, 12(2), pp. 179–97.

THOMPSON, JAMES D. Organizations in action; social science bases of administrative theory. New York: McGraw-Hill, 1967.

TSURUMI, Y. Multinational management: Business strategy and government policy. Cambridge, Mass.: Ballinger, 1977.

U.S. FEDERAL TRADE COMMISSION. Report of the Federal Trade Commission on the merger movement: A summary report, Washington, D.C.: U.S. Government Printing Office, 1948.

VERNON, R. Sovereignty at bay: The multinational spread of U.S. enterprises. New York: Basic Books, 1971.

WILKINS, MIRA. The maturing of multinational enterprise: American business abroad from 1914 to 1970. Cambridge, Mass.: Harvard University Press, 1974.

WILLIAMSON, O. E. The economics of discretionary behavior: Managerial objectives in a theory of the firm. Englewood Cliffs, N.J.: Prentice-Hall, 1964.

_____ Corporate control and business behavior. Englewood Cliffs, N.J.: Prentice-Hall, 1970.

_____ Markets and hierarchies: Analysis and antitrust implications: A study in the economics of internal organization. New York: Free Press, 1975.

_____ "Franchise Bidding for Natural Monopolies—in General and with Respect to CATV," Bell J. Econ., Spring 1976, 7(1), pp. 73–104.

_____ "Transaction Cost Economics: The Governance of Contractual Relations," J. Law Econ., Oct. 1979, 22(2), pp. 233–61.

_____ "On the Governance of the Modern Corporation," Hofstra Law Rev., Fall 1979, 8(1), pp. 63–78.

_____ "Organizational Innovation: The Transaction-Cost Approach." Discussion Paper No. 82, Center for the Study of Organizational Innovation, University of Pennsylvania, Sept. 1980.

_____ "Antitrust Enforcement: Where It's Been; Where It's Going." Discussion Paper No. 102, Center for the Study of Organizational Innovation, University of Pennsylvania, May 1981.

_____ AND TEECE, D. J. "European Economic and Political Integration: The Markets and Hierarchies Approach," in *New approaches to European integration.* Edited by P. SALMON. Forthcoming.

_____; WACHTER, MICHAEL L. AND HARRIS, JEFFREY E. "Understanding the Employment Relation: The Analysis of Idiosyncratic Exchange," *Bell J. Econ.*, Spring 1975, 6(1), pp. 50–280.

[13]

Excerpt from *Multinationals: Theory and History*, Peter Hertner and Geoffrey Jones (eds.)

3 General Theories of the Multinational Enterprise: Their Relevance to Business History[1]

Mark Casson

Introduction

In the past few years there has been a spate of new theories which claim to be general theories of the multinational enterprise (MNE).[2] The object of this chapter is to assess the logical coherence of these theories and to examine their relevance to the history of the MNE. It is suggested that there are several weaknesses that are common to all the theories. To begin with, they are far too steeped in the special institutional forms of foreign involvement which have prevailed in the post-war period. As a result, the concept of the MNE which underpins current theories remains too narrow to make analytical study of the economic history of the MNE an especially rewarding subject. Thus the theories presuppose a static configuration of independent nations, each with a liberal constitution, and with its production organised largely by private companies and corporations. The theories do not consider in detail the position of nations with colonial or dominion status, nor the consequences for international business of political instability caused, for example, by international territorial disputes. Neither do they take account of the fact that throughout history there has been unappropriated frontier territory, such as that represented today by the Antarctic, the oceans and the atmosphere.

Theories of the MNE, being themselves the product of liberal thought applied to economics, presume a liberal political framework. This means that, if applied uncritically, they give a distorted view of MNEs' economic relations with illiberal economies—whether the socialist countries of Eastern Europe, or fascist dictatorships elsewhere.

The legal privileges afforded by a liberal constitution encourage business leaders to clothe their activities in a corporate 'shell'. The legal shell provided by incorporation may well, however, disguise the true locus of economic power within the firm.[3] The theories' preoccupation with the firm and its arm's -length contractual alternatives make them difficult to apply to earlier times in which the extended family, the partnership, the merchant guild and the cartel were also important forms of economic organisation (as some still are today).

The Concept of Ownership Advantage

The current economic theory of the MNE began mainly as an attempt to explain post-war US corporate investment in Western European industry. The theory was mainly concerned with manufacturing industry rather than services such as banking. Initially, two main analytical questions were posed: Firstly, why do the investing firms produce in Europe rather than in the US? Secondly, how can they compete with indigenous producers, given the additional costs of doing business abroad?

The answer to the first question is that the investments were import-substituting. Sourcing the foreign market by local production was made profitable by the avoidance of transport costs and tariffs. In some cases it also provided access to cheaper labour. Although labour productivity may have been lower in Europe—due partly to the lower scale of production—labour was relatively cheap in Europe, because the combination of the dollar shortage and nominal wage stickiness in the US[4] made the US own-product wage very high. The answer to the second question lies in the technology gap: the cost to US firms of doing business abroad was offset by lower production costs and better product quality achieved through superior technology and more professional management practices. This is the essence of the Hymer-Kindleberger theory of the MNE: it synthesises what Dunning calls the location and ownership advantages of international production.

Both Hymer and Caves emphasised the monopolistic nature of the ownership advantage,[5] Hymer pointing to privileged access to proprietary technology, and Caves to special skills in the design and marketing of differentiated products. Other writers emphasised non-monopolistic advantages, e.g. Aliber, who argued that stockholder preferences for strong currency assets gave an advantage to all firms whose parent company was based in a strong currency area.[6]

The importance of the distinction between monopolistic and non-monopolistic advantages is not always recognised in applications of the Hymer-Kindleberger theory. 'Advantage' is a relative concept—someone always has an advantage *relative* to someone else—and it is important to specify who that someone else is. When a foreign firm enjoys a monopolistic advantage, such as a proprietary technology, it enjoys an advantage not only over indigenous firms but over all firms everywhere. On the other hand, a foreign firm which enjoys a non-monopolistic advantage may enjoy an advantage only over indigenous firms. This means, for example, that in an industry

43

where there are no indigenous firms, none of the foreign firms need have any kind of advantage relative to the other firms actually operating in the industry. In applied work on multinationals, therefore, it is incorrect to assume that each multinational in the industry must have some kind of advantage relative to the others. This is true if the advantages are monopolistic, but untrue of they are not.

A third question was also posed by Hymer and Kindleberger,[7] namely, Why do US firms not license their ownership advantages to European firms? Consideration of this question showed that ownership and location factors were not themselves sufficient to explain international production: some disincentive to license is also required. A number of disincentives have been suggested; though different, they are related to each other. First, if the advantage is advertised for sale, it will attract attention: imitation will be encouged, and the appropriation of monopoly rents made that much more difficult.[8] Secondly, buyers will be reluctant to pay the full value of the advantage as they will be uncertain of exactly what is on offer, or what its quality is.[9] Thirdly, transfers of technology between employees of the same firm may be less costly than transfers of technology between employees of different firms, because the employees share a common corporate culture, and this makes it easy for them to learn from one another. This last idea is rarely articulated, but underpins much of the discussion in the literature.

Buckley and Casson went further by suggesting that this question was merely a special case of the question of why multinational firms exist anyway. In other words, why is multinational organisation of economic activity preferred to a network of arm's-length contractual arrangements between individual factor-owners and individual consumers in different countries? Following McManus, Buckley and Casson appeal to the Coase theorem for the answer.[10] They show that a necessary and sufficient condition for the existence of an MNE is that there is a net benefit to internalising an intermediate product market linking activities located in different countries.[11] In this context, the concept of an intermediate product market is a very broad one. It includes markets in raw materials, semi-processed products, components, and also wholesale products ready for final distribution. It includes markets in technology and all kinds of know-how. Finally, it includes markets in price commitments and production commitments; these commitments are used both to establish collusion in oligopolistic industries, and to reduce costs through rationalisation in industries utilising indivisible assets. Different motives for internalising lead to different patterns of backward, forward, horizontal and conglomerate integration. It is the relation between the motive for internalisation and the resulting pattern of integration that yields the major predictions of internalisation theory.

An immediate consequence of this result is that a monopolistic advantage is not necessary to explain why an MNE exists, any more than it is necessary to explain why a uninational firms exists. For example, when profit-tax rates are not harmonised between two countries, firms in an industry whose product is mined in one country and processed in another have an incentive to internalise the raw material market in order to minimise tax liabilities through transfer pricing. The same result would ensue if tax rates were harmonised but economies from vertical integration were operating. In neither case is monopolistic advantage required.

In a definitive statement of his recent work, Dunning[12] asserts that three different types of advantage are necessary to explain the behaviour of MNEs: ownership advantage, internalisation advantage and location advantage. Some writers identify Dunning's ownership advantage with a monopolistic advantage, but this is incorrect. It was established above that a monopolistic advantage is not always necessary where MNEs are concerned. Dunning's ownership advantage concept includes any advantage that an MNE possesses over rival indigenous firms. It includes, for example, the advantage of transfer pricing referred to above. Ownership advantage thus includes some of the advantages of internalisation. This means that in some cases, Dunning's statement that both ownership and internalisation advantages are necessary becomes almost a tautology. By grouping together under the one heading both monopolistic and non-monopolistic advantages, and internalisation and non-internalisation advantages, the ownership advantage concept is in danger of obscuring the crucial analytical issues.

The problem seems to be that internalisation was first introduced into the theory to explain the disincentive to licensing a monopolistic advantage[13] and some writers continue to regard this as the only role of internalisation. They speak of 'internalising an advantage, as though internalisation had its everyday connotation of 'keeping to oneself'. They fail to recognise that in the theory of the firm it is markets that are internalised and not the advantages themselves. The internalisation of a market for a monopolistic advantage is a special case of the internalisation of markets in general. Internalisation is nothing if it is not a general theory of how market failure leads to the creation of firms.[14] From this perspective, internalisation theory does not leave any gaps that an ownership advantage is needed to fill.

Nevertheless a paradox arises here. Empirical work on the MNE regularly points to the importance of ownership advantages—even in

45

pre-war investments, where vertical integration was an important factor too. The evidence also suggests that managers rarely perceive licensing as a crucial issue—the advantages of internalising the market for know-how are usually believed to be heavily outweighed by the costs. The resolution of this paradox may lie in identifying another question, namely, why it is that certain firms are persistently successful and grow large while other firms are only short-lived or always remain small.

Dunning is on firmer ground when he argues that the *success* of MNEs *vis-à-vis* non-MNEs rests on their possession of ownership advantages. The question of success and failure is, in fact, absolutely crucial, and the discovery of a convincing answer would have major policy implications. According to our interpretation, therefore, the major contribution of Dunning's theory is its assertion that possession of an ownership advantage is a necessary condition for sustained profitability and growth.

This interpretation of Dunning is supported by a reconsideration of the two questions posed at the beginning of this section. It is worth noting that while the first question of the Hymer-Kindleberger theory concerns managerial choice between two alternative strategies of sourcing a foreign market, the second question is not directly concerned with managerial choice, but with the ability of the firm to survive in a foreign market environment. The fact that the latter question is concerned specifically with competition from indigenous producers does not alter the fact that the basic issue is the survival of the firm. Questions of managerial choice and questions of survival are logically quite distinct. Internalisation theory represents an extension of the theory of choice to encompass the choice, within each market, of the appropriate contractual arrangement. Ownership advantage, however, is not concerned with choice, but with the performance of the firm once managerial choices have been made. Its proper place is not within the subdivision of the theory that deals with choice, but with the subdivision that deals with the success, and the consequent growth, of the firm.

The Concept of Internalisation

It might appear that our critique of the ownership advantage concept indicates support for Rugman's view that internalisation alone constitutes the general theory of the MNE.[15] Rugman's work is notable for its lively and readable presentation of the major analytical concepts. Unfortunately, however, Rugman's use of the internalisation concept is not always consistent. Internalisation has different connotations in different branches of economics. *Internalisation of a market* refers to the

46

replacement of an arm's-length contractual relationship (i.e. the external market) with unified ownership (i.e. the internal market), while *internalisation of an externality* refers to the creation of a market of any kind where none existed before.

The first concept of internalisation is used in industrial organisation theory and the second in the economics of welfare. Writers who discuss the welfare implications of alternative forms of industrial organisation need always to keep this distinction in mind. Rugman, unfortunately, confuses the two concepts at crucial points in his analysis.

There is some disagreement in the welfare literature as to whether the internalisation of an externality involves the creation of a market of *any* kind[16] or whether it involves the creation of a market specifically through the unification of ownership.[17] If the former interpretation is used then internalisation of an externality does not imply the creation of an internal market, whereas if the latter interpretation is used then it does. However, *neither* interpretation implies that the internalisation of a market removes an externality. It *may* do so, but equally it may not. Only if the external market is missing altogether is the creation of an internal market practically certain to lead to the avoidance of an externality.

It is possible that the replacement of external markets by internal ones may increase efficiency, but there is no guarantee that it will do so. Rugman defines an externality as a divergence between private and social costs, and it is quite possible that internalisation may increase this divergence and not reduce it. Thus an MNE which maximises monopoly profits by restricting the output of high-technology goods, or uses vertical integration as a barrier to entry, may well *create* externalities, according to Rugman's definition. Internalisation of a market is not, therefore, equivalent to the removal of an externality.

Although Rugman is seeking a general theory, he is actually very restrictive in his interpretation of the internalisation of a market. He identifies internalisation of a market with centralisation of control, failing to recognise that when ownership is unified, control can still be decentralised using shadow prices or other kinds of flexible budgetary control within the ownership unit. He also claims that research and development must be centralised within the MNE, a claim that seems contrary to his emphasis elsewhere upon the benefits of the international division of labour within the MNE.

In recent work, Rugman discusses applications of internalisation theory to the oil and drugs industries.[18] His examples suggest that the distinctions drawn above may be unduly pedantic, since in these cases markets internalised within the firm are indeed missing altogether outside it. This, however, is an empirical issue, and further research

47

must be done before support can be given to Rugman's policy recommendations on such practical grounds.

It is quite possible, in fact, to extend internalisation theory in new directions, but not along the lines that previous authors have suggested. There is one particular extension that is of special interest to the economic historian, and which also illustrates vividly the way in which multinational organisation may damage social efficiency. By internalising collusive agreements on price and output, the MNE may render collusive arrangements more readily enforceable, and so provide a more powerful mechanism for exploiting international monopoly power than an international cartel.[19]

Suppose, for example, that, in the absence of anti-trust policy, it is planned to create a world monopoly through collaboration between oligopolistic firms producing in different countries. A suitable arm's-length contractual arrangement would be a collusive agreement between the oligopolists; if the arrangement were long-term it could lead to the institution of an international cartel. The main administrative problem for cartel members would be the avoidance of covert price-cutting and the violation of production quotas by the others. Unified ownership effected through an MNE would reduce the incentives to default on the collusive agreement, and would also make it easier to effect adjustments in prices and quotas, as protracted negotiations would be avoided. The main disadvantage of the MNE would be that, being a more overt use of monopoly power, it would be more likely to attract political hostility. Additionally, the agglomeration of capital would be so large that shareholdings would be highly diversified and it would therefore be difficult for the owners to discipline the management.

It may be objected that, in the absence of entry barriers, neither the cartel nor the MNE could exploit its monopoly power in the long run. This is correct, but there are sufficient industries characterised by natural monopoly stemming from economics of scale to render this objection a fairly weak one. The issue of the transition from international cartel to MNE in naturally monopolistic industries is a subject that has so far received little attention, and one that should repay further study.

Modelling Transaction Costs

Internalisation is a powerful analytical concept, but to render it operational it is necessary to make specific assumptions about the costs of alternative institutional arrangements. Very little effort has been made in this direction. The appropriate methodology is to specify transaction cost functions, and then to determine which institutional arrangement has the lowest cost under given circumstances.[20] Given profit maximisation, rational transactors will choose the arrangement with lowest cost.

The specification of transaction cost functions is not, however, an easy matter. To set up a transaction, traders must invest in acquiring information. Some of the information is needed simply to make contact, some to secure the most favourable terms in the bargain, and some to reduce the risk of default. Information, once acquired, may prove useful in subsequent trades. This means that transaction costs—or some component of them—represent an investment; not all transaction costs are a recurrent cost. Matters are further complicated by the fact that not only is information required for trade, but trade itself generates information. This means that each trade reduces the marginal transaction cost incurred by a subsequent trade in the same product, or with the same person, i.e. there are economies to repeated trade.

Because of 'learning by trading', two traders seeking a long-term relationship will normally commence with a trial or one-off trade. If this is mutually satisfactory they will progress to recurrent spot trade, which may increase in regularity as mutual confidence grows. If the traders are looking for a long-term partner at the outset then, where the initial transaction is concerned, the value of the commodity itself may be very small compared with the value of the information that the initial trade conveys.

Another feature of transaction costs is that it is often difficult to quantify the variables on which they depend. 'Psychic distance'—generated by differences in language and culture—raises transaction costs by impeding information flow between the two parties, but an adequate measure of psychic distance is difficult to devise.

The concept of psychic distance is usually applied to *direct* communication between two parties. It must be recognised, however, that information relevant to trade can also be obtained at second hand. For example, information about product quality may be obtained through social contacts with people who have prior experience of the product; information about a trader's integrity and his ability to pay may be obtained from people with personal knowledge of him. Of course, the value of second-hand information is very much a matter of confidence in the person who acts as the contact: respect for a contact is required before one can accept his assessment of someone else. Thus psychic distance is essentially a social phenomenon, in the sense that it depends not only upon channels of direct communication between the two parties, but also upon indirect channels mediated by other people. This suggests that a major factor reducing the psychic distance between

49

transactors is common membership of a social group.

An important corollary relates to the role of reputation in promoting trade. Reputation is achieved when a favourable opinion percolates widely through the network of social contacts, so that many people are willing to place confidence in the person or the product. As a result, people are willing to trade without further acquisition of information, so that the marginal cost of transacting is reduced. Effective creation of a reputation involves skilful use of social contacts, and an astute knowledge of how the network of social communication is structured, so that contacts can be developed at crucial points. Reputation, in other words, tends to be acquired by people with a good understanding of the structure and the customs of the group (or groups) to which they belong. They can achieve this reputation either for themselves, personally, or for the product that they supply.

Reputation reduces the relative cost of arm's-length trade. If buyer and seller have great confidence in each other, there is little reason for one to acquire control over the other in order to monitor product quality or to guard against default. The converse of this is that the need for internal markets is greatest where reputation is lacking. In a new industry, for example, producers may have little confidence in the quality of the inputs they are purchasing, and so may integrate backwards to secure quality control. They may also have little confidence in the ability of retailers to promote their product effectively, and so may resort to direct selling in place of wholesale supply. Similar reasoning suggests that arm's-length trade will be most common in countries with strong cultural homogeneity. Thus for example, the relatively high ratio of wholesale to retail sales in Japan compared to Western Europe and the US may be attributed in part to a greater degree of trust—coupled with the cultivation of personal reputation—that seems to exist amongst the Japanese.

As an industry matures and reputations are built up, arm's-length trade becomes easier to organise. The firms that survive will have acquired a reputation. As a result, intermediate products can be traded between the subsidiaries of different firms: markets that were closed against outside suppliers become opened up, even though outside suppliers may be used only to 'top-up' intra-firm supplies. Individual managers may even be able to acquire reputations within their firms, sufficient to allow them to 'buy out' their subsidiaries and operate on an arm's-length basis with the parent establishment.

The analysis of reputation also has a bearing on our earlier discussion of ownership advantage. The fact that MNEs internalise markets should not obscure the obvious fact that they are involved in arm's length trade in both final product and factor markets. Where customers

50

are concerned, a reputation for product quality may be the basis for a monopolistic advantage—especially where a brand name is used to indicate quality. Where factor suppliers are concerned, reputation may confer an important ownership advantage in the capital market. The typical MNE enjoys an international reputation, and is therefore able to borrow funds from sources in several countries. When the cost of capital differs internationally, the MNE's reputation gives it an important advantage over purely indigenous firms.

The Synthesis of Internalisation and the Orthodox Theory of Trade

The current economic theory of the MNE has developed independently of orthodox trade theory. Attempts by trade theorists to develop a theory of the MNE by grafting capital movements onto the Heckscher-Ohlin-Stolper-Samuelson (HOSS) model have signally failed. This is because the HOSS model stands firmly in the neoclassical tradition. There are no transaction costs in the HOSS model, and so there are no grounds for distinguishing between direct and indirect investment. This is a point altogether ignored by Kojima.[21] Yet it is clearly unsatisfactory for the theory of the MNE to remain divorced from mainstream trade theory, and a number of efforts have been made to integrate them.

The simplest way to integrate the theory of transaction costs—i.e. internalisation theory—with the HOSS model is to recognise that the case for multinational operations rests upon the relative and not the absolute costs of transacting.[22] Suppose that, apart from transaction costs, the HOSS assumptions apply. If it is assumed that, although certain institutional arrangements may be costly, the cheapest method of transacting is always a costless one, then the HOSS approach to the location of production remains valid. So long as the MNE plans efficiently, it will mimic the location of production that would prevail under arm's length contracts, as described by the HOSS model. (This result is analogous to the theoretical equivalence of competitive general equilibrium and idealised central planning that was discovered in the 1930s.)

The result is, of course, of limited interest because of the strong assumptions upon which it is based. It becomes more interesting when the HOSS model is modified to allow for technology gaps and for intermediate product trade. With these modifications, the basic insight of the HOSS model—that trade in final products can substitute for factor movements—is augmented by two further insights: (1) that technology transfer can substitute either for trade in final products or for factor movements; and (2) that intermediate product trade can substitute for trade in final products and also for technology transfer and factor movement.

51

Insight (1) encompasses the case where the export of technology through foreign direct investment substitutes for the export of high-technology products, as occurs in the 'maturing product' phase of the product cycle.[23] In this way the modified HOSS model can shed light on the global implications of import-substituting high-technology investment, as discussed in the section on ownership advantage.

Insight (2) encompasses the case of internationally rationalised production, exemplified by an assembly line supplied with components from a number of different locations. The potential for rationalised production in manufacturing has existed since the development of mass production and interchangeable parts in the early part of the century, but because of political instability and obstacles to trade in the inter-war period, it was not until the creation of customs unions and free trade areas in the 1960s and 1970s that the potential has been fully exploited.

It is not difficult to integrate the modified HOSS model with the modern theory of international finance. Both theories, being neoclassical, emphasise that markets facilitate functional specialisation. Each new market that is created permits a further separation of functions. The introduction of an international market in risk capital and an international market in loanable funds demonstrates that the provision of risk-bearing and the provision of 'abstinence' or 'waiting' can be separated from the organisation of production and trade.[24] This result has two important consequences.

Firstly, it demonstrates that a firm can obtain a controlling equity stake in a foreign plant merely by exchanging its debenture debt for equity debt in the foreign country. As a result, what is called foreign direct investment may involve no international movement of capital at all. Foreign direct investment may occur simply at the expense of foreign indirect investment, leaving the total stock of foreign investment completely unchanged.

Secondly, it means that when financial markets are globally integrated, a firm may produce in one set of countries, be funded by debenture-holders in another set of countries and have its risks borne by equity-holders in yet another set of countries. This has serious implications for people who wish to talk of 'US' multinationals or 'British' multinationals, since an important element in multinationality is that ownership, funding and production operations can each have quite distinct patterns of multinationality.

The main problem with the attempted synthesis of transaction costs and neoclassical theory is that the synthesis concedes too much to the neoclassical position. The focus in neoclassical theory is upon markets, and upon the functional specialisation that markets permit: the firm is of no intrinsic interest. All the theory requires is a representative firm that can be regarded as a 'black box'. The 'black box' must have an upward-sloping long-run supply curve of output and downward-sloping long-run derived demand curves for factors, and that is all.

The synthesis achieved with transaction cost theory makes it possible to predict, in principle, the institutional arrangement that will prevail within the black box, but only at the expense of assuming that the institutional arrangement will be one in which the management function is totally trivial. The triviality of management follows both from the fact that the institutional arrangement is by assumption costless, and also from the fact that since the firm's environment is purely neoclassical, all relevant information about the environment is encapsulated in freely available market prices (or a fully known demand curve in the case of product monopoly). In the neoclassical world, the invisible hand of the market does practically all the managing that is required. One cannot have an economic theory of the MNE that includes both the neoclassical theory of location and a realistic theory of management.

The neoclassical theory has enjoyed the undivided attention of a majority of British and American economists for well over a century. It would seem most fruitful at this stage to embrace the idea that the management and the organisation of the firm are of such intrinsic interest that the neoclassical approach should be put to one side for the moment, so that research can be focused more closely upon the firm.

Entrepreneurship and the Dynamics of Ownership Advantage

The moral of our review of the literature is that there is no really satisfactory general theory of the MNE. The best way to further enhance the relevance of the theory seems to be not to 'purify' or 'generalise' it, but to focus upon specific gaps in it.

This section and the next discuss two such gaps in the theory, and outline possible ways in which they could be filled. This section raises the question of how ownership advantages are created, and what factors determine the pace at which they are dissipated. The next section discusses political factors, and in particular the role of source-country governments acting as 'protectors' of their MNEs.

It is a commonplace that, where entrepreneurship is concerned, there is a gap in conventional economic theory.[25] Theories of the MNE are no exception to this. The entrepreneur fills the gap labelled 'fixed factor' in the neoclassical theory of the firm. Entrepreneurial ability is analogous to a fixed factor endowment because it sets a limit to the efficient size of the firm. The fact that neoclassical theory reduces the entrepreneur to a mere 'fixed factor' illustrates well the essentially static nature of its approach.

53

The same criticism may be applied to the 'ownership advantage' approach. Ownership advantage may be interpreted as a measure of the net wealth accruing from past entrepreneurial activity[26] but it tells us nothing about how this entrepreneurial activity was actually carried on, and offers little clue about the circumstances under which it is likely to continue in the future. Why is it, for example, that in the past 500 years technological and commercial advantages have passed from Italy to the Netherlands, and then to England, Germany and the United States? Why did US advanced technology appear exactly when it did, and why has it diffused so slowly to developing countries as compared to Western Europe? Why has it diffused much more rapidly to Japan? Current theories are too static to handle issues of this kind.

It is possible to develop a dynamic theory of ownership advantage using the economic theory of the entrepreneur. The theory views the economy as an evolutionary system[27] whose future is very uncertain, so that decisions have to be made on the basis of mere speculations about their consequences. Even the *probable* consequences of decisions cannot be estimated objectively: there are often insufficient precedents with which to estimate the relative frequencies of different outcomes.[28] People therefore hold different opinions about what is the best policy to pursue. Decisions upon which opinions differ may be termed judgemental decisions, and a person who specialises in taking judgemental decisions is defined as an entrepreneur[29]. The entrepreneur is of importance to the historian because at turning points in the evolutionary process it is his judgement which most often prevails.

There is one aspect of this theory that is particularly relevant to the MNE, and that is the idea that the most crucial entrepreneurial judgements take place on 'the frontier'.

Schumpeter defines the entrepreneur as someone who innovates by carrying out 'new combinations'.[30] Leibenstein emphasises judgement in identifying 'gaps' to be filled, and Penrose in finding 'interstices' to explore.[31] Kirzner emphasises the importance of alertness to opportunity.[32] This activity of exploring new opportunities takes place on the frontiers of knowledge. Other activity takes place on the territorial frontier: voyages of discovery to new lands, for example, or expeditions to prospect for mineral deposits. In historical terms, the exploitation of the frontiers of technology and territory seem to have gone hand in hand. In eighteenth- and nineteenth-century Britain, the industrial revolution at home was accompanied by the commercial exploitation of new colonial territories abroad. In the late nineteenth-century United States, the exploitation of the mid-Western frontier was paralleled by inventive activity in the Eastern states. Several other examples could be given from earlier periods.

The historical parallel between territorial and technological frontiers is matched by a theoretical parallel. It is a feature of any frontier that the environment in which people operate is not properly mapped out or fully understood. Since people do not have a proper model of the 'frontier territory', it is difficult for them to make choices which are 'optimal' in the usual sense of that word.[33] People may not know exactly where the frontier is, nor how far it extends, nor how many rival 'prospectors' there are and where exactly they are 'located'. It is difficult for people to plan rationally under these circumstances, and even more difficult to imagine how any kind of equilibrium distribution of frontier activity could emerge.

Another feature of frontiers is that property rights are usually ambiguous and ill-defined. As the frontier moves forward, the law moves along behind. It usually consolidates the position that has already been attained. The theory of the entrepreneur analyses the kind of situation that frontiersmen—working in a legal vacuum—are likely to generate. Where people on the frontier are drawn from a unified social group, they will tend to appropriate the frontier in accordance with custom. Custom cannot, however, anticipate all eventualities. It may dictate, for example, that priority of discovery confers ownership, but fail to indicate just how much of a newly discovered territory may be fairly appropriated. Custom may recognise the rights of individuals to keep newly discovered information secret, but may equally recognise the rights of others to extract the information by subterfuge, if they can.

Where there is a mixture of social groups on the frontier, it is more likely that force and not custom will govern appropriability, and that the strongest group will consolidate its position through the laws that it finally imposes upon the others.

Neoclassical theory provides little guidance on the factors influencing the allocation of resources when neither law nor custom prevails. The theory of games[34] analyses some of the strategic issues involved, but does so in an essentially static manner.

Successful frontier activity requires a combination of skills: the ability to identify profit opportunities, the judgement to evaluate them, and the tactical awareness to exploit them properly.

The identification of profit opportunities involves synthesising information from diverse sources. Identifying a potential innovation, for example, requires the entrepreneur not only to make contact with the inventor, but also to know something about the activities which the invention may displace. Skill in making social contacts is invaluable in obtaining information of this kind, and to exercise this skill it is often important for the entrepreneur to gain entry to the right social group.

55

Judgement is required because imponderables always have a crucial effect on the profitability of an innovation. There are diminishing returns to collecting 'objective' information: sooner or later the entrepreneur must rely upon subjective assessments. Entrepreneurs who have acquired a varied background—through travel or migration, for example—are most likely to develop judgement of this kind.

Tactical awareness is important in securing exclusive rights to the opportunity, and thereby appropriating the maximum reward from it. Dynamic considerations suggest that a particularly successful appropriation strategy is likely to be the 'pre-emptive strike'. Once a discovery is made, the entrepreneur quickly extracts all the economically relevant information from what he has found, and uses it to guide him towards further discoveries before others learn of his find and draw similar conclusions for themselves. An entrepreneur with a good 'track record' may attract a following of potential imitators, and may have to resort to diversionary tactics to put them 'off the scent'. At the same time he will attempt to consolidate his position by erecting 'barriers to entry'—which in this context could be anything from physical defences to announcements of threatened reprisals against imitators. Where resources are difficult to defend, the entrepreneur may attempt to monopolise more easily defensible resources which are complementary to them, for example if the entrepreneur has discovered a new technology, he may attempt to monopolise the raw material sources on which the exploitation of the technology depends. This may be more effective than attempting to defend his know-how through a patent since, even if a patent is available, his patent application will merely advertise his discovery to potential imitators.

The theory of the entrepreneur makes it possible to identify the kind of skills which favour business success. The 'frontier' concept indicates that these skills are most likely to belong to the social extrovert, the migrant and the military officer. This in turn provides a link with the kind of cultural values most likely to encourage entrepreneurship.[35]

Cultures which promote entrepreneurship are most likely to prove viable in the long run. Cultural differences may explain, for example, why foreign entrepreneurs often persistently identify opportunities that are missed by indigenous entrepreneurs. The foreign culture may accord higher status to the skills that make for entrepreneurial success. Even when the indigenous population is inventive, it may be foreign entrepreneurs that adopt the inventions and appropriate the economic rewards. Cultural differences may also explain why in some countries indigenous entrepreneurs are so much slower to learn from foreign example than in others. The very narrow background of the indigenous entrepreneurs in some countries may make the practices of the foreign entrepreneurs seem quite alien to them: their inclination is to resist the innovations, rather than to imitate them.

Specific instances of the role of entrepreneurship in the growth of the MNE have been given elsewhere.[36] Tactical behaviour by MNEs is exemplified by their exploration activities in the oil and mineral industries, and by the way that they have used their control of transport networks to create barriers to the entry of rival firms. A number of studies have suggested that the cultural impact of the MNE has been one of the most enduring effects of foreign direct investment.

The MNE and the Nation-state

In current economic theories of the MNE the *multinational* aspect receives much less attention than the *enterprise* aspect. An extreme position on this is taken by Williamson, who discusses the theory of the MNE as though it were merely a special case of the theory of the firm.[37]

It was, in fact, political concern about the threat to national sovereignty that sparked off post-war interest in the MNE.[38] Economic theories of the MNE assume a fixed configuration of nation-states. Taking the nation-state for granted, they inquire into the viability of the enterprise. This is the thrust of the Hymer–Kindleberger approach: given the costs of operating across national borders, what are the economic advantages of doing so? But this question can be turned around the other way. Given the economic advantages of operating on a global scale, what is the rationale for continuing to split up the world into different nation-states? Is the nation-state really viable in a world where the barriers to organisation over distance have been substantially reduced by jet travel and modern telecommunications?

With the world split up into different nation-states, each claiming sovereignty over some particular territory, an individual entrepreneur may, within limits, choose the state from which he takes citizenship. Although he is likely to be born a citizen of one particular country, he does not necessarily have to remain a citizen of that country if economic incentives suggest otherwise. The same point applies to a legal entity such as a firm. Differences in legislation mean that the privileges offered to firms—joint stock organisation, limited liability and, above all, rights to confidentiality—may differ between states. A firm registered under one jurisdiction may change to another by arranging to be taken over by a holding company registered elsewhere.

With both individuals and firms having a choice of national allegiance, it seems reasonable to postulate an international market for the services of nation-states. The 'product' is the bundle of services provided by the nation-state. The 'payment' is principally the tax obligations imposed by the state. The 'price' is therefore the value of the services provided per unit of taxation.

The privileges of corporate organisation are just one element in the package offered by the government. Fair adjudication when the company is in the right—coupled, perhaps, with the opportunity for bribery and corruption when the company is in the wrong—is also very valuable. The private costs of the adjudication process are an important component of transaction costs, and so the minimisation of these costs is a major consideration. Freedom of contract, and immunity for *ad hoc* interventions by the government executive are important too; when the executive does intervene, for example by regulating markets, it should be in response to rent-seeking lobbying by the company.[39]

For the MNE, however, the quality of the protection afforded for its assets is almost certainly the paramount consideration. A colonial power, for example, is able to offer much better protection to firms in its dependent territories than are other nations. This suggests that an enterprising businessman seeking to operate in the colonies would seek citizenship of the colonising nation, if he did not have it already, and would register his company under the jurisdiction of the colonial government. Likewise, if sovereignty over a colonial territory changes, it may be advantageous for entrepreneurs to seek new protectors by changing their corporate identity.

The net benefits conferred by a protector cannot be assessed without taking account of the tax liabilities involved. When entrepreneurs can shop around for protection, protectors must compete for custom by offering protection on reasonable terms. Imperial or colonial powers may demand high taxes to support high levels of military spending. Nations with little economic strength must compete by offering important legal privileges and low taxation: for example, attracting banking by offering exceptional confidentiality, offering flags of convenience to shippers who wish to operate with low safety standards, tax havens for those who wish to exploit opportunities for transfer pricing, and so on.

It is inevitable that from time to time rival protectors come into conflict with each other. Protectors, for example, may make rival claims to the same territory. This is particularly likely on the frontier. As noted earlier, unappropriated frontier territory is especially attractive to entrepreneurs. To begin with, entrepreneurs are operating in a legal vacuum, being entirely self-reliant where protection is concerned. Secrecy, subterfuge and the rule of force determine the appropriation of frontier territory, especially where the rival entrepreneurs are drawn from different social groups. In due course, each entrepreneur will appeal to his protector to consolidate his position by helping him to defend the territory he has acquired. If the territory is valuable, for example rich in minerals, he can expect vigorous protection because of the potential tax revenues involved. There is, however, a clear incentive for each protector not merely to consolidate established positions but to attempt to expropriate property held under weaker protection. Where valuable resources are at stake, nations may easily be drawn into war. This is likely to lead to mutual expropriation of existing foreign investments even if these are nowhere near the frontier. Instability on the frontier may therefore spill over to raise protection costs elsewhere, and damage the climate for foreign investment as a whole.

This discussion of the economic role of the nation-state may seem somewhat fanciful but, in other contexts, economic theory already reaches well into the domain of public choice.[40] The view that nation-states operate in a market environment underlines the fact that nation-states are not permanent institutions. Like enterprises, some grow, while others survive only a short time. The recent economic history of Europe illustrates this very well. The break-up of the Austro-Hungarian empire made some European companies into MNEs overnight.[41] These MNEs promoted advances in armaments technology and the growth of strategic industries in the interwar period. Rival prospecting for raw materials to supply these industries led to international tension in the years before the Second World War. After the war, the map of Europe was redrawn again, and greater emphasis was placed on European political union under the aegis of the US as superpower. The conversion of military technology to civilian uses, when combined with US marketing skills, gave the US the economic power to sustain this role. It was under this protection that US companies acquired the confidence to invest in Europe on a large scale.

The Place of Theory in Business History
Although this chapter is critical of several aspects of current theory, theory is still of considerable relevance to the business historian. It is important, however, to appreciate its scope and limitations. It is obvious that economic theory cannot derive laws analogous to those in physics, which involve simple exact relationships between measurable quantities, which are valid throughout space and time.

In any economic situation—such as the growth of a particular firm—there are a multitude of specific factors at work, and these can obscure the influence of general factors. The influence of general factors can be easily discerned only when information on a number of different economic situations is pooled. The best way to isolate their influence is to identify for each factor two groups of cases: one group where theory predicts that the factor will have had a significance influence and the other group where theory predicts that it will not. It is then possible to

59

compare the *average* behaviour in the two groups to see if the evidence reveals an effect of the magnitude and direction expected from the factor.

Another way of expressing the same idea is to say that economic theory is concerned with representative economic units, such as Marshall's representative firm. No single firm is ever fully representative: the only way of approximating representative behaviour is by taking a group of actual firms. Where the group has been selected from a larger population, the members of the group need to be selected so that the group reflects the same variety in behaviour as does the population as a whole. The historian needs to beware of the possibility that the kind of firms that make available archival material may be unrepresentative of firms in their industry as a whole—they may, for example, be more profitable, or longer-lived, than the typical firm. A statistician would say that a sample of firms selected on the basis of access to archives is unlikely to be a random sample of the firms in the industry, and that the results obtained from the sample may therefore present a biased picture of the population. For various reasons, business historians appear to be attracted to the study of successful firms, and this is sometimes justified on the grounds that the successful firms are the dominant firms in their industry. It should not be forgotten, however, that unless these firms enjoy a total monopoly of their respective industries, they will not be *representative* of the firms within them.

Research in business archives is very time-consuming, and it is therefore appropriate to inquire into the minimal number of cases that must be studied in order to put an economic theory to the test. A simple answer is that if the economic theory suggests that n distinct factors influence behaviour then 2^n cases should be studied. In the most elementary case, where just one factor is involved, the minimum number of cases is two. If, for example, theory asserts that higher profits leads to faster growth, then it is necessary to compare the growth of two firms, one of which is more profitable than the other. If the more profitable firm does indeed grow faster, then the theory is tentatively confirmed. If it does not grow faster, then the theory is tentatively rejected. With just two cases, however, specific factors may be masking the effects of profits, and the result may be spurious. To reduce this problem, additional cases must be considered.

If theory predicted that growth depends upon both profitability and the firm's degree of multinationality, then four cases would need to be studied: a profitable multinational firm, a profitable non-multinational firm, an unprofitable multinational firm, and an unprofitable non-multinational firm. Information on the non-multinational firm is

60

necessary to provide a 'control' or 'norm' with which the behaviour of the multinational can be compared. Likewise information on the unprofitable firm is necessary to provide a 'control' for the profitable firm. The use of controls is developed further in the theory of experimental design and analysis of variance.[42]

To summarise, it is evident that in the history of any particular business, specific factors exert an important influence upon its development. If, for example, the founder of a British firm has a cousin in Sydney, that may tip the balance in favour of locating his first overseas investment in Australia. It cannot be inferred from this, however, that in a sample of, say, twenty companies, the location of the initial overseas investment is determined by the migration of favourite cousins. It is likely that in a sample of twenty companies, factors such as transport costs, tariffs and the size of the market will appear more important, even though in any one case their effects may be only dimly discerned.

Conclusion

The economic theory of the MNE is a lively area of academic enterprise, and further developments can be expected to bring the theory closer to the needs of the business historian. In the meantime, there is enormous scope for applying the current theory to data generated by business historians. Once it is appreciated that economic theory is concerned with general influences on the behaviour of the representative firm, rather than with all the influences at work on each individual firm, it should be possible for business historians to gain new insights from application of the theory.

Notes

1. The author is grateful to John Cantwell, Tony Corley, John Dunning, Leslie Hannah, Geoffrey Jones, Steve Nicholas and Alan Rugman for their comments on the earlier version; however, the author alone is responsible for the views expressed.
2. The theories are related, though by no means identical. They include Dunning's eclectic theory as set out in J.H. Dunning, 'Trade, Location of Economic Activity and the Multinational Enterprise: a Search for an Eclectic Approach' in B. Ohlin, P.O. Hesselborn and P.M. Wijkman (eds), *The International Allocation of Economic Activity* (London, 1977) and J.H. Dunning, *International Production and the Multinational Enterprise* (London, 1981); Rugman's generalised internalisation theory, in A.M. Rugman, *Inside the Multinationals: The Economics of Internal Markets* (London, 1981); and Kojima's macroeconomic theory of foreign direct investment, in K. Kojima, 'A Macroeconomic Approach to Foreign Direct Investment', *Hitotsubashi Journal of Economics* (1973), pp. 1–21 and K. Kojima, *Direct Foreign Investment: A Japanese Model of Multinational Business Operations* (London, 1978). Kojima's approach is rather different from the other two, and as it has already been critically examined by P.J. Buckley, 'A Macroeconomic versus International Business Approach to Direct Foreign Investment: A Comment on Professor Kojima's Interpretation', *Hitotsubashi Journal of Economics* (forthcoming), only

passing reference is made to it here. There is also the synthesis between internalisation theory and neoclassical location theory originally proposed by P.J. Buckley and M. Casson, *The Future of the Multinational Enterprise* (London, 1976) and elaborated in M. Casson, *Alternatives to the Multinational Enterprise* (London, 1979). Finally, Williamson appears to suggest that his markets and hierarchies approach, as outlined in O.E. Williamson, *Markets and Hierarchies: Analysis and Antitrust Implications* (New York, 1975), already embraces the MNE as a special case, see O.E. Williamson, 'The Modern Corporation: Origins, Evolution and Attributes', *Journal of Economic Literature* (1981), pp. 1537–68. This does not by any means exhaust the list of contending theories. However, there is sufficient variety in the theories already mentioned to bring out the most important issues involved.

There are now many reviews of the economic theory of the MNE: see particularly P.J. Buckley, 'A Critical Review of Theories of the Multinational Enterprise', *Aussenwirtschaft* (1981), pp. 70–87, and P.J. Buckley, 'New Theories of International Business: Some Unresolved Issues' in M. Casson (ed.), *The Growth of International Business* (London, 1983); A. Calvert, 'A Synthesis of Foreign Direct Investment Theories and Theories of the Multinational Firm', *Journal of International Business Studies* (1981), pp. 43–60; R.E. Caves, *Multinational Enterprise and Economic Analysis* (Cambridge, 1982); J.H. Dunning, *International Production and the Multinational Enterprise*; and J.-F. Hennart, *A Theory of Multinational Enterprise* (Ann Arbor, 1982). There is even a second-generation literature reviewing the reviewers: N.M. Kay, 'Multinational Enterprise: A Review Article', *Scottish Journal of Political Economy* (1983), pp. 304–12.

3. M. Wilkins, 'The Significance of Foreign Investment in US Development, 1879 to mid-1914', *University of Reading Discussion Papers in International Investment and Business Studies* (1982).
4. R.J. Gordon, 'Why US Wage and Employment Behaviour Differs from that in Britain and Japan', *Economic Journal* (1982), pp. 13–44.
5. S.H. Hymer, *The International Operations of National Firms: A Study of Direct Investment* (Cambridge, Mass., 1976); R.E. Caves, 'International Corporations: the Industrial Economics of Foreign Investment', *Economica* (1971), pp. 1–27.
6. R.Z. Aliber, 'A Theory of Direct Investment' in C.P. Kindleberger (ed.), *The International Corporation* (Cambridge, Mass., 1970).
7. S.H. Hymer, op. cit.; C.P. Kindleberger, *American Business Abroad* (New Haven, Conn., 1960).
8. S.P. Magee, 'Multinational Corporations, Industry Technology Cycle and Development', *Journal of World Trade Law* (1977), pp. 297–321.
9. P.J. Buckley and M. Casson, op. cit.
10. J.C. McManus, 'The Theory of the Multinational Firm' in G. Paquet (ed.), *The Multinational Firm and the Nation State* (Toronto, 1972); R.H. Coase, 'The Nature of the Firm', *Economica* (1937), pp. 386–405.
11. P.J. Buckley and M. Casson, op. cit.
12. J.H. Dunning, *International Production and the Multinational Enterprise*.
13. J.J. Boddewyn, 'Foreign Direct Divestment Theory: Is it the Reverse of FDI Theory?', *Weltwirtschaftliches Archiv* (1983), pp. 345–55.
14. R. Sugden, 'Why Transnational Corporations?', *Warwick Economic Research Papers*, no. 222 (1983).
15. A.M. Rugman, *Inside the Multinationals: The Economics of Internal Markets* (London, 1981); A.M. Rugman, 'Internalisation and Non-equity Forms of International Involvement' in A.M. Rugman (ed.), *New Theories of the Multinational Enterprise* (Beckenham, 1982).
16. This is suggested by E.J. Mishan, *Elements of Cost-Benefit Analysis*, 2nd edn (London, 1976), Chapter 16.
17. Y.-K. Ng, *Welfare Economics: Introduction and Development of Basic Concepts*, (London, 1983), p. 175.

18. A.M. Rugman, 'The Determinants of Intra-industry Direct Foreign Investment', *Dalhousie Discussion Papers in International Business*, no. 25 (1983); A.M. Rugman, 'Transfer Pricing in the Canadian Petroleum Industry', mimeo (1983).
19. M. Casson, 'Multinational Monopolies and International Cartels' in P.J. Buckley and M. Casson, *Theory of the Multinational Enterprise: Selected Papers* (London, 1984).
20. M. Casson, 'Foreword' in A.M. Rugman, *Inside the Multinationals: The Economics of Internal Markets* (London, 1981); S. Nicholas, 'The Theory of Multinational Enterprise as a Transactional Mode', Chapter 4, this volume.
21. K. Kojima, 'A Macroeconomic Approach to Foreign Direct Investment'; K. Kojima, *Direct Foreign Investment*.
22. M. Casson, *Alternatives to the Multinational Enterprise* (London, 1979).
23. R. Vernon, 'International Investment and International Trade in the Product Cycle', *Quarterly Journal of Economics* (1966), pp. 190–207.
24. M. Casson, 'The Theory of Foreign Direct Investment' in J. Black and J.H. Dunning (eds), *International Capital Movements* (London, 1982).
25. W.J. Baumol, 'Entrepreneurship in Economic Theory', *American Economic Review* (Papers and Proceedings), 58 (1968), pp. 64–71.
26. S. Hirsh, 'An International Trade and Investment Theory of the Firm', *Oxford Economic Papers* (1976), pp. 258–70; P.J. Buckley, 'New Theories of International Business: Some Unresolved Issues' in M. Casson (ed.), *The Growth of International Business* (London, 1983).
27. R.R. Nelson and S.G. Winter, *An Evolutionary Theory of Economic Change* (Cambridge, Mass., 1982).
28. F.H. Knight, *Risk, Uncertainty and Profit* (Chicago, 1921, 1971 ed. by G.J. Stigler).
29. M. Casson, *The Entrepreneur: An Economic Theory* (Oxford, 1980).
30. J.A. Schumpeter, *The Theory of Economic Development* (Cambridge, Mass., 1934).
31. H. Leibenstein, *General X-efficiency Theory and Economic Development* (New York, 1978); E.T. Penrose, *The Theory of the Growth of the Firm* (Oxford, 1959).
32. I.M. Kirzner, *Competition and Entrepreneurship* (Chicago, 1973); I.M. Kirzner, *Perception, Opportunity and Profit* (Chicago, 1979).
33. H.A. Simon, *Reason in Human Affairs* (Oxford, 1983).
34. J. von Neumann and O. Morgenstern, *Theory of Games and Economic Behaviour* (Princeton, NJ, 1944).
35. F. Redlich, 'The Military Enterpriser: A Neglected Area of Research', *Explorations in Entrepreneurial History* (1956), pp. 252–6.
36. M. Casson, 'Entrepreneurship and Foreign Direct Investment' in P.J. Buckley and M. Casson, *Economic Theory of the Multinational Enterprise: Selected Papers* (London, 1985).
37. O.E. Williamson, 'The Modern Corporation: Origins, Evolution and Attributes', *Journal of Economic Literature* (1981), pp. 1537–68.
38. J.J. Servan-Schreiber, *The American Challenge* (New York, 1968); R. Vernon, *Sovereignty at Bay: The Multinational Spread of US Enterprises* (New York, 1971).
39. A.O. Krueger, 'The Political Economy of the Rent-seeking Society', *American Economic Review* (1974), pp. 291–303.
40. D.C. Mueller, *Public Choice* (Cambridge, 1979).
41. A. Teichova, 'Outline of Certain Research Results concerning Multinationals in Interwar East-Central Europe', paper presented to the Florence Conference on Multinationals: Theory and History, 19–21 September 1983.
42. M.D. Intriligator, *Econometric Models, Techniques and Applications* (Amsterdam, 1978).

63

[14]

British-Based Investment Groups Before 1914*

By S. D. CHAPMAN

Research by economic historians into new forms of business organization in the nineteenth century has cast the British role in a poor light. The British had shown little enthusiasm for joint-stock organization for much of the century or for the *crédit-mobilier* type of financing industrial development. The multi-national corporation was, it appears, largely an American phenomenon, with only late and limited indigenous development in Britain. The multi-divisional corporation was again entirely a creation of American managerial creativity. The trust was, as we have long known, an outcome of German dynamism.[1] Even the British banking scene continued to be dominated by family dynasties, while overseas investment in business enterprise, both colonial and foreign, was more restrained than historians had long thought.[2] The consequence appears to be that the small-to-middling business remained the most characteristic form of enterprise, even in the "leading sectors", for longer than the early writers led us to suppose. In a wide range of manufacturing and service industries the characteristic structure featured a multiplicity of diverse specialists whose leadership was addicted to family and (if possible) dynastic control.[3]

The evidence for this situation has been extensively researched and is quite convincing. However, so far as the British position in the world economy is concerned, some misgivings need to be recorded. Could the world's largest and most dispersed empire, created—so we are persuaded—primarily from economic motives,[4] be entirely sustained in all its diverse activities by traditional entrepreneurial and family enterprise? Was there nowhere any increase in scale commensurate with the mighty growth of empire and world markets? Most research has been focused on manufacturing industry, yet the traditional British genius was said to be mercantile rather than manufacturing, a sector that has attracted relatively little attention or money for research, and it would

---

* This is a revised version of a paper discussed at the 'City and Empire' Seminar at the Institute of Commonwealth Studies, London, on 11 Oct. 1984. For specific help I would like to acknowledge the contributions of Prof. K. N. Chaudhuri, Dr R. P. T. Davenport-Hines, Dr R. Greenhill, Dr Pat Herlihy, Prof. A. G. Hopkins, Dr Stephanie Jones, Mr S. Thompstone, and Dr A. C. M. Webb.

[1] There is a large literature on this subject but see especially, P. L. Cottrell, *Industrial Finance, 1830-1914* (1980); J. M. Stopford, 'The Origin of British-based Multinational Manufacturing Enterprise', *Business History Review*, XLVIII (1974), pp. 303-35; A. D. Chandler, 'The Growth of the Transnational Industrial Firm in the US and UK', *Economic History Review*, 2nd ser. XXXIII (1980), pp. 396-410; and H. W. Macrosty, *The Trust Movement in British Industry* (1907).

[2] D. C. M. Platt, 'British Portfolio Investment Overseas before 1870: Some Doubts', *Econ. Hist. Rev.* 2nd ser. XXXIII (1980), pp. 1-16. S. D. Chapman, *The Rise of Merchant Banking* (1984).

[3] See e.g. L. Hannah, *The Rise of the Corporate Economy* (1976) chs 1, 2.

[4] A. Hopkins and P. J. Cain, 'The Political Economy of British Expansion Overseas, 1759-1914', *Econ. Hist. Rev.* 2nd ser. XXXIII (1980), pp. 463-90.

be sensible to look for evidence of new kinds of organizational response to the boundless opportunities of the great age of imperialism.[5]

I

The far-reaching changes in mercantile organization in the last quarter of the nineteenth century remain indistinct. It is known that the introduction of the telegraph revolutionized international communications and that in London and Liverpool the general merchant and the commission merchant were superseded by specialized commodity brokers acting as principals. Unfortunately the standard works on this subject do not attempt to analyse market membership, though they leave some impression of family firms and dynasties.[6] Deficiencies in British entrepreneurship were offset by the migration of foreign entrepreneurs—especially Germans, Greeks, and Americans—to British commercial centres.[7]

This outline probably accounts for the more important part of the British response, but not the whole of it. The specialized commodity brokers were in direct and daily contact with world suppliers, but they were not themselves suppliers from foreign and colonial sources, much less the generators of materials of international trade. That function was originally performed by general merchants and commission agents, but as the chain of middlemen contracted they were often under pressure to look elsewhere for business. At the same time, the overall demand for raw materials and foodstuffs was increasing by leaps and bounds. In this situation a number of general merchants and original suppliers with established reputations evolved into investment groups, a form of organization defined neither by contemporaries nor by the writers of numerous commissioned histories, nor indeed by economic historians.

Historically, an investment group is simply an entrepreneurial or family concern whose name and reputation was used to float a variety of subsidiary trading, manufacturing, mining or financial enterprises, invariably overseas and often widely dispersed. The real economic strength of the group was concealed from the public, and is still largely concealed from historians, by the practice of preserving the parent organization as a partnership or private company, while the activities it owned or controlled were often registered abroad and run by junior partners or managers there, sometimes under quite different names and local legislation. It was a device that developed from various starting points to maintain effective economic power in a few hands, but its very size and diversity made it much more than a family business in the accepted sense. At the same time, it was able to avoid the clumsy leadership of such manufacturing giants as Imperial Tobacco and the Calico Printers Association that were federations of jealous family interests.

---

[5] The main exception to this generalization is Blair Kling, 'Origins of the Managing Agency System in India', *Journal of Asian Studies*, XXVI (1966).

[6] T. Ellison, *The Cotton Trade of Great Britain* (1886); G. L. Rees, *British Commodity Markets* (1964); P. Chalmin, *Negociants et chargeurs: La saga du négoce international des matières premières* (Paris, 1983); P. Griffiths, *The History of the Indian Tea Industry* (1967), ch. 43.

[7] S. D. Chapman, 'The International Houses', *Journal of European Economic History*, VI (1977), pp. 5-48.

This essay attempts to assemble the little that is known about this phenomenon by surveying some of the major areas of international trade: India, China and the Far East, Russia, South Africa, Latin America, and Australia. Leaving the details aside for a moment, it is not difficult to identify the economic logic behind the organization of trade. In the course of the revolution in communications that extended worldwide during the last three decades of the nineteenth century general merchants were increasingly caught in a scissor movement, for while the chain of mercantile links contracted, the financial sector (the traditional escape route of successful merchants) was dominated increasingly by the merchant and international banks—in which the great merchant houses were themselves partners or investors. Several prominent first-class houses disappeared in the 1870s and 1880s. Meanwhile, the rate of interest continued at higher—often much higher—levels abroad than in Britain. The old-established firms were familiar with local investment conditions and opportunities in the countries in which they had won their fortunes and reputations, while London merchant banks, company promoters, stockbrokers, and the investing public at large were wary of unproved foreign and colonial ventures, especially those in mining and manufacturing.[8] Partners who accumulated capital during their years of overseas service would leave it invested in the organization, and when they were promoted to the home partnership or retired from business it was invariably more profitable to leave it there. The business also attracted the loyalty and capital of family connexions, friends, and a wider circle of adherents both at home and in the overseas bases.

A more specific reason for the investment group, later rationalized in South Africa, was that of spreading high-risk investments. It was widely accepted that the risks of deep-level mining were so high in relation to fluctuating market demand, and capital needs were so immense, that the initial burden had to be shouldered by an exploration company or financial group. Having proved an economic reef, the finders might then appeal to a wider investment public, in practice rewarding themselves by maintaining control over groups of mines and other properties they did not own.[9] However, South African investment groups were by no means the first or only such concerns, as we shall see, to promote investment groups.

This identification must be related to the explorations of other historians in this jungle. The activities of mercantile investment groups should be distinguished from portfolio investments of the kind described by Charles Jones and others.[10] The present paper deals with the diversification and redeployment of mercantile capital, most characteristically in the course of the evolution of the business, or when assets were acquired by default of debtors, or to find an outlet for surplus capital. Portfolio investment simply represents wealthy individuals or firms seeking optimum returns from diversified share holding. The phrase "British-based" in the title of this essay also

[8] S. D. Chapman, *Rise of Merchant Banking* (1984) esp. ch. 1. J. W. McCarty, 'British Investment in Overseas Mining, 1880-1914', (unpublished Ph.D. thesis, University of Cambridge, 1961).

[9] S. H. Frankel, *Investment and the Return to Equity Capital in the South African Gold-Mining Industry, 1887-1965* (Oxford, 1967), p. 23.

[10] Charles Jones, 'Great Capitalists and the Direction of British Overseas Investment in the late 19th Century', *Business History*, XXII (1980), pp. 152-65.

needs a word of explanation. By no means all the firms listed were British, but all had a base (office) in Britain and conducted a large part of their trade or financial operations (or both) through London. Since foreign merchants made a major contribution to British overseas trade and finance in the nineteenth century, their exclusion from consideration would result in distortion.[11]

II

The investment groups serving the Orient originated in the special circumstances that surrounded British trade to India, China, and the Far East. The monopoly of the British East India Co. began to be eroded in the 1780s, when various former employees began to trade on their own account. In course of time the most successful of these concerns was Paxton, Cockerell, Trail & Co. which was started about 1781 in Calcutta, and presently fell under the control of an ex-naval officer called John Palmer. The abundance of money in Calcutta in 1822 caused the interest on the Company's debt to be progressively reduced from 8 to 4 or 5 per cent and led investors to deposit large sums with the agency houses, to which they responded by taking deposits only on fixed terms. Overflowing with deposits, the agency houses invested heavily in indigo factories, sugar plantations, ships, agricultural and building speculations, docks, and loans to mercantile firms in Singapore, Java, Manila, and other places, as well as to their local customers. It was estimated that by 1830 the total liabilities of the six agency houses amounted to £17m, of which Palmers accounted for £5m.[12]

As is well known, Palmers became bankrupt in 1830, followed at intervals by the five other leading houses possessing similar investments. However, the system they created was too useful to perish, and never lost the respect of the Indian communities. The partners carried on their bankrupt firms for many years afterwards, and in the course of the next generation the system was taken up by other British merchant houses, including some based in Liverpool and Glasgow.[13] Experience showed that because of the risks connected with distance, war, and financial crises, satisfactory trading results in the India trade could only be achieved by employing a large capital and "a very extended range of operations". Given a large capital and high degree of liquidity, it was easy to make money by accepting deposits at 6 per cent and lending to indigo planters and manufacturers at 10 per cent.[14]

Possibly the most successful investment group operating in the Far East was the Scottish house, Matheson & Co., which for many years was closely associated with, and in 1912 entirely bought out by, Jardine Matheson & Co. of Hong Kong and Jardine Skinner & Co. of Calcutta. Jardines' fixed capital investments began with a silk filature in Shanghai in 1870 and a sugar-refining plant in Hong Kong in 1878. In the same decade they were employing mining engineers to test and report on potential sites in China, Malaya and Korea

---

[11] Chapman, 'International Houses'.

[12] *Select Committee on Foreign Trade, Third Report* (P.P. 1820, II), p. 218. Bodleian Library Palmer MSS, especially D107. J. W. Maclellan, 'Banking in India and China: A Sketch', *Banker's Mag.* LV (1893), pp. 50-8, 214-18, 730-7.

[13] For case studies see W. E. Cheong, *Mandarins and Merchants* (1979), p. xii.

[14] *Select Committee on Manufactures* (P.P. 1833, VI), pp. 138, 196, ev. of G. G. de H. Larpent.

and built the first railway line in China. In the 1880s they set up and ran a shipping line and controlled Hong Kong's dockyards. Meanwhile, Mathesons bought Rio Tinto mines in 1873 and pioneered gold mining in the Transvaal. Several copper mines followed. In the 1890s, acting as agents of Platt Bros. of Oldham, Jardines built cotton-spinning mills at Shanghai and Hong Kong to meet the incipient Japanese competition. Along the way they regularly extended their banking and insurance interests. When Matheson & Co. was incorporated in 1908 the issued capital was given as £200,000, but the capital invested in the various subsidiary companies controlled by them was many times that amount; the mining interests in which they shared mounted to at least £7m. Most of this capital, so far as is known, was subscribed to joint-stock companies managed by Matheson, such as the Indo-China Steam Navigation Co. (1881), the Ewo Bank of Peking (1870), the Hong Kong Fire Insurance Co. (1868), the Jardine Spinning & Weaving Co. (Hong Kong, 1897), and the British & Chinese Corporation (1898), a joint venture with the Hong Kong & Shanghai Bank (in which Mathesons were major shareholders) formed to build railways in China.

There are at least three substantial business histories devoted to Jardine Matheson & Co. but none of them makes a serious attempt to analyse the policy behind this proliferation of enterprise or to estimate its overall value. The financial records of Jardine Matheson & Co. deposited at Cambridge tail off in the 1880s, and the present company declines to release further information. However, some notion of the size and diversity of the organization may be conveyed by the adjacent diagram showing Matheson & Co.'s investments on the eve of World War I.[15]

Fortunately, other business histories are a little more forthcoming, particularly that on Matheson's principal rival, Butterfield & Swire. The historians of this aggressive firm confirm that the difficult trading conditions in the Far East in the 1870s acted as the major stimulus to the development of a diversified business in which the components would feed each other. John Swire's extension from China shipping to sugar refining, insurance and dockyard development were prompted not only by the example of Jardine Matheson, but by the need to sustain his fleet at work. For most of his career he was short of capital so drew in friends as shareholders; in 1876 the partnership capital was £0·75m but over £4·0m was committed to the other interests.

The agency houses whose main interests were in India evidently followed a different course from those whose primary links were with China. Probably the best documented case is James Finlay & Co., a Glaswegian house founded in 1745 and originally strong in the cotton trade and industry. When Sir John Muir took over the leadership in the 1860s, the traditional policy underwent dramatic revision. Muir decided that cotton gave insufficient employment to the partners' capital and turned to tea as a trade with more growth potential. Another agency house, Cockerill & Co., had already demonstrated the possibilities with the £0·5m Assam Tea Co. (1839) so the investment was in no way a

[15] The full bibliography on Mathesons and 29 other investment groups included in this study is contained in the Appendix. Subsequent footnotes are therefore limited to supplementary references. Capital invested in mining has been calculated as follows: RTZ £3·5m, Transvaal Gold Co. £0·3m, Mountain Copper Co. £1·25m, Panuco Copper Co. £0·33m, Caucasus Copper Co. £1·4m. C. E. Harvey, *Rio Tinto Co.* (1981), p. 19, Standard Bank Archives, Johannesburg, Inspection Reports, Pilgrim's Rest, 1884-90; McCarty, thesis, ch. 5.

Structure of the Matheson Investment Group c. 1914

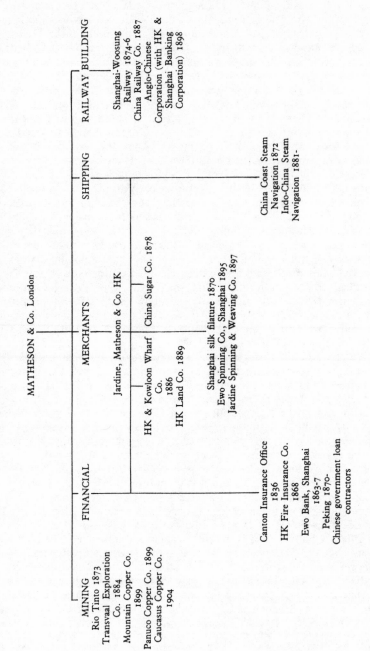

Sources: See Appendix.
Abbreviation: HK = Hong Kong.

236   S. D. CHAPMAN

speculative one.[16] From the tea estates the Finlay partners went on to investments in Indian jute mills (from 1873), shipping (from 1882) and cotton mills (from 1902). In much the same way, when Henry Neville Gladstone, a son of the prime minister, took over Ogilvy, Gillanders & Co., another old Scottish house, in the 1880s, he saw that the old shipping agency and consignment businesses could no longer be relied on as a mainstay and the firm shifted its capital to the development of Indian industries, particularly indigo factories, jute mills, railway development, coal mining and syndicates for the mining of copper, diamonds and gold. In the early years of this century they spread their interests to include two Russian petroleum companies and the Russian Collieries Co. It is interesting to note that a leading merchant bank characterized the senior partner as a representative rather than an outstanding business man. Similar details are available on Wallace Bros., who floated a string of subsidiary joint-stock companies beginning with the Bombay Burma Trading Co. in 1863 (intended to exploit the teak business) and from this success moving on to Arracan Ltd. (Siamese trade) in 1885 and the Indo-Java Rubber Planting and Trading Co. (1906). The Company's official history records that the Dutch East Indies and Malaysia were explored for investment possibilities in oil, gold, coffee and rubber. Rather similar but less well documented investments can be found in the development of Mackinnon, Mackenzie & Co. and Binney & Co. (now the Inchcape Group), E. D. Sassoon & Co. (Anglo-Persian Jews originally competing with Mathesons for the opium trade), R. & J. Henderson, the Borneo Co. agents, and Guthrie & Co. who borrowed £200,000 from the King of Siam to sustain their rubber estate investments. A careful analysis of British investment in Malayan plantation rubber in its main period of growth between 1904 and 1922 shows the major role of the agency houses.

However, by this time the local depositors in India and the Far East had evidently given way to much stronger financial support from the home country, at any rate in secure investments in the British colonies. The few partnerships that were running in the traditional way might now be regarded as something of a curiosity in the City. The transition from the old system to the new was eased, at least among firms in the vanguard, by the growing size of partners' capital left in the business, and by the growing flow of funds from the agency, banking and insurance business.

Certainly investment groups came in various forms and guises from around the turn of the century. Arthur Lampard of Harrisons & Crosfield, originally a firm of tea importers, became a leader in the development of rubber plantations when his Far Eastern tours opened his eyes to the potential. His firm had only modest capital and, initially, limited interest, so most of a long series of issues were made through the Stock Exchange. Marcus Samuel launched his Shell Transport & Trading Co. with the support of seven other Far Eastern trading houses to form what was originally called the "Tank Syndicate". The Samuels subscribed £1·2m out of the original (1897) capital of £1·8m but reserved entire control to themselves, a characteristic feature of investment groups; this was still true in 1918 when Shell's assets reached £11·0m.

[16] H. A. Antrobus, *A History of the Assam Co.* (Edinburgh, 1957).

III

Although the investment group is most familiar in India, China and the Far East (albeit disguised by the phrase "agency house"), it also appeared in most other sectors of British overseas trade. Latin America and Australia were not the most fertile ground for this form of capitalism but, perhaps because of the difficulties, the surviving records and literature relating to the groups operating there are rather more informative.

The best known name was, of course, Antony Gibbs & Sons, originally a small merchant house exporting textiles to Spain and South America, then from the 1840s to 1860s holders of the well-known Peruvian guano monopoly. The development of the business is most strikingly epitomized in the words of Vicary Gibbs, who was senior partner at the turn of the century. Leaving aside the period from 1808 to 1845, when he wrote "the business was being gradually worked up", Gibbs divided his firm's history into two periods. In the first, from 1845 to about 1870, he believed that the business was still concentrated on a very few lines, "all who were engaged in it, both chiefs and juniors, were active working partners"; most of the business was simply consignment trade which was "enormously profitable", between £80,000 and £100,000 annually, so that "the borrowed capital formed only a small proportion of the capital of the firm". In the second period, which he knew better from personal experience, he saw great contrasts:

> The business became extraordinarily various and widespread. There was no active working head, and latterly even junior members went into Parliament. Consignment business had practically ceased and the firm was forced into all sorts of enterprises of which it had no experience. But for the one business left which the firm understood viz. Nitrate, the business as a whole was extraordinarily speculative and unprofitable. The borrowed capital formed a very large proportion of the capital of the firm. . . .[17]

The variety of business developed in the second period has not yet been fully written (though there is ample documentation), but it certainly included nitrate factories and railways (in Chile), shipping, copper mines, various Australian interests, and a large portfolio of stocks and securities. Vicary Gibbs thought the business had come closely to resemble a trust company.

Gibbs's experience in South America was in itself unique, yet it exhibited features that were familiar to many established merchant houses of the period. Prosperity and high profits in the middle decades of the century were succeeded by severe competition in which a new generation, casting about for easier ways of supporting gracious life-styles and public service, was willing to defy the conventional wisdom of mercantile forebears by making long-term commitments to new ventures in developing countries. Living beyond their means or aspirations, the new merchant adventurers used their names to recruit capital from connexions and clients to float a variety of overseas development projects. In general, only the success stories have (so far) been recorded, but in Gibbs's case liquidity crises are on record in 1876, 1884, 1890, 1894 and 1920. Australia in particular swallowed up more capital than the partners and their clients could easily afford.[18]

[17] Guildhall Library, Antony Gibbs & Co. MSS 11,024/1, memo of Apr. 1902.
[18] Guildhall Library, Antony Gibbs & Co. MSS 11,042/2, 12 Dec. 1883, 8 Jan. 1891.

238   S. D. CHAPMAN

Other British investment groups active in South America appear to have been less speculative and to have initiated joint-stock enterprises in a more formal way. Balfour, Williamson & Co., founded in Liverpool as forwarding agents in 1851 and subsequently prominent in the grain trade with California, set up the Pacific Loan & Investment Co. in 1878 to extend their interests on the west coast of the USA, and in Chile and Peru. Initially most of the investments were connected with the grain trade (notably flour mills, warehouses, elevators and wharves) but interests were also taken in fruit farms, a coal mine and iron-ore deposits. Trading connexions were encouraged to deposit money with the London house, which in turn advanced credits to Chilean nitrate companies on a large scale. "No matter where the ownership lay, management was always the responsibility of Balfour Guthrie", the US organization, according to the firm's official historian, Wallis Hunt. The Chilean operation (Williamson Balfour) made issues for the South American companies and accepted seats on their boards. In the first decade of this century, these investment activities were greatly increased to include petroleum and cement, and the flour-milling side was built up. The partners' "responsible capital" in 1913 was £2·0m, but figures scattered through Hunt's book indicates that they controlled investments worth at least £4·475m in 1913.

The evolution of Knowles & Foster seems to have followed a similar pattern but on a much more limited scale. The firm started in the Brazilian trade in 1826 and diversified in the period when Thomas Foster Knowles was the most active partner (1878-1939). The best-known venture was the Rio Flour Mills Co., incorporated in 1886 with an initial capital of £0·25m. The mill company, part of whose capital was owned in Brazil, in time launched its own subsidiary shipping company and cotton mill; the capital reached £0·6m in 1912 and £0·8m in 1919. It is an interesting commentary on the source material that while Gibbs and Knowles & Foster were included in W. Skinner's standard work *The London Banks*, Balfour Williamson was not.

During the last quarter of the nineteenth century, two merchant houses with offices in London, Bunge and Dreyfus, came to dominate both the Russian and the Argentinian grain trade. Bunges were an old Dutch mercantile family who traded through Rostov, while Louis Dreyfus was an Alsatian Jew who started in Basle in 1852, then reached out to the Balkans and Odessa. Bunge & Borne opened in Buenos Aires in 1858 and Dreyfus soon afterwards. Though both firms still play a major role in the international economy, the reasons for their success have evaded the most dedicated scholars. However, for the present purpose it is probably adequate to note that they exhibit the characteristic features of an investment group, a modest capital at the home base concealing a massive and increasingly diversified overseas operation; Bunge moved into flour, rubber and petroleum, while Dreyfus seems to have concentrated on shipping. Contemporaries were highly impressed by their size and enterprise, but details of their capital and profits could only be estimated.

IV

During the first three-quarters of the nineteenth century a large part of British overseas trade, especially that to the Continent, was conducted by continental merchant houses with branches in London, Manchester, Leeds, Liverpool, and other commercial centres. The "international houses", as they have been called, provided a great deal of the enterprise, capital and specific expertise needed to translate British production techniques into commercial success, especially in the markets of Europe and Asia Minor. They were largely of German and "Greek" (Ottoman Christian) origin, but included a sprinkling of Dutch, French, Italian and other merchants. One of their most singular achievements, still uncharted, was to link the UK economy with the great Russian market which, for very different reasons, was short of indigenous mercantile enterprise. Many of the German houses originated in Hamburg, where they had traditional trading links with the Baltic ports as well as England, while the Greeks had long-standing connexions with the Russian Black Sea ports.[19]

As France, Germany and other parts of the Continent industrialized, their potential as export markets fell away, and the merchant houses that had prospered in European trade shifted their interests further afield.[20] But Russia continued to be a major sector for capitalist development, and several of the most successful merchant houses promoted investment groups there. The most diversified of these was probably Wogau & Co. whose structure was so complicated by 1914 that it seems best to represent it in a diagram. The firm was founded in Moscow in 1839 by M. M. Wogau of Frankfurt, and the London branch was opened by his partner E. A. Schumacher in 1865. In its early years the firm was largely interested, it seems, in the trade in tea, sugar, cotton and other commodities of international trade, but in the last quarter of the century it joined the vanguard of Russian industrialization by investment in a remarkable range of industries, including sugar refining, paper milling, metals, chemicals and building materials. In 1914 the concern in all its diverse activities was still run entirely by the descendents of the founders, but a large part of the capital consisted of deposits left in the business by relatives at 6 per cent interest. The London branch had now evolved to the status of a leading merchant bank with a capital of about £1·0m, a median figure for accepting houses whose bills were regarded as first class.[21]

However, the largest investment group active in Russia was undoubtedly that built up by Ludwig Knoop, "the Arkwright of Russia". Knoop came from Bremen but began his career with De Jersey & Co., a Manchester firm specializing in the export of yarns and (later) machinery to Russia. When they went bankrupt in 1847, Knoop effectively took over the organization, along with the Russian agency for Platt Bros., the textile machine-builders. Most of his enterprise was focused on building, equipping and managing cotton mills in Russia, but he was also active in the cotton trade with the US and in banking. It is said that Knoop was instrumental in setting up some 122 spinning concerns in Russia by the 1890s, that at the end of the century the Knoop family were on the boards of ten manufacturing companies and in addition held shares in another 15 undertakings. The house's capital in 1914

[19] Chapman, 'International Houses'.
[20] E.g. Ralli Bros. to India, Kessler to the USA, Reiss Bros. to Indonesia. Further examples are given in the author's 'International Houses'.
[21] Capital of accepting houses in Chapman, *Rise of Merchant Banking*, p. 55.

240 S. D. CHAPMAN

Structure of Wogau & Co. Moscow and London, in 1914

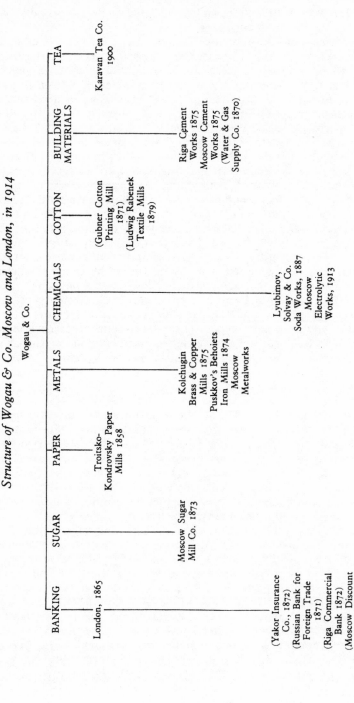

Wogau & Co.

BANKING — London, 1865

(Yakor Insurance Co., 1872)
(Russian Bank for Foreign Trade 1871)
(Riga Commercial Bank 1872)
(Moscow Discount Bank 1869)

SUGAR — Moscow Sugar Mill Co. 1873

PAPER — Troitsko-Kondrovsky Paper Mills 1858

METALS — Kolchugin Brass & Copper Mills 1875
Puskkov's Behoiets Iron Mills 1874
Moscow Metalworks

CHEMICALS — Lyubimov, Solvay & Co. Soda Works, 1887
Moscow Electrolytic Works, 1913

COTTON — (Gubner Cotton Printing Mill 1871)
(Ludwig Rabenek Textile Mills 1879)

BUILDING MATERIALS — Riga Cement Works 1875
Moscow Cement Works 1875
(Water & Gas Supply Co. 1870)

TEA — Karavan Tea Co. 1900

Source: Materialy po Istorii SSSR VI (*Documents on Monopoly Capitalism*), (Moscow, 1959) pp. 697–706. Firms in brackets are those in which Wogaus had a participation rather than full ownership.

was £1·2m but an attempt to embrace all their interests in one concern
envisaged a capital of £8·0m.

Wogaus and Knoops were pace makers, but a number of other firms
evidently had comparable interests, albeit on a more modest scale. Brandts,
best known in London as merchant bankers, had interests in sugar and
cotton mills as well as shipping and a meat refrigeration plant in Argentina.
Hubbards, one of the few survivors of the old Anglo-Russian merchants, were
also interested in cotton mills, forestry, and other ventures. The Russian
petroleum and mining industries attracted a good deal of west European
capital in the first decade of this century, but to maintain a balanced view it
should be added that this was more often raised by financial syndicates.[22]

The Anglo-Russian grain trade was originally in the hands of Greek firms
with offices in London, such as the Rallis, Rodocanachis, Scaramangas and
Negropontis, but in the second half of the last century their leadership in this
sector flagged. In *Merchants of Grain* (1979), Dan Morgan suggests this was
because Dreyfus and other Jewish merchants had easier access to the capital
required for warehouses, docks and ships to conduct the fast-growing trade.
This is not convincing because the leading Greek houses were much richer
than the firms that superseded them: by the turn of the century Rallis had a
capital of £4·2m in the Far Eastern trade. However, the only clear evidence
of a Greek firm creating an investment group in Russia refers to Rodocanachis,
who ran cotton spinning and weaving factories, a flour mill, brewery, pottery,
wire factory and steamship company. The explanation for the change of course
by the Greeks seems to be the rise of Jewish middlemen in the Russian grain
trade who built a closer relationship with their co-religionists.

V

At first glance the South African mining investment groups may appear to
be an entirely different species from those considered in the Far East, South
America and Russia, but closer inspection reveals close connexions and
parallels. It was not simply that investment groups in the sectors already
discussed were moving into mining and real estate, and would have moved
further faster had their geologists made more economic discoveries. Nor was·
it just a matter of South African adoption of the practice of a partnership or
private company controlling a range of private companies whose total capital
far exceeded that of the parent. Even more significantly, the earliest effective
gold-mining company in South Africa, the Transvaal Gold, Exploration &
Land Co. was initiated, financed and controlled by Matheson & Co. The
London partners were encouraged by the success of Rio Tinto Copper, which
they had floated in 1873, and made them the biggest importers of copper. The
new venture started at Pilgrim's Rest in 1882 with a capital of £100,000, which
had built up to £300,000 before the end of the decade. We have seen
that initially Mathesons were merchants, as were other firms that became
prominent in South African mining in the early years, notably Jules Porges &
Co. of Paris, Barnato Bros. and J. B. Robinson. As these firms grew wealthy

[22] For British examples of such syndicates see Guildhall Library, Gibbs MSS 11,117, and McCarty,
thesis, ch. 5.

they became even more like other major merchant houses, with offices in London and increasingly diversified investments including banking.[23]

Only Rhodes always insisted he was a "digger" but his enterprise also owed something to the influence of British business in India, at any rate by way of exemplar. In a triumphant letter written in 1888, just after the consolidation of the Kimberley diamond mines into the De Beers' Company, he wrote "we have now got the powers we required, and with the enormous back country daily developing we have every chance of making it another East India Company . . . . Africa is on the move. I think it is a second Cinderella".[24] Rhodes' subsequent career shows that the vision was not simply imperial flag-waving; rather was it recognition of the possibility of using De Beers' profits and the almost unlimited legal powers conferred in the articles of association to insure against further discoveries and to create a diversified investment group. At the very same period that Rhodes was forging De Beers, his partner, Rudd, was raising capital for the launch of Consolidated Gold Fields of South Africa, intended as a holding company to develop Rand mines, but in 1888 also used to support De Beers. As one of his associates wrote, Rhodes "disliked the feeling of not having a finger in every pie; besides, he was never averse from making money whenever there was a chance".[25] If his attempts to diversify do not look so impressive in the formal records, this is largely because the London board of De Beers repeatedly vetoed his bold projects, the City financiers fearing that he would pour their investors' money into unproven and open-ended projects such as those in Rhodesia and German South-West Africa.[26]

Apart from the emphasis on mining, the principal difference between South African investment groups and those operating in other sectors of international trade was the source of capital. In India, China, Russia and some of the Latin American republics, British firms made considerable use of local capital deposited with them, and it is easy to suppose that this was not available in empty countries like the Transvaal, Cape Colony (Kimberley), Rhodesia and Namibia. In point of fact, British investors were for long wary of mining shares, and the initial capital for the Rand gold mining industry was, with few exceptions, generated internally.[27] However, this capital was inadequate to sustain the sinking and equipping of deep level mines—estimated in 1889 at £0·5m each—and Alfred Beit (the financial genius behind both De Beers and Rand Mines Ltd) turned to the Continent. As a result of the popularity that De Beers shares had enjoyed in Paris, Berlin and Vienna, the same groups that had introduced these shares to the respective stock exchanges were glad to father the gold shares offered to them by Wernher, Beit & Co. Indeed, these stockbrokers were so eager to participate in the Rand promotions that

[23] On Mathesons' Transvaal interests see A. F. Williams, *Some Dreams Come True* (Cape Town, 1948), pp. 492-3 and Standard Bank Archives, Johannesburg, Inspection Reports, Barberton, 10 Sept. 1888, 21 Nov. 1889 etc.

[24] Rhodes House Library, Oxford, MSS. Afr. t14, 317-20.

[25] Consolidated Gold Fields of S.A. Ltd., *The Gold Fields, 1887-1937* (1937), p. 20. J. B. Taylor, *A Pioneer Looks Back* (1939), p. 122.

[26] S. D. Chapman, 'Rhodes and the City of London: Another View of Imperialism', *Historical Journal* XXVII (1985), forthcoming.

[27] A. C. M. Webb, 'Witwatersrand Genesis' (unpublished Ph.D. thesis, Rhodes University, 1981), ch. 1.

Wernher Beit did not have to resort to issuing prospectuses and soliciting public subscriptions. Other promoters also found themselves on an easy wicket; Barnato boasted at a civic reception in London in 1895 that he had never issued a prospectus. The shareholders were more like holders of bank deposits than of franchises under a constitution.[28]

From the earliest years of South African diamond and gold mining, the group system and the autocracy of a handful of pioneer financiers together conspired to create a situation in which a few familiar names controlled chains of mining, land, transport and other combines. The problem is to put figures on this situation and to identify the exact nature of control, partly because of the usual problems of business secrecy, but also because of the extraordinarily volatile nature of the market in mining shares. The most reliable group figures seem to be those assembled by the General Manager of the Standard Chartered Bank in 1895. Admittedly that was a boom year, but the £8·0m entered for Barnato Bros. seems a sober figure when compared with Barnato's own estimate of £20m at this date. J. B. Robinson was reckoned to be of equal size, and Luebeck, Neumann & Co. who were really stock dealers, rather smaller.

The only significant difference between the South African investment groups and those surveyed in other sections of this paper is that, in general, the former were founded later and their development was telescoped into a much shorter period of time. Perhaps their most interesting feature as investment groups, apart from precocious development, is that they brought together British enterprise, French and German capital, and American engineering expertise, an unusual if not unique combination in this period. The view that the mines of Kimberley and Johannesburg were somehow controlled by Rothschilds and other London financial interests is, in the light of recent evidence, no longer tenable; South African investment groups were as much the product of specific local trading conditions and decisions as others mentioned in earlier sections.[29]

VI

Clearly the information assembled in this survey is incomplete; it is based on the records of only 30 investment groups and few of them are well documented. Nevertheless, it is felt that most of the leaders of this development have been identified and a fairly wide geographical coverage achieved so that it is possible to make some provisional assessment of the significance of the phenomenon. At least, recognition of the species should lead to the identification of further and perhaps more telling examples and consequent revision or refinement of the features that can be described at this stage.

The sources cast little light on the problems of management and organization, but there can be no serious doubt that the investment group was primarily a device to maintain the wealth and power of the family (or families) that controlled the particular business. Nevertheless, outside expertise was introduced, sometimes with far-reaching results—for instance James Bryce in

[28] Taylor, *A Pioneer*, pp. 109-10; S. Jackson, *The Great Barnato* (1970), p. 170.
[29] Chapman, 'Rhodes'.

Wallace Bros. (for his unique knowledge of Burma), William Keswick in Mathesons for his managerial ability, and Herman Eckstein to promote the development of Wernher Beit's Rand Mines Ltd. The traditional development of the successful merchant house featured young partners investing their early careers in overseas stations, returning to a "home" partnership as they attained entrepreneurial maturity. This arrangement, evidently assumed by investment groups, assured a regular testing and turnover of the partners (or directors). Management recruitment within the family was not always a narrow choice, for Victorian families were large and selection was not confined to sons and sons-in-law of the partners.[30] Historians of particular houses have noted some positive virtues of the system from the management point of view. Thus, Sir Percy Griffiths writes in his attractive survey of the Inchcape Group that "Managerial expertise in India was in short supply and the system enabled a limited number of experienced managers to apply their professional skill in more than one field. There can be little doubt that such a system was almost essential to the economic growth of nineteenth century India." The historian of Wallace Bros. offers some insights, recording that from 1878 "the management was so constituted that the responsibility of the several managers in any branch was in the nature of a partnership", while the central partnership kept detailed records on the recruitment and progress of all its staff. But there are also clear indications of management weakness in comparable firms. Jardine Skinners were complaining of management recruitment problems even in 1891, which prompted the observation that "you may find that you have ultimately to recruit Germans, of whom there is an almost unlimited supply". Incompetent management carried another agency house (Binneys) into bankruptcy in 1906, while at different times Hubbards, Gibbs, Butterfield & Swire and the British & Chinese Corporation (Jardine Matheson) are known to have suffered from inadequate management. In South Africa there was no shortage of young upper-class adventurers from England, but many of the mining engineers had to be drawn from the USA, and the "problem of finding competent managers proved an enduring one".[31] Nevertheless, this does not significantly change the overall conclusions of Chandler and others about the managerial consequences of British nepotism; rather do they reinforce the American interpretation, showing how the traditional system was maintained through a period of rapid growth in the scale of international trade and investment.

However, it may be necessary to revise another accepted interpretation of British business history in the Victorian age, that of antipathy to the joint-stock company, for the investment group system evidently allowed the traditional family control to acquire many of the advantages of the joint-stock

[30] Guildhall Library, Wallace Bros. records, contain the only full record of staff recruitment and promotion for an investment group. There are stray comments on recruitment in various works, e.g. in M. Keswick, ed. *The Thistle and the Jade* [Mathesons] (1982), p. 38; R. Henriques, *Marcus Samuel* (1960), pp. 63-6, C. Drage, *Taikoo* [Butterfield & Swire] (1970), p. 224, and Hubbard (Anglo-Russian Mills), MSS at Guildhall Library.

[31] In addition to the bibliography in the Appendix, see C. B. Davis, 'Financing Imperialism', *Bus. Hist. Rev.* LVI (1982), pp. 244-9; R. P. T. Davenport-Hines, 'Business Representation in China, 1900-1930' (forthcoming); J. T. Hammond, *Autobiography* (New York, 1935), p. 231, and A. C. M. Webb, 'Some Managerial Problems Faced by Early Witwatersrand Mining Companies' (forthcoming).

system without losing control. Like so many others in British economic history, this interpretation is largely based on manufacturing industry, and finance and trade often proceeded from rather different assumptions—if only because the family owners were often of Scots or foreign origin. But the important factor was that the English legal framework for the creation of joint-stock companies was generous after 1865 and colonial legislation or case law made it even more so. This is most evident in the case of South Africa, where Cecil Rhodes was able to do much as he liked, but is also significant in the important case of China.[32] For ambitious entrepreneurs on the new frontiers of economic development, whether in India, China, Argentina, Russia, or South Africa, the opportunities were often too good to miss; the family name attracted (or retained) the necessary capital while the joint-stock system contained any possible loss. The art of those who controlled the investment group was of knowing how to use other people's money profitably. The system also offered advantages to the investor, for the Stock Exchange was not much interested in developments in distant parts of the world, and the family business offered a relatively cheap and secure way of acquiring the high rates of return from foreign investments.

But probably the most interesting finding in this area of research relates to the scale of business at the time. One of the most striking features of the investment group system is that it deliberately concealed the true magnitude of its operations behind the modest financial data of the parent company, and this has also deceived historians. The data on investment groups assembled in the Appendix to this survey have many gaps, and experience suggests they will be difficult to plug, but the figures are sufficient to make an initial comparison. Hannah's list of the 50 largest companies of 1905 includes two dozen firms with a capital of £4·0m or more, mostly in beer, textiles and shipbuilding, and all in manufacturing.[33] The preliminary survey in this work already offers more than half that number and comparisons between firms hint at several more that might qualify for this division. Peering into the future of research in this area, it is not too much to suppose that the 1905 manufacturing list might be equally matched in scale by a list of overseas investment groups based in or partly conducted from Britain. When we add the African chartered companies,[34] it is clear that the growth in scale of British enterprise in the period has already been seriously underestimated.

Unfortunately the sources available at present do not allow any calculation of the economies of scale of such investment groups, but the published work contains some indications that size and integration would be cost-saving.[35] We may surmise that trade generated the work for shipping, warehouse and financial services on the one side, and, through agencies for British engineering and machinery manufacturers, unrivalled appreciation of investment opportunities in the overseas countries in which they operated. No doubt there was, in

[32] Rhodes House MSS. and *Economist*, 25 Feb. 1893 (article on 'vendors' shares). A. Feuerwerker, *China's Early Industrialisation* (New York, 1970), pp. 1-19.

[33] Hannah, *Corporate Economy*, p. 183.

[34] A. G. Hopkins, 'Imperial Business in Africa', *Journal of African History*, XVII (1976), pp. 24-48, 267-90.

[35] E.g. in S. Marriner and F. E. Hyde, *The Senior* (Liverpool, 1967) and the bibliography of South African investment groups.

some group or other, "empire building" for its own sake or to flatter the founder, but no evidence of this has emerged so far. The emphasis, rather, is on necessary decentralization and decision making, a system of organization that was no doubt more efficient than the factious federations of family firms characteristic of many large industrial giants of this period.

A full history of investment groups would identify and explain their chronology and geographical dispersion, but on the basis of present evidence it is not possible to be precise about growth patterns. Originating in the early years of the century, the group gathered momentum through the century, with extra impetus imparted by the American Civil War (a major stimulus to Indian cotton growing and production), the difficult trading conditions of the 1870s in the Far East (due to the decline in the market for silk, indigo, and opium), the preference for imperial (as distinct from foreign) investments in the 1890s (following the Baring crisis), and the period 1910-15, when Russian investments were particularly favoured. Although the investment group has been identified in locations round the world, it appears to have been strongest in India and the Far East, and did not make any appearance in North America, Europe and in domestic industry. The explanation seems to lie in the collapse of the old kind of merchant house in many sectors of British trade in the wake of the Napoleonic War, giving way to the overseas commission merchant (or agent) financed by the London merchant bankers. This duality became more evident as rapid communications—especially the telegraph—extended, but something akin to the old type of merchant house survived, particularly in oriental trade (as the "agency house") and in Continental overseas trade (as the "international house"), and both retained strong representation in London.[36] In British industry the investment group was slow to overtake the traditional family business: the first appears to have been that formed by Soloman Barnato Joel of Barnato Bros., the London–South African investment group, in 1919.[37]

The final point must relate to investment groups and the City of London financial establishment at large. In one sense the families who owned these concerns *were* the City establishment, for 20 out of the 30 examined appear in W. Skinner's *The London Banks* (1914), and the others were closely connected with the same interests. For instance, Balfour Williamson & Co. called themselves merchant bankers, Harrison & Crosfield were a leading issue house, and De Beers' London board was dominated by Lord Rothschild's right-hand man, Sir Carl Meyer. Moreover, various partners or directors of these groups also appeared as directors of imperial, international and clearing banks and of major insurance companies.[38] There was no clear line demarcating investment groups with financial functions from merchant banks active in the promotion of public utilities and overseas shares.[39] Indeed, the only

---

[36] S. D. Chapman, 'British Marketing Enterprise: The Changing Roles of Merchants, Manufacturers and Financiers, 1700-1860', *Bus. Hist. Rev.* LIII (1979), pp. 205-34 and 'International Houses'.

[37] Stanhope Joel, *Ace of Diamonds: The Story of Soloman Barnato Joel* (1958), pp. 142-5. Wernher Beit and the Exploration Co. had diversified their investment portfolios from the 1890s, but not so as to control non-mining groups outside South Africa.

[38] Directors' and partners' names appear in Skinner, *The London Banks*, and these names may then be checked in Skinner, *Directory of Directors*.

[39] E.g. Erlangers were active in promoting railways in South Africa and Rhodesia in partnership with Paulings, the railway contractors: G. Pauling, *The Chronicles of a Contracter* (1926), Speyers were said to control the whole of London's omnibus service and the underground electric railways. See A. Moreton Mandeville, *The House of Speyer* (1915).

realistic distinction seems to be between them and what may be called the English *haut banque*—Rothschilds, Barings, Kleinworts, Schroders, Morgans and other leading accepting houses, whose reputation depended on their liquidity.[40] Most of these firms were also active as issuing houses, but limited their interest to safe stock, which in the context of this essay often meant investments whose value had been demonstrated by the investment groups. In other words, the groups still performed a mercantile function in the sense that they were the "local" experts with capital and supporting services in the countries or sectors of world trade in which they specialized.

University of Nottingham

[40] Chapman, *Merchant Banking*, esp. ch. 5.

248   S. D. CHAPMAN

APPENDIX.
Investments and Capital (in £m) of 30 Leading British-Based Investments Groups, c. 1900–1914

Group	Overseas base	Activities	Partners' Capital	Group Capital
FAR EAST				
Palmer & Co.	Calcutta 1781	B, D, Im, S, Sm	0·4 (1830)	5·0 (1830)
Binney & Co.	Madras 1799	Co, Cm, K, Sm, Su, Wm	0·12 (1906)	
Ogilvy, Gillanders	Calcutta 1824	Cu, Dm, G, Jm, K, RW, Su, S	0·75 (1907)	
Matheson & Co.	Canton 1832	(See chart 1)	0·2 (1906)	1·72 (1891)
E. D. Sassoon & Co.	Bombay 1833	B, Br, Cm, L, S, TW	1·25-1·50 (1909)	6·7 (1920)
Boustead & Co.	Singapore 1831	B, P, R, T	0·3-0·5 (1908)	
Finlay & Co.	Bombay 1862	B, Cm, K, S, Su, T	1·0 (1909)	4·36 (1898)[1]
Guthrie & Co.	Singapore 1821	B, OP, R	0·45 (1912)	
Jardine, Skinner	Calcutta 1840	Im, Jm, Pm, K, Sm, T		1·66 (1914)[5]
Mackinnon Mackenzie	Calcutta 1847	Jm, K, S, T		1·16 (1880)
Wallace Bros.	Bombay 1847	B, Cm, D, F, R, RW	0·8 (1911)	3·2 (1909)
Ralli Bros.	Calcutta 1851	B, Cm, K		4·2 (1902)
Henderson	Singapore 1856	F, G, K, Jm, Pm, R	0·5 (1908)	0·3 (1913)[2]
Butterfield & Swire	Shanghai 1867	H, S, Su	0·75 (1896)	4·15 (1900)
M. Samuel & Co.	Yokohama 1878	B, P, S	1·29 (1903)	3·0 (1903) 11·0 (1918)
Harrison & Crosfield	Malaya	Ru, T, To	0·2 (1901)	
LATIN AMERICA				
Antony Gibbs	Lima 1822	B, RW, S, Z	0·44 (1900)	2·0 (1900)
Bunge & Co.	Buenos Aires 1858	FM, P, R, S, W	1·6-2·0 (1910)	
Dreyfus & Co.	Buenos Aires 1880	B, S, W	0·6 (1903)	1·9 (1902)[3]
Balfour Williamson	Valparaiso	Ce, Fm, Fe, K, P	2·0 (1913)	4·5m+ (1913)
Knowles & Foster	Rio de Janeiro 1886	B, Fm, K		0·6 (1912)[4]
RUSSIA				
Brandt	Archangel 1805	B, Cm, Sm	0·75 (1904)	
Hubbard	St Petersburg 1816	B, Cm, F, K, P	0·3 (1900)	0·73 (1900)
Wogau	Moscow 1839	(See chart 2)	1·0 (1915)	3·67 (1915)
Knoop	Moscow 1840	B, Cm	1·2 (1915)	8·0 (1915)
Rodocanachi	St Petersburg 1851	B, Br, Cm, Fe, Fm, S	0·4 (1913)	
SOUTH AFRICA				
Robinson	Kimberley 1871	B, Dm, G		8·0 (1895)
Wernher Beit	Kimberley 1873	B, Dm, G		13·0 (1895)
Barnato Bros.	Kimberley 1873	B, Dm, G	0·96 (1897)	8·0 (1895)
De Beers	Kimberley 1874	Dm, G, Rw	3·95 (1896)	14·5 (1896)
Neumann, Leubeck	Johannesburg c. 1888	B, Dm, G		2·5 (1895)

Notes
(1) Overseas base refers only to the earliest or principal overseas location; in fact almost all investment groups operated simultaneously from several overseas centres of trade.
(2) Much information on capital is drawn from bank records which convey orders of magnitude, possibly erring on the conservative side.

Key to Investment Group activities:

B	Banking	OP	Oil palm plantation
Br	Breweries	Pm	Paper mills
Ce	Cement works	P	Petroleum
Co	Coffee plantation(s)	R	Rubber estates
Cm	Cotton mill(s)	RW	Railways(s)

BRITISH-BASED INVESTMENT GROUPS   249

Cu	Copper mine(s)	Sm	Sugar mills
Dm	Diamond mine(s)	S	Shipping
Fe	Iron works	T	Tea estates
Fm	Flour mill(s)	To	Tobacco plantation
G	Gold mine(s)	TW	Tramways
H	Harbours and/or docks	W	Warehousing
Im	Indigo mills	Wm	Woollen mill(s)
Jm	Jute mill(s)	Z	Soda factories

References
1 Tea estates only.
2 Borneo Co. only, nominal valuation.
3 Russia only, Argentinian interests probably much greater.
4 Rio Flour Mill Co. only
5 B.I. shipping line only.

SOURCES
(order of appearance in text)
Abbreviations: KB Info Bks=Kleinwort Benson Information Books, Guildhall Library.
                Skinner=W. Skinner, *The London Banks* (1865-1914), *Directory of Directors*.

India, China and the Far East
PALMER & Co.
J. W. Maclellan, 'Banking in India and China, A Sketch', *Banker's Mag.*, LV (1893), p. 52.
Bodleian Library, Palmer MSS. D107 (bankruptcy).
A. Tripathi, *Trade and Finance in the Bengal Presidency, 1793-1833* (Calcutta, 1956).

MATHESON & Co.
E. Lefevour, *Western Enterprise in Late Ch'ing China: A Selective Survey of Jardine Matheson & Co.'s
     Operations, 1842-95* (Harvard, 1968).
Maggie Keswick, ed. *The Thistle and the Jade* (1982)
Cambridge University Library, Jardine Matheson MSS. Jardine Skinner MSS.
McCarty, thesis, ch. 5.
C. E. Harvey, *The Rio Tinto Company, 1873-1954* (1981).

OGILVY, GILLANDERS & Co.
J. S. Gladstone, *History of Gillanders, Arbuthnot & Co. and Ogilvy, Gillanders & Co.*
KB Info. Bks II p. 165.

JAMES FINLAY & Co.
[C. Brogan] *James Finlay & Co., 1750-1950* (Glasgow, 1951).
John Scott and Michael Hughes, *The Anatomy of Scottish Capital* (1980), ch. 1.

E. D. SASSOON & Co.
Cecil Roth, *The Sassoon Dynasty* (1941).
Stanley Jackson, *The Sassoons* (1968).
KB Info. Bks UK III p. 131.
Nottingham University Archives, Brandt Circulars..

WALLACE Bros.
A. C. Pointon, *Wallace Bros.* (Oxford, 1974).
A. C. Pointon, *The Bombay Burma Trading Corporation* (Southampton, 1963).
Wallace Bros. MSS, Guildhall Library.

GUTHRIE & Co.
KB Info. Bks UK II pp. 47, 121, 151. Skinner.
G. C. Allen and A. G. Donnithorne, *Western Enterprise in Far Eastern Economic Development: China and
     Japan* (1954).

R. & J. HENDERSON
KB Info. Bks. UK III p. 166.
P. Griffiths, *A History of the Inchcape Group* (1977), pp. 130-6.
Borneo Co. MSS, Inchcape Group, London.

HARRISON & CROSFIELD
Harrison & Crosfield, *One Hundred Years as East India Merchants, 1844-1943* (1943).
KB Info. Bks UK I p. 98.

250 S. D. CHAPMAN

EDWARD BOUSTEAD & Co.
KB Info. Bks UK II p. 46.
Skinner.

BUTTERFIELD & SWIRE
S. Marriner and F. E. Hyde, *The Senior: John Samuel Swire, 1825-98* (Liverpool, 1967).
C. Drage, *Taikoo* (1970).

M. SAMUEL & Co.
R. Henriques, *Marcus Samuel* (1960).
F. C. Gerretson, *History of the Royal Dutch, 1953-7*, II, pp. 145-6.
KB Info. Bks UK II pp. 170-1, gives £1·2m as partners' capital.
Guildhall Library, Antony Gibbs & Co. Info Bks, MS 11,069C gives Shell's capital as £1·8m in Oct. 1897,
    £2m in June 1900, £3m in Feb. 1903.

JARDINE, SKINNER & Co.
University of Cambridge, Jardine Skinner MSS.

MACKINNON, MACKENZIE & Co.
P. Griffiths, *A History of the Inchcape Group* (1977).
G. Blake, *B. I. Centenary* (1956).
Inchcape Group Archives, London.

BINNEY & Co.
Griffiths, *Inchcape.*
Binney & Co. MSS. Inchcape Group, London.

RALLI Bros.
[Jack Vlasto], *Ralli Bros. Ltd.* (1951).
Chapman, 'The International Houses'.
Baring Bros. 'Characters Book I', pp. 131-2.
Jardine Skinner MSS. In-Letters 13.

Latin America
ANTONY GIBBS
J. A. Gibbs, *The History of Antony & Dorothea Gibbs* (1922)
W. Maude, *Antony Gibbs & Sons Ltd* (1958).
Guildhall Library, Papers of Antony Gibbs & Sons, esp. 11,942/1, 11,042/2, pp. 1-29.
John Mayo, 'British Commission Houses and the Chilean Economy, 1851-80', *Journal of Latin American
    Studies*, XI (1979), pp. 283-302.
W. M. Matthew, *The House of Gibbs and the Peruvian Guano Monopoly* (1981)

KNOWLES & FOSTER
[Anon.], *The History of Knowles & Foster, 1828-1948* (1948).
R. Graham, 'A British Industry in Brazil', *Bus. Hist.* VIII (1966), pp. 13-38.
The 'group capital' entered for this firm refers only to Rio Flour mills.

BALFOUR, WILLIAMSON & Co.
Wallis Hunt, *Heirs of Great Adventure: The History of Balfour, Williamson & Co. Ltd.* (1951).
University College London, Balfour Williamson MSS.

Russia and Latin America
BUNGE & Co. LOUIS DREYFUS & Co.
J. R. Scobie, *Revolution on the Pampas* (Austin, 1964).
Dan Morgan, *Merchants of Grain* (1979).
M. P. Federov, *Khlebnaya Torgovlya u Glaneyshikh Russkikh Portakh i Kenigsberge* (The Grain Trade in
    the Main Russian Ports and in Konigsberg) (Moscow, 1888).
P. Chalmin, *Negociants et Chargeurs: La saga du négoce international des matières premières* (Paris, 1983).
Nottingham University Archives, Brandt Circulars.
KB Info. Bks, France, Belgium & Holland II pp. 8, 104, III p. 114, UK II p. 97.

Russia
WOGAU
Documents on Monopoly Capitalism VI (Moscow, 1959), pp. 597-706.
Brandt Circulars, Nottingham University Archives.

KNOOP
S. Thompstone, 'Ludwig Knoop, The Arkwright of Russia', *Textile History*, XV (1984), pp. 45-73.

Nottingham University Archives, Brandt Circulars, for financial details.
Baring Bros. Character Books VIII (1870-83), p. 189.

BRANDTS
C. Amburger, *William Brandt and the Story of his Enterprises* (Typescript n.d., *c.* 1950).

J. HUBBARD & Co.
T. H. S. Escott, *City Characters under Several Reigns* (1922), ch. XIV.
Guildhall Library, Anglo-Russian Cotton Co. MSS. 10,364/1, 2.
J. Mai, *Das Deutsche Kapital in Russland* (Berlin, 1970), p. 70.
KB Info. Bks. UK III, p. 139.

RODOCANACHI, Sons & Co.
P. Herlihy, 'Greek Merchants in Odessa in the 19th Century', *Harvard Ukrainian studies*, III/IV (1979-80),
     pp. 399-420, and information from Dr Herlihy.
Chapman, 'The International Houses'.

South Africa
DE BEERS
R. V. Turrell, 'Rhodes, De Beers and Monopoly', *Journal of Imperial & Commonwealth History*, X (1982),
     pp. 311-43.
C. Newbury, 'Out of the Pit: The Capital Accumulation of Cecil Rhodes', *Journal of Imperial and
     Commonwealth History*, X (1981), pp. 25-49.
Consolidated Gold Fields of S.A. Ltd., *The Gold Fields, 1887-1937* (1937).
J. B. Taylor, *A Pioneer Looks Back* (1939).

WERNER, BEIT & Co.
A. P. Cartwright, *The Corner House* (Cape Town, 1965).
R. V. Kubicek, *Economic Imperialism in Theory and Practice: The Case of South African Gold Mining
     Finance, 1886-1914* (Duke, 1979).

BARNATO Bros.
H. Raymond, *B. I. Barnato: A Memoir* (1897).
S. Jackson, *The Great Barnato* (1970).
Statist, XLII (1898), p. 457 for Barnato family wealth.

ROBINSON
L. Weinthal, *Memories, Mines and Millions* (1929).

NEUMANN, LUEBECK & Co.
Kubicek, *Economic Imperialism.*
Standard Bank Archives.
Skinner.

[15]

Economic History Review, 2nd ser., XLI, 2(1988), pp. 259-282

The free-standing company, 1870-1914: an important type of British foreign direct investment[1]

By MIRA WILKINS

The 'free-standing company' is a novel phrase that redefines a particular type of British foreign direct investment, which although familiar to all students of British capital exports in the period 1870-1914, is none the less inadequately analysed in the extensive literature on British overseas investment.[2] This article seeks to fill this gap in the literature, by employing a new typology that focuses on the individual firm as an operating entity.

A recent estimate shows the proportion of overseas assets in British national wealth was 30 per cent just before World War I.[3] Some of this overseas investment was strictly financial in character (in the form of loans to foreign governments and capital for private firms abroad), but some of it was foreign 'direct investment', defined here (following the U.S. Department of Commerce) as investments abroad made for business purposes with the investors intending to control or having the potential to control the foreign operations.

Foreign direct investments differed from bank loans or other 'portfolio' investments where the relationship between the investor and the recipient was at arm's length. In the latter case, the foreign lender (investor) evaluated the borrower and made the loan or provided the equity capital; thereafter, the money was at the disposal of the recipient. By contrast, what characterized the foreign direct investor was the power retained to control and run the business abroad.

While the existence of British direct investments overseas in this

---

[1] I have discussed my ideas on free-standing companies with Alfred D. Chandler, John McKay, Geoffrey Jones, Tony Corley, Les Hannah, Ra Lundström, Phil Cottrell, Christopher Platt, Jean-François Hennart, Rondo Cameron, John Dunning, Stanley Chapman, and Lou Wells, all of whom have contributed significantly in clarifying my views. Likewise, the work of Oliver Williamson, Kenneth Arrow, and Mark Casson has been important in my thinking, as has that of R.C. Michie and P.L. Payne. This paper was presented at two seminars—one at Florida International University and the other at the Wharton School, University of Pennsylvania. In both cases, I want to thank the participants for their stimulating comments.

[2] The literature on British overseas investment 1870-1914 is enormous. The notes to Pollard, 'Capital exports', provide a good start in bibliography. See also Edelstein's superb Overseas investment. In this paper, I use the words 'foreign' and 'overseas' as synonymous, that is, to cover British investments outside England, Wales, Scotland, and Ireland.

[3] Edelstein, Overseas investment, p. 25.

period has long been acknowledged,[4] its quantitative significance has been understated and is still not clear. In 1970 Dunning concluded that only 10 per cent of British overseas investments on the eve of World War I were direct investments. By 1983 substantial new research led Dunning to suggest that 35 per cent was probably a more reliable estimate.[5]

Research on the history of British foreign direct investment has taken two distinct directions, both identifying the sizeable extent of such stakes. On the one hand, there have been the students of multinational enterprise, who knew how American companies behaved and assumed British ones followed the American model. These authors studied businesses with headquarters and operations in the United Kingdom which made direct investments abroad to sell or to manufacture in foreign lands, or alternatively to obtain sources of supply overseas. On the other hand, some researchers on British foreign investment knew nothing of or ignored the American model. They found that there were many British-managed companies overseas and described them as foreign direct investments.

The research revealed many British multinationals operating in the same pattern as their American counterparts. But there were also enterprises domiciled abroad, managed by British migrants who had been born and brought up in Britain but who resided overseas; such enterprises might not have a British head office or a British parent company. The individual Briton who settled abroad did *not* create a foreign direct investment, since there remained no obligation to anyone in Britain, whereas the expatriate who went abroad for years, who considered himself British and who then returned home, retaining an interest in his overseas business, became thereby on his return a foreign investor. In those instances where the expatriate tapped British capital markets, establishing a company or companies in England or Scotland, the British *company* became the foreign direct investor.[6]

---

[4] Paish wrote of 'private capital employed abroad' that could not be documented. Paish, 'Great Britain's capital', p. 187, and *idem*, 'Export of capital'. Sometimes this has been called 'direct investment', i.e. investment bypassing British money markets. On the variations in definition see Wilkins, 'Modern European economic history', p. 585. Platt, *Britain's investment overseas*, pp. 54, 60, 115, 137, and 139, wants to increase the amount of foreign direct investment in the British overseas investment estimates. On direct investments, see also Remer, *Foreign investments*; Brayer, 'Influence of British capital'; Clements, 'British-controlled enterprise'; Spence, *British investments*; and Rippy, *British investment*.

[5] Dunning, *Studies*, p. 2, used the 90 per cent portfolio (10 per cent direct) investment figure, which has frequently and mistakenly been repeated as gospel. His newer tentative estimates are in *idem*, 'Changes', p. 87. Platt's 16 per cent estimate is equally impressionistic (Platt, *Britain's investment overseas*, p. 60). Dunning and Platt defined 'direct' investments differently, with the former using a more encompassing definition. The new research includes Dahl, thesis; Coram, thesis; Jackson, *Enterprising Scot*; McFarlane, 'British investment'; Stopford, 'Origins'; Wilson, 'Multinational'; Paterson, 'British direct investment'; Kerr, *Scottish capital*; Stone, 'British direct and portfolio investment'; Svedberg, 'Portfolio-direct composition'; Nicholas, 'British multinational investment'; Jones, 'State and business practice'; Jones, ed., *British multinationals*.

[6] Remer, *Foreign investments*, dealt with both resident and non-resident British direct investment, as did Coram, thesis. Methodologically, this is wrong. Here again, it is useful to accept the U.S. Department of Commerce definition that a 'foreign investment' must be by a *nonresident*; otherwise, there is no ongoing 'foreign' obligation. Since America was a country of immigrants, not emigrants, students of the history of U.S. business abroad rarely had to deal with the expatriate investor, although some cases bore a resemblance to British expatriates' behaviour. It is true that emigrants (and expatriates) transferred capital (especially human capital), but the absence of any continuing obligation to *owners* in Britain meant the lack of an ongoing foreign direct investment. If the British expatriate raised money in Britain without forming a British company, such *investments* would be portfolio ones by definition.

THE FREE-STANDING COMPANY 1870-1914 261

Of key importance, such research showed that there were thousands of companies registered in England or Scotland to conduct business overseas, most of which, unlike the American model, did *not* grow out of the domestic operations of existing enterprises that had headquarters in Britain. Some of these thousands of companies had their origins in expatriates' behaviour. Most were what I have called free-standing companies.[7] Typically, they were included in studies of British portfolio investment, because usually their formation involved capital markets.[8] Yet they were direct investments, since they were designed to conduct business operations abroad, to manage and to direct the specific business.[9]

Students of multinational enterprise have paid little attention to them, since they failed to conform to the expected model. Likewise, in the literature on British portfolio investments, capital exports, and overseas finance, authors have frequently ignored the foreign investment carried out by these 'firms', referring to the *owners of the securities* of the British enterprise as the overseas investors. Thus, the real foreign investors (the companies) often became invisible. Accordingly, their role in overseas investment has been inadequately understood. The free-standing company was, however, probably the most typical mode of British direct investment abroad. The purpose of this article is to analyse and to explain the institutional dimensions and performance of these companies, considering the free-standing company as a governance structure.[10]

I

In London, and to a far lesser extent in other British cities, notably Edinburgh, Glasgow, and possibly Dundee, between 1870 and 1914 thousands of free-standing companies were organized to engage in business overseas,[11] though their precise number is unknown. Such companies represented a

---

[7] See Wilkins, 'Defining a firm', pp. 84-91. Many free-standing companies were neither 'expatriate' investments as defined by Stopford ('Origins', pp. 305-8), nor did they fit the U.S. model of foreign direct investment.

[8] Paish in Wilkins, ed., *British overseas investments*; Hall, *London capital market*; Simon, 'The pattern'; Davis and Huttenback, 'Export of British finance' and *idem, Mammon*.

[9] Both Svedberg, 'Portfolio-direct composition', and Paterson, *British direct investment*, recognized this.

[10] The phrase 'governance structure' is from Williamson, *Economic institutions*, p. 13.

[11] The basic files on these companies are in the Companies Registration Office, England and the Companies Registration Office, Scotland. The files of defunct English companies are at the Public Record Office. They are often cited with registration number and the designation, BT 31. See also the *Stock Exchange year book, Burdett's official intelligence* and its successor, *Stock Exchange official intelligence*; Ashmead, *Twenty-five years*, is helpful on the overseas mining companies. Guildhall, London, has Stock Exchange records and added data on these firms. Ostrye, *Foreign investment*, pp. 96, 129-67 lists roughly 1,800 free-standing companies set up to operate in the North American west, 1870-1914. The U.S. Federal Trade Commission, *Report on cooperation*, II, pp. 537-74, contains a 'partial' list of more than 2000 'British-organized or controlled companies whose properties were located outside of the United Kingdom, United States, and Canada'. Most of these companies were organized and registered in Britain. Michie, *Money, mania*, p. 154, noted that 'The most prominent feature of Scottish joint-stock company promotion in the second half of the [nineteenth] century was the growing number of concerns, in an increasing variety of fields, that were formed to operate outside of Scotland', that is, overseas. His book contains useful data on such firms.

sizeable proportion of the proliferation of British joint-stock companies.[12] Each of the companies set up to conduct business abroad was registered in England or Scotland as a joint-stock, limited liability company.[13] Each had a board of directors and stockholders who might or might not be British; a memorandum of association and articles of association defined corporate objectives and functions; and their capital was denominated in sterling. Usually the enterprises operated (or were intended to operate) directly abroad, although they might be holding companies, owning securities of a subsidiary or subsidiaries that operated overseas, a distinction which for the purpose of this article made no difference.[14]

The companies were to operate in numerous countries at various stages of development, inside and outside the Empire, worldwide, although usually, initially at least, on a bi-national basis, that is, with a headquarters in the United Kingdom and operations in only one foreign country (for example, Anglo-Brazilian, Anglo-Australian, or Anglo-Russian). While each typically operated in only a single economic sector, the companies were to be found in such widely differing activities as agriculture, timber, cattle raising, mining, oil production, manufacturing, transportation, public utilities, banking, land-mortgages, and land development.[15] Sometimes a company acquired an existing business overseas, and sometimes it commenced afresh.

Legally, the companies were separate units, corporate persons. At times, an existing British firm might establish a legally distinct corporation for overseas activities.[16] If an existing British business did so as an extension of its home operations, while juridically free-standing the new corporation would not be free-standing by the definition employed here. A free-standing company, at origin, was administratively as well as legally independent— that is, its management strategy was not subordinated to, nor coordinated with, that of a British parent company operating at home in the same industry. Similarly, specifically excluded from the free-standing category are subsidiaries or affiliates of a multinational enterprise whose headquarters was overseas.[17] In short, the thousands of free-standing companies considered here were legally separate units which were neither controlled by an operating

[12] As of 1914, Hall found that of the 5,337 companies registered in England and Scotland *and* listed in the *Stock Exchange official intelligence*, 1,976 (or 37 per cent) were operating mainly or wholly overseas. Hall, *London capital market*, p. 201. This number is in no way a proxy for the far larger number of companies registered in England and Scotland, 1870-1914, to do business abroad, since many had come and gone, and many were never listed in the *Stock Exchange official intelligence*.

[13] The free-standing *companies* considered herein were *legally domiciled* in Britain.

[14] The description is based mainly on material cited in notes 4, 5, 8 and 11 above. If they were holding companies, they typically had 'double boards' of directors: a board in London and one (or more) abroad. Many companies when set up never did any business; they were stillborn (in these cases, the formulation should be 'were intended to operate').

[15] Very few operated in more than one host country initially. Figures given in Paish, 'Export of capital', pp. v-vi, on 'countries to which Great Britain has supplied capital' and 'purposes for which capital has been subscribed' provide a rough breakdown by country and economic sector.

[16] Liability questions (foreign operations had higher risk and were more prone to bankruptcy), tax considerations, U.S. antitrust law (if the business operated in America), raising outside capital, joint-venture arrangements, and continuity were among the various reasons why an existing British firm might start up an affiliated *British* limited company for business abroad.

[17] To conduct business in Britain and perhaps elsewhere, foreign-based multinationals often formed companies registered in the U.K. Jones, 'Foreign multinationals'; Wilkins, *Emergence*.

THE FREE-STANDING COMPANY 1870-1914　　　　263

enterprise in Britain nor functioned as an operating extension of a foreign multinational enterprise.[18]

Typically, the purpose of a free-standing company was to obtain capital by bringing together profitable or potentially profitable operations overseas with British investors seeking financial opportunities superior to those at home—though frauds were not infrequent. By presenting a new corporation in Britain, the founders sought to attract British savings. The costs of the promotion, legal fees, and other payments have been estimated at from 17 to 33 per cent of the amount raised,[19] which leads to the question why so many companies of this type were floated. It seems to have been assumed that no sensible Briton would invest in the totally unknown, and that foreigners should not be trusted to manage British investments.[20] The free-standing companies would provide an institutional framework that minimized such risks, managed the savings of British investors, and could attract foreign as well as British investment.[21] William Lazonick has suggested that they gave the 'borrower' privileged access to capital.[22] Most were not, however, simply financial intermediaries. They differed from contemporary investment companies in that the latter in many cases operated solely within Britain as institutional portfolio investors,[23] whereas the free-standing company's administration was committed to managing a specific business overseas. Since these companies were expensive to establish, often their capital structure was inflated to cover formation and other costs.[24]

In raising capital the British limited liability company enjoyed two major advantages over a company in the recipient country. The first was that the investor in the British firm enjoyed liquidity; he could sell his sterling-denominated shares (or bonds) with ease if he was unhappy with the overseas

[18] If a U.S. (or other foreign) multinational formed a British-registered company *to acquire the American* (the original) business, if the legal *headquarters* moved to Britain, this new British company *would* qualify as free-standing, since it did not arise out of the *operations* of any existing company possessing headquarters in Britain nor did it develop out of the *operating requirements* of a foreign multinational.

[19] Wilkins, *History of foreign investment*. Some companies were not floated, and thus incurred no such large expense. These typically served to manage the monies of a small group of individuals.

[20] Payne, *Early Scottish limited companies*, p. 49, makes the point (citing Michie) that investors are not ready to release their funds 'to an anonymous foreigner'. My argument is that the British free-standing company was an alternative to such arm's-length release.

[21] Spence, *British investments*, p. 219, found that 'probably a majority of Anglo-American companies registered in London or Edinburgh had at least some foreign shareholders on their roster'. Many had American owners, i.e. holdings of 'vendors'. But others were cosmopolitan. Still others, he found, were controlled by continental European investors. On this matter, see also U.S. Federal Trade Commission, *Report on cooperation*, II, p. 537. Apparently, two very large companies involved in public utilities (electric power and tramways) in Argentina were organized and registered in Great Britain, but attracted German ownership. See ibid., I, p. 282, and II, pp. 543-4.

[22] Comments made at the Business History Conference, Wilmington, Dela., 13 March 1987.

[23] Often investment companies had no 'operations' abroad. Their 'foreign' portfolio investments were made *in Britain*. Sometimes, however, they did operate abroad, appointing agents in a foreign country and actually managing a network of lenders. Kerr, *Scottish capital*, quite properly considers such companies as direct investors. Financial intermediaries can be direct investors; in their operations, they are 'producing' a service for their customers. See Michie, 'Crisis and opportunity', pp. 125-47, showing how the investment company—the British Assets Trust—'managed' money, international investments; all this firm's investments were portfolio ones; it had 'agents' in America.

[24] Commentators on these companies have noted that the assets acquired were frequently overvalued. In the American case, promoters offered U.S. owners what seemed like preposterous sums. The inflated 'cost' of the assets was then reflected in the nominal capital.

project—assuming that the whole affair was not a sham. The existence of a British company, traded on British markets, with the securities denominated in sterling, thus encouraged the investments of British individuals and financial intermediaries.

The second, and probably more important, advantage of the free-standing British company as a conduit of British capital was that the British company was designed to provide the institutional apparatus for the management of the specific business investment.[25] The investment instrument was subject to British law. The directors of the free-standing company—the representatives of the shareholders—were mandated to monitor the overseas operations, to be sure that the investors' money was not misused. Those at the British headquarters were expected to select the managers of the business abroad, to receive reports, and to ensure prudent and efficient management of operations. As the managing director of one free-standing company wrote in a private letter: 'We [the London board members] are the men who stand to be shot at in the event of anything going wrong'.[26] The board of directors were charged with providing responsible management of the capital entrusted to their care.

While the free-standing companies were set up to manage the business investments abroad, their British head offices normally comprised a corporate secretary and the board of directors (whose members participated in other activities in Britain), and little else. This was why many of these companies could, in fact, be referred to as 'little more than a brass nameplate some place in the City',[27] representing an enterprise that could disappear as suddenly as it had emerged.

The limited size of the typical head office was ultimately the crucial feature that distinguished these companies from contemporary U.S. multinationals. American businessmen of this era learned at home about multi-regional operations over the vastness of the United States; American companies became large multi-functional, multi-regional enterprises that developed management talents. Domestic business was a training ground for multi-national enterprise, whereas the compact, geographically small domestic market in Britain provided an unsuitable basis for developing skills in business administration comparable with those learned by American managers.[28] The free-standing company, therefore, served as an alternative in many instances to the extension of the British home-based operating enterprises abroad, though the need to manage the business overseas was still there and provided a formidable challenge, and one that the free-standing companies often failed to meet.

---

[25] Powell wrote that the São Paulo Railroad was an English company, of English registration, under London management, owning and working a railroad in Brazil. This was a preferable investment to the Armavir-Touapse Railway, where the 'locus' was wholly Russian, since both that railway and its management were within the dominion of the czar, and bondholders were 'merely creditors'. Powell, *Mechanism*, pp. 144-5.

[26] Frank Spencer, managing director, Pillsbury-Washburn Flour Mills Company, Ltd., London, to William de la Barre, 7 May 1907. De la Barre Papers, Minnesota Historical Society, St Paul, Minnesota.

[27] Nicholas, 'British multinational investment', p. 606.

[28] Wilkins, *Emergence*; Chandler, *Visible hand*; Wilkins, 'History of European multinationals'.

II

Although the companies were free-standing, they were not always entirely independent of one another. They were in clusters (based on varied rationales and interest groups), consisting of numerous overlapping circles of individuals and enterprises. While the resulting governance structure sometimes approximated to a multinational enterprise, in most cases the connections within the clusters were too partial and too weak to be so designated.[29] The loose clusters were united by founders, directors, and suppliers, many of whom were also shareholders; as a result there were conflicts of interest.[30] Despite difficulties of definition and the insuperable difficulty of quantification, it is possible to list ten interrelated cluster sets. Identical patterns prevailed in the Empire and the rest of the world. Common to all clusters, because of the free-standing companies' limited head office facilities and absence of internal 'know how', was the provision of services. The clusters may be categorized as follows:

Promoters: free-standing companies were designed to link British capital to overseas opportunities. Promoters identified these opportunities; the promoter might serve as an intermediary setting up the company, and never owning its securities. More often, he was the equivalent of an underwriter, obtaining securities for resale,[31] or he might be a principal in the transaction, expecting to continue to hold the new company's securities. The promoter of a British free-standing company might be English or Scottish, or a national of the host or a third country.[32] Early in the period he would often contract for a property, and only purchase and sell it to the new company if the flotation was successful. By the late nineteenth century promoters more frequently purchased mines, acquired concessions, bought factories, and offered them in Britain through the free-standing company. Since typically the promoter was the purchaser of the property, the words vendor (to the new company) and promoter were in these cases synonymous, as the vendor would sell the property to the new British company.[33] The promoter might be a finance company (especially in relation to mining), an investment trust company, or an agency house.[34] Irrespective of whether the promoter was an individual or individuals, a finance company, an investment trust or

[29] At one point Vernon described the multinational enterprise as a cluster of firms, but his cluster had a common administrative organization, a defined headquarters; it was one that arose out of the operations of a single firm. Wilkins, 'Defining a firm', p. 81. The clusters described herein are entirely different. On clusters, see McKay, 'House of Rothschild (Paris)'; Chapman, 'British-based investments'; Payne, *Early Scottish limited companies*, p. 49; Scott and Hughes, *Anatomy*; Hall, *London capital market*, pp. 111ff; Porter, *Victorian shipping*, esp. pp. 152-60; Jones, 'Who invested'.

[30] Hennart noted this in conversation; apparently none of the British participants saw anything inappropriate in these arrangements.

[31] When Davis and Huttenback, *Mammon*, studied these firms' owners, they considered companies that were at least several years old to eliminate the 'investments' of the mere promoter.

[32] O'Hagan, *Leaves*; Hall, *London capital market*, p. 98; Sprague, *Money mountain*, pp. 212-5.

[33] The original owners, the first-stage vendors, would very likely be paid for the property by funds raised in the flotation and sometimes in securities of the new company; thus, it was not atypical for the original owners to have a continuing role, as shareholders, bondholders, and sometimes as local management—or even, on occasion, sometimes as members of the London board. Hall, *London capital market*, pp. 27-8.

[34] Firms such as Bewick, Moreing & Co. handled mine finance. On this company, see Nash, *Herbert Hoover*. On agency houses as promoters, Stillson, 'Financing', p. 592.

266   MIRA WILKINS

agency house, each exercised the entrepreneurial function of connecting the overseas project to potential investors; the skill acquired in doing this for one venture enabled the promoter to repeat it many times, creating the cluster of companies.[35]

British investment trust companies: these financial intermediaries were formed to obtain higher returns for middle-class investors than those available in the home economy. Some investment trusts which had operations abroad could qualify as free-standing companies.[36] Some viewed the shares in free-standing companies as excellent investments. Sometimes the investment trust company actually acted as a promoter (and underwriter); at other times, it was simply involved as a shareholder, frequently with a coterie of other investment trust companies. Groups of investment trust companies that invested in free-standing companies in tandem often possessed interlocking directorates, and also directors that interlocked with the free-standing companies as well. The pattern of investment is partly explained by a desire to spread risks and partly by a wish to let 'friends' share in a profitable opportunity. By providing capital in this way the investment trust company became a portfolio investor in the free-standing company.[37]

Solicitors: law firms were instrumental in establishing free-standing companies, with the clients of partnerships, such as Ashurst's, Linklater's, and Freshfield's, probably forming another set of clusters.

Accountants: firms of accountants called on to verify the accounts of free-standing companies also generated a distinctive cluster set, which was frequently linked, or overlapped, with those joined by promoters, investment trusts, and law firms.[38]

Members of Parliament or other 'ornamental' directors: prestige for a flotation and lustre for a prospectus could be secured by placing a titled aristocrat or prominent Member of Parliament on the board of directors.[39] Certain promoters called on the same men to enhance the image of different companies.

Geographical locations: British businessmen participating in trade or investments in a country or region tended to make unrelated (or only remotely related) investments in the same geographical area. Their involvements through directorships and shareholdings in free-standing companies formed yet another cluster set, the common element being the availability of information.[40]

Mining engineers: mining finance houses provided engineers for evaluation

---

[35] For one such cluster, see the list of the 1888-91 issues of the Trustees', Executors' and Securities' Insurance Company in *Investors' Review*, 1 (1892), p. 34-5.

[36] See note 23.

[37] Data in the Stillman Papers, Columbia University, New York. See also *Investors' Review, passim.*

[38] Wilkins, *History of foreign investment.*

[39] For example, in 1894 Sir H.S. King, M.P., was on the board of the American Freehold Land Co., the Canadian Agricultural Coal and Colonization Co., the Queensland Investment and Land Mortgage Co., and the Indian and General Trust Co. *Investors' Review*, 3 (1894), pp. 200-1. See Jefferys, *Business organisation*, p. 423, on 'ornamental' directors, who were 'decoys on the front page of the prospectus'.

[40] The Coats family, for instance, had investments in thread in America—multinational enterprise type investments—but members of the family were also directors and shareholders in free-standing companies in other industries (timber and mining) in the United States. Jackson, *Enterprising Scot*, pp. 221, 229.

THE FREE-STANDING COMPANY 1870-1914   267

and management purposes, which is how such leading firms as Bewick, Moreing, & Co. and John Taylor & Sons became associated with sets of mining enterprises in many parts of the world.

Non-mining industry networks: typically, the board of directors of a free-standing company contained a man (or men) active in the same or in a closely associated economic sector. The board membership (and often stockholdings) was based on familiarity with the industry and capability in assessing opportunities, an eagerness to determine what competitors were doing, and the potential for complementarity (i.e. the free-standing companies could become alternatives to vertical integration by British firms). The first of these three rationales can be perceived from the standpoint both of the promoter and of the director (*qua* stockholder). For example, the appointment of a prominent British brewer to the board of a South African brewery at its promotion would appear to the potential, less well-informed, investor to be a well-informed endorsement, increasing the attraction of shareholding.[41] Extending this example, from the directors' and shareholders' standpoints, experienced brewers were in a position to assess the profitability of a brewery investment (for *themselves* as well as for others). Thus, they wanted to be involved. So, too, a stock raiser in Scotland could judge for himself the financial viability of raising cattle in the United States. Hennart found that individual Cornish tin producers were directors of, and investors in, free-standing companies mining tin in Malaya, their participation being related in large part, it seems, to their knowledge of the industry, which enabled them to recognize profitable opportunities;[42] analysed in terms of transaction costs, information reduced costs substantially.

The second basic reason for the industry clusters is connected with possible competition; board membership made it feasible, for example, for the stock raiser in Scotland to obtain superior intelligence about potential competition from America.[43] In a number of instances, the development of new businesses abroad might offer rivalry to existing British industries or to British investments in third countries. Men in the same sector sought to be involved not only to profit from the potential competitive activity, but also to remain informed and *possibly* to influence the course of events by controlling, stabilizing, and neutralizing the competition.

The third reason is associated with complementarity. Pillsbury-Washburn Flour Mills Ltd., a typical free-standing company, was promoted in London. On its board was Sydney T. Klein, whose trading company handled part of the British flour trade for this American miller. Unlike the typical multinational enterprise, Klein's *trading house* was not integrating backwards into U.S. production. Klein was at the same time the principal figure in his trading house and a director and substantial stockholder in the large Pillsbury

---

[41] On the British-owned *American* breweries, Wiman (in 'British capital', p. 228) wrote that the British parent companies were 'officered by men of prominence and position, whose presence in a board of directors is a guarantee to capitalists that thorough investigation has taken place, and that the business will be honestly and efficiently administered'.

[42] Hennart, 'Internalization', pp. 131-43, esp. p. 141. He never uses the phrase 'free-standing companies'.

[43] Scottish stock raisers invested in American cattle companies at the time when U.S. meat exports to the United Kingdom were rising rapidly.

company, though he had no exclusive rights. Through his position on the Pillsbury board Klein presumably had an insider's advantage.[44]

Many free-standing companies were producers abroad, selling their output in Britain. When this was the case, they were often in industries that provided *inputs* for businesses in Britain. The British customer wanted knowledge, which with the free-standing company could be acquired without vertical integration of the British enterprise. Casson has suggested that when economies of scale are dissimilar at different stages of the production, and by implication the distribution, process, vertical integration is often undesirable.[45] This insight and others on asymmetrical production units would seem relevant in explaining why, for example, individuals served on boards of free-standing companies while their own companies did not integrate backward. Also, in some cases, British capital goods producers appear to have wished to *sell* to the free-standing firms. In his study of British free-standing companies in the Queensland gold-mining industry in the late 1880s, Lougheed found 'that some English engineering firms bought into several of the companies in order to sell them mining equipment'.[46] Presumably shareholders received preferential treatment over independent suppliers.

The business interests of members of the boards and shareholders of the free-standing companies (interests directly linked with their own British firms) were different from relationships characterizing multinational enterprise, since there was no clear, overall, administrative direction provided by the businessman's company, although it might be involved in marketing contracts, construction contracts, banking arrangements, and other specific functional interlocking associations.[47]

Trading companies: like the ties produced by mining engineers, the linkage associated with the trading company is to some extent a subset of the industry connection. Trading houses were often allied with what Chapman has called 'investment groups'.[48] Firms such as Balfour, Williamson & Co. of Liverpool[49] and Matheson & Co. of London[50] were intimately linked with British-incorporated free-standing companies. Cottrell notes that in the decade before 1914 many London 'mercantile firms' entered the new issue market: 'Eastern agency houses established [rubber] plantation companies and provided their protégés with local management and financial services.'[51] The merchants, Harrison & Crosfield, for example, promoted new issues in London for tea estates and tobacco companies in Java and India, as well as for Borneo timber, Japanese silk concerns, and Malayan rubber enterprises.[52] For the tea, tobacco, and rubber properties, the trading companies served

[44] Wilkins, *History of foreign investment*.
[45] Casson, *Multinationals*, p. 56.
[46] Lougheed, 'British company formation', p. 78.
[47] See Jefferys, *Business organisation*, p. 423.
[48] Chapman, 'British-based investment groups'.
[49] See Hunt, *Heirs*.
[50] Chapman, 'British-based investment groups', p. 235.
[51] Cottrell, *British overseas investment*, p. 33.
[52] Stillson, 'Financing', p. 592; Chapman, *Rise of merchant banking*, p. 144; on Scottish trading companies and tea plantation companies, see Michie, *Money, mania*, p. 158.

as suppliers of management services. Very often, in the course of their existing commercial business, trading companies saw opportunities abroad and assisted in the formation of British-registered free-standing companies. Stillson found that in Malaya the same agency houses that floated the companies' new issues and provided management of the rubber estates also 'serviced the financing'.[53] In short, free-standing companies were often grouped around the activities of a particular mercantile house.

Merchant banks: Chapman noted that 'There was no clear line demarcating investment groups with financial functions from merchant banks active in the promotion of . . . overseas shares.'[54] Merchant banks acted as promoters and as trading houses. Likewise, merchant bankers, such as the Rothschilds, engaged in the metals trades, were at centre stage *vis-à-vis* clusters of free-standing mining companies.[55] There appear to have been two tiers of British merchant banks: the large ones that only handled the best-quality issues and the smaller ones that might be less prudent. The various roles of merchant banks in relation to free-standing companies need much more study.[56]

For the most part, each of the ten cluster sets described above seems to have had a functional relationship to the free-standing units—emphasizing a particular function (or functions), rather than, as in the prototype U.S. multinational enterprise, offering an entire package, including product, process, marketing ability, technological know how, capital, *and* management. What seems evident is that the basic reason for the clusters lay in the severe limits to home office decision-making and governance of the free-standing company. For example, in the case of a typical American multinational enterprise the decision to invest abroad involved not only a consideration of financial requirements, but also the provision of operating and administrative needs. Growing out of conditions that arose in domestic business operations, the decision to invest was made by experienced senior managers in the home office, whose knowledge of the same industry in the large and diverse U.S. domestic market could be transferred abroad *within* the firm.

Lacking a comparable home office and in-house expertise, the free-standing company none the less faced establishment as well as operating and administrative requirements. Moreover, if the board of directors was to exercise control and to monitor activities, some institutional apparatus was necessary. The required functions were undertaken by the principals in the cluster sets.

One explanation for the many frauds and shortlived ventures was that the promoter abandoned the company after taking a profit from promotion and start-up, leaving minimal revenue-producing assets. Not all failures were

[53] Stillson, 'Financing', p. 592.

[54] Chapman, 'British-based investment groups', p. 246.

[55] The Rothschilds' Exploration Company furnished mining engineers for various Rothschild projects. Spence, *Mining engineers*, pp. 22–3, 137, 265. See also Turrell and Van Helten, 'The Rothschilds'.

[56] Stillson, 'Financing', p. 594, points out that from 1905 to 1914 the bulk of British investment in British-registered companies with Malayan rubber plantations was *not* attracted by agency houses, but rather the British companies were floated by 'London issuing houses'. At one point, Stillson describes the latter as intermediaries between British wealth-holders and promoters (p. 591) and at another as either merchant bankers or promoters themselves (p. 595). The line between the finance house and the merchant bank was often thin, both playing a role in investment banking.

attributable to sharp practice, but a responsible systematic approach to management could avoid disaster. The free-standing company had to find outsiders for this purpose. In addition to the inclusion of professional statements in the prospectus, accountants were asked to make periodic investigations, and at times were involved at the board's request in a quasi-managerial role in the overseas operations, one example of which was the connection between Price, Waterhouse and the British breweries in Chicago.[57] In a similar manner, mining engineers not only offered reassuring information for the prospectus, but stayed on as mine managers, while trading companies acted as 'managing agents'. When a British trading company, such as Balfour, Williamson, invested in U.S. oil production, coal mining, and flour milling, managerial services were provided. In this instance, the trading firm was behaving as a prototype multinational enterprise, investing in diversified operations related to its general trading activities. In some instances trading companies developed industry-specific managerial expertise.[58] Most important, if the free-standing company was generating profits, interested parties sought to remain involved to ensure effective management.

The services rendered to the free-standing companies were often highly profitable to the service sector enterprises; many promoters flourished.[59] In 1909 an observer remarked on overseas business which 'gave a great amount of employment in the city of London and other cities for directors, managers, clerks, solicitors, and accountants, etc.'. Mining finance firms found opportunities for themselves and their friends. Trading houses, extending activities beyond the mere movement of commodities, perceived that the added connections *vis-à-vis* overseas investments not only expanded their commerce but offered important sources of earnings.[60] Merchant banks became involved in marketing metals and through their loose connections with free-standing firms obtained information on the size of reserves and other crucial data affecting present and future prices, the effects of which on some occasions were to stabilize metal prices.[61] In sum, the principals in the clusters might participate both in the initiation and in the continuation of the free-standing companies. The needs of the free-standing company were the basis of the clusters. How service sector individuals and firms were utilized frequently became a way of determining whether the free-standing company proved profitable, how long it lasted, and what became of it.

III

What happened to the thousands of free-standing companies registered in England and Scotland in the years 1870-1914? Among the approximately 2,000 free-standing companies remaining in existence in 1914[62] the profitable

[57] Wilkins, *History of foreign investment.*

[58] Stillson, 'Financing', pp. 593-4, suggests that in the 1920s and early 1930s the London issuing houses became less important in the financing of Malayan rubber, and the Malayan agencies, which appear to have developed the managerial expertise, relatively more significant.

[59] Not all promoters were successful. See Michie, 'Options, concessions', pp. 154-7.

[60] Crammond, 'Comments'.

[61] On the London Rothschilds see Wilkins, *History of foreign investment.*

[62] See note 12.

THE FREE-STANDING COMPANY, 1870-1914 271

ones included those that developed their own in-house managerial organiz-ations, and those still under the aegis of a mining engineering firm or a trading company's management. Those that were unprofitable or earning low returns included numerous companies which never developed effective management, but nonetheless continued to exist.[63] For every company still in existence in 1914 far more had vanished, their termination taking varied forms. In many instances dissolution of a free-standing company left productive assets abroad in the hands of nationals or British expatriates (the British registration had been deemed superfluous). Sometimes the overseas assets went to a multinational enterprise possessing superior managerial resources. Often a dissolved company would be replaced by a differently structured free-standing one, the assets transferred from the first to a second free-standing unit. Sequences of free-standing companies holding the same overseas assets were common, but derived from different circumstances. Sometimes the solicitors felt the articles of association were not broad .enough; in some instances the succession related to ownership changes (and was a means of rewarding previous owners); on occasion, promoters believed a new company would be more attractive to the investing public, while at other times restructuring followed bankruptcy of the prior company. At times winding up left no assets and nothing remained to liquidate; many free-standing companies were abortive. While far from precise the evidence suggests that the number of free-standing companies with continuity, flourishing as successful, profitable enterprises, represented a very small percentage of the total number established. The mortality rate of the overseas companies seems to have greatly exceeded that of their purely domestic counterparts.[64]

In view of such a high mortality rate, why were lessons not learned? Why was British investment so readily forthcoming for so many years? Several reasons may be adduced. As some enterprises were profitable, the potential for success existed; free-standing companies were presented in such a way as to generate confidence, even though the prospectus might cloak the reality; nominal, projected returns always looked attractive; and few investors appreciated the managerial difficulties inherent in these ventures.

The character of these firms and their performance through time may be illustrated by examples selected from different industries and countries, providing substance for the earlier generalizations and showing how, in specific terms, the clusters related both to the companies' persistence and to their performance through time. The examples also reveal the managerial

[63] Often, they were formally dissolved years later. Some were lucrative for the managing agent, but *not* for the shareholders.

[64] That these companies had a higher mortality rate than domestic ones is suggested in Payne's study of Scottish companies, at least in regard to overseas mining companies. Payne, *Early Scottish limited companies*, table 23, pp. 101ff. Shannon, 'Limited companies', shows the high mortality rate of *all* registered companies. Between 1875 and 1883, for example, of the 9,551 companies registered, 35 per cent were 'abortive' (p. 382). Of those continuing in business, 34 per cent eventually became insolvent (p. 387)! Shannon separates out some of his data by home, colonial and foreign, but most of his figures are not divided in this manner, so his tabulations do not aid in segregating domestic from overseas business.

dilemma: how did a company established afresh provide adequate management to a business abroad?

In May 1871 the Spanish government offered for sale the Rio Tinto Mines.[65] Why? It wanted to raise monies 'to relieve the state of burdensome obligations'. There was little interest until the German merchant, Heinrich Doetsch, who had extensive trading and mining interests in southern Spain, went to London, seeking out financiers 'with appropriate experience and resources in the promotion of a new venture, to purchase, modernize and operate the Mines'. He met with Hugh Matheson of Matheson & Co., from the same family associated with Jardine Matheson & Co., the large trading company in the China trade. Matheson had taken part in other 'promotions', in Persia for example, and in 1873 he formed a syndicate to raise money to buy the mine, after which the Rio Tinto Company Ltd. was floated on the British market. Respectable 'financiers' and a Member of Parliament were put on the board, though Matheson himself was the key figure. Doetsch, whose firm Sundheim & Doetsch received a cash commission of £80,000 from the new Rio Tinto Company for arranging the flotation, became vice-chairman. Matheson & Co. would act as commercial agents for Rio Tinto throughout the world (except in continental Europe) and receive a commission on sales and purchases; others involved were similarly rewarded for services supplied, for example, Clark, Punchard and Co. received a contract for building railway facilities to the mine.[66]

Matheson & Co. continued to participate in many other business projects.[67] For a long while after its establishment Rio Tinto did not handle its own marketing, and according to Harvey's account, only Doetsch and Matheson were 'willing to devote the greater part of their energies to the handling of Rio Tinto business'.[68] Eventually, however, an administrative organization emerged, enabling the Rio Tinto Company Ltd. to become an entity in its own right.

In origin Burmah Oil was also a free-standing company. The promoter, who connected the opportunity in Burma with the monies in Britain, was the Scottish-born East Indian merchant, David Cargill. The 'concept of its creation' came when Cargill and Kirkman Finlay met at the Rangoon office of Galbraith Dalziel & Co., managing agents of the then Rangoon Oil Company Ltd. (a free-standing company, registered in Edinburgh in 1871).[69] Finlay was one of those roving young Scots, who before going to Burma had been in Angola seeking his fortune overseas. Both Cargill and Finlay were associated with trading companies; they used the existing Rangoon Company as the basis for the search for oil in Burma. Finlay returned to Scotland in 1879 and became Cargill's right-hand man in 'the Glasgow office'.[70] While Corley is not specific, the Glasgow office seems to have been that of Cargill's trading company rather than of the Rangoon Oil Company

[65] What follows is based on Harvey, *Rio Tinto*.
[66] Ibid., pp. 4-11, 26-35, 43, 48n., 49.
[67] Chapman, 'British-based investment groups', p. 235; see also Jones, *Banking and empire*, pp. 11-2
[68] Harvey, *Rio Tinto*, p. 102.
[69] Corley, *Burmah Oil Company*, pp. 15, 17, 13.
[70] Ibid., pp. 18, 22.

THE FREE-STANDING COMPANY, 1870-1914 273

Ltd., though they may have been one and the same. Nothing existed in Glasgow related to the oil business except a head office. For ten years until 1886 the record of oil operations in Burma was a lossmaking one. In that year Cargill established the Burmah Oil Company Ltd., registered in Edinburgh, a typical free-standing company. The goal was to attract outside financial resources to be applied to the potentially profitable opportunity in Burma. A new company would be preferable to the loss-ridden Rangoon Oil Company Ltd.[71] Corley noted that 'in structure the new company was merely one branch of an East India mercantile house, or rather a group of more or less interrelated businesses, and Cargill must have needed much agility of mind to keep separate all the various strands, from tea plantations in Ceylon to oil wells in Burma'. Finlay was alone in the organization, in devoting all of his time to oil, and soon moved from Glasgow to London where he became concerned with the 'marketing, staff and technical aspects from the London office'.[72] Corley has outlined the growth of the business, with the trading company initially taking the lead in getting the concession, starting drilling operations (the trading company had 'no technical expertise to call on'), beginning refining, and all along encountering the problems of staffing the new venture. The company called on Boverton Redwood, the foremost oil consultant in Britain; Ferrier has described him as 'a kind of single-handed oil personnel agency' for the British oil industry.[73] Over time, Burmah Oil Company Ltd. began to form its own managerial organization. By the end of the nineteenth century, the company owned tankers,[74] though trading companies were still employed to handle marketing. As time passed, this free-standing company had to create its own administrative structure in order to survive.

Still another set of free-standing companies was organized by William Knox D'Arcy, the son of an Irish solicitor whose family had emigrated to Australia. While living in Australia in the 1880s D'Arcy had been approached by three Australian brothers to assist them in developing a gold mine in that country. D'Arcy (as promoter) formed a free-standing company in Britain and floated the company, retaining shares in the business, a shrewd decision which by the mid-1890s made him a wealthy man; until 1910 the Mount Morgan Mine was one of the largest gold mines in the world. Returning to England, he served as chairman of the London board of the Mount Morgan Gold Mining Company, Ltd: 'He kept in close touch with his Australian affairs', although the Australian business seems to have been run from Australia.[75]

The United States was host to some successful British free-standing

---

[71] Ibid., p. 30. This is a good example of sequences of companies. Instead of using the Rangoon Oil Company Ltd., a new company with a more promising future was set up.

[72] Corley, Burmah Oil Company, pp. 32-3.

[73] Ibid., pp. 35, 39, and Ferrier, British Petroleum Company, I, p. 32. See also Jones, State and the emergence, pp. 97-8, on Boverton Redwood.

[74] Corley, Burmah Oil Company, p. 49.

[75] On William D'Arcy and the Mount Morgan mine, see Ferrier, British Petroleum Company, I, p. 31 (the quoted passage); Western Range Cattle Industry Study Collection (WRCIS), Library of Congress, Acc. 11,090, Reel 22; Spurr, ed., Political and commercial geology, p. 251; Hall, London capital market, p. 112.

companies. Certain gold-mining companies were very profitable, owing to supervision by mining engineering firms with headquarters in Britain. Most companies associated with Balfour, Williamson's American trading affiliate prospered. One important free-standing company set up by Balfour, Williamson became part of the Royal Dutch-Shell Group.[76] In these cases the clusters provided the early basis for management and for success.[77] Otis Steel Co. Ltd. also did well, but not because it was a free-standing company. In the early twentieth century it was dissolved as a free-standing entity, and the British shareholders became portfolio investors in an American-based enterprise.[78] All those which flourished eventually developed, or took over and used, middle management administrative structures; many gave up their British incorporation, which became superfluous.

Of the formidable number of British free-standing companies investing in the United States (and apparently elsewhere too), shortlived ventures far outnumbered the longlived, healthy ones.[79] For example the American Association Ltd. and its various associated ventures proved a major fiasco. Initially organized in 1887 as a free-standing company to acquire mineral land in the American south, the establishment of the American Association Ltd. was followed by a whole cluster of other British companies. These included the Middlesborough Town Company, Ltd., and its successor the Middlesborough Town Lands Company, Ltd., the Coal and Iron Bank of Middlesborough, Ltd., the Middlesborough Hotel Company, Ltd., the Cumberland Gas Company, Ltd., the Middlesborough Electric Company, Ltd., the Middlesborough Street Railroad Company, Ltd., the Middlesborough Water Company, Ltd., and the Watts Steel and Iron Syndicate, Ltd.

In May 1889, Middlesborough, Kentucky, had 50 inhabitants, rising to 15,000 two years later as a new iron and steel town was formed. Press reports indicated that by 1889 some $10 million in British monies had been subscribed, and the promoters were seeking more. Then came the 1890 Baring Crisis, the U.S. panic of 1893, and the collapse of the whole project. America was left with furnaces and a steel plant; British investors in the free-standing companies lost everything. The American Association Ltd. was bankrupt, as were all the other companies. In November 1893 the *Investors' Review* commented that 'what actual cash capital these various joint-stock ghosts managed to extract from the British public it would be impossible . . . to say'.[80] The promoters of the American Association Ltd. were involved also in other U.S. and foreign undertakings.[81] Some associated

---

[76] California Oilfields, Ltd.

[77] Wilkins, *History of foreign investment*. The Scottish investment trust companies, which can be called free-standing companies, did very well. See Kerr, *Scottish capital*, passim.

[78] Wilkins, *History of foreign investment*. A British accountant joined the board of the *American* company to represent the British shareholders.

[79] On the numerous failures, see Spence, *British investments*, pp. 230-2. Ashmead, *Twenty-five years*, tells a similar story of lack of success in the United States and worldwide.

[80] Wilkins, *History of foreign investment*, and *Investors' Review*, 2 (1893), pp. 606-8.

[81] Prominently involved, for example, was Dillwyn Parrish of 2 Copthall Buildings in the City. Parrish was not only a participant in numerous American activities from railroads to attempting brewery promotions, to investment trusts, but in 1892 he was a director of the Rothschilds' Exploration Co. Ltd., the Adventurers of Mexico Ltd., the Delagoa Bay and East African Railway Co. Ltd., and the Foreign Pilsen Electric Light and Power Co. Ltd.! For his directorships, see *Directory of directors 1892*.

THE FREE-STANDING COMPANY, 1870-1914   275

with this venture seem to have wanted to sell equipment to it, while iron and steel producers planned to make money through construction contracts. British investors in this group of companies suffered severe losses mainly because of inadequate administration of the American Association Ltd., and of the Middlesborough companies.[82]

At much the same time in a different region within the United States a British free-standing company was established to take over the Hammond Company, one of America's leading meat packers. The British company was floated; the promoter prospered; but here again there was virtually no direction or administration from Great Britain; despite the lack of effective governance the company survived but lost rank; then, in time, it returned to American control; the company's properties were purchased by American meat packers, and the free-standing company was dissolved.[83]

In all branches of activity, industrial, mining, or cattle ranching, in numerous instances British free-standing companies doing business in the United States failed to create satisfactory managerial organizations, with the consequence that holders of the companies' securities faced losses. While financial returns were unsatisfactory to their British owners, these enterprises did, however, contribute to American productive resources.[84] Sometimes free-standing companies established in America would go through dissolutions, only to be followed by reconstructed ventures which in turn also failed.[85] Sometimes, the free-standing company was fraudulent from the start,[86] paying no dividend at all—or only one to enable the promoter to sell stock as the price rose.[87] Many were wound up within a few years of formation,[88] and some, failing to raise capital, were aborted before birth.[89]

Paterson has documented the poor performance of British free-standing companies in Canada.[90] He concluded that 'decision-making authority far removed from the area of economic activity was bound to slow down the process of reaching economic decisions. It was also likely to lead to less well-informed decisions, because of unfamiliarity with local Canadian conditions. When this failure to delegate responsibility was coupled with the unwillingness to engage local expert opinion, the results usually led to unprofitability.'[91] All of this is true and legitimate, but it neglects the fundamental difficulty; the free-standing firm could employ engineers to make surveys and could

[82] Wilkins, *History of foreign investment*.

[83] Ibid.

[84] Ibid.

[85] Ibid. See also Spence, *British investments*, *passim*.

[86] The most famous, or as Spence puts it, 'infamous' free-standing company scandal in America was the Emma Silver Mining Co. Ltd., which from start to finish was fraudulent. Spence, *British investments*, ch. viii.

[87] Wilkins, *History of foreign investment*.

[88] For example, the 'Gold Queen' Ltd., formed in 1888, was wound up in 1892; the Old Lout Mining Co., Ltd., formed in 1888, was wound up in 1894; and the Ni-Wot Gold Mines Ltd., also formed in 1888, was liquidated in 1894. Reel 52, WRCIS. The Mines Intersection Syndicate Ltd. formed in 1897 was wound up in 1898. Reel 64, WRCIS.

[89] The Boulder Valley Collieries Co., Ltd., registered in 1874 did no business whatsoever. Reel 40, WRCIS.

[90] Although he does not use the term 'free-standing companies', the business failures which he documents were almost all of that variety. Paterson, *British direct investment*, pp. 80–103.

[91] Ibid., pp. 101-2 and 112.

use service sector agencies; but it had no real home office to draw on to make the required decisions. The lean governance structure, the absence of home office experience to transfer to Canada, created the principal disability. As Paterson notes, those few ventures which proved successful developed managerial hierarchies, administrative structures.[92]

One more example of 'failure' seems appropriate. McKay has described the activities of Palmer Harding, an English contractor who obtained a concession for a horse tramway line in Rouen in 1877. Harding set up a French company, but failed to get 'administrative approval' to sell the shares to French investors; accordingly, an English holding company (a free-standing firm) was established, with inflated capital, to raise money in Britain. The company languished.[93] Subsequently, the French Thomson-Houston applied its considerable experience and made a success of an electric tramway.[94]

These illustrations suggest that in countries lacking indigenous management, for example in Spain and Burma, British free-standing companies eventually provided the administrative requirement, whereas in other parts of the world the British free-standing firm had no advantage in creating or furnishing management; in Canada, British settlers seem to have run the very few successful, efficiently managed British free-standing companies; likewise, in Australia, the same appears true. Indeed, often the free-standing company became only a means of enriching the promoter. Passive investors tempted by the prospects of profits were incapable of providing management. In the United States and Canada the British contribution was often solely financial; the British free-standing company had no sustained advantage. Americans, especially, either possessed or could obtain the technology, and could run the projects. The free-standing company became an albatross. Why should Americans pay for a board of directors that generated only cost and no benefit to the ongoing business? Moreover, the free-standing form became prey (and this was especially true of mining companies) to the unscrupulous, who gained by providing a 'service' in setting up the company and perhaps selling equipment to it, but retained no interest in its continuing success or failure. In the French example, the British free-standing 'holding company' added nothing except capital. When an experienced French company (an affiliate of an American multinational) took over the venture, it became highly successful.

A distinction has already been drawn between less developed and developed host countries, managerial creation via the free-standing company tending to take place more often in the former. The disappearance of the British free-standing parent company, leaving resources in national hands, so prevalent in the United States seems to have occurred in the case of British

[92] Ibid., p. 103. These ventures were typically run by Britons who settled in Canada. In 1893 the managers of the British Columbia Canning Co., Ltd. and the Anglo-British Columbia Packing Co., Ltd. were both long-time residents in the province.

[93] McKay, *Tramways and trolleys*, pp. 133-4.

[94] Ibid., p. 134. The French Thomson-Houston was an affiliate of the American company, General Electric. See ibid., pp. 127ff. and Wilkins, *Emergence*, pp. 58-9 and 94.

THE FREE-STANDING COMPANY, 1870-1914 277

stakes in Russia as well,[95] and by 1870-1914, according to Feis 'In British India the demand that the London boards be abolished increased in firmness.'[96] An important question to consider is whether the British head office developed crucial managerial functions. In the more successful companies this was the case, but in many others it was not, and accordingly the British-registered company was erased, leaving an operating company in the host country with some British portfolio investments. The presence of a shortlived British free-standing company that failed to provide anything beyond capital did not necessarily mean that economic activity abroad was also shortlived.[97]

The British free-standing company concept is useful in dealing with agriculture, banking, and certain railway investments, as well as with those in the economic sectors discussed in the specific illustrations above. While in broad terms free-standing companies participated in every economic sector, such companies tended to be absent from the high-technology industries of this era, notably the electrical and chemical industries. Public utilities and certain low-technology electrical manufacturing industries did attract such companies, but not businesses with the most advanced technology.[98] There was no free-standing company in the car industry. It appears that advanced technology could not be effectively transferred via this type of intermediary and that the lean governance structure was the constraint.[99]

The many free-standing firms in Britain were designed to match abundant British capital, under British management and control, with profitable opportunities. So many proved shortlived because international business involved not only capital export but diffusion of known products and processes and the successful transfer of a management package. The free-standing company with its tiny home office had either to find or to create that package; otherwise it was doomed to dissolution.

IV

The most typical British direct investment abroad between 1870 and 1914 appears to have been that which began as a free-standing company, a form which proved extremely effective in raising capital in Britain for business overseas. Was the free-standing company equally successful in providing management, technology, and business know-how? American enterprise abroad in the main had no problem in this respect; U.S. businessmen took experience at home and extended it, modifying and making changes as

---

[95] Based on discussions with V. Bovykin, A.A. Fursenko, and B. Ananyich.

[96] Feis, *Europe*, p. 28.

[97] The evidence on U.S. portfolio investments suggests that as information channels improved, British investors felt less hesitancy in investing in some companies registered abroad.

[98] Eastman Kodak Co., Ltd. was a British free-standing company for a few years, though tax matters changed this. However, the form was not viable for this innovative firm.

[99] It might be argued, however, that British business was generally deficient in high technology industries. None the less, there were British businesses abroad in high technology activities, for instance Marconi in the electrical industry. This took the form of the 'typical' multinational enterprise, not the free-standing company form. In the car industry, which lagged far behind the American industry before 1914, no British foreign direct investment occurred—of either variety.

needed, but developing foreign operations from a given knowledge of both product and process. This was the case with certain British firms as well. Some (not all) British free-standing companies that emerged out of expatriates' or foreign nationals' endeavours had local management in place. Some that arose from a trading company genesis could call on the trading house's managers. But many, and perhaps most, British free-standing companies had no company-specific experience on which to rely. At first, therefore, they had to engage existing service sector individuals and firms that both identified the opportunities and furnished the initial supervision.

At least initially, the service companies were infrequently industry-specific. The trading company, for example, was excellent as a conduit of information on trading conditions, but it lacked ongoing experience in the production of raw materials or manufactured products; that is, a trading company did not, at the start, know how to manage goods-producing units. Accordingly, industry-specific service functions multiplied; trading companies learned and became specialized. Management of productive activities was required if the free-standing company was to generate returns to its shareholders. Some free-standing companies became highly successful; most of these ultimately had to shed their reliance on the outsiders' services and develop their own company-specific managerial expertise. In some instances, service sector firms were able to provide the basis for the transition; in other cases, service sector firms created within their own organizations the needed expertise. Many more free-standing companies failed to find or install competent management, or to exploit service sector companies effectively, and were wound up.

Research on the free-standing company as an operating entity is still in its infancy. The paradigm should provide insights into the establishment, operations, and performance of British cotton textile plants in India, British meat packers in Argentina, and British nitrate firms in Chile.[100] It assists us in understanding much of British overseas banking,[101] and implies a need to rethink the nature of British capital exports that did not go into government loans. Far more research is needed to trace the relationships between the free-standing companies and existing British businesses. What were the competitive and complementary associations? Can the free-standing company be seen as an intermediate solution for some British businesses—between integration and arm's-length alternatives? Was the solution selected because of managerial constraints? Did the free-standing company succeed in activities where the prototype multinational enterprise had no advantage? How do we identify such activities?[102] The free-standing company approach may aid us in learning more about the efficiency of British enterprise overseas and the course of technology transfer. It may also give help in evaluating the costs

---

[100] It helps, for example, in understanding the behaviour of John Thomas North and his promotion of a battery of Chilean nitrate companies. See Greenhill, 'Nitrate and iodine', pp. 236-7.

[101] The Imperial Bank of Persia is a splendid example of a free-standing company. Jones, *Banking and empire*.

[102] For example, a multinational enterprise producing rubber tyres had a major advantage in doing so worldwide, but no advantage in growing rubber. A free-standing company not only had no advantage in manufacturing rubber tyres, but would be at a disadvantage. However, both types of organization needed to learn afresh about rubber plantations.

THE FREE-STANDING COMPANY, 1870-1914 279

and benefits of British overseas business. Little is known about the history of most of these companies after 1914; more information is needed on how they survived during the remainder of the twentieth century.[103]

Likewise, more research is required on the transition and the mix between British-registered companies and those registered abroad (without a British parent). There seem to be systematic patterns relating to British registration and overseas registration, which poses the question why a company should have been registered in England or Scotland rather than only abroad. Tentatively, it seems that overall management from a British head office with no British registration was virtually impossible, although all kinds of specific functional relationships could persist.[104]

The free-standing company concept directs our attention to the institutional dimensions of overseas direct investments and the conduct of operations abroad, to the rationale behind particular business forms, to the nature of the business interconnections that started and maintained British foreign direct investment, and to the critical role of management in determining the success or failure of direct investment. It questions whether the fragmented functional management by various service sector units could be prolonged and could alone provide a basis for continuity.

This analysis suggests that it is the company rather than the investors in the company that should be studied as the principal actor in the foreign direct investment process. Most significant was the finding that fundamental to the free-standing company was its inherently weak managerial structure at origin, causing it to depend on outside providers of services. This initial lean governance structure was responsible for the short life or failure of many of the British businesses operating overseas. Attention should be directed to the company, to the management of its business abroad, and to the development of productive activity overseas within the firm. To be sure, part of the substantial British direct investment abroad in this era was made by traditionally defined multinational enterprises, but far more seems to have been by British-registered free-standing companies. While not entirely unique to Great Britain, this type of institution was certainly far more in evidence there between 1870 and 1914 than in any other country.[105] The reason is obvious. Britain was the world's largest creditor nation—and its nationals chose not to send their wealth abroad unsupervised. Though frequently not up to the task, the free-standing company was designed to provide that supervision. Between 1870 and 1914 the free-standing company

---

[103] Tignor, *Egyptian textiles*, mentions some free-standing companies operating in Egypt, from the turn of the century into the 1950s.

[104] Lewis suggests that 'Foreign ownership [and] the location of boards of directors in London' enhanced British exports—but that 'externally registered entities' were not a necessary condition for either Argentinian or Brazilian imports. Trade in this context is the 'functional' relationship. Lewis, 'Railways and industrialization', p. 219.

[105] Free-standing companies with headquarters in the United States operated in the sugar industry of Cuba, in mining in Latin America, and in other circumstances. Their relative importance in U.S. direct investment, 1870–1914 was, however, miniscule in comparison with their role in the United Kingdom. Free-standing companies with headquarters on the European continent also existed and require further investigation. Recent research suggests they were nowhere near as important as in the British case.

280   MIRA WILKINS

was not only of major importance in the history of British foreign direct investment, but was central to the history of all British capital exports.

Florida International University

Footnote references
Ackerman, C.W., *George Eastman* (Boston, 1930).
Ashmead, E., *Twenty-five years of mining, 1880-1904* (1909).
Brayer, H.O., 'The influence of British capital on the western range cattle industry', *J. Econ. Hist.*, Supplement, 9 (1949), pp. 85-98.
Casson, M., *Multinationals and world trade* (1986).
Caves, R.E., 'International corporations: the industrial economics of foreign investment', *Economica*, 38 (1971), pp 1-27.
Caves, R.E., *Multinational enterprise and economic analysis* (Cambridge, 1982).
Chandler, A.D., 'The growth of the transnational firm in the United States and the United Kingdom: a comparative analysis', *Econ. Hist. Rev.*, 2nd ser., XXXIII (1980), pp. 396-410.
Chandler, A.D., *The visible hand* (Cambridge, Mass., 1977).
Chapman, S.D., 'British-based investment groups before 1914', *Econ. Hist. Rev.*, 2nd ser., XXXVIII (1985), pp. 230-51.
Chapman, S.D., *The rise of merchant banking* (1984).
Clements, R.V., 'British-controlled enterprise in the west between 1870 and 1900 and some agrarian reactions', *Agric. Hist.*, 27 (1953), pp. 132-41.
Coram, T.C., 'The role of British capital in the development of the United States, c. 1600-1914' (unpublished M.A. thesis, University of Southampton, 1967).
Corley, T.A.B., *A history of the Burmah Oil Comany, 1860-1924* (1983).
Cottrell, P.L., *British overseas investment in the nineteenth century* (1975).
Crammond, E., 'Comments' in *J.R.S.S.*, LXXII (1909), p. 482.
Dahl, A.J., 'British investment in California mining, 1870-1890' (unpublished Ph.D. thesis, University of California, 1961).
Davis, L.E. and Huttenback, R.A., 'The export of British finance, 1865-1914', in A.N. Porter and R.F. Holland, eds., *Money, finance and empire, 1790-1960* (1985), pp. 28-76.
Davis, L.E. and Huttenback, R.A., *Mammon and the pursuit of empire* (Cambridge, 1986).
Dunning, J.H., *American investment in British manufacturing industry* (1958).
Dunning, J.H., 'Changes in the level and structure of international production: the last one hundred years', in M. Casson, ed., *The growth of international business* (1983), pp. 84–139.
Dunning, J.H., *Studies in international investment* (1970).
Dunning, J.H. and Archer, H., 'The eclectic paradigm and the growth of UK multinational enterprise', paper presented at Business History Conference, Wilmington, Dela., 1987.
Edelstein, M., *Overseas investment in the age of high imperialism: the United Kingdom, 1850-1914* (New York, 1982).
Feis, H., *Europe: the world's banker, 1870-1914* (New York, 1965).
Ferrier, R.W., *The history of the British Petroleum Company*, I (1982).
Greenhill, R., 'The nitrate and iodine trades, 1880-1914,' in D.C.M. Platt, ed., *Business imperialism, 1840-1930* (Oxford, 1977), pp. 231-83.
Gruber, W., Mehta, D. and Vernon, R., 'The R & D factor in international trade and international investment of U.S. industries', *J. Pol. Econ.*, 75 (1967), pp. 20-37.
Hall, A.R., *The London capital market and Australia, 1870-1914* (Canberra, 1963).
Harvey, C.E., *The Rio Tinto company* (Penzance, 1981).
Hennart, J.-F., 'Internalization in practice: early foreign direct investments in Malaysian tin mining', *J. Int. Bus. Stud.*, 17 (1986), pp. 131-43.
Hunt, W., *Heirs of great adventure*, 2 vols. (1951, 1960).
Jackson, W.T., *The enterprising Scot: investors in the American west after 1873* (Edinburgh, 1974).
Jefferys, J.B., *Business organisation in Great Britain, 1856-1914* (New York, 1977).
Jones, C., 'Great capitalists and the direction of British overseas investment in the late nineteenth century: the case of Argentina', *Bus. Hist.*, 32 (1980), pp. 152-69.
Jones, C., 'The state and business practice in Argentina, 1862-1914', in C. Abel and C.M. Lewis, eds., *Latin America, economic imperialism, and the state* (1985), pp. 184-98.
Jones, C., 'Who invested in Argentina and Uruguay?', *Bus. Archives* 48 (1982), pp. 1–23.
Jones, G., *Banking and empire in Iran* (Cambridge, 1986).

Jones, G., 'Foreign multinationals and British industry before 1945', Econ. Hist. Rev. (forthcoming).
Jones, G., The state and the emergence of the British oil industry (1981).
Jones, G., ed., British multinationals: origins, management and performance (Aldershot, 1986).
Kerr, W.G., Scottish capital on the American credit frontier (Austin, 1976).
Kindleberger, C., American business abroad (New Haven, 1969).
Lewis, C.M., 'Railways and industrialization: Argentina and Brazil, 1870-1929', in C. Abel and C.M. Lewis, eds., Latin America, economic imperialism and the state (1985), pp. 199-230.
Lougheed, A.L., 'British company formation and the Queensland mining industry, 1886-1890', Bus. Hist., 25 (1983), pp. 76-82.
McFarlane, L.A., 'British investment in midwestern farm mortgages and land, 1875-1900: a comparison of Iowa and Kansas', Agric. Hist., 47 (1974), pp. 179-98.
McKay, J., 'The house of Rothschild (Paris) as a multinational industrial enterprise, 1875-1914', in A. Teichova et al., Multinational enterprise in historical perspective (Cambridge, 1986), pp. 74-86.
McKay, J., Tramways and trolleys (Princeton, 1977).
Michie, R.C., 'Crisis and opportunity: the formation and operation of the British Assets Trust, 1897-1914', Bus. Hist., 25 (1983), pp. 125-47.
Michie, R.C., Money, mania and markets: investment, company formation and the stock exchange in nineteenth-century Scotland (Edinburgh, 1981).
Michie, R.C., 'Options, concessions, syndicates, and the provision of venture capital, 1880-1913', Bus. Hist., 23 (1981), pp. 147-64.
Nash, G., Herbert Hoover (New York, 1983).
Nelson, R.R. and Winter, S.G., An evolutionary theory of economic change (Cambridge, Mass., 1982).
Nicholas, S., 'British multinational investment before 1939', J. Eur. Econ. Hist., 11 (1982), pp. 605-30.
O'Hagan, H.O., Leaves from my life, 2 vols. (1929).
Ostrye, A.T., Foreign investment in the American and Canadian west, 1870-1914: an annotated bibliography (Metuchen, N.J., 1986).
Paish, G., 'The export of capital and the cost of living', Statist Supplement, LXXIX (14 Feb. 1914), pp. i-vii.
Paish, G., 'Great Britain's capital investments in individual colonial and foreign countries', J.R.S.S., LXXIV (1911), pp. 167-87.
Paterson, D.G., British direct investment in Canada (Toronto, 1976).
Payne, P.L., The early Scottish limited companies, 1856-1896 (Edinburgh, 1980).
Platt, D.C.M., Britain's investment overseas on the eve of the First World War (New York, 1986).
Pollard, S., 'Capital exports, 1870-194; harmful or beneficial?' Econ. Hist. Rev., 2nd ser., XXXVIII (1985), pp. 489-514.
Porter, A., Victorian shipping, business and imperial policy (Woodbridge, Suffolk, 1986).
Powell, E.T., The mechanism of the city (1910).
Remer, C.F., Foreign investments in China (New York, 1933).
Rippy, J.F., British investment in Latin America (Minneapolis, 1959).
Scott, J. and Hughes, M., The anatomy of Scottish capital: Scottish companies and Scottish capital, 1900-1979 (1980).
Shannon, H.A., 'The limited companies of 1866-1883', Econ. Hist. Rev. 4 (1933), repr. in E.M. Carus-Wilson, ed., Essays in economic history (New York, 1966), pp. 380-405.
Simon, M., 'The pattern of new British portfolio foreign investment, 1865-1914', in A.R. Hall, ed., The export of capital from Britain, 1870-1914 (1968), pp. 15-44.
Spence, C.C., British investments and the American mining frontier, 1860-1901 (Ithaca, N.Y., 1958).
Spence, C.C., Mining engineers and the American west (New Haven, 1970).
Sprague, M., Money mountain: the story of Cripple Creek gold (Boston, 1953).
Stillson, R.T., 'The financing of Malayan rubber', Econ. Hist. Rev., 2nd ser., XXIV (1971), pp. 589-98.
Stone, I., 'British direct and portfolio investment in Latin America before 1914', J. Econ. Hist., 37 (1977), pp. 690-722.
Stopford, J., 'The origins of British-based multinational manufacturing enterprises', Bus. Hist. Rev., 48 (1974), pp. 303-45.
Spurr, J.E., ed., Political and commercial geology and the world's mineral resources (New York, 1920).
Svedberg, P., 'The portfolio-direct composition of private foreign investment in 1914 revisited', Econ. J., 80 (1978), pp. 763-77.
Tignor, R.L., Egyptian textiles and British capital, 1930-1956 (forthcoming).
Turrell, R. and Van Helten, J.J., 'The Rothschilds, the Exploration Company and mining finance', Bus. Hist., 28 (1986), pp. 181-205.
Vernon, R., Storm over the multinationals (Cambridge, Mass., 1977).
U.S. Federal Trade Commission, Report on cooperation in American export trade, 2 vols. (Washington, D.C., 1916).
Wells, L.T., The product life cycle and international trade (Boston, 1972).

282   MIRA WILKINS

Wilkins, M., 'Defining a firm: history and theory', in P. Hertner and G. Jones, eds., *Multinationals: theory and history* (Aldershot, 1986), pp. 80-95.

Wilkins, M., *The emergence of multinational enterprise: American business abroad from the colonial era to 1914* (Cambridge, Mass., 1970).

Wilkins, M., 'The history of European multinationals: a new look', *J. Eur. Econ. Hist.*, 15 (1986), pp. 483-510.

Wilkins, M., *The history of foreign investment in the United States to 1914* (Cambridge, Mass., forthcoming).

Wilkins, M., *The maturing of multinational enterprise: American business abroad from 1914 to 1970* (Cambridge, Mass., 1974).

Wilkins, M., 'Modern European economic history and the multinationals', *J. Eur. Econ. Hist.*, 6 (1977), pp. 575-95.

Wilkins, M., 'Multinational enterprises', in H. Daems and H. van der Wee, eds., *The rise of managerial capitalism* (Louvain, 1974), pp. 213-35.

Wilkins, M., ed., *British overseas investments, 1907-1948* (New York, 1977).

Wilkins, M. and Hill, F.E., *American business abroad: Ford on six continents* (Detroit, 1964).

Williamson, O.E., *Economic institutions of capitalism* (New York, 1985).

Wilson, C., 'The multinational in historical perspective' in K. Nakagawa, ed., *Strategy and structure of big business* (Tokyo, n.d. [1976]), pp. 265-86.

Wiman, E., 'British capital and American industries', *North Amer. Rev.*, 150 (1890), pp. 220-34.

[16]

The Growth of the Transnational Industrial Firm in the United States and the United Kingdom: A Comparative Analysis[1]

By ALFRED D. CHANDLER

THIS article is an exercise in comparative institutional history. It examines the beginnings and continuing growth of a powerful economic institution, the modern transnational industrial corporation, in two quite different economies. Such a comparative analysis has the advantage of pointing to basic institutional similarities and, at the same time, suggesting how institutions are affected by differing economic needs and opportunities as well as by differing culture attitudes and values. And, although the similarities in the history of the large industrial firm in the two countries are significant, it is the differences that are particularly striking.

This analysis is based on a comparative study that I have been carrying out with Prof. Herman Daems on the rise of large-scale industrial enterprise in the United States, Britain, and the Continent. Our plan has been to make use of lists of over 100 of the largest industrial firms (ranked either by assets or market value of securities outstanding) in the United States, the United Kingdom, Germany, and France for three sets of years: those immediately after World War I, those just prior to the onslaught of the great depression, and those immediately following World War II.[2]

These lists document what I found to be the case for the United States.[3] The largest firms clustered in a few capital-intensive and energy-intensive groups of industries whose products are distributed in volume in national and international markets. In all four countries the largest enterprises were found primarily in the chemical, machinery, and metal-making industries. In Britain, as might be expected from its industrial history, there were more large textile firms. In the United States there were more large petroleum enterprises. In both the United States and the United Kingdom there were many large companies in the food industries, but in Germany and France there were almost none. In no country,

[1] The Tawney Memorial Lecture for 1979.

[2] I wish to acknowledge with gratitude the valuable assistance received from Margaret Ackrill, who compiled the three lists of the 200 largest firms in Britain; from Peter Grant, who categorized these lists into S.I.C. categories and provided data on ownership, sales branches, and factories; and from other scholars, who compiled comparable lists for Germany and France. I am also indebted to the Alfred P. Sloan Foundation, the German Marshall Fund, and the Research Division of the Harvard Business School for the financial support they provided for this research.

[3] For the United States, see my *Visible Hand: The Managerial Revolution in American Business* (Cambridge, Mass. 1977), pp. 370, 503-12. The findings for Britain, Germany, and France are presented in Alfred D. Chandler, Jr. 'The Place of the Modern Industrial Enterprise in Three Economies', a paper presented at International Symposium in Economic History held at the University of East Anglia, 19-22 Sept. 1979.

however, were there more than one or two large firms in the apparel, furniture, lumber, leather, and printing and publishing industries.

Because of the nature of this clustering we decided to focus our research efforts on the individual histories of the largest firms in three industries: chemicals (including soap and allied industries, paint, pharmaceuticals, explosives, and fertilizers as well as industrial chemicals); machinery (including electrical machinery and transportation equipment), where the large firm clusters in all major economies; and food (including drink and tobacco), where many large enterprises appeared in the United States and the United Kingdom. These industries provide a spread in production from simple to the most complex technologies and in distribution from mass consumer to highly specialized industrial markets. The companies in these three industrial groups plus those in petroleum, rubber, and glass, whose experience parallel closely that of the chemical firms, accounted in the 1970s for 81·3 per cent of the 256 companies in the world employing more than 30,000 workers in 1973, and for approximately 80 per cent of the world's 800 largest industrial companies in the same year. Of this 80 per cent nearly all were transnationals.[1] A review of their history from their beginnings until World War II can, therefore, tell us much about the institutional development of today's market economies.

The composite history of the largest firms in these industries in the United States and the United Kingdom makes it absolutely clear that modern industrial enterprise did not become large merely by expanding the company's industrial plant or factory.[2] Instead, these enterprises grew by adding new units of production and distribution, by adding sales and purchasing offices, by adding facilities for producing raw and semi-finished materials, by obtaining shipping lines, railroad cars, pipelines, and other transportation units, and even by building research laboratories. Growth through the addition of new units came in two ways: either the enterprise itself built new offices, plants, and opened mines, all of which were normally paid for out of retained earnings, or it obtained them through the acquisition of or merger with other enterprises. (And nearly all of these acquisitions and mergers were financed by the exchange of stock.)

Either route to growth meant the hiring of managers. Managers were needed not only to administer the activities of the new units but also to co-ordinate and monitor these units and to allocate resources to them for the firm's future production and distribution. Thus the growth of the firm led to the creation of multiunit enterprises administered through managerial hierarchies. Such growth also meant that in many industries the productive assets became concentrated in a few large business enterprises.

One of the most striking differences between the history of big business in the two countries is that these managerial hierarchies became larger and appeared much more quickly in the United States than they did in the United Kingdom.

---

[1] Based on an analysis of *Fortune*'s large 800 industrials in the United States and abroad in 1973.

[2] The information on the growth of the large American firm comes from Chandler, op. cit. particularly chs. 7–11. That on Britain comes from a wide variety of business histories and biographies, company-sponsored commemorative volumes, memoirs, annual and other corporate reports, and financial news in specialized and daily newspapers. As Prof. Daems and I have not yet completed the review of the machinery industries, the examples used in this article will be taken primarily from the food and chemical industries.

ALFRED D. CHANDLER

In neither case did large multi-unit industrial firms appear before the 1880s. They came only after new forms of transportation and communication—the railroads, steamships, telegraph, and cable—had been improved enough to make possible high-volume production and distribution, the basic characteristic of the modern industrial firm. From the 1880s such enterprises appeared in the United States with unprecedented speed and took their place in the economy in a revolutionary way. In Britain they came in a slower, more evolutionary manner. Let us review these differing processes of growth in the two countries.

I

In the United States the first firms to grow large in the 1880s did so by integrating forward into wholesaling and backward into direct purchasing and then into the control of raw and semi-finished materials. They explicitly carried out a strategy of vertical integration. They did so, however, only in four subsets of industries, each of which had somewhat similar characteristics. The large multi-unit firm appeared in the production of low-priced, branded, packaged products where manufacturers adopted large batch and continuous-process technologies of mass production; in the processing of perishable products for the national market; in the making of new mass-produced machines that required specialized marketing services to be sold in volume; and, finally, in the manufacturing of volume-produced machinery and chemicals which were standardized, but technologically complex, and which called for somewhat different specialized marketing services.

During the 1880s pioneering enterprises of the first of these four groups included American Tobacco producing cigarettes; Washburn and Pillsbury both making flour; Quaker Oats in breakfast cereals; Heinz, Campbell Soup, Borden's Milk, and Libby, McNeil & Libby in canned goods; Procter & Gamble in soap; Sherwin-Williams in paints; and Parke Davis, Colgate, and Squibb in proprietary drugs. The managers of these enterprises continued to use the wholesaler to handle the physical distribution of goods, but they took over branding, advertising, and they scheduled the flows of the goods from the factories to the new mass markets.

In the same decade, meat packers, including Armour, Swift, Morris, Hammond, Cudahy, and Swartschild & Sulzberger, and brewers, including Pabst, Miller, Schlitz, and Anheuser-Busch, began to build national, and often international, networks of branch houses with refrigerated warehouses and distribution facilities, as well as to obtain fleets of temperature-controlled railroad cars and ships. Similar networks were formed in the 1890s by the precursors of United Fruit to produce and sell bananas on a mass scale. These firms often bypassed the wholesalers completely, for the latter were unable to provide extensive refrigerated facilities or to schedule with the necessary precision the flow of these perishable products over thousands of miles from the initial processing to thousands indeed tens of thousands of local butchers, grocers, and other retailers. At the same time, like the producers of semi-perishable products, they created extensive purchasing organizations to ensure a continuous flow of raw materials into their mass-producing facilities.

The third group, the makers of newly invented machinery produced by assembling interchangeable parts, also bypassed the wholesalers. To sell their relatively complex and costly products in the volume at which they could be produced, these manufacturers had to provide demonstrations, continuing service and repair on machines sold, and credit to consumers. Moreover, the weekly delivery of thousands of machines on schedule required careful co-ordination, as did ensuring a high-volume flow of a wide variety of materials through the factory. Nearly all these firms quickly built world-wide marketing organizations. The pioneers were the makers of sewing machines. The most successful of these, the Singer Sewing Machine Co., was the innovator in direct canvassing of consumers, that is, it moved into retailing as well as into wholesaling. Others, particularly the makers of agricultural implements, such as McCormick Harvester, Deering Harvester, John Deere, and J. I. Case, preferred the less expensive alternative of using franchise dealers supported by a strong, well-organized wholesale organization that permitted dealers to market aggressively and to provide necessary services. The manufacturers of new machines, including Fairbanks Scales, Remington Typewriter, National Cash Register, A. B. Dick Mimeograph Machines, Burroughs Adding Machine, and Computer-Tabulator-Recorder (the predecessor of I.B.M.), also came to rely on the franchise dealer. Nearly all of these enterprises either built or perfected their sales departments in the 1880s.

During the same decade, makers of standardized heavy machinery created comparable world-wide organizations. Normally, they staffed these with college-trained engineers because of the technological complexity of their products and the uses to which they were put. These firms included the forerunners of General Electric and Allis Chalmers, as well as Westinghouse Electric, Westinghouse Air Brake, Western Electric, Otis Elevator, Worthington Pump, Babcock & Wilcox, and Mergenthaler Linotype. The fast-moving technology of the machinery-makers, particularly that of the manufacturers of electrical equipment, required close co-ordination among salesmen, product designers, and manufacturing managers. Early in the twentieth century, this kind of co-ordination became significant in the growth of the American Solvay Process Co., Union Carbide, and other new large chemical producers.

As they were building these organizations at home, the large American firms often moved overseas. They first set up branch offices and warehouses on foreign shores. Then, as demand grew and as local tariffs appeared or as shipping costs increased and scheduling of flows across oceans became complex, the enterprise built plants abroad which it soon began to supply from near-by sources. By 1914 at least 41 American companies, clustered in machinery and in food industries, had built two or more operating facilities abroad.[1] The largest number of these were in Canada; but by 1914 23 had factories in Britain and 21 in Germany, with a small number scattered in other countries. That the largest number of factories outside of Canada was built in Britain, still a free-trade country, indicates that transportation costs and scheduling problems were as important considerations for direct investment abroad as was the desire to get within the tariff barriers. In

[1] Mira Wilkins, *Emergence of Multinational Enterprise* (Cambridge, Mass. 1970), pp. 212–16, and Chandler, op. cit. p. 368.

this way, then, American entrepreneurs had created, within less than a generation, giant multinational enterprises whose names are all well known today.

All these integrated enterprises developed much the same type of organizational structure to administer their operating units. At some, the new structure came quickly in a planned manner; at others more slowly and in an *ad hoc* way. All had large central offices, housed in multi-storeyed buildings, where salaried middle managers supervised, through functionally defined departments, the work of the many lower-level operating managers. The Production or Operating Department administered the operations of a number of factories, works or plants. The Sales Department managed the branch offices in the United States and abroad. The Purchasing or Essential Materials Department watched over the buying or production of raw and semi-finished materials. The Financial Department had its accounting, auditing, and treasurer's offices. A smaller Traffic Department handled shipments to, from, and through the enterprise. Often an Experimental or Research Department worked on improving products and processes. In addition, Legal, Personnel, and Real Estate Departments were formed. Finally, where the companies had factories or other direct investments abroad, they had begun to set up their international departments by World War I.

The top management consisted of the Vice-Presidents in charge of the major functional departments, the President, and the Chairman of the Board. Legally constituted as the Executive Committee of the Board, the senior executives monitored the performance of the functional departments, defined policies for the enterprise as a whole (of these the policies to determine the co-ordination of flows of materials through the enterprise were of particular importance), and allocated the resources, both capital and personnel, needed to maintain and expand the activities of the firm. Because most of these enterprises had financed their expansion from retained earnings, the founders and their families normally continued to own the controlling shares of stock. So they continued to sit on the Board and often to take an active part in top management. No family, however, could provide the lower and middle level managers required to administer one of these business giants, whose managerial staff by World War I numbered often over 100 and in some cases even 300 or 400.

As I have suggested, the British story is different. In the United Kingdom large integrated enterprises first appeared about the same time and in some but not all of the same industries as in the United States, but they grew more slowly. They flourished in the consumer sectors of the chemical and food industries where low-priced, packaged products were sold in Britain's rapidly growing urban markets. They came, too, in the processing and distribution of perishable goods—meat, dairy products, and beer—but on a smaller scale than in the United States. They were fewer, however, in the machinery industries, where in general firms still produced relatively uncomplicated machines for the older industries—such as textiles, mining, metal-making, and food. Until the expansion of the automobile and the appliance industries in the 1920s, almost no British-owned firm mass-produced consumer durables. The leading producers of standardized machines in Great Britain remained the subsidiaries of such American companies as Singer Sewing Machine, International Harvester, Ford, United Shoe Machinery, General Electric, Westinghouse, and Western Electric.

In Britain nearly all the producers of low-priced, packaged, and brand products followed the same strategy of growth. These included the makers of chocolates (Cadbury, Rowntree, and Fry), biscuits and confectionery (Peek Frean, Huntley & Palmers, and Barratts), jams and sauces (Crosse & Blackwell, Lea & Perrins, and H.P. Sauce), condiments (J. & J. Colman and Cerebos), meat products (Bovril and Liebig's Extract), soft drinks (Schweppes), soap, starch, and toilet articles (Gossage, Reckitt, and Yardley), paints (Pinchin Johnson, Lewis Berger, and Goodlass, Wall), and pharmaceuticals (Beecham and Sangers). Nearly all were small family partnerships that were well established before the new transportation and communication facilities opened national and overseas markets. As more distant markets began to be reached, firms branded their products, started to advertise nationally, and, most important of all, sent out an army of salaried salesmen, or "travellers", to obtain orders from wholesalers and the larger retailers and to be responsible for the delivery of the orders on schedule. These family firms, however, rarely set up a network of branch offices, as did their American counterparts. The sales force continued to be supervised from the factory. Only in the 1920s did Cadbury, Crosse & Blackwell, and others begin to build a network of warehouses and depots and to own and operate their own lorries and other transportation facilities.

Most of these firms had branch offices staffed by salaried managers overseas before they had them at home. Nearly all began to sell overseas first in what were to become the white Commonwealth nations—Australia, New Zealand, Canada, and South Africa. Only a few looked to the Indian subcontinent. In the twentieth century more ventured into the United States and continental Europe. Occasionally, before World War I and more often in the 1920s, overseas sales grew to a size that warranted building factories abroad. The reason for building overseas plants appears to have been tariffs in the United States and on the Continent, and also in some Commonwealth nations, rather than the need to reduce shipping costs or to improve the scheduling of flows.

Growing demand at home and abroad brought a gradual enlargement of the firm's main factory and with it an expansion of its buying organization. Unless materials were needed in quantity and on relatively precise schedules, the firms continued to rely on existing middlemen to obtain raw and semi-finished materials from overseas. However, early in the twentieth century some makers of chocolate, soap, margarine, and meat products did consider it necessary to acquire plantations, agencies, and trading companies in distant lands in order to have assured sources of supplies.

The histories of these individual firms varied of course. Some moved overseas earlier than others; some entered the American and continental markets with more energy and enthusiasm than their competitors. In nearly all cases, however, the growth of the enterprise came gradually over a period of two or even three generations.

Such evolutionary growth permitted a family to continue to own and to manage the firm it had founded. The travellers and buyers continued to be supervised from small offices usually housed in or next to the factory. Before the coming of the aeroplane, the managers of overseas sales branches, purchasing offices, and plantations were too far away to make practical the close supervision and scheduling which American firms had developed for their branches within the continental United States. After all, San Francisco was only three days from Chicago, and New York one; while South Africa was three weeks from London, and Australia six. So British enterprise-builders were under less pressure than their American colleagues to hire middle and top managers. As late as the 1930s, the great majority of the leading firms making packaged, branded goods continued to be run by one or two families. The Cadburys, Frys, Rowntrees, Colmans, Reckitts, Ranks, Lyles, Barratts, Beechams, Sangers, Courtaulds, Albrights, and Wilsons, and the families who owned Crosse & Blackwell, Peek Frean, Huntley & Palmers, Gilbeys Gin, Cerebos, Liebig, Bovril, Carreras, Yardley, Pinchin Johnson, and Goodlass, Wall, and Borax Consolidated continued to manage their firms into the third and even fourth generations. Thus, in the 1930s the Chairman of Barratts, long owned by the Barratt and Sennett families, had quite properly the name of J. Barratt Sennett. When a line ran out, the succession usually went to a collateral branch. Until the 1930s, close to 80 per cent of the companies studied in the food and chemical industries had family members on the Board and in active positions of top and middle management.

Thus, the continuance of the family firm in Britain was encouraged by the existence of a well-established distribution network both at home and in the long-distance trades serving small but fast-growing overseas markets and sources of supply. The invisible hand of the market worked more effectively in the United Kingdom than in the United States. Nevertheless, these factors cannot alone account for its longevity. The career of William Lever, a driving entrepreneur, and the success of American machinery companies such as Singer, General Electric, Westinghouse, and United Shoe Machinery suggest that there was in Britain a potential for the more tightly controlled, integrated firm with its own sales branches, buying offices, and transportation facilities—that is for the visible hand of administrative co-ordination. By building such organizations, Lever in soap and the American firms in machinery quickly became the leading enterprises in their industries in Britain.[1] Surely, many of the family firms could have created comparable powerful enterprises, if they had wanted to invest in the facilities and personnel.

II

Differences in the second route to size—that by merger and acquisition—were as significant as in the first route—that by direct investment in marketing and purchasing facilities. And the differences in the second route suggest a more fundamental cause for the continuation of the family firm in the United Kingdom. That was simply that the family wanted to retain and manage its birthright. In the United States mergers brought administrative centralization and industrial rationalization. In Britain they remained federations of autonomous family enterprises. Until the 1930s, British mergers rarely brought economies of scale or other advantages of administrative co-ordination and control.

[1] Charles Wilson, *History of Unilever*, 2 vols. (1954), I, chs. 3–4, esp. pp. 42–3, 50–2. On p. 52 Wilson refers to the Newcastle, Leeds, and Port Sunlight Branches. For Singer see Robert B. Davies, 'Peacefully Working to Conquer the World: The Singer Manufacturing Company in Foreign Markets, 1858–89', *Business History Review*, XLIII (1960), 299–346. United Shoe Machinery, Westinghouse, and General Electric, including its subsidiary British Thomson Houston, are mentioned in F. A. McKenzie, *The American Invaders* (1902), pp. 49–51, 81–5, 157–64.

In the United States a successful merger went through the following steps. First came legal consolidation, which gave a central office complete legal power over the activities of the constituent companies. Initially this took the form of creating a trust, and after the 1890s a holding company. Then came administrative centralization and industrial rationalization. Some of the manufacturing facilities of the constituent companies were enlarged, more were eliminated, and a few new ones built. Then the administration of these facilities was placed under control of a single production or operating department. Next the consolidated centralized enterprise normally embarked on a strategy of vertical integration by moving forward into marketing by setting up a branch office and distribution network, and backward by obtaining its own purchasing offices and sources of raw and semi-finished materials.

The first modern mergers came in the United States in the 1880s, when existing trade associations—loose federations of small, single-function firms—created during the economically depressed years of the 1870s, realized that they were not able to control price competition within an industry. The first of these associations to turn to legal consolidation and administrative centralization were those in the refining and distilling industries, where new continuous-process techniques of mass production were first introduced and where, therefore, pressure for rationalization first appeared. Thus the earliest national merger came, not surprisingly, in the oil industry. As soon as John D. Rockefeller and his associates formed the Standard Oil Trust in 1882, the American petroleum-refining industry was rationalized with the concentration of two-fifths of the world's production of refined oil in only three refineries. As a result, the unit cost of producing a gallon of kerosene was reduced from $1\frac{1}{2}$c to $\frac{1}{2}$c.[1] Next, Standard Oil built a national and indeed an international marketing network, and in the late 1880s it began to produce crude oil for the first time. In the 1880s the Cotton Seed Oil, Linseed Oil, and National Lead Trust (the last was a producer of white lead for paint) followed Standard Oil's example, with the Sugar and Whisky Trusts taking a little longer than the others to centralize and to integrate. In the 1890s mergers using the holding-company form became increasingly popular, and culminated during the years 1898 to 1903 in the nation's largest and still most significant merger movement. Among the best known examples of consolidated centralized mergers of this period in the three sets of industries studied were National Biscuit, Corn Products, and Standard Milling in food; DuPont and General Chemical in chemicals; and General Electric and International Harvester in machinery.

Again, the organizational response was quite similar. The pioneering firm, Rockefeller's Standard Oil Trust, devised a complex system of committees, and staff officers operating out of the massive headquarters at 26 Broadway in New York City. Nearly all the other successful mergers, however, moved to a functional organization similar to that used by the firms that had grown large through building their own marketing and purchasing networks from retained earnings. In addition to their primary departments of production, sales, purchasing or essential materials, and finance, each with its own staff and often with its own advisory committees, these consolidations formed departments for traffic,

[1] Ralph W. Hidy and Muriel E. Hidy, *Pioneering in Big Business* (New York, 1955), pp. 108–21.

research and development, personnel, and legal matters. Because the organizers of the merged firm usually were, at least initially, involved in rationalizing what was often a large part of a major American industry, because they drew their managerial personnel from a number of companies, and because they had to institute industry-wide accounting, auditing, and other control systems, they created larger central or corporate offices than those firms which had attained their size by reinvesting retained earnings. For these reasons nearly all of the techniques of modern top management—those developed to co-ordinate, to monitor, and to allocate resources to the operating units—were devised in the corporate offices of these integrated consolidations. It was there that present-day procedures of budgeting, forecasting, and control had their beginnings.

Whatever the initial route to size—by merger or by reinvesting retained earnings—most large industrials continued to grow through acquisitions. Normally the personnel and facilities acquired were melded into the existing functional core organization of the acquiring firm. This was true even where, as in the case of International Harvester, the trade names and dealer organizations of the constituent companies were for a time retained. Only after the invention of the multidivisional form with its autonomous operating divisions administered by a large, general corporate office[1] were acquired companies permitted to continue to operate as autonomous administrative units with their internal organizations relatively unchanged.

Therefore, mergers in the United States, although at first considered as a means to control competition, in most cases became instruments to improve industrial productivity through rationalization and centralization. In Britain, on the other hand, the goal of mergers remained primarily to restrain competition. The internal organizations of constituent companies were little changed; their autonomy was not challenged, so little rationalization occurred. In the late nineteenth century, mergers which normally used the legal form of a holding company were mostly large horizontal combinations including as many as 30 to 50 firms.[2] In these mergers price and output of the group were determined by the representatives of the constituent firms sitting on the Board of Directors or by a smaller management committee. Such mergers occurred largely in the older textile and iron and steel industries. In the food, chemical, and machinery industries the most common type of merger was that of two or three of the industry's leaders who joined to co-operate with each other in purchasing materials, especially materials coming from abroad; to divide overseas markets; and, to a lesser extent, to stabilize prices at home. Such were the motives for the mergers between Cadbury and Fry that formed British Chocolate & Cocoa in 1918; Peek Frean and Huntley & Palmers that formed Associated Biscuits in 1921, and those forming Crosse & Blackwell, Reckitt & Colman, and Tate & Lyle. In none of these mergers was the independence of the constituent companies impaired. The same was true for a number of brewery mergers such as Watney, Combe, Reid in London; Bass, Ratcliffe & Gretton in Burton-on-Trent, and Scottish

---

[1] This structure was invented in the early 1920s primarily to administer firms that carried out a new strategy of diversifying into different product lines.

[2] Peter Mathias, 'Conflicts of Function in the Rise of Big Business: The British Experience', in Harold F. Williamson, ed. *Evolution of International Management Structures* (Newark, Del. 1975), pp. 40–3.

Breweries in Edinburgh, and also true for the merger of Dewar and Buchanan that formed Scottish Whisky Brands.

The largest and certainly the best known of this type of merger was Imperial Tobacco. This company, formed as a direct response to an attack from James B. Duke's American Tobacco Company, was a combination of one large firm, W. D. & H. O. Wills and 12 smaller ones.[1] Its formation, however, brought little rationalization to the British tobacco industry. Imperial's subsidiaries did lose their legal identity in becoming "branches", but they remained administratively autonomous. They did co-operate in purchasing their tobacco—largely from the United States and Turkey—and in obtaining cigarette paper and other supplies. The "branches", however, continued to produce, sell, and advertise their own products and, indeed, to compete with one another. An Executive Committee of the Board, consisting of representatives of the families of the four largest members of the federation, set pricing policies, controlled advertising expenditures, and reviewed the capital expenditures of the constituent enterprises. The central office remained small; in fact it was housed in rooms attached to Wills's largest factory, a striking contrast to American Tobacco's multi-storey office building at 111 Fifth Avenue, New York. This organization, which lasted relatively unchanged until the 1960s, permitted generations of Wills, Players, Butlers, and Mitchells to compete decorously with one another in the British market.

If mergers did not bring administrative centralization, nor did more gradual growth by acquisition. The companies acquired were not incorporated into the central organization of the acquiring company, as was the case in the United States, but were left to operate quite autonomously. This was true of Ranks Ltd. the largest flour millers in Britain, which acquired an impressive number of mills in the second and third decades of the century. As the company's official history explained: "As each mill consolidated its position and strengthened its hold on a particular trade so it tended to be self-contained, each branch (of the company) naturally striving to do the best for itself."[2] Pinchin Johnson in paints expanded in much the same way in the 1920s, as did the Distillers Co. Ltd. and Lever Brothers somewhat earlier.

Lever Brothers provides a useful example of the process of growth through acquisition in Great Britain. Between 1910 and 1921 William Lever carried out the consolidation of the soap industry in a piecemeal fashion by acquiring nearly all of his competitors by means of exchange of stock.[3] Lever did not attempt, however, to administer these companies through a single centralized administrative hierarchy. All he did was to assign one of the directors of his enterprise to supervise a number of the new "associated companies", as they came to be called.[4]

As a result, acquisition brought little rationalization. The Lever purchasing organization did begin to buy for the associated companies at home and abroad, but there was no systematizing of production or distribution. During the 1920s

---

[1] B. W. E. Alford, *W. D. & H. O. Wills and the Development of the U.K. Tobacco Industry* (1973), pp. 309–14, 330–3.

[2] Hurford James, *The Master Millers: The Story of the House of Rank* (1956), pp. 64–8.

[3] Wilson, op. cit. I, chs. 8–9, 18.

[4] In 1917, in answer to a request from Lever, each of his directors defined their duties. Their replies are summarized in a file in the Unilever archives entitled 'Management and Labour'. The letters are in the L C 6391 file.

the Lever combine included 49 different soap-making sub-companies with 48 different sales organizations.[1] This condition remained, even though one executive pointed out that administrative centralization could bring a saving of £2 per ton in distribution costs alone. Lever and his salaried directors favoured, in Lever's words, "healthy" but not "frenzied" competition between the associated companies.[2] Committees were formed to set pricing policies and to control advertising expenditures. Nevertheless, relatively unrestricted competition continued between Lever Brothers and the other large subsidiaries. Rationalization and centralization did not become effective until the early 1930s after the formation of Unilever, a combination of Lever and Dutch margarine-makers in 1929.[3] The failure to centralize and rationalize may account for the drop in Lever's share of the British soap market from 67 to 60 per cent between 1920 and 1929 (and to 51·5 per cent in 1935), and for the entry into the British market in strength of the American giants, Procter & Gamble and Palmolive-Peet.[4] At Lever, as in nearly all other acquisitions and mergers in Britain until the 1930s, the result was federation rather than centralization.

In Britain, the historical record makes clear that mergers were specifically arranged to maintain family control. In most cases the constituent firms remained legally and administratively autonomous entities managed by descendants of the founder's family. Sons took over from fathers. The consolidated company permitted its members to co-operate in the purchasing of raw materials and in overseas marketing, and it stabilized the domestic market by preventing uncomfortable price competition and high advertising costs. Representatives of the family on the Board worked out policies by negotiation.

Only severe financial and competitive pressures caused federations of British firms to move towards a centralized management structure before the 1930s. The mergers and acquisitions that resulted in United Alkali in the 1890s and Spiller's and Union Cold Storage in the 1920s provide the relatively rare examples in the industries studied. United Alkali was a merger of 40 producers of alkali by the Le Blanc process which had become obsolete with the development of the new far more efficient Solvay process.[5] In attempting to meet the overwhelming competition of the new technology, United Alkali centralized control, rationalized its production, set up a research laboratory, and diversified into new products. However, because it remained saddled with an obsolete process, it never was able to acquire sufficient funds or personnel to exploit its improved managerial controls or the findings of its research laboratory. Spillers, the second largest processer of wheat, began to centralize and rationalize its domestic production and its overseas marketing in 1927 after substantial losses and passing of dividends had frightened the families whose firms dominated the federation into calling on the well-known accounting firm of Price, Waterhouse to reorganize their enterprise.[6] The resulting changes in middle management were not, however, accom-

[1] Wilson, op. cit. II, 302, 345.
[2] W. Lever to F. A. Cooper, 14 Oct. and 11, 24 Nov. on the subject of competition within the firm in file L C 1482.
[3] Wilson, op. cit. I, 299-304; II, 354-7.
[4] H. R. Edwards, *Competition and Monopoly in the British Soap Industry* (Oxford, 1962), pp. 183-6.
[5] I am greatly indebted to Yuichi Kudo for information on United Alkali.
[6] *The Times*, 25 Jan., 5 Feb., 9 May 1927.

panied by major ones at the top, where the same families continued to dominate. Finally, in the meat-packing trade, where retailers rather than manufacturers played a major role in developing the early integrated enterprises, and where American competition, particularly in Argentine imports, drove down sharply the share of the British market held by British firms, merger was followed by centralization and rationalization.[1] Even so, the Vesty family, the architects of the final consolidation, The Union Cold Storage Company, has continued to dominate the top management of Britain's one large integrated meat-packing enterprise until today.

This review of the processes of merger and acquisition in Britain makes clear the importance of the merger that formed Nobel Industries, for it was the first to be followed quickly by rationalization and administrative centralization.[2] The merger brought together in 1918 four makers of dynamite and other explosives— two family firms (Kynoch and Bickford Smith), a federation of such firms (Curtis's & Harvey), and Nobel Explosives, Britain's largest explosive company which had acquired in the fashion of Lever Brothers a number of subsidiaries and which, as was so rare in Britain, had been long run by salaried managers instead of owners. The members of its Organization Committee first looked at the experience of comparable firms in Britain—the Calico Printers, Bradford Dyers, J. & P. Coates, Metropolitan Carriage, United Steel, and others. They found that, although the majority of these firms had centralized their purchasing and were moving towards centralizing other activities, each still remained, in the committee's words, "an aggregation of a number of companies".[3] The organizers turned instead to the United States. There, as the committee's report pointed out, "the policy of large American amalgamations, after passing through a phase of some sort of loose agreement: a pool, a trust, a holding company, has crystallized into the complete merger in which the separate management and personnel of the individual units disappear, even if the units themselves retain their nominal existence, a single executive and operating staff is created in which the entire control is centralized." The committee's specific model was an old Nobel ally, the E. I. DuPont de Nemours & Company. The organizing committee travelled to the DuPont headquarters in Delaware, studied the company's lengthy reports on organization, discussed structure and accounting with senior DuPont executives, and came home impressed—at least the salaried managers of the old Nobel Explosives Company returned impressed. Arthur Chamberlain, the chairman of Kynoch, the second largest firm coming into the merger and a member of one of Britain's best known industrial families, had doubts. He urged his colleagues to "go slowly in altering the inherited and accepted notions of British Industrial

---

[1] The meat-packing story can be pieced together from James T. Critchell and James Raymond, *A History of the Frozen Meat Trade* (1912), [U.S.] Federal Trade Commission, *Food Investigation: Meat Packing Industry*, summary and pt. 1 (Washington, 1919), *The Times*, 17 June 1913, 30 March 1917, and stock-exchange year books.

[2] W. J. Reader, *Imperial Chemical Industries, A History, Vol. I The Forerunners, 1870–1926* (1970), pp. 254–6, ch. 17.

[3] This and the following quotation are from the 'Report of the Committee on Organization to the Chairman and Directors of Explosives Trades, Limited', 21 April 1919, in the I.C.I. archives. The report further stated that "the keynote of the American system appears to be: (1) Complete centralization of control. (2) Reliance on individuals and not upon committees. (3) Full authority and responsibility for each individual within his own sphere. (4) The employment of younger men in positions of importance."

Management and instead of jumping to complete control at once, only adopt it if and when distinctive trades' control has shown a weakness."[1] However, the managers had their way. The centralized structure was adopted. In the resulting rationalization of production and distribution the names of several old and respected family firms disappeared. Within a short time Arthur Chamberlain retired. The new organization at Nobel Industries provided the model for that of Imperial Chemical Industries, the much larger merger which it helped to instigate in 1926. It was a model, too, for a number of other British mergers during the depressed economic years of the early 1930s, when continuing financial and competitive pressures forced federations to centralize and rationalize. It was only in the 1930s, therefore, that mergers in Britain began to create extensive managerial hierarchies, and then only in a relatively few, though important, cases.

III

This comparative analysis of the growth of the large industrial firm in the two countries emphasizes how much more quickly managerial enterprise appeared in the United States than it did in the United Kingdom. Normally, it took a British firm three generations to reach the size and managerial strength that a comparable American enterprise achieved in one. Certainly the continuance of the family firm helps to account for differences in the processes of growth. But did the continuance of the family firm and the slower appearance of the managerial enterprise make any real difference? Did the continuance and the delay have an appreciable effect on the performance of the large industrial firm in Britain and of the British economy as a whole?

I think that it did. In the first place, the failure to build up managerial hierarchies may have deprived British industrialists of some of the cost advantages and therefore market power of large-scale enterprise. Although sophisticated in merchandising consumer goods, British manufacturers moved slowly into their mass production, for that required new methods of organizing distribution as well as production. Their delay in adopting the new methods made it possible for American firms to obtain a significant share not only of international markets but also of the British market itself in canned goods, frozen meat, proprietary articles such as toothpaste and pills, as well as in such durables as sewing machines, typewriters, cash registers, and other office machinery. The failure of the local heavy-machinery firms to develop marketing organizations within Britain also made it easier for the Americans to take over the British market for volume-produced standardized producers' goods, such as harvesters, electrical equipment, elevators, shoe machinery, and printing presses.

Second, delays in building managerial hierarchies meant that the British were slow in adopting modern management methods. The American managers in the first years of the twentieth century and even earlier, as they were perfecting the basic techniques of mass production and mass distribution, were also devising new methods of inventory and quality control. In addition they worked out cost-accounting procedures based on standard volume and capacity that permitted middle managers to monitor systematically and continuously the work of the

[1] Quoted in Reader, op. cit. 1, 393.

operating units under their command. They also perfected scheduling procedures necessary to maintain a high and steady flow of material through an enterprise's plants and departments. Such accounting and control methods, so important in improving a firm's competitive ability by reducing unit costs, only began to be adopted in Britain extensively in the 1930s. In many cases such methods were borrowed directly from the United States.[1]

More serious was the longer delay in adopting top-management procedures—procedures so essential for the continuing efficient use of an enterprise's resources. In the United States such procedures had been initially devised in the large corporate office of the consolidated mergers—offices that were so rare in Britain. There, senior executives drew up organizational plans that defined the functions of managerial positions, drew the lines of authority, responsibility and communication, and differentiated between a line and staff activities. They developed accounting and budgetary procedures to permit top management to monitor systematically the performance of their middle managers and to allocate resources for future activities of the enterprise. These men also devised short-term forecasting of financial and market conditions necessary for co-ordinating flows of goods through the enterprise, and long-term forecasting necessary in the evaluation of capital appropriations for facilities that would not come into production for two or three years. To aid in this monitoring and planning, they also invented sophisticated formulas for determining the rate of return on total investment. I have run across little evidence of the systematic use of such basic top-level organizational and control procedures even in the largest British multinational firms until after World War II. Such methods were imported into Britain, largely by American consultants, only in the 1950s and 1960s.

Finally, the differing processes of the growth of the firm affected the recruitment and training of managers in both countries. In the United States during the 1880s and 1890s the need for trained production and marketing specialists, particularly in the technologically advanced machinery, electrical, and chemical firms, quickly brought state and private universities and the new technical schools, like the Massachusetts Institute of Technology, into offering a variety of courses in mechanical, electrical, and chemical engineering. A decade later the continuing demand for functional specialists in the consumer as well as in the producer goods industries led the nation's most prestigious universities—Harvard, California, Chicago, Dartmouth, and Pennsylvania, to name a few—to create new courses and even schools of business where professional training was given in finance, production, marketing, and even policy-making. In Britain, however, there was little such training. Top managers came from the owners. The few middle managers could be recruited from the company's ranks, from its travellers, buyers, or production supervisors. So there was little demand for engineering courses—particularly for those in chemical or electrical engineering—and even less for business schools.

This lack of engineering and business training can hardly be blamed on the supposed bias of British universities and British undergraduates against trade. When large firms, such as I.C.I. and Unilever, first began to recruit college

---

[1] A good example of such borrowing is that done by Boots. See Stanley Chapman, *Jesse Boots of Boots the Chemist* (1974), pp. 144–54.

graduates, they had little difficulty in getting the men they wanted from Oxford, Cambridge, and other universities.[1] Until there was a significant demand for managers, however, the British could hardly be expected to provide facilities to train them. After World War II, when managerial hierarchies became larger and more numerous in Britain, the educational system responded by expanding engineering and inaugurating business schools.

This lack of contact between the industrial enterprise and the university had a particularly debilitating effect on technologically advanced industries. In the United States, and also in Germany, managers on both the production and distribution sides of these industries kept their ties with the universities and institutions in which they had been trained.[2] They looked to their former professors not only to supply them with a steady flow of new recruits but also for a flow of technological advice about process and product. Their contacts were often with the scientists as well as with the engineers in the educational departments involved. This close relationship between theoretical and applied science permitted the Americans and the Germans to develop a commanding lead in many of the most important new technological processes and products of what has come to be called the Second Industrial Revolution.

The lack of engineers and managers and of sophisticated technological skills and management techniques may have made little difference in the production and distribution of branded, packaged consumer goods, except possibly perishable products. It did, however, make a vital difference in the chemical, machinery, and electrical equipment industries. These were precisely the industries which became organized through managerial enterprise; for in these industries trained managers and engineers and carefully defined organizational and control systems have been essential to reducing the cost of production, to providing delivery to specification and on schedule, and to assuring continuing specialized marketing services. And it was in just these industries that the Americans and the Germans successfully invaded the markets of the world and of Britain itself.

The British failure to participate fully in the growth of the new industries and to meet the competition from the United States and the Continent has often been explained as entrepreneurial failure. A better term may be managerial failure: that is, the continuing existence of the family firm helped to deprive Britain of a class of trained managers and sets of technological and managerial skills that became increasingly essential, not only to technically advanced industries but also to the operation of modern urban, industrial economies. Possibly, Britain is still paying for that deprivation.

Harvard University

---

[1] Both Wilson and Reader make this point.
[2] As indicated in David Noble, *America By Design* (New York, 1977), chs. 7–9.

[17]

PROFESSOR OF ECONOMICS
FLORIDA INTERNATIONAL UNIVERSITY

American-Japanese Direct Foreign Investment Relationships, 1930–1952*

¶ One of the leading experts on the history of multinational enterprise, Mira Wilkins here sets forth the history of American multinational investment in Japan and Japanese multinational investment in the United States during two crucial decades. The tumultuous years from 1930 to 1952 forced these companies to deal with the vastly different challenges of depression, war, and peace. Professor Wilkins explains how they adapted to their changing environment. She also provides noteworthy support for the view that cross-investment was not symmetrical.

American multinational enterprises in the pre-World War II years were active in Japan. Likewise, and less well-known, Japanese multinational businesses were present in the United States. The investment interests and their consequences were diverse; there was no symmetry; but both sets of investments were significant. American-Japanese direct foreign investment relationships are more important today than in the past. The Japanese now rank among the largest direct investors in the world.[1] It is thus useful to understand the antecedents. This article reveals the extent, nature, and impact of the cross-direct investments, before, during, and immediately after World War II. The reader will find many surprises. There is much here that has hitherto been undocumented — gaps in our knowledge of American-Japanese business interactions that are being filled for the first time.

From the earliest American business investments in Japan in the late nineteenth century, U.S. business interests mounted. By 1930, according to U.S. Department of Commerce figures, they peaked at $61.4 million; the level of investments dropped in 1936 to $47 million and four years later in 1940 to $37.7 million. At the eve of Pearl Harbor, a U.S. Treasury Department census concluded the investment totaled $32.9 million.[2]

Business History Review, Vol. LVI, No. 4 (Winter, 1982). Copyright © The President and Fellows of Harvard College.

* This article was originally presented as a paper delivered at the University of California, Los Angeles, in 1978 as part of a seminar series financed and sponsored by the Luce Foundation. I have made a few changes, but have updated the references and incorporated the wise suggestions of two anonymous reviewers and of Albro Martin.

[1] See Lawrence Krause and Sueo Sekiguchi, "Japan and the World Economy," in Hugh Patrick and Henry Rosovsky, eds., Asia's New Giant (Washington, D.C., 1976), 447.

[2] The figures for 1930 are from the U.S. Department of Commerce, Bureau of Foreign and Domestic

It is not clear when the first Japanese business investments were made in the United States. We know of one investment in 1879 and another in 1880. We have, however, few figures on the growth of Japanese stakes in the United States. The U.S. Commerce Department found the level of such direct investments in 1937 to be $41 million. As of June 1941, the U.S. Treasury determined that the value of the assets of Japanese-controlled enterprises in the United States equaled $35.1 million.[3]

In this article I am going to confine myself to American-Japanese business relations that involved *direct* foreign investment. I am not going to be concerned with trade *per se* or all investment flows. Rather, I want to look at foreign investment that was for the purpose of running a business abroad — what we now call multinational enterprise.

AMERICAN BUSINESS IN JAPAN

There seems little doubt that U.S. business investments in Japan in 1930 were larger than Japanese investments in the United States. Yet U.S. direct investments in Japan in 1930 were less than one per cent of total U.S. direct investments abroad and only 14.6 per cent of U.S. direct investments in Asia. American companies had larger direct investments in 1930 in China, the Philippines, and the Netherlands East Indies than in Japan, and their direct investments in Canada, England, Germany, France, as well as in Chile, Argentina, Venezuela and Brazil far exceeded those in China.[4]

In short, in terms of U.S. direct investment worldwide in 1930 Japan played a very small role in multinational corporate strategy. Nonetheless, what happened there was far from insignificant. U.S. direct investment in Japan was part of a multinational pattern. U.S. companies that were multinational in their characteristics were present in Japan.[5]

It is fascinating to see how in the modern sectors, U.S. and Japanese business interacted in Japan and how in the process Japanese business was able to innovate and at the same time to absorb the technology of

Commerce, *A New Estimate of American Investments Abroad*, Trade Info. Bull. 767 (Washington, 1931), 20; for 1936 from the U.S. Department of Commerce, *American Direct Investments in Foreign Countries-1936*, Eco. Ser. 1 (Washington, 1938), 16–17; for 1940 from U.S. Department of Commerce, Bureau of Foreign and Domestic Commerce, *American Direct Investments in Foreign Countries-1940*, Eco. Ser. 20 (Washington, 1942), 16; for 1941 from U.S. Department of Treasury, Office of the Secretary, *Census of American-Owned Assets in Foreign Countries* (Washington, 1947), 71. All of these pamphlets are conveniently reprinted in *Estimates of United States Direct Foreign Investments* (New York, 1976).

[3] The figure for 1937 is in U.S. Department of Commerce, Bureau of Foreign and Domestic Commerce, *Foreign Long-Term Investment in the United States 1937–39*, Eco. Ser. 11 (Washington, 1940), 22. The June 14, 1941 figure is in U.S. Department of Treasury, *Census of Foreign-Owned Assets in the United States* (Washington, 1945), 63. These two pamphlets are conveniently reprinted in Mira Wilkins, ed., *Foreign Investments in the U.S.* (New York, 1977).

[4] My calculations based on *A New Estimate* (Trade Info. Bull. 767), passim.

[5] For background on multinational corporate behavior see Mira Wilkins, *The Emergence of Multinational Enterprise, American Business Abroad from the Colonial Era to 1914* (Cambridge, 1970) and Mira Wilkins, *The Maturing of Multinational Enterprise: American Business Abroad from 1914 to 1970* (Cambridge, 1974).

American private enterprise. This was the case in automobiles, electrical products and electrical machinery, non-electrical machinery, and certainly oil refining. Even though the level of direct foreign investment was not high, the influence, sometimes through demonstration effect, sometimes through direct participation, was substantial.

In 1930, the key U.S. automobile companies, Ford Motor Company and General Motors, had business in Japan. Each of these firms was in every sense a multinational enterprise. In 1930 neither manufactured in Japan; both, with an eye to reaching the Japanese market, *assembled* "knocked down" cars there. They had done so since 1925 and 1926, respectively.[6] In 1930, only 458 motor vehicles had been manufactured in Japan, all by Japanese producers. Imported cars and trucks assembled in that country totaled 18,663. The majority of these appear to have been assembled by Ford and General Motors, with Ford in the lead. Of the large U.S. tire makers, only Goodrich manufactured in Japan. It was in a joint-venture with Japanese capital.[7]

By 1935, Japanese producers made almost twelve times the cars and trucks built in 1930, although only 5,355 units. Ford Motor Company that year sold in Japan 13,744 cars and trucks. Nissan (the maker of Datsun) and Toyoda were the leaders in the purely Japanese industry.

Nissan became in the interwar period the largest of the "new" zaibatsu. Nissan originated in mining. Its founder Fusanosuke Kuhara in 1912 had incorporated the Kuhara Copper Mines, which prospered during the first world war and spawned the independent Hitachi Electric Works in 1920. When the price of copper fell in the early 1920s, Kuhara Copper Mining was on the brink of bankruptcy. It was acquired by Yoshisuke Ayukawa* in 1926,** who reorganized it and developed it into the Nissan group. Ayukawa, a relative of Kuhara, and a producer of steel pipes and cast iron, had studied in the United States. He organized a holding company, Nihon Sangyo (shortened to Nissan) and established new companies in fisheries, chemicals, and oils and fats. Hitachi Electric Works was brought into the group, and the new Nissan Motors was

[6] Unless otherwise noted, comments on the U.S.-Japanese automobile industry are based on materials put together for Mira Wilkins, "The Role of U.S. Business," in Dorothy Borg, ed., *Pearl Harbor as History* (New York, 1973), 360–361; Mira Wilkins and Frank Ernest Hill, *American Business Abroad: Ford on Six Continents* (Detroit, 1964), 254–256. Data in Acc. 390, Box 85, and Acc. 38, Boxes 29, 38, and 41, Ford Archives, Dearborn, Mich., have been very useful. We have also found helpful Hideichiro Nakamura, "The Activities of the Japan Economic Federation," in *Pearl Harbor as History*, 415–416.

[7] B.F. Goodrich had in 1917 made an agreement with Baron Furukawa and established the Yokohama Rubber Co., making tires and various industrial products. With the 1923 earthquake everything was destroyed. In 1929, the company was reestablished. Goodrich put up most of the financing, and in 1930 had a 57 per cent interest in the Yokohama Rubber Company. Furukawa, however, provided the management. The business expanded in the 1930s; American engineers would turn up to show "how to make better tires," but their number was rarely more than four. The Japanese were in charge. Interview in Japan, September 1965. See also J. Crawford, "Memorandum on the Visit of Messrs. Caywood and Aspell of B.F. Goodrich Rubber Co. to Mr. Ford's office," Oct. 15, 1936, Acc. 390, Box 85, Ford Archives, Dearborn, Mich.

* In Ford records the name is translated Yoshiyuki Aikawa.
** Johannes Hirschmeier and Tsunehiko Yui, *The Development of Japanese Business 1600–1973*, 168, give the date as 1928.

established in December 1933. The Nissan group by the mid-1930s controlled more than eighty enterprises.[8]

By contrast, Toyota had its origins in the nineteenth century firm founded by Sakichi Toyoda, which made Toyoda power looms and received financing from Mitsui Bussan. Toyoda Automatic Loom Works had expertise in machinery. It established an Automotive Division, which marketed the first "Toyoda" trucks in 1935.[9] Other Japanese companies also started to make vehicles.[10]

In the mid-1930s, a large number of small and medium sized shops making automobile parts had come into being in Japan due to the demand for replacement parts for Fords and Chevrolets. Nissan Motors had initially provided parts for Ford. The suppliers would serve and in the case of Nissan become the basis for Japanese industry. Likewise, Ford and General Motors appointed dealers. These would later act for Japanese industry.[11]

As Japanese businesses began to manufacture vehicles, both General Motors and Ford Motor Company, to defend their market position, considered going beyond mere assembly into production in Japan. General Motors in 1935 hoped to make Chevrolets there in a joint-venture with Nissan. Ford Motor Company purchased 91.5 acres, fronting the water in Yokohama, to build its own manufactory.

In June 1936, Ford applied for permits to build on its land and to assemble and manufacture at its newly-planned facilities. The Ford manager wrote Dearborn that the new Automobile Control Law made it more necessary that a foundry be built. The Japanese legislation provided that licenses to manufacture cars and trucks would go only to firms whose shareholders were 50 per cent or more Japanese.

By July 30, it was clear that the government intended to license only Toyoda and Nissan as manufacturers. Ford's expansion was blocked. Nissan dropped its plans for a joint-venture with General Motors. In September, Ford and General Motors were assigned import quotas based on their last three years imports (Ford for 12,360 units; G.M., 9,470 units). At the same time, Toyoda and Nissan were officially licensed as "manufacturers." In August, 1937, the Automotive Division

[8] K. Nakagawa, "Business Strategy and Industrial Structure in Pre-World War II Japan," in Keiichiro Nakagawa, ed., *Strategy and Structure of Big Business* (Tokyo, 1976), 29–30, and Johannes Hirschmeier and Tsunehiko Yui, *The Development of Japanese Business 1600–1973* (Cambridge, 1975), 168; Shotaro Kamiya, *My Life with Toyota* (n.p., Japan: Toyota Motor Sales Co., 1976), 30, gives the December 1933 date.

[9] Hirschmeier and Yui, *Japanese Business*, 153, 170. The Toyoda loom was a triumph of Japanese technology. W.W. Lockwood, *The Economic Development of Japan* (Princeton, 1954), 332. See *ibid.*, 219, on where Toyota Motor Car Co. fits in the Mitsui empire (1946). Kamiya, *My Life with Toyota*, 37 (on early history of Toyota).

[10] Mitsubishi Economic Research Bureau, *Japanese Trade and Industry* (London, 1936), 307.

[11] H.R. Hesser to C.E. Sorensen, Apr. 10, 1935, Acc. 390, Box 85, Ford Archives, and interview B. Kopf, Mexico City, Dec. 11, 1961, on suppliers. Masaru Udagawa, "Japan's Automobile Marketing," paper delivered at Business History Conference, Shizuoka, Japan, Jan. 1980.

of Toyoda Automatic Loom Works became the new Toyota Motor Company.*

Meanwhile, Ford sought a Japanese partner. In 1936, Ford explored the possibility of a merger with Furukawa or Mitsubishi interests. Nissan wanted to buy Ford out; but this did not occur because Ford did not want to give up the market, and, more important, because it seemed doubtful that Nissan could "get permission to remit such a large sum of money as would be involved in this case."

Nissan's Ayukawa had become an active participant in Manchurian developments. In 1937 he suggested a joint-venture between Ford and Nissan in Manchuria. Ford made good profits in 1937 in Japan. Its manager in Japan could not remit the profits to the United States because of "blocked" currency and he recommended the investment in Manchuria. Officials in Dearborn for public relations reasons vetoed this idea in February 1938. The American public look askance at Japanese aggression in China. There is evidence, too, that the Japanese government would not have approved this venture. Until June, 1938, Ayukawa hoped to involve U.S. capital in the development of Manchuria. Then, as the Japanese military advanced in China, he abandoned this plan.[12]

In 1937 and 1938, vehicle manufacture in Japan (mostly trucks) mounted. The Japanese could easily copy American products. They did not require American partners. Toyoda in 1935 had employed G.M.'s assistant manager, Shotaro Kamiya, who preferred to work for a Japanese manufacturer (but was schooled by an American company). Ford's land at Yokohama went unused. After 1938, the Japanese government reduced the import permits for Ford and General Motors. In 1939, Ford was still discussing a merger with Nissan, but neither Nissan nor Toyota needed the U.S. enterprises. The Japanese manufacturers flourished. By 1940–1941, Ford and General Motors sales had dwindled. Only skeleton organizations of the U.S. automobile companies remained in Japan. It should, however, be noted that in 1940, neither Nissan Motor Company nor Toyota ranked among Japan's fifty largest industrial firms.[13] These new vehicle manufacturers were still fledgling enterprises.

---

*The earliest vehicles were "Toyodas," after the family name. The company decided "Toyota" sounded clearer and was better for advertising purposes. Toyota became the *product's* name in October 1936 and the motor car company's name in August 1937. It was Kiichiro Toyoda, who established Toyota Motor Company. Kamiya, *My Years with Toyota*, 41, 109.

[12]The chronology is based on correspondence in Acc. 390, Box 85, Ford Archives. Kamiya, *My Life with Toyota*, 41. See also Yukio Cho, "An Inquiry into the Problem of Importing American Capital into Manchuria" in *Pearl Harbor as History*, 389.

[13]In 1938 and 1939, Ford also had negotiations with Toyota for a possible joint-venture. See B. Kopf to J. Crawford, Sept. 1, 1938, Acc. 390, Box 85 and Kopf to Crawford, Nov. 4, 1938, Acc. 38, Box 41, and 1939 correspondence in Acc. 390, Box 85, Ford Archives. See also Kamiya, *My Life with Toyota*, 71–72. K. Nakagawa, "Business Strategy," 27 (on company rank).

AMERICAN-JAPANESE DIRECT FOREIGN INVESTMENT   501

Just as the U.S. automobile companies were squeezed out by the emerging Japanese industry, the same was true of the one U.S. tire manufacturer in Japan. The military put pressure on Yokohama Rubber Co. to become independent from B.F. Goodrich. Corporate expansion in the 1930s was financed in Japan, and Goodrich's share in Yokohama Rubber Co. dropped from 57 per cent in 1930 to 9 per cent in 1941. Indeed, in the late fall of 1941, Baron Furukawa took over Goodrich's shares and made a custodial agreement.[14]

Similarly, growing Japanese industry, accompanied by nationalism and militarism, resulted in General Electric's position in Japan being sharply reduced. In 1905, General Electric had acquired controlling interest in Tokyo Electric Co., Ltd. G.E. licensed this firm to use its electric light bulb technology. In 1910, G.E. obtained a minority holding in Shibaura Engineering Works, a manufacturer of heavy electrical power equipment, which was backed by the house of Mitsui.[15]

G.E. contributed technology to both ventures, which prospered during World War I and in the 1920s. In the early 1930s — after the Japanese invasion of Manchuria — the Board of Directors of Tokyo Electric desired to reduce the "foreign" influence. The company decreased its capital stock, gradually reacquiring G.E.'s holdings, which were cut from 57 per cent in 1931 to 32.5 per cent in 1936. On July 1, 1939, Tokyo Electric and Shibaura merged to form Tokyo Shibaura (or Toshiba). At first, General Electric's share was 32.8 per cent, but this figure was soon to be more than halved. Toshiba was Japan's eighth largest industrial company in 1940.[16]

Westinghouse had made a licensing arrangement with Mitsubishi Electric Manufacturing Co. in 1923, in exchange for a small minority interest. In the 1930s its share in this business also dropped dramatically.[17]

Another aspect of the electrical industry involved telephone and communication equipment. Here the American ties came to be with the Sumitomo group. Nippon Electric had long had links first with Western Electric and then, after 1925, with I.T.T., through its subsidiary International Standard Electric (ISE). When in 1925 ISE acquired control of Nippon Electric, it also obtained an indirect interest in Sumitomo Wire and Cable Co. In 1932 ISE acquired a direct minority holding in the Sumitomo firm. Here, too, there was substantial technological interchange. And here, too, in the 1930s, "under military pressure," I.T.T.'s stake in Nippon Electric and in Sumitomo Wire and Cable Co. fell.[18]

[14] Interview in Japan with Goodrich personnel, Sept. 1965.
[15] Toshiba, *History of Toshiba* (Tokyo, 1964), 97ff. (I have had a translation made of parts of this Japanese-language history). See also Wilkins, *The Emergence*, 94.
[16] Toshiba, *History*; K. Nakagawa, "Business Strategy," 27.
[17] *Ibid.*, 31.
[18] In 1899, Western Electric acquired an interest in Nippon Denki Kabushiki Kaisha (Nippon Electric Co.).

The technological interactions between U.S. and Japanese business in the electrical industry were extensive. Japanese sources indicate that as early as 1937, the quantities of electricity generated in Japan exceeded that of Britain. Transformers produced by Toshiba were said to have the largest capacity in the world. Nippon Electric became Japan's leading telephone manufacturer.[19]

In other industries there was U.S.-Japanese business cooperation. Mitsui Bussan had a subsidiary, Sanki Engineering. Sanki Engineering handled construction work, electrical engineering, and plumbing. Carrier Air Conditioning — an American firm — went into a joint-venture with Sanki, forming a subsidiary, Toyo Carrier, in 1930 to manufacture air conditioners (owned 50-50). Two years later, Otis Elevator entered into a joint-venture with Sanki Engineering (owned 60-40) to produce elevators.[20]

National Cash Register Co. established a small Japanese assembly plant in 1934. The next year, its Japanese affiliate merged with a competitor into Nippon Cash Register Co., 70 per cent owned by NCR and 30 per cent by Fujiyama interests. The new enterprise manufactured; NCR gave technical advice on the training of mechanics and service. Japanese managers ran the business. IBM organized a subsidiary in Japan in 1937 and the following year started a small operation manufacturing IBM cards.[21]

IBM continued in operation up to 1941, but because of Japanese government restrictions National Cash Register, while it retained a sales organization in Japan, stopped producing registers. In 1940 NCR sold its factory to Toshiba. Victor Talking Machine — makers of phonographs — had a 68 per cent interest in a factory in Japan in 1931. By 1941, it had sold out to Japanese producers.[22]

In every industry, Japanese industrial initiative crowded out the American multinationals. The pattern was particularly evident in oil. In the 1930s, only two U.S. oil companies had significant investments in Japan. One was Associated Oil (later Tidewater), which in 1931 entered into a joint-venture with Mitsubishi in oil refining and marketing. The other was Standard-Vacuum Oil Company, known as Stanvac, formed in

---

Nippon Electric was the first industrial company in Japan in which foreign capital participated in the equity, under the revised treaties and new laws (July 1, 1899). In 1920 Sumitomo Wire and Cable Co. bought 5 per cent of the shares of Nippon Electric and Nippon Electric acquired 35 per cent of the shares of Sumitomo Wire and Cable Co. When in 1925 Western Electric sold its entire international business to I.T.T., its interest in Nippon Electric was 55.5 per cent. In the early 1930s the association with Sumitomo interests was temporarily strengthened. Thus, in the 1930s, I.T.T. had interests in Nippon Electric and Sumitomo Wire and Cable. See data in Western Electric Archives, N.Y.; letter Howard F. Van Zandt, I.T.T. to Mira Wilkins, Oct. 12, 1965; interview, Iwadare, Kamakura, Japan, Oct. 1, 1965; on Western Electric's sale of its foreign operations to I.T.T., see Wilkins, *Maturing*, 70.

[19] A. Okochi, "A Comparison of Choice of Technology," in Nakagawa, *Strategy and Structure*, 166.
[20] Interview Mr. Motomoro, Mitsui & Co., Tokyo, Oct. 1965; data from MITI.
[21] Interview National Cash Register, Tokyo, Sept. 1965, and interviews IBM, Tokyo, Sept. 1965. In 1935 Nippon National Cash Register Sales Company became the sales subsidiary of Nippon Cash Register Co.
[22] Wilkins, *Maturing*, 250; interview Tokyo, Sept. 1965.

1933 and jointly-owned by Standard Oil of New Jersey (now Exxon) and Socony-Vacuum Oil Co. (now Mobil).[23] Of the two, Stanvac was far more important. Of the $6.9 million U.S. direct investment in petroleum in Japan in 1941, fully $5.5 million was Stanvac's.[24]

The story of Stanvac's difficulties in marketing in Japan in the 1930s has been told elsewhere.[25] In oil, as in other industries, the Japanese did not want to be dependent on outsiders — yet they hoped to capture what advantages the outsiders could provide. Stanvac — while operating under adverse conditions — was allowed to continue in Japan, since it served a vital function. Stanvac officials sought to curb their investment in the 1930s as tensions mounted.

In sum, on the eve of World War II, despite the new entries, U.S. direct investment in Japan was barely more than half its 1930 level. Total U.S. direct investment abroad had sunk from $7.8 billion in 1930 to $7 billion in 1940 (1941 totals are not available).[26] The worldwide fall was small compared with what was happening in Japan. The reason for the decline of direct investment in Japan lay mainly in the "domestication" of American manufacturing in Japan. Table 1 indicates the drop in the equity interest of major U.S. participants in joint-ventures in Japan, 1931–1941. Table 2 shows the downward trend in investment 1930–1941. It also shows that in 1941 the largest part of the investment was in manufacturing. Petroleum refining and distribution ranked second in 1941.* Companies that remained 100 per cent American-owned were by 1941 shadows of their former substance.

U.S. business in Japan had been copied, absorbed, manipulated, and molded to Japanese requirements — by the rules of the Japanese state and by the initiative of Japanese business leaders.

JAPANESE BUSINESS IN THE UNITED STATES

Meanwhile, what was happening with Japanese enterprise in the United States? My assumption was that the stake would be minimal compared with U.S. direct investment in Japan.[27] I was thus surprised to discover that by 1941, as U.S. direct investment in Japan declined,

[23] Wilkins, *Maturing*, 211–213.

[24] Irvine H. Anderson, Jr. *The Standard-Vacuum Oil Company and United States East Asian Policy 1933–1941* (Princeton, 1975), 214.

[25] See Anderson, *Standard-Vacuum* and Wilkins, "The Role of U.S. Business," 362–367.

[26] See Note 2 above.

[27] This assumption was based on my reading of the literature on Japanese multinational enterprises, for example, Yoshi Tsurumi, *The Japanese Are Coming* (Cambridge, Mass., 1976); M.Y. Yoshino, *Japan's Multinational Enterprises* (Cambridge, Mass., 1976); Kiyoshi Kojima, *Japanese Direct Foreign Investment* (Rutland, Vt., 1978). It was an assumption shared by all my academic colleagues, based primarily on the absence of documentation of the earlier Japanese role in the United States.

*The rise in investment in distribution, 1940–1941, indicated on Table 2, may be a result of different classifications made by the U.S. Commerce Department and the Treasury Department. On the other hand, it may be a consequence of a shift in certain U.S. investments from manufacturing to distribution.

TABLE 1

KEY U.S. INDUSTRIAL CORPORATIONS AND UTILITIES WITH DIRECT INVESTMENTS IN JAPAN — 1931–1941

Corporation	Activity	Percentage U.S. Ownership in Japanese Enterprises 1931	1941
Associated Oil Co. (see Tidewater)			
Carrier Corp.	Manufactured air conditioners	50%	46%
Columbia Co.	Manufactured records	67	3
Eastman Kodak	Sales outlet	100	100
Ford Motor Company	Assembly of automobiles	100	100
General Electric	Manufactured electrical products	57 - 32(2 cos.)	15
General Motors	Assembly of automobiles	100	100
Goodrich (B.F.)	Manufactured tires	57	9
International General Electric Co. (see General Electric)			
International Standard Electric Co. (see International Telephone & Telegraph Corp.)			
International Telephone & Telegraph Corp.	Manufactured telephone equipment	59	20
Libbey-Owens Glass	Manufactured glass	30	17
Singer Sewing Machine	Sales outlet	100	100
Radio Corporation of America (see also Victor Talking Machine)	Radio connections	100	100
Socony-Vacuum (as of 1933 Standard-Vacuum Oil Co.)	Oil distribution	100	100
Tidewater	Oil refining	50	25
U.S. Steel	Sales outlet	100	100
Victor Talking Machine	Manufacturing	68	0
Westinghouse	Manufacturing	9	4

Source: Information from Record Group 151, National Archives, Washington, D.C., Ministry of International Trade and Industry, Tokyo; and records of the companies involved.

AMERICAN-JAPANESE DIRECT FOREIGN INVESTMENT   505

TABLE 2
U.S. DIRECT INVESTMENT IN JAPAN 1929–1941 BY SECTOR
(in millions of dollars)

	1929	1930	1936	1940	1941**
Total	$60.7	$61.4	$46.7	$37.7	$32.9
Manufacturing	40.3	n.a.	25.6	24.2	18.2
Petroleum	8.1	n.a.	*	*	6.9
Distribution	10.6	n.a.	5.2	3.5	4.1
Finance	*	n.a.	*	*	.8
Miscellaneous	1.7	n.a.	15.9	10.0	2.8

* included in miscellaneous;
** numbers do not add up because of rounding
n.a.: not available

Source: Developed from U.S. Department of Commerce data (1929–1940) and U.S. Department of Treasury data (1941) in *Estimates of United States Direct Foreign Investment*, New York: Arno Press, 1976.

the dollar value of direct investment by Japanese in the United States came to be larger than that of U.S. investment in Japan ($35.1 million v. $32.9 million). Japanese predominance was *not* true in 1936–1937, but even then the figures of $47 million and $41 million (U.S. direct investment in Japan in 1936 and Japanese direct investment in the United States in 1937) were not as far apart as one might expect. Table 3 gives a summary of Japanese direct investment in the United States in 1937 by sector. I do not have good 1941 figures in this format, but all evidence indicates no substantial change in the composition of the investment. The nature of the Japanese investment in the United States was unlike that of U.S. direct investment in Japan. Note that more than half was in finance and the second largest sector was distribution. Obviously, more study of pre-World War II Japanese business in the United States is in order. What follows are some tentative, early findings.[28]

A number of Japanese banks had branches and agencies in the United States, mainly in New York and California, although at least one bank had Seattle and Honolulu branches. According to a 1944 U.S. government report, these Japanese banks were mainly concerned with "financing foreign trade, particularly U.S. exports to Japan; . . . the rendering of financial assistance to Japanese-owned enterprises in the United States; the buying and selling of foreign exchange; and similar activities.

[28] I have depended heavily on the published Annual Reports of the Alien Property Custodian. The Alien Property Custodian was responsible for Japanese properties in the United States seized during World War II. The Annual Reports have been conveniently assembled in U.S. Office of the Alien Property Custodian, *Annual Reports 1942–1946* (New York, 1977). I will henceforth cite these reports as APC, *Annual Report*, and add the appropriate dates. In 1980 Nobuo Kawabe completed a Ph.D. dissertation at Ohio State University entitled "Japanese Business in the United States Before World War II: The Case of Mitsubishi Shoji Kaisha, the San Francisco and Seattle Branches." His work used the confiscated records — in English and Japanese — of the two Mitsubishi branches, which he located in Record Group 131 (Records of the Alien Property Custodian), at the Washington National Record Center in Suitland, Maryland. Kawabe's study is the first business history using this collection. He plans further research in these records.

They also transacted a considerable amount of purely domestic business. The largest bank, the Yokohama Specie Bank of New York, acted as fiscal agent of the Japanese Government in the United States."[29]

In 1930, U.S. "portfolio investments" (investments in securities — mainly bonds — that did not carry control) far exceeded U.S. direct investments in Japan.[30] It is not clear how important the Japanese banks in the United States were in channeling U.S. capital into Japanese securities. This needs more investigation.[31]

TABLE 3

JAPANESE DIRECT INVESTMENTS IN THE UNITED STATES 1937–1941 BY
SECTOR
(in millions of dollars)

	1937	1941
Total	41.0	35.1
Manufacturing	.9	n.a.
Distribution	16.5	n.a.
Transportation	1.8	n.a.
Finance	21.8	n.a.

n.a.: not available

Source: Data from U.S. Department of Commerce and U.S. Department of Treasury, included in Mira
Wilkins, ed., *Foreign Investments in the United States*, New York: Arno Press, 1977.

By 1941, sixteen large multinational Japanese banks had direct investments in the United States, including the Yokohama Specie Bank. The Bank of Japan had a New York branch; there were New York agencies of the Mitsui Bank, the Mitsubishi Bank, and the Sumitomo Bank. The Japanese-owned Bank of Chosen also had a New York agency.[32] In California, there was the Sumitomo Bank of California. Under New York and Washington state laws, foreign banks could participate in international banking but not accept deposits.[33]

Of all the pre-World War II Japanese banks in the United States, the largest was the Yokohama Specie Bank, Ltd., incorporated in Japan in 1880. This bank became Japan's chief foreign exchange bank;[34] it had branches worldwide. Its New York branch had been established in 1880.

[29] APC, *Annual Report, 1943–1944*, 58.
[30] They were $383 million, compared with $61.4 million in direct foreign investments. See U.S. Department of Commerce, *A New Estimate*, 20.
[31] John G. Roberts, *Mitsui: Three Centuries of Japanese Business* (New York, 1973), 241, suggests that many of the loans "were negotiated by Mitsui."
[32] Lockwood, *Economic Development*, 516–517, describes the Bank of Chosen as playing a major role in the development of Korea. It conducted banking and currency operations for the Japanese Army and colonial government as well as financing Japanese business. It served as fiscal agent for the Kwantung Army. Lockwood says "It also financed a whole series of puppet regimes and companies on the continent. It was even so versatile as to engage in large-scale smuggling of silver, opium, and textiles in the Tientsin area, where the Japanese were trying to break down Chinese administrative authority in 1935–1936."
[33] APC, *Annual Report, 1942–1943*, 99ff, and APC, *Annual Report 1943–1944*, 218, 221.
[34] Lockwood, *Economic Development*, 249.

Subsequently, it opened a San Francisco branch, as well as a subbranch in Los Angeles, a branch in Seattle, and another one in Honolulu. All its branches conducted foreign banking operations; only the California and Hawaiian branches received deposits. In the 1930s the branches of the Yokohama Specie Bank financed over half of Japan's imports from the United States.[35]

In addition, three Japanese insurance firms were present in the United States, mainly for the purpose of issuing marine insurance.[36] Although the dollar value of the investment in "finance" (banks and insurance companies) was larger, the number of Japanese enterprises in "distribution" in the United States far exceeded those in finance. Japan had hundreds of trading companies. The large ones had interests in the United States.

The most important one, Mitsui Bussan (in English, Mitsui Trading) had by 1876 established an overseas marketing organization for selling Japanese coal in China, Hong Kong, and Singapore. In time, this distribution network had grown and new products were included reflecting the expansion of the business activity. The distribution web extended to London, Paris, Bombay, Sydney, as well as New York and San Francisco. Mitsui's first New York branch opened in 1879, only to close in the early 1880s; it reopened in 1897, and its business grew dramatically thereafter.[37] By 1907, Mitsui Bussan was handling 100 articles and, by 1914, more than one-quarter of Japan's foreign trade. In 1931, with added competition, it still participated in as much as 12.5 per cent of Japan's entire foreign trade, and during the 1930s, its percentage of Japanese foreign trade seems to have increased, rising even more sharply in 1940–41.[38] By 1941, in the United States, Mitsui & Co., Ltd., had branches in New York, San Francicso, and Seattle.[39] Yet, its business was by no means confined to these cities. For example, in the 1930s, Mitsui & Co. (along with Mitsubishi) acted on behalf of International Mineral and Chemical Co., a Florida phosphate rock and fertilizer producer, to sell the latter's output in Japan.[40]

Mitsui & Co. also served as a transmitter of American technology to Japan. Economist Eleanor Hadley indicates that Mitsui & Co. was "Japan's principal acquirer of America's aviation technology" in the

[35] APC, *Annual Report, 1943–1944*, 87–88.
[36] *Ibid.*, 58.
[37] There are good data on Mitsui in K. Nakagawa, "Business Strategy," 6–7. See also [Mitsui & Co.]. *The 100 Year History of Mitsui & Co., Ltd., 1876–1976* (Tokyo, 1977), 32, 34, 295.
[38] R. Iwata, "Marketing Strategy and Market Structure in Three Nations: the United States, the United Kingdom, and Japan," in Nakagawa, *Strategy and Structure*, 190, gives the percentage of Japanese foreign trade of Mitsui Bussan, 1897–1932. Eleanor M. Hadley, *Antitrust in Japan* (Princeton, 1970), 154, gives the percentages for 1936–1945. Using these figures, in the 1930s Mitsui Bussan had a high of Japanese export trade in 1932 (15.9%) and a low in 1936 (9.7%). It held a high of Japanese import trade in 1937 (16.9%) and a low in 1932 (10.2%). In 1941, it was handling 12.8% of Japanese imports.
[39] APC, *Annual Report 1942–1943*, 101.
[40] Interview Mitsui & Co. U.S. Inc., Sept. 22, 1975.

pre-war years.[41] In addition, Mitsui & Co. participated in foreign trade that did not involve Japan at all. Thus, it sold Singapore rubber and tin in the United States.[42]

Mitsubishi Shoji Kaisha (in English, Mitsubishi Trading Co.), founded in Japan in 1918, like Mitsui Bussan, established branches around the world. Mitsubishi opened American branches in Seattle (1919), New York (1921), and San Francisco (1926). The main business of these branches by 1940–1941 was the export of steel, steel scrap, machinery (built to Japanese specifications), petroleum, fats and fertilizers from the United States to Japan, and the import of silk from Japan into the United States. In addition, Mitsubishi's U.S. branches exported to Japan raw cotton and other items and (from the United States and Canada) pulp and newsprint; they imported canned crab meat, canned tuna fish and other canned seafoods, as well as canned pineapples and canned oranges (a new product on the U.S. market). Sometimes, the branches traded on their own account. Sometimes, they acted as agents for other Japanese businesses (in cultured pearls, for example). Sometimes, they appear to have acted as agents for U.S. firms (which were exporting). Each branch office rented space and kept its inventory in public warehouses.[43]

Other Japanese trading companies with branches in the United States included Asano Bussan Co. Ltd., Ataka & Co., Iwai & Co., Okura & Co. (Trading) Ltd., Showa Tsusho Kaisha Ltd., and Taiyo Trading Co. These firms all had New York branches; Asano had branches in Los Angeles and Seattle as well.

There were also Japanese transportation companies involved with American trade. Kawasaki Kisen Kaisha (Kawasaki Steamship Line), with branches in New York, San Francisco, and Seattle, was one. Mitsubishi's important steamship line, Nippon Yusen Kaisha (N.Y.K.) had seven American branches. Osaka Shoshen Kaisha (controlled by Sumitomo interests) had a New York branch. Additional Japanese shipping enterprises included the Yamashita Line and the Kokusai Kisen Kaisha Ltd., both with New York branches. The Mitsui Line was a department of the trading company. In the 1930s, Japan was a major mercantile nation. Its own merchant fleet carried about 63 per cent of its imports and 73 per cent of its exports. Japan ranked third — after Britain and the United States — as a maritime nation.[44]

[41] Hadley, *Antitrust in Japan*, 152.

[42] *Ibid.*, 154. For further data on Mitsui's international trade in the 1930s, but with nothing on its direct investments in the United States, see Roberts, *Mitsui*, 259–263.

[43] APC, *Annual Report 1943–1944*, 81–82. For details, see Kawabe, "Japanese Business," which deals with Mitsubishi Shoji Kaisha and its predecessor, Mitsubshi Goshi Kaisha, which apparently had a New York branch in 1917.

[44] APC *Annual Report 1942–1943*, 100, 101, 104, 106; APC, *Annual Report 1943–1944*, 32; Professor K. Enatsu was immensely helpful to me in sorting out the key companies; Lockwood, *Economic Development*, 229, 349, 546, and Mitsubishi, *Japanese Trade and Industry*, 468–470, on Japanese shipping. *The 100 Year History*, 100–101, 126 (Mitsui).

AMERICAN-JAPANESE DIRECT FOREIGN INVESTMENT   509

A well-known Japanese enterprise in pre-war America was Yamanaka. Three firms, each named Yamanaka and Company, Inc., and each wholly-owned subsidiaries of Yamanaka and Company of Osaka, sold oriental art and antiques in the United States, primarily (80–90 per cent) Chinese works. The business of the parent firm in Osaka was about 200 years old and by the 1930s Yamanaka and Company was a multinational enterprise with branches or subsidiaries in China, Europe, and the United States. Its U.S. subsidiaries were located in Boston, Chicago, and New York. Its New York business had been established around the turn of the century. There, its showroom (made up of 14 display rooms) was on Fifth Avenue. In season, it opened branch stores at the fashionable resorts of Bar Harbor, Newport, and Palm Beach. As noted, it dealt mainly in Chinese art and antiques — from sculpture, to furniture, brocades, paintings, and porcelain. Some works dated back to the Shang-Yin period (1766–1122 B.C.).[45]

Banks and trading companies dominated Japanese investment in the United States. We need to know more about their activities and their management. They seem to have played an important role in U.S.-Japanese trade and financial relationships. The evidence indicates that a large percentage of U.S.-Japanese trade was financed by Japanese banks, insured by Japanese insurance companies, arranged by Japanese trading firms, and carried on Japanese ships. All of these enterprises needed representatives in the United States to carry on these functions. Our data herein barely touch the surface on this subject.

NATIONAL RESPONSES TO WORLD WAR II

President Roosevelt on July 26 (but effective June 14), 1941 — as Japanese troops moved into Indo-China — froze Japanese assets in the United States.[46] All financial and import-export transactions between Japan and the United States came under U.S. government control.[47] The Japanese retaliated, freezing U.S. assets in Japan.[48]

After Pearl Harbor and American entry in World War II, the U.S. Treasury Department began to take over enemy assets. As of March 11, 1942, President Roosevelt established the Office of the Alien Property Custodian. The Alien Property Custodian was to acquire the properties of any business enterprise in the United States owned by nationals of an enemy country. This included resident and nonresident-owned businesses. A large number of Japanese firms came under the control of the Alien Property Custodian.

[45] APC, *Annual Report 1943–1944*, 83–84.
[46] APC, *Annual Report 1942–1943*, 152.
[47] Wilkins, "The Role of U.S. Business," 373.
[48] Wilkins, "The Role of U.S. Business," 360.

In Japan, after Pearl Harbor, U.S. properties passed into Japanese hands. During the war years, these properties were managed and operated to meet Japan's military objectives. Since most of the U.S. businesses in Japan had been Japanese managed, they carried on accordingly. IBM was put under Japanese government control and continued in business making IBM cards, with a reduced staff.[49] Under Sumitomo management, Nippon Electric Co.'s plants all functioned during the war, except for one facility that was two-thirds destroyed. Deprived of U.S. technological assistance, NEC had difficulties.[50]

Where there were joint-ventures in Japan, U.S. shares were placed in custody. Goodrich's shares in Yokohama Rubber were held, for example, in a custodial account.[51] In October 1942, the Finance Ministry ordered the Fujiyama holding company to buy the 70 per cent American (National Cash Register) interest in Nippon Cash Register Co., thus releasing that firm "from enemy control."[52] Toshiba placed General Electric's shares in the custody of Trustees appointed by the company. According to a business history, Toshiba "disposed of these shares in the market by ordinance" in 1943.[53]

In the United States, the Office of the Alien Property Custodian at once started the process of "vesting" property in business enterprises, where the ownership was by nationals of enemy countries and constituted actual or potential control of the enterprise.[54]

Certain of the "vested" firms were liquidated. Even before the formation of the Office of the Alien Property Custodian, U.S. Treasury officials concluded that the business of the Japanese banks and insurance companies in the United States "was rarely such that they could be profitably continued in time of war, and none of them were [sic] essential to the communities in which they were located." Thus, they were closed, and liquidation began under Treasury Department supervision.[55]

The largest Japanese property in the United States to be "liquidated" was the Yokohama Specie Bank. Table 4 gives the total assets of its U.S. branches, which in 1942–1943 approximated $55.6 million. It represented the largest Japanese financial interest in the United States.[56] In all the Alien Property Custodian liquidated 28 banks and insurance companies of which 19 were formerly owned by Japanese nationals.[57]

As for trading companies, Treasury officials started liquidating some of them before the Office of the Alien Property Custodian was estab-

[49] Interviews with IBM officials in Japan, Sept. 1965.
[50] Interview Mr. Iwadare, Kamakura, Japan, Oct. 1965.
[51] Interview in Tokyo, Sept. 1965.
[52] Data from NCR, Tokyo, Sept. 1965.
[53] Toshiba, *History*.
[54] APC, *Annual Report 1943–1944*, 9.
[55] *Ibid.*, 58, 52.
[56] *Ibid.*, 87–88.
[57] APC, *Annual Report 1942–1943*, 56. The rest were primarily German.

AMERICAN-JAPANESE DIRECT FOREIGN INVESTMENT   511

lished.[58] The decision was made by the Alien Property Custodian to liquidate all so-called "orphan enterprises — enterprises which are so dependent upon enemy affiliations that they have no independent place in the American economy. Importing concerns and agencies of foreign transportation companies are examples."[59]

The process of liquidation of the trading companies was lengthy and problematic.[60] At the Mitsubishi branches, the Alien Property Custodian found 45,000 cases of canned oranges, which were sold subject to Office of Price Administration and War Production Board regulations.[61] It was more difficult to sell off a huge continuous steel billet mill owned by Mitsubishi, which in 1941 was being built on order for export to Manchuria and was valued at about $725,000.[62] Table 5 gives the 1942, 1944, and 1945 balance sheet of Mitsubishi Shoji Kaisha Ltd.'s U.S. branches. It shows the efforts of the Alien Property Custodian to reduce the level of inventories and increase the cash holdings.

The Alien Property Custodian (James E. Markham) seems to have been overawed at the 57,000 art and antique items in the Yamanaka collection. Its stores had been closed by agents of the U.S. Treasury Department on December 7, 1941. Guards were posted to protect the valuable possessions, and in January 1942 the Treasury Department allowed the stores to reopen to begin to liquidate the assets. When the Alien Property Custodian took charge, he set up an orderly procedure, trying to give museums the opportunity to acquire the art objects. Finally, the Boston store was closed in July 1943, the Chicago store in March 1944, and the New York store that same spring. The whole inventory, including some items which had been in stock for thirty-five years, was sold. As of June 30, 1944, the balance sheets showed $628,786 undistributed cash and $416,218 accounts receivable.[63]

In the process of liquidating the Japanese firms in the United States, the Alien Property Custodian found a variety of pieces of property that proved helpful to the U.S. war effort. Included were three large-scale maps "showing in minute detail the cities of Osaka, Nagoya and Yokohama" (found among the property of a firm called Japan Products Co. Inc.). The maps were forwarded to the U.S. Army Intelligence. The Custodian retrieved from the files of Mitsui & Co., Ltd. books, maps, plans, and machinery specifications, which "yielded valuable information." Two Japanese typewriters, discovered among the assets of the Pacific Trading Company, were turned over to U.S. Army Intelligence and then flown to General MacArthur's headquarters.[64]

[58] APC, *Annual Report 1943–1944*, 82.
[59] *Ibid.*, 52.
[60] APC, *Annual Report 1942–1943*, 56, and APC, *Annual Report 1943–1944*, 82.
[61] APC, *Annual Report 1943–1944*, 82.
[62] *Ibid.* and APC, *Annual Report 1944–1945*, 83.
[63] APC *Annual Report 1943–1944*, 84–86.
[64] *Ibid.*, 57.

TABLE 4
TOTAL ASSETS OF UNITED STATES BRANCHES OF YOKOHAMA SPECIE BANK LTD.

Branches	Assets	Date Audit
New York	$33,475,735	9-28-42
San Francisco	11,826,016	10- 3-42
Los Angeles	2,543,949	10- 3-42
Seattle	4,271,005	9-30-42
Honolulu	3,479,604	5-10-43
Total	$55,596,309	

Source: Office of Alien Property Custodian. *Annual Report 1943–1944.* p. 87.

TABLE 5
MITSUBISHI SHOJI KAISHA, LTD., UNITED STATES BRANCHES, CONSOLIDATED COMPARATIVE BALANCE SHEETS,[1] AUGUST 28, 1942, MARCH 31, 1944, AND JUNE 30, 1945

	Aug. 28, 1942[2]	Mar. 31, 1944	June 30, 1945
ASSETS[3]			
Located in the United States:			
Cash	$1,830,176.30	$2,031,705.11	$2,039,610.74
Receivables	159,017.77	19,033.66	2,697.03
Inventory	1,310,186.37	1,125,379.87	951,097.85
Investments	4,073.21	2,935.21	1,935.21
Fixed assets	1,265.55	331.25	—
Intangibles	—	—	21.00
Deferred charges	10,455.00	1,024.20	—
Claims and deposits	190,498.09	153,274.68	104,208.86
Total assets in the United States	3,505,672.29	3,333,683.98	3,099,570.69
Located in allied and neutral countries	272,392.05	2,112.28	2,112.28
Located in enemy and enemy-occupied countries[4]	2,741.23	—	—
Total assets	3,780,805.57	3,335,796.26	3,101,682.97
LIABILITIES AND NET WORTH			
Liabilities:			
Owing to residents of the United States[5]	3,659,200.21	3,594,499.45	3,595,300.66
Owing to residents of allied, neutral and enemy-occupied countries[4]	42,758.91	41,766.98	41,766.98
Owing to residents of enemy countries	74,310.56	74,116.51	77,833.69
Owing to Custodian (vested)	—	—	—
Total liabilities	3,776,269.68	3,710,382.94	3,714,901.33
Net worth[6]	4,535.89	(374,586.68)	(613,218.36)
Total liabilities and net worth	3,780,805.57	3,335,796.26	3,101,682.97

[1] These balance sheets are prepared on the basis of financial data supplied by the branches. They are not the official balance sheets of the branches.

[2] The date of vesting.

[3] Receivables and claims are classified according to location of debtors; deposits according to location of depositories; and securities according to location of issuers.

[4] The phrase "enemy-occupied countries," as here used, includes all countries that have been occupied by the enemy at any time during the war.

[5] Federal income tax claims against the branches for the years 1934 to 1942; court actions, several of which are stayed *pendente bello;* and other circumstances have given rise to contingent liabilities of approximately $2,000,000.

[6] The ownership interest in the branches consist of accounts to the credit of the head office of Mitsubishi Shoji Kaisha, Ltd. By reason of vesting all United States property of Mitsubishi Shoji Kaisha, Ltd., all such interests are vested in the Custodian.

Source: Office of the Alien Property Custodian. *Annual Report 1944–1945.* 83.

AMERICAN-JAPANESE DIRECT FOREIGN INVESTMENT   513

Many of the German enterprises taken over by the U.S. Alien Property Custodian were continued in operation and put to work directly contributing to the U.S. war effort. There was, however, an absence of formerly-owned Japanese enterprises in vital war businesses.[65] The reason, of course, lay in the composition of Japanese investment (refer again to Table 3). Japanese business in the United States was mainly in banking and trade.

By June 1945, the Alien Property Custodian had vested 169 Japanese companies with assets of almost $104 million.[66] When the war was over, after consultation, the Secretary of State, the Secretary of Treasury, and the Alien Property Custodian agreed that "the complete elimination of German and Japanese ownership of properties in the United States was in the national interest."[67]

POST-WAR DEVELOPMENTS

As for the victors' investments in Japan, returning Americans in 1945 wanted to see what was left of their interests and to unscramble the complexities resulting from the various wartime dispositions of corporate shares.

The early policy of SCAP (Supreme Commander for the Allied Powers) was to eliminate industrial concentration in Japan.[68] The very groups that U.S. businesses had had joint-ventures with in the pre-war years were to be dissolved. SCAP was also cautious about permitting U.S. companies to resume operations in Japan. As is well known, in 1947–1948, the policy of SCAP toward Japanese recovery began to change, and there was a retreat from the earlier trust-busting approach. There came to be a recognition of the need for Japanese economic recovery.

The first U.S. enterprises to start business in post-war Japan did so during the occupation. Coca Cola built its initial bottling plant in Japan to supply U.S. forces stationed there. The military "footed the bill."[69] IBM was asked to run the installation of the GHQ under the occupation. Its pre-war company personnel returned.[70]

During the occupation, Stanvac began to look at the prospects of reentry and Caltex (a joint-venture marketing company of Standard Oil of California and Texaco) wanted to invest anew. In November 1945 a

[65] *Ibid.*, 47–49.
[66] APC, *Annual Report 1944–1945*, 37.
[67] *Ibid.*, 2. (The statement was signed by Joseph Grew as Acting Secretary of State, H. Morgenthau, Secretary of Treasury, and James Markham, Alien Property Custodian.)
[68] On the policies, see Hadley, *Antitrust in Japan*.
[69] Interview W.H. Roberts, Coca Cola, Tokyo, Sept. 1965.
[70] Interview IBM officials, Tokyo, Sept. 1965.

Petroleum Advisory Group was established. It investigated, regulated, and controlled the supply and distribution of petroleum in Japan. It was made up of leading U.S. and foreign oil men. Its goal came to be the return of the oil business to private ownership. The process was slow. But by 1950, in accord with the new policy of letting Japan rebuild, Japanese refineries were being reopened. Caltex and Stanvac interests became associated with Japanese companies. In 1950 middle eastern crude oil began to flow in to fill the needs of the refineries. The Korean war, starting in June of that year, created new demands on the Japanese oil industry.[71] During 1950, petroleum product sales in Japan were divided: Caltex-Nippon Group (30.6%), Standard Vacuum Oil Co. (22.1%), the Shell Group (19%), Idemitsu (8.6%), and Mitsubishi Oil (6.5%).[72] Only Idemitsu was exclusively Japanese. On April 1, 1951, SCAP controls came off the Japanese petroleum industry.

Meanwhile, on May 10, 1950, the Japanese Diet enacted a Law Concerning Foreign Investments. It was designed to create a "sound basis" for foreign investment in Japan. Under this law, in 1950 and 1951, a number of pre-war U.S. investors were permitted to resume business (see Table 6). IBM was one of the first companies to be "validated" under the new law. "Validation" meant a company could remit profits to the United States. Validation also specified the amount of capital that could be repatriated. IBM came back into Japan on a 100 per cent basis. It was exceptional. IBM-Japan had been 100 per cent owned by IBM before the war. The fact that IBM had run the installations of the GHQ during the occupation gave IBM an advantage, as, of course, did its technological superiority. It started operations with funds accumulated in Japan during the war, at first only manufacturing cards.

Other companies re-entered with Japanese partners. B.F. Goodrich went back in with Furukawa interests; Tidewater resumed its connections with Mitsubishi interests; National Cash Register returned in concert with the Fujiyama group.* There were also *de novo* entries into joint-ventures, for example, Monsanto Chemical.[73]

Years later, the Chairman of the Sumitomo Bank explained to the author, "In the pre-war period, we wanted control of our industry for military reasons; today we have no intention of waging a war but we still want control in Japanese hands."[74] The statement could have been made in 1950–1951. With the door ajar, U. S. direct investment in Japan

[71] See Report of Petroleum Advisory Group, May 31, 1951. See also Yoshi Tsurumi, "Japan," in Raymond Vernon, ed., *The Oil Crisis* (New York, 1976), 114–115.
[72] Figures from records of Caltex, Tokyo.
[73] My files contain a translation of the Foreign Investment Law. My data on reentries are based on information collected in Japan, Sept.–Oct. 1965.
[74] Interview Mr. Shozo Hotta, Tokyo, Sept. 1965.

* Data from MITI indicates that in 1950–1951 a total of 45 foreign companies were authorized to do business in Japan and only two were 100 per cent foreign owned.

AMERICAN-JAPANESE DIRECT FOREIGN INVESTMENT   515

increased. From a mere $12 million in 1949, it reached $69 million in 1952 (see Table 7).

It is not clear when the Japanese reentry into investment in the United States began. The major pre-war investors were in a state of dissolution or disorganization. The Alien Property Custodian in the United States had done its job thoroughly. In Japan, the Yokohama Specie Bank had closed its doors. In its place a new commercial bank was established in 1946 in Japan under the name, The Bank of Tokyo Limited. It inherited the business and personnel of the Yokohama Specie Bank. In time, it would develop worldwide operations.[75]

Until August 1947, the Occupation handled Japanese international trade; then Japanese private firms once again resumed exports and imports.[76] Under the Foreign Exchange and Foreign Trade Control Law of 1949, every Japanese investment abroad had to be approved by the Japanese Ministry of Finance.[77] The Japanese were watching their balance of payments. In 1950 a survey of foreign investment in the United States found the level of Japanese interest so low that it was included under the rubric "other areas."[78]

In the early 1950s, as Japanese-U.S. trade began to increase, so did Japanese foreign investment.[79] Before 1954, Fuji Shoji Kaisha America, Inc., Tokyo Boeki Kaisha, Inc. and Tozai Koeki Kaisha, Inc. had U.S. operations. These merged on July 11, 1954, into Mitsubishi International Corporation, incorporated in New York, February 11, 1954.[80] Mitsui interests — shattered only temporarily by the actions during the occupation — reestablished their trade outposts in the United States.

By 1952, when Japan regained political independence, the tentative resumption of two-way direct investments had taken place. U.S. investment in Japan in current dollars already exceeded its pre-war high; in constant dollars (taking into account inflation), the level was still substantially below that of 1930. As for Japanese investment in the United States, there was as yet no real indication of its future formidable growth.

CONCLUSION

In conclusion, the war had created a discontinuity in the investment history of U.S. business in Japan and of Japanese business in the United

[75] Bank of Tokyo, *Profile* (Tokyo, n.d.), 10–11.
[76] Yoshi Tsurumi, *The Japanese Are Coming* (Cambridge, 1976), 135.
[77] K. Bieda, *The Structure and Operation of the Japanese Economy* (Sydney, 1970), 227.
[78] U.S. Department of Commerce, Office of Business Economics, *Foreign Business Investments in the United States*, Washington [1962], 34. Reprinted in Wilkins, ed., *Foreign Investments in the United States*.
[79] Bieda, *The Structure*, 229. Tsurumi, *The Japanese*, 142, *implies* that there may have been investment abroad in 1950.
[80] This information appears in the Office of the Secretary of State records in Florida! I checked the Secretary of State records in New York and they had no records of the registration of the predecessor companies. The regrouping first occurred in Japan. See Alexander K. Young, *The Sogo Shosa* (Boulder, Colo., 1979), 37.

TABLE 6
AMERICAN COMPANIES APPROVED FOR INVESTMENT* IN JAPAN
IN 1950–1951

Company	Japanese Company	Held by U.S. Investor
1950 IBM	IBM	100%
B.F. Goodrich	Japanese Zeon Co./	33/
	Yokohama Rubber Co.	35
Caltex	Kao Oil Co.	50
Tidewater Associated Oil Co.	Mitsubishi Oil Co.	49
National Cash Register	National Cash Register	70
Stanvac	Toa Nenryo Kogyo Co.	51
1951 Monsanto Chemical	Mitsubishi Chemical Industries	50
Caltex	Nippon Oil Refinery	50
International Standard (ITT)	Nippon Electric	33

* Excludes participations of under 30 million yen.

Source: List of Joint-Ventures in Japan, Japan Industry Series, II, Trade Bulletin Corporation, Tokyo 1964, and data from MITI.

TABLE 7
VALUE OF U.S. DIRECT INVESTMENT IN JAPAN, 1949–1952
(in millions U.S. dollars)

1949	$12
1950	19
1951	45
1952	69

Source: *Survey of Current Business*, January 1954, p. 7.

States. Before World War II, U.S. companies in Japan had significant impact on the creation of modern Japanese industry, assisting directly and by demonstration effect in the process of Japanese industrialization. While the dollar amounts invested in Japan by American multinationals declined 1930–1941, the impact of these U.S. enterprises did not. Japanese firms absorbed what the Americans presented. By contrast, Japanese business in the United States was more associated with *Japanese* development than U.S. economic growth. While American companies in Japan were in the technologically-advanced sectors and preeminently in manufacturing, Japanese business in America aimed at aiding Japanese commerce by providing needed financial, insurance, trading, and shipping intermediaries. The Japanese investment was primarily in the service sector. A large portion of the pre-World War II U.S.-Japanese trade was financed and handled by Japanese multinationals with their branches and subsidiaries in the United States. In writing this, it seems almost obvious. Many observers have noted that the

Japanese — with their very limited natural resources — were compelled to engage in international trade. Why, indeed, should they not develop foreign business *investments* to facilitate that activity? Yet, the "obvious" has never before been documented, and frequently the obvious becomes so only *ex post facto*.[81] In any case, by 1941, Japanese business investment in the United States was larger than U.S. business investment in Japan.

After 1941, many U.S. establishments in Japan could be used for Japanese wartime needs. While miscellaneous items in the files of some Japanese companies were helpful, American government authorities resolved to liquidate the Japanese businesses in the United States because by their very nature they did not have an independent life and could not be converted to U.S. military requirements.

When World War II was over, U.S. executives found the bricks-and-mortar and often the management of their pre-war investments still intact. They could repair war damages and resume where they left off — subject to severe occupation-imposed and Japanese government restrictions. The Japanese interests in the United States could expand on their "generalized" past experience (knowledge of international business), but not based on an established set of properties. This had little to do with victory versus defeat. Rather, the reasons lay in the character of the pre-war investment. The Japanese had to, and did, start afresh.

In this article, I have compared U.S. investment in Japan with Japanese investment in the United States, 1930–1952. The results have proved extremely fruitful. New information has been uncovered. Moreover, the data should contribute importantly to the developing theory of multinational enterprise, in showing (1) that multinational investment expansion has long been a two-way street, (2) that it is based on advantage (in this case U.S. advantage in manufacturing, Japanese in finance and trade), and (3) that cross-investments are not symmetrical.[82] This paper will hopefully stimulate scholars to pursue the history of Japanese multinational enterprise, their strategies and structure, in the United States and worldwide.

[81] In 1969, when I was preparing an article on American business relations with Japan in the 1930s for Dorothy Borg's *Pearl Harbor as History* (see Note 6 above), I could not find American businessmen that carried on certain specific trading, shipping, insuring, and financing functions. I posed my dilemma to a number of specialists on Japanese-American relations. The functions had to exist. Why couldn't I find the U.S. companies that pursued them? No one suggested to me that Japanese investors in the United States might be undertaking these roles; this never occurred to me or any of my colleagues. Until I prepared the present article, I remained mystified. The mystification is now gone. Japanese investors undertook these business activities.

[82] In a 1960 Ph.D. dissertation, first published in 1976, Stephen Hymer suggested symmetry in cross-investments. Stephen H. Hymer, *The International Operations of National Firms* (Cambridge, 1976). I have demonstrated in Mira Wilkins, "Cross Currents: American Investments in Europe, European Investments in the United States," *Business and Economic History* (edited by Paul Uselding), VI, 2nd ser., 1977, 22–35, the absence of such symmetry in early U.S.-European cross-investments; this is very apparent in the U.S.-Japanese case.

[18]

"Giants of an Earlier Capitalism": The Chartered Trading Companies as Modern Multinationals

ANN M. CARLOS and STEPHEN NICHOLAS

¶ Much has been written about late-nineteenth-century multinationals and their relationship to the transnational firms of the present, but both historians and economists have largely discounted the relevance of the earlier chartered trading companies to this discussion. In an article emphasizing transaction cost analysis and the theory of the firm, Professors Carlos and Nicholas argue that the trading companies did meet the criteria of the modern MNE— the growth of a managerial hierarchy necessitated by a large volume of transactions and of systems to control those managers over space and time.

Economists have tended to view the growth and expansion of multinational firms primarily as an American phenomenon with roots in the post-1950 period. Offering a corrective to the economists' view of both the timing and the location of the international firm, economic historians have found that the multinational was as much a European, particularly a British, as an American development and that the late nineteenth century was the seedbed of the new transnational corporation.[1] Surprisingly, the early sixteenth- and seventeenth-century trading companies—the English and Dutch East India companies, the Muscovy Company, the Hudson's Bay Company, and the Royal African Company—which traded goods and services across national boundaries and had a geographical reach rivaling today's largest multinational firms, have been generally ignored.

This failure does not result from the lack of good data on the early trading companies; detailed business histories exist for each company. These early companies were characterized by cross-border transactions through sales or production branches in two or more countries. Indeed, the historian of each of the individual trading companies implicitly treats his firm as a multinational, and K. N. Chaudhuri has explicitly recognized that the East India Company had a premodern organization.[2]

ANN M. CARLOS is currently a visiting fellow at the Hebrew University of Jerusalem; as of July 1990 she will be associate professor of economics at the University of Colorado, Boulder. STEPHEN NICHOLAS is senior lecturer in economics at the University of New South Wales.

We would like to thank David Meredith and two anonymous referees for helpful comments.

[1] For a survey of the recent historical literature, see Mira Wilkins, "The History of European Multinationals: A New Look," *Journal of European Economic History* 15 (Winter 1986): 483–86.

[2] K. N. Chaudhuri, "The English East India Company in the 17th and 18th Centuries: A Pre-Modern Multinational Organization," in *Companies and Trade*, ed. L. Blusse and F. Gaastra (The Hague, 1981), 29–46.

Business History Review 62 (Autumn 1988): 398–419. © Copyright 1988 by The President and Fellows of Harvard College.

Despite the work of these historians, data on the charter companies have not been utilized to compare fully the early companies with their late-nineteenth-century successors or to integrate the trading companies into the evolution of the modern multinational. The neglect of the early trading companies springs from the implicit belief that they were outliers, offering little of historic or economic interest. In fact, Charles Wilson compared the trading companies to dinosaurs, with small central administrative and controlling offices atop large bodies.[3] The extinction of all but a few trading companies by the twentieth century completed the analogy.

SIMILARITIES AND DIFFERENCES

This article argues that the early trading companies shared important characteristics with today's modern multinationals. Although at first glance the nineteenth-century multinational looks much more like its late-twentieth-century counterpart than do the charter companies, appearances are misleading. The three business structures all developed in the same way. Nineteenth-century international firms began as trading multinationals when they replaced merchant houses and agents with sales branches abroad. Only after gaining experience as trading multinationals did the firms establish overseas production facilities. The charter companies also began as trading companies with sales branches, but many established production plants abroad early in their existence. The Muscovy Company, for example, opened a rope house in Russia, where it employed English craftsmen to make cordage, only four years after the company's formation in 1553.[4] In Bengal, the Dutch East India Company established a plant to refine saltpeter as early as 1641, a print works for textiles ten years later, and by 1717 the company employed over four thousand silk spinners in Kaimbazar.[5] Although the nineteenth-century multinational became much more involved in production than the early charter companies, the difference was one of degree, not of kind.

Both the early trading companies and the late-nineteenth-century multinationals arose for the same reason: to economize on the high number of recurrent transactions. Yet business historians have focused exclusively on the late-nineteenth-century industrial transnational firm as the modern multinational enterprise in embryo. Two criteria, the degree of administrative control and the frequency of transacting, have been used to date the origins of the modern multinational to the last decades

---

[3] C. Wilson, "Multinationals, Management and World Markets: A Historical View," in *Evolution of International Management Structures*, ed. H. F. Williamson (Newark, Del., 1975), 111.

[4] T. S. Willan, *The Early History of the Russia Company* (New York, 1956), 40.

[5] O. Prakash, *The Dutch East India Company and the Economy of Bengal, 1630–1720* (Princeton, N.J., 1985), 112–17.

of the nineteenth century. As Mira Wilkins argued, the growth of "communications and transportation facilities made it possible (for the first time in world history) to extend the span of managerial control over substantial distances."[6] One of the few historians of multinationals to consider the early charter companies, Wilkins recognized that the trading companies shared many similarities with the modern corporation, but she thought that they failed to satisfy either criterion. Drawing on the work of Alfred Chandler, Wilkins argued that the volume of transactions was not great enough to bring about a managerial hierarchy until the late-nineteenth-century revolution in transport and communication. The railroad, telegraph, steamship, and cable allowed managers to coordinate at a distance.[7] According to Chandler, today's "small industrial enterprises handle a far greater volume of transactions than did those giants of an earlier capitalism—the Hudson's Bay Company, the Royal African, even the East India Company."[8]

This is almost certainly wrong. The early trading companies were characterized by a large volume of transactions, and they innovated in mechanisms of administrative control to increase their information and to reduce the costs of transacting internationally. In these two critical respects, the early trading companies were indeed analogues to the modern multinational. A transaction is defined as the transfer of a good or service across a technologically separate interface, where one activity stops and another begins.[9] Thus, a transaction is an interchange of a good or service between two or more contracting parties. Clearly, the interchange can occur inter- or intra-firm and can involve either a separate contract for each transaction or multiple interchanges within one contract. For example, the firm may subcontract the production of a good by specifying one formal inter-firm contract, or the firm may enter into an employment contract, under which many intra-firm transactions are undertaken by employees.

The volume of transactions is central to the argument that the charter companies were analogues to the modern business corporation. Some extremely large contemporary multinationals do engage in millions of transactions daily, but these firms do not represent the typical twentieth-century multinational, which engages in many fewer transactions. The volume of transactions of the nineteenth-century multinationals, which historians have been willing to define as the precursors of the modern multinational, was also much smaller than that of twentieth-century giants. The typical late-nineteenth-century British multinational was a

---

[6] Wilkins, "History of European Multinationals," 488.

[7] Ibid.; Alfred D. Chandler, Jr., "The Emergence of Managerial Capitalism," mimeo, 1981, 1–3.

[8] Alfred D. Chandler, Jr., "The Growth of the Transnational Industrial Firm in the United States and United Kingdom: A Comparative Analysis," *Economic History Review* 33 (Aug. 1980): 401–9.

[9] Oliver Williamson, *The Economic Institutions of Capitalism* (New York, 1985), 1.

single-product, one-plant firm, producing in one foreign market.[10] In contrast, the early trading companies had a higher volume of transactions than most nineteenth-century British multinationals and than many of today's international firms.

If one looks at only a fraction of the transactions, the invoicing of goods between the factory at Batavia (present-day Jakarta, Indonesia) and the head office of the Dutch East India Company, the volume of transactions filled "more than 500 fat volumes from the 17th century."[11] These volumes include neither the intra-Asian trade, which was more extensive than the trade with Europe during part of the seventeenth century, nor the transactions between the company's factors and local merchants in the Middle East, India, Batavia, and Japan, nor the transactions covering the flow of trade goods from Europe to Asia. In addition, there were transactions surrounding the building, chartering, and sailing of ships, the building and maintenance of "factories" (warehouses or outposts, not production units), and payment for goods and services. Both the English and the Dutch East India companies engaged in hundreds of thousands of transactions every year, and even the smaller Hudson's Bay Company was involved in tens of thousands of transactions between the Indians and the local factor, the local factor and the ships' captains, and the ships' captains and the principals in London. This large volume of transactions occurred before the advent of the steamship, telegraph, or other modern means of transportation and communication.

According to Chandler and Wilkins, it was the volume of transactions that forced the replacement of owner-managers by teams of salaried managers organized into hierarchies, which differentiated the modern transnationals from earlier firms. If our hypothesis that the early charter companies experienced a large volume of transactions is correct, then partners, unable to handle the high number of transactions themselves, would have been impelled to create a team of managers to coordinate the firms' activities in far-flung outposts. This is exactly what happened.

For the Hudson's Bay Company, each factory was managed by a chief factor, who carried out the trade with the Indians, managed the day-to-day operations of the post, and oversaw the general workers, or servants. One chief factor, answerable to the Court of Directors in London through the correspondence committee, was appointed with control over all the factories on the Bay.[12] The English East India Company's Court was served by subcommittees for accounts, buying, private trade, presidencies, shipping, and treasure; the Dutch East India Company had com-

---

[10] Calculated from a sample of 448 pre-1939 British multinationals. In the sample, 31 percent of the largest 1918–39 multinationals (those with paid-up capital greater than £4.5 million) had only one overseas branch.

[11] K. Glamann, *Dutch-Asiatic Trade, 1620–1740* (The Hague, 1981), 269.

[12] E. E. Rich, *Hudson's Bay Company, 1660–1760* (The Hudson's Bay Record Society, 1958), chap. 7.

mittees for receipts, equipment of ships, accounting, commerce, and correspondence.[13] The home-based managers of the Dutch company corresponded with the Batavia Government, and those of the English company corresponded with President and his Council in each of the company's separate trading regions in Asia; these in turn controlled the local managers in the branch factories.[14]

Thus, if we accept Chandler's argument that the existence of a managerial hierarchy is a defining characteristic of the modern business enterprise, we must reject his suggestion that managerial hierarchies are entirely modern.[15] In this crucial aspect, the trading companies of the seventeenth century were analogous to the modern multinational, the same in kind but different in degree.

Although there are striking similarities between the early chartered companies and the modern multinational, their differences also must be explicitly recognized. They operated in different historical environments, both economically and politically. K. N. Chaudhuri argued that "the organization and the conduct of the East India trade could not be strictly separated from the conduct of national foreign policy," and K. G. Davies found that the Royal African Company "preserved English interests, the company carrying the national burden."[16] The early trading companies differ also in that the head office managers were usually owners with a minority share, whereas today's senior managers may be shareholders, but they usually hold an insignificant number of total shares. These trading firms operated in a pre-industrial world, where a system of capitalist international trade had to be grafted onto a premodern system of artisan and peasant production.[17] Given their economic environment, the ability of these firms to develop hierarchical structures is all the more remarkable.

This article integrates the charter companies into the historical work on the evolution of the modern multinational and into the recent theoretical literature on the origin and growth of firms. We focus on two elements that made the early trading firms analogues to the modern multinational: first, the institution—the managerial hierarchy—that developed to economize on transaction costs arising from a high volume of transactions and second, the mechanisms that the managerial hierarchy used to control its managers at a distance. Drawing on the transaction cost literature used to explain modern multinationals, we briefly specify a model for the existence of international firms. Next we apply

---

[13] K. Chaudhuri, *The Trading World of Asia and the English East India Company, 1660–1760* (New York, 1978), 267, 26–27; Glamann, *Dutch-Asiatic Trade*, 5.

[14] Chaudhuri, *Trading World*, 27; Glamann, *Dutch-Asiatic Trade*, 186.

[15] Chandler, "Emergence of Managerial Hierarchy," 1; Alfred D. Chandler, Jr., *The Visible Hand: The Managerial Revolution in American Business* (Cambridge, Mass., 1977), 7.

[16] Chaudhuri, *Trading World*, 455; K. Davies, *The Royal African Company* (London, 1957), 264. Of course, some present-day multinationals, such as the United Fruit Company, have exercised a quasi-political function.

[17] Chaudhuri, *Trading World*, 455.

this model to the charter companies to show how the trading firms economized on transaction costs related to a large volume of repetitive transactions in the international market. Finally, we employ the theory to analyze the internal control structures used to monitor and assess the behavior of the companies' managers.

THE CHARTERED TRADING COMPANIES

The sixteenth and seventeenth centuries saw the evolution of the joint-stock company, of which the chartered trading company was an important example. In this article we focus on five of the companies chartered during the period and involved in long-distance trade—the Muscovy Company, chartered in 1553 and disbanded in 1746; the East India Company, chartered in 1600 and wound up in 1858; the Dutch East India Company, chartered in 1602 and dissolved in 1799; the Hudson's Bay Company, chartered in 1670 and still operating; and the Royal African Company, chartered in 1672 and disbanded about 1712.

Our sample, spanning a hundred years between the first company chartered and the last, is broadly representative of the seventeenth- and early-eighteenth-century joint-stock trading companies. These companies captured trade to virtually every known corner of the globe, from Russia to India, from Africa to Canada. The companies differed in size and in the quantities of goods traded; the two East India companies were the largest in terms of the value of business conducted, and the Hudson's Bay Company was the smallest.

The sizes of the head offices also varied. Both the Royal African and the Hudson's Bay companies had small central offices, growing from six to twenty permanently salaried managers (excluding the Court) by 1700, whereas the Dutch and English East India companies employed over 350 head office administrators by the mid-eighteenth century. Few late-nineteenth-century British multinationals had an administrative staff greater than the Hudson's Bay or Royal African companies, and few British interwar multinationals could claim a head office administrative staff of 350 people.[18] As late as 1968, a survey in *Management Today* reported that 66 percent of the top 120 British companies had no hierarchy other than the chairman and managing director.[19] Even at a large American multinational—Standard Oil, on the eve of dissolution in 1911—the general administration of the entire company numbered just over one thousand individuals, and Jersey Standard had fewer than three hundred

[18] Recently, T. R. Gourvish has reemphasized family control in British firms, the lack of administrative hierarchies, and the absence of innovations in managerial structures before 1950. T. Gourvish, "British Business and the Transition to a Corporate Economy: Entrepreneurship and Management Structures," in *Enterprise, Management and Innovation in British Business, 1914–1980*, ed. R. P. T. Davenport-Hines and Geoffrey Jones (London, 1988), 18–45.

[19] D. F. Channon, *The Strategy and Structure of British Enterprise* (London, 1973), 212.

THE DUTCH EAST INDIA HOUSE, AERIAL VIEW

This early-eighteenth-century engraving shows the expanse of warehouse and office space
occupied by the Dutch East India Company on the Hoogstraat in Amsterdam. (Reproduced
from J. C. Overvoorde and P. de Roo de la Faille, De Gebouwen van de Oost-Indische
Compagnie en van de West-Indische Compagnie in Nederland [Utrecht, 1928], 21.)

administrators, fewer than the Dutch East India Company 160 years
before.[20]

Although the chartered trading companies differed in certain
characteristics—date of charter, size, and location of trade—they were
remarkably similar in the way they organized their business. The seventeenth and early eighteenth centuries were periods of experimentation
in business form, yet all of these companies chose the same methods
to lower the costs of doing business internationally. They chose to
become vertically integrated firms rather than to conduct their business through the market. They chose this route not because a private
market did not exist, but because operating by managerial fiat inside
the hierarchical firm was less costly than using the market.

TRANSACTION COSTS AND THE ECONOMICS OF AGENCY

The new institutional economics argues that firms arise as institutions for transacting in goods and services when the costs of managerial
coordination are less than the costs of using the market.[21] Transaction

---

[20] Ralph Hidy and Muriel Hidy, *Pioneering in Big Business, 1882–1911* (New York, 1955), 580.
[21] See Williamson, *Economic Institutions*; Peter Buckley and Mark Casson, *The Future of the Multinational Enterprise* (London, 1976); Mark Casson, *Alternative to the Multinational Enterprise* (London, 1979);

CARLOS AND NICHOLAS: TRADING COMPANIES 405

EAST INDIA HOUSE, c. 1840

From modest beginnings, the English East India Company soon outgrew its quarters, and several additions and renovations were made during the eighteenth and nineteenth centuries to house goods and staff. The company's meeting rooms and warehouses eventually covered a full block between Leadenhall and Lime streets. (From an engraving by W. Wallace, reproduced in William Foster, The East India House: Its History and Associations [Edinburgh, 1924], facing p. 146.)

costs in arms-length markets include the costs of gaining information and of negotiating, monitoring, and enforcing contracts for the exchange of goods and services. Firms economize on transaction costs by replacing the price mechanism in the market with fiat inside the firm. Internalization of these market transactions takes the form of vertical integration. According to Chandler, the increase in the frequency and volume of transactions brought about by the expansion of markets made administrative coordination more efficient and profitable than market coordination.[22] In this section we analyze the costs of transacting in the markets in which the trading companies functioned, and we show how the trading companies used managerial coordination to economize on these costs.

The degree of hierarchy is a function of the frequency and volume of transacting, but hierarchical coordination by salaried managers poses

John Dunning, *International Production and the Multinational Enterprise* (Winchester, Mass., 1981); Diane Hutchinson and Stephen Nicholas, "Theory in Business History: New Approaches to Institutional Change," *Journal of European Economic History* (forthcoming, 1989). The transaction cost approach is from the same generic literature as that employed by Douglass North. See North, *Structure and Change in Economic History* (New York, 1981).

[22] Chandler, *Visible Hand*, 8.

its own costs related to the economics of agency. Such costs are particularly evident in long-distance trade, where it is especially difficult to ensure that managers will use their discretionary powers to the best advantage of the company. Agency problems arise when incomplete information and uncertainty are explicitly recognized.[23] Asymmetries in information meant that the principal or managers in London or Amsterdam had different quality information than their agents (managers) in India, Batavia, or Hudson Bay. Informational asymmetries give rise to hidden action, typically the amount of effort put into task completion by the agent, and hidden information, which relates to observations available to the agent but not to the principal. The principals at home thus cannot determine whether their managers abroad act opportunistically by failing to use their better information in the way best calculated to serve the principals' interests. Nor can principals simply evaluate the work of their agents on the basis of results. An energetic agent may have fewer sales than an inactive one, for example, because of fluctuations in demand caused by poor harvests and famine.

Hidden action and hidden information make the employment relationship between the principal at home and the managers abroad a decision problem under uncertainty. Since no employment contract can specify for the agent a set of actions to meet every contingency, companies use a number of mechanisms to reduce the costs of agency. First, the remuneration package in the employment contract uses fixed and incentive fee payments to reduce opportunism and maximize effort. In addition, managers must promise in their contracts to work hard and in the interests of the principal. Since it is costly to write and enforce contracts, firms also establish systems to monitor the behavior of managers and to supplement information on outcomes.

Having created large hierarchies of salaried managers, the trading companies employed all these methods to overcome the costs of agency. Further, they created information by requiring written records of decisions and notification of compliance to orders from home and by implementing rules and procedures that regularized action.

ECONOMIZING ON TRANSACTION COSTS

The trading companies were vertically integrated firms that undertook the entire range of activities from the procurement of commodi-

---

[23] For recent work on agencies see Kenneth J. Arrow, "The Economics of Agency," in *Principals and Agents: The Structure of Business*, ed. J. Pratt and R. Zeckhauser (Boston, Mass., 1984), 27–51; N. Strong and M. Waterson, "Principals, Agents and Information," in *The Economics of the Firm*, ed. R. Clarke and T. McGuinness (New York, 1987), 18–61; M. Jensen and W. Meckling, "Theory of the Firm: Managerial Behavior, Agency Costs and Ownership Structure," *Journal of Financial Economics* 3 (Nov. 1978): 305–11; S. Ross, "The Economic Theory of Agency: The Principal's Problem," *American Economic Review* 63 (May 1973): 134–49; Williamson, *Economic Institutions*, chs. 2, 3, 8; E. Fama and M. Jensen, "Separation of Ownership and Control," *Journal of Law and Economics* 26 (June 1983): 301–26.

ties in distant lands to their wholesaling in Europe. These transactions included the purchase of trade goods for export from Europe, the requisitioning of ships and manpower for the transportation and subsequent sale of these goods abroad, and finally the procurement of imports, which required grading and standardization for shipment and sale in Europe. Each of these cycles of activity normally took eighteen months to two-and-a-half years to complete, making it important for the company to have good information about the level of supply and demand and about the preferences and tastes of consumers. These activities could have been undertaken by separate firms transacting through the market, but as this section shows, it was the efficient processing of information about transactions in each of these areas that gave the early trading companies their advantage over the market.

In the seventeenth-century international economy, with markets separated by time and space, market information was highly imperfect. In such a world the domination of the market by many individual traders would have led to large fluctuations in both price and quantity. In fact, as Davies points out, when the Royal African Company collapsed in 1712, "separate traders . . . neglected small colonies, starved Barbados, and by competition in Africa helped to force up prices."[24] The need to equate supply and demand in markets with imperfect information is integral to our understanding of why trading companies existed. As Chaudhuri rightly argued in regard to the English East India Company, "with supplying and consuming markets separated by thousands of miles and served by slow means of communication, it was of utmost importance that a systematic solution should be found to the problem of maintaining equilibrium between supply and demand."[25] The frequent and recurrent nature of transacting led to the rise of a specific governance structure, the trading company, which used hierarchies of salaried managers to economize on the market. By collecting and processing information about different markets, the charter companies drew up the "indents," or lists of commodities to be procured, in both Asia and Europe, giving the companies an enormous advantage over the market as the means of equating supply and demand.

From the beginning the Courts of Directors organized trade on the basis of a committee system. For example, the Amsterdam chamber of the Dutch East India Company had four committees in 1602: for the signing on of the crews, for victualling, for procuring ships, and for merchandise.[26] The Court had to gather information by monitoring the official correspondence with the foreign outposts. This correspondence specified stock levels, amounts of advances, debts, and credits; it also

---

[24] Davies, *Royal African*, 312.
[25] Chaudhuri, *Trading World*, 37.
[26] J. R. Bruijn, F. S. Gaastra, and I. Schoffer, *Dutch-Asiatic Shipping* (The Hague, 1987), 19.

contained letters and reports on the nature of the trade, import and export invoices for all goods, including cost-price data, and samples collected, which were sent to the European head offices.[27] In addition to this official intelligence, the companies relied on informal, unofficial reports sent privately and confidentially by their servants.[28]

This great flow of information quickly overwhelmed the Court of Directors, limiting their ability to process the data and to make decisions. One solution to this problem was the growth of the subcommittee system, staffed by salaried managers from the home office. Within a decade of its formation in 1600, the English East India Company had evolved the correspondence subcommittee as the "central problem-scanning body . . . which first read all letters and reports."[29] Four years after its formation, the Dutch East India Company formed a committee to process data on receipts and accounts, and in 1649 it created a separate correspondence committee "as a means for relief, especially of the very time-consuming and important task of reading and answering reports and letters from India."[30] Both the Royal African Company and the Hudson's Bay Company had a subcommittee system from the beginning.[31] The administrative organization created at home by the charter companies was mirrored in the system of local head and subordinate factories in the Indies, North America, Russia, and Africa.

For each of these early trading companies the basic administrative structure solidified quickly, although there were improvements as the committee structure evolved over time. According to Chaudhuri, as early as the 1620s the English East India Company had established a stable administrative organization in the Indies; "By 1640 the company had almost fully developed the institutional and commercial framework for its trading needs, and the structure of its operations in the restoration period and even in the early eighteenth century appears to have contained very little modification to the basic system created during the early seventeenth century."[32] The rapid establishment of subcommittee organization demonstrates not only the managers' adaptation to a high volume and frequency of transactions, but also their ability to learn from other trading firms. The Dutch East India Company organization of 1602 reflected the structure of the *voorcompagnieen*, and joint directorships in the English chartered companies provided a mechanism for the transfer of managerial expertise between firms.[33]

[27] A. Ray and D. Freeman, *"Give Us Good Measure": An Economic Analysis of Relations between the Indians and the Hudson's Bay Company before 1763* (Toronto, 1978), 81–87; Chaudhuri, *Trading World*, 28, 58, 74–75; Prakash, *Economy of Bengal*, 262–65; Glamann, *Dutch-Asiatic Trade*, 89.
[28] Chaudhuri, *Trading World*, 75; Willan, *Russia Company*, 23–24.
[29] Chaudhuri, *Trading World*, 29.
[30] Glamann, *Dutch-Asiatic Trade*, 5.
[31] Davies, *African Company*, 158.
[32] K. Chaudhuri, *The English East India Company: The Study of an Early Joint Stock Company, 1600–1640* (New York, 1965), 15–20.
[33] Bruijn, Gaastra, and Schoffer, *Dutch-Asiatic Shipping*, 6. The *voorcompagnieen* were the predecessors of the Dutch East India Company.

CARLOS AND NICHOLAS: TRADING COMPANIES 409

The committees began to ask for more detailed and specific information on markets, tastes, and local politics in addition to the standard reports. The Muscovy Company wanted to know what export goods were the most acceptable, and the East India Company sought detailed and precise information on the nature of demand, leading the company to issue a standing order that "Lists be yearly sent us, of the several sorts of goods and their quantities that are vendible."[34] Similarly, the Hudson's Bay Company wrote to Governor John Bridgar in 1683, "we expect to receive a very exact account from you of all our concerns and particularly of what goods you have traded and what remains with you of all sorts of provisions and stores as well as of goods and Merchan[d]ises which you must carefully observe to do every year that we may the better know how to supply you."[35] These information flows reduced risk and uncertainty, attenuating the costs of transacting through the market.

As trade grew, the frequency and repetition of transactions called into existence a managerial hierarchy, which used the regular and detailed flows of information to coordinate the movement of goods by administrative fiat. The companies had to establish a causal relationship between the sale price in Europe and the cost price abroad, given the customs duties, freight costs, and fixed costs related to their factories. On the basis of the information flows, the companies in Europe made investment decisions, instructing the factories abroad what quantity and quality of goods to purchase. Like today's modern corporation, the trading companies forecast future demand on the basis of historical levels of demand and prices, and these projections formed the basis for the orders placed in their annual lists of goods for procurement abroad. The factors of the Muscovy Company, for example, were told the prices of the goods sent so they could judge the best price for them in Russia, and the English East India Company sent printed sales books of auction prices to India to help their factors determine buying prices.[36] The Hudson's Bay Company set the standards of trade, specifying the actual prices to be paid for furs.[37]

In addition, all the companies established rules on procurement, which remained in force for up to eighteen months, the turn-around time on communications with Asia. Each ship of the English East India Company brought back exact details about the stock in the warehouses and the amounts contracted for but not delivered, so the London auctions could be planned.[38] Similarly, the trading companies had to estimate the future demand for European goods in distant export markets, and they faced the problem of matching the supply of export goods to

[34] Willan, *Russia Company*, 31; Chaudhuri, *Trading World*, 221.
[35] Ray and Freeman, *"Give Us Good Measure"*, 87.
[36] Willan, *Russia Company*, 31; Chaudhuri, *Trading World*, 299–300; 457.
[37] Rich, *Hudson's Bay Company*, 145.
[38] Chaudhuri, *Trading World*, 303.

HUDSON'S BAY COMPANY
TRADE TOKENS

*These tokens, called "beavers"
because of their representation of
the value of beaver pelts, became
an accepted medium of exchange
throughout the territories in
which the Hudson's Bay Company traded. (Reproduced from
sketches in Beckles Willson,* The
Great Company, being a History
of the Honourable Company of
Merchants-Adventurers Trading
into Hudson's Bay *[Toronto,
1899], 458.)*

the tastes and demands of Asian, African, and North American consumers. How well the companies' orders in the list of goods for export
and import were filled depended, in the first instance, on the system
of procurement.

To procure exports, the companies employed a number of modes,
including spot markets (where goods were bought and delivered "on
the spot"), customary arrangements with independent traders, and long-
term contracts with manufacturers. In Europe, the companies were able
to use the already well-established marketing networks for the purchase
of copper, iron, woolen cloth, coral, ivory, knives, guns and gunpowder,
amber, and crystal beads. Nevertheless, many of the companies sought
ways of reducing the costs of using spot markets. For example, the Royal
African Company instituted forward contracts for iron and copper that
specified the quantities, quality, prices to be paid, and the dates of deliv-

ery.[39] Both the Hudson's Bay Company and the Royal African Company put out tenders, and encouraged the establishment of local production.

The charter companies, particularly those trading in Asia and Russia, dealt with a much larger range of commodities in the import trade than in exports; the English East India Company required over two hundred pages in its ledger book simply to list the goods purchased. Abroad, each company had to use differently organized and much less familiar trading networks than those utilized in Europe. Both the Hudson's Bay and the Muscovy companies created a new market, whereas the other companies plugged into trading systems already in existence. But in each case it was the frequent and recurrent nature of transacting and the type of trade goods that allowed the companies to invest in specialized physical capital in the form of factories (outposts). Of course, the factories fulfilled military and diplomatic functions, providing protection for the companies' men and goods and flying the flag in distant and hostile lands; but more significantly, this forward integration reduced the costs of transacting below those of market trading. The factory acted as both a symbolic and a physical bond, representing the companies' long-term commitment to a new market as well as providing a building for holding inventories of trade goods to supply the foreign market and to fill the yearly shipments to Europe.[40] Only for the Royal African Company did the costs of factories outweigh their benefits. The volume of the company's trade and the type of cargoes—slaves and perishable foodstuffs—did not argue for the establishment of factories, but political rather than economic considerations seem to have been paramount in the Royal African's case.[41]

The frequency of transacting explained not only the need for physical capital in outposts, but also for the investment by the charter companies in specialized human capital. Skilled traders, expert in trade negotiations, foreign languages, assessing the quality of goods and determining their proper handling, storage, and loading, allowed the trading companies to reduce their transacting costs below that of the market. Since there were, for example, four different kinds of cloves, the Dutch East India Company found that it required detailed knowledge for the purchase of spices, and the Muscovy Company sent specialized craftsmen, with a knowledge of wood and furs, to oversee the purchase of those goods in Russia.[42]

The Asian factors and expert buyers employed spot markets, but they too reduced the costs of market transacting by entering into agreements with customary traders and middlemen and by contracting for imports

---

[39] Davies, *African Company*, 171.
[40] The only case in which European companies did not establish factories was in the trade with Imperial China, where supercargoes were used to trade with the Hong.
[41] Davies, *African Company*, 240.
[42] Glamann, *Dutch-Asiatic Trade*, 16; Willan, *Russia Company*, 39.

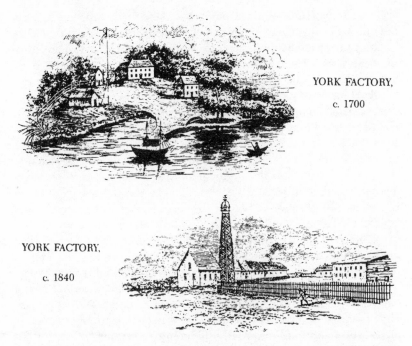

YORK FACTORY,

c. 1700

YORK FACTORY,

c. 1840

One of the early Hudson's Bay Company outposts, York factory was on the western side of the Bay and served as a jumping-off point into the interior. The later sketch shows the development of the factory. The early tents have been replaced by sturdier buildings, which housed warehouses and a trading post as well as factors. (Reproduced from sketches in Beckles Willson, The Great Company, being a History of the Honourable Company of Merchants-Adventurers Trading into Hudson's Bay *[Toronto, 1899], 355 and 502.)*

directly with local manufacturers. In Bengal, the Dutch East India Company wrote contracts with local merchants for the supply of textiles, specifying the quantity, price, delivery date, and advance that the company would supply to the weaver.[43] The local merchants also oversaw production. In by-passing the market, the company had to assess the reputation of the merchant and guard against bad debts, poor workmanship, and late delivery. To overcome these problems of opportunism by the local merchants, the company terminated the contracts of agents who cheated, kept cash advances to merchants low, inspected looms to ensure quality, and reduced agreed prices for poor quality and late delivery.[44] The English East India Company avoided the problems of dealing with local merchants by making contracts directly with Bengali weavers.[45] Direct contracting meant that the company had to invest in a local factory and arrange to transport the cloth from the weaver to

[43] Prakash, *Economy of Bengal*, 98–110.
[44] Ibid., 108–12.
[45] Chaudhuri, *Trading World*, 353.

the factory, and from the factory to the seaport, tasks that had been part of the merchants' job.

Finally, the trading companies replaced the market by vertically integrating into production. In Russia, the Muscovy Company established a factory for making cordage, employing English craftsmen. As a result, though the company often complained about the poor quality of other export goods, it reported that its cordage was always good.[46] Both the Dutch and the British East India companies owned saltpeter and silk spinning factories in India.[47] Transaction cost theory suggests that when the frequency of transacting in a particular product is high and product quality difficult to assess, then local production should replace subcontracting. Indeed, the chartered companies undertook local production under precisely these circumstances.

After the companies' managers had procured the trade goods abroad, the scheduling of the fleets required the transmittal of detailed instructions regarding loading and sailing, if supply and demand were to be equilibrated in Europe. In each outward letter the English East India Company sent orders for the efficient disposition of ships, specifying sailing times and giving orders for the maximum utilization of space and capacity.[48] The Muscovy Company set down a precise sailing schedule, with ships leaving London at the beginning of May, reaching Russia about 1 June, staying for thirty days before leaving Russia to return home by August.[49] Similarly, the English East India Company scheduled sailings to ensure that their ships would catch the global trade winds, and they set 13 January as the date beyond which the servants in India were not, at least theoretically, allowed to delay sailings.[50] Careful scheduling of sailings was particularly important for the Hudson's Bay Company, because "experience had already taught that if the ships left London later than 25th May they would be too late for the return voyage to be made in the same year, there would be no furs for sale and captains and crews would have to be paid for the whole year."[51]

Besides coordinating sailings, the managers also supervised the loading of ships. The Dutch East India Company "continually supervised the effective use of the tonnage, not least the ballast, and made complaints when the Batavian government e.g. used old iron instead of merchandise."[52] Particularly important were the instructions for the loading of the mixed commodities that were sent by Asian and African traders. The East Indian companies were anxious to prevent the product deterioration that had occurred in the early years of the trade, when

[46] Willan, *Russia Company*, 40, 78.
[47] Prakash, *Economy of Bengal*, 112–17.
[48] Chaudhuri, *Trading World*, 71–72.
[49] Willan, *Russia Company*, 49.
[50] Chaudhuri, *Trading World*, 72.
[51] Rich, *Hudson's Bay Company*, 91.
[52] Glamann, *Dutch-Asiatic Trade*, 25.

silks arrived discolored from moisture, coffee was placed in ships carrying pepper, which contaminated the coffee and reduced prices by 8 to 10 percent, and pepper was used as ballast, enduring rough handling that reduced its value.[53]

In all of these functions the trading companies were institutions for economizing on the costs of using the market. Called into existence by frequent and recurrent transacting, their administrative hierarchies reduced risk and uncertainty by collecting information, and they replaced the market as the device for transacting in long-distance trade. In the place of decentralized and fragmented trading relations, the charter company imposed a bureaucratic and hierarchical organization. But trading company organization did not eliminate costs, since the need to monitor and assess the performance of the companies' salaried managers generated costs of its own.

MANAGING THE MANAGERS

The primary activity of the companies' managers abroad was trading, but they also supervised the work force of general servants, oversaw the sailing and loading of ships, and carried out quasi-political and diplomatic functions as representatives of European governments. In the area of trade, the problems of hidden action, hidden information, and opportunistic behavior loomed large, requiring the principals in Europe to monitor and assess the performance of their agents abroad. To attenuate opportunism and to encourage the managers to work in the best interests of the company, the principals wrote a generous employment contract for their managers. Besides a wage component, the companies provided housing, food, and transportation.[54] The English East India Company, Chaudhuri found, motivated its senior servants by "high and generous salaries."[55] The Agent-General of the Royal African Company in 1680 received £600 per year, free board and lodging, plus a gratuity of £200 at the end of three years' service in exchange for abstaining from private trade.[56] The method of payment varied among the companies: the Hudson's Bay and Dutch East India companies held money in London and Amsterdam on their agent's accounts; the Muscovy Company paid some wages in rubles; and the Royal African paid its men from the gold collected in Africa.[57]

---

[53] Ibid., 149, 193; Chaudhuri, *Trading World*, 368.

[54] Ann Carlos and Stephen Nicholas, "Managing the Manager: The Hudson's Bay Company and the Economics of Agency," mimeo, 1988, 10–11; Willan, *Russia Company*, 37–38.

[55] Chaudhuri, *Trading World*, 32.

[56] Davies, *African Company*, 252.

[57] Bruijn, Gaastri, and Schoffer, *Dutch-Asiatic Shipping*, 150; Willan, *Russia Company*, 249; Davies, *African Company*, 253.

CARLOS AND NICHOLAS: TRADING COMPANIES   415

In addition to providing a high real wage component, most companies, at least in the beginning, permitted private trade. Designed to call forth a high level of effort, private trade also encouraged opportunism— managers' maximization of their private welfare at the expense of the company. Vertical integration merely internalizes transaction costs between contracting parties in the market, thus decreasing, but not eliminating, these costs. Opportunism by the firms' managers was quickly recognized as a problem. After only two years of operation in Canada, the Hudson's Bay Company banned private trade; the Royal African Company, after first curbing private trade, abolished it after eight years of operation.[58] According to J. S. Willan, the Russia Company was concerned about "horedom, incontinency, drunkeness and idellness," but the greatest evil was private trade.[59] In 1710 the Dutch East India Company accused the Bengali factories of putting aside the most profitable assortment of textiles for their own benefit, and the English East India Company complained that the inter-Asian trade was poorly developed because of private trade.[60] Private trade, then, was a major area of conflict between the companies' "official objectives and the private interests of its agents."[61]

In response to the problem, the trading companies either curtailed or abolished private trade. The Hudson's Bay Company, the Royal African Company, and the Muscovy Company tried to end private trade by requiring their managers to take an oath promising not to trade privately, by assigning pursers on ships, searching all vessels, and reading their servants' private correspondence to detect violations, and by requiring bonds from their managers as insurance against private trade.[62] Despite these steps, none of the companies was successful. In 1691, nine years after it banned private trade, the Royal African Company wrote, "We have reason to complain that our factors and some of the chiefs manage private trade, which is the way to encourage interlopers and ruine our stock by bearing the charge without having the advantage."[63] All three companies continued to monitor the private trade of their agents by carefully marking and checking outward and inward cargoes and by offering rewards to ships' captains who detected illegal goods.

Both the Dutch and English East India companies allowed private trade, but they tried to restrict it within acceptable limits. When the English East India Company increased its trade with China, the freedom of its servants and ships' captains to purchase tea privately was

[58] Carlos and Nicholas, "Managing the Manager," 11; Davies, African Company, 111.
[59] Willan, Russia Company, 37.
[60] Glamann, Dutch-Asiatic Trade, 147; Chaudhuri, Trading World, 208.
[61] Chaudhuri, Trading World, 269.
[62] Davies, African Company, 256; Willan, Russia Company, 27, 37, 247; Carlos and Nicholas, "Managing the Manager," 12–14.
[63] Davies, African Company, 255.

TRADING AT CANTON, 1785

Most European trading companies first used supercargoes—agents who traveled back and forth with shipments of goods—rather than resident factors in dealing with China. Neverthe-less, the companies gradually built warehouses, offices, and other facilities, and in the late eighteenth century supercargoes began to remain behind in China to manage the procure-ment of goods for the next year's sailings. (Colored lithograph by W. Daniell, reproduced in Hosea B. Morse, The Chronicles of the East India Company Trading to China, 1635–1834 *[Cambridge, Mass., 1926], 2: facing p. 144).*

severely curtailed.[64] The chief factor was responsible for obtaining a high level of effort from the company's servants and for ensuring that private trade did not dominate official trade. Chief factors who failed in these functions were dismissed, jeopardizing their bonds and, in the case of the Hudson's Bay Company, where no alternative employment existed, paying their own way home.[65] To identify the shirkers, the companies relied on the information flows used to regulate supply and demand. The Hudson's Bay, East India, and Royal African companies set down precise regulations governing every aspect of the keeping of accounts and correspondence, enabling the companies to monitor its agents care-fully.[66] The irregular accounts kept by the Bencoolen factory, for exam-ple, convinced the Court of the English East India Company that the managers there were corrupt.[67]

In addition, the companies examined order lists and manifests of goods received to calculate the difference between quantities ordered and those actually delivered, and they used the size of the gap as an inverse measure of performance.[68] The companies in the Asian trade used the ratio of capital to tonnage to assess performance, and the Hudson's Bay

[64] Chaudhuri, *Trading World*, 386.
[65] Carlos and Nicholas, "Managing the Manager," 20–21; Chaudhuri, *Trading World*, 302.
[66] Carlos and Nicholas, "Managing the Manager," 16.
[67] Chaudhuri, *Trading World*, 65.
[68] Ibid., 61, 304.

CARLOS AND NICHOLAS: TRADING COMPANIES 417

Company calculated each post's ratio of trade goods to furs to evaluate profitability.[69] Bad debts and the actual quantity of goods delivered also identified possible opportunism. The Dutch and English East India companies used the amount of outstanding credit on advance contracts to local merchants to assess performance, and the Hudson's Bay Company kept a careful watch on the "overplus," the difference between the actual price paid to the Indians and the "Official Standard."[70]

Inventory lists and surveys also allowed the principals in Europe to monitor their agents. When the Dutch East India Company experienced low stocks of pepper in Europe, the company complained that its agents in Batavia had failed to utilize the available tonnage efficiently. In the 1620s, the company found that it had stockpiled between five and seven years' supply of cloves, a problem attributed to oversupply by its agents in Batavia.[71] Performance in some areas could be assessed directly by whether the ships sailed on time, their load factor, and the care used in loading mixed cargoes. The companies gave their managers abroad regular reprimands over failures in each of these areas, with dismissals and demotions for recidivist factories.

Returns were a powerful information source for controlling managers, and they could be used either as a relative or as an absolute standard. The growth of the Bengal factories of the Dutch East India Company was restricted because of poor returns, for example, whereas the Coromandel factory was encouraged to expand.[72] On the basis of its poor performance relative to other factories, the Bengal Council was dismissed by the East India Company in 1732.[73] The Royal African Company measured performance by output, calculating the charge for the whole voyage according to the number of live slaves landed in the West Indies, no separate charge being made for the London-African run.[74] There were, of course, other absolute standards for judging performance. When the Bengal President of the East India Company was found to have large borrowings from Calcutta cloth merchants, which turned him into an agent acting for them and subordinating the company's interests, his service was terminated in 1739.[75] The Royal African Company dismissed its chief merchant at Sherbro in 1705 when he saved his own belongings, and neglected the company's, during a French attack; two years later the chief factors at Sekondi, Dixcove, and Anomabu were dismissed on similar charges of inefficiency and pusillanimity.[76]

[69] Carlos and Nicholas, "Managing the Manager," 18.
[70] Glamann, *Dutch-Asiatic Trade*, 147; Chaudhuri, *Trading World*, 457; Carlos and Nicholas, "Managing the Manager," 15–18.
[71] Glamann, *Dutch-Asiatic Trade*, 87, 93–95.
[72] Ibid., 66.
[73] Chaudhuri, *Trading World*, 302.
[74] Davies, *African Company*, 198.
[75] Chaudhuri, *Trading World*, 302.
[76] Davies, *African Company*, 256. Sherbro is in modern Sierra Leone; Sekondi, Dixcove, and Anomabu are along the coast of present-day Ghana.

CONCLUSION

The defining characteristic of modern business enterprise is a hierarchy of salaried managers who make basic decisions over production, distribution, and prices. Their innovations in this new form of business organization—the managerial hierarchy—make the sixteenth- and seventeenth-century trading companies analogues to the modern multinational. The managers who controlled the early trading companies grappled with the problem of coordinating the flow of goods, services, and information over long distances and with the need to extend head office control over the company's managers abroad. The same necessity confronted the managers of the late-nineteenth-century multinationals, who derived central functional and multidivisional forms of organization to counteract similar problems. The managers of the largest international firms today still search for new structures to overcome the problems of coordinating goods and people at a distance as they innovate into global product and area divisions. The charter companies shared a common business organization with modern firms, and they are important both historically and economically.

The rise of managerial hierarchies in both the early trading companies and today's multinationals was the result of the frequency and volume of transacting. The market, with imperfect information and uncertainty, is not a costless institution for transacting the exchange of goods and services. When the transaction frequency is high, then teams of managers can coordinate the flow of goods and information more cheaply than the market. This transaction cost explanation of the operation of firms applies to the development of the charter companies of the sixteenth and seventeenth centuries as much as to their modern counterparts in the nineteenth and twentieth centuries.

Applying the transaction cost approach, we argue that in an uncertain world, where information was imperfect, the charter companies had to equate supply of foreign goods to European demand and of European goods to the needs of consumers in Canada, Africa, and Asia. With markets separated by time and space and linked only by slow and uncertain means of communciation, the salaried managers economized on the market by collecting and processing information on tastes, commodities, and prices to ensure an equilibrium in supply and demand. A sophisticated committee system collated information, sent out orders for trade goods, organized the shipping schedules, and determined the prices for goods. Vertical integration in the form of the charter company replaced the market as a system for exchanging goods and services internationally. However, though it economized on the market, the managerial hierarchy itself generated costs—those of monitoring and assessing the performance of its managers abroad. These early multinationals experimented in high real wage labor contracts, bonding of managers, and the use of incentives to motivate and control overseas factories.

The early trading companies are often viewed as failures. Some, like the Royal African Company, had checkered careers and failed, but the Hudson's Bay Company, formed in 1670, remains a successful firm even today, claiming to be the world's oldest surviving multinational. The English and Dutch East India companies were large and successful firms for nearly two hundred years, and the extent of economic and political power that they held remains unsurpassed even by today's large multinationals. Conversely, not all modern multinationals have been unqualified successes. Recent work on pre-1939 British multinationals has assessed their performance as "poor," uncovering evidence of deficient top management and inadequate home office control.[77] The charter companies did not always successfully control overseas managers, but the early trading companies developed incentive contracts, oaths and bonds, and information flows on work performance, which are standard mechanisms for evaluating managerial effort in modern multinationals. For over two hundred years the great charter companies successfully brought into equilibrium the demands of Europe for spices, textiles, furs, tea, and coffee with the supply of these goods in Canada, Russia, Africa, and Asia. This success was the work of a "modern" business organization, committees of salaried managers, and in this crucial respect the trading companies were analogues to today's multinationals.

[77] Geoffrey Jones, ed., *British Multinationals: Origins, Management and Performance* (Brookfield, Vt., 1986), 18–19.

Part IV
Case Studies

[19]

The Growth and Performance of British Multinational Firms before 1939: The Case of Dunlop*

By GEOFFREY JONES

I

On the basis of a case study of the Dunlop Rubber Company this article examines two aspects of the growth of British multinational enterprise before the Second World War. First, why did British manufacturing firms establish factories in foreign countries? Second, what did firms gain from this strategy? The first question has attracted some comment, although generalizations have continued to rest on a combination of inadequate secondary literature and a few scholarly business histories of large firms.[1] The second question has received hardly any attention. The Macmillan Committee on Finance and Trade in 1931 seems to have assumed that both the private and social rates of return from foreign direct investment exceeded those from portfolio investment overseas, and this was probably the general view in business circles in the interwar period.[2] However, there was no systematic attempt to measure the gains to British firms of their foreign direct investments until the investigation by Prof. Reddaway of the performance of a sample of British multinational firms over the period 1955-64.[3]

Dunlop grew from a small firm launched in Dublin in 1889 to the eighth largest British company, measured in terms of estimated market value, in 1930.[4] The firm became the largest tyre and rubber goods manufacturer in Britain. Dunlop also made substantial foreign direct investments. The firm acquired its first foreign factories in the 1890s alongside other early British multinationals such as Lever Brothers and J & P Coats.[5] Within three years

* I would like to thank Profs Leslie Hannah and Mira Wilkins and Mr M. E. Falkus for their helpful comments on earlier drafts of this article, Dunlop Ltd. for allowing access to their archives, and the Nuffield Foundation for its financial support.

[1] C. Wilson, 'The Multinational in Historical Perspective', in K. Nakagawa, ed. *Strategy and Structure of Big Business* (Tokyo, 1977), pp. 265-303; J. M. Stopford, 'The Origins of British-based Multinational Manufacturing Enterprises', *Business History Review* (1974) pp. 303-35; P. Buckley and B. Roberts, *European Direct Investment in the USA before World War I* (1982); S. Nicholas, 'The Motivation and Direction of U.K. Direct Investment, 1870-1939', *Journal of European Economic History* (1982), pp. 605-30; Geoffrey Jones, 'The Expansion of British Multinational Manufacturing', in T. Inoue and A. Okochi, eds. *Overseas Business Activities* (Tokyo, 1983), pp. 125-53. There are numerous definitions of multinational enterprise. In this article the term is defined widely as a company which owns, controls, and manages income-generating assets in more than one country.
[2] L. Hannah, *The Rise of the Corporate Economy* (1976), p. 134.
[3] W. B. Reddaway, *Effects of United Kingdom Direct Investment Overseas: An Interim Report* (Cambridge, 1967); *Final Report* (Cambridge, 1968).
[4] Hannah, *Rise of the Corporate Economy*, p. 120.
[5] See Geoffrey Jones, 'The Expansion of British Multinational Manufacturing'.

36   G. JONES

of its foundation the firm had established manufacturing facilities in France, Germany, and the United States. During the interwar years the firm acquired further overseas factories. Table 1 gives an outline of the main chronological stages in the firm's foreign manufacturing expansion.[6]

Table 1. *Growth of Dunlop's Foreign Manufacturing Subsidiaries, 1892-1939*

Country	Date of first factory	Date factory sold or lost	Date factory re-established
France	1892(a)	–	–
Germany	1892(a)	1915	1919
United States	1893	1898	1923
Japan	1909	–	–
Canada	1927(b)	–	–
Australia	1928(b)	–	–
South Africa	1935	–	–
Eire	1935	–	–
India	1936	–	–

(a) Minority shareholding. Full control in France 1909, Germany 1910.
(b) Date of acquisition from previously independent local Dunlop company.

Despite the obvious interest and importance of Dunlop's history, remarkably little has been published about any aspect of the company, and nothing about its development as a leading British-based multinational.[7] This article examines Dunlop's multinational growth and performance before 1939, and draws for the first time on evidence from the surviving business archives of the firm.

II

Why did Dunlop establish factories in foreign countries before 1914? The views of economists such as C. P. Kindleberger and S. Hymer, who regarded multinational growth as coming from firms in oligopolistic positions in their home markets seeking to appropriate quasi-monopoly returns in other markets by manufacturing in those countries, provide a useful starting point from which to answer this question.[8] Most of the British firms making multinational investments in this period were in industries which from the late nineteenth century experienced changes in marketing methods or technology which encouraged the growth of oligopolistic market structures. Lever Brothers, J & P Coats, Nobel Explosives, and Courtaulds all fell into this category, and Dunlop's experience was broadly similar. The firm's initial growth rested on John Boyd Dunlop's discovery of the pneumatic tyre principle in 1888, which was patented in 1889. It was on this basis that J. B. Dunlop, Harvey du Cros and others formed the Pneumatic Tyre and Booth's Cycle Agency Co. Ltd. In 1890 the firm purchased two other important patents—the Welch

---

[6] This article does not consider supply-oriented investment, notably Dunlop's acquisition of large rubber estates in Malaya before 1914.

[7] There is some background material in Sir Arthur du Cros, *Wheels of Fortune: A Salute to Pioneers* (1938), P. Jennings, *Dunlopera* (1961), E. Tompkins, *The History of the Pneumatic Tyre* (1981), and Kathleen E. Dunlop, "The History of the Dunlop Rubber Co. Ltd. 1888-1939 (unpublished Ph.D. thesis, University of Illinois, 1949).

[8] C. P. Kindleberger, *The International Corporations* (Cambridge, Mass. 1970); S. Hymer, *The International Operations of National Firms* (Cambridge, Mass. 1975).

and Bartlett patents—concerned with methods of attaching pneumatic tyres to bicycle rims.

These patents placed the company, which in 1896 was floated on the Stock Exchange as the Dunlop Pneumatic Company, in a very strong position in the British bicycle tyre trade in the 1890s. Business rapidly expanded during the great "bicycle boom" in Britain during the middle of that decade, and there was a steady diversification in the firm's manufacturing activities. During the first years of its existence the company did not manufacture cycle tyres. The component parts of the tyres—the outer strips for forming the tread of the tyre, the air tubes, and the canvas—were purchased from rubber manufacturers, and assembled at the firm's factory at Coventry. During the late 1890s, however, Dunlop, aware that the Bartlett and Welch patents were due to expire in 1904, formulated a policy of acquiring its own rubber mills. This policy was designed both to enable the company to make its own rubber for its tyres, and provide a basis for diversification into the manufacture of general rubber products. In 1900 Dunlop purchased a general rubber goods business, and a year later acquired its own rubber mills. These two businesses were combined in a subsidiary called the Dunlop Rubber Company Ltd. This became the manufacturing company in the group, with the Dunlop Pneumatic Tyre Company functioning as the selling company. This arrangement continued until 1912, when the Dunlop Pneumatic Tyre Company (the 'Parent Company', as it was known) became entirely a holding company and all trading activities were vested in the Dunlop Rubber Company.

Dunlop's expansion, therefore, rested on the possession of patented technology. Yet it should be emphasized that, during the period of initial foreign investment, the company did not feel itself to be in a secure oligopolistic position. The early years of the company's history were dominated by disputes and uncertainties over patents. The first blow came when it came to light that J. B. Dunlop had not discovered the pneumatic tyre. He had been preceded by Robert William Thompson who had patented a pneumatic tyre in 1845. This invention had sunk into obscurity, and J. B. Dunlop appears to have been unaware of Thompson's work.[9] After the re-discovery of Thompson's patent, the English courts invalidated Dunlop's master patent in 1892. The rest of the 1890s saw prolonged litigation over other rubber patents.[10] The situation of other early British multinationals was not dissimilar. Lever Brothers, for example, did not hold a secure oligopolistic grip on the British market before it began to establish factories abroad.[11] The concept of advantage, rather than oligopoly, seems a more helpful one for understanding the basis on which firms undertake multinational investment.

Given Dunlop's possession of an "advantage" to exploit, why did the firm choose foreign manufacture rather than the more obvious strategy of export to capture overseas markets? The attractiveness of the relatively high income markets of the United States, France and Germany, each of which experienced "bicycle booms" on the British pattern in the 1890s, needs no further elaboration. A number of factors, however, made export to these markets difficult.

[9] P. Schidrowitz and T. R. Dawson, *History of the Rubber Industry* (Cambridge, 1952), p. 214.
[10] W. W. Woodruff, *The Rise of the British Rubber Industry during the Nineteenth Century* (Liverpool, 1958), pp. 72-3, 155.
[11] Wilson, 'The Multinational in Historical Perspective', p. 296.

38   G. JONES

The most important was patent legislation in various countries, which required working the inventions if the patent was to be maintained. In both France and Germany it soon became apparent to the British company that some local manufacture would be required in order to secure patents. The company, however, preferred to minimize any capital commitment in overseas ventures, so local partners were found. In France, the Pneumatic Tyre Company was associated with Messrs Clement and Company of Paris, one of the leading cycle firms in France.[12] The British company initially exported cycles with tyres attached, which were sold through Clement. In April 1891, however, Clement's lawyers advised that it was necessary "to make the tyres in France as the law would not be satisfied with the putting on only".[13] In the following year a higher duty on imported cycles reinforced the pressure for local manufacture. By autumn 1892, plans were advanced for a Compagnie Française des Pneumatiques Dunlop. Clement and other French interests contributed the money, while the Pneumatic Tyre Company granted the company the use of its patents in exchange for a one-third shareholding and royalties. Events took a similar course in Germany, where the company was advised in 1892 that "German patent law required the valves for use in Germany should be manufactured there".[14] In Germany, the Pneumatic Tyre Company went into business with a local firm owned by Heinrich Kleyer.

The third country which attracted the Pneumatic Tyre Company's attention in the early 1890s was the expanding and prosperous market of the United States. Harvey du Cros arrived in New York on Christmas Day 1890.[15] By 1 January 1891 he had made a licensing agreement with an Alfred Featherstone of Chicago, whereby the latter assembled Dunlop tyres in return for a royalty of 10s. per tyre.[16] In the case of the United States tariffs provided a stimulus to local manufacture. The McKinley Act of 1890 increased the *ad valorem* duties on imported cycles and parts from 35 per cent to 45 per cent. However, the desire to establish a strong patent position in a large market was the most important motive behind the firm's decision to make a direct investment.[17] In 1892 two of Harvey du Cros's sons, Alfred and George, were sent to visit Featherstone's factory at Chicago, after spending the previous eight months learning how to make tyres. A year later their brother, Harvey du Cros Jnr., arrived in the United States, after being manager of the Coventry business. The licensing agreement with Featherstone was terminated, and Harvey du Cros Jnr. formed and became the President of a new company, the American Dunlop Tyre Company, which had a factory in New York and supplied American cycle manufacturers.[18]

However, the experiment of a wholly-owned foreign manufacturing subsidiary was not retained for long. In 1898 the American business was sold to the Canadian manager of the American Dunlop Tyre Company, and in 1899 the

[12] A. E. Harrison, 'The Competitiveness of the British Cycle Industry, 1890-1914', *Economic History Review*, 2nd ser. XXII (1969), p. 289. Sir Arthur du Cros, *Wheels of Fortune*, p. 98.
[13] Dunlop Archives, (hereafter D.A.). Pneumatic Tyre Co. Board Minutes, 1 April 1891.
[14] Ibid. 30 March 1892.
[15] du Cros, *Wheels of Fortune*, p. 98.
[16] D.A. Pneumatic Tyre Co. Board Minutes, 1 January 1891 and 15 September 1891.
[17] D.A. evidence of Mr Guedala, Dunlop Investigation Evidence, 1922.
[18] Ibid. Evidence of Harvey du Cros, Vol. 18.

Rubber Goods Manufacturing Company secured a controlling interest in the Dunlop Tyre Company. By then the company was allegedly "the most important maker of bicycle and vehicle tyres in America".[19] It is not altogether clear why the British company sold the business, but the decision was probably related to the collapse of the cycle boom in Britain and the United States after 1897,[20] and the desire of the Dunlop company in England to raise capital for its expansion into rubber manufacture.

Dunlop's only other market-oriented foreign direct investment before 1914 was in Japan. Tariffs, or the fear of tariffs, was the primary motive in this case. During the early 1900s Dunlop became interested in Japan's potentialities as a market. In late 1906 plans for a Japanese Dunlop company were under consideration when rumours reached the British company that some commercial interests in Japan planned to start their own rubber mills which would secure Japanese government protection.[21] A company was launched almost immediately, Dunlop as usual providing the technology in return for a part of the equity. In 1909 a factory at Kobe began production, apparently specializing in tyres for rickshaws.

In several other markets Dunlop relied entirely on licensing agreements with local companies, rather than becoming involved in local manufacture itself. Licensing agreements were concluded with companies in Canada in 1894, Australia in 1899, and Russia in 1910.[22]

III

Before assessing the results of Dunlop's multinational investments before 1914, it is necessary to observe the transformation in the market for tyres during the 1900s by the development of the motor car. The manufacture of motor vehicles advanced rapidly in France, Germany, and especially the United States. This growth provided a huge new market for tyres, which became one of the largest rubber products. The United States Rubber Company, for example, was primarily a producer of footwear in the early 1900s, but the expanding demand for tyres led it to acquire, in 1905, the Rubber Goods Manufacturing Company, the owner of the American rights of the Dunlop tyre.[23]

The development of car manufacture was much slower in Britain than in the United States and Dunlop's entry into the car tyre market was also rather retarded. The French firm, Michelin, was probably responsible for the first application of the pneumatic tyre to a motor car in 1895, and in the late 1890s car tyres were imported into Britain from the Continent. However, in 1900 Dunlop began the manufacture of car tyres, and in 1906 a wheel-manufacturing plant was built. Further product diversification came in 1910, with the production by Dunlop of its first aeroplane tyre and its first golf ball. Yet

[19] V. Clark, *History of Manufacturers in the United States, 1860-1914* (Washington, 1928), p. 772.

[20] Harrison, 'The Competitiveness of the British Cycle Industry', p. 292; A. E. Harrison, 'Joint-Stock Company Flotation in the Cycle, Motor-Vehicle and Related Industries, 1882-1914', *Bus. Hist.* XXIII (1981), p. 168.

[21] D.A. Dunlop Rubber Co. (hereafter Dunlop), Board Minutes, 13 November 1906.

[22] Ibid. Board Minutes, 4 April 1913 and 19 April 1923.

[23] C. B. Babcock, *History of the United States Rubber Company* (Indiana, 1966), pp. 72-4.

40   G. JONES

it is hard to escape the conclusion that Dunlop was losing international competitiveness in the decade before 1914. Dunlop's major European rivals, Michelin of France and the Continental Company of Germany, grew rapidly, and this growth was based on a responsiveness to changing market conditions and innovations in technology which the British firm was slow to emulate. "At one time the Company led the industry and initiated all new developments", a Memorandum explained to the Board in January 1917, "but through one cause or another the company had fallen behind in this respect in recent years".[24]

It soon became apparent that the type of international expansion adopted by Dunlop in the 1890s was unsuited to the changing market conditions of the 1900s. While patent legislation and tariffs would have blocked a successful export trade to France, Germany, Japan, and the United States, Dunlop's particular investment strategy proved unsatisfactory. In France and Germany local shareholders handicapped the parent company's control over the subsidiaries. Both the French and German Dunlop companies had conservative managements, which the British company was powerless to change, yet it was prevented from directly exporting its products to those markets. The German management in the early 1900s resisted the British company's requests that it should diversify from merely producing valves by adding the manufacture of complete tyres, arguing that it was "idle for the German company to endeavour to enter into competition with the Continental Company who held the bulk of the tyre trade in Germany."[25] Similarly, the French company failed to diversify its product range on the lines of the British company, and exercised poor quality control over its products. A report produced by the British company in 1912 remarked that "our manufacture was absolutely discredited in France."[26] Both continental subsidiaries were confined to cycle tyre production, and failed to penetrate the rapidly growing motor tyre business. Although it has not been possible to re-constitute the financial results of the two subsidiaries, clues from Board minutes and other internal evidence suggest that the returns were meagre. In the five years between the acquisition by the British company of French Dunlop in 1909 and the outbreak of War, the firm accumulated trading losses of over £200,000.[27] Eventually, after a lengthy and unexplained delay, Dunlop bought out the local shareholders. In 1909 the French, and in the following year the German, companies became wholly owned subsidiaries of Dunlop, and attempts began to improve the range and quality of these firms' products.

This solution was less easy in countries where licensing agreements had been concluded. Although the Australian Dunlop Company lacked the resources to make motor tyres, it resisted the overtures of the British Dunlop Company which urged the need for a closer understanding.[28] The situation, however, was most serious in the United States. The 1898 agreement had sold Dunlop's right to trade in the United States in tyres "for use on cycles and other

[24] D.A. Dunlop Board Minutes, 17 January 1917.
[25] Ibid. 30 July 1920.
[26] D.A. See A. Dutreux, Report on the French Business, November 1912: File: French Income Stock.
[27] D.A. French Income Stock and Dunlop Rubber Company, File 5176.
[28] D.A. Dunlop Board Minutes, 6 January 1909.

vehicles".[29] This sweeping phrase prevented the company from re-entering the United States after the market for car tyres began to expand. In 1909 Dunlop managed to secure the raising of the embargo on its trading in America, but the company was still prohibited from using the name Dunlop.[30] The fact that Dunlop was prevented from using its well-known trade name in the largest tyre market in the world was a major handicap for the company. Michelin, Dunlop's great French rival, had established an American factory in 1907.[31] Moreover, the company's weakness in the United States had damaging implications in other markets. During the 1900s the American car industry began exporting cars all over the world. These cars were not only fitted with American-made tyres, but American cars were also fitted with tyres of sizes used in the United States but not made for British cars. The world-wide strength of the American automobile industry rendered Dunlop's failure to establish itself as a large-scale American tyre producer the greatest source of weakness in Dunlop's international marketing position for the next 30 years.

IV

The First World War was good for the tyre business. The demand for tyres rapidly increased in all the advanced economies. Even Dunlop's loss-making French company became profitable. A spirit of confident optimism in the industry during the War led Dunlop to plan a large-scale programme of international expansion. Unfortunately, by 1921 this plan lay in apparent ruins and Dunlop faced imminent bankruptcy.

The most immediate effect of the War on the Dunlop organization was the loss of the German company. In common with other British companies such as Lever Brothers and the Gramophone Company, Dunlop's German company was sequestrated by the German authorities during the War. In 1915 Dunlop's investment in the company, valued at £278,000, was written off shortly before the company was sold to German interests.[32] However, the former German management purchased most of the stock, and they remained friendly to their British parent. Throughout the War the Dunlop Board in London received news of the German company's affairs via a Dutch intermediary. As soon as the War ended, representatives of the British and German companies met to discuss the reunion of their firms.[33]

It was during the War that Dunlop's Board formulated a strategy for re-entering the American market. The attractions of an American factory had become clear by 1914. Unfortunately the Board once again opted for capital-minimizing tactics to secure their goal, with near-ruinous results.

It is impossible to understand subsequent events without digressing briefly into the internal politics of Dunlop's management during the War. Before 1914 the company had been dominated by the du Cros family. Old Harvey

[29] D.A. Dunlop Investigation, evidence of Harvey du Cros, Vol. 18.
[30] Ibid. Evidence of L. Bergin, Vol. 1.
[31] I am grateful to Prof. Mira Wilkins for this information.
[32] D.A. Dunlop Board Minutes, 27 April 1915.
[33] Ibid. 11 April 1919.

42   G. JONES

du Cros died in 1909 but his sons occupied almost all the senior positions in the company, with Sir Arthur du Cros as the main voice. In 1912 the du Cros family floated the Dunlop Rubber Company as an independent public company, keeping their shareholding in the Pneumatic Tyre Company (the 'Parent Tyre Company'). About the same time, Sir Arthur came into contact with James White, a financier of sorts and at that time an undischarged bankrupt.[34] During the War Sir Arthur used White's services to manage various share issues. White's power in the company grew steadily, especially after August 1917, when he and various associates formed a "Pool" to purchase shares from the Parent Tyre Company, with the intention of reselling them at a profit. White and his associates soon exerted their powers as owners of the Ordinary shares of Dunlop Rubber, and during 1918 White challenged the influence in Dunlop of his old ally, Sir Arthur du Cros. By an agreement in February 1919 Sir Arthur was made titular President for life, and pensioned off with a huge £150,000 lump sum payment and a lucrative long-term "advisory" agreement. Although White was still not a member of the Board, he secured the election of a number of his nominees, and his control, for a time, was absolute.

These rather unusual managerial developments affected the company's foreign operations. After the outbreak of War, Dunlop officials continued their negotiations with U.S. Rubber with the aim of recovering their trading rights in the United States. In 1916 an agreement was reached whereby Dunlop was allowed to trade under the name of Dunlop in consideration of a royalty of £20,000 ($100,000). This opened the way for the company to resume manufacturing in the United States. Characteristically, however, Sir Arthur du Cros proposed that Dunlop itself should not put up any money for a new American company, but that the finance should be raised elsewhere.[35]

James White soon became involved in this scheme. White had already ventured into the area of Dunlop's foreign companies. In 1917 he formed a company known as the Tyre Investment Trust, and he used this medium to purchase holdings in Dunlop Canada and Dunlop's Far Eastern company. The Tyre Investment Trust then made a series of advisory and information exchange agreements with the main Dunlop company. During 1918 White became involved in the American plan, which had been in abeyance since the United States entered the War. He purchased from Dunlop the right to trade in the United States for £20,000, and a new company—the D.A. Trust—was formed, as the vehicle for the entry into American manufacturing.

The plans to enter the American market were strengthened by the support of Sir Harry McGowan, the Chairman of Nobel Explosives. McGowan was determined to diversify out of the explosives industry after the end of the War, and he was particularly interested in the motor industry and in the potentialities of the United States.[36] McGowan became a member of the Dunlop "Pool", and in March 1919 he joined the Board of Dunlop. In July 1919 he went to the United States, with the specific aim of trying to forge a link

---

[34] D.A. Sir Arthur du Cros to Harvey du Cros, 23 March 1916, File 5005. For a brief account of the career of 'Jimmy' White, see Hubert A. Meredith, *The Drama of Money Making* (n.d.).

[35] D.A. Dunlop Board Minutes, 11 July 1916.

[36] W. J. Reader, *Imperial Chemical Industries: A History*, 1 (1970), p. 328.

between Dunlop and General Motors, the giant American car manufacturer in which Nobel was soon to acquire a large equity stake and a seat on the Board. General Motors, however, gave 85 per cent of its tyre business to the American tyre manufacturer Goodyear, and evinced little interest in doing business with the British company. Despite this setback, McGowan was convinced that Dunlop must establish itself in the United States. He was characteristically impressed by the American rubber manufacturers, especially U.S. Rubber, "If we could get the use of their methods for England", he wrote in August 1919, "we could sweep this market, and we would find it a very profitable business".[37] By July 1920 White and McGowan had formulated an ambitious plan to unify, as McGowan told the Dunlop Board in July 1920, "Dunlop interests as far as possible throughout the World".[38] The Dunlop Rubber Company, D.A. Trust and the Tyre Investment Trust were to be joined in one dynamic, and happy family.

Within a few months the bubble burst. Although McGowan was a serious industrialist, White was primarily a financier concerned to make profits from share dealings. White's arrangements for the financing of the American company were completely inadequate. While a company capitalized at £10 millions was projected by the Dunlop Board, and commitments in the United States undertaken commensurate with that size of capital, by the middle of 1920 White had only found, or claimed to have found, £4 millions. During the autumn of 1920 the beginning of the collapse of the postwar boom in the United States, and the contraction of credit facilities, exposed the fragility of White's financial arrangements. By November 1920 the Dunlop Board was informed of the "urgent need for further funds to prevent suspension of payment in America".[39]

This American crisis coincided with a series of other crises in Dunlop's affairs, a combination of the legacy of James White and the serious recession which also hit the United Kingdom. After the Armistice, White vigorously supported a policy of expansion on all fronts. In particular, he had insisted that the company undertake considerable forward purchases in the rubber and cotton markets in order to meet the expected rise in demand for its products. The cautious advice of Dunlop's own rubber experts was overruled. During the summer of 1920 both the prices of cotton and rubber, and Dunlop's demand for these raw materials, began to decline sharply, and the company was left with huge and expensive commitments in the forward markets. There was also a fiasco with a new range of tyres. By the middle of the War it was widely recognized in the company that its standard type of motor tyre, the doubled-wire grooved pattern, was obsolete compared to the American tyres with rubber non-skid treads which flooded Europe after the outbreak of War. Dunlop's response was constrained by wartime shortages, and the hybrid eventually produced, the Magnum tyre, was a shoddy and unreliable product. By August 1921 it was estimated that Dunlop had had to pay out £75,000 to dissatisfied customers.[40] James White was elected to Dunlop's Board on 21

[37] D.A. H. McGowan to L. Bergin, 12 August 1919, File 5222.
[38] D.A. Dunlop Board Minutes, 5 July 1920.
[39] Ibid., Board Minutes, 19 November 1920.
[40] D.A. Dunlop Investigation, evidence of L. Bergin, Vol. 1.

October 1920, but he resigned on 10 November, leaving Dunlop with a disastrous legacy. In August 1921 the company announced a loss of £8 millions on the year's trading.

V

Dunlop, however, did not collapse. The short-term financial situation was saved with the assistance of F. A. Szarvasy, of the British Foreign and Colonial Corporation. Early in 1921 White's nominees on the Dunlop Board were removed, and eventually a powerful new Chairman, Sir Eric Geddes, was recruited. The various consultancy agreements between the Dunlop company and members of the du Cros family were cancelled, and in 1924 a large capital reconstruction was carried through, the issued capital being written down from just under £20 million to £9·4 million.[41]

The 1920s saw the transformation of Dunlop Rubber's product range and organization. In the early 1920s Dunlop was still almost entirely dependent on the manufacture of tyres and golf balls. After 1924 Geddes launched a policy of product diversification. The acquisition of several rubber firms, especially Macintosh in 1926, gave Dunlop a share of the British general rubber goods and footwear market. As a result, while in 1920 90 per cent of the firm's turnover had been in tyres for motor cars, by 1928 this had fallen to 72 per cent.[42] The next year Dunlopillo latex foam was patented, and in 1933 commercial production of Dunlopillo products began. This product diversification, in turn, prompted Geddes to reform the management structure of Dunlop. A number of product sections or divisions were formed, for plantations, cotton mills, wheels and rims, boots and shoes, and over the next decade this structure became increasingly sophisticated.

The interwar years saw considerable international expansion by Dunlop. The German company was acquired again after the War, and the activities of it and the French Dunlop rapidly expanded during the 1920s. The decision was taken to proceed with the projected American Dunlop Company. In 1927 Dunlop acquired a shareholding in the Australian Dunlop Company, and in the following year the Tyre Investment Trust's shareholding in the Far East and Canadian companies were acquired. Numerous national selling companies were also formed in the 1920s, especially on the Continent and in South America. During the 1930s Dunlop's multinational manufacture was further extended. Factories were opened in South Africa and Eire in 1935, and in India in 1936.

The reasons for this renewed multinational investment differed from those which explained Dunlop's initial foreign ventures. Patent legislation had prompted most of the firm's early investment decisions. After 1920, the most significant influence on Dunlop's international policy was the action, or anticipated action, of major foreign competitors. This was a reflection of Dunlop's changed position in the world rubber industry. Before 1914 Dunlop's main international competitors had been French and German firms, but

---

[41] James White committed suicide in 1927. Sir Arthur du Cros retained his large investment in the Parent Tyre Company, but his fortunes were wrecked after the collapse of the Hatry Group in 1929.
[42] D.A. Dunlop Board Paper No. 1477, 25 October 1929.

after 1918 competition from the American rubber companies also became a major factor. During the 1920s these firms threatened Dunlop's own domestic market. The British Government's imposition of a 33⅓ per cent import duty on tyres in 1927 led to a number of American companies, including Goodyear, Firestone, and Goodrich, and Pirelli of Italy, establishing factories in the United Kingdom. In these conditions, the behaviour of Dunlop began to resemble that of a classic international oligopolist, with foreign investment decisions being substantially affected by the behaviour of its fellow oligopolists.

As for the consequences of Dunlop's postwar multinational investments, the firm was even less successful than before 1914, but for different reasons. While under the du Cros and White regimes management failure by the parent company was clearly at the root of the firm's difficulties, after 1920 a variety of exogeneous factors combined to thwart a much improved management performance.

The most ill-fated of Dunlop's foreign ventures was the American company. Before 1914 Dunlop had suffered by exclusion from the American market: after 1921 it suffered from being a manufacturer in, and for, that highly competitive market.

During 1922 the Dunlop Board decided to proceed with a properly financed manufacturing venture in the United States and the plans were made for a factory at Buffalo, in New York State. By the time the factory was built, however, the prospects for profit in the American tyre market had deteriorated. By the middle of 1923, selling prices had fallen by 50 per cent, while costs remained constant. Various technical changes led to growing excess capacity in the American tyre industry. The industry became fiercely competitive. The number of tyre companies in the United States fell from 300 in 1922, and to 26 in 1935. At first, the parent company gained some benefits from its American manufacturing subsidiary. In particular, the exchange of cost data between Dunlop's United Kingdom factories and the new American factory led to a drive for efficiency at the British factories.[43] However, such advantages were soon overwhelmed by the continuing losses of the American company, shown in Table 2, which by the end of 1936 had reached over £4 millions.[44]

Table 2. *Trading Profits (and Losses) of American Dunlop, 1923-1936*
(£ Sterling)

Year	Profit (or Loss)	Year	Profit (or Loss)
1923	(392,781)	1930	(447,567)
1924	(414,464)	1931	(344,885)
1925	(943,030)	1932	(327,830)
1926	7,311	1933	(192,386)
1927	(67,343)	1934	(66,844)
1928	(524,899)	1935	(158,052)
1929	(223,554)	1936	(165,925)

The depressing financial results of American Dunlop demonstrated the failure of Dunlop's American strategy. Throughout the 1920s the Dunlop

[43] Ibid. No. 2850, 5 December 1935.
[44] Ibid. and No. 3176, 22 January 1937.

46   G. JONES

Board never wavered from the belief that it was vital for the company to maintain a large manufacturing operation in the United States. A manufacturing company in the United States was seen as an important tool in the struggle against the major American tyre manufacturers. "The big market of the world is the United States", the Dunlop Board was reminded in 1928, "and there our competitors are strong and we have not yet grown to the size we would like. There is always a danger so long as that situation lasts that we may be attacked in our strong market and very seriously damaged, whilst our competitors could carry the results of competition of that kind without suffering any appreciable set-back themselves".[45] Moreover, Dunlop's international marketing position was increasingly undermined by the failure of British manufacturers to penetrate many markets outside the United Kingdom. "The preponderance of American cars throughout the world", an internal memorandum concluded in July 1929, "is our greatest weakness as we are not supplying the big American producers with first equipment tyres".[46]

Dunlop's attempts to secure a share of the American first equipment business were undermined by the falling prices of the industry, combined with the traditionally strong links between the large American car manufacturers and the large American rubber companies. Dunlop had entered the market too late to forge any special links with the motor industry giants. Between 1921 and 1927 the wholesale price index of a tyre in the United States fell from 103·5 to 31·5.[47] As Table 3 indicates, Dunlop's first equipment business with manufacturers steadily diminished as American tyre manufacturers engaged in cut-throat price competition.[48]

Table 3. *Dollar Sales of Dunlop America, 1924-34 ('000s US $)*

Year	Retail	Dealer, Distribution and Sports	Export	Manufacturers	Total
1924	–	–	–	–	7,380
1925	–	–	–	–	14,386
1926	–	8,798	1,010	6,003	15,811
1927	–	8,598	1,398	1,677	11,673
1928	–	9,719	983	2,030	12,732
1929	174	8,314	837	742	10,049
1930	2,485	3,083	302	280	6,150
1931	3,013	2,648	118	–	5,779
1932	1,737	2,816	29	–	4,582
1933	1,772	2,327	50	106	4,255
1934	3,438	2,007	109	30	5,584

By the end of the 1920s Dunlop was faced with massive surplus capacity at its factory in Buffalo. During 1929 an average of 17,000 tyres were produced each week, but the factory had a capacity to produce 10,000 tyres a day. Various expedients were suggested to relieve the situation. At one stage a plan to switch some business from the British factories to America was under

---

[45] D.A. Dunlop Board Paper No. 1227, 21 October 1928.
[46] Ibid. No. 1424, July 1929.
[47] J. D. Gaffey, *The Productivity of Labor in the Rubber Tire Manufacturing Industry* (New York, 1940), p. 131.
[48] D.A. Dunlop Board Paper 2850, 5 December 1935.

consideration but this was discarded on the grounds that it "would have a very bad effect on the Company's reputation in England if it became generally known".[49] During the early 1930s Dunlop began to open chain stores selling exclusively Dunlop products. By 1934 this policy had begun to boost retail sales, although only when prices were held below a profit-making level, and sales never generated a sufficiently large turnover to reduce the crippling overhead burden. By the late 1930s the only possibility of relief was seen in the introduction of sports and Dunlopillo products into the American market.[50]

Dunlop's Canadian company had an equally miserable experience in the 1930s, and for the same reasons. The plant operated for much of the decade at below capacity, and at a loss.

The performance of Dunlop's continental subsidiaries was also unsatisfactory, a problem shared by many British enterprises with subsidiaries on the Continent in the interwar period. The French company made annual war-related profits of over £170,000 in the four years ending July 1917 to July 1920, but this was wiped out over the subsequent four years by losses in excess of £670,000.[51] A major handicap was that Michelin monopolized the wheel business in France, as it possessed the French patent for disc wheels until 1928, and thus supplied practically all the tyres for French car manufacturers.

Despite this poor performance, however, the decision was taken in 1923 to expand the capacity of the French business. The motivation behind this policy lay in Dunlop's international business strategy, rather than in any interest in the French market or even in making profits in France. As in the case of the American company, Dunlop's relations with other large tyre companies were a decisive influence. In the early 1920s Dunlop faced serious competition from Michelin, which had secured a substantial share of even the British market. Dunlop's French subsidiary was regarded as "assurance for the Company's general business throughout the World."[52] If Dunlop did not possess a stake in the French market, the Board was told in June 1924, "our principal competitor, having no serious competition, would be enabled to increase his prices in the French market and make corresponding decreases in the English market, and that would have a most serious effect on this Company's business as a whole."[53]

During the late 1920s the threat from Michelin receded, and the French company began to be regarded in a more strictly commercial light. Michelin's business in Britain declined, while Dunlop established itself as a significant force in the French tyre market. At the 1928 Paris Motor Show 41·75 per cent of the tyres exhibited on cars were Dunlop compared to 42·69 per cent belonging to Michelin.[54] Dunlop's sales by value increased by 15 per cent during 1927, and 44 per cent in 1928. In the light of this progress, the activities of Dunlop in France were extended. It was decided in 1929 to build a cotton

[49] Ibid. No. 1424, July 1929.
[50] Ibid. No. 2850, 5 December 1935.
[51] D.A. Dunlop French Income Stock and Dunlop Rubber Company, File 5176.
[52] D.A. Dunlop Board Paper 1369, 26 April 1924.
[53] Ibid. No. 332, 13 June 1924.
[54] Ibid. No. 1242, 26 October 1928.

mill in France, and in 1930 to diversify into wheel manufacture in order to secure a larger share of the car manufacturers' business.[55]

During the 1930s, however, the fortunes of Dunlop in France took a more unfavourable turn. As in many continental markets the Depression cut the demand for tyres. During the early 1930s French motor vehicle production declined, and Dunlop's regular growth in tyre sales ceased after 1930. The tyre factory had to be put on a four-day week in January 1932. Michelin's response throughout the 1930s to depressed market conditions was to cut prices, rather than to enter the kind of market stabilization schemes favoured by the British company. Nevertheless, throughout the 1930s Dunlop made small profits in its French business.

As for Dunlop in Germany, it seems to have been simply assumed after 1918 that the business should be retrieved. The political disturbances in the early 1920s and the great inflation in 1923, however, prompted a prolonged debate about whether the German company should be wound up. It was eventually decided to remain in Germany, primarily because the cost of getting out was probably greater than staying in. Not only would redundancy payments have had to be paid to the company's German workers, but there was no sign of a buyer for the German property. In May 1923 it was definitely decided to keep the German company going, provided it did not make further losses. There were two further motives behind this decision, apart from the costs of closing the German factory. First, there was a belief that there was a "large potential demand". Second, it was hoped that the German factory might produce lower cost products for Dunlop's international trade than the British and French factories.[56]

By 1925 the decision to resume manufacturing in Germany seemed amply justified, as the tyre market expanded. By the end of 1925 the firm's profits were sufficiently large for them to be regarded as a source of embarrassment, which might "create a bad impression with our Workpeople and also with the Authorities".[57] To meet this problem, in December 1925 the capital of German Dunlop was raised from 5 to 9 million marks, and it was raised again in 1929 to 12 millions. By that date Dunlop was in possession of the second largest tyre factory in Germany.

After 1929, however, first economic and then political factors combined to render Dunlop's investment in Germany unprofitable. During 1929 the fortunes of German Dunlop took a downturn, and over the three years 1929 to 1931 lost 1·5 million marks. The company's fortunes improved in 1932 with the general economic recovery in Germany, but political uncertainties continued to cloud the company's fortunes. It was, therefore, with some relief that the company's German management welcomed the Nazi acquisition of power in May 1933. The awkward problem of Dunlop's position as a foreign-owned company in a nationalistic state was relieved by the decision of the Nazi State Commissar in Hanau (where the Dunlop factory was located), who declared that it could "be regarded by all good Germans as a definitely German company without any Jewish influence in the Management".[58]

[55] Ibid. No. 1571, 21 February 1930.
[56] D.A. Dunlop Board Paper No. 69, 18 May 1923.
[57] Ibid. No. 621, 27 November 1925.
[58] Ibid. No. 2294, 26 May 1933.

The honeymoon period was soon over. Even before the Nazi victory, nationalistic pressures had begun to worry Dunlop's German management. By the end of May 1933 it was being suggested, "in view of the national feeling in Germany" that the company should actually sell off part of its equity to German interests.[59] The question of shareholding, however, soon became academic as the government tightened its control over all companies, domestic and foreign owned. In April 1934 a *Fuehrer* was appointed for each German industry. Within months, German Dunlop had been ordered to buy only locally-made goods, and to join the official price cartels. By May 1934 imports of rubber and cotton were controlled by the government. The worst problem of all, however, was the blocking of remittances of profits and interest payments from Germany to Britain. In December 1934 came a decree that any dividend above 6 per cent had to be invested in state bonds, to be repaid to shareholders after four years.[60]

Dunlop Germany found its sales booming during the mid-1930s, but both product-mix and profits were strictly controlled by the state. Moreover, Dunlop's investment in Germany became a hostage, preventing the company from doing little except follow the state's decrees, in the vain hope of better times to come. At the end of December 1936, for example, the company decided to establish further capacity in Germany. This decision was not taken in any hope of the British company securing any profit from the investment, but because "friendly relations with the Government depend upon our willingness to contribute at least as much relatively as other Companies to the motorization of Germany".[61] In the following year, the authorities forced Dunlop to switch from natural rubber to synthetic rubber over a period of two years, a move which caused considerable capital expenditure.[62]

Dunlop's German experience was a vivid demonstration of the increased politicization of the environment in which Dunlop and other British multinational companies operated in the 1930s. "Every country", a Dunlop Board memorandum observed in June 1932, "is becoming more national in its ideas".[63] In Japan, Dunlop's experience was broadly similar to that of Germany. In 1928 Dunlop acquired full control of the Japanese Dunlop Company from the Tyre Investment Trust, and an increase in tariff protection at the end of the decade seemed set fair to make this a profitable investment. However, the growth of military influence in the Japanese government soon began to make the Japanese market look less attractive. Dunlop's response to the growth of nationalistic pressures in Japan was to take on some local colour. In January 1931 the Board agreed to sell 40 per cent of the equity of the Japanese company to local interests, so as to place the Company "in the position of being accepted by the Japanese authorities as a really local Company".[64] Various unforeseen obstacles, however, delayed the implementation of this scheme. in preparation for the admission of outside interests into the Japanese company, its relations with other Dunlop Far Eastern companies

[59] Ibid. No. 2296, 26 May 1933.
[60] Ibid. No. 644, 21 December 1934.
[61] Ibid. No. 3147, 18 December 1936.
[62] Ibid. No. 3201, 26 February 1937.
[63] Ibid. No. 2083, 24 June 1932.
[64] Ibid. No. 1765, 23 January 1931.

had to be put on a revised footing. Moreover, when the company's Japanese workers heard that part of their company might be sold, they demanded a discharge allowance, even though only a transfer of shares was involved.[65]

By the mid-1930s Dunlop was in the frustrating position of having an expanding turnover and profit position in Japan, almost entirely due to military demand, yet the political environment was so hostile that the only rational course was to retrieve as much money as possible from the Japanese investment. By January 1937 a sale of 49 per cent of the equity of the Japanese company had been agreed, and at the suggestion of the Japanese buyers it was also agreed that a further 6 per cent of the equity should be placed with Japanese nominees "so that it may definitely appear that more than a 50 per cent holding is in Japanese hands".[66] The sum involved was £245,000, but tight exchange control laws presented a continuing problem. Schemes were considered to try to obtain the money at a discount, "it being Dunlop's definite policy to get back some of our investment from Japan".[67] It did not prove possible to arrange a sale before 1941, though Dunlop continued to receive some dividends from its subsidiary.

Dunlop built new foreign manufacturing facilities in India, Eire, and South Africa in the 1930s. In all three cases the behaviour of competitors was the decisive factor in making the investment decision, although other influences were also of some importance. In India, the growth of nationalist feeling from the early 1920s led to a consideration of ways to strengthen the firm's local identity. The *swadeshi* movement prompted the company to consider establishing a local rupee capital company instead of selling its products through an agency. The logic of taking this step was reinforced by the Government of India's preference for giving business to Indian-registered companies. A large proportion of Dunlop's business was done with the government or other public bodies. An Indian selling company, therefore, was established, and during the 1930s, in common with several British companies, Dunlop began to consider erecting a factory in India.[68] Although senior management was concerned over nationalism, it was the expanding Indian tyre market which provided the incentive, and the desire to pre-empt the anticipated moves of a rival company, the trigger to the investment decision. In May 1935 Dunlop became convinced "that one of our competitors—and probably Goodyear—will decide to establish such a factory, and India being a part of the Empire, we do not consider that this risk should be incurred".[69] In 1936 a factory was opened at Calcutta.

There were similar factors at work in the decision to establish factories in Eire and South Africa. During the 1930s the Eire government sought to expand the industrial capacity of the country. British companies with a large export trade to the Irish Free State, such as Dunlop and Cadbury's, were put under heavy pressure to establish local factories. In November 1933 Dunlop was informed by the Irish government that if it did not build a factory, it

[65] D.A. Dunlop Board Paper No. 2503, 27 April 1934.
[66] Ibid. No. 3175, 22 January 1937.
[67] Ibid. No. 3335, 23 July 1937.
[68] For the growth of British foreign direct investment in India in this period, see B. R. Tomlinson, 'Private Foreign Investment in India, 1920-1950', *Modern Asian Studies*, 12 (1978), pp. 655-77.
[69] D.A. Dunlop Board Paper 2724, 3 May 1935.

would ask another firm which would be given "a monopoly of the tyre business of the Irish Free State".[70] In the face of this threat, Dunlop's Board gave way and reached an agreement with the government. In July 1934 Dunlop was granted a licence to manufacture tyres and waterproof goods for a period of fifteen years, and in return imports of these commodities were to be restricted in such a way that when Dunlop's "factory [was] in full operation, imports of tyres will only be allowed in those types, sizes or classes which [Dunlop] do not manufacture".[71] In 1935 this scheme was extended into various footwear products. As in India, a need was recognized to give the company a local identity, and local capital was admitted into the subsidiary.

The decision to erect a factory in South Africa in 1935 was partly based on the attractiveness of the rapidly growing South African economy, but once again it was the activities of rival companies which provided the trigger. In this case, the rival was the American company, Firestone, which established a factory at Port Elizabeth. An additional attraction of the South African investment was that it fitted into Dunlop's plan for co-operation with another American tyre manufacturer, Goodyear. In March 1932 Geddes visited the United States, and made an arrangement with Goodyear which involved the "very closest collaboration . . . on all points of interest in the export markets for the year 1933".[72] This kind of arrangement was a common business reaction to the economic vicissitudes of the 1930s, and was found in many industries. In 1934 this co-operation was extended to a series of reciprocal manufacturing agreements, based on the general understanding that "wherever either Dunlop or Goodyear have a factory (other than in the USA, Canada, and GB) they will favourably consider the question of manufacturing for the other party in that territory".[73] As part of this arrangement, Dunlop agreed to manufacture for the American company in South Africa, and Goodyear to manufacture for Dunlop in Argentina.

It is often forgotten that, given the limited development of management accounting in interwar Britain, most firms had only a crude knowledge of their costs and other internal financial information. Dunlop was in a better position than most firms in this respect, for in 1929 it had recruited a former Professor of Accounting at the London School of Economics, F. R. M. de Paula, as Controller of Finance. De Paula pioneered new methods of internal audit and costing at Dunlop. Though crude by later accounting standards, his calculations made clear the general point that during the 1930s the overseas factories detracted from, rather than added to, the overall profitability of the group. In 1936 the company calculated its rate of return on capital invested in some of its foreign subsidiaries. The United States and Canada yielded negative rates of return. Dunlop's French and German companies yielded small returns of 3·9 per cent and 4·6 per cent respectively, although it was impossible to repatriate any profits from Germany. The Japanese company earned 9·2 per cent, but it became increasingly difficult to repatriate those profits. The new South African company delivered a handsome 12·6 per cent

[70] Ibid. No. 2387, 24 November 1933.
[71] Ibid. No. 2540, 27 July 1934.
[72] Ibid. No. 2200, 22 December 1932.
[73] Ibid. No. 2541, 27 July 1934.

during its first year of operation. The highest returns on capital employed, however, were found in Dunlop's home investments. In the early 1930s the return on capital employed at the Fort Dunlop tyre division in Birmingham was estimated at over 35 per cent.[74] A further calculation in 1936 estimated that £6·5 millions, or 53 per cent of the total issued share capital of the Dunlop Rubber Company, was invested in "unproductive" (defined as non-revenue earning) foreign subsidiaries. This included £3·1 million in the American company, £500,000 in Canada, £620,000 in Australia, £450,000 in Germany, and £1·8 million in the overseas plantations (which were rendered unremunerative by the falling world rubber prices of the early 1930s).[75]

VI

This article has explored the multinational growth of Dunlop, one of the pioneer British multinational manufacturing companies, and among the largest before 1939. While A. D. Chandler and others have pointed towards tariffs as the major factor prompting British multinational growth before 1939,[76] Dunlop's experience does not conform to this generalization. Dunlop's foreign investment decisions varied according to time and market. The primary force behind the foreign expansion in the 1890s was the desire to exploit and protect patented technology in important markets. The situation was different in the interwar years, when Dunlop faced large international competitors. Manufacturing investments continued to be located in large markets, but for reasons that were not always related to those markets. Dunlop's international policies were substantially influenced by the behaviour, or anticipated behaviour, of the other large international rubber companies. This is a recognized feature of multinational behaviour in the contemporary world.[77] Government policies, including tariffs, were the second most important influence on the company's decision-making in this sphere. Neither the factory in Eire would have been built, nor the German factory expanded, without such pressure.

As for Dunlop's performance as a multinational manufacturer, it is clear that the firm's foreign subsidiaries did not produce great financial returns to their parent, and with the exception of the American company in the 1920s there is little evidence of any technological or organizational benefits being transferred from subsidiaries to parent company. Both before 1914 and in the interwar years the British company regarded its foreign subsidiaries' performance as unsatisfactory, though it needs to be borne in mind that in most cases export was not an alternative to local manufacture. The reasons for the poor performance of Dunlop's foreign investments before 1921 are to be found within the firm. The initial strategy of licensing and minority shareholdings proved very unsatisfactory. While a painful "learning process" might be anticipated when a firm begins manufacturing abroad, in Dunlop's case the Du Cros management seemed very slow to correct its mistakes. The

---

[74] D.A. Dunlop Board Papers for 1937.
[75] Ibid. No. 3026, 1936.
[76] Alfred D. Chandler, 'The Growth of the Transnational Industrial Firm in the United States and the United Kingdom: A Comparative Analysis', *Econ. Hist. Rev.* 2nd ser. XXXIII (1980), p. 401.
[77] See F. T. Knickerbocker, *Oligopolistic Reaction and the Multinational Enterprise* (Boston, 1973).

BRITISH MULTINATIONAL FIRMS   53

legacy of this early period continued to handicap Dunlop after 1921. In particular, the fact that Dunlop only launched its American factory in 1922 meant that it was not well placed to survive the intense competitive struggle seen in the American rubber industry over the next two decades. However, most of Dunlop's difficulties in the interwar years do seem to have been exogenous to the firm. The Geddes management successfully revived the French and German companies in the 1920s, and struggled energetically to reduce the American losses. However, during the 1930s the combination of world-wide depression, competition, and surplus capacity in the United States, and exchange controls in Germany and Japan, acted as major constraints on profitability.

Without more case studies it is difficult to ascertain the extent to which Dunlop's experience was representative of other British mulitnationals before 1939. An extreme contrast to Dunlop's performance was the brilliant success of Courtaulds' American Viscose Company, at least before the late 1930s. Yet not even Courtaulds was immune from adversity, for the firm's subsidiaries on the continent and elsewhere lost money in the interwar years.[78] The performance of the foreign subsidiaries of the other firms which have been researched in detail is similarly mixed. Before 1914 Lever Brothers' factories in Belgium and Canada were very profitable, but those in the United States and Australia were long-term loss-makers.[79] A study of Cadbury's foreign direct investments in the interwar years has revealed substantial long-term losses in Canada and Australia, balanced by large profits in New Zealand.[80] Reddaway reported the same diversity of experience in his study of British multinationals in the period 1955-64.[81] Further case studies may eventually permit generalizations linking performance with particular markets, products, periods or strategies, as well as comparisons with continental and American multinationals. One conclusion already seems clear. British multinational investment before 1939 was not always a licence to print money.

London School of Economics

[78] D. C. Coleman, *Courtaulds* (Oxford, 1969), II, pp. 374-8, 384-428.
[79] C. Wilson, *History of Unilever* (1954), I, pp. 191, 194-8, 202-6. D. K. Fieldhouse, *Unilever Overseas* (1978), pp. 64-7.
[80] Geoffrey Jones, 'Multinational Chocolate: Cadbury Overseas, 1918-1939' (*Business History*, forthcoming).
[81] W. B. Reddaway, *Interim Report*, p. 36.

[20]

MULTINATIONAL CHOCOLATE: CADBURY OVERSEAS, 1918–39

By GEOFFREY JONES

I

There are still comparatively few archivally based case studies of the historical development of British multinational firms.[1] Many generalisations on this subject rest precariously on the foundation of a few oft-quoted examples and a morass of often dubious secondary literature. There are, for example, a number of assertions about the preference of British firms for making investments in the British Empire and Commonwealth. By the 1950s 70 per cent of British foreign direct investment was located in the Commonwealth, primarily in Australia, Canada, New Zealand and South Africa.[2] This 'Empire preference' seems to have originated in the inter-war years. The reasons for the geographical direction of British multinational investment in this period have never been systematically explored, but various writers have cast the Empire as a 'haven of sanity and security' and a 'safe-haven' for British firms. An implication is that the British firms which invested in the Empire did so to avoid the competitive rigours found elsewhere, and followed the 'path of least resistance'.[3]

This article looks at the experience of one classic inter-war Empire investor, Cadbury. Cadbury built up a large export trade in chocolate and confectionery before 1914, but did not undertake any overseas manufacture. After 1918 the firm established or acquired factories in Canada (1920), Australia (1921), New Zealand (1930), the Irish Free State (1933) and South Africa (1937). Almost nothing has been published about the firm's multinational growth, or indeed about any aspect of its performance before the Second World War.[4] This article, drawing on surviving material in the firm's archives, examines the origins and development of the multinational investments of Cadbury in the Empire before 1939.

II

By the time Cadbury Brothers established its first foreign factories the firm held a strong position in the British chocolate and confectionery market, and had large export sales. The growth of Cadbury from a small family firm to a large manufacturing company did not rest on a single product innovation, such as Courtauld's purchase of the artificial silk patent.[5] Instead, the firm's growth came in a series of stages. In 1831 John Cadbury had begun manufacturing cocoa and chocolate for drinking. The firm became Cadbury Brothers in 1847, but went into decline in the late

1850s. The firm's first major breakthrough came in 1866 when the second generation of Cadbury Brothers introduced an improved cocoa into Britain. Previous cocoa powders had contained all the cocoa butter found in the cocoa bean, and various additives such as treacle had had to be added to make them palatable. Cadbury imported a cocoa press developed in Holland, which removed some of the cocoa butter. Cadbury Cocoa Essence was advertised – at a time when there was a growing public debate about food adulteration – as 'Absolutely Pure and therefore Best'. Cadbury Brothers' second innovation came when the firm began using surplus supplies of cocoa butter to make eating chocolates, challenging the previous dominance of the British market by Continental firms. Milk chocolate, however, remained virtually a monopoly of Swiss manufacturers, who had first developed the product in 1876. In 1905, however, Cadbury Dairy Milk Chocolate (widely known both inside and outside the firm as simply 'CDM') was launched, based on a recipe developed to suit English tastes. The product was of exceptional quality and was a great sales success. In 1906 Bournville Cocoa, which had a stronger chocolate flavour than Cocoa Essence, was launched. CDM and Bournville Cocoa provided the basis for the firm's rapid pre-war expansion.

The strong position of Cadbury in the British market was shared with two other leading manufacturers, J.S. Fry of Bristol, founded in 1761 (when Joseph Fry purchased the chocolate patent of Walter Churchman), and Rowntrees of York, founded in 1862. Before the First World War, two major trends in the industry had been the increasing co-operation between the three Quaker firms on levels of advertising expenditure, sales policies and prices, and the relative decline of Fry under the long chairmanship between 1886 and 1913 of Joseph Storrs Fry II. The War accentuated both trends. In early 1917 Cadbury and Fry held the first 'Cheltenham Conference', which fixed minimum home and export prices for cocoa, chocolate and confectionery. Rowntrees joined the conference in 1918. In May 1919 Cadbury and Fry merged their financial interests in a new holding company, the British Cocoa and Chocolate Company Ltd. Cadbury dominated the new company, although Fry retained their own board, organisation and products, and part of the capital of Fry was held by outside interests. In March 1918 Rowntrees also discussed a merger with Cadbury, but the negotiations were subsequently discontinued.[6] Rowntrees approached Cadbury again in 1921 and 1930 with merger proposals, which Cadbury declined on both occasions.[7] However, by 1930, even without Rowntrees, the British Cocoa and Chocolate Company Ltd. had become the twenty-fourth largest British manufacturing company in terms of estimated market value of capital.[8]

Cadbury established a large export trade before 1914, which was organised through a series of agents in various foreign markets. The firm began exporting its products during the 1870s. By 1897 the firm had agents or depots in Australia, Canada, France, India, South Africa and Turkey.[9] By 1900 exports represented 10 per cent of the value of Cadbury domestic sales of cocoa, and 22 per cent of the value of the firm's domestic chocolate sales. By 1911 the percentages were 18 per cent and 36 per cent respectively.[10] Most of these exports went to Australasia, South Africa and India. Between 1911 and 1914 nearly 60 per cent of Cadbury exports (by value) went to Australia, 13 per cent to South Africa and 10 per cent to India. National tastes in chocolate and confectionery vary widely, and the Cadbury product offered a peculiarly British taste. Cadbury products were eaten and drunk by British descendants, whether immigrants or, as in the case of India, expatriates. On the Continent, or even in the United States, Cadbury found it almost impossible to develop a market for its products.

There was no question of Cadbury engaging in overseas manufacture before 1914. The formation of the Australian Federation in 1901 provoked some fears at Bournville about protection. Edward Cadbury visited Australia during that year, and gave '£50 to the funds of the Free Trade party'.[11] However, Cadbury held such a large share of the Australian, and other Empire, markets, and tariffs remained sufficiently low, that local manufacture was ruled out. In May 1911 the Board 'definitely decided not to consider a suggestion by one of their Australian representatives that they should manufacture in Australia'.[12] The firm's only foreign direct investment abroad was the purchase in 1897 of two estates in Trinidad on which cacao beans were planted. The aim was to secure information on the cultivation of cacao, and most of the firm's requirements were met by 'direct buying' from producers on the Gold Coast.[13] Cadbury policies, therefore, were in marked contrast to those of several Continental chocolate and confectionery firms which made foreign direct investments before 1914. The German chocolate manufacturer Stollwerke, for instance, established a large factory in the United States before the war. In a related field, the Swiss combination formed in 1905, the Nestlé & Anglo-Swiss Condensed Milk Company, built up a widespread multinational empire in the milk food industry, with factories in Britain, the United States, Australia, Norway, Germany and Spain. Nestlé marketed chocolates for the Swiss company Peter, Cailler & Kohler from 1904, although it did not manufacture chocolate itself until 1929 when it acquired the Swiss chocolate firm.

III

The British chocolate manufacturers were impelled to establish their first foreign factories by the repercussions of the First World War. The War seriously damaged the large British chocolate and confectionery export trade. At first the damage was slight, but from the beginning of 1917 it became progressively harder to obtain export licences for such non-essential commodities. In 1913 Cadbury had exported to Australia cocoa worth £75,542 and chocolate worth £231,479. By 1918 these figures had fallen to £9,608 and £34,480 respectively.[14] Moreover, there was evidence that this decline in trade would not prove temporary. The Cadbury market during the war was taken over by local manufacturers, especially the firm of MacRobertson's, and it was known that the Australian government was sympathetic to these local firms. After the end of the war the government did institute tariffs and a licensing system designed to limit exports. There were similar developments in Canada, where by 1918 the once dominant share of Fry in the chocolate and confectionery trade had disappeared, although the firm retained an important share of the cocoa market.[15] Competition from American companies, and growing protectionism, put Fry in Canada in a similar position to Cadbury in Australia.

These developments lay behind the decisions to establish the first overseas factories. In December 1916 Fry approached Cadbury with the idea of establishing a joint cocoa and chocolate factory in Canada, but Cadbury turned down the proposal because of the strength of American competition in the market. Fry later considered going alone, but by 1919 had settled on a joint venture with a Canadian company.[16] In the same year Cadbury decided to start local manufacture in Australia.

Cadbury and Fry adopted different investment strategies for their respective foreign ventures. In Australia, Cadbury and Fry allied themselves with James Pascall Ltd., a small British confectionery firm. The idea of the joint venture to exploit a foreign market had several precedents in the pre-war British chocolate and confectionery industry. Several firms had established joint depots or representatives in foreign countries with each other. Cadbury established a depot in Buenos Aires with the Cambridge jam manufacturer Chivers, while Fry and Reckitts of Hull shared an agent for South Africa. The economics of an industry where exports to many markets were relatively small and where it made sense to share overheads encouraged such arrangements, and they were facilitated by the Nonconformist religious beliefs of the families controlling a considerable number of firms in the industry. The formation in 1920 of a joint venture company, Cadbury-Fry-Pascall Ltd. (CFP) to construct and operate a factory in Australia built on this tradition in the industry. Originally 50 per cent of the capital was allotted to Cadbury, and 25 per cent each to Fry and Pascall, but it was eventually decided that expenses would be charged 10/16 for Cadbury, 5/16 for Fry and 1/16 for Pascall. By the end of 1922 nearly £500,000 had been spent on the factory, and by the end of 1924 the three firms had invested £700,000 in the Australian venture.

In Canada Fry also opted for a joint venture, but with the Canadian subsidiary of an American firm. The chosen firm was Messrs Lowney of Boston, which owned a 70 per cent share in a factory at Montreal. An investigation of the Lowney Canadian company found it to be a 'successful business with definite profits'.[17] On 4 November 1919 Fry and Lowney reached an agreement. A complicated organisation consisting of three different boards was formulated. A holding company was created, the Canadian Cocoa and Chocolate Company Ltd., which held the shares of the two operating companies. The American Lowney Company had three directors on the holding company's board, and Fry two. Beneath the holding company were two manufacturing companies, Lowney and a newly-established J. S. Fry and Sons (Canada) Ltd. Fry paid up 50 per cent of J. S. Fry and Sons (Canada)'s authorised capital of $1 million, and this was to be used for the acquisition of a site for a factory in Canada. Fry were not, therefore, strictly buying themselves into a going manufacturing concern. Instead, the agreement committed them to build their own new factory, but in alliance with the Lowney Company. It also placed Fry as the minority shareholder in the whole concern.

The financial performances of the Australian and Canadian subsidiaries were very poor during the 1920s. Table 1 outlines profits, or rather losses, earned by CFP for its British shareholders during the 1920s.

TABLE 1
CFP NET PROFITS (OR LOSSSES) 1923–30[18]
(£ STERLING)

1922/23 (year end 30 June)	(£38,000)
1923/24	(£21,600)
1924/25	(£33,300)
1925/26	(£31,300)
1926/27	(£33,600)
1927/28	£6,000
1928/29	(£17,800)
1929/30	(£6,000)

By the end of 1927 CFP had accumulated large losses, and a brief upsurge in profits in the late 1920s was reversed by the onset of the Depression. Although comparable profit and loss figures for the Canadian investment of Fry have not survived, it is clear that the subsidiary made losses throughout the 1920s and was a source of considerable worry to its parents.[19] Overall, by 1929 the cost to Cadbury and Fry of establishing the Australian and Canadian firms, plus the cost of meeting their subsequent losses, probably exceeded £1.5 million. This compares with the Hannah estimate of the market value of the whole British Cocoa and Chocolate Company Ltd. of £10.3 million in 1930. Australia and Canada may have been havens of 'sanity and security', but this was clearly no guarantee that a subsidiary would be a commercial success.

The fundamental difficulty in both Australia and Canada throughout the 1920s was one of turnover. The Australian company factory was forced to manufacture well below capacity, with the result that its costs of production were extremely high. The factory was planned with a capacity of 2,000 tons per annum, but for most of the 1920s sales were only sufficient to keep the factory working at 50 per cent capacity.[20] Fry faced a similar problem in Canada. The firm's Breakfast Cocoa held 50 per cent of the Canadian cocoa market during the 1920s, but failed to capture a significant share of the chocolate and confectionery market. The large market for cheap 5 or 10 cent chocolate bars was dominated by five or six local producers, plus American and even British imports.

The loss-making predicament of the Australian and Canadian subsidiaries was undoubtedly partly a function of the falling incomes of the two Dominions in the wake of falling primary product prices. However, three more specific factors can be isolated. The first was the strength of local competition. Australia was far from being a virgin territory for British manufacturers even before the First World War. While local entrepreneurs did not possess the resources to establish manufacture in the more capital – and technology – intensive industries such as artificial silk, they had made considerable progress in the consumer goods sector, and these firms were quite capable of offering effective competition to the subsidiaries of British firms. Lever Brothers' Australian soap factory, for example, made almost no progress against its local competitor during the 1900s.[21] Cadbury faced the same problem. The local chocolate manufacturers who had taken over the Cadbury market share during the war proved hard to dislodge. The leading Australian firm, MacRobertson's, produced a wide range of goods, of an equal quality to those of CFP. CFP's attempts to compete over a wide front with MacRobertson's resulted in the firm manufacturing small quantities of a large number of product lines, which further forced up costs. In Canada Fry faced aggressive competition from American and other British firms. Rowntree in this period still relied on imports rather than local manufacture, but their local management adopted highly aggressive selling strategies which Fry regarded as very 'unQuakerly'. 'Their methods of business', a member of the Cadbury family remarked after a visit to Canada in 1927, 'are not those one would expect from the York House'.[22]

The second factor which handicapped the Australian and Canadian subsidiaries was the adoption of a number of mistaken or inappropriate managerial strategies. This was in part a reflection of the tendency of firms making their first direct investment in a foreign country to experience a painful learning process.

In Australia, the decision to build the factory at Claremont, near Hobart in Tasmania, proved costly. Melbourne had originally been considered the most promising location. However, partly because it was believed that Tasmania's climate was more conducive to good chocolate manufacture, and partly because the island gave more scope for a garden factory on the lines the firm had built in Bournville in the late nineteenth century, a site near Hobart was chosen.[23] Transport costs were generally high in Australia, which had several geographically dispersed centres of population, but the Hobart site made them particularly high for CFP. Hobart's population was tiny, and only three per cent of Australia's population lived in the whole of Tasmania during the 1920s. The products for the rest of the population had to be shipped by sea, at distances varying from 470 miles to Melbourne to over 2,300 miles to Perth. In contrast, CFP's largest competitors had factories in one or other of the main consumption centres – MacRobertson in Melbourne and Nestlé in Sydney.

Cadbury also had difficulties getting the right kind of local management. The management of CFP was initially placed in the hands of the man who had acted as the Cadbury agent in Australia before 1914. He failed, however, to make the transition from being a successful selling agent to running a manufacturing company, and his failure contributed to getting CFP off to a bad start. In 1924 he was retired and replaced by someone who had been head chemist at Bournville for the previous twenty years. This was also, however, not an ideal appointment, as the new man's expertise was not in marketing, the weak point of the company.

The dual parentage of CFP caused additional difficulties. Chocolate and confectionery recipes were closely guarded secrets, and Cadbury were particularly anxious that Pascall should not learn the secrets of their products which were being manufactured in Australia. Consequently, they refused for several years to manufacture their flagship brand, CDM, in Tasmania in case the 'special process' became known to Pascall.[24] Pascall reacted with some frustration to this policy, one of the Pascall family reflecting in 1924 that, on past experience, it was 'more likely that a process would become known to MacRobertson's of Melbourne than to our own people at Claremont'.[25] A further difficulty was that the Pascall holding in CFP prevented the company from exporting its products to New Zealand, which continued to be supplied directly from the United Kingdom. Cadbury regarded the possibility of the Tasmanian factory's supplying New Zealand as a chance to reduce the factory's surplus capacity. Pascall, however, held a very strong position in the New Zealand market, and had no desire to encourage the sale of Cadbury-Fry products in that country.[26]

There were many echoes of CFP's managerial and strategic problems in Canada. Fry appointed their old sales agent as chief manager, and as in Australia this proved an unsatisfactory decision. The man refused to co-operate with Lowney. Moreover, in order to penetrate the cheaper chocolate market he produced a chocolate made from oatmeal and flour, which was so awful 'that it had only to be tried once to be avoided in future'.[27] Tons of the product had to be withdrawn from the market, at great cost both to the firm's finances and to its reputation.[28]

Fry also ran into problems with its partners. At the end of 1922 it became clear that Lowney of Boston were in financial difficulties. By July 1923 all the firm's assets were in the hands of the First National Bank of Boston, and Fry found themselves as the junior partner of this American bank in the Canadian venture. For the next six months there was an anxious debate in England about future strategy. Some members of the Cadbury Board felt that the Canadian investment was better written off.[29] Eventually, however, it was decided that the dangers of having the Fry name controlled by someone else were sufficiently great that it was worth buying J. S. Fry and Sons (Canada)'s freedom from the Canadian Cocoa and Chocolate Ltd. After hard negotiations with the Boston bank, Fry re-purchased full control of its Canadian subsidiary for just over £205,200.[30]

A third factor which helps to explain, or at least put into perspective, the performance of the Australian and Canadian subsidiaries, is that the affairs of the foreign subsidiaries were low down in the British parent company's priorities in the inter-war years. Managerial attention and capital resources were primarily focused on two areas of the firm's activity in Britain. First, during the 1920s, a programme of mechanisation and rationalisation was initiated at the Cadbury Bournville factory complex. This resulted in a considerable rise in labour productivity and fall in production costs by the 1930s, and was an underlying factor in allowing Cadbury to achieve a major breakthrough in the British market during the 1930s with their '2 oz for 2d.' campaign with CDM.[31]

Secondly, substantial resources were allocated to reinvigorate Fry. At the time of the merger with Cadbury, Fry possessed seven separate small factories in central Bristol. Cadbury dictated the removal of Fry to a central site, Somerdale, located in the nearby countryside. The cost of this relocation during the 1920s was substantial, especially as the still largely autonomous Fry management failed to reverse the firm's decline. During the decade sales of Fry products slumped both in Britain and in the export markets. After 1922 Cadbury received no dividends on its Fry shares, while after 1926 it had to start giving money to Fry in order to pay dividends to outside shareholders. The price of failure was a slow erosion of Fry autonomy. In 1929 the Export Offices at the two firms were amalgamated. In the same year Cadbury took over the management, and most of the shares, of J.S. Fry & Sons (Canada) Ltd., and an Overseas Factory Committee was established to supervise both the Canadian and the Australian manufacturing companies. Subsequently, Cadbury purchased most of the Fry holding in the Australian subsidiary.[32] In 1935 Cadbury completely bought out the outside shareholding in Fry and it became a wholly-owned subsidiary.

The extension and modernisation of the Bournville factory and the decline of Fry had two consequences for the overseas subsidiaries. On the one hand, the managerial attention of the parent company was largely preoccupied with domestic matters during the 1920s. On the other, the expected or realised gains made from the improvements at Bournville encouraged the Cadbury management to take a long-term view of the prospects of the overseas subsidiaries. Although there was disappointment about the losses in the 1920s, the view was taken that the long-term prospects were good. 'In the Australian and Canadian businesses', a memorandum written in 1927 noted, 'the B.C. and C. Company have an insurance for the future. While the Home firms are able to pay a substantial dividend it appears ... comparatively unimportant to receive dividends from the businesses abroad.'[33]

IV

The end of the 1920s saw Cadbury, so widely quoted as a classic Empire investor, engage in a curious flirtation with Germany. Cadbury had never experienced any success in its attempts to sell its goods to the Continent.

As early as 1877 a depot had been opened in Paris, but its main purpose was to bring the prestige of a Paris address to the firm rather than sell chocolate. During the early 1920s Cadbury regarded the Continent as an impenetrable market. In December 1921 it was decided to re-open a depot in Paris, but this made few sales and in 1923 it was closed, confirming Cadbury opinion 'that on the whole it is undesirable to push trade on the Continent'.[34]

During 1928, however, Cadbury began to consider a link with a German chocolate company. Cadbury were anxious to enter the high class confectionery and boiled sugar goods market in Britain, and it was believed that a link with a German firm might provide the production and marketing expertise for this strategy. It was also thought that a link with a Continental chocolate firm might provide Cadbury with a key for the penetration of certain 'difficult' export markets, such as the United States. A further consideration was that Rowntrees were rumoured to be considering a German factory. Lastly, there were tentative thoughts that the Continental market might substitute for an apparently saturated home market – 'an opportunity for expansion ... which is apparently being denied to us in England'.[35] By July 1928 Cadbury had located a small firm producing high-class cocoa, chocolate and confectionery products, Burk & Braun, which lacked capital for expansion and seemed ideal for a partnership with Cadbury. A scheme developed for the formation of a new German company jointly owned by Cadbury and Burk & Braun. This arrangement was preferred to a majority holding, 'which would entail responsibility for the control of a business in a foreign country'.[36]

As negotiations developed, Cadbury plans to make a quasi-direct investment in the German company receded. This was partly because of worries over assuming managerial responsibilities, but even more because the Cadbury management was disturbed by the morality of business in Germany. During 1928 members of the Cadbury Board had visited Burk & Braun, and had been impressed by the firm's factory and the two partners, who seemed to have 'a very happy family life'.[37] An accountant's report, however, discovered that the German firm was not as straightforward in its dealings with the German fiscal authorities as Cadbury wished. It was decided that until Burk & Braun were 'prepared to keep accounts and render returns on the English standard', a partnership was out of the question.[38]

Burk & Braun declined the invitation to reform their accounts, and so Cadbury insisted on a more flexible arrangement. In 1928 Burk & Braun were given a loan of £25,000 at five per cent for five years. At any time within these five years, the British Cocoa and Chocolate Company had the option of calling upon Burk & Braun to convert their business into a limited company in which the British Cocoa and Chocolate Company would have the right to take up to 50 per cent of the controlling capital.[39] Over the next few years the German company attempted to increase the Cadbury commitment, whilst the latter were only prepared to expand their loan. In June 1929 Burk & Braun were granted a further loan of £10,000 at eight per cent. In September 1929 the German company asked for further funds. This request hardened the attitude of Cadbury. It was decided to lend Burk & Braun yet a further £15,000 at eight per cent, but all idea of a partnership was finally abandoned. There were to be no further loans, and the company were instructed 'to keep their accounts in such a manner as to give a true statement of the company's position'.[40]

The investment in Burk & Braun was not a great success. None of the Cadbury objectives were achieved, and even the arrangements for exchange of information had little effect. During the early 1930s Burk & Braun were badly hit by the German Depression, and it seemed for a time that the whole investment would be lost. Despite this, the Joint Board of Cadbury and Fry resolved that they were 'not prepared to face taking over the responsibility for this business and would, if necessary, submit to the loss of the money already abandoned rather than make a further investment'.[41] Burk & Braun did not in fact collapse, but German exchange-control regulations soon prevented regular repayments of the loan. By the outbreak of the Second World War Cadbury were owed £37,414. In August 1940 this was written down to a nominal sum of £5 in the British Cocoa & Chocolate Company books.[42] Cadbury's burnt fingers on the Continent were, at least, not unique. A number of leading British companies and banks lost larger sums in inter-war Europe, and indeed even after 1945 the Continent has proved a difficult area for many British multinationals.[43]

V

The unfortunate German experience strengthened the Cadbury resolve to concentrate its activities on the Empire. During the 1930s the firm established factories in New Zealand, the Irish Free State and South Africa. These ventures were more successful than both the earlier Australian and Canadian investments, and the ill-fated German adventure.

Two factors prompted Cadbury to undertake further foreign investments. The most important was the further spread of protectionism, and other pressures for local manufacture. Cadbury were consistently reluctant to embark on further foreign manufacture, but equally saw it as an unavoidable step if tariffs went too high. '`The Board do not think it advisable at the present time to build any factories for the manufacture of Cocoa or Chocolate abroad,' the Cadbury board minuted in March 1928; 'it is, however, thought desirable to make certain preparations in case of sudden increase in tariff in South Africa, New Zealand or the Irish Free State which would make it impossible to export'.[44] Decisions to undertake local manufacture followed tariff increases. In 1928 the New Zealand Government increased the duty on chocolate from 3d. in the pound in weight to 25 per cent *ad valorem*, and a decision to establish a factory followed a year afterwards.[45]

In the Irish Free State rising customs duties prompted discussions about local manufacture from 1927 onwards. In 1928 some consideration was given to the idea of having Cadbury products manufactured under licence, but no final agreement was reached.[46] By the 1930s Cadbury were losing money on their Irish exports, but a concern to maintain production at the British factories postponed for a time a decision on a local factory.[47] In 1932, however, rumours of a 150 per cent rise in cocoa and chocolate duties, and pressure from the Irish Government, finally persuaded Cadbury to build a factory. In August a new Irish company, Fry-Cadbury (Ireland) Ltd., was formed, and ten months later the Irish factory began production.

South Africa was the last country to acquire a Cadbury factory before the Second World War. Both Cadbury and Fry had long-established links with the country. Fry had exported their products to South Africa since the early nineteenth century, and in 1885 had appointed a local agent. In 1880 Cadbury cocoa appeared in the country, and in 1894 the firm dispatched a representative to Cape Town. Until the mid-1920s, however, no interest was shown in local manufacture. Duties were low, and Cadbury and Fry held a very large share of the cocoa and plain chocolate markets. The overall market size was also small. A decision by Rowntrees in 1926 to establish a factory in South Africa in partnership with a local firm stimulated the first thoughts at Cadbury about local manufacture. A report in 1927 concluded that 'if the duty goes up on cocoa and block chocolate, or if the Rowntree combination affects our position, we might consider a small plant at Cape Town', but no further steps were taken.[48] During 1929, however, Cadbury sales began to fall due to 'increased competition'.[49] An arrangement was made under which Rowntrees manufactured certain Cadbury products at their South African factory, in return for which Cadbury Fry Pascall manufactured certain Rowntrees products in Australia.

During the early 1930s rumours of increased tariffs rose. The agreement with Rowntrees did not work altogether satisfactorily, with Cadbury suspecting that Rowntrees delayed the production of certain of their new lines. In 1935 it was finally decided to look for a site for a factory, as 'an insurance against the possibility of export being at a prohibitive cost'.[50] At first Cape Town, with its large local market, was the favoured area, but at the beginning of 1936 considerations of milk supply, climate, and good port facilities for importing West African cocoa beans, led to a site being purchased at Port Elizabeth. In 1937 the construction of a small, £30,000 factory was begun, designed to serve as a basis in case more extensive manufacture became necessary.

The contributory stimulus towards local manufacture in the three countries was, as seen in the case of South Africa, the behaviour of competitors. In the United Kingdom, Rowntrees were the main competitors of Cadbury, and from the mid-1920s they established foreign factories in various countries. A Rowntree factory was established in the Irish Free State in 1926, and in Canada and South Africa Rowntrees purchased shares of local concerns. Rowntrees were thus well placed to compete with Cadbury-Fry sales in these markets. Nestlé provided even more vigorous competition. The firm completely took over its Swiss chocolate supplier in 1929, and expanded rapidly in the world chocolate market in the 1930s using its already large milk food production facilities. In 1932 Nestlé were considered by Cadbury as their 'chief competitor' in world markets.[51]

The foreign investments of the 1930s were more successful than those of the 1920s. The New Zealand subsidiary, Cadbury Fry Hudson Ltd., was profitable from the beginning. Table 2 outlines the growth in the firm's sales and profits.

TABLE 2

SALES AND PROFITS OF CADBURY-FRY-HUDSON 1930–45[52]

(£000 STERLING)

Years	Net Sales	Profits after Tax
1930–33	1,176	29.1
1934–37	1,560	77.7
1937–41	2,438	82.2
1942–45	3,554	141.3

During the early 1930s the dividends from Cadbury-Fry-Hudson helped to meet the losses from the Canadian and Australian factories, and the company's rising turnover prompted several factory extensions during the 1930s. Again, although the statistics seem to have been lost, it is clear that both the Irish and the South African factories were making profits within a year of beginning production.

The reasons for the greater success of the three new investments of the 1930s were partly exogenous to Cadbury. Living standards in South Africa, for example, rose sharply in the 1930s with a 70 per cent expansion in Gross National Product between 1932 and 1937. However, two other factors were important. The first was that Cadbury avoided some of the mistakes seen in Australia and Canada in the 1920s. In New Zealand, it was decided to ally with a local firm, ideally a confectioner with expertise in the making of chocolate centres. Conveniently, Cadbury were approached by a local firm, R. Hudson & Company of Dunedin, with a proposal to form a joint manufacturing firm. In March 1930 Cadbury purchased a controlling share of Hudson's assets for £17,000, and a new company was formed – Cadbury-Fry-Hudson Ltd., with a capital of £400,000. Cadbury were entitled to 50 per cent of the dividends earned by the company. Cadbury transferred the right to manufacture its chocolate to the new company, but only the selling agency for Bournville Cocoa, which was to continue to be exported from Britain.

The decision to retain the Hudson family in senior positions in the company undoubtedly enabled the company to benefit fully from Hudson's familiarity with local market conditions. Moreover, an effort was made to avoid the difficulties that had damaged the relationships between Fry and Lowney and even Cadbury, Fry and Pascall in Australia. In 1933, for example, it was agreed that Hudsons' Milk Chocolate would be made to the Cadbury recipe and process up to the stage at which a differing flavour was added. This reduced considerably the degree of duplication in the firms' manufacturing processes.[53] Meanwhile, in Ireland and South Africa, Cadbury opted for wholly-owned subsidiaries, which removed the dangers of inter-parent tensions of the kind seen in Australia and Canada.

A second factor which assisted the profitability of the three new subsidiaries was the trend towards cartelisation in many markets during the 1930s. Competition between chocolate manufacturers gave way to market-sharing agreements and reciprocal manufacturing arrangements. In 1930 Cadbury-Fry-Hudson, for example, reached an agreement with Rowntrees whereby it manufactured certain Rowntrees products for New Zealand, and similar arrangements were made later with Sharp's, the toffee manufacturers. These agreements helped to reduce considerably the firm's manufacturing and selling overheads.

The 1930s saw some recovery in the fortunes of the Australian and Canadian subsidiaries. Initial mistakes were corrected, and changed market conditions enabled the companies to move into profitability by the end of the decade. The first years of the decade, however, began extremely badly for the companies as they floundered in the trough of the Depression and the sharp downturn in living standards caused by the collapse of the primary product markets. CFP's total sales in value fell by nearly 40 per cent, and in tonnage by 30 per cent between 1929 and 1931. Losses mounted, with a £23,000 loss in 1930/1, £6,000 in 1931/2, and £16,000 in 1932/3. CFP was also badly affected by the currency instability of the period. Exchange losses exceeded £250,000 between 1929 and 1932. A report on the year 1932/3 observed that prices were so low that it was 'quite impossible to manufacture any lines competitive in quality and price at a profit'.[54] In May 1933 it was decided to write the capital of the company down. The value of CFP's 212,750 £1 ordinary shares was written down to 1/- each, writing off CFP's accumulated debt of £192,356 and writing down the value of the factory.[55] In a generous gesture to relieve the substantial loss this involved for the small firm of James Pascall, Cadbury purchased £4,000 ordinary shares in Pascall.

By the time of the capital write-down, CFP were already on the way to recovery. Apart from the recovery in the Australian economy, two factors were particularly important. First, as elsewhere, the problem of low turnover was to some extent solved by agreements to manufacture or sell other firms' products. During 1931 CFP reached an agreement with Rowntrees to manufacture certain of their lines in Australia, and in the same year an agreement was made whereby CFP acquired the selling agency of the White Signet Company, a firm which manufactured cheap confectionery. By 1932/3 sales of White Signet and other firms' products were 30 per cent of total CFP sales turnover, significantly reducing the overhead costs of the firm's sales organisation.

Secondly, the competitive nature of the market was reduced. Mac-Robertson's declined in vitality as Mr MacRobertson aged (he was 79 in 1938). CFP and Nestlé came to dominate the cocoa and chocolate markets, and they and Rowntrees were closely allied in price and other agreements. This was a reversal of Cadbury policy of the 1920s. During the early 1920s the parent company had vetoed CFP's plans to join a local price cartel, the Manufacturing Confectioners Association. Strong moral objections to such cartels had been expressed. 'The association is an organisation, possible in a protective country, which aims at a complete and absolute price ring', a member of the Cadbury family observed in May 1924. 'The interests of the consumer and distributor are subservient to those of the manufacturer, and the corrective influence of outside or foreign competition is practically absent owing to the tariff barrier.'[56] A more practical objection, however, was that if CFP entered such a cartel when its turnover was so low it might be prevented from ever securing a sufficient share of the market to reduce its crippling overheads.[57] During the 1930s MacRobertson's decline enabled Cadbury to participate in cartels with more confidence, and the policy did not hinder expansion. The value of CFP's sales doubled from £300,000 in the five years after 1933.[58] In July 1938 the Cadbury Board agreed a £40,000 factory extension for CFP, 'owing to the expansion of trade in recent years'.[59]

The legacy of CFP's first ten years, however, still hung over the company. In 1936 Cadbury were owed £533,550 by CFP, quite apart from its original investment and missed dividend payments.[60] Cadbury resolved that, once CFP had started to make profits, the repayment of this loan should take first priority over dividends. As this ruled out the payment of dividends in the foreseeable future, Cadbury decided to buy out their junior partners in CFP. Cadbury purchased Pascall's £20,000 shares in CFP at 10/- per share. As part of the arrangement, CFP paid Pascall a royalty of 0.5 per cent on the continuing Pascall section of the CFP trade, and Pascall resolved neither to manufacture nor to sell in Australia apart from CFP.[61]

The experience of Cadbury in Canada broadly paralleled that in Australia. An investigation in 1930 highlighted the highly unprofitable nature of the business and its declining turnover. Cadbury assumed the management of the Canadian companies, in place of Fry. As the Fry failure to make any headway in the chocolate market had been a major factor in the firm's disappointing performance, it was decided to have a full-scale launch of Cadbury products, especially CDM, on the market.[62] In December 1929 the Joint Board authorised an additional £50,000 to be spent on the Canadian company, £20,000 of which was for a CDM plant at the Montreal factory, and £30,000 for a three-year advertising campaign to introduce CDM to Canadians.[63]

The campaign was, at first, a success, but sales soon began to plummet with the onset of the Depression and increasingly fierce competition for the remaining market. In June 1931 it was decided to concentrate on cocoa and moulded chocolate only, abandoning the luxury confectionery fancy-box trade.[64] By February 1932 the Montreal factory was completely idle, as Fry cocoa sales slumped alongside those of CDM.[65]

The crisis at the beginning of 1932 led to another commission from Bournville being sent to Canada, charged with ascertaining whether there was a 'reasonable chance' of placing the Canadian company on a 'firm profit-making basis', or whether the whole venture would have to be closed down. The report particularly identified the 'hopeless disproportion between Cocoa and Chocolate sales' as a major cause of the company's difficulties, and recommended a Five Year Plan to reverse the situation. The plan suggested a progressive sales effort, involving a capital expenditure of £50,000, designed to create a balance between cocoa and chocolate sales by increasing Cadbury chocolate sales from £50,000 to £150,000 per annum, while holding Fry sales at £200,000.[66]

The recovery took longer than in Australia. The firm's overheads were reduced by the securing of contracts with other companies. During 1931 the firm made an agreement to manufacture Sharp's toffee in Canada, and also to manufacture (as opposed to just sell) Pascall products. In 1933 a contract was secured to provide the covering chocolate for the products of a large B-class confectionery company. The contract, however, was secured on unremunerative terms, and failed to compensate for declining cocoa sales. As a result, the Canadian company lost £32,000 in 1934, the year the Australian company moved into profitability.[67] The mid-thirties, however, saw some recovery in Canadian living standards, and an increase in chocolate sales, and after 1936 small profits were earned by the subsidiary.[68] By 1938 both the Australian and the Canadian subsidiaries were profitable.

VII

This article has examined the multinational growth of Cadbury between 1918 and 1939. The company generally fits the widely accepted thesis that tariffs were a major factor prompting British multinational growth in this period.[69] Cadbury erected factories in overseas markets as a last resort when valuable export markets were threatened by tariffs. Only the Burk & Braun investment deviated from this pattern, and Cadbury soon retreated from its uncomfortable German entanglement. The behaviour of the international competitors of Cadbury, however, also acted as an important influence on the firm's foreign investment decisions. The spread of Rowntree factories abroad was watched closely, and Cadbury followed its York competitor into South Africa and the Irish Free State.

The experience of Cadbury does not so easily fit generalisations about the 'safe haven' of the Empire in the inter-war years. On the other hand, Cadbury products were unsuccessful on the Continent and in the United States, and only long-term experimentation with new recipes would have changed the situation. Cadbury only eschewed competition in regions where it had no chance of competing, and it was perfectly good strategy to concentrate on Empire markets. On the other hand, the firm's subsidiaries established in Canada and Australia in the 1920s faced very tough competition. The markets were not virgin territory, nor were they 'easy'.

There was a noticeable variation in the performance of the five foreign manufacturing companies. The Australian and Canadian subsidiaries performed well below their parents' expectations over a long period, while the New Zealand, Irish and South African companies were profitable soon after they were established. This picture supports evidence from other companies that the performance of British multinational investments before 1939 was very mixed, with some firms being disappointed by their foreign investments and others receiving considerable gains from them.[70] The reasons for the varying performance of the foreign subsidiaries of Cadbury were both exogenous and endogenous to the firm. The depressed market conditions in inter-war Australia and Canada did not present great opportunities for chocolate manufacturers, but the subsidiaries were also handicapped by initial errors in business strategy and managerial policies. To a certain extent these mistakes were not repeated in the later investments, suggesting the firm underwent a learning process. A major factor affecting performance, however, was the degree of competition in a market. The Australian and Canadian companies in the 1920s were faced with highly competitive market conditions, while the New Zealand, Irish and South African companies operated in the more favourable context of market-sharing and reciprocal manufacturing agreements.

Business History Unit, London School of Economics

NOTES

I would like to thank Cadbury Schweppes Ltd. for permission to consult their archives; Mr Basil Murray, the Archivist of Cadbury, for his valuable assistance and helpful advice; and the Nuffield Foundation for its financial support.

1. A major exception is D.K. Fieldhouse, *Unilever Overseas: The Anatomy of a Multinational* (London: Croom Helm, 1979). See also Geoffrey Jones, 'The Growth and Performance of British Multinational Firms before 1939: the case of Dunlop', *Econ. Hist. Rev.*, 2nd series, XXXVII, No. 1 (1984). Many business histories also contain information about their firm's foreign investments, for example, D.C. Coleman, *Courtaulds: An Economic and Social History*, 3 vols. (Oxford: OUP, 1969, 1980). There are several fine recent studies of British multinationals in the extractive sector. See in particular Charles E. Harvey, *The Rio Tinto Company: An Economic History of a Leading International Mining Concern, 1873–1954* (Penzance: Alison Hodge, 1981), R.W. Ferrier, *The History of the British Petroleum Company*, I (Cambridge: CUP 1982), and T.A.B. Corley, *A History of the Burmah Oil Company, 1886–1924* (London: Heinemann, 1983).
2. W.B. Reddaway, *Effects of United Kingdom Direct Investment Overseas* Interim Report (Cambridge: CUP, 1967); Final Report (Cambridge, CUP, 1968), passim.

3. J.M. Stopford, 'The Origins of British-based Multinational Manufacturing Enterprises', *Bus. Hist. Rev.*, XLVIII, No. 3 (1974), p. 327; S. Nicholas, 'The Motivation and Direction of U.K. Direct Investment 1870–1939', *J. of Europ. Econ. Hist.*, Vol. 11, No. 3 (1982), p. 626.

4. The best account of the development of the Cadbury business remains Iolo A. Williams, *The Firm of Cadbury 1831–1931* (London: Constable, 1931). A.G. Gardiner, *Life of George Cadbury* (London: Cassell, 1923) has some information on the firm's early history. There are also a number of shorter books sponsored by the company, including T.B. Rogers, *A Century of Progress 1831–1931* (Bournville: Cadbury Brothers, 1931) and Cadbury Brothers Ltd. *Industrial Record 1919–1939* (Bournville: Cadbury Brothers, 1947).

5. See Coleman, op.cit.

6. Memorandum No. 72 for Joint Board, 9 April 1930, Cadbury Archives, Bournville (hereafter CB).

7. Ibid., Private Letter to Mr Seebohm Rowntree, 7 May 1930; Joint Board Minute, 23 November 1921.

8. L. Hannah, *The Rise of the Corporate Economy* (London: Methuen, 1979), p. 120. Hannah estimated the market value of the British Cocoa and Chocolate Company in 1930 at £10.3 million.

9. Edward Cadbury: General Note Book, June 1897, CB 2372(b).

10. Ibid., Cadbury Brothers Committee of Management 1900; Cadbury Brothers Board Minutes, 1911.

11. Ibid., Special Meeting, Cadbury Brothers Board Minutes, 19 July 1901.

12. Ibid., Minute of 9 May 1911.

13. Williams, op.cit., pp. 146-61.

14. Cadbury Brothers Board Minutes, Remarks on Export Trade 1916, 17 January 1917, CB.

15. Ibid., Joint Board Memorandum No. 291, 26 June 1919.

16. Ibid., J.S. Fry & Sons Board Minute, 4 March 1919, CB No. 433.

17. Ibid., Joint Board Memorandum No. 291, 26 June 1919.

18. Ibid., The profit figures are located in various reports in the Cadbury-Fry-Pascall Minute Books 1920–30.

19. Ibid., P.S. Cadbury Report on Visit to Canada, February 1927, CB No. 1280.

20. Ibid., Reports in Australia Committee Minute Books.

21. Fieldhouse, op.cit., pp. 64-8.

22. P.S. Cadbury Report on Visit to Canada, February 1927, CB No. 1280.

23. Ibid., Joint Board Memorandum No. 21, 17 September 1919.

24. Ibid., Minute 18 June 1924, Australian Committee Minute Book File.

25. Ibid., Mr Pascall to Edward Cadbury, July 1924.

26. Ibid., Notes by T.A. Cooper on Tasmania, CB No. 2141.

27. Ibid., Joint Board Memorandum No. 104, 1925.

28. Ibid., F.T.W. Saunders to Cecil Fry, 7 March 1928, CB No. 1280.

29. Ibid., Joint Memorandum No. 272, 'Points Against' by Walter Barrow, 7 December 1923.

30. Ibid., Joint Board Memorandum No. 104, 1925.

31. *Industrial Record, 1919–1939*, op.cit., pp. 16-40.

32. Cadbury Board Minute File No. 743, 17 December 1931, CB.

33. Ibid., P.S. Cadbury, Report on Visit to Canada, February 1927, CB No. 1280. In the long-term this view proved correct.

34. Ibid., Joint Board Minutes, 28 February 1923.

35. Ibid., Joint Board Memorandum, Nos. 115 and 133, 1928.

36. Ibid., Joint Board Minute, 19 September 1928.

37. Ibid., Joint Board Memorandum, No. 115, 6/7 September 1928.

38. Ibid., Joint Board Memorandum, No. 133, 2 October 1928.

39. Ibid., Joint Board Minute, 17 October 1928.

40. Ibid., Joint Board Minute, 11 September 1929.

41. Ibid., Joint Board Minute, 4 November 1931.

42. Ibid., Cadbury Board Minute, 12 August 1940.
43. See, for example, Geoffrey Jones, 'Lombard Street on the Riviera: The British Clearing Banks and Europe 1900–60', *Bus. Hist.*, Vol. XXIV, No. 2 (1982); Coleman, op.cit., Vol. II, pp. 374-9. For the more recent experiences of a British firm, see W. J. Reader, *Metal Box: A History* (London: Heinemann, 1976), especially chapters 8 and 15. Cadbury had a further unsatisfactory experience in Germany in the 1960s. Two German firms were purchased, Schierbeck and Hanseaten Schokolade Werke, and Cadbury/Fry Gmbh established in 1961. The subsidiary performed badly, failing to find a market for its products, and in 1968 Cadbury's German factory was closed.
44. Ibid., Cadbury Board Minute, 28 March 1928.
45. Ibid., Joint Board Minute, 17 April 1929.
46. Ibid., Joint Board Minute, 11 July 1928.
47. Ibid., Joint Board Minute, 7 May 1930.
48. Ibid., Cadbury Board Minute File No. 654, 30 August 1927.
49. Ibid., Report on Export Trade 1929, No. 127, 31 January 1930.
50. Ibid., Cadbury Board Minutes, 18 December 1935.
51. Ibid., Report on Export Trade 1929, No. 127, 31 January 1930.
52. Ibid., Cadbury Fry Hudson Ltd., CB 2351.
53. Ibid., Cadbury Board Minute, 23 January 1933.
54. Ibid., Cadbury Board Minute Files, No. 119, 30 June 1933.
55. Ibid., Joint Board Minute, 17 May 1933.
56. Ibid., P. S. Cadbury, 20 May 1924, Australian Committee Minute Book File No. 414, CB.
57. Ibid., Minute Book File No. 417, 19 March 1926.
58. Ibid., Joint Board Memorandum No. 214, April 1938.
59. Ibid., Cadbury Board Minute, 6 July 1938.
60. Ibid., Cadbury Board Minute Files, No. 326, 29 May 1936.
61. Ibid., Cadbury Board Minute, 24 March 1937.
62. Ibid., Report on Visit to Canada by Mr Tatham, October 1929, CB 1280.
63. Ibid., Joint Board Minute, 4 December 1929.
64. Ibid., Cadbury Board Minute, 17 June 1931.
65. Ibid., Joint Board Memorandum No. 14, 21 January 1933.
66. Ibid., Cadbury Board Minute Files, No. 122, 18 February 1932.
67. Ibid., File 543, October 1934.
68. Ibid., Cadbury Board Minute Files, Overseas Factories Committee Reports.
69. A. D. Chandler, 'The Growth of the Transnational Industrial Firm in the United States and the United Kingdom: A Comparative Analysis', *Econ. Hist. Rev.*, 2nd series, Vol. XXXIII, No. 3 (1980), p. 401.
70. See, for example, 'The Growth and Performance', op.cit.; Courtaulds had an outstandingly profitable foreign subsidiary, the American Viscose Company, established in 1910, but its Continental factories established in the 1920s were much less successful. Coleman, op.cit., Vol. II. The measurement of 'success' or 'failure' of a multinational investment is, however, a complex task. A full measure of performance, for example, would need to take into account the effect of a firm not undertaking the foreign direct investment.

[21]

ITT's International Business Activities, 1920-40 : The Remarkable Advance and Setback of a "Pure International Utility Company"*

by ABO Tetsuo

I

The overseas expansion of firms, especially of multinational enterprises, can be classified into several distinct types depending on the industries they belong to and on their individual characteristics. Usually, however, models describing the growth or organizational structures of multinational enterprises (hereafter abbreviated as "MNEs") tend to abstract from the concrete peculiarities of these various types of foreign expansion, pointing out only those aspects common to these various types of expansion in an extremely generalized manner. My contention here is by no means to deny the usefulness of such model building. Indeed, many of these models can serve as an effective guide for the concrete analysis of specific MNEs. It should be pointed out at the same time, however, that some of the specifics cast away by general models are often too important for specific analysis. And especially when model-builders build their models "theoretically," they are inclined to be concerned primarily with generalization and deductive reasoning, referring to fragmentary experimental facts by way of illustration.

I for one am of the opinion that in analyzing the multifarious development of MNEs, their impact on individual national economies and on the world economy as a whole, and national and international restraints on their activities — that is to say, in understanding the significance of MNEs' activities today in their totality — it is imperative for us to base our analysis on concrete facts. For this purpose it is especially important to accumulate as many detailed case studies as possible on typical and larger MNEs in major industries. It is on the basis of these case studies that we can construct a set of deep penetrating theories capable of analyzing the dynamic processes of the development of MNEs and that we can eventually grapple with the vivid picture of the world-wide deployment of MNEs in its totality. Unfortunately, however, such case studies available thus far are extremely limited, with a series of outstanding works by Professor Mira Wilkins being notable exceptions.[1]

The case study of the International Telephone and Telegraph Corporation in the interwar period to be undertaken in this paper — along with other similar ones I have already made on Ford Motors and General Motors (in the automotive industry), on EXXON and SOCAL (in the petroleum industry), and General Electric (in the electrical products industry)[2] — is a modest attempt to contribute toward the accumulation of much needed case studies. One factor that has motivated me to publish a case study on ITT in English is that I was unable to locate any in-depth analyses of the corporation in the interwar period when I sorted out materials on major United States-based MNEs even at the Harvard Business School's Baker Library during my one-year stay in the United States in 1980-81. I hope the following case study on ITT, though brief due to space limitations, will be of some value.

II

Along with American Foreign Power Co.,[3] another utility company that came into being during the 1920s, ITT is a company of a very peculiar kind, established and operated from the outset to be active mainly in foreign territories. Unlike other international or global firms which went abroad on the basis of their production and marketing activities in their home countries, it set out in overseas operations without having roots in the home country, and when it eventually came to hold approximately 20 per cent of its assets within the United States, these were mainly for the sake of international operations. Thus ITT is unique not only because it does not immediately fit conventional theories of foreign direct investments, but also because it is a utility company that expanded abroad on a large scale. And given such uniqueness, it seems to provide a very interesting topic for the study of MNEs in the interwar period.

There is available neither a systematic history of ITT compiled by the company nor an autobiography of an influential person in the company's management that bears witness to its activities in the period concerned. In undertaking my analysis in the following pages, therefore, I have no choice but to thread together whatever materials are available, i.e., a very limited number of studies, magazine and newspaper articles, various issues of the *Annual Report of the International Telephone and Telegraph Corporation* (hereafter abreviated as *Report*), and the *Moody's or Poor's Public Utilities*. Fortunately, however, each issue of the *Report*, reflecting the company's nature, places main emphasis on its international activities and deals in considerable details with its activities because of its need for fund-procurement in the American securities markets. I will, therefore, base my analysis mainly on various issues of ITT's *Report.*

ITT had a heavily international character from the very moment of its inception. Sosthenese Behn, who established the company in 1920 together with his elder brother and who continued to preside over it as its dictatorial chairman or president until 1956, had a Danish father and a French mother, received education in Corsica and Paris, and then obtained United States citizenship. Behn's family parentage and the history of his earlier life seem to have had a certain bearing upon the nature of his company's business activities. Indeed, the cosmopolitan nature of Americans, of which he was an extreme representative, seems to have been an important factor underlying the company's all-out cosmopolitan nature. The Behn brothers were acting as sugar factors in Porto Rico when they by chance seized a telephone company on the island in payment of a bad debt. Realizing that telephone service would be very promising, the brothers soon purchased a telephone company in Cuba. Following the end of World War I, they established in 1920 the International Telephone and Telegraph Corporation. This naming, liable to be mixed up with the American Telephone and Telegraph Corporation, which had already monopolized telephone services within the United States, was deliberately chosen so as to make the new company appear as, and eventually grow into, an international version of the famous ATT, even though at the time there was no connection between the two.[4] It should be pointed out, however, that following its purchase of a telephone company in Cuba, ITT before long came to have certain relationship with ATT as the two agreed to hold half each of the capital stocks of the Cuban American Telephone and Telegraph Co. established in 1921 for the purpose of laying a submarine cable connecting the Cuban system with the telephones of the mainland United States. And Behn made use of this tie with ATT as an invaluable asset contributing to his company's credibility.[5]

Behn's characteristic behavior pattern formed the core part of ITT's persistent and aggressive drive — especially in its earlier days — to procure the funds necessary for the expansion of its overseas activities in the financial markets within the United States. Indeed, in expanding its network of overseas telephone and telegraph subsidiaries, in supplying equipment to these subsidiaries, in allocating manufacturing and servicing subsidiaries internationally, and in connecting its overseas systems each other by cables, ITT depended on the American financial markets for much of the funds necessary for purchasing pre-existing foreign companies and for establishing new ones. And accordingly, ITT not only paid a great deal of attention to the trends of dividend rates and stock prices but also took great trouble in maintaining and reinforcing its ties with the financial circles, which were of vital significance to its very survival. Though I cannot afford to go into detail here, the rapid progress of ITT was closely related to the abundant supply of cheap money in the American financial markets during the 1920s and especially to the active floatation of foreign bonds and securities there in the latter half of the 1920s.

In 1923, ITT established a subsidiary within the United States, the International Telephone Securities Corporation, whose expected role it was to take care of issuing ITT securities. In the same year, when the securities markets were not generally favorable for issuing securities to raise money for overseas businesses, the well-known medium-standing investment house E. B. Smith & Co. and another investment banker brought out an issue of 50,000 shares of ITT common stocks (totalling over $3.4 million). In the following year, the representatives of these two investment houses joined the company's board of directors along with two National City Bank executives, C.E. Mitchell and A.G. Hoyt. To mention in passing, G.H. Gardiner from a law firm affiliated with the Morgan group joined the directorates in 1923.[6] Needless to say, these factors contributed tremendously to enhancing ITT's credibility among American investors at large.

In the following year, ITT succeeded in concluding its first big deal, a contract granted by the Spanish dictatorship for the creation and operation of a general telephone service in Spain. It established a Spanish corporation, the Compañía Telefónica Nacional de España, in order to rehabilitate the Spanish telephone system from its state of disorder and to further develop it under this concession. In the same year, ITT issued approximately 90,000 shares of new capital stocks (totalling about $7.5 million) and put a major portion of the proceeds (a little less than $5 million) in its Spanish subsidiary. What is worthy of attention here is that the subsidiary's stocks, worth more than three times the amount invested and lent by the parent company, were accepted for issuance within Spain by a group of Spanish banks. Although it is impossible to ascertain on the basis of the ITT *Report* the exact share of the Spanish subsidiary's common stocks represented by the parent company's investments, this seems to have been about 80% according to the *Fortune* magazine.[7] It should be pointed out, however, that the consolidated balance sheet of ITT's *Report* entered these investments under the heading of investments and loans to "affiliated and allied companies," thereby differentiating the Spanish company from ITT's wholly-owned subsidiaries.[8] Thus, in exchange for forsaking the complete ownership and control of the Spanish company, ITT relieved itself of the burden of raising an enormous fund for it, while securing a large concession in Europe. Along with explicitly stipulating the terms giving the Spanish state an option to take over the telephone system, with compensation, 20 years after the conclusion of the contract. ITT displayed in the organizational set-up of the Spanish company and its relationship with the parent company a concrete manifestation of its persistent policy of "nationalization," i.e., localization.[9]

Immediately after its launching, this large undertaking in Spain created a series of chain reactions in various spots in Europe, with the first important deals taking place as early as 1925. These were due to the fact that ITT was obliged, by the Spanish dictatorship's "nationalization," i.e., localization, policy, to secure local manufacturing subsidiaries in order to locally manufacture the telephone apparatus necessary for operating the Spanish system. In an attempt to meet this requirement, ITT purchased in 1925 all the capital stock of International Western Electric Co., an international division of the largest American producer of electric products, Western Electric Co., which was the manufacturing wing of ATT, and renamed the acquired company the International Standard Electric Co. (or ISE for short). ISE was a large international firm having a global network of plants manufacturing electric products and telephone apparatus, centered mainly in Europe. It had wholly-owned subsidiaries in Spain, England, Belgium, France, Italy, and the Netherlands, had controlling interests in subsidiaries in Japan and China, and had minority interests in affiliated companies in a score of other countries. Its annual gross sales in 1925 amounted to approximately $33 million and were expanding rapidly. The total number of its employees as of the end of 1925, 17,000, accounted for approximately 63% of all ITT employees (see Table 3). In a sense, ITT by acquiring this company as a division to supply equipment for its international operations, prepared itself well in advance for the subsequent expansion of its telephone and telegraph services.

To add in passing, prior to the purchase of International Western Electric, Behn first asked ATT, the parent company of Western Electric, to let International Western start supplying telephone apparatuses to ITT's operation in Spain; and it was only after this request was turned down that Behn decided to purchase International Western itself and that its purchase offer won ATT's consent. There was one circumstance that reputedly made this purchase deal possible. Western Electric at the time was anticipating an anti-trust law suit and found it imperative to rid itself of International Western. At any rate, one might be able to say that with the conclusion of this deal, ITT took on the characteristics of ATT's offshoot in the area of international operations. As a matter of fact, thereafter the ATT group and the ITT group came to divide between them the American market and the international market through overt as well as tacit agreements. Of the staggering price of $30 million paid to buy up International Western, a large portion, $25 million, was paid in ITT gold clause bonds (redeemable in 20 years and carrying an annual interest of 5.5%), which ATT turned over to J. P. Morgan & Co. for sale on the market. This fact alone clearly reveals how heavily ITT relied at the time on the American securities markets for funding its expansion. Perhaps in close connection with this deal, two executives of J. P. Morgan & Co. joined ITT's directorates in 1926.[10]

In the year 1925, ITT also acquired a controlling interest in the Compagnie des Téléphones Thomson-Houston, a company in Paris manufacturing telephone apparatuses and supplies, from its French parent company affiliated with General Electric, the Compagnie Française pour l'Exploitation des Procédés Thomson-Houston. (And in the following year, it acquired all the remaining capital stock of this French telephone apparatus manufacturer.) In Mexico, too, ITT acquired a controlling interest in the Mexican Telephone and Telegraph Co., which operated a general telephone service in one district of Mexico and a long-distance telephone service throughout the country.[11] As a result of these aggressive purchasing deals, ITT expanded its activities quite phenomenally from 1924 to 1925, as is evident from Tables 1 and 3.

Table 1.   Consolidated Balance Sheet of ITT. 1921-40[a]

Unit: $1,000.

	Assets			Liabilities			
	Total assets[b]	Plant, property, etc.[c]	Other investments[d]	Total liabilities[b]	Paid-up capital[e]	Funded debts[f]	Current liabilities
1921	32,563	25,655	2,789	32,563	18,792	9,548	1,153
1922	32,896	27,062	1,136	32,896	18,487	9,520	1,418
1923	30,519	24,239	1,539	30,519	15,538	9,052	1,457
1924	38,325	26,655	3,097	38,325	16,952	8,990	4,555
1925	99,184	47,734	10,077	99,184	39,047	33,896	10,757
1926	130,982	58,774	22,544	130,982	60,944	33,724	15,640
1927	238,884	114,504	41,768	238,884	138,409	44,184	19,452
1928	389,914	225,273	44,910	389,914	182,859	93,517	43,056
1929	535,204	336,882	51,994	535,204	235,200	136,584	54,035
1930	604,403	394,688	67,640	604,403	254,469	187,599	46,835
1931	615,190	420,819	83,038	615,190	252,572	188,853	63,050
1932	566,153	407,204	82,616	566,153	252,325	189,727	57,214
1933	584,611	408,674	85,829	584,611	250,787	194,615	58,518
1934	581,043	410,149	70,740	581,043	250,782	192,890	60,224
1935	513,757	308,721	111,648	513,757	225,358	141,689	50,912
1936	525,472	304,343	139,412	525,472	138,940[g]	140,035	56,929
1937	558,613	315,063	140,506	558,613	138,065	167,163	47,429
1938	537,280	323,559	99,516	537,280	140,781	183,875	39,919
1939	503,674	321,180	114,090	503,674	140,781	155,378	29,703
1940	426,389	235,597	168,815	426,389	136,968	142,604	9,774

Source: *Annual Report of the International Telephone and Telegraph Corporation.* various
issues.

Notes: a. All the figures are as of the year of their first publication but are not the ones
revised later.
   b. Inclusive of items other than those shown in this table.
   c. Inclusive of patents and licences.
   d. Consist of securities investments in and advances to the affiliated and allied companies and special subsidiaries which are not incorporated in the consolidated
balance sheet.
   e. Inclusive of preferred stocks held by subsidiaries, and up to 1924 inclusive of
that part of capital stocks of subsidiaries which were held by a small number
of stockholders in the form of common stocks.
   f. For 1932 and thereafter, inclusive of long-term bonds issued by subsidiaries.
   g. In the year 1936, paid up capital decreased drastically due to rewriting down
of the stated value of common stocks from $33.33 to $20 a share. (see *Report*,
1935, p. 21, note 1). The resulting increment in capital surplus was entered under
the headings of "capital surplus" and "reserve for revaluation of assets," which
are not shown in this table (see *Report*. 1936, pp. 19 and 23).

Let us first turn to Table 1, in which major items of the company's consolidated balance sheet are shown. Total assets, which stood at a little less than $40 million in 1924, jumped more than two and half times to close to $100 million in 1925, while the two items of the assets account, "plant, property, etc." and "other investments" (i.e., investments and advances to affiliated and allied companies), showed sizable increases of $21 million and $7 million respectively, reflecting the series of acquisitions. However, the item in the assets account that showed the largest increase in 1925 was "liquid assets" (not shown in the table) which, for the same reason, increased by as much as $30 million from 1924, mainly in the form of cach, accounts and notes receivable, and inventories. Turning to the capital and liabilities account, on the other hand, it stands to reason that paid-up capital increased 2.3 times or by $22 million, but it is quite noteworthy that the funded debts increased at a far greater rate, i.e., 3.8 times or by $25 million, the amount which was due for the payment of the purchase of International Western. To add a note of caution, ITT's share in the assets of the Companñia Telefónica Nacional de España, which became affilaited with ITT as a result of ITT's acquisition of a majority interest in it in 1924, is included in the 1925 balance sheet under the heading "other investments."

Staying with this table, let us trace the trends of assets and liabilities in the latter half of the 1920s. Total assets, after showing a considerably large increase of a little over $30 million in 1926, expanded dramatically in the years from 1927 to 1929, increasing by $100-150 million per annum or by a staggering total of $400 million. Approximately 60 to 70 per cent of these increments were accounted for by increases in fixed assets, i.e., plants, property, etc., suggesting that ITT in this period was all the more active in its telephone business and telephone-related manufacturing activities. One noteworthy item is that although ITT's liquid assets increased substantially by $76 million in the period from 1925 to 1929, reaching a total of $100 million, the ratio of liquid assets to the total assets decreased rapidly from about 37% to about 21% in the same period. Turning now to the capital and liabilities account, it is interesting to note that whereas the paid-up capital and the funded debts were just about the same levels as in 1925, their subsequent rates of increase until 1929 were significantly different, with the former increasing 6 times and the latter 4 times, and consequently the former grew more than 1.7 times as large as the latter. It should be pointed out, however, that as far as the years 1928 and 1929 are concerned, the two items grew by more or less the same amounts, $40-50 million per annum. The funds required for rapid expansion of the company's assets in this period were procured mainly through stock issues (and common stocks without exception when issued within the United States), but were also supplemented to a considerable extent through the floatation of long-term bonds. All in all, the fact that the securities markets increasingly acquired the characteristics of the stock exchange markets in the years 1928-29 does not seem to have significantly affected the company's funding practices. At this juncture, let us compare the total of stocks and long-term bonds newly issued each year by ITT with total annual American foreign direct investments funded by the issuing of securities (shown in Table 2). The ratio of the former to the latter, although fluctuating somewhat from year to year, increased rapidly from about 30% in 1925 to around 60% in 1927 and 1928 (after declining to about 9% in 1926) and then tailed off to 38% in 1929, as might be expected. At any rate, ITT evidently had significant shares in American foreign direct investments funded by the issuing of securities in the latter half of the 1920s.

Let us turn next to Table 3 and look into the activities of ITT mianly on the basis of the trends of the income-or-loss account. It is immediately clear from each series of data shown

Table 2. American Foreign Direct Investments, 1919-39

Unit: $1,000,000.

	Foreign direct investments[1]	Foreign direct investments financed by issuance of securities[2]		Foreign direct investments[1]	Foreign direct investments financed by issuance of securities[2]
1919	94	25	1929	602	252
1920	154	64	1930	294	142
1921	111	46	1931	222	92
1922	153	68	1932	16	–
1923	148	64	1933	–32	1
1924	182	78	1934	17	–
1925	268	153	1935	–31	–
1926	351	225	1936	12	–
1927	351	148	1937	–35	–
1928	558	152	1938	–16	–
			1939	– 9	–

Source: H.B. Lary et al., *The United States in the World Economy*, Washington, D.C.: G.P.O., 1943, Table III, p. 216.
Notes: 1. The figures for 1919-29 are inclusive of, but those for 1930-39 exclusive of, reinvestments of the profits earned overseas.
2. The figures are taken from note 7 to Table III of the source cited above.

Table 3. ITT's Consolidated Income-or-Loss Account, and the Numbers of Its Employees and Stockholders, 1921-40[a]

Units: $1,000 and persons.

	Income-or-loss account		No. of employees	No. of stockholders
	Gross earnings	Net income[b]		
1921	3,590	1,248	1,352	846
1922	4,246	1,314	1,453	1,296
1923	4,703	1,661	1,600[c]	1,665
1924	5,841	3,384	7,500[c]	2,202
1925	17,037	4,668	27,237	2,774
1926	22,681	7,105	41,249	4,164
1927	37,229	14,413	49,826	11,682
1928	81,235	14,596	85,000[c]	16,568
1929	100,341	17,732	94,939	53,594
1930	104,473	13,750	n.a	n.a
1931	89,308	7,654	66,980	n.a
1932	67,527	–3,935	57,186	n.a
1933	73,960	694	54,106	n.a
1934	79,258	2,080	57,989	n.a
1935	52,272	5,787	62,335	n.a
1936	52,990	4,009	71,000	7,800
1937	63,624	10,236	71,248	n.a
1938	67,519	7,039	77,955	n.a
1939	55,668	4,894	n.a	n.a
1940	27,870	–162	n.a	n.a

Source: *Report, op. cit.,* various issues.
Notes: a The figures are as of the years of their first publication, but are not the ones revised later.
b Net income is before deduction of dividends.
c The employment figures for 1923, 1924 and 1928 have been estimated from graphs.

in the table that the years 1925 and 1929 were the turning points. One thing to be noted here is that whereas gross earnings increased approximately three times in 1925 from $5.8 million to $17.0 million, net income increased only about 1.4 times from $3.4 million to $4.7 million. The gap between the rates of increase in gross earnings and in net income is ascribable to the fact that the large scale acquisitions of the preceding year did not immediately result in an increased net income. Subsequently around 1927 the gap became somewhat smaller, but in 1928 and 1929 the rate of increase in net income fell farther behind that in gross earnings. While it is generally true that when a company expands rapidly there tends to emerge a time-lag between the growth of its gross earnings and its net income, a more convincing reason behind the widening gap seems to be that ITT overtaxed itself by carrying out too ambitious a policy of expansion in the late 1920s.[12]

ITT's rapid expansion is more pronounced when looked at in terms of its employment figures (also shown in Table 3). ITT employees, who numbered around 1,600 in 1923, increased more than 4.5 times to approximately 7,500 in 1924, and then in 1925 the number jumped again by 20,000 to over 27,000, or 3.6 times the 1924 figure. Thus, between 1921 and 1925, ITT's workforce expanded as much as 20 times, far in excess of the rates of increase in total assets and gross earnings in the same period (these were, respectively, 3 times and a little less than 5 times). By the late 1920s, however, these gaps in the rates of increase were reduced; while the employment figure continued to grow steadily until 1929, when it reached 95,000, its rate of increase from 1925 to 1929 (3.5 times) was considerably smaller than the rate of increase in total assets in the same period (5.4 times). At any rate, ITT's employment figure, which was close to 100,000 in 1929, was comparable with those of two large firms, General Motors and Standard Oil of New Jersey in the same year, which, respectively, stood at around 23,000 and 13,000.[13] Indeed the size of ITT's workforce was at once amazing and a bit too impressive for a young company with only a decade-long history, as the events in the 1930s would soon testify.

I would like to say a few words about the trend of the increase in the number of stockholders shown in Table 3, a trend considerably different from that of the increase in paid-up capital shown in Table 1. Whereas paid-up capital increased two times in 1921-25 and 12.5 times in 1921-29, the number of stockholders increased at far greater rates of 33 times and 64 times, respectively. Needless to say, underlying the rapid increase in the number of stockholders was the fact that ITT absorbed and made use of bits of funds extended by an increasingly large number of small and medium stockholders. In this sense, too, the rapid growth of ITT in the 1920s was a typical result of the growth of the securities markets that was taking place at the time.[14] For ordinary investors, ITT securities might have been on an equal standing with the securities floated by utility companies active within the United States. One supporting piece of evidence for this is that, as noted above, the new issues of ITT stocks and bonds did not show signs of decreasing even in the year 1929. One thing of interest in this connection is that ITT established in 1925 an "employees' stock subscription plan" as a means of encouraging its employees, within certain limits, to invest in the company and of mobilizing funds so vital for financing its further growth.[15]

III

In the foregoing discussion, I have first noted that ITT's acquisition of an operational concession in Spain and its establishment of ISE in 1924-25 were a turning point in its development. I then proceeded to present an overview of its business activities throughout the 1920s referring to tables showing its financial position and other major indices. At this point, I would like to return to the main thrust of the paper and look into some of the important aspects of ITT's international expansion in the latter half of the 1920s and the period up to 1931 following the establishment of ISE.

After reorganizing the Spanish manufacturing company in 1926 under the control of ISE, in 1927 ITT made a series of purchases in quick succession. It first acquired a controlling interest in All America Cables Inc., a company operating cables connecting New York and Central and South America, and then bought up telephone companies located in strategic cities of the area, i.e., in Uruguay, Chile, Brazil, and Argentina. The purpose of these purchases was obviously to bring the telephone companies isolated and scattered in Central and South America under the control of ITT and to incorporate them into the All America Cables network, thereby connecting them with each other and with New York. Needless to say, this network was linked with those in Cuba, Porto Rico and Mexico to form an international telephone network covering all of the Americas, extending from Central and South America, to the Caribbean and the United States. Furthermore, this pan-American network was linked with Europe via ITT's New York-London line. At that juncture, ITT met competition from Cables and Wireless, Ltd., a British company operating a direct line between Rio de Janeiro, Brazil, and London which was nearly half the length of the ITT line that detoured through New York. Although ITT beat the British company in terms of waiting time, it was not able to compete in terms of rate, and had to go along, at least for the time being, with the price cuts the British company initiated.

Yet Behn's mind remained firmly set on further expansion. He was, in a manner of speaking, concerned more about perfecting his global strategy than about local competition such as this. By that time, his company had installed a trans-Andean cable making possible for the first time direct communications between Buenos Aires and San Tiago and had gained control of 55% of all the telephones in South America. He was planning to extend the company's activities into Asia, especially to Singapore and China, and was also eager to strive into the burgeoning area of wireless telephone. At least as far as the Americas were concerned, ITT's telephone networks covered virtually both continents, except for those areas covered by ATT, which had monopoly control in the United States and a certain influence in Canada, and those covered by Western Union, which exercised a certain amount of control in Canada and Mexico.[16]

Furthermore in 1928, in addition to establishing wireless telephone and telegraph subsidiaries in Argentina, Brazil and Chile, and acquiring a controlling interest in a British manufacturer of telegraph apparatuses, ITT established the Postal Telegraph and Cable Corporation within the United States as the largest undertaking of the year. This company, a private American company without any direct connections with the United States Postal Services and its official post offices, established itself as a holding company by buying up the Mackay Co., which had been active in the field of telegraph services, and by incorporating its operations. Through its two-staged holding company system, ITT incorporated in its network a cabling subsidiary linking the United States, Canada, England, and France, another cabling subsidiary linking San Francisco,

Hawaii, the Philippines, Shanghai, and Japan, and still another subsidiary, the Postal Telegraph, offering similar telegraph services on a nation-wide scale within the United States. ITT thereby expanded its activities in the new area of telegraph services both within and without the United States.[17]

The year 1929 also saw the expansion of ITT's activities, mainly centered in Central and South America, throughout the world. In Europe, it obtained a controlling interest in a company producing telephone and telegraph apparatuses located in Berlin (which it did not bring under ISE). All in all, however, ITT was not able to expand its telephone and telegraph business into Europe except for Spain (and except for the acquisition of one company in Rumania in 1931), but managed to establish its bases in the major European countries only for the production of apparutuses and the operation of cable services. In Central America, on the other hand, through its subsidiary, All America Cables, ITT bought up a cable company doing services linking Haiti, Santo Domingo, and Venezuela, and acquired concessions to engage in wireless telephone and telegraph services in Peru and Colombia. In South America, ITT bought up what became the largest telephone company under its control, the United River Plate Telephone Co. in Argentina. With this purchase, the number of telephones in the possession of the entire ITT system increased by 260,000 at once, bringing the total to nearly 600,000. In keeping with this development, ITT-Sud America was established as a subsidiary in charge of providing technical and financial backup for ITT's operations throughout South America.[18] Another important accomplishment by ITT in the same year was the opening of its International Telegraph Research Institute in New York and similar research institutions in London and Paris (the latter two under ISE), thereby consolidating its own set-ups to promote research and development in all areas of business activity. This seems to imply that ITT, after having emerged as the world's largest international telephone and telegraph company in such a short period, mainly through buying up pre-existing companies and technological know-how, was now trying to alter the course of its development.

On the eve of the world depression, ITT's international operations had already grown both in scope and contents to form what might be aptly called a world telecommunication empire, and the company was preparing for new growth ahead. However, precisely because of its nature as an internationally active utility company, ITT suffered far more seriously from world-wide political and economic upheavals than any other global firm. It should be pointed out, however, that at least in terms of its assets including plants and properties, the company continued to grow, though slowly, until around 1931. The critical turning point in ITT's business activities came when foreign exchange rates of various countries fell sharply following the suspension of the gold standard by England in the autumn of 1931. In the light of this, I will take the years 1930 and 1931 as an extention of ITT activities in the 1920s and treat the period after 1932 as constituting a new phase.

Let us now turn to the period up to 1931. Total assets in 1930 grew by a considerable amount, $70 million, over the year before, although the rate of increase was not as large as previously; and increases in fixed assets and other investments in the same year even exceeded this amount. However, due to the collapse of stock markets, ITT was able to procure only $20. million of this increment through stock issues and had to raise the balance by way of issuance of long-term bonds. From 1930 to 1931, there was a tentative recovery of the bond market, including foreign bond markets, which took up the slack stock market, and ITT with the enormous credibility it had earned in financial circles was still able to procure funds in the bond markets where interest rates had fallen sizeably. In fact, the securities issued by ITT in 1930 totalled $70 million, accounting for approximately half the total American foreign direct investments made in that year financed through security issues (see Table 2 above). In 1931, ITT's total assets increased by $10 million, and its fixed assets and other investments increased by margins of more than $30 million (with the balance offset by decreases in liquid assets, mainly cash and inventories). However, the increase in total assets was not funded by the floatation of long-term bonds but by increased current liabilities.[19]

Turning next to the income-or-loss account of Table 3, it is clear that in 1930 gross earnings showed a slight increase and stayed above $100 million, and the net income of approximately $14 million, though somewhat smaller than the year before, was close to the level of 1927-28. In 1931, however, these accounts began to suffer a decline, with gross earnings falling by 15% from the preceding year and net income by a far greater proportion of 45%. The decline in gross earnings was due partly to the overall stagnation of business, mainly in the postal telegraph sector, within the United States – although the telephone sector was continuing to grow even if at a slow tempo as shown in Figure 1 below – and partly to the effects of the foreign exchange restrictions imposed by foreign countries which curtailed the remittances received from foreign subsidiaries. (N.B.: Foreign exchange losses are not taken into account in the gross earnings statistics). On the other hand, the major reason for the significant decline in net income was that long-term bonds, which had suddenly expanded in 1928-30, had to be amortized annually at constant rates regardless of the cyclic fluctuations of business from one year to the next. For all that, ITT was still able to earn a net income of $7.7 million in 1931, more than 40% of the amount it earned in 1929. Obviously this was largely due to the fact that ITT had its major bases of business not in the United States, which at the time was hit more seriously than any other country in the world by the Great Depression. This situation, however, would turn totally to ITT's disadvantage beginning the following year, as I will discuss shortly. In passing, despite the increase in its total assets, ITT's employment figure decreased in 1931 to 67,000, or 70% of the 1929 figure.[20]

Given this situation, it was natural that ITT slowed the rhythm at which it launched new undertakings in 1930-31. And yet, the year 1930 still saw some additions to the ITT empire. These included the expansion of its pre-existing systems in Peru and Shanghai through new purchases; the acquisition in Rumania of a concession to operate in all areas of electric communications, excepting telegraph, and the establishment of a new telephone company there on the basis of this concession; and the establishment of the International Marine Radio Co., a subsidiary for marketing and installing radio communications apparatuses for marine vessels and aircraft, whose purpose was to cultivate a new market for wireless services. But the expansionary actions virtually came to a halt in 1931, the only exception being the buying up, through Mackay Co., of the Federal Telegraph Co., formerly a subsidiary of a radio company and manufacturer of radio and wireless apparatuses. This was the first manufacturing company bought up by ITT within the United States. It seems safe to say that, aside from these new additions, ITT had to shift the major emphasis of its activities to the partial reinforcement and expansion of its pre-existing structure and facilities and to the cultivation of new markets based on more sophisticated services – or, in present-day language, to the development of soft-ware technology and know-how.[21]

At this point, based on Table 4, let us summarize the sectorial and regional distribution of ITT's business activities as of the end of 1931. In terms of the share of ITT investments in and loans to its subsidiaries in various sectors, the telephone service sector was naturally the largest, absorbing 60% of the funds, followed by the manufacturing and marketing sector and the cable and wireless telegraph sector, each absorbing around 20% of the funds. Data on the distribution of funds on a country-by-country basis are available only for the telephone service

Table 4. A Sectorial and Geographical Breakdown of ITT Investments in and
Advances to Subsidiaries, 1931 and 1940[1]

Units: $1,000 and %.

	1931[2]			1940		
	Investments & advances	%	%	Investments & advances	%	%
Subsidiaries in telephone & cable services	n.a	60.0	100.0	210,231	67.04	100.00
Argentina	n.a		41.4	90,911		43.2
Brazil	n.a		1.8	6,383		3.0
Chile	n.a		7.6	22,053		10.5
Peru	n.a		1.3	4,137		2.0
Cuba	n.a		6.5	10,241		4.9
Porto Rico	n.a		1.2	2,084		1.0
Mexico	n.a		7.8	10,416		5.0
China	n.a		3.2	2,054		1.0
Spain	n.a		24.7	50,080		23.8
Rumania	n.a		3.2	11,871		5.7
Mfg. & marketing subsidiaries	n.a	21.3		52,399	16.71	
Subsidiaries in cable & wireless telegraph service	n.a	18.0		28,310	9.03	
Other subsidiaries	n.a	0.7		22,668	7.22	
Total	n.a	100.0		313,608	100.00	

Source: *Report, op. cit.*, 1931 and 1940.
Notes: 1. ITT investments in and advances to affiliated companies are also included.
2. For the year 1931, only the percentage breakdowns are available.

sector. Leading in this sector was Argentina which, with a large subsidiary purchased in 1929, absorbed an immensely large 41.4% of sectorial funds. Coming next was Spain with approximately a 25% share. Spain was followed with considerable margins by Mexico, Chile, and Cuba, each with a share in the 6 to 8% range; then by China and Rumania, in the 3 to 4% range; and finally by Brazil, Peru, and Porto Rico, in the 1 to 2% range. One thing should be kept in mind here: the percentage breakdown of investments and advances shown above does not necessarily correspond to the number of telephones held in each country, because investments in and advances to affiliated and allied companies such as the one in Spain, in which ITT had only a partial interest, are also included. For instance, out of the total of more than 772,000 telephones owned by ITT in 1931, the number held in Argentina, 250,000 or 32.4%, and that in Spain, 242,000 or 31.4%, were not much different. All that can be said definitely about the other areas of activity is that manufacturing and marketing were mostly undertaken in Europe by ISE as mentioned earlier and that cable and wireless services were mainly concentrated in the United States.

IV

Such was the overall picture of ITT's global telecommunications empire when it expanded geographically to its utmost limits. Beginning in 1932 — or more accurately in the autum of 1931 — ITT was forced to stand on the defensive, to concern itself primarily with the question of how to keep its gigantic, extensive and diversified international structure alive in an international environment undergoing violent upheavals induced by the World Depression. In particular, it showed several crucial weaknesses in coping with the situation that emerged following the collapse of the restructured gold standard. In the first place, not only did ITT's financing scheme, which had functioned so well during the 1920s, cease to be operative with the collapse or stagnation of the securities market, but the burden of the excessive funding of the 1920s was also multiplied by the restrictions foreign governments imposed on remittances from its overseas subsidiaries. This financing scheme was such that ITT would raise operational funds in the American securities market and pay them back with profits remitted from its overseas subsidiaries. Thus, even if the inflow of remittances was reduced or totally stopped, the deadlines for debt servicing, at least those for the amortization of the bonds, came at regular intervals. In the second place, the violent fluctuations in foreign exchange rates affected ITT's financial position seriously, if not always negatively. In particular, it had no way of avoiding exchange losses caused by the devaluation of the currencies of those countries into which it had branched out.

And in the third place, especially because of its nature as an internationally active utility company, ITT was very vulnerable to restrictions placed on its overseas subsidiaries by local governments and to outright take-overs. Given the rising tide of nationalism and the ever intensifying political and military strains that characterized the international scene of the 1930s, it was not always possible for ITT, a private company, to expect to keep uncontested control of the nerve segment of a certain country's communications system. In this connection, there is no denying that ITT's persistent policy of promoting the "nationalization," i.e., localization, of overseas ventures by local residents was apt to invite the intervention of local governments. All of these problems were of course shared to one extent or another by many other MNEs, including those in the automotive and petroleum industries. But the nature and style of ITT's business activities made all of these problems a life-or-death question. I must admit, on the other hand, that ITT was not totally without means of protecting itself. It tried to put its organizational characteristics to the best possible use, mobilizing whatever means available to minimize the extent of the setback. I would like to trace in the following discussion some of the major steps ITT took in its desperate effort for survival.

ITT's business activities in the 1930s are clearly reflected in the trends of the income-or-loss account in Table 3. As I have noted above, gross earnings and especially net income had already begun to decline drastically in 1931, by 15% and 45%, respectively; in 1932, the former decreased further by $22 million, or 24%, and the latter by $12 million, or 15%, giving rise to a large net loss of $4 million. The large decrease in net income relative to the decrease in gross earnings is ascribable to the heavy costs of the annual redemption of bonds, which amounted to $5.8 million for the parent company alone, and to more than $11 million for the entire ITT system including subsidiaries. More precisely, the other cost items, including operational and marketing costs, depreciations of facilities, and interest on bank loans and taxes decreased along with gross earnings, and thus net income before payment of principals and interests for bonds, though decreasing at the very large rate of 58% far in excess of the rate of decrease of gross earnings, still showed a surplus of $18 million in 1931 and $7.4 million in 1932. Moreover, the payment of dividends — which is not directly related to the income-or-loss account as it is deducted from net profits in the surplus fund account — was suspended throughout the 1930s beginning in 1931. As for exchange losses, which amounted to $2.5 million in 1931 and $2.2 million in 1932, these were not reckoned up in the income-or-loss account but were treated as a deductable item in the surplus fund account.[22]

Thus ITT was faced with a growing gap between the costs of refunding the enormous liabilities it had accumulated in the course of its rapid expansion in the past and a sharp reduction in current income from its overseas subsidiaries. For several years thereafter it continued to be annoyed when the time came to pay principal and interest on bonds each year. But the question was not simply a matter of declining income: it was also a matter of liquidity. To be more specific, although the ITT system as a whole held $12 million in cash as of the end of 1932, nearly $4 million of this amount was frozen by foreign governments and unavilable for the payment of debts. Within the United States, too, from around 1931, Behn, aggressive businessman though he was, found it increasingly difficult to obtain money on loan for debt servicing. Like any other firm in this situation, ITT had no recourse but to fall back on what may be called a set of passive rationalization schemes including wage reductions, personnel curtailment, and the scaling down of operations, i.e., the "conservation of cash resources."[23]

As a result of these rationalization schemes, each of which contributed to reducing costs on the order of $100,000, and also due to a slight upturn of economic activities in the United States and abroad, ITT's financial positions improved somewhat in 1933 and thereafter. What is noteworthy about this process of modest recovery is that although gross earnings did not increase much or even decreased slightly, net income was maintained at a more or less stable level (see Table 3). It is also worth noting that although ITT was annoyed during the first half of 1933 by the financial panic in the United States, in the second half of the year, the ITT system as a whole earned a large profit of $9.5 million accruing from the revaluation of its liquid assets. This reputedly contributed to a great extent to bringing its gross earnings and net income for the year back into surplus again. This, along with the relaxation of control on foreign exchange outflow undertaken by several countries in the same year, mitigated the parent company's liquidity position at least for the time being.[24]

It should be kept in mind, however, that in dealing with the liquidity question, ITT also had recourse to interesting methods devised to make use of its international structure. One such method, the "Shanghai formula," consisted of letting the Shanghai subsidiary procure funds for use by the parent company in repaying its debts in the United States. In 1932-33, the Shanghai company raised seven million Chinese dollars through local bond issues and loans and transferred five million of this amount to the parent company in partial repayment of its outstanding debts to the head office, thereby contributing to the improvement of the latter's liquidity position. Pleased with the success of this formula, ITT used it frequently from then on not only with the Shanghai company but with subsidiaries elsewhere, as I shall point out later. These factors contributed to the improvement of the parent company's liquidity position and also helped it recover its credibility with American banks to some extent, enabling it to start renewing short-term bank loans again.[25]

It was precisely when ITT's financial position appeared to be regaining stability and equilibrium, if on a reduced scale, that the Spanish Civil War broke out in the summer of 1936, throwing ITT into what proved to be its most serious crisis during the 1930s. ITT found itself in a very delicate position. It was viewed by the Francoists as an enemy siding with the People's Front government; it was also suspected by the Loyalists as a potential ally of their enemy and was thus "defended" by 200 government soldiers. The building housing the headquarters of its Madrid company was chosen as one of the main targets of bombing by the Francoists. When a neutral force proposed that the company building be protected, Franco rejected the proposal on the grounds that a communications center was an important military target. It is reported, however, that Franco, wanting to take over the telephone system unharmed, did not seriously intend to destroy it. Yet, on the other hand, the government forces threatened to blow up the company building when they retreated from Madrid, and ITT thus continued to sit on thorns. Amidst the political upheavals and against all the odds, ITT reputedly tried its best to keep its Spanish operation alive by taking a neutral stance at all times. And after the People's Front government was finally defeated and the Civil War came to an end in 1939, ITT's Spanish subsidiary was saved from being taken over by the Francoists through the intervention of the American State Department.[26]

However, the losses incurred during the Civil War by the Spanish company, which previously accounted for a quarter of ITT's total income, put Behn in a straitjacket. As a matter of fact, even prior to the outbreak of the Spanish Civil War, Behn had been driven into a corner because the Postal Telegraph, a subsidiary in the United States, had incurred an enormous loss close to $15 million over a period of several years, and by 1935 it had been forced to rehabilitate itself under Section 77B of the Bankruptcy Act. In its effort to cope with this financial crisis, ITT resorted to an extremely drastic measure in 1936, cutting the face value of ITT's common stocks by more than one third, from $33.33 to $20 per share. As a result, ITT reduced its paid-up capital from approximately $225 million to approximately $139 million (see Table 1 above), transferred the approximately $87 million difference to such items as "reserve for revaluation of assets" and "capital surplus," and thus raised spare money with which to overcome the crisis situation.[27] Needless to say, however, this drastic measure did not create the cash the company required at regular intervals for the redemption of its bonds and bank loans, and money for this purposed had to be raised by other means.

In the first place, ITT set out to put the Shanghai formula into effect on a large scale in 1937, selling $30 million worth of bonds of the large and prosperous Argentine subsidiary, United River Plate, through banking syndicates in Argentina, Sweden, and Switzerland in the currencies of the respective countries. Most of the money raised was used to reduce the subsidiary's outstanding debts to ITT. Then ITT took over the guaranteed notes of its subsidiaries held by New York banks amounting to $20.9 million and to reduced the notes to $9.7 million. It also set aside another portion in a special account to meet the 1939 bond maturity. In 1938, ITT resorted to the same scheme in a somewhat more interesting way. The parent company arranged for the sale by its European manufacturing and marketing subsidiary, ISE, of $15 million worth of bonds in Switzerland and the Netherlands. The parent company absorbed much of the proceeds, i.e., $9 million, by way of selling ISE equity in several of its European subsidiaries (such as those in France and England). Given the fact that ITT owned ISE 100 per cent, these transactions did not affect ITT's control over its subsidiaries in substance but simply changed the form of control into a somewhat indirect one intermediated by ISE, a holding company. The year 1938 also saw the application of the Shanghai formula on a smaller scale to subsidiaries in Buenos Aires, Argentina, and Lima, Peru. The parent company itself also held, in 1938, a series of small-lot sales of its securities in Zurich, Amsterdam, Brussels, and London.[28]

One might say that ITT was able to resort to these measures by taking advantage of its international corporate structure to the fullest extent. In actuality, however, these were no more than desperate measures taken under the pressure of necessity: ITT, unable to meet its past liabilities by issuing refunding bonds in the current American securities markets, barely managed to convert its old debts into new ones by turning to the securities market abroad where the terms of bond issues were not necessarily favorable. Needless to say, one condition that allowed ITT to avail itself of this method was that up till the early 1930s, the ITT system had been structured in a way such that the parent company alone issued bonds in the securities markets but the majority of the subsidiaries would not, on their own. In this respect, the aforementioned measures might be regarded as the ones employed to readjust this structure. And the process of this readjustment was characterized by the fact that some part of the capital funds that had flowed out of the United States during the 1920s was recycled back to the United States through the internal transfers of one international corporate system. At any rate, however, there is no denying that these measures were resorted to under the pressure of necessity. Moreover, quite suggestive of the extent of the hardships the company was facing in its international activities during this period, it even dared to resort to a very special form of barter transactions by receiving petroleum in payment for its sales of telephone apparatuses in East Europe where foreign exchange restrictions were extremely severe, then changing the petroleum into tobacco or grains, and finally into American dollars.[29]

Despite these efforts, it became utterly hopeless during 1939 for ITT to raise on its own the funds required to pay $37.5 million worth of long-term bonds and $9.7 million worth of the notes payable it had taken over as mentioned above, both of which fell due on 1 January 1939. Coming on the scene at this juncture as lender of last resort was the Export-Import Bank of America. As is well known, the Export-Import Bank was established as a government-funded financial institution with the purpose of assisting American firms with their international, mainly trade-related, activities in light of the stagnant international economic environment following the World Depression.[30] In December 1938, the Bank decided to grant ITT's request for emergency rescue loans on the grounds that — as Chairman J.H. Jones of the Reconstruction Finance Corporation, the superior government-affiliated agency financing the Bank, emphasized — it was a matter of high policy that the United States not lose its important international communications enterprise. Even though the Export-Import Bank did not offer the entire amount requested by ITT but underwrote $10 million of a ten-year, $15 million serial loan, the Bank's decision induced New York banks, which had been reluctant to extend loans to ITT, to agree at long last to supply the rest.[31]

The intervention by the Export-Import Bank was of qualitative significance in the sense that it not only enabled ITT to remain alive but also helped it overcome the chief weakness in its financial structure. This is because once ITT was assured of the possibility of paying off the liabilities which it had accumulated inside the United States, it would find it relatively easy to let its foreign subsidiaries service and pay off their own debts, which they had been gradually incurring, from out of their own revenues in local currencies without being bothered by converting such revenues into dollars and remitting the dollars to the parent company.[32] To put it differently, its subsidiaries had become more autonomous than previously, and ITT had reached a higher stage of development as an MNE. At the same time, however, this fact, along with the international situation of the time in which nationalism was on the rise, seems to have accelerated the tendency toward decentralization of the ITT system as a whole. In spite of this, it is worth special notice that in its debt-passing, ITT managed to keep intact its equity in its subsidiaries, reflecting the strong tenacity of Behn in retaining control over them.

The year 1939 turned out to be a relatively calm one for ITT. Having gone through the radical revamping described above, its operations were apparently returning to a stable path. Yet the apparently favorable performance owed mainly to the military boom in France, England, and elsewhere. The ITT system derived as much as 40% of its total revenues from the dividends of ISE, which was manufacturing and marketing mainly in Europe. By nature, this war boom was a prelude to Nazi Germany's invasions into neighboring countries on the European continent and to the subsequent outbreak of World War II in the autumn of this year, and as such it was destined to be short-lived. In fact, the dividends received from ISE in 1940 plummeted to one sixth the amount of the preceding year and to zero in 1941. On top of this came the reimposition of foreign exchange restrictions by South American countries, causing ITT to run up a deficit in 1940 which grew further in 1941 (see Table 3 above). Thus, in 1940, after only two years of "stability," ITT was again faced with a shortage of debt servicing funds amounting to $2 million.

This time Behn, in spite of all his entrepreneurial talents, apparently had to fall back on the last resort available to him, i.e., selling off of some of ITT's subsidiaries. Early in 1940, by coincidence, Spanish bankers offered to buy ITT's 80% common equity in the Spanish Telephone Co. at a price of $60 million, which was $36 million more than the equity's value on ITT's books. Moreover, ITT had not received any revenue from the Spanish company since 1936. All in all, therefore, the terms of the offer were exceptionally favorable to ITT. Yet, the United States Department of State repeatedly refused to grant ITT permission to conclude the deal on the grounds that German money was behind the offer, but in return, the State Department assured the company of greater aid from the Export-Import Bank. Not only did the Export-

Import Bank agree to offer a new loan of $1.5 million; it also agreed, along with other holders of the company's ten-year notes, to postpone a payment of $400,000 amortization for 1940 until 1948.[33] For the second time, ITT managed to tide over a crisis without having to play its last card.

It should be pointed out, however, that the ITT system had in effect already been shrinking considerably due partly to the fact that for several years ITT had for all practical purposes been out of touch with its German subsidiaries and partly to the fact that it sold its Rumanian subsidiary to the Rumanian government several days before it was taken over by the German army in January 1941.[34] The scaling down of the ITT system is evident from the consolidated balance sheet shown in Table 1. The company's total assets had been on the decline with minor fluctuations from the peak value of approximately $620 million in 1931, reached approximately $500 million by 1939, and declined further to $430 million by 1940. Over the same period, its fixed assets had also decreased following more or less the same trend from $420 million to $320 million and then to $240 million.

In this connection it is also interesting to take note of trends in the number of telephones held by company subsidiaries engaged in telephone services, the most important sector of ITT operations. It is immediately clear from Figure 1 that the number of telephones owned by ITT had grown at a fast tempo, peaking at around 750,000 in 1930, and that thereafter the rate of increase slowed down appreciably. Needless to say, a completely different picture could be drawn for the late 1930s depending on how one evaluates the number of telephones held by the Spanish subsidiary in the period from 1936 to 1939. As noted above, the Spanish company was outside the control of the parent company during this period, and thus the exact number of telephones in its possession is unknown, except for an estimate for 1937 indicated by broken lines in the figure. Supposing the total number of telephones to have increased along the line joining those for 1935 and 1940, both of which are known, and that for 1937 inclusive of the estimated number for the Spanish company, then it seems that the number of telephones in ITT's possession, including those of the Spanish company, increased at a faster rate in the latter half of the 1930s than in the earlier half.

As a result, as shown in Table 4, the share of the telephone service sector in the parent company's investments in and advances to its subsidiaries, inclusive of the Spanish one, rose from 60% in 1931 to 67% in 1940. In contrast, the cable and wireless telegraph sector's share decreased by half due mainly to Postal Telegraph's bankruptcy; the manufacturing and marketing sector's share, too, decreased drastically. As for the distribution of investments in the telephone service sector on a country-by-country basis, there was not much drastic change excepting that the shares of Argentina and Chile increased slightly, and those of Cuba and Spain decreased by small margins and that, as pointed out already, the Rumanian subsidiary totally broke away from the ITT system in 1940.

V

I have thus far traced the rapid development of ITT in the 1920s as an international telephone and telegraph enterprise and the hard struggles for survival it waged subsequently in the 1930s. The company's composition, which helped it grow as a peculiar type of interna-

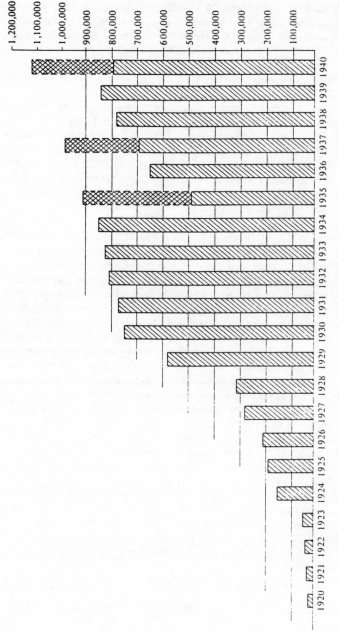

Figure 1. The Number of Telephones Possessed by ITT, 1920-40

Source: For the years 1920-39, ITT's *Annual Report*, 1935, p. 43; for the years 1936-40, the number given in each issue of the *Report* has been graphically represented.

Note: The numbers for the years 1936-39 are exclusive of those held in Spain, which are unknown due to the Spanish Civil War and the subsequent state of disorder. Only an estimated number is available for 1937 for the Spanish company. ⬚ represents the telephone held in Spain.

tional firm in the 1920s, suddenly turned to its disadvantage in the 1930s, pushing it into a tight corner and forcing it to backtrack somewhat. However, even while on the defensive, ITT coped with the situation in an exceptionally resourceful manner and managed somehow or other to keep functioning as an international utility company at least until the outbreak of World War II. But the company's resistance had its limits. Once the war started, its business performance changed completely. On the one hand, its overseas activities crumbled first in Europe and then in Asia, leaving only its operations in Latin America barely going in a very precarious way. On the other hand, the manufacturing subsidiaries in the United States were flooded with orders for electric communications apparatuses placed by the military.[35] Expanded production activities in the United States not only helped the company make up for losses incurred abroad, albeit not entirely, but also drastically changed the company's nature. In 1944 and 1945, ITT sold its two largest foreign telephone subsidiaries, i.e., the Spanish and the Argentine companies, to the respective local governments, and in 1949 it saw its Shanghai subsidiary confiscated by the newly established socialist government of China. Thus, in the immediate aftermath of the war it had no choice but to make a fresh start by concentrating, for the time being, on the manufacturing and marketing of electric products inside the United States and looking forward to the resumption of production by its manufacturing subsidiaries in Europe. It is therefore safe to say that with the conclusion of the war, ITT's history as an international utility company also came to an end.[36]

In many respects, ITT underwent experiences that are quite unique for an MNE. One factor that makes ITT stand out among MNEs is that as an international utility company it rode the tide of the securities boom of the 1920s in the United States, along with American utility companies operative inside the country, established a multiple-layered holding-company system on a global scale by purchasing pre-existing firms, and in the 1930s, when securities speculation ceased to work for it, it suffered a serious setback. As a matter of fact, in this context, the rise and fall of ITT is similar to that of American Foreign Power Co., also a utility company active internationally. Just as securities speculation triggered the consolidation of nation-wide networks of power grids and telephone and telegraph services within the United States, so did it mediate the process of expansion and the propagation of similar facilities abroad. Of special significance in the case of telephone and telegraph services is that ITT not only promoted these services and the manufacture of necessary apparatuses in each of the countries into which it branched out, but it also integrated the telephone and telegraph systems of individual countries into a literally global network. And given the considerably poor relations of mutual communications that existed at the time among the governments of various countries, an internationally operative private firm like ITT seems to have been better adapted to and far more capable of installing a global communications network than the state machinery of any country. Needless to say, in the establishment of a global communications network, a not insignificant role was played by an individual named Behn, a rare international entrepreneur.

Another unique aspect of ITT is that from its inception, it began as a company engaged in the international operation of telephones and telegraph services, the parent company having virtually no managerial base within the United States including technological know-how. It was only after it started operating telephone services internationally that it bought up a series of manufacturing subsidiaries, mainly abroad, which were necessary for its business, and allocated them internationally. A course of development such as this is quite extraordinary for an MNE, and the case of ITT is very significant in that it offers a concrete example of development along this path. In this regard, the American Foreign Power Co. was different, as it had some roots in the United States. It was established by the holding company of a public utility affiliated with the General Electric group, Electric Bond & Share Co., and was desinged to engage mainly in the cultivation of overseas markets for General Electric's products. It should be kept in mind, however, that even ITT eventually established relations with ATT, and came to act as, so to speak, the latter's international division.

The extremely rapid pace of growth that characterized ITT in its earlier days had inherent in it a very serious problem. That ITT, along with the American Foreign Power Co., was subsequently forced during the late 1930s and World War II to backtrack and scale itself down cannot be explained away simply in terms of the generally unfavorable international business climate prevailing at the time. I have already pointed out that ITT's financial operations scheme proved totally disadvantageous during this period. Far more important, however, is that ITT was active in telephone and telegraph services, a utility sector with pivotal importance to any country's political and economic system, just as the supply of electricity, the field of the American Foreign Power Co., was of pivotal importance. It is precisely because of this that ITT, by paying greatest concern to promoting the "nationalization," i.e., localization, of its subsidiaries, grew into an MNE in the true sense of the word and that it was able to extract special aid from the American State Department and the Export-Import Bank without difficulty. And yet it is this very same point that basically explains why ITT, with the end of World War II, was not allowed to revive itself again as an internationally active utility enterprise.

A multinational company, in my understanding, is a large modernized firm which has grown to acquire production, marketing, managerial, and administrative techniques and know-how on a global scale; in the very process of its global expansion, it constantly faces the need to adapt itself to the natural and social environment, in particular modern nationalism, of the country into which it expands; while trying to find its way toward further growth, it is consequently obliged to devise a variety of "localization" schemes; and in that sense it is indeed a living entity with ceaseless tensions and strains. And this pressure for "localization" worked especially heavily upon ITT, an international utility company.

Notes

*   This paper is one of the results of the research I conducted during my one-year stay in the United States – mainly at Florida International University – from fall 1980 to summer 1981 as a Fellow of the American Council of Learned Societies. In preparing the paper, I have benefitted a great deal from the important materials on ITT and other MNEs which Professor Mira Wilkins of the above-mentioned university generously provided me and from the penetrating suggestions concerning studies of MNEs I received from her in her seminars and through private discussions with her. Needless to say, whatever flaws that may still remain in the paper are entirely mine.

1.   See, for instance, her major works: M. Wilkins and F. E. Hill, *American Business Abroad: Ford on Six Continents*, Wayne University Press, 1964; M. Wilkins, *The Emergence of Multinational Enterprise*, Harvard University Press, 1970; and *do.*, *The Maturing Multinational Enterprise*, Harvard University Press, 1974.

2.   ABO Tetsuo, "American Automobile Enterprises Abroad during the Interwar Period: Case Studies

on Ford and General Motors with Emphasis on the Process of their 'Multinational' Adaptation to Local Climates," *Annals of the Institute of Social Science,* University of Tokyo, No. 22, 1981; *do.,* "Nyudiiru no Taigaikeizai: Sono Keizai Gaiko to Daikigyo no Kokugaijigyo Katsudo" (Foreign e-conomic policies and the overseas business activities of large enterprises), in the Institute of Social Science, University of Tokyo, ed., *Fashizumu-ki no Kokka to Shakai, 3: Nachisu-keizai to Nyudiiru* (State and society during the period of fascism, 3: The Nazi economy and the New Deal), Univer-sity of Tokyo Press, 1980. All of these papers, along with a piece on General Electric, are incorpo-rated in my forthcoming book tentatively titled *Ryo-taisenkan-ki Amerika Taigaitoshi no Kenkyu* (Studies on American foreign investments during the interwar period), scheduled for publication by the University of Tokyo Press in early 1983.

3.   For general analysis of the activities of the American Foreign Power Co., see ITAGAKI Hiroshi, "1920-nendai Amerika Koeki-kigyo no Kaigai Toshi (1), (2)" (Investment of United States utility corpo-rations in Latin America in the 1920s, (1), (2)), *Journal of Saitama University Social Science,* Vol. 27, 1979, and Vol. 29, 1981.

4.   For the description of the paragraph, see *Fortune,* December 1930, p. 35; and A. Sampson, *The Sovereign State: The Secret History of ITT,* London, etc.: Hodder & Stoughton, 1973, pp. 23-25. It should be pointed out additionally that there is one factor that seems to have interested Behn into the telephone and telegraph business: he served as Colonel in the United States Army's Communi-cations Corps during World War I. See Sampson, *ibid.*

5.   *Fortune, op. cit.,* p. 36; and *Annual Report of the International Telephone and Telegraph Corpora-tion* (hereafter abbreviated as *Report*), 1921, p. 5 ff.

6.   For the description of the paragraph thus far, see *Report,* 1929, p. 9; and *Fortune. ibid.,* p. 37.

7.   *Fortune, ibid.,* p. 42.

8.   Various issues of ITT *Report* regarded the Spanish company as a subsidiary in a broad sense, but treated it somewhat differently from other subsidiaries by excluding this company from the consolidated balance sheet. It should be pointed out that whereas the parent company's investments in and loans to the Spanish company amounted to a little less than $5 million, the value of stocks issued by the latter in Spain was approximately $17 million, of which $14 million was in the form of preferred stocks, the balance being in the form of common stocks. It appears, therefore, that most of the com-mon stocks (approximately 80%) were bought up with the parent company's investments mentioned above. (On this point, see *Report,* 1924 and 1925.) In connection with the issuing of stocks by the Spanish subsidiary, Marqués de Urguijo, the nation's foremost banker-financier, joined the parent company's directorate. (See *Fortune,* op. cit., p. 45.)

9.   For more detail on this point, see *Boston News Bureau,* October 6, 1924 (thanks are due to Professor M. Wilkins for showing me this piece from her file); *Fortune, op. cit.,* pp. 41-42; and *Report,* 1924, p. 11, and 1925, p. 7.

10.   On the purchase of International Western Electric, which was renamed ISE, see the *New York Times,* August 15, 1925 (again my thanks are due to Professor Wilkins for showing me this piece from her file); Sampson, *op. cit.,* pp. 24-25; R. Newfarmer, *Transnational Conglomerates and the Economics of Dependent Development: A Case Study of the International Electrical Oligopoly and Brazil's Elec-trical Industry,* Greenwhich: JAI Press Inc., 1980, p. 70; *Report,* 1925; and *Fortune. op. cit.,* pp. 36 and 124.

11.   *Report,* 1925.

12.   Various issues of *Report* fail to explain why the rate of increase in net income fell behind that in gross earnings. As shown in Table 3, for instance, from 1927 to 1928, gross earnings more than doubled, increasing from $37 million to $81 million, but net income did not increase much and remained in the range of $14-15 million for both years. In the consolidated balance sheets for the two years, this significant gap is ascribable mainly to the difference in the combined cost items of "operational, marketing, and general costs, taxes, and depreciations" for the two years (i.e., $20 million for 1927 and $58 million for 1928). But as to why the figures differed this much, no explanation is available (see *Report,* 1927, p. 28, and 1928, p. 34).

13.   For the workforce of General Motors, see *Moody's Industrial,* 1930, and for that of Standard Oil of New Jersey, see H.M. Larson, et al., *New Horizons 1927-1950,* New York, etc.: Harper & Row Publishers, 1971, Appendix 2, Table 6, p. 819.

14.   In investing in ITT's or in any other company's stocks at the time, small and medium investors were primarily motivated by expected capital gains rather than by dividends, and, accordingly, ITT's dividend rate was kept around 6% per annum throughout the 1920s. On the other hand, as shown in the table below, the stock prices after 1923, when data become available, continued to increase rapidly until 1929, except for 1926 when they declined slightly.

Changes in ITT's Stock Prices, 1923-29

Unit: $ per share with
face value of $100.

	1923	1924	1925	1926	1927	1928	1929
Maximum	$71\frac{1}{2}$	94	144	133	$158\frac{7}{8}$	201	279
Minimum	64	64	$87\frac{1}{2}$	111	$122\frac{1}{4}$	$139\frac{1}{2}$	$197\frac{1}{4}$

Source: *Poor's Public Utilities,* 1930, p. 2213.

In this connection, it is worth pointing out that there is one factor that seems to have been quite effective in attracting ordinary investors. This is that when issuing new stocks, ITT entitled the current stockholders to purchase new stocks at a price below the current price in amounts proportional to their current holdings. This arrangement might have made the sales of new stocks easier than otherwise and provided ordinary investors with incentive to own ITT stocks. For instance, in April 1925, ITT allotted approximately 90,000 new stocks to its stockholders at $83 per share and at a ratio of one new stock for every two pre-existing stocks. This price was lower than the minimum stock price for the year by several dollars, and, needless to say, it was more than 60 dollars lower than the year's maximum price.

15.   An employee was allowed to purchase one stock for every $600 of his annual salary, up to a maximum of 50 stocks. In 1928, for instance, 8,600 employees, or approximately 10% of the total workforce, were in possession of a total of 21,000 shares, which accounted for approximately 1.5% of the total stocks outstanding at the time (see *Report,* 1925, p. 17, 1928, p. 26, etc.).

16.   On the developments in 1926-27, see *Report,* 1927; *Fortune, op. cit.,* pp. 120 and 123; and Wilkins, *The Maturing..., op. cit.,* pp. 129-31.

17. In buying up Mackay Co., many of the securities (common stocks, preferred stocks, and bonds) of this company were acquired in exchange for securities of the Postal Telegraph and Cable Corp., and then ITT owned the latter's common stocks. As in cases of other utility firms in the United States, ITT managed to expand its areas of activity in an efficient manner by bringing many subsidiaries under its control through its two-stage holding company set-up. On this point, see *Report*, 1928; and *Fortune*, *op. cit.*, pp. 43 and 118.

18. Since the purchase of United River Plate in Argentina was made in cash, nearly 730,000 stocks were newly issued, of which about 70% were allotted to present stockholders (in the form of non-par stocks, at $50 per share and at the ratio of one share for every 10 shares held). In contrast, in the case of the establishment to the Postal Telegraph and Cable Corp., ITT only acquired the new subsidiary's common stocks and thus was able to raise the funds for this purpose by issuing only about 22,000 new stocks (see *Report*, 1929).

19. *Report*, 1930, p. 30; and 1931, p. 26.

20. For the description of the paragraph, see *Report*, 1930 and 1931; and *Fortune*, September 1945, pp. 148 and 191.

21. *Report*, 1930 and 1931. It should be pointed out that in June 1931, ITT signed a contract to purchase L.M. Ericson Telephone Co., Ltd. of Stockholm, one of its major rivals in the manufacturing of telephone apparatuses in Europe and Latin America, at $11 million. However, ITT cancelled this large-scale deal because immediately following the signing of the contract, an accounting scandal involving L.M. Ericson's parent company, Kreuger & Toll, was exposed. Although the deal to buy up Ericson did not materialize, ITT thereafter kept holding a 30% interest in it and putting three executives on its directorates. See *Fortune*, *op. cit.*, 1945, pp. 191-92.

22. On these points, see the facts shown in the pertinent tables in the text and *Report*, 1931 and 1932.

23. For a description of the paragraph, see *Fortune*, *op. cit.*, 1945, pp. 191-92.

24. Unlike the handling of the exchange losses in 1931-32, the exchange margins on this occasion seem to have been computed into the income-or-loss account, although I cannot say this for sure because the 1933 *Report* fails to provide detailed breakdowns of the surplus account. See *Fortune*, *ibid.*, p. 192.

25. *Ibid.* pp. 192 and 195.

26. For a description of the paragraph, see *ibid.*, pp. 195-96; and Sampson, *op. cit.*, p. 29.

27. *Report*, 1935; and 1936, pp. 19-23; and *Fortune*, *op. cit.*, 1945, p. 196.

28. *Fortune*, *ibid.*, pp. 196 and 198; and *Report*, 1937 and 1938.

29. For ITT's bartar transactions, see *Fortune*, *ibid.*, p. 198.

30. For an analysis of the Export-Import Bank, see my "Nyudiiru no Taigaikeizai ....," *op. cit.*, p. 381; and F. C. Adams, *Economic Diplomacy: The Export-Import Bank and American Foreign Policy, 1934-1939*, University of Missouri Press, 1976.

31. *Fortune*, *op. cit.*, 1945, pp. 198 and 201.

32.   From the end of 1936 through the end of 1939, for the ITT system as a whole, debts in dollars decreased by approximately $46 million while debts in foreign currencies increased by approximately $44 million (see *Fortune, ibid.*, p. 201).

33.   *Fortune, ibid.*, pp. 201 and 203.

34.   For a general descriptions of ITT's relations with Nazi Germany, see Sampson, *op. cit.*, p. 27 ff. For the selling off of the Rumaninan subsidiary, see *Fortune, op. cit.*, 1945, p. 203.

35.   *Fortune, ibid.*, pp. 204 and 207.

36.   ITT sold its Spanish subsidiary to the Spanish government at $88 million and its Argentine subsidiary to the Argentine government at $95 million. It should be pointed out, furthermore, that after the war, ITT first of all concentrated on expanding its businesses within the United States and on expanding the manufacture of electrical products, particularly in Europe, thereby transforming itself into a large MNE active in the areas of electrical products manufacturing and communications services. And by 1963, it had grown to hold the largest number of employees among all the United States-based MNEs (see Wilkins, *The Maturing ..., op. cit.*, pp. 304 and 423-24). Ever since, it has been continuously transforming itself into a "conglomerate," extending its activities even into areas other than electrical products manufacturing and communications services. On this point, see ITAGAKI Hiroshi, "1960-nendai no Amerika ni okeru Godo-undo: Konguromaritto-kigyo ITT o chusin ni" (Concentration of firms in the United States during the 1960s: An analysis with emphasis on ITT, a conglomerate), *Shoken Kenkyu* (The Study of Security), Vol. 48, 1976.

Part V
Hosts to Multinationals

Economic History Review, 2nd ser., XLI, 3 (1988), pp. 429-453

Foreign multinationals and British industry before 1945[1]

By GEOFFREY JONES

Since the late nineteenth century Britain has been the recipient of substantial investment by foreign-owned multinational enterprises. Foreign-owned companies had a significant impact on certain sectors of British industry, and the positions they acquired in those sectors point towards the existence of serious managerial, entrepreneurial, and technological inadequacies within indigenous British business. This article examines the role of foreign multinationals in British manufacturing and utilities before 1945. Section I looks at the dimensions of this investment; section II discusses the reasons which led foreign companies to establish or acquire factories in Britain, and section III examines the impact of these companies on the British economy.

I

A considerable number of foreign companies established or acquired manufacturing operations in Britain between 1850 and 1945.[2] No full listing of these companies exists, but this study has established 125 such investments, the details of which are given in appendix 1. It should be stressed that marketing and sales companies are excluded, although it was usual for foreign firms to establish such companies before they began manufacturing in Britain, and that the analysis is confined to initial investments. Appendix 1 has been compiled from a wide range of sources, each entry having been checked from at least two different sources. Given that a firm's inclusion in the list depended on the availability of reliable information, the sample cannot claim to have been 'randomly' selected. Nevertheless the data set appears well distributed with respect to industries and dates of foundation, although there is probably a bias towards larger, American, and publicly-quoted firms, about which more information is available. Two earlier estimates give much larger numbers of foreign multinational investments in Britain, but as they do not list the companies concerned it is impossible to verify them. Dunning estimated that around 240 American companies established factories in Britain before 1939. Appendix 1 lists 67 American investments, or 28 per cent of the Dunning estimate. Law located 162

[1] I would like to thank John H. Dunning, Howard Gospel, Hans Chr. Johansen, Jonathan Liebenau, Ragnhild Lundström, Mike Robson, Mira Wilkins, the participants in seminars at Cambridge, Edinburgh and Glasgow, and two anonymous referees for their help in preparing this article.

A multinational is defined broadly in this article as an enterprise possessing a controlling interest in income-generating assets or productive activities outside its national boundaries.

[2] Dunning, *American investment* was a pioneering study of this subject. Wilkins, *Emergence* and *idem, Maturing* provided valuable new information on American companies in Britain.

430   GEOFFREY JONES

foreign companies which established plants in Britain between 1918 and
1944. Appendix 1 lists a total of 71 investments in the same period, or 44
per cent of the Law figure.[3] It would seem safe to conclude that appendix
1 includes at least one-third of total multinational investments in British
industry before 1945; that it contains a high proportion of the larger
investments; and that it provides a respectable, if not perfect, sample on
which to base inferences about the population of foreign multinationals in
Britain as a whole.

Table 1 summarizes the data on the timing and nationality of the 125
multinational investments in appendix 1.

Table 1. *Date of establishment of first factory in Britain by foreign
companies, 1850-1939*

Decade	USA	Germany	Sweden	Other	Total
1850-9	2	—	—	—	2
1860-9	2	1	—	—	3
1870-9	—	—	—	1	1
1880-9	—	1	—	1	2
1890-9	6	2	1	—	9
1900-9	13	6	1	5	25
1910-9	3	—	4	5	12
1920-9	24	1	5	10	40
1930-9	17	6	2	6	31
Total	67	17	13	28	125

From the middle of the nineteenth century a trickle of foreign companies
began manufacturing in Britain. The 1900s saw the first large wave of such
investment, and there was an even greater number of investments in the
1920s. Although international investment in general slumped in the 1930s,
new foreign multinational investment in Britain remained substantial. The
United States was the leading multinational investor. Of the sample of 125
investments between 1850 and 1939 54 per cent were American, and the
American preponderance grew over time. Between 1850 and 1919, 48 per
cent of the 54 investments were American. The other large investors came
from Germany (19 per cent), Sweden (11 per cent), and Switzerland (10 per
cent). There were also one or two investments by companies from Denmark,
the Netherlands, France, and Italy. Between 1920 and 1939, 58 per cent of
the 71 investments were American. Germany and Sweden followed with 10
per cent each, a smaller number of investments being recorded for companies
from Denmark, the Netherlands, France, Italy, Czechoslovakia, Australia,
and Canada.

The first 'multinational' manufacturing investments in Britain were
probably those of Samuel Colt, the American gun manufacturer, who
established a factory in London in 1853, and J. Ford and Co. who established
an Edinburgh factory to manufacture vulcanized rubber in 1856. Both
companies disinvested within a few years, and the first sustained American

---

[3] Dunning, *American investment*, pp. 32-44; Law, *British regional development*, p. 174.

FOREIGN MULTINATIONALS AND BRITISH INDUSTRY 431

investment was that of Singer, which established a sewing machine factory at Glasgow in 1867.[4] Meanwhile, the German electrical firm of Siemens founded a London factory to manufacture sea cables in 1863. Although the British branch of the firm possessed some managerial independence, it can be regarded as a subsidiary of the German parent.[5] In the decades before 1914 a steady stream of American companies established factories in Britain in a wide range of industries. There was a particular emphasis on electrical equipment and telecommunications, but American firms also invested in office machinery, matches, cameras, records, food and—with the establishment of a Ford assembly plant at Manchester in 1911—motor cars.

Although American companies were the most numerous multinational investors, continental firms were also active. By 1914 there were subsidiaries of prominent German firms such as Mannesmann and Hoechst manufacturing in the electrical, chemical, and pharmaceutical sectors in Britain. One Swiss company was an early multinational investor in Britain; in 1872 the Anglo-Swiss Condensed Milk Company, which despite its name was a wholly owned Swiss firm, established a factory. Nestlé, Anglo-Swiss's national rival, established a British factory in 1901 before the two firms merged in 1905.[6] By 1914 Hoffman La Roche, in pharmaceuticals, and the largest Swiss chemicals company, Gesellschaft für chemische Industrie (Ciba), had established or acquired British factories. Swedish companies invested before 1914 in the electrical and telecommunications sector. L.M. Ericsson established a joint venture in 1903 with the British-owned National Telephone Company to manufacture telephone equipment, while Jönköping and Vulcan built a match factory in London in 1910.[7] Among other European investments before 1914 were those undertaken by the Danish margarine manufacturer, Otto Monsted, who established a factory in Manchester in 1888,[8] and Adolphe Clément, a leading French car manufacturer who in 1903 formed a joint venture with British interests known as Clément-Talbot, which assembled and later manufactured 'Talbot' cars in a London factory; another French car manufacturer, Lorraine-Dietrich, established a factory in Birmingham in 1903.[9] In 1914 Pirelli of Italy joined with the British-owned General Electric Company to found the Pirelli General Cable Works, with a factory at Southampton to manufacture cables and electrical equipment.[10]

The First World War did nothing to impede the expansion of foreign multinationals in Britain. After 1919 the numbers of American companies investing in Britain increased. Three leading American tyre manufacturers established British factories. In the motor industry, Ford began the construction of a giant new plant at Dagenham near London in the late

[4] Wilkins, *Emergence*, pp. 29, 30, 39-42; Blakemore, 'Colt's London armoury'; Davies, *Peacefully working*, pp. 42-4; Hounshell, *From the American system*, pp. 18-25, 92-6.
[5] Scott, *Siemens brothers*, chs. 3 and 4.
[6] Heer, *World events*, pp. 57, 67, 79, 89.
[7] Lundström, 'Swedish multinational growth', pp. 137, 143; Lindgren, *Corporate growth*, p. 168.
[8] H.C. Johansen, 'Danmark pa de multinationale selskabers landkort for 1914' (unpublished paper, 1986).
[9] Laux, *In first gear*, pp. 44, 105, 165. Maxcy, *The multinational motor industry*, p. 64.
[10] B. Bezza, 'L'activité multinationale de la Pirelli, 1883-1914', paper presented to a conference on 'The early phase of multinational enterprise in Germany, France, and Italy', held at the European University Institute, Florence, 17-19 Oct. 1984.

1920s and General Motors acquired a British producer, Vauxhall, in 1925. The 1930s saw some American disinvestment but also new investment in a wide range of sectors, including food, chemicals, and electrical appliances.[11]

Non-American companies also continued to be active investors in Britain, especially in the 1920s. A number of Swedish firms, of which perhaps the most important was Elektrolux (later changed to Electrolux), the manufacturer of domestic electrical equipment, established factories in Britain in this period, while two Dutch viscose yarn companies (Enka and Breda) erected British plants.[12] There was also substantial Dutch investment in margarine manufacture. From 1917 the rival Dutch companies Jurgens and Van den Bergh's established or acquired a large number of margarine factories in Britain.[13] In the late 1920s there was a spate of French direct investments. In 1927 Renault built a British car factory and Michelin established a tyre factory in Britain. In the same year Poulenc Frères (which became Rhône-Poulenc in 1928) secretly acquired May & Baker, the British fine chemicals company.[14] There was also a Czechoslovakian direct investment when Bata, which dominated Czech shoe production in the interwar years, established a footwear factory in East Tilbury. The interwar years also saw the first Australian and Canadian direct investments in Britain.

All German direct investments were sequestrated during the First World War, and there was little significant German direct investment in British industry during the 1920s. The capital-starved German economy had little cash for foreign investments and generally opted for alternative strategies such as licensing and participation in international cartels. German investment in Britain in the 1920s was usually confined to small distribution companies, often joint ventures. Bayer Products Ltd, for example, was established in 1923 to distribute fine chemicals marketed under the Bayer name. It was jointly owned by I.G. Farbenindustrie and Sterling Products Inc. of the United States. There were some unsuccessful attempts by German firms to re-acquire the British subsidiaries which they had lost. German Siemens acquired 15 per cent of the capital of British Siemens in 1929, and the two companies reached a comprehensive technological licensing agreement, but the British company never fell under German control.[15] The 1930s saw more new German direct investment, sometimes in joint ventures with British or American interests.

The nationality of certain multinational investments was obscured by the fact that foreign parents managed their British subsidiaries through companies registered in third countries. Pirelli's British companies, for example, were owned and managed by Société Internationale Pirelli S.A. of Switzerland. A noteworthy variant on this pattern before 1914 was the Nobel-Dynamite Trust, an Anglo-German holding company founded in 1886, which owned the leading British explosives manufacturer, Nobel's Explosives. Although a majority of the share capital was probably German, the Trust was registered

---

[11] Wilkins, *Maturing*, chs. 4 and 8.
[12] Lundström, 'Swedish multinational growth', p. 139; Coleman, *Courtaulds*, II, p. 265.
[13] Wilson, *Unilever*, II, pp. 174, 254, 257, 259-60.
[14] Slinn, *May & Baker*, pp. 97-9.
[15] Scott, *Siemens Brothers*, p. 92. See also Teichova, 'The Mannesmann concern', p. 107.

in England, had an Anglo-German board of directors, and cannot be accurately counted as a German *direct* investment in British manufacturing.[16] It has been excluded from appendix 1.

A number of American and continental companies had multi-plant operations in Britain even before 1914. To the Anglo-Swiss Condensed Milk Company's original Chippenham factory, established in 1872, were added factories in Aylesbury and Middlewich in 1874, and Staverton in the early 1900s. Singer built another factory at Clydebank in 1885. Monsted built a second factory in London in 1895, and Mannesmann a second factory at Newport in 1913.

It is difficult to quantify the amount of capital which foreign companies invested in British industry before 1945. Dunning has estimated total inward direct investment in Britain at US$200 million in 1914 and $700 million in 1938.[17] If half of these totals was in manufacturing, it would suggest that foreign investment in British industry was around £20 million in 1914 and £87.5 million in 1938. These estimates cannot be verified by independent data, but seem about the right order of magnitude. From the late 1920s there is hard evidence on the size of American investment in British manufacturing. In 1929 this was estimated (in book value) by the U.S. Department of Commerce at $268.2 million (£55.2 million). A more thorough survey by the same source in 1932 put the figure at $165 million (£48.5 million), and in 1940 at $275.3 million (£68.3 million).[18] The size of non-American direct investment in British manufacturing is a mystery, but the wartime sequestration of German assets in Britain provides some evidence on German investment. A Board of Trade estimate in the First World War suggested the amount of German equity in identified manufacturing subsidiaries in Britain was just under £1.7 million.[19] During the Second World War the British government took over 130 companies in which German-owned shares had more than 50 per cent of the voting rights, but the total issued capital of these firms was only £676,929.[20] German direct investment in British manufacturing in 1939 is unlikely to have exceeded £0.25 million.

Not only was the amount of foreign direct investment in British industry before 1945 modest, but the place of foreign subsidiaries in Britain's corporate structure was also limited. In 1980, 402 of Britain's 1,000 largest firms were foreign-owned. The available listings of the 50 largest British manufacturing companies (by estimated market value) in 1905, 1919, and 1930 indicate that in terms of corporate size the significance of foreign-owned companies was much less at those dates.[21] In 1905 only the American-owned British Westinghouse (electrical engineering) was included in the largest 50 companies. By 1919 there were no foreign subsidiaries, for in 1918 British

[16] Reader, *ICI*, 1, pp. 126-7, 179-82.

[17] Dunning, 'Changes in the level and structure of international production', p. 188.

[18] Dunning, *American investment*, pp. 32, 44. Wilkins, *Maturing*, p. 185. I have converted dollars into sterling at £1 = $4.86 in 1900 and 1929, $3.40 in 1932 and $4.03 in 1940.

[19] P.R.O., Board of Trade files, BT 8/11, Shares etc. held in British companies by alien enemies under Section 3 (ii) Trading with the Enemy Amendment Act 1914.

[20] BT/80/12, Departmental meeting, 17 June 1945.

[21] Hannah, *Rise of the corporate economy*, pp. 102-3, 187-90, 116.

Westinghouse had been acquired by British interests. In 1930, 4 of the largest 50 firms—Ford, Associated Electric Industries (AEI), Boots, and Mond Nickel—were under American ownership, while another, the British Match Corporation, was 30 per cent Swedish controlled and 70 per cent British.

The role of foreign companies in certain industries and products was, however, highly significant. Foreign influence was the most extensive in the electrical engineering and other electrical industries. Before 1914 the heavy plant side of British electrical machinery production was dominated by British Siemens and American interests, especially British Thomson Houston (a subsidiary of the General Electric Company of America) and British Westinghouse, a subsidiary of US Westinghouse Electric. In 1918 Vickers and Metropolitan Carriage Wagon and Finance acquired British Westinghouse and it was incorporated in a new British-controlled company, Metropolitan Vickers Electrical Company (Metrovic). However, in 1928 the General Electric Company of America (through its subsidiary formed to control overseas operations, the International General Electric Company) arranged a merger of British electric interests, including Metrovic and British Thomson Houston, to form Associated Electrical Industries (AEI). The whole of Metrovic's assets thereby passed to American control.[22] Elsewhere in the industry, the English Electric Company had been formed in 1919, partly on the basis of the dynamo and electrical engineering parts of the old Siemens business. At the end of the 1920s American interests took control of the company, though this was not disclosed to the public at the time.[23] During the 1930s, therefore, two of the three leading British electrical engineering companies were foreign controlled, although by 1936 a majority of AEI's shares were back in British hands. The manufacture of telephones and telephone equipment was also an area where the subsidiaries of foreign multinationals were very active. In the late 1930s this sector was dominated by the American-owned STC, Swedish-owned Ericsson and British Siemens (which had a minority German shareholding at that stage). In addition, in 1920 the American Theodore Cary group acquired the Automatic Telephone Manufacturing Company, the largest indigenous telephone equipment manufacturer, although in 1935 this company was sold back to British interests.[24]

In the interwar years foreign-owned companies also established a prominent position in the expanding domestic electrical appliances sector. The American-owned Hoover and Swedish-owned Elektrolux were the leading manufacturers in the United Kingdom of vacuum cleaners and refrigerators.[25] Before the merger in 1931 of the Gramophone Company and Columbia Graphophone to form Electrical and Musical Industries (EMI), American interests also had a prominent role in the gramophone and recording industry. During the interwar years foreign interests were at times important in electrical

---

[22] There is a clear account of the corporate structure of the pre-1914 industry in Byatt, *The British electrical industry*, pp. 136-58. For the shifts in ownership see Jones and Marriott, *Anatomy of a merger*, esp. chs. 3 and 5; Davenport-Hines, *Dudley Docker*, pp. 157-8, 178-80.

[23] Scott, *Siemens Brothers*, p. 87; Jones and Marriott, *Anatomy of a merger*, ch. 7.

[24] Dunning, *American investment*, p. 40.

[25] Corley, *Domestic electrical appliances*, pp. 31-5.

FOREIGN MULTINATIONALS AND BRITISH INDUSTRY

utilities. In 1928 an American corporation acquired a group of British electricity supply companies, making it 'one of the largest suppliers of electricity in Britain'.[26] In 1936, however, this group was sold back to British interests. Less significant was the purchase in the late 1930s by an Italian group of five British electricity supply companies controlled by a holding company.[27]

The motor car industry was another area where foreign multinationals were active. Ford's construction of a plant at Manchester in 1911 was followed by a period of dominance of the British motor car industry until the early 1920s. After 1923 Ford rapidly lost its position to the British firms of Austin and, especially, Morris, with the American-owned company failing to develop models appropriate to the British market and handicapped by inappropriate selling arrangements. Ford's new Dagenham plant and a managerial re-organization only partially revived the company's British fortunes. By 1939 Ford and Vauxhall (owned by General Motors) controlled about a quarter of British production in the motor industry.[28]

Before the First World War the subsidiaries of foreign multinationals were also significant in the chemical industry. The 1907 Patent Act, which specified that a foreign patent taken out in Britain had to be worked there, led the German and Swiss dyestuffs manufacturers to establish British plants, but the British government did not enforce the requirements of the Act strictly and these ventures remained small. However, Hoechst's Ellesmere Port factory produced almost all of Britain's production of indigo, which amounted to 50 per cent of domestic demand. This factory was also equipped to make certain drugs, especially the anti-syphilic 'Salvarsan', which were made nowhere else in Britain before 1914.[29] The Clayton Aniline Company, one of the few British dyestuffs manufacturers before the First World War, was purchased by the Swiss firm Ciba in 1911.[30] After the War, and particularly after the formation of Imperial Chemical Industries in 1926, the chemical industry in Britain made considerable progress and foreign-owned firms were of importance only in certain limited sectors. In the 1930s, for example, Clayton Aniline still held an important place in dyestuff production, manufacturing 19 per cent of the total value of dyestuffs produced in Britain in 1937.[31] The American firm Monsanto, which established manufacturing operations in Britain in 1920, was a leading producer of new kinds of phenolic and plastic materials.

Foreign companies also acquired strong positions in a wide and diverse range of consumer products. Singer dominated sewing machine production. The British subsidiary of Eastman Kodak shared with the British firm Ilford the domination of the British photographic materials industry.[32] Dutch

---

[26] Hannah, *Electricity before nationalization*, p. 228.

[27] Ibid., p. 290. P.R.O., Ministry of Power, POWE 14/15 Memorandum of 16 May 1940.

[28] Wilkins and Hill, *American business abroad, passim*; Church and Miller, 'The big three'.

[29] Hertner, 'German multinational enterprise', p. 124; Reader, *ICI*, 1, p. 266.

[30] Haber, *Chemical industry*, pp. 166-7. On the German and Swiss dyestuff companies in Britain see also *Hoechst in England*; Abrahart, *Clayton Aniline Company*; and Hertner, 'Fallstudien zu deutschen multinationalen Unternehmen', p. 27.

[31] Gribben (ed.), *Survey of international cartels*, p. 85.

[32] Edgerton, 'Industrial research in the British photographic industry'.

utilities. In 1928 an American corporation acquired a group of British electricity supply companies, making it 'one of the largest suppliers of electricity in Britain'.[26] In 1936, however, this group was sold back to British interests. Less significant was the purchase in the late 1930s by an Italian group of five British electricity supply companies controlled by a holding company.[27]

The motor car industry was another area where foreign multinationals were active. Ford's construction of a plant at Manchester in 1911 was followed by a period of dominance of the British motor car industry until the early 1920s. After 1923 Ford rapidly lost its position to the British firms of Austin and, especially, Morris, with the American-owned company failing to develop models appropriate to the British market and handicapped by inappropriate selling arrangements. Ford's new Dagenham plant and a managerial re-organization only partially revived the company's British fortunes. By 1939 Ford and Vauxhall (owned by General Motors) controlled about a quarter of British production in the motor industry.[28]

Before the First World War the subsidiaries of foreign multinationals were also significant in the chemical industry. The 1907 Patent Act, which specified that a foreign patent taken out in Britain had to be worked there, led the German and Swiss dyestuffs manufacturers to establish British plants, but the British government did not enforce the requirements of the Act strictly and these ventures remained small. However, Hoechst's Ellesmere Port factory produced almost all of Britain's production of indigo, which amounted to 50 per cent of domestic demand. This factory was also equipped to make certain drugs, especially the anti-syphilic 'Salvarsan', which were made nowhere else in Britain before 1914.[29] The Clayton Aniline Company, one of the few British dyestuffs manufacturers before the First World War, was purchased by the Swiss firm Ciba in 1911.[30] After the War, and particularly after the formation of Imperial Chemical Industries in 1926, the chemical industry in Britain made considerable progress and foreign-owned firms were of importance only in certain limited sectors. In the 1930s, for example, Clayton Aniline still held an important place in dyestuff production, manufacturing 19 per cent of the total value of dyestuffs produced in Britain in 1937.[31] The American firm Monsanto, which established manufacturing operations in Britain in 1920, was a leading producer of new kinds of phenolic and plastic materials.

Foreign companies also acquired strong positions in a wide and diverse range of consumer products. Singer dominated sewing machine production. The British subsidiary of Eastman Kodak shared with the British firm Ilford the domination of the British photographic materials industry.[32] Dutch

[26] Hannah, *Electricity before nationalization*, p. 228.
[27] Ibid., p. 290. P.R.O., Ministry of Power, POWE 14/15 Memorandum of 16 May 1940.
[28] Wilkins and Hill, *American business abroad, passim*; Church and Miller, 'The big three'.
[29] Hertner, 'German multinational enterprise', p. 124; Reader, *ICI*, I, p. 266.
[30] Haber, *Chemical industry*, pp. 166-7. On the German and Swiss dyestuff companies in Britain see also *Hoechst in England*; Abrahart, *Clayton Aniline Company*; and Hertner, 'Fallstudien zu deutschen multinationalen Unternehmen', p. 27.
[31] Gribben (ed.), *Survey of international cartels*, p. 85.
[32] Edgerton, 'Industrial research in the British photographic industry'.

companies were predominant in margarine manufacture in the second half
of the 1920s. By 1939 a Canadian, Garfield Weston, had the largest bakery
business in Britain.[33]

The market share of foreign multinationals was never a static phenomenon,
and the national ownership of a significant number of firms fluctuated over
time. The shifts in ownership in the electrical engineering industry have
already been mentioned, but there were many other examples. Boots in the
interwar years ceased to be a British company by becoming the subsidiary
of an American multinational, but then reverted to being a British company.[34]
The Gramophone Company made exactly the same transition in ownership
between 1920 and 1931.[35]

'Anglicization' of British subsidiaries of foreign companies was fairly
common. In 1901 Diamond Match of the United States acquired a majority
shareholding in the leading British match company, Bryant & May, but by
1914 control was back in British hands.[36] When the British-registered British
American Tobacco Company (BAT) was formed in 1902 two-thirds of its
capital was owned by the American Tobacco Company, but by 1923 British
interests had secured both managerial and financial control.[37] In 1927 the
Swedish Match Company, whose manufacturing presence in Britain dated
back to the Jönköping and Vulcan factory in 1910, merged its British
interests with the leading British manufacturer, Bryant & May, to form a
new holding company, the British Match Corporation, which was 70 per
cent British controlled. Swedish Match hoped that its 30 per cent stake
would give it control over this company, but in fact managerial control
remained in British hands.[38] A peculiar variant of this pattern was the
merger of the Dutch margarine manufacturers with Lever Brothers in 1929
to create Unilever, in which British and Dutch interests both held 50 per
cent.[39] The cluster of Dutch margarine factories in Britain thereby passed
into Anglo-Dutch ownership.

II

Modern theories of the multinational enterprise suggest that the explanation
for foreign direct investment in British industry before 1945 must be found
on several different levels. A firm will invest in a foreign country only if it
has an advantage of some kind over domestic competitors. Such 'ownership-
specific' advantages can lie in a variety of factors, including superior
management structures, better technology or marketing skills, or easier
access to finance. A firm can exploit these advantages by exporting to, or
licensing in, foreign markets, but under certain conditions it is more
beneficial for a firm to internalize its advantages through an extension of its
own activities across national boundaries. Generally, the greater the ownership

[33] Hunt, 'Weston', pp. 753-4.
[34] Chapman, *Jesse Boot*, ch. 7.
[35] Jones, 'The Gramophone Company', pp. 91-8.
[36] Hildebrand, *Expansion*, p. 25.
[37] Cochran, *Big business in China*, pp. 3, 164.
[38] Hildebrand, *Expansion*, p. 85.
[39] Wilson, *Unilever*, II, pp. 301-8.

advantages of enterprises the more the incentive they have to exploit these themselves. To explain fully the preference for investing abroad over, say, exporting, another group of 'location-specific' factors also needs to be considered. These factors include market size and growth, and trade barriers in host countries.[40]

The foreign multinationals which invested in British industries can be seen as possessing strong ownership-specific advantages which enabled them to compete successfully with indigenous firms. There were several sources of advantage, but Chandler has argued powerfully that the most important was management structure. In industries such as electrical machinery, and chemicals before the 1920s, British entrepreneurs failed to develop the large integrated enterprises administered by extensive managerial hierarchies which their American counterparts had adopted. In these industries American companies had considerable advantages over their British competitors, enabling them to build factories and prosper in the British market.[41] The reasons why many British entrepreneurs preferred to retain personal family management remain uncertain. However, significant influences included the slower growth of the British market compared to the American; the British education system; the lack of anti-trust legislation; and perhaps a hostility to change among many British industrialists.[42]

Many foreign multinationals also possessed technological advantages over their British competitors. In general terms the success in Britain of continental and American electrical, telecommunication, chemical, and pharmaceutical companies reflected their superior research and development methods, and more generally, the greater scientific and technological strengths of their home economies. The technological advantages of foreign companies were often highly visible: American companies, for example, were frequently more receptive to instrumentation than British companies. H.J. Heinz installed automatic controls in their London factory in 1929 before British food canners introduced any form of control. American multinationals also demonstrated an ability to differentiate between products by brand advertising and selling methods which were often—but not always—superior to those of British competitors.[43] Such advantages were important in explaining the success in Britain of the American quick and instant food manufacturers.

Easier access to capital supplies was a much less important advantage for foreign firms. There is some evidence that foreign companies provided capital to industries which British financial institutions would not fund. In 1890 the dyestuffs manufacturer Levinstein's of Manchester turned to the German firms, Bayer and Agfa, for funds after failing to raise capital in Britain.[44] However, even those historians convinced of institutional failure in the British financial sector can find little evidence that British industry as a whole was short of funds before 1914.[45] Certainly the motor car industry

---

[40] Hood and Young, *Economics of multinational enterprise*, ch. 2 provides a good introduction to theories of the multinational enterprise. See also Dunning, *International production*, chs. 2-4.

[41] Chandler, 'Emergence of managerial capitalism', pp. 496-7.

[42] Coleman and Macleod, 'Attitudes to new techniques'.

[43] Dunning, *American investment*, pp. 264-5.

[44] Reader, *ICI*, 1, pp. 261-2.

[45] Elbaum and Lazonick, 'An institutional perspective on British decline', p. 3.

before 1914 experienced little difficulty in raising capital from public issues on the London Stock Exchange, and British firms found it easier to raise capital than their American counterparts, such as Ford, which were excluded from public equity markets until after 1918.

This discussion of the advantages of foreign companies would support a thesis of entrepreneurial and management 'failure' in certain industries at certain times in Britain. There were market opportunities which foreign interests perceived and exploited, but which indigenous entrepreneurs did not. However, this argument does not support a general hypothesis of entrepreneurial failure over all sectors of British industry, for Britain itself was a major home country of multinational investment before 1945, and beyond. From the late nineteenth century British multinationals such as Dunlop, J. & P. Coats, and Courtaulds established worldwide networks of foreign factories which reflected *their* advantages over foreign competitors.[46]

The possession of ownership-specific advantages represents a necessary but not a sufficient condition for multinational investment. A number of location-specific advantages need to be considered. Britain possessed the highest per caput income in Europe, a high population density, and excellent transport, which made it an attractive market for many products. The large British market was particularly attractive to firms based in such countries as Sweden and Switzerland, and most of these companies were large exporters to Britain before they established plants. Some 75 per cent of the production of Anglo-Swiss Condensed Milk was sold in Britain before it established its first British factory in 1872. Similarly, the Swedish telephone manufacturer, L.M. Ericsson, sold 50 per cent of its output in Britain prior to its establishment of a joint venture with the National Telephone Company in 1903.[47]

Why did foreign companies switch from exporting to manufacture in Britain? It is well established that the desire to 'jump' tariff barriers was a major factor which led many British companies to establish factories abroad.[48] Britain before 1914 was still a free trade country, but there were a number of more general trade barriers which prompted foreign investment. Fear of tariffs being imposed at some future date may have influenced some companies, such as Western Electric in the late 1890s.[49] Britain had some import duties designed to encourage domestic manufacture. It was because of a discriminatory duty on manufactured tobacco that the American Tobacco Company acquired a British company in 1901, which led to a brief foray into domestic manufacturing before a wide-ranging cartel agreement was reached with the dominant British firm, Imperial Tobacco.[50] Some foreign companies established British plants in order to take advantage of imperial preference, and thereby penetrate the protected markets of Australia, Canada, and other Dominions. The desire to sell to Australia was also the explicit reason behind Jönköping and Vulcan's decision to establish a match factory

---

[46] Jones, ed., *British multinationals*.
[47] Heer, *World events*, p. 56; Lundström, 'Swedish multinational growth', p. 143.
[48] Jones, 'Origins, management and performance', pp. 8-9.
[49] Young, *Power of speech*, p. 12.
[50] Wilkins, *Emergence*, pp. 91-2.

in Britain in 1910. Australia levied only 50 per cent of the standard import duty on matches of British origin.[51]

After 1914 the growth of British protectionism meant that many factories were established in Britain in order to avoid tariff barriers. The McKenna duties of 1915, which imposed a 33 per cent duty on imported 'non-essentials', such as motor cars, originating outside the Empire, led to a rapid rise in the proportion of local content in Ford vehicles assembled at its Manchester factory, and the continuation of the duties after 1918 eventually led to Ford's decision to construct the huge Dagenham plant in the late 1920s. The same reason prompted General Motors' acquisition of Vauxhall in 1925.[52]

Patent legislation, as already observed, was also an influence prompting British manufacture in some sectors. The 1907 Patent Act not only led the German and Swiss dyestuffs manufacturers to establish British factories but has also been credited with prompting American direct investment in the cinematic film, safety razor, and cash register industries.[53]

A range of other factors prompted individual firms to manufacture in Britain. Sometimes local inputs were important in manufacturing processes. The Swiss condensed milk manufacturers needed access to fresh milk supplies. The peculiarity of British weights and measures was an influence. The decision of SKF, the Swedish ball and roller bearings company, to start manufacture in Britain in 1910 was apparently influenced by the use of the inch system in the United Kingdom.[54] The ability to raise finance in the City of London and London's role in international trade were important. The English language helped to make Britain the first choice for many American companies locating in Europe. According to one estimate, in 1931 almost 40 per cent by number of the American-owned manufacturing plants in Europe and over 40 per cent by value were located in Britain.[55] Lower labour costs do not appear to have been a major location-specific advantage. Singer was initially attracted to Glasgow 'because of the low cost and docile labour as well as the good shipping facilities',[56] but this seems to have been an exception. The fact that most foreign investment was not in labour-intensive industries is significant in this context.

III

Foreign multinational investment affects a host economy in diverse ways. It can be regarded as transferring 'resources' of various kinds into that economy. It can also influence the corporate structure, the regional distribution of industry, and the balance of payments. This section looks, briefly, at each of these points for the British economy before 1945.

Foreign multinationals can make an important contribution by filling a

[51] Lindgren, *Corporate growth*, pp. 46, 168.
[52] Wilkins, *Maturing*, pp. 73-5.
[53] Dunning, *American investment*, p. 33.
[54] Lundström, 'Swedish multinational growth', p. 148.
[55] Southard, *American industry in Europe*, p. 134.
[56] Hounshell, *From the American system*, p. 93; Davies, *Peacefully working*, pp. 44-5.

resource gap in a host economy between desired investment and domestic savings. However, it would appear that the actual transfer of capital into Britain by foreign companies before 1945 was small and it is unlikely that foreign direct investment played an important role in industrial capital formation. Expansion was often financed by ploughed back profits. Singer used re-invested British profits to build a new factory at Clydebank in 1885.[57] It was also common for foreign firms to borrow or sell part of their equity in Britain. The French car manufacturers, Renault and Citroen, borrowed from British banks in the 1920s to finance British subsidiaries.[58] During the 1930s the British subsidiaries of a number of American companies disposed of part of their equity to British investors, including Woolworths, American Radiator Company, and Monsanto.[59] In 1928 Ford offered 40 per cent of the equity of Ford of England to the British public, and subsequently raised more than £4.5 million in the early 1930s to finance the construction of the Dagenham factory.

A more significant 'transfer' may have been of managerial and entrepreneurial skills. Many contemporaries argued that American subsidiaries in Britain were better managed than their indigenous competitors. 'The names Ford, Vauxhall, Singer, Kodak, Hoover, Standard Telephone, are bywords for efficiency [and] good management', observed the city editor of the News Chronicle in 1945, going on to contrast these firms with the 'inferiority' of 'inefficient British industries.'[60] American companies can be seen as transferring their managerial advantages into the British economy, and in the process stimulating their indigenous competitors to adopt improved methods. Ford of England in the 1920s was not a well-managed company, but the firm's use of time study experts in the early 1930s helped to diffuse to Britain the benefits of American experience in management.[61]

There are a number of caveats to this argument. Many foreign multinational operations in Britain were not models of superior management. The American-dominated AEI conformed in the 1930s to the typical British management pattern of a loose confederation of subsidiaries with weak central control. Some multinational subsidiaries emitted clear signals of management failure rather than organizational superiority. British Westinghouse, for example, performed poorly before 1914, primarily because of poor management and a failure to adapt American methods to British conditions, and the company could not even make money during the First World War when other electrical companies in Britain made large profits.[62] In 1919 the Swiss firms, Geigy and Sandoz, acquired one-sixth stakes each in Clayton Aniline, formerly wholly owned by Ciba, and over the following decade there were constant disputes between the partners over the running of the British venture.[63]

[57] Davies, Peacefully working, p. 79.
[58] Fridenson, 'Growth of multinational activities', p. 161.
[59] Wilkins, Maturing, pp. 171, 184-5.
[60] News Chronicle, 7 Sept. 1945.
[61] Foreman-Peck, 'American challenge', p. 878.
[62] Byatt, British electrical industry, pp. 151, 195; Davenport-Hines, Dudley Docker, p. 156.
[63] I would like to thank Jonathan Liebenau and Mike Robson for allowing me to see the results of their research in the Ciba and Sandoz archives in Switzerland.

FOREIGN MULTINATIONALS AND BRITISH INDUSTRY 441

The number of instances in which foreign companies had their British operations 'anglicized' might also suggest that British managements were sometimes more than competitive with their foreign counterparts, although this may also have reflected the problems of controlling foreign subsidiaries in the pre-1945 period. However, it is clear that in some industries, such as tobacco at the turn of the century, the British response to foreign intruders was so strong that the foreign companies were forced to withdraw or reach a compromise with local interests.[64] In the motor industry British companies overcame an early American lead, although doubts have been raised whether this was indicative of 'superior' British management methods.[65]

One criticism of the impact of multinationals on host countries is that they can reserve managerial and skilled jobs for home country nationals and thereby limit the 'spin-off' benefits of improved managerial techniques. However, many American companies in Britain before 1945 employed British nationals in senior positions. A number of companies, such as Firestone and Gillette, employed entirely British staff, although, as a writer in 1931 noted, 'a portion of it may have had training in the American company'.[66] Ford and General Motors in Britain were both headed by British managers in the 1930s. The willingness of American corporations to appoint British nationals to senior positions can be explained in part by similarities of language and culture, although even some of the continental companies conformed to this pattern. The senior management of Renault's British subsidiary in the interwar years, for example, was British.[67]

Britain may also have benefited because a number of foreign multinationals before 1940 chose to base their international operations in the United Kingdom. Before 1914 the London office of the Nestlé and Anglo-Swiss Condensed Milk Company was responsible for the Swiss firm's sales in Asia, Australia, and Latin America.[68] During the interwar years it was common for American corporations to use their British subsidiaries to control and sometimes to own subsidiaries in other countries, especially but far from exclusively in the British Empire. The most striking example was Ford's decision in 1928 to place all its European and Middle Eastern operations under the control of Ford of England.[69] This phenomenon meant a net gain to Britain in terms of expertise in managing international businesses, as well as in the creation of numerous head office management posts.

Perhaps the most frequently cited transfer associated with multinational enterprise is technology. There are potential benefits to a host country of technology transfer by a multinational, but in practice the size of the gain depends upon such matters as the terms under which the technology is transferred and its suitability. Before 1945 Britain again appears to have been a gainer in this area. In electrical engineering, American and German firms transferred new technologies into Britain, although in some instances—

---

[64] Alford, *Wills*.
[65] Lewchuk, 'Return to capital', p. 18.
[66] Southard, *American industry*, p. 146.
[67] Fridenson, 'Growth of multinational activities', p. 158.
[68] Heer, *World events*, p. 100.
[69] Wilkins, *Maturing*, pp. 139-40; Wilkins and Hill, *American business abroad*, pp. 143-4.

442   GEOFFREY JONES

such as that of British Westinghouse before 1919—these were inappropriate
to the domestic cost structure.[70] During the interwar years some foreign
firms invested in research and development in Britain. In 1928 Kodak's
British subsidiary established what may have been the first American
industrial research laboratory abroad. By 1939 this laboratory was larger
than the entire scientific effort of Kodak's British competitor, Ilford, and it
was also engaged—unlike Ilford—in fundamental research work.[71]

Yet it was far from axiomatic that foreign companies introduced superior
technologies. Initial optimism about the beneficial influence of American
investment in electrical utilities in the interwar years, for example, soon gave
way to alarm about high costs and prices.[72] Nor did the motor car industry
provide substantial examples of technology transfer. Ford remained dependent
on its American parent in matters of design. Moreover, Ford's Dagenham
factory was isolated from the principal centres of British car production,
which limited any technological 'spin-off' to domestic firms.[73] Many foreign
subsidiaries, such as Clayton Aniline, undertook no serious research and
development in Britain. Although imported technology was important for
British industry in the interwar years, the major conduits through which
this technology was acquired were licensing agreements (as held by ICI and
Metal Box) and the acquisition of American machinery (by Austin and
Morris, for example) rather than inward direct investment.[74] British
companies in the interwar years often demonstrated considerable skill in
acquiring and applying foreign technologies acquired in such ways.

Multinationals create employment and can also introduce innovatory labour
management practices. Before 1914 foreign multinationals were not large
employers. By the eve of the First World War the manufacturing subsidiaries
of American companies may have employed 12-15,000 people.[75] A listing of
the 100 largest manufacturing employers in 1907 includes only 3 foreign
companies: Singer (ranked 31st with 7,000 workers); British Westinghouse
(ranked 47th with 5,000 workers); and Siemens (ranked 61st with 4,150
workers).[76] Some of the foreign ventures were very small indeed. Ford in
1914 had a workforce of 1,500, Clayton Aniline employed 300 workers,
while the Hoechst and BASF subsidiaries at Liverpool had only 57 and
37 workers respectively. In the interwar years employment by foreign
multinationals increased. In 1932 American-owned manufacturing establishments employed over 66,000 people.[77] The continental companies were
usually smaller operations, although some were at least medium-sized
employers. British Enka and Clayton Aniline, for example, had workforces
of 2,600 and 1,200 respectively in the early 1930s. A listing of the 100

---

[70] Byatt, *British electrical industry*, p. 195.
[71] Wilkins, *Maturing*, p. 84; Edgerton, 'Industrial research'.
[72] Hannah, *Electricity*, pp. 231-3.
[73] Wilkins and Hill, *American business abroad*, p. 291; Church, 'Effects of American multinationals',
p. 117.
[74] Reader, *ICI*, II, pp. 506-13; Reader, *Metal Box*, p. 54; Foreman-Peck, 'American challenge',
p. 871. For the pre-1914 period see Saul, 'American impact'.
[75] Dunning, *American investment*, p. 36.
[76] Shaw, 'Large manufacturing employers of 1907'.
[77] Dunning, *American investment*, p. 44.

FOREIGN MULTINATIONALS AND BRITISH INDUSTRY   443

largest manufacturing employers in 1935 includes eight American-owned companies: AEI (ranked 11th with 30,000 workers); Singer (43rd, 8,103); National Cash Register (46th, 8,000); STC (52nd, 7,911); Ford (55th, 7,128); Vauxhall (64th, 6,726); English Electric (67th, 6,091); and Kodak (91st, 4,400). Employing a workforce of 60,000, the Anglo-Dutch Unilever was Britain's largest manufacturing employer.[78]

Foreign multinationals exercised an influence on labour management policies in Britain before 1945, although the paucity of evidence makes generalization difficult. It does seem that American-owned companies may have been more successful than British firms in pursuing the division of labour and simplifying work. The fact that many of their plants and facilities in Britain were new would help to explain this. They also brought with them ideas of scientific management, were quick to introduce work study, and probably tolerated fewer restrictive practices.

In the matter of employment practices, American companies were more sophisticated in some ways than British companies, relying on higher day wages rather than piecework.[79] On the other hand, British companies may have been ahead in terms of providing such fringe benefits as pensions and sick pay.[80] However, it was·the appearance in Britain in 1927 of the largest American insurance company, Metropolitan Life of New York, which, responding to the needs of its American clients in Britain such as Kodak and General Motors, introduced American-style group life and pension contracts.[81]

Few American firms in Britain decided to join employers' organizations because this meant recognizing trade unions. Companies such as Ford and Pressed Steel held out against recognition until 1944 when government pressure helped secure recognition. Even after American subsidiaries had accepted unions, they often continued not to join employers' organizations, opting to deal with unions independently within the firm.[82] Their labour policies, on occasions, showed scant regard for conventional practice in Britain. British Westinghouse in the 1900s followed the Pittsburgh practice of employing works police to patrol factories to see that everyone was hard at work. Not surprisingly, the company had a poor labour relations record.[83]

Among other effects of foreign multinationals on Britain was the regional impact of foreign investment. Between 1945 and the 1970s British government policy helped to steer many foreign companies towards the peripheral regions of Scotland, Wales, and the north of England. However, locational distribution of inward direct investment before the Second World War was quite different. Before 1914 the investments shown in appendix 1 were quite widely dispersed throughout England, although Wales and Scotland never attracted many factories. Between 1850 and 1919, out of the 53 recorded investments only 3 were in Scotland and 1 in Wales. After the First World

[78] Johnman, 'Large manufacturing companies of 1935'.
[79] For the experience of the motor car industry, see Lewchuk, 'Fordism'.
[80] I owe this point to Howard Gospel.
[81] Hannah, *Inventing retirement*, pp. 34-7.
[82] Gospel, 'Employers' organizations'.
[83] Byatt, *British electrical industry*, p. 195.

War, London and the south east became the usual location. This generalization is supported by Law's larger sample of 162 multinational investments in British industry between 1918 and 1944, of which 70.3 per cent were in the south east (mostly London), 11.7 per cent in the north west, and 6.8 per cent in the west midlands. A mere 3.7 per cent were in Scotland, 0.6 per cent in Wales, and none in Northern Ireland.[84] This geographical concentration on the south east must have had a significant impact by introducing new products and methods into that region, and increasing its capacity for innovation in the interwar years.

A second trend was a greater willingness of non-American firms to invest outside the south east. Both before and after the First World War, German companies showed some preference for the north of England. Swedish companies showed interest in areas to the north of London, and the west midlands. Two of the three Canadian multinational investments in the interwar years were initially in Scotland. The different industries in which American and continental companies were engaged was an important factor in explaining variations in geographical distribution.

Foreign multinationals may also have an impact on the market structure of host economies. Multinationals appear most commonly in concentrated industries, and there is some evidence that their presence may increase oligopolistic tendencies in markets. In Britain, however, the impact of foreign companies before 1945 was often to enhance rather than to limit competition. It is true that some product markets, such as that for sewing machines, were totally dominated by a foreign company. However, the merger boom of the 1920s led to certain sectors of British industry being controlled by one or two large British companies. In some of these industries foreign subsidiaries provided the main competition to the local giants, especially as their foreign ownership often made them less vulnerable to takeover by British firms. In the late 1920s, for example, ICI attempted to gain control of Clayton Aniline, 'so as to give ICI a closer approach to monopoly in the British dyestuffs industry', but the Swiss parent company resisted these overtures.[85] Sometimes, however, a foreign threat encouraged British firms to work together— as with the creation of Imperial Tobacco in 1901—and thus increased the degree of oligopoly.

Finally, much attention in post-1945 Britain has focused on the balance of payments effects of foreign multinationals. Before 1945 most foreign subsidiaries in Britain manufactured largely for the home market using local materials, which suggests a neutral impact on the balance of trade. Some foreign-owned companies did have an export business even in this early period. Clayton Aniline exported the bulk of its British production before 1914 to its Swiss parent, and Jönköping and Vulcan's London factory despatched all its matches to Australia before 1915.[86] In the interwar years Ford of England entered the export market. Dagenham manufactured many of the components of Ford cars produced in Germany until the advent of Hitler in 1933, and British-made Ford tractors were sold to many countries,

---

[84] Law, *British regional development*, pp. 174-7.
[85] Reader, *ICI*, II, pp. 187-8.
[86] Haber, *Chemical industry*, p. 149; Lindgren, *Corporate growth*, p. 169.

including the United States.[87] Overall, it is impossible to generalize on the balance of payments impact from such scattered anecdotal evidence.

IV

The overall significance of foreign multinationals in British industry before the Second World War was limited. Few foreign-owned companies featured in the lists of the largest companies or the largest employers even in the 1930s. Yet the foreign impact on such industries as electrical engineering, telephone equipment, motor cars, domestic electrical appliances, and a range of foodstuffs and consumer products was clearly visible. Many of the fastest growing and/or high technology industries of pre-1945 Britain were sustained by substantial foreign direct investment. Foreign companies invested in Britain because they had a range of managerial, entrepreneurial, and technological advantages over local competitors, sufficiently large to encourage and facilitate their exploitation by direct investment. In industries such as rayon, where British companies possessed appropriate managerial structures and modern technologies, the impact of foreign multinationals on Britain was small, while British-based multinationals were active as direct investors in foreign markets. Location-specific factors such as trade barriers encouraged foreign firms to exploit their advantages by local manufacture in Britain rather than by exporting or licensing.

Given the diversity in the range of multinational activity as well as the data limitations, it would be facile to offer a definitive judgement on the impact of multinational enterprise on the British economy before 1945. Britain avoided the worst problems which can arise from multinational activity, such as technological dependency and threats to sovereignty. Foreign companies introduced new technologies, products, and marketing methods into British industry, and sometimes increased competition in oligopolistic markets. They created employment and probably improved some labour management practices. Capital flows into Britain, on the other hand, do not seem important. Nor did the British subsidiaries of American companies always provide models of managerial perfection for their domestic competitors to emulate. Contemporaries sometimes over-estimated the managerial superiority of the foreign companies in their midst. Overall, however, the evidence suggests more gains than losses to British industry from foreign multinational investment.

The ability of foreign companies to acquire leading positions in parts of British industry indicates inadequate indigenous management structures, enterprise, and technology in those sectors. The continuing attachment to the family firm was possibly an underlying cause of these problems. However, generalizations about British business failure even in these sectors need careful qualification. In chemicals and some other industries British companies proved to be skilled at acquiring superior foreign technologies under licence, keeping foreign enterprises at arm's length. The advantages of foreign companies in Britain were often not sustained. In the motor industry British

[87] Wilkins and Hill, *American business abroad*, pp. 247, 304.

446   GEOFFREY JONES

firms in the interwar years overcame early foreign predominance. British managements on occasion captured the upper hand in joint ventures. Several subsidiaries of foreign companies were 'anglicized'. British entrepreneurs sometimes responded well once challenged. Reluctance to change, to introduce new methods, structures, and products has been a long-term problem for much of British manufacturing industry in the twentieth century. Foreign companies sometimes provided a catalyst which challenged British business to renewed vitality. It was, perhaps, in eliciting such responses that foreign multinationals had their most beneficial impact on British industry before 1945.

London School of Economics

Appendix I: some foreign multinationals in British manufacturing and utilities before 1945

   This appendix gives details of direct investments by foreign companies in British manufacturing and utilities before 1945. Each entry has been checked from more than one source, but the data on some entries are incomplete and the list cannot be regarded as comprehensive.

   There were frequent changes of name by foreign parents and British subsidiaries over the period covered. In general the name of companies at the time of the initial investment has been given. If the name of the British subsidiary has been left blank, it can be assumed to have a title similar to its parent.

   The 'start date for manufacturing' column gives the date when a foreign company acquired a British manufacturing company, or established a manufacturing operation in Britain. Occasionally firms made two investments which were entirely separate from one another (e.g. American companies no. 6, 12, 24, 33). These have been counted as *two* investments—for example, the total number of American investments is 67, even though only 63 firms are given. Companies established by foreign individuals are excluded, such as the British office manufacturing company established by the American immigrants, Burroughs and Wellcome in 1896. Purely marketing or sales companies are excluded. It was often difficult to give an exact date when a British company came under foreign 'control'. The U.S. Department of Commerce considers a foreign company 'controls' a domestic company if it holds at least 10 per cent of its equity, but I have preferred to use more subjective measures of when British companies came under, or passed from, foreign ownership and managerial control.

   The 'date when manufacture ceased' column gives the date when a foreign company ceased to own and control a British manufacturing operation. If this operation was still in existence in 1945 the column has been left blank. The letters after the dates categorize the fate of the venture. Categories A, S, and W represent a transfer from foreign to British ownership and control; A = acquired by, or control shifted to, a British company, or the British partner in a joint venture; S = sequestrated by the British government; W = foreign company withdrew from British manufacturing, either by

FOREIGN MULTINATIONALS AND BRITISH INDUSTRY 447

liquidating its British company, ceasing manufacturing, or selling the venture to individual (non-corporate) British investors; M = merged with another foreign company.

The 'plant location' column gives the location of the *initial* manufacturing plant in Britain. The location of later factories, and re-locations—such as Ford's move from Manchester to Dagenham—are not recorded. London is used loosely to cover a wide geographical area in and around the capital. The 'product' column gives the main product manufactured by the British subsidiary.

This appendix has been compiled from sources given in the footnotes, supplemented by *Moody's manual of investments*, reports of the Monopolies Commission, the *Stock Exchange year book*, and various British trade directories, especially the *Red book of commerce*.

1:1 United States companies

Parent	British subsidiary	Start date for manu-facturing	Plant location	Date when manufacture ceased	Product
1 S. Colt	Colt	1853	London	1857W	firearms
2 J. Ford	North British Rubber Co.	1856	Edinburgh	1868W	rubber
3 Singer	Singer Sewing Machines	1867	Glasgow		sewing machines
4 R. Hoe & Co.	R. Hoe & Co.	1867	London		printing press
5 American Radiator	National Radiator	1895	Hull		radiators
6 Diamond Match	Diamond Match	1896	Liverpool	1901W	matches
Diamond Match	Bryant and May	1901	London	1914W	matches
7 Western Electric	Fowler Waring Cable (STC 1925)	1898	London		telecommuni-cations
8 United Shoe Machinery	British United Shoe Machinery	1899	Leicester		boots and shoes
9 Kodak	Kodak	1899	Harrow		cameras
10 Westinghouse Electric	British Westinghouse	1899	Manchester	1917A	electrical machinery
11 GEC	British Thomson Houston	1901	Rugby	1928M	electrical machinery
12 American Tobacco	Ogdens	1901	Liverpool	1902W	tobacco
American Tobacco	British American Tobacco	1902		1923A	tobacco
13 Parke, Davis	Parke, Davis & Co.	1902	London		patent medicine
14 Columbia Graphophone	Columbia	1905	Surrey	1923A	record cylinders
15 H.J. Heinz	H.J. Heinz	1905	London		food
16 Horlicks Food Company	Horlicks Malted Milk Co.	1907	Slough		soft drinks
17 Mergentheler Linotype	Linotype & Machinery	1909	Manchester		typesetting machinery
18 Ford	Ford	1911	Manchester		motor cars
19 American Chicle		1900s	London	1923W	chewing gum
20 Chicago Pneumatic Tool	Consolidated Pneumatic Tool	1900s	Fraserburgh		pneumatic tools
21 Gillette	Gillette	1900s	Slough		safety razors
22 United Drug		1912	Notts		pharmaceuticals
23 Electric Storage Batteries	Chloride Electric and Storage Company	1900s	Manchester		storage batteries
24 National Lead	William Harvey & Co.	1916	Liverpool	1929A	tin smelting
National Lead	British Titanium Products	1933	Billingham		titanium

448   GEOFFREY JONES

Parent	British subsidiary	Start date for manu-facture	Plant location	Date manu-facture ceased	Product
25 Drug Inc.	Boots	1920	Nottingham	1933W	pharmaceuticals
26 Theodore Cary	Automatic Telephone Manufacturing	1920	Liverpool	1935W	telephone equipment
27 Monsanto	Monsanto Chemicals	1920	Wales, Sunderland		chemicals
28 Victor Talking Machine	Gramophone Co.	1921	Middlesex	1931A	records, gramophones
29 Quaker Oats Co.	Quaker Oats Co.	1920s	London		food
30 Shredded Wheat Co.	Shredded Wheat Co.	1920s	Welwyn		food
31 Otis Elevator	Wayood Otis	1924	London		lifts
32 B.F. Goodrich	British Goodrich	1924	Burton	1934W	rubber goods
33 General Motors		1924	London		motor cars
General Motors	Vauxhall	1925	Luton		motor cars
34 Goodyear	Goodyear Tyre and Rubber	1927	Wolver-hampton		tyres
35 Firestone	Firestone Tyre and Rubber	1928	London		tyres
36 American Home Products	W.L. Dodge, St Jacobs Oil, and others	1926-9	London		pharmaceuticals
37 American Tobacco	J. Wix & Sons	1927	London		cigarettes
38 American Timken	British Timken	1927	Birmingham, Northampton		roller bearings
39 Wm Wrigley Jr	Wrigley Products Ltd.	1927	London		chewing gum
40 Chesebrough Manufacturing Company		1920s	London		proprietary medicines
41 Colgate		1920s	London		toiletries and soap
42 Sterling Products	Scott and Turner	1928	Newcastle		pharmaceuticals
43 Utilities Power and Light	Edmundsons	1929	various	1936W	electricity, utilities
44 IBM	International Time Records	1929	London		office equipment
45 International Nickel	Mond Nickel	1929	Swansea		nickel refining
46 Yale and Towne	H. and T. Vaughan	1929	Staffs		locks & keys
47 Chrysler		1928	London		motor cars
48 American Can	British Can	1929	London	1931A	cans
49 Proctor & Gamble	Thomas Hedley and Sons	1930	Newcastle		soap
50 Hoover	Hoover	1931	Middlesex		domestic electrical appliances
51 Standard Brands	Standard Brands	1932	Liverpool		baking powder
52 Bristol's		1932	Dorset		industrial instruments
53 General Motors	Frigidaire	1933	London		refrigerators
54 Corn Products	Brown and Polson	1930s	Paisley		food
55 N/A	British Laundry Machine Co. Ltd.	1930s			laundry machines
56 York Shippley	York Shippley	1930s	London		refrigerators
57 Mars		1934	Slough		chocolate
58 Du Pont (+ICI)	Nobel Chemical	1935	London		chemicals
59 Dennison Manufacturing	Dennison Manufacturing	1930s	London		packaging

FOREIGN MULTINATIONALS AND BRITISH INDUSTRY   449

Parent	British subsidiary	Start date for manu-facturing	Plant location	Date manu-facture ceased	Product
60 Champion Spark Plug	Champion Sparking Plugs	1937	London		sparking plugs
61 Armstrong Cork	Armstrong Cork	1938			cork
62 United States Rubber	North British Rubber Co.	1938	Edinburgh		rubber goods
63 E.W. Bliss	E.W. Bliss (England)	1939	Derby		metal-working machinery

1:2   German companies

1 Siemens & Halske	Siemens Brothers	1863	London	1916S	electrical machinery
2 Vereinigte Rheinisch-Westphalische Pulverfabriken	Chilworth Gunpowder Co.	1885	London	1915S	explosives
3 Bayer+Agfa	Levinstein Ltd	1890	Manchester	1895A	dyestuffs
4 Mannesmann	British Mannesmann	1899	Llandore	1916S	seamless tubes
5 Bosch	Bosch Magneto	1907	London	1916S	ignitors
6 Hoechst/Casselle/Kalle	Meiser Lucius & Brüning	1907	Liverpool	1916S	dyestuffs
7 BASF/Dreiband	Mersey Chemical	1907	Liverpool	1916S	dyestuffs
8 V.G.F.	British Glanzstoff	1908	Flint	1916S	cuprammonium yarn
9 Osram (+GEC)	Osram Lamp Works	1908	London	1916A	electrical machinery
10 Bayer	Bayer	1900s		1916S	pharmaceuticals
11 J.P. Bemberg	British Bemberg	1926	Doncaster	1939S	cuprammonium yarn
12 Nitsche and Gunther Optische Werke	Nitsche and Gunther	1932	London	1939S	spectacle frames
13 AEG (+Westinghouse)	Westinghouse Ticket Machine	1934		1939S	machinery
14 I.G. Farben (+ ICI)	Trafford Chemical	1938	Manchester	1939S	dyestuffs
15 I.G Farben (+ Aluminium Corp)	Magnesium Metal Corporation	1936		1939S	magnesium
16 I.G. Farben (+ Metallgesellschaft)	British Carbo-Union	1930s		1939S	activated carbons
17 Krupps	Tool Metal Manufacturing	1939		1939S	hard metal

1:3   Swedish companies

1 ASEA	Fuller Wenström Manufacturing Co.	1898	London		electrical equipment
2 L.M. Ericsson (+ National Telephone)	L.M. Ericsson Manufacturing	1903			telephone and office equipment
3 Jönköping & Vulcan	J. John Masters (after 1919)	1910	London	1927A	matches
4 SKF	Skefco Ball Bearing Co.	1910	Luton		ball bearings
5 Landis and Gyr	Landis and Gyr	1912	London		electrical equipment
6 Jungner	Batteries Ltd.	1918	Redditch		accumulators/mining lamps
7 AGA	Gas Accumulator Co.	1920s	London		beacons, railway equipment

450   GEOFFREY JONES

Parent	British subsidiary	Start date for manu-facture	Plant location	Date manu-facture ceased	Product
8 C.E. Johansson	C.E. Johansson	1920s	Coventry	1923M	precision gauges
9 ESAB	Anglo-Swedish Electric Welding	1920s			electric welding
10 Elektrolux	Elektrolux	1926	Luton		domestic electrical equipment machines
11 Separator	Chadburn Ship Telegraph Co.	1923			
12 Wicander	C.A. Greiner	1937	Middlesex		cork, linoleum
13 Atlas Diesel		1939	London		diesel engines

1:4   Danish companies

1 Monsted		1888	Manchester	1914A	margarine
2 Aarhus Oliefabrik	Erith Oil Works	1900s	London	1918A	vegetable oils
3 Hellesen's-enke		interwar	London		dry cell batteries
4 F.L. Smith		interwar	Luton		rotary kilns

1:5   Swiss companies

1 Anglo-Swiss Condensed Milk		1872	Chippenham		condensed milk
2 Nestlé		1901	Tutbury		condensed milk
3 Hoffman La Roche		1909	Welwyn		pharmaceuticals
4 Ciba	Clayton Aniline	1911	Manchester		dyestuffs
5 Sandoz		1911	Bradford		dyestuffs

1:6   Dutch companies

1 Jurgens		1917	Purfleet	1929A	margarine
2 Van Den Bergh's		1917	London	1929A	margarine
3 Enka	British Enka	1925	Liverpool		viscose yarn
4 Breda	Breda Visada	1928	Littleborough		viscose yarn
5 Phillips	Mullard Radio Valve	1924	London		domestic electrical equipment

1:7   French companies

1 Clément	Clément-Talbot	1903	London	1919A	motor cars
2 Lorraine-Dietrich		1907	Birmingham		motor cars
3 Renault	Renault	1927	London		motor cars
4 Compagnie Générale des Etablissements Michelin	Michelin Tyre Co.	1927	Stoke		tyres
5 Poulenc Frères	May & Baker	1927	London		fine chemicals

1:8   Italian companies

1 Pirelli (+ 50% GEC 1918)	Pirelli General Cable Works	1914	Southampton		cables
2 Pirelli	Pirelli Ltd	1924	Burton-on-Trent		tyres
3 N/A	Lincolnshire and Central Electricity Supply	1936	various	1940S	electrical utility

Note Pirelli's investments were controlled by Société Internationale Pirelli S.A. of Switzerland.

FOREIGN MULTINATIONALS AND BRITISH INDUSTRY 451

Parent	British subsidiary	Start date for manu- facture	Plant location	Date manu- facture ceased	Product
1:9 Canadian companies					
1 Northern Aluminium	Northern Aluminium	1928	Birmingham		aluminium
2 Massey-Harris		1930s	Manchester		agricultural implements
3 George Weston Ltd		1934	Edinburgh		biscuits
4 Hiram Walker		1937	Dumbarton		whiskey and spirits distillers
1:10 Australian companies					
1 Nicholas	Aspro	1925	Slough		pharmaceuticals
1:11 Czech companies					
1 Bata Company	British Shoe Co. (Bata) Ltd	1933	Tilbury	1939W	footwear

Footnote references

Abrahart, E.N., *The Clayton Aniline Company Ltd* (Manchester, 1976).
Alford, B.W.E., *W.D. and H.O. Wills and the development of the U.K. tobacco industry, 1786-1965* (1973).
Blakemore, H.L., 'Colt's London armoury', in S.B. Saul, ed., *Technological change: the United States and Britain in the nineteenth century* (1970), pp. 171-95.
Byatt, I.C., *The British electrical industry, 1875-1914* (Oxford, 1979).
Chandler, A.D., 'The emergence of managerial capitalism', *Bus. Hist. Rev.*, 58 (1984), pp. 473-503.
Chapman, S.D., *Jesse Boot of Boots the chemists* (1974).
Church, R. and Miller, M., 'The big three: competition, management, and marketing in the British motor industry, 1922-1939', in B. Supple, ed., *Essays in British business history* (Oxford, 1977), pp. 163-86.
Church, R., 'The effects of American multinationals on the British motor industry, 1911-83', in A. Teichova, M. Lévy-Leboyer, and H. Nussbaum, eds., *Multinational enterprise in historical perspective* (Cambridge, 1986), pp. 116-30.
Cochran, S., *Big business in China* (Cambridge, Mass., 1980).
Coleman, D.C., *Courtaulds: an economic and social history*, 2 vols. (Oxford, 1969).
Coleman, D.C. and Macleod, C., 'Attitudes to new techniques: British businessmen, 1800-1950', *Econ. Hist. Rev.*, 2nd ser., XXXIX (1986), pp. 588-611.

452   GEOFFREY JONES

Corley, T.A.B., *Domestic electrical appliances* (1966).
Davenport-Hines, R.P.T., *Dudley Docker* (Cambridge, 1984).
Davies, R.B., *Peacefully working to conquer the world* (New York, 1976).
Dunning, J.H., *American investment in British manufacturing industry* (1958).
Dunning, J.H., *International production and the multinational enterprise* (1981).
Dunning, J.H., 'Changes in the level and structure of international production: the last one hundred
    years', in M. Casson, ed., *The growth of international business* (1983), pp. 84-139.
Edgerton, D.E.H., 'Industrial research in the British photographic industry, 1879-1939', in J. Liebenau,
    ed., *The challenge of new technology* (Aldershot, 1988), pp. 106-34.
Elbaum, B. and Lazonick, W., 'An institutional perspective on British decline', in B. Elbaum and
    W. Lazonick, eds., *The decline of the British economy* (Oxford, 1986), pp. 1-17.
Foreman-Peck, J., 'The American challenge of the twenties: multinationals and the European motor
    industry', *J. Econ. Hist.*, XLII (1982), pp. 865-81.
Fridenson, P., 'The growth of multinational activities in the French motor industry, 1890-1979', in
    P. Hertner and G. Jones, eds., *Multinationals: theory and history* (Aldershot, 1986).
Gospel, H.F., 'Employers' organisations: their growth and function in the British system of industrial
    relations in the period 1918-39' (unpublished Ph.D. thesis, University of London, 1974).
Gribben, J.D., ed., *Survey of international cartels* (1976).
Haber, L., *The chemical industry during the nineteenth century* (Oxford, 1958).
Haber, L., *The chemical industry, 1900-1930* (Oxford, 1971).
Hannah, L., *Electricity before nationalisation* (1979).
Hannah, L., *The rise of the corporate economy* (1983).
Hannah, L., *Inventing retirement* (Cambridge, 1986).
Heer, J., *World events, 1866-1966: the first hundred years of Nestlé* (Rivaz, 1966).
Hertner, P., 'Fallstudien zu deutschen multinationalen Unternehmen vor dem Ersten Weltkrieg', in
    N. Horn and J. Kocka, eds., *Law and the formation of the big enterprises in the nineteenth and early
    twentieth centuries* (Göttingen, 1979), pp. 388-419.
Hertner, P., 'German multinational enterprise before 1914: some case studies', in P. Hertner and
    G. Jones, eds., *Multinationals: theory and history* (Aldershot, 1986), pp. 113-34.
Hildebrand, K.-G., *Expansion, crisis, reconstruction, 1917-1939* (Stockholm, 1985).
Hoechst in England, 1901-1914 (Frankfurt, 1971).
Hood, N. and Young, S. *The economics of multinational enterprise* (1979).
Hounshell, D.A., *From the American system to mass production, 1800-1932* (Baltimore, 1984).
Hunt, S., 'Williard Garfield Weston', in D.J. Jeremy and C. Shaw, eds., *Dictionary of business biography*,
    vol. 5 (1986), pp. 752-8.
Johnman, L., 'The large manufacturing companies of 1935', *Bus. Hist.*, XXVIII (1986), pp. 226-45.
Jones, G., ed., *British multinationals: origins, management and performance* (Aldershot, 1986).
Jones, G., 'The Gramophone Company: an Anglo-American multinational, 1898-1931', *Bus. Hist. Rev.*,
    59 (1985), pp. 76-100.
Jones, G., 'Origins, management and performance', in *idem*, ed., *British multinationals: origins, management
    and performance* (Aldershot, 1986), pp. 1-23.
Jones, R. and Marriott, O., *Anatomy of a merger. A history of G.E.C., A.E.I. and English Electric* (1970).
Laux, J.M., *In first gear: the French automobile industry to 1914* (Liverpool, 1976).
Law, C.M., *British regional development since World War I* (Newton Abbot, 1980).
Lewchuk, W., 'Fordism and British motor car employers, 1896-1932', in H.F. Gospel and C. R. Littler,
    eds., *Managerial strategies and industrial relations: an historical and comparative study* (1983), pp. 82-
    110.
Lewchuk, W., 'The return to capital in the British motor vehicle industry, 1896-1939', *Bus. Hist.*, XXVII
    (1985), pp. 3-25.
Lindgren, H., *Corporate growth. The Swedish match industry in its global setting* (Stockholm, 1979).
Lundström, R., 'Swedish multinational growth before 1930', in P. Hertner and G. Jones, eds.,
    Multinationals: theory and history (Aldershot, 1986), pp. 135-56.
Maxcy, G., *The multinational motor industry* (1981).
Reader, W.J., *Imperial Chemical Industries: a history*, 2 vols. (1970, 1975).
Reader, W.J., *Metal Box: a history* (1976).
Saul, S.B., 'The American impact on British industry, 1895-1914', *Bus. Hist.*, III (1960), pp. 19-38.
Scott, J.D., *Siemens Brothers, 1858-1958* (1958).
Shaw, C., 'The large manufacturing employers of 1907', *Bus. Hist.*, XXV (1983), pp. 42-60.
Slinn, J., *A history of May and Baker, 1834-1984* (Cambridge, 1984).
Southard, F.A., *American industry in Europe* (New York, 1931).
Teichova, A., 'The Mannesmann concern in east central Europe in the interwar period', in A. Teichova
    and P.L. Cottrell, eds., *International business and central Europe, 1918-1939* (Leicester, 1983), pp. 103-
    37.

FOREIGN MULTINATIONALS AND BRITISH INDUSTRY 453

Wilkins, M. and Hill, F.E., *American business abroad: Ford on six continents* (Detroit, 1964).
Wilkins, M., *The emergence of multinational enterprise* (Cambridge, Mass., 1970).
Wilkins, M., *The maturing of multinational enterprise* (Cambridge, Mass., 1974).
Wilson, C., *The history of Unilever*, 2 vols. (1954).
Young, P., *Power of speech: a history of Standard Telephones and Cables, 1883-1983* (1983).

[23]

Excerpt from *Historical Studies in International Corporate Business*, Alice Teichova, Maurice Levy-Leboyer and Helga Nussbaum (eds.)

14 The Japanese cotton spinners' direct investments into China before the Second World War

TETSUYA KUWAHARA

Introduction

The Japanese cotton industry depended heavily on overseas markets for its growth since the beginning of its development. Japanese major cotton spinners exported about 40% of their total sales in 1914. The exports of Japanese cotton spinners were almost completely confined to the Chinese market before the First World War. They had established a dominant position there, especially in the area of cotton yarn and coarse cotton cloth. They exported 500,000 bales of cotton yarn (worth about 56.5 million yen) to China. This amounted to 55% of the total imported yarns to China in 1914. They also exported coarse cotton cloth (sheeting, drill and T-cloth) for a total of 24.7 million yen which was 57% of the total amount imported to China in 1913.

During the First World War the Chinese modern cotton industry began expansion of its production capacity on a large scale while imports from Lancashire decreased and the price of cotton goods rose considerably.[1] Then the Chinese market became self-sufficient in the areas of coarse cotton yarns (cotton yarns of 20 count and downward) and coarse cotton cloth. Imports of cotton yarns to China decreased from 901,000 bales in 1914 to 377,000 bales in 1918. Chinese imports of sheeting and drill decreased from 3,054,000 pieces and 1,759,000 pieces respectively in 1915 to 2,268,000 pieces and 952,000 pieces in 1918. This change in the Chinese coarse cotton goods markets had a serious impact on the Japanese cotton industry which had established a dominant position there. They continued to lose their market share of coarse cotton goods to the local cotton spinners during and after the First World War. Most major Japanese cotton spinners then embarked on building local mills.[2] At the same time the Japanese cotton spinners also had a chance of entering new overseas markets such as the fine cotton cloth markets in China and the cotton goods markets of other underdeveloped areas where these demands had been met previously with imported Lancashire cotton goods.

152   Tetsuya Kuwahara

Table 14.1. *The four largest cotton firms (December 1918)*

	Total assets (1919) (thousand yen)	Spindles (December 1918) (thousand)	Looms (December 1918)
Toyo Cotton Spinning Company	84,316	512 (16%)	12,961 (32%)
Kanegafuchi Cotton Spinning Company	72,940	485 (15%)	7,323 (18%)
Dainippon Cotton Spinning Company	69,738	569 (18%)	3,561 (9%)
Fuji Gasu Cotton Spinning Company	48,525	298 (9%)	1,642 (4%)
Total	275,519	1,864 (58%)	25,487 (63%)
All Japan (43 companies in December 1918)	—	3,228 (100%)	40,391 (100%)

Source: Dainippon Boseki Rengokai (Japanese Cotton Spinners' Association) (ed.), *Menshi Boseki Jigo Sankusho (Reference Book for Japanese Cotton Spinning)* (Osaka, the second half of 1918).
K. Nakagawa *et al.* (eds.) *Nihon Keieishi no Kisochishiki (Basic Knowledge of Japanese Business History)* (Tokyo, 1974), p. 452.

This chapter examines the four largest Japanese cotton firms in terms of their assets at the end of 1918. They are the Toyo Cotton Spinning Company, the Kanegafuchi Cotton Spinning Company, the Dainippon Cotton Spinning Company and the Fuji Gasu Cotton Spinning Company (table 14.1) The number of spindles of these four was 1,864,000, which is 58% of all spindles installed in Japan.

The direct investments into China by these four Japanese cotton firms are analysed comparatively from the viewpoint of their product-market structures and their entrepreneurship. The product-market structure stands for the composition of products and their positions in markets, and is constructed through a series of strategies for corporate growth. When the environment changes, firms are required to formulate new strategies which result in new product-market structures. Entrepreneurship signifies the ability and energy of top management to recognise and respond to new external conditions by adopting the product-market structure.

Dainippon Cotton Spinning Company: no alternatives except for local production[3]

The Amagasaki Cotton Spinning Company (339,848 spindles, 2,703 looms) merged with the Settsu Cotton Spinning Company (214,000 spindles, 560 looms) in June 1918 and changed its name to Dainippon Cotton Spinning Company which made it the largest firm in terms of number of spindles. While Amagasaki was the largest producer of the middle count and high count cotton yarn, Settsu had specialised in coarse cotton yarn. Through this merger Dainippon became a major producer of coarse cotton yarn.

Settsu's growth had heavily depended on the Chinese coarse cotton yarn market, having been the second largest exporter of coarse cotton yarns to that market in the period from 1903 to 1910. Its proportion of exports to total production was as high as 60% in 1914. This was based on high quality and productivity achieved by the company. Settsu's export increased to 72,123 bales (48% of the total production) in 1914. During the First World War Settsu gradually lost its established share of the Chinese market. Its export decreased to 14,178 bales (18% of the total production) during the first five months of 1918.

Dainippon Cotton Spinning Company inherited this formidable problem through the merger with Settsu. The president, Kikuchi, who had also taken up the presidency of Settsu in June, 1915, recognised changing needs, and immediately after the merger, Dainippon dispatched a mill manager to Tsingtao to investigate a prospective mill site. In October 1918, Dainippon considered buying a local cotton spinning mill, the Oriental Cotton Spinning Company in Shanghai. In March and April of 1919, Kikuchi travelled in Shanghai, Hankao and Tiengtao and other cities in China to search for placing direct investments there. While Dainippon was trying to acquire mill sites in Shanghai and Tsingtao, he announced a plan for investments in China at the general meeting of shareholders in June 1919. The Shanghai mill was late in beginning construction because of difficulties in the acquisition of a suitable site. Construction of the Tsingtao mill began in November 1919. The mill commenced partial operations in November 1921 and full operations with 58,000 spindles in the first half of 1923. The Shanghai mill was completed and began full operations in the latter half of 1923. Ninety per cent production capacity was applied to the manufacture of coarse cotton yarns and 10% to that of middle count yarns. Through these two local mills the company defended its market position in China which had been established by the Settsu Cotton Spinning Company before the First World War.

Concomitant with the decrease in exports of coarse cotton yarns, the domestic spinning division suffered the problem of excess capacity. In order to increase the consumption of coarse cotton yarn within the company, the

154   Tetsuya Kuwahara

weaving section was enlarged. The number of looms was increased from 3,561 at the time of the merger to 9,504 by 1926. The weaving division had consumed 9% of the total production of cotton yarns in 1918, but this rose to 26% in 1926. Dainippon increased the output of coarse cotton cloth such as sheeting, most of which was exported to overseas markets.

The Kanegafuchi Cotton Spinning Company: some prejudice with regard to direct foreign investment[4]

Even before the First World War Kanegafuchi Cotton Spinning Company had built a diversified product-market structure as a result of the concatenation of preceding strategies. Kanegafuchi had grown to a big business by expanding the export of coarse cotton yarn to China after the Sino-Japanese War. It exported 78,065 bales (49% of total production) mainly to China, which was equivalent to 25% of the total of Japanese export to China in 1903. The rapid acquisition of a share in the Chinese market was based on the large-scale production facilities acquired by a series of mergers. For the purpose of more stability and growth, Kanegafuchi diversified its products to cotton cloth and fine yarns. While exporting sheeting to China after the Russo-Japanese War, Kanegafuchi took a leading role in import substitution of shirting in the domestic market. The product-market structure of 1914 is shown in table 14.2. In 1914 when Kanegafuchi's export of cotton yarn reached a peak of 93,688 bales, the estimated amount of coarse cotton yarn exported to China was 73,894 bales (25% of the total production). The estimated amount of coarse cotton cloth exported to China was as high as 8.3% of the total production in terms of cotton yarn consumed within the firm in 1914.

During the First World War, Kanegafuchi suffered badly, losing its established position in the Chinese market as the Chinese cotton industry began to develop rapidly on a large scale. Kanegafuchi exported only 12,007 bales of coarse cotton yarn in 1919 and 3,885 bales in 1921. Furthermore it began losing its established position in coarse cotton cloth in China.

On the other hand Kanegafuchi was given the opportunity of entry into new overseas markets where it replaced Lancashire goods. Also in the domestic market the demand for middle count cotton yarn increased. Due to the emergence of these new market opportunities, Kanegafuchi increased the production of middle count cotton yarn and fine cotton cloth. The output of middle count cotton yarn increased from 54,036 bales (19% of the total production of cotton yarn) in 1914 to 124,194 bales (44%) in 1919. And the production of thin cloth of Kanegafuchi's total production rose from 7% to 20% in the same period. This was executed not only by building new mills but also by utilising excess capacity arising from the decline in exports of coarse cotton goods to China. Kanegafuchi, moreover, constructed dying,

Table 14.2. *Product-market structure of Kanegafuchi Cotton Spinning Company in 1914*

Product Market	Coarse cotton yarn (20 count and downward)	Middle count cotton yarn (higher than 20 count)	Total
Within the company	41,736 bales (14%)	16,554 bales (6%)	58,290 (20%)
Domestic market	114,494 (39%)	24,375 (8%)	138,869 (47%)
Foreign market	81,203 (28%)	12,485 (4%)	93,688 (32%)
Total	237,433 (82%)	53,414 (18%)	290,847 (100%)

Note: The bales of cotton yarn consumed within the firm are estimated on a basis of production volume of coarse and fine cotton cloth.
Source: Dainippon Boseki Rengokai (Japanese Cotton Spinners' Association) (ed.), *Dainippon Boseki Rengokai Geppo* (*Monthly Report of Japanese Cotton Spinners' Association*) (Osaka), February 1914–January 1915.
Dainippon Boseki Rengokai (ed.), *Menshi Boseki Jijo Sankusho* (*Reference book for Japanese cotton spinning*), 1914.

bleaching and printing mills on a large scale in Osaka to increase its outlets for the cotton cloth. The mill began dying operations in 1917, bleaching in the latter half of 1919, and printing in April 1924. The cotton cloth thus produced was exported.

Even if Kanegafuchi was successfully acquiring new market opportunities, it was still necessary to defend their established share in China for the sake of their corporate growth. But Kanegafuchi was slow to respond. Sanji Muto, the managing director of Kanegafuchi, believed that direct foreign investment was detrimental to the Japanese economy, because he thought it would result in the elimination of employment opportunities, in the decline of related industries, and in the decay of local communities. Muto thus could not accept direct investment into China as a legitimate policy. Meanwhile his Japanese competitors embarked on the construction of local cotton spinning mills in China. Muto finally recognised the need to emulate these competitors and to defend Kanegafuchi's share against them. Kanegafuchi thus broke new ground for a cotton spinning mill in Shanghai in March 1921. The first mill in Shanghai with 20,000 spindles for coarse cotton yarn was completed in October 1922, the second with 18,000 spindles for 42 count doubling cotton yarn in November 1923. A Tsingtao mill was completed with 40,536 spindles for coarse cotton yarn and 860 looms for sheeting in March 1925.

156   Tetsuya Kuwahara

Kanegafuchi, moreover, purchased the Lao Kom Mow Cotton Spinning and Weaving Company and thus acquired 45,000 spindles and 850 looms in Shanghai in May 1925. At the end of 1925, Kanegafuchi held 131,576 spindles and 1,527 looms in China. This was the largest share among the local firms established by the Japanese cotton spinners during and after the First World War.

Toyo Cotton Spinning Company: preference for export to local production[5]

While Settsu and Kanegafuchi had been the largest exporters of coarse cotton yarn to China, the Toyo Cotton Spinning Company had established a major position in the Chinese market of coarse cotton cloth such as sheeting and drill. The Toyo Cotton Spinning Company had been reorganised as a new company through the merger of the Osaka Cotton Spinning Company and the Mie Cotton Spinning Company. Toyo held 10,136 looms (40% of the total Japanese looms owned by spinning firms) and 441,796 spindles (17%). Both companies had pioneered the export of Japanese coarse cotton cloth to North China, Manchuria and Korea. They took over the market share which had been held by Lancashire and American cotton goods, and established a leading position there after the Russo-Japanese War. Besides the export of cotton cloth, Osaka and Mie increased their export of coarse cotton yarn from about 1911 onwards. The export peak of 60.7 thousand bales (17% of the total production of cotton yarn) was reached in 1914.

During the First World War Toyo suffered a sharp decrease in its exports of coarse cotton cloth and yarns to China, while the Chinese output of machine woven cotton cloth increased from 58 million square yards in 1905–7 to 354 million square yards in 1923, and the hand woven cotton cloth rose from 375 million square yards to 1,591 million square yards in the same years. This increase of production of coarse cotton cloth was based on the development of the spinning industry there. Then Japanese export of sheetings and drills to China decreased respectively from 3,356,000 pieces in 1913 to 1,856,000 pieces in 1920, and 1,667,000 pieces to 433,000 pieces in the same years. As a response to the impact on the weaving division, Toyo shifted the export market from China to South East Asia, the Middle East and Africa where there were large markets for coarse cotton cloth. Thus the major destination for the export of Japanese coarse cotton cloth changed to areas outside China after the First World War. Seventy-two per cent of the total export of Japanese sheeting was destined for markets outside China in 1921. For the Chinese market Toyo increased exports of fine cotton cloth such as shirting and jeans.[6]

On the other hand, there was no export market for cotton yarn outside

China. Thus Toyo's spinning division had no alternative for maintaining its overseas market share but to produce locally in China. The strategic need to build mills there was recognised by Toyo's managers, but Toyo did not take positive action towards local production when faced initially with the loss of its share in China. This can be explained by the fact that cotton yarn did not play such an important role in Toyo's exports as it did in the product-market structure of other major cotton spinner. Even at the peak year of Toyo's exports to China, cotton yarn was equivalent to only 8% of its sales, while the export of cotton cloth to China amounted to 19% of Toyo's total sales. The export of cotton yarn of Toyo was 17% which was the lowest among the major cotton spinners. The average for exports of all Japanese cotton spinners was 34% in 1914.

But when the Japanese competitors began the construction of local mills in China, Toyo felt that its competitive position was threatened. This threat generated a galvanising force in Toyo to take action in China. The Toyo Cotton Spinning Company began to construct a local spinning mill in Shanghai in October 1921, when the Dainippon Cotton Spinning Company had already begun trial operations in their local mill in Tsingtao. The Shanghai mill was completed with 45,600 spindles for coarse cotton yarn in the latter half of 1923.

The Fuji Gasu Cotton Spinning Company: mobilised on the standpoint of national interests[7]

Fuji Gasu Cotton Spinning Company which had established a position in the middle count cotton yarn market in the Kanto (Tokyo) district through merging with the Tokyo Gasu Cotton Spinning Company (Tokyo Gasu Boseki Kaisha), the largest producer of gassed yarn in Japan in 1906. It then became the third largest cotton spinning company in Japan. Fuji Gasu had a 39% market share in gassed yarn, 17% in middle count doubling yarn and 11% in middle count yarn in the domestic market in 1909. When some major cotton spinners which had specialised in coarse cotton yarns entered into the high and medium count cotton yarn markets in the Kanto area, Fuji Gasu entered into the coarse cotton yarn market on a large scale as a countervailing response to these competitors. Fuji Gasu completed the Koyama No. 4 Mill in 1910, and increased production of coarse cotton yarn steadily. The coarse cotton yarns which were mostly sold in the domestic market totalled 58% of the production of the firm in 1917.

Through establishing a position as a major firm in the domestic markets, Fuji Gasu developed managerial skills which allowed it to be not only domestically but also internationally competitive with such resources as blending techniques for raw cotton, combining processes of spinning and weaving facilities and labour management.

158   Tetsuya Kuwahara

Fuji Gasu accomplished these achievements under the leadership of its managing director, Toyoharu Wada. After the remarkable success of Fuji Gasu, Wada began a wider engagement in business activities around 1910. He assisted in organising new companies and reorganising failing ones in a variety of industrial fields. He helped form the Nihon Kogyo Club (Industrial Club) in March 1917. He believed himself to be a leader in the Japanese cotton spinning industry and expected to play a role in protecting and promoting the national interest.

As soon as the Chinese cotton spinning and weaving industry began to make great progress during the First World War, Wada perceived the possibility of losing the established position of Japanese cotton spinners there. He saw the new situation as a symptom of decline of the Japanese cotton spinning industry with a consequent depression of the Japanese economy. As a result he recognised the need to have local plants in order to defend their established position. Motivated by the national interest, he worked on several projects with local cotton spinning and weaving businesses in China. In October and November 1916, for example, he inspected the Soy Chee Cotton Spinning Company of Shanghai for sale on the spot. He also organised the Sina Sen-i Kogyo Kumiai, an association for Chinese textile industries concerned with the cotton growing, spinning and weaving businesses in China; he organised Nikka Boshoku Kaisha (Japan China Cotton Mill) in Shanghai in July 1918; he invested in Nisshi Boshoku Kaisha, the Japan China Cotton Spinning and Weaving Company formed in Shanghai in November 1919; and he assisted in concluding three loan agreements between Toa Kogyo Kaisha (a Japanese investment company for Chinese industries) and three Chinese cotton mills in 1921–2. Nikka Boshoku Kaisha was the first local production base which the Japanese established during and after the First World War. The company was organised mainly through the capital of cotton merchants in Osaka, starting with a factory which had previously been bought by a Japanese merchant. For the reorganisation of the mill Wada not only gave directions himself but also sent engineers and technicians of the Fuji Gasu Cotton Spinning Company and other Japanese spinning firms with which he was concerned to the local mill.

In the process of channelling Japanese investment into the Chinese cotton industry, he mobilised the managerial resources of Fuji Gasu Cotton Spinning Company. Fuji Gasu began the mill construction in Tsingtao in October 1921. The mill was completed in April 1924; with 30,720 spindles it produced coarse cotton yarn. Fuji Gasu invested 30 % of the total share capital in Manshu Boseki Kaisha (Manchuria Cotton Spinning Company) in March 1923. Their mill opened in the first half of 1925, with 31,000 spindles and 504 looms for coarse cotton yarn and sheeting. Through these local mills

Japanese cotton spinners' investments into China   159

in China, Fuji Gasu entered the Chinese coarse cotton yarn and cloth market, a market to which it had previously paid little attention.

Conclusion

Most of the major Japanese cotton spinners established local production bases in China in order to defend their market shares, which they had acquired through exporting.[8] Most of the local mills produced coarse cotton yarns. Large Japanese export companies established larger mills than smaller exporters. Only a few local mills produced coarse cotton cloth. While the export of coarse cotton yarns could only be possible to the Chinese market, Japanese coarse cotton cloth could find alternative markets overseas outside China. Thus the coarse cotton cloth exporters were able to shift their market from China to more distant areas.

Beside them, a few Japanese cotton spinners such as Fuji Gasu Cotton Spinning Company built local production bases in China to secure their market for cotton goods there. Fuji Gasu mobilised its managerial resources aggressively in order to acquire a share there.

While proceeding to invest directly in China, most Japanese cotton spinners at the same time diversified their products for the home market. This solved the problem of excess capacity which arose as a result of the loss of the Chinese market. They increased their own weaving looms to increase consumption of coarse cotton yarn within the company. Also, production of middle count yarns was increased, replacing output of coarse cotton yarns. Thus the product-market structures of Japanese cotton spinners became more diversified.

To compete successfully with the Chinese cotton spinners, Japanese-owned local mills were required to have some advantages over them. Managerial resources transferred to the local mills were expected to carry this additional advantage even after compensating for the cost of operations abroad. Having the competitive managerial resources such as the technological expertise for cotton blending, for repair and maintenance of spinning and weaving machinery, and the organisational capability of labour management, these local mills could stay ahead of the Chinese owned mills in cost and quality. The sales agencies and distribution networks that had been established in China by Japanese merchants were also favourable to the local mills.

The different strategies in the investment behaviour of Japanese cotton spinners in China was also influenced by the varying quality of entrepreneurship of each firm. Kanegafuchi's slow response to the needs for establishing production units abroad can be traced to the managing director Muto's prejudice towards direct foreign investments overseas, whereas president

160   Tetsuya Kuwahara

Table 14.3. *Processes of Japanese cotton spinners' direct investments into China*

Names of firms	Relations with the Chinese markets prior to the local production		Entrepreneurship
	Coarse cotton yarn exported to China in 1914 (proportion of it to total production)[a]	Coarse cotton cloth exported to China in 1914 (proportion of it to total production)[a]	
Dainippon Cotton Spinning Company	Settsu only: 65,600 bales (44%) total of Settsu and Amagasaki: 66,300 bales (32%)	Settsu only: none total of Settsu and Amagasaki: 1,100 bales (0.5%)	Recognition of almost no alternatives except for local production
Kanegafuchi Cotton Spinning Company	73,900 bales (25%)	24,200 bales (8%)	Muto Sanji's partial prejudice on direct foreign investments
Toyo Cotton Spinning Company	23,700 bales (7%)	54,800 bales (16%)	Preference for export to direct investment
Fuji Gasu Cotton Spinning Company	800 bales (0.9%)	4,600 bales (5%)	Toyoji Wada's aggressive mobilisation of managerial resources on the standpoint of national interests

Notes: The data source is the author's papers, cited in this chapter.
[a] The volume is estimated by the following method in cases of Dainippon, Kanegafuchi and Fuji Gasu:
– coarse cotton yarn export = each firm's export volume of coarse cotton yarn × 91%; 91% is the proportion of the Japanese export to China to Japan's total export of cotton yarn.
– coarse cotton cloth export = total production volume (converted into cotton yarns) × 2/3 × 87%; 2/3 is the export ratio of width coarse cotton cloth; 87% is the proportion of Japanese sheeting export to China to Japan's total export of sheeting in 1914.

Direct investments into China after the First World War

Motive	Location and year of commencement of construction	Mill size and product lines[b]	New strategies of the domestic division during and after the First World War
Defending the market position of its major export item	Tsingtao, November 1919 Shanghai, April 1921	120 thousand spindles – 90% of them for coarse cotton yarn and 10% for middle count yarn	Downward integration into the weaving section for increased consumption of coarse cotton yarn within the mills. The weaving looms increased from 3,561 in June 1918 to 9,504 in 1926.
Defending the market position of its major export item	Shanghai, March 1921 Tsingtao, May 1922 Shanghai, May 1925 (purchased)	124 thousand spindles and 1,295 looms – 51% of spindles for coarse cotton yarn, 23% for middle count cotton yarn, and 27% of spindles and looms for coarse cotton cloth (on a basis of 79 thousand spindles and 860 looms at March 1925)	Shift of product lines from coarse cotton yarn and cloth to middle count yarn and to fine cotton cloth such as shirtings. Proportion of middle count and high count yarn of total production increased from 19% in 1914 to 52% in 1924.
Defending the market position of its minor export item	Shanghai, October 1921	46 thousand spindles for coarse cotton yarn	Shift of export markets for coarse cotton cloth from China to the other undeveloped areas – from coarse cotton yarn to middle count yarn and to fine cotton cloth. The production of fine cloth (shirtings, jeans, calico) increased from 43 million yards in 1915 to 84 million yards in 1919.
New entry into the local market	Tsingtao, October 1921 Liao Yang, Manchuria, 1923 (a mill to be constructed by Manchuria Cotton Spinning Company)	41 thousand spindles and 168 looms[c] for coarse cotton yarn and cloth	

[b] The proportion of volume of product lines is obtained on a basis of the production facility.

[c] The total of Tsingtao mill and 30% of the production facilities of Manchuria Cotton Spinning Company.

Source: Yokohama Shi (ed., 'Yokohama Shi Shi' (History of Yokohama City), *Shiryo Hen* (Book of Statistical Data), vol. 2, 1962.

Export volume of Toyo Cotton Spinning Company is estimated on a basis of value amount.

162   Tetsuya Kuwahara

Wada mobilised Fuji Gasu's managerial resources for acquiring local mills in China because of his own understanding of what was best for national interests.

NOTES

1 Tetsuya Kuwahara, 'The business strategy of Japanese cotton spinners: overseas operations 1890–1931' in Akio Okochi and Shin-ichi Yonekawa (eds.), *Textile industry and its business climate: Proceedings of the Fuji Conference*, (Tokyo, January 1982), in English.
2 The investment amount of Japanese-owned cotton spinning and weaving industry in China was 300 million yen whose proportion to total Japanese investments into China except for Manchuria was 36 per cent in 1936. Naosuke Takamura, *Kindai Nihon Mengyo to Chugoku (The modern Japanese cotton industry and China)* (Tokyo, 1982), p. i.
3 For more details refer to the following paper: Tetsuya Kuwahara, 'Zaika Bosekogyo no Seisei: Dainippon Boseki Kaisha no Jirei o chushin to shite' ('Formation of Japanese owned cotton spinning firms in China: case of Dainippon Cotton Spinning Company) *Keizai Keiei Ronso (Review of Economics and Business Administration)*, 16: 3, Kyoto Sangyo University, 1981.
4 Tetsuya Kuwahara, 'Senzen ni okeru Nihon Boseki Kigyo no Kaigai Katsudo: Kanegafuchi Boseki Kaisha no Jirei' (Overseas operations of Japanese cotton spinners in the pre-Second World War period: case of Kanegafuchi Cotton Spinning Company), *Roddokai Ronshu (Rokkodai Review)*, 22: 1 (Kobe University Graduate School, April 1975). Also see Tetsuya Kuwahara, 'Zajka Bosekigyo no Seisei: Kanegafuchi boseki Kaisha no Jirei' ('Japanese cotton spinners' direct investments into China: case of Kanegafuchi Cotton Spinning Company'), unpublished.
5 Tetsuya Kuwahara, 'Senzen ni okeru Nihon Bosekikigyo no Kaigai Sijo Senryaku: Toyo Boseki Kaisha no Jirei' ('Overseas market strategies of Japanese cotton spinners in the pre-Second World War period: case of Toyo Cotton Spinning Company'), *Keizai Keiei Ronso*, 17: 3, (Kyoto Sangyo University, December 1982). *Toyo Boseki Kaisha (Toyo Cotton Spinning Company)*. *Toyo Boseki Hyaku Nen Shi (One Hundred Years of Toyo Cotton Spinning Company)*, (Osaka, 1986), vol. 1, pp. 216–227.
6 The numerous values in this paragraph are from the following sources. N. Takamura, *Kindai Nihon Mengyo to Chugoku (Modern Japanese cotton industry and China)* (Tokyo, 1982), p. 127. Yokohama Shi (ed.), *Yokohama Shi Shi (History of Yokohama City)*, Book of Statistical Data, vol. 2 (Yokohama City, 1962), p. 174. Statistics of the Chinese Maritime Customs quoted in M. Yasuhara, *Shina no Kogyo to Genryo (Manufacturing industries and raw materials in China)* (*Shanghai*, 1919), vol. 1, 19, chapter 4, section 1, and Ki-ichi Nishikawa, *Menkogyo to Menshi Menpu (Cotton industry and cotton yarns and cloth)* (Shanghai, 1924), pp. 259–61.
7 Tetsuya Kuwahara, 'Zaika Bosekigyo no Seisei n: Kansuru Seihin Sijo Kozotek Kigyosha Seinoteki Bunseki: Fuji Gasu. Boseki Kaisha c Toyoj Wada' ('Japanese cotton spinners' direct investment into China Before the Second World War: Fuji Gasu Cotton Spinning Company and Toyoji Wada'), *Kyoto Sangyo Daigaku Ronshu, International relations series*, no. 12, (Kyoto Sangyo University, March 1985).
8 The processes of Japanese cotton spinners' direct investments into China are summarised in table 14.3.

[24]

ARTICLES

The Prewar Japanese Automobile Industry and American Manufacturers

By Masaru Udagawa
Hosei University

Introduction

The use of automobiles in Japan began to grow during the economic boom that followed World War I. The growth continued in the aftermath of the great earthquake of September 1923, which destroyed South Kanto, including Tokyo and Yokohama. In the reconstruction following the earthquake, automobiles played an especially important role transporting goods and people in the city. The usefulness of automobiles was thus widely recognized by the early 1920s.[1]

Against this background, there emerged not only entrepreneurs who began producing automobiles, but also well-established companies that expanded their business into automotive manufacturing. The industry seemed to enjoy an auspicious beginning, yet most early auto makers failed to grow. Ironically, in the midst of plentiful opportunities for market expansion, many either went bankrupt or withdrew from the industry. The only firms that survived were Tokyo Ishikawajima Zosensho Jidoshabu (Automobile Division of Tokyo Ishikawajima Shipyards), Tokyo Gasu Denki Kogyo Jidoshabu (Automobile Division of Tokyo Gas and Electric), and DAT Jidosha Seizo (DAT Automobile Manufacturing).

The failure of the early Japanese auto industry is attributable to the "Big Three" American manufacturers, who quickly recognized the increasing demand for automobiles in the 1920s and lost no time in making inroads into the Japanese market. Ford founded Japan Ford in Yokohama in 1925, with 4 million yen in capital, which was increased to 8 million yen in 1929. General Motors founded Japan GM in Osaka in 1927, investing 8 million yen. Chrysler was represented by Kyoritsu Jidosha Seisakusho (Kyoritsu Automobile Works), a concern in Yokohama established in 1928 with capital of 200,000 yen. When the Big

Three commenced production using the "knock-down" assembly method, the Japanese makers, as yet lacking mass production and marketing techniques, could not compete. Table 1 shows how swiftly the U.S. manufacturers infiltrated Japanese markets.

This article has two purposes. The first is to review Japanese government policies which sought to foster the domestic industry in the face of a market monopoly by the American corporations. The second is to examine, from the vantage point of business history, the choices Ford and GM made in response to those policies, and the consequences of their choices.[2]

The Japanese Government's Automotive Policies

Before World War II, the Japanese government implemented three major policies to build the automotive industry. The first was the Gunyo

Table 1 Motor Vehicles Supplied in Japan: 1916—1935   (unit: vehicles)

| Year | Domestic Made | Imports | Knock-Down Kits (KD) | | | |
			KD Imports	Japan Ford	Japan GM	Kyoritsu Automobile
1916	—	218	—	—	—	—
1917	—	860	—	—	—	—
1918	—	1,653	—	—	—	—
1919	—	1,579	—	—	—	—
1920	—	1,745	—	—	—	—
1921	—	1,074	—	—	—	—
1922	—	752	—	—	—	—
1923	—	1,938	—	—	—	—
1924	—	4,603	—	—	—	—
1925	376	1,765	3,437	3,437	—	—
1926	245	2,381	8,677	8,677	—	—
1927	302	3,895	12,668	7,033	5,635	—
1928	347	7,883	24,341	8,850	15,491	—
1929	437	5,018	29,338	10,674	15,745	1,251
1930	458	2,591	19,678	10,620	8,049	1,015
1931	436 (2)	1,887	20,199	11,505	7,478	1,201
1932	880 (184)	997	14,087	7,448	5,893	760
1933	1,681 (626)	491	15,082	8,166	5,942	998
1934	2,247 (1,170)	896	33,458	17,244	12,322	2,574
1935	5,094 (3,913)	934	30,787	14,965	12,492	3,612

Sources: Nissan Jidosha Kabushiki Kaisha, ed., *Nissan Jidosha Sanju Nenshi* (A 30-Year History of Nissan Motor), Nissan Jidosha Kabushiki Kaisha, 1965. p. 16.

Notes: 1. Figures in parentheses are numbers of small cars.
2. Total number of KD imports and total of breakdown for KD imports differ but follow the statistics on record.

Jidosha Hojo Ho (Military Automobile Subsidies Law) of 1915. This
was enacted at the request of the Army, which was impressed by the
the military's use of automobiles during World War I. It consisted of the
following points:

1) identify auto makers capable of producing 100 units per year and,
   by giving them subsidies, facilitate their production of large trucks
   to be designated for the military as "protected vehicles;"
2) subsidize the procurement and maintenance of these trucks; and
3) in an emergency, requisition the trucks for military use with compensation paid at a fixed rate.[3]

Although the Military Automobile Subsidies Law was applied only
to large trucks, it boosted the industries that began automobile production amid the wartime economic boom. Moreover, it helped defend
domestic automobiles against the intrusion of U.S. manufacturers in
the early 1920s since Tokyo Ishikawajima Shipyards, Tokyo Gas and
Electric, and DAT Automobile Manufacturing were the only companies
licensed in accordance with the new law.

The second policy was initiated by the Ministry of Commerce and
Industry. After World War I, due to an unfavorable balance of trade,
Japan suffered a large deficit in international payments. The domestic
companies' slump and increased imports of automotive products from
U.S. manufacturers became serious problems, and in September 1929 the
Ministry of Commerce and Industry referred the matter, "Jidosha
kogyo o kakuritsu suru hosaku ikan" (What is the right method to
establish an automobile industry?), to its consultative organ, the Committee to Promote Domestic Industry. This action was in line with the
Ministry's campaign to promote the home industry through buying
domestic goods. On the committee's recommendation, the Ministry
created in May 1931 the Committee to Establish an Automobile Industry, consisting of scholars, the bureau chiefs of government ministries
charged with automotive manufacturing, and the presidents of the three
Japanese automobile companies mentioned above. The new committee's
deliberations resulted in a ministerial policy containing the following
three points:

1) design a standard model for mid-size trucks and buses, weighing
   from 1.5 to 2 tons, and pay a premium to produce such vehicles;
   such vehicles;
2) attempt a merger of the three domestic auto makers to strengthen
   production of standard models; and
3) raise tariffs on automotive imports.[4]

In March 1932, the first standard model vehicle was built on a trial basis (the model was named the Fuji in 1933 and renamed the Isuzu the following year). Thereafter, the Ministry of Commerce and Industry requested that the three Japanese auto makers merge to form a new company. As a result, in March 1933, Jidosha Kogyo (Automobile Industries), with capital of 3.2 million yen, was created through the merger of DAT Automobile Manufacturing and Ishikawajima Jidosha Seisakusho (Ishikawajima Automobile Works, formerly Automobile Division of Ishikawajima Shipyards, which had become independent in 1929). Four years later, in 1937, the Automobile Division of Tokyo Gas and Electric merged with the new company.

Concurrently, in June 1932, the government changed tariff rates for automotive imports, raising the *ad valorem* duty for parts from 30 percent to 40 percent and converting the specific duty of 100 *kin* (1 *kin* = 600 grams) levied on engines into a 35 percent *ad valorem* duty. In the Franco-Japanese tariff agreements of that year, the old rates of 35 percent for automobiles and 25 percent for parts were unified into a flat rate of 35 percent.[5]

But Automobile Industries failed to take a primary place in the subsequent history of Japanese auto manufacturing. Nor did the Isuzu model become the strategic vehicle to preclude imports. The Isuzu could not achieve its goal partly because it was a mid-size vehicle designed to avoid outright competition with inexpensive Fords and Chevrolets sold in the mass market at the time.[6] Furthermore, after the outbreak of the Manchurian Conflict in September 1931, the Ministry of the Army gradually replaced the Ministry of Commerce and Industry as the decision maker in automotive industry policies.[7]

In the wake of the Manchurian Incident, the Ministry of the Army requisitioned trucks throughout Japan and discovered that, unlike the Fords and Chevrolets, the domestic vehicles performed poorly and broke down easily. Anticipating a military operation on the Chinese mainland, which might threaten the import of foreign cars into Japan, the Army began to demand a new strategy for building the automobile industry. The purpose was to boycott foreign auto makers and take steps to produce trucks comparable to the Fords and Chevrolets for mass markets.[8]

In January 1934, negotiations began between the Ministry of Commerce and Industry and the Ministry of the Army, but the former, which had planned to mass produce the Isuzu model, declined the requests made by the Army. Its high-ranking officials, moreover, voiced support for the continuation of the U.S.-Japan Treaty of Commerce and Navigation as well as for the plan for the first Nissan-GM joint venture (discussed below). The Foreign and Finance Ministries were also opposed to the radical position of the Ministry of the Army. The Consultative Council of the Ministries Charged with the Automobile Industry, created by the Ministry of Commerce and Industry in August 1934, also failed to reach a consensus, and the activities of the council were suspended in December of the same year.[9]

It was impossible, however, to resist the Army, whose power was growing daily. Personnel changes within the Ministry of Commerce and Industry carried out in October 1935 brought the so-called reformist bureaucrats to key positions of policy making. Since these officials supported government control of the economy and a more sophisticated industrial structure, the Ministry of Commerce and Industry under their leadership discontinued its opposition to the automotive policies of the Army. The two ministries began discussing the third and last of the three prewar automotive policies which this article examines, the Jidosha Seizo Jigyo Ho (Automobile Manufacturing Business Law).[10]

On August 9, 1935, the Cabinet approved the Army's position, contained in "Jidosha Kogyo Ho Yoko" (Outline for an Automobile Manufacturing Business Law). The law enacted, in accordance with this outline, had seven points:

1) Companies which produce more than 3,000 automobiles with an engine capacity of more than 750 cc and companies which produce parts for these automobiles must get a license from the government.

2) More than half of the shares of licensed companies must be owned by Japanese, or by Japanese companies which are governed by Japanese law and in which votes must be held by Japanese.

3) Licensed companies are exempted for five years from income taxes, business revenue taxes, local taxes, and import taxes for machinery, equipment, and materials which are necessary for the production of automobiles.

4) In order to make it easier to raise capital, a special exemption from the Commerce Law is given to licensed companies in the case of capital increase and issuance of bonds.

5) In order to protect Japanese automobile and parts manufacturers from foreign competitors, it is possible to restrict imports of those products and to impose a dumping tax.

6) The Japanese government has authority to order and control the following matters: proposals of business plans, closing of businesses, mergers, dissolution, and the production of military automobiles and parts.

7) Companies which were operating before August 9, 1935, are

permitted to continue but cannot freely expand their production capacity beyond the level of the above date.[11]

It is clear from the above that the Automobile Manufacturing Business Law had two purposes. One was to foster the domestic auto industry under the supervision and with the assistance of the government. The other was to protect Japanese markets from the two major foreign auto manufacturers, Japan Ford and Japan GM, which represented the greatest obstacles to the growth of the domestic auto industry.

The Response of Ford and GM

After the Manchurian Incident, when various operations to create a strong auto industry in Japan began at the Army's behest, both Ford and GM, which virtually monopolized the Japanese market, had to adapt to the changed situation. Due to their different business objectives and management styles, the American corporations manifested two contrasting modes of behavior.

Table 2 shows Japan GM's profits between 1927 and 1934. Comparable information for Ford during the same period is not available, but its profits were probably as high as GM's.[12]

General Motors

GM's *Annual Report* for 1929 states its overseas operating objectives as follows:

> The policy which the Corporation is following in the development of its overseas business ... consists of making General Motors a local institution in each country in which it is operating, rather than a foreign concern doing business in that country. This is

Table 2 Japan GM's Profits

Year	Capital (Yen)	Profits (Yen)	Profit/Capital Ratio (%)
1927	8,000,000	664,700	8.3
1928	"	3,278,500	41.0
1929	"	3,125,900	39.1
1930	"	1,789,000	22.4
1931	"	1,094,900	13.7
1932	"	1,352,700	16.9
1933	"	2,117,500	26.5
1934	"	2,629,300	32.9

Source: "Nissan-GM Dai-Ichiji Kosho Kankei" (The First Nissan-GM Negotiation) in the Akikawa Family Archives.

accomplished by recognizing the customs of the country, and harmonizing the Corporation's procedures and policies with such customs. So far as possible, native personnel is employed. The Corporation's products are adapted in the fullest possible measure to the local taste. Experience has shown that in that way the most effective result can be obtained [sic] .[13]

Accordingly, GM allowed considerable managerial independence to its subsidiaries abroad. When, moreover, its assembly manufacturing system was challenged in foreign countries through market restriction, discriminatory tariffs, and preferential treatment of domestic products, GM is reported either to have purchased native automobile companies or to have become their affiliate in order to continue operations. In fact, GM adopted these policies in Japan.

GM believed in those days that Japan GM faced the most difficult business environment of all its overseas subsidiaries.[14] Its two choices were either to "continue to import components from American source [s] and assemble cars and trucks in Osaka in a constantly diminishing volume until a shut-down of the plant became inevitable; or . . . seek affiliation with Japanese interests to the end of establishing a sufficiently 'nationalized' activity." Of the two, "the latter . . . seemed to offer the better prospect of continuing returns, on a diminishing scale, and of postponing the ultimate day of total exclusion."[15]

In 1932, therefore, in view of the possible merger of the three Japanese auto manufacturers, R.M. May, the executive director of Japan GM, unofficially notified the Ministry of Commerce and Industry that he was prepared to participate in such a merger.[16] Although nothing came of May's proposal at this time, it was noticed by the Nissan combine, which was planning to take a decisive step into the automobile business.[17] Yoshisuke Aikawa, the founder of the Nissan combine, believed that the auto industry could become truly "national" by creating a mass production system aimed at building cars for the masses. As a shortcut to this end, Aikawa thought "the fundamental strategy" lay in "tying up with one of the American Big Three" and importing its technology.[18] In February 1933, therefore, after ascertaining that May's position reflected that of GM itself, Nippon Sangyo (Japan Industries, hereafter Nissan), which was the Nissan combine's holding company, issued a proposal to GM for cooperation. On April 26 of the following year, an agreement was reached between the two that each would own 49 percent of the shares in the other's subsidiaries, namely, Japan GM and Jidosha Seizo (Automobile Manufacturing) which was founded in

1933 and renamed Nissan Motor the following year.

Immediately after the agreement was reached, Nissan obtained a statement from the Factory Bureau Chief of the Ministry of Commerce and Industry that cooperation between it and GM was "most welcome." It further obtained from the Chief of the Foreign Exchange Bureau of the Ministry of Finance unofficial permission to forward a remittance to GM for the purchase of Japan GM's shares. The authorities within the Ministry of the Army, however, did not agree to the proposed Nissan-GM cooperation since they were pressing for automotive industry policies under their auspices.

Nissan thereupon requested a GM concession, explaining that the terms of cooperation agreed upon between them would not be supported by the Ministry of the Army and that the government would not approve an agreement without the Army's support. Consequently, on October 4, 1934, GM accepted the following proposals made by Nissan:

1) Nissan would own 51 percent of Japan GM's stocks;
2) as to the shares of Nissan Motor, if GM so desires, Japan GM, under Nissan's control, could own them independently of General Motors in the United States.

Despite these concessions on GM's part, however, the Ministry of the Army refused to support the revised proposal, forcing the dissolution of the first Nissan-GM cooperation plan. Aikawa gave up negotiations with GM and the first round of negotiations was broken off on December 31, 1934.[19]

The second series of negotiations between Nissan and GM began in June 1935, this time at GM's initiative, a step taken after it became clear that the government would approve the Army's policies toward the automotive industry in the form of the previously mentioned Outline for an Automobile Business Law. GM first proposed cooperation under the conditions agreed upon in the first plan, namely, that it transfer 51 percent of Japan GM's shares to Nissan to realize joint GM-Nissan management. Nissan asserted that the times had greatly changed since the first negotiations and that GM, if it truly wanted to cooperate with Nissan, should go beyond the transfer of shares and accept a merger of Japan GM and Nissan Motor to create a new company.[20]

GM realized that once the Automobile Manufacturing Business Law was enacted. Japan GM's future would be jeopardized. At GM's suggestion. H.B. Phillips of the General Motors Export Company, who headed the negotiations in Japan, conferred with the Vice Minister of Commerce and Industry on October 1, 1935. GM accepted Nissan's position after securing through Phillips the following promise from the Vice Minister:

Phillips: According to the proposed law, either one company or
several companies may be licensed. In determining the
number of licensees, what criteria will the Japanese
government apply?

Vice-Minister: In the automobile industry, there is naturally a certain
index of efficiency to be a profitable business. I do
not have a clear notion as to the capability of the
facilities of such a business in terms of the number
of vehicles it can produce. Nonetheless, it seems to
me that such an index does exist. Therefore, in my
opinion, if you divide the total number of vehicles
needed in Japan, say 25,000, by this index .you get
an answer such as two companies or three. Thinking
in this vein, more or less, we are planning now to
license, for the time being, two companies, one an
exclusively Japanese company and the other a joint
Japanese and foreign enterprise.

Phillips: Will GM's cooperation with Nissan be agreeable to
the Japanese government as a whole and receive
support in the future as well?

Vice-Minister: As you may perhaps already know, within the Army,
the desire to create an automobile industry by the
Japanese in a purely Japanese way has been extremely
intense. For myself, if I were asked whether or not
an auto industry can be built by the Japanese, I would
answer it can. For Nissan Motor has already succeeded
in manufacturing automobiles, though small ones.
But, according to Mr. Aikawa, while the Japanese can
make automobiles by themselves, they can do it "better, smoother, and quicker" if they tie up with GM. I
agree with this view completely. Personally I am of the
opinion that credit should be given to either Ford or
GM or both for having contributed much to Japan
regarding automobiles. I don't find it amusing to kick
out GM and Ford right away now that Japan has today
become capable of walking on her own feet. Besides,
the Ministry of Commerce and Industry does not favor
doing everything excessively nationalistically. It wishes
instead to keep some threads of international cooperation. You may understand, if you desire, that these
sentiments found an expression in the writing of "The

89

Phillips: Outline for an Automobile Manufacturing Business Law."

Phillips: Will a joint Nissan-GM enterprise be treated completely the same, without discrimination, as a purely Japanese company?

Vice-Minister: Yes.[21]

To anticipate the conclusion, the second Nissan-GM cooperation plan ended in a deadlock. In November 1935, upon commencement of the writing of the plan to establish a new company through the merger of Nissan Motor and Japan GM, GM expressed discontent over five points: 1) evaluation of Nissan Motor's assets at the time of merger; 2) Nissan Motor's past financial policy; 3) its management of inventory; 4) selection of board members for the new company; and 5) the investment plan of the new company. Moreover, GM suspended Phillips' authority to conclude a merger contract with Nissan. Nissan emphasized that the most important thing was to establish a new company and obtain a license in compliance with the Automobile Manufacturing Business Law. Regarding the attitude of the Ministry of Commerce and Industry, in Nissan's judgment, this step was possible only then, not later.

GM declined to respond immediately. Instead, it proposed to use GM's headquarters in New York for the final negotiations, which started in January 1936. According to Genshichi Asahara, a Nissan director who represented the company, the outcome of the negotiations was as follows:

General Motors in the end abandoned the idea of a joint company because, in addition to uncertainty about the investment, it was worried about the Japanese military's strong desire for domestic automobiles. Besides, after Hitler's seizure of the Opel factories in Germany, it feared that a joint company in Japan might be doomed to the same fate. In New York, we became convinced that it was impossible to found a joint company. This was why in New York we issued a memorandum with GM, announcing that creation of a joint company in Japan was postponed because the times were not appropriate.[22]

In short, GM concluded that a joint venture in Japan at that time would have to be undertaken on a grand scale as well as on terms unfavorable to it in order to get permission under the Automobile Manufacturing Business Law. Furthermore, judging from the stance of the military authorities, GM was uncertain about the safety of a joint company. The second series of negotiations for a Nissan-GM cooperation thus was fruitless, leaving the four year attempt at a joint venture as no more than "wishing for the impossible."

Ford

Unlike GM, Ford insisted on its own automobile manufacturing capacity in Japan. Useful in understanding Japan Ford's view of the state of the industry after the Manchurian Incident is the following report dated March 28, 1935, and submitted by Benjamin Kopf, the general manager of Japan Ford. In the last two or three years, he wrote, "when the country seriously felt that it might become embroiled in warfare with one or more of the largest Western powers . . . desperate efforts [were] made to bring forth a complete, self-sufficient motor industry, almost regardless of cost; but it is intended that this industry shall be in the hands of the Japanese exclusively." In the future, Kopf continued, "restrictive measures of diverse kinds will be enforced against foreign (imported) vehicles, and the only way for us to retain this important market is to take timely steps to manufacture locally before we are shut out of the market." [23]

Ford's main office in Dearborn, Michigan, was of the same opinion. [24] To build production facilities for manufacturing steel, engines, and other components, as well as for assembly, Ford planned to purchase 82 acres of reclaimed land owned by the city of Yokohama. When the plan became known to the Army in April 1934, the military demanded that the Yokohama city government call off the sale. The Army argued:

> Presently, the government and various ministries are designing auto industry policies. To sell the city's reclaimed land to Ford and assist a foreign country at this time is to sabotage domestic manufacturing of automobiles indispensable in war. Japan will then have no auto industry of its own. This is a serious problem, which will affect the future of the country. [25]

Nonetheless, Ford did not abandon its plan to build new production facilities in Japan. On July 24, 1935, despite the Army's persistent obstruction, Ford succeeded in purchasing 90 acres of land also in the reclaimed area of Yokohama but owned by Tokyo Wan Umetate (Tokyo Bay Reclamation), a subsidiary of the Asano zaibatsu. The sale was carried out despite the Army's opposition because Tokyo Bay Reclamation acted on its own judgement that "Ford will build factories and provide technology. Even if a war breaks out, they cannot take the factories back to America." [26]

Having purchased land, Ford began implementing the plan to build new facilities. The idea was to execute the corporation's business policies before the Automobile Manufacturing Business Law was announced. Ford's bullish behavior appears to have been based on the following grounds. Although the Japanese machine industry had grown, it still fell far short of a mass production system for automobiles. To meet demand, then, the continuation of foreign business in Japan seemed unavoidable. In this case, it was strategic to build a large factory before the Automobile Manufacturing Business Law was promulgated, insuring favorable business conditions in the future.

In fact, while the Outline for an Automobile Manufacturing Business Law was being written, the government unofficially asked Automobile Industries, Tokyo Gas and Electric, and big zaibatsu such as Mitsui, Mitsubishi, and Sumitomo, whether they intended to apply for a license. All of them said they did not.[27] As for Nissan and Toyoda, which later became licensees, it seemed that it would be several years before their automobile output would reach the mass production level. Presumably bluffing, Japan Ford's Kopf is reported to have remarked that the would be happy to "meet this wonderful car which owes its existence to a legal measure."[28]

Ford also acted bullishly because it had acquired information that the Ministry of Foreign Affairs and the Cabinet's Bureau of Legislation were reluctant to support the proposed Automobile Manufacturing Business Law because it conflicted with the U.S.-Japan Treaty of Commerce and Navigation.[29] Moreover, Navy authorities regarded Japan Ford as a semi-domestic company.

Having thus analyzed the situation, Ford announced in November 1935 the following plan for a new plant:
1) to double the capital of Japan Ford (to 16 million yen) and transfer new shares *en toto* to the Ford dealers in Japan; and
2) to found a Ford manufacturing plant in Yokohama and produce bona fide "Japanese Ford" vehicles a few years later.[30]

Ford probably conceded share ownership to the dealers because opposition was expected from various quarters against Ford-owned capital. Management control was to remain with Ford until genuinely "Japanese Fords" were produced.

The situation developed contrary to Ford's expectations and to its disadvantage. On May 23, 1936, the Automobile Manufacturing Business Law passed the 69th session of the Imperial Diet without revision. Ford therefore was forced to extensively revise the plan for its production system. Besides announcing the policy to use Japanese parts, it instructed Japan Ford to apply to the Kanagawa prefectural government for a permit to build a new plant capable of producing three times as much as the assembly plant in existence. The reason given for the application, submitted on June 9, 1936, was as follows:

> The automobile industry is still infant-like. The small number of vehicles presently made in Japan is markedly inferior to our company's products in efficiency, durability, and fuel consumption. The expansion of our company, therefore, should contribute greatly to the expansion of the Japanese auto industry. Moreover, the several tens of factories that currently produce parts for Ford vehicles will have more business along with an expanded Ford. Furthermore, if in the future Japan should enter into war with a third country, practical and inexpensive Ford vehicles will be to Japan's advantage. From all points of view, the expansion of our company will be in Japan's best interest. Besides, our company is called "Japan Ford Automobile Company, Inc." and the parts the company uses are all made in Japan. The only thing foreign about us is the capital. We think that our company on the whole does not conflict with the Automobile Manufacturing Business Law.[31]

The Kanagawa authorities believed there was "not only no precedent for rejecting this type of application, but also the laws relevant to this application contained provisions favorable to it."[32] Except for the heads of the automotive bureaus and sections of the Ministry of Commerce and Industry and the Army, many officials believed that Ford's plan to build a new factory should be approved.[33] Yet, the national government and military officials contended that since the Automobile Manufacturing Business Law had been enacted, foreign automobile companies could not be permitted to expand. Citing Article I, "The purpose of this law is to foster the automobile manufacturing industry in the Empire in order to complete national defense and develop industry," they overruled the opinions supporting Ford's plan and upheld the view that "foreign countries cannot complain but will accept Japan's position," which was that the Automobile Manufacturing Business Law was enacted for the sake of national security.[34] They requested the Kanagawa authorities to postpone issuing the license to Ford, and pressed for enforcing both the Automobile Manufacturing Business Law and supplementary rules and regulations. On July 11, 1936, they succeeded in having an Imperial edict issued to bring the law into effect. In consequence, Ford's application for a permit to build a plant was rejected, costing Ford an opportunity to implement local production.

Epilogue

As soon as the Automobile Manufacturing Business Law was enacted, Toyoda Jidoshokki Seisakusho (Toyoda Automatic Loom Works) and Nissan Motor applied and were granted licenses.[35] In contrast, Japan Ford and Japan GM were ordered by a "bulletin" from the Ministry of Commerce and Industry, dated September 22, 1936, to keep production under 12,360 and 9,470 vehicles, respectively.[36] Their business was further restricted when the Japanese government raised import tariffs, changed the Foreign Exchange Control Law, and enacted the Law Regarding Temporary Measures for Import and Export Goods, all in preparation for a wartime economy. To continue doing business and ensure the security of their assets in these difficult circumstances, both Ford and GM were compelled to develop a new business strategy.

After the miscarriage of the cooperation plan with Nissan, GM began negotiations for a joint venture with Toyoda and Sumitomo. This effort failed, however, owing to GM's insistence on using its own components for major parts and its refusal to export the vehicles jointly produced by GM and a Japanese enterprise.[37] Consequently, GM, sooner than Ford, decided to withdraw from Japan completely.[38]

In contrast, when its plan for a new factory failed, Ford changed its strategy and sought either cooperation or a joint venture with a Japanese company.[39] It approached Mitsubishi, Furukawa, Nissan, and Toyoda. Among these, Nissan signed a contract with Ford in August 1937, agreeing that the components imported by Nissan Motor be assembled at Japan Ford's plant.[40] This contract benefited both Japan Ford, whose production was restricted by the Japanese government, and Nissan Motor, which was under pressure to increase production in response to the outbreak of the Sino-Japanese War (1937). On the basis of this contract and an assumed future merger, Japan Ford's manager, Benjamin Kopf, and Nissan's Yoshisuke Aikawa planned a joint venture in Manchukuo.[41]

Kopf repeatedly advised Ford's main office that the proposed joint venture was not only a profitable investment for Japan Ford but also the last resort if Ford was to continue to do business in Japan. The main office concluded, however, that in view of U.S. public opinion after the Panay Incident of December 12, 1937, it was inappropriate to bring business into Manchukuo in this manner.[42] Inside Nissan Motor, too, the opinion opposing a joint venture with Ford prevailed on the grounds that it was doomed to the same fate as the plan to cooperate with GM.[43] Despite the impassioned efforts of Kopf and Aikawa, the Nissan-Ford cooperation plan was abandoned.

In 1939, another attempt was made to merge Nissan Motor, Toyota Motor, and Japan Ford. This would have created a company with capital of 60 million yen, but it also failed because the parties concerned could not muster enough support within the Army.[44] In the meantime, the business environment of both Japan Ford and Japan GM continued to deteriorate, and in 1940 these companies terminated their operations.

This article has focused on the Japanese government's automotive industry policies, especially on the Automobile Manufacturing Business Law and the response of U.S. auto manufacturers in Japan. Worthy of note is that the law facilitated the exclusion of Ford and GM, which had monopolized the Japanese automobile market. The law also afforded a basis of development for Toyota and Nissan Motor by giving them the status of licensed companies. In this sense, the enactment of the Automobile Manufacturing Business Law was an extremely significant event in the history of automotive manufacturing in Japan.

Notes

1) Nippon Jidosha Kogyokai, ed., *Nippon Jidosha Kogyo Shiko* 2 (Outline of the History of the Japanese Automobile Industry, Vol. 2) (Nippon Jidosha Kogyokai), 1967, p. 8 ff.

2) Kyoritsu Automobile Works was Chrysler's assembly facility. It was founded with capital invested jointly by Chrysler's four importing agents. I chose not to examine this company in this study because it was much smaller than both Japan Ford and Japan GM, and Chrysler left its management to the discretion of these licensed agents instead of bringing in company officers to implement the parent company's policies.

3) Nippon Jidosha Kogyokai, ed., *Nippon Jidosha* 2, pp. 173–174.

4) Shokosho Komukyoku, ed., "Honpo Jidosha Kogyo Seisaku no Ryakushi" (A Short History of the Japanese Government's Automobile Industry Policies) in "Jidosha Kogyo" (Unpublished papers held in the Archives of Tsusho Sangyo-sho [MITI].)

5) Nissan Jidosha Kabushiki Kaisha, ed., *Nissan Jidosha Sanju Nenshi* (A 30 Year History of Nissan Motor) (Nissan Jidosha Kabushiki Kaisha), 1965, p. 26.

6) Shokosho Komukyoku, ed., *Jidosha Kogyo Kakuritsu Chosa Iinkai Keika Gaiyo* (Outline of the History of the Investigation Committee

to Establish an Automobile Industry) (Shokosho Komukyoku), 1932, p. 17.

7) Toyota Jidosha Hanbai Kabushiki Kaisha, ed., *Motarizeishon to Tomo ni* (Along with Motorization) (Toyota Jidosha Hanbai Kabushiki Kaisha), 1970, p. 11.

8) Masaru Udagawa, "Historical Development of the Japanese Automobile Industry, 1917–1971: Business and Development," *Keiei Shirin* (The Hosei Journal of Business), Vol. 19, no. 4 (January 1983), p. 35.

9) Matsuyoshi Iwasaki, *Jidosha Kogyo no Kakuritsu* (Establishment of the Automobile Industry) (Ito Shoten), 1941, p. 168. See also "Honpo Jidosha Kogyo."

10) Jidosha Kogyo Shinkokai, ed., *Nippon Jidosha Kogyoshi Gyosei Kirokushu* (The Sources of Japanese Automobile Industry Policies), (Jidosha Kogyo Shikokai), 1979, p. 17; Masaru Udagawa and Seishi Nakamura, "Japanese Business and Government in the Interwar Period: Heavy Industrialization and the Industrial Rationalization Movement" in Keiichiro Nakagawa, ed., *Government and Business* (University of Tokyo Press), 1976, pp. 96–97.

11) Tsusho Sangyo-sho, ed., *Shoko Seisakushi 18: Kikai Kogyo* 1 (The History of Commercial and Industrial Policies, Vol. 18: The Machinery Industry, No 1), (Shoko Seisakushi Kanko Iinkai), 1976, p. 465.

12) For reference, it may be noted that Japan Ford's profits in 1939 and 1940 were ¥4,616,725 and ¥1,045,880, respectively. See Okurasho, ed. *Dai-Niji Taisen ni okeru Rengokoku Zaisan Shori* 1 (Confiscated Assets of the Allied Powers During World War II, Vol. 1) (Okurasho), 1966, p. 119.

13) Frederic G. Donner, *The World-Wide Industrial Enterprise: Its Challenge and Promise* (New York: McGraw-Hill), 1967, pp. 19–20.

14) General Motors Overseas Operations, *The War Effort of the Overseas Division* (New York: General Motors Overseas Operation), 1944, p. 88.

15) *Ibid.*, p. 18.

16) Masahisa Ozaki *Jidosha Nihonshi* 1 (The History of Japanese Automobiles, Vol. 1) (Jikensha), 1955, p. 331.

17) Nissan is one of the new zaibatsu that expanded very rapidly after the Manchurian Incident. By 1937, it had developed into a business combine ranking just below the Mitsui and Mitsubishi zaibatsu. For more information on Nissan, see Masaru Udagawa, *Shinko Zaibatsu* (The New Zaibatsu) (Nihon Keizai Shinbunsha), 1984,

Chapter 1.

18) Jidosha Kogyo Shinkokai, ed., *Nippon Jidosha Kogyoshi Kojutsu Kirokushu* (Recordings of Oral Interviews on the History of the Japanese Automobile Industry) (Jidosha Kogyo Shinkokai), 1975, p. 112.

19) For the foregoing discussion on the first Nissan-GM negotiations, I used "Nissan GM Dai-Ichiji Kosho Kankei" (The First Nissan-GM Negotiations) and "Zeneraru Motasu to no Teikei Keikaku" (The Plan for Cooperation with General Motors), both from the Aikawa Family Archives. For more information, see Masaru Udagawa, "Nissan Zaibatsu no Jidosha Sangyo Shinshutsu ni tsuite: Nissan to GM to no Teikei Kosho o Chushin ni 1, 2" (The Development of the Automobile Industry of the Nissan Zaibatsu with Emphasis on the Nissan-GM Negotiations for Cooperation 1, 2), *Keiei Shirin* (The Hosei Journal of Business), Vol. 13, no. 4 and Vol. 14, no. 1 (January and April), 1977.

20) Iwasaki, *Jidosha Kogyo*, p. 170.

21) For the history of the second series of negotiations for Nissan-GM cooperation, I consulted "GM-Nissan Gappei Mondai" (The Problems of a GM-Nissan Merger) in the Aikawa Family Archives.

22) Jidosha Kogyo Shinkokai, ed., *Nippon Jidosha Kogyoshi Zadankai Kirokushu* (Symposium on the History of the Japanese Automobile Industry) (Jidosha Kogyo Shinkokai), 1973, p. 62.

23) Mira Wilkins, "The Role of U.S. Business," in Dorothy Borg and Shumpei Okamoto, eds., *Pearl Harbor as History: Japanese-American Relations, 1931–1941* (New York: Columbia University Press), 1973, p. 361.

24) Mira Wilkins and Frank E. Hill, *American Business Abroad: Ford on Six Continents* (Detroit: Wayne State University Press), 1964, p. 253.

25) Nippon Jidosha Kogyokai, ed., *Nippon Jidosha Kogyo Shiko* 3 (Outline of the History of the Japanese Automobile Industry, Vol. 3) (Nippon Jidosha Kogyokai), 1969, p. 37.

26) *Ibid.*, p. 38.

27) *Ibid.*, p. 32.

28) Ryozo Yanagida, *Jidosha Sanju Nenshi* (A 30 Year History of Automobiles) (Sansuisha), 1944, p. 354.

29) Nippon Jidosha Kogyokai, ed., *Nippon Jidosha* 3, p. 32.

30) Ozaki, *Jidosha Nihonshi* 1, pp. 383–384.

31) The Ford-related sources in "Jidosha Kogyo" in the Tsusho Sangyo-sho Archives.

97

32) *Ibid.*

33) Ozaki, *Jidosha Nihonshi* 1, p. 386. See also C.S. Chang, *The Japanese Auto Industry and the U.S. Market* (New York: Praeger Publishers), 1981, p. 24.

34) Jidosha Kogyo Shinkokai, ed., *Gyosei Kirokushu*, p. 23.

35) In August 1937, the Toyoda Automatic Loom Works separated its automobile division and created an independent company, Toyota Motor. Note that the original company name, "Toyoda," was modified to "Toyota" for the independent automobile company. In April 1941, Tokyo Jidosha Kogyo (Tokyo Automobile Industries) was also issued a license. This was formerly known as Automobile Industries, and is the predecessor of Isuzu Jidosha (Isuzu Motors) and Hino Jidosha (Hino Motors).

36) Tusho Sangyo-sho, ed., *Shoko Seisakushi* 18, p. 422.

37) Shotaro Kamiya, *My Life with Toyota* (Toyota Motors Sales Company), 1967, p. 71.

38) Incidentally, the labor problems that arose within Japan GM also contributed to GM's decision to withdraw. See Ozaki, *Jidosha Nihonshi* 1, p. 386.

39) Wilkins and Hill, *American Business*, p. 255.

40) Nissan Jidosha, ed., *Nissan Jidosha*, p. 77–78.

41) Nippon Sangyo, which was the Nissan combine's holding company, moved to Shinkyo, the capital of Manchukuo, in November 1937. At the same time, it adopted a new name, Manshu Jukogyo Kaihatsu (Manchuria Heavy Industry Development) and acquired monopoly rights for industrial development in Manchuria. Aikawa, the president of the company, tried to bring in American capital to develop Manchuria. For details, see Udagawa, *Shinko Zaibatsu*, pp. 65–80 and Yukio Cho, "Inquiry into the Problem of Importing American Capital into Manchuria: A Note on Japanese-American Relations, 1931–1941" in Borg and Okamoto, eds., *Pearl Harbor as History*, pp. 388–391.

42) Chihiro Hosoya, Makoto Saito, Seiichi Imai, and Michio Royama, eds., *Nichi-Bei Kankeishi–Kaisen ni itaru Junen 3: Gikai Seito to Minkan Dantai* (The History of Japanese-American Relations: The Ten Years Before the War, vol. 3: The Diet, Political Parties, and Private Groups) (University of Tokyo Press), 1971, p. 249. This is one of four volumes of the proceedings of the conference on Japanese-American Relations, 1931–1941, which was held at Lake Kawaguchi, Japan, in July 1969. The English edition of the Kawaguchi papers was published under the title *Pearl Harbor as History*, but did

not contain the discussion on the papers presented at the conference that I cite here. The American gunboat *Panay* was sunk by the Japanese naval air force while it was patrolling the Yangtze River.

43) Jidosha Kogyo Shinkokai, ed., *Kojitsu Kirokushu*, p. 113.
44) Kamiya, *My Life with Toyota*, pp. 71–72.

Translated by Atsuko Hirai, Wellesley College

[25]

Excerpt from *Historical Studies in International Corporate Business*, Alice Teichova, Maurice Levy-Leboyer and Helga Nussbaum (eds.)

12   J. & P. Coats Ltd in Poland

EMMA HARRIS[1]

In 1918, J. & P. Coats Ltd of Paisley, the Scottish multinational thread manufacturers, were faced with the loss of one of the major components of their European empire: the Russian operation controlled through the Nevsky Thread Manufacturing Company of St Petersburg, which on the eve of the First World War had accounted for some 90% of Russian thread production, and which had from the 1890s yielded large profits to the parent company. Of the 150 million strong Russian market, only the populations of Poland and the Baltic states (c. 10 million) were still accessible; and of Coats' six main manufacturing units in Russia, only two tattered remnants had – so far – escaped the Bolsheviks: the Strasdenhof mill at Riga, and the Łódzka Fabryka Nici T.A. at Łódź, now in the shakily-reborn independent Polish state. Radical readjustments were therefore required. We should note that in 1918 all decisions on the future of the Łódź mill rested with Paisley alone: J. & P. Coats Ltd, while maintaining the polite fiction of being 'only share-holders' in subsidiary companies, was a highly-centralised operation. Correspondence with the Łódź company may indeed have been conducted throughout in courtly language of suggestion and advice, but this was merely a gloss on a management structure in which all decisions on investment, production patterns, employment policy, supplies and sales (the last through Coats' marketing arm, the Central Agency) were taken from headquarters departments at Paisley. Łódź could not purchase so much as a coffee boiler for the canteen without headquarters' approval.[2]

The Łódź mill – employing 64,000 spindles and 850 workers in 1914 – had after its take-over by the Nevsky company in 1900 been closely integrated into the Paisley-directed Nevsky manufacturing and sales network. It produced spooled thread and Nevsky tickets for Poland and Russian markets, and grey thread for other Nevsky mills. During the war, it had been closed under compulsory German administration, but although subjected to requisitions which included machine parts, damage was not particularly extensive, and the capital outlay required to reinstitute production was in the region of £100,000. Loss of established markets and production linkages

136   Emma Harris

were far more serious problems for the company in 1918. Although this was the only large-scale thread mill in the Polish territories, the thirty million strong Polish market was exhausted, and the Southern and Western territories which had previously formed part of the Austro-Hungarian and German empires enjoyed established supply connections with other Coats mills and brands. Indeed, during the 1920s, the Polish market for finished thread was to prove capable of absorbing only about 20 % of the Łódź mill's spinning capacity.[3] Moreover, Poland in the first phase of its inter-war history – through border disputes, the Polish–Soviet war, internal political instability and labour unrest, inflation and the German tariff war, down to Piłsudski's coup in May 1926 – represented a superficially unattractive proposition to all but the most speculative of foreign capital.

In this situation, Coats' policy in Poland in the first years after the war can most readily be interpreted in terms of continued expectations in the Russian market. The company was by no means resigned to the loss of its Russian interests, and like other British firms with long-standing ties in Russia, saw Poland at least to 1921 as a potential stepping-stone towards renewing these contacts at an appropriate future date. Until the conclusion of the Polish–Soviet war in the late autumn of 1920, Coats' strategy amounted to a cautious reservation of options on renewed use of its manufacturing base in Poland should occasion in Russia arise; from October 1920, the company's activities rapidly accelerated in response to the Polish victory; and only from late 1921 can signs be detected of longer-term adjustment to an exclusively Polish context.

The timing of the initiation of an investment programme at Łódź strongly suggests that the decision was taken against a background of Russian expectations. Coats' first purposeful approach to the Łódź company in May 1919 coincided with the opening stages of the Polish–Soviet war, and was apparently made in direct response to an appeal by the MacAlpine commission, which in March 1919 forwarded to Paisley a report on the mill, 'strongly urging the advisability of sending a representative with plenary powers and money as soon as possible, with a view to the resumption of operations'. While MacAlpine's concern was based on a desire to prevent Bolshevism developing behind the lines while the Polish army was away fighting it at the front[4] – a sentiment that Coats might have applauded but were hardly likely to back financially – the possible opportunities afforded by a satisfactory outcome to the war were not ignored in Paisley. Thereafter, the pattern of the company's activity at Łódź to the autumn of 1920 was designed not to reinstitute production, but cautiously to set in place a structure which could be swiftly activated when required. Thus after an exploratory mission to the mill in May 1919, a young man named Samuel Harvey was sent out as mill manager, specifications for replacement machine parts were taken, and orders placed with British suppliers. But the pace of deliveries to October 1920 betrayed no impatience to begin manufacture. The spinning mill machinery, which required relatively few replacement parts, some of which could be supplied locally, was not operational until June 1920. Re-fitting of the twisting mill, which called for a higher level of investment, was carried out even more dilatorily: parts for the frames were ordered in November 1919, but between June and September 1920, materials for only 14 of the 48 frames were dispatched, while in contrast the remaining 34 sets were to be delivered between October 1920 and January 1921. Parts for the polishing machinery were not ordered until December 1920.[5]

The minimal production instituted from June 1920 when the spinning machinery became operational further indicates that this was only a holding operation. Employment in the spinning mill stood at 15 in June, and by October had reached only 41; it was not until early in 1921 that a viable work force was recruited. Recruitment for the twisting mill did not begin at all until November 1920.[6] While Coats were prepared to provide some thread imports to retain their hold on the Polish market, the limited spinning that did take place at Łódź was intended to offer the appearance rather than the substance of activity, to placate the somewhat uncertain quantity of the new Polish government. The raw cotton dispatched to Łódź at this stage was sent in answer to a telegram from the mill in January 1920, reporting an urgent request from the Polish Industry Ministry that they start production as soon as possible; the telegram concluded: 'Send some cotton to show the authorities our earnest endeavour.' In September 1920, following further official approaches, Paisley showed renewed concern, writing: 'It is unfortunate that the Department of Industry has had occasion to ask an explanation ... We think it extremely important that you should endeavour to give the authorities the satisfaction they desire.'[7] Coats' lack of enthusiasm for immediate market prospects can also be observed in their attitude in July 1920 to an enquiry about loan spinning from a neighbouring Łódź mill: Paisley regretted that 'we are not inclined to entertain your proposal'.[8]

Coats' wariness of irrevocable commitment in this turbulent period is highlighted by the pattern of their behaviour during the concluding stages of the Polish–Soviet war, when Poland faced defeat. Contingency plans had been drawn up: in what was obviously a prearranged code, Łódź wired in early August, 'Harvey health worse. Send instructions in case of death', to which Paisley replied in a series of telegrams ordering sales of cotton and yarn 'against sterling if possible'. Even after the Polish victory at Warsaw in August Coats cut off supplies to Łódź while Polish military requisition was still in the offing. It was not until October 1920 that the situation was noted to be 'considerably more settled', and sales of yarn stocks were discontinued.[9]

For roughly a year after this, however, Coats' revanchist hopes took more concrete form. An interesting message sent to Łódź after the Polish victory suggests specific plans: 'Herbert Cooper ... should hold himself in readiness

138   Emma Harris

to leave for Russia at fairly short notice'.[10] Certainly from October 1920 Coats abandoned their policy of caution and began full institution of production at the Łódź mill. A special meeting 'to discuss matters relating to the Łódź Thread Manufacturing Company' was held at Glasgow on 19th October; here a decision was taken to send raw cotton to Łódź, and the first post-war investment in new machinery for the mill was approved.[11] Increased urgency in supplying parts of the twisting frames meant that by January 1921 all were operational, and the mill commenced spooling sixcord thread; all polishing machine parts had been supplied by May 1921, when some glacé thread manufacture was begun.[12] By mid-1921 this had resulted in a build-up of relatively large stocks of spooled thread at the mill: nearly 20 000 gross, with a current monthly sales average of less than 2000 gross. In view of Coats' tight control of the production: sales ratio, this must at least in part be explained in terms of preparations for the Russian market, a conclusion moreover borne out by the fact that this was largely 'second-grade thread' which was not suitable for marketing under Coats' own-brand labels in Poland.[13] Paisley soon however showed signs of unease, in June advising the curtailment of sixcord production with reference to the Polish market; by October there was a note of agitation from headquarters, who telegraphed: 'Reduce production in all departments in accordance with sales. Keep in touch with Warsaw agents.'[14]

From now on, while not entirely abandoning plans for the Russian market, Coats began to develop a role for the Łódzka Fabryka Nici T.A. outside this framework. At first this was to be expressed through greater interest in the Polish market, although gradually, as the Polish inflation developed from 1922, and domestic sales (given imported raw materials) became ever more unattractive, emphasis was increasingly placed on export of semi-products.

Growing acceptance of the exclusively Polish context can be traced in attempts – mainly unsuccessful – from 1921 to find local suppliers of auxiliary materials;[15] in the accession of the company to the Łódź Association of Textile Manufacturers;[16] and perhaps most evidently in the new share issue of April 1922, annulling shares previously held by the Nevsky company.[17] Łódź finished thread production was now planned on the basis of demand in the Polish market, with extension in some lines into the Baltic states. Although there was as yet no serious competition for Coats brands in this market, Paisley was sensitive to indications of Polish demand, proposing for example from October 1922 the introduction of 'a cheaper quality of knittings...for the Polish market'. A policy was also developed of substitute production at Łódź of other Coats brands established in certain regions of Poland – notably Harland's Eiserngarn in Galicia.[18] A long-term approach was moreover now adopted to domestic brand reputation and future competition, reflected in quality control and a strategic pricing and ticketing

J. & P. Coats Ltd in Poland   139

policy. In 1921, Paisley recalled that Łódź brands had not enjoyed a high reputation in Poland before the war: 'It may be necessary to sell…at prices, say, 10% lower than for goods of British manufacture, and it must also be borne in mind that the Łódź brands must be in a position to meet eventual foreign competition.' For the marketing of Łódź's large stock of second quality goods in 1921, Paisley advocated the use of a ticket that did not show the name of the manufacturer; and for Lithuania in 1923, they favoured a ticket which did not show the country of origin ('We understand that Polish designations are not very popular in Lithuania').[19]

The evolution of company policy over the period can be traced in their approach to the Polish military market. Whereas in mid-1920 – anxious to preserve their hold on the civilian market, and clearly not placing much faith in the new Polish authorities – Coats had actually complained that the Polish government had bought most of the company's imports to Poland 'for their own purposes'[20], by November 1920 their attitude had shifted perceptibly and they bridled at indications of long-term competition. While Coats had been making haste slowly in 1920, the Scheibler/Grohmann partnership had re-activated the tiny Łowicz Thread Mill. On 5 November Coats wrote to Łódź:

We note that the military authorities are negotiating with the Łowicz Thread Mill for delivery of Thread….As there may be a danger of this Polish mill later being subventioned, we should like to be kept fully informed so that we may claim entirely similar treatment. It may be that this is only a case of the officials concerned having been bribed, and steps should be taken to find out who they are and what can be done to support our interests.[21]

Whatever was done, from 1921 the Warsaw Commissariat began to renew its approaches to the Central Agency, and from 1922 to the end of our period, the bulk of Commissariat supplies came from the Łódź mill, accounting for c. 10–15% of its finished thread production (minimum military sales: 1922 – 3000 gross; 1923 – 5118 gross; 1924 – 12600 gross). In the first years, Coats gave priority to these orders and stressed the importance of retaining this market.[22]

Gradually, however, as inflation developed, a more cavalier attitude evolved. In the years to 1926, Coats exploited their position of virtual monopoly on supply of thread suitable for the military: Department VII of the Commissariat noted in 1923 that 'the Łodzka Fabryka Nici is the only firm in Poland capable of producing high-quality thread up to military requirements', and the Polish inflation made this an unattractive market to foreign producers without a manufacturing base in the country.[23] Coats therefore did not hesitate to bring pressure to bear upon the Commissariat in 1922–4 on the question of the types of thread ordered and method of payment. In June 1922, Paisley had instructed: 'You should persuade them to take as much as possible in (Black) Troika…in order to reduce your large

140   Emma Harris

stocks in this brand.' Apparently, this directive was successfully implemented, for the contract signed in March 1923 was questioned by the Chief
of Military Administration, who demanded to know 'why Department
VII...had purchased black thread now, when all parts of the uniform
stipulated for the army are khaki'. Since his objections delayed the signing
of the second part of the contract, Węgliński, the director of the Warsaw
Central Agency, visited the Chief in person and threatened 'that if the
contract were not confirmed on that very day, the firm would break off
negotiations'. The Chief therefore signed.[24] Later in 1923, by again
threatening to withdraw supplies, Coats ensured in the worst period of
inflation that the War Ministry would pay their accounts in Sterling, or
sterling equivalent on the day of delivery, in contravention of the original
contract, which laid down fixed prices.[25]

Even as general demand somewhat recovered, the Polish and Baltic
finished thread market could absorb only 80,000 to 100,000 gross spools, or
c. 20% of the Łódź mill's spinning capacity.[26] Having turned their back on
the Nevsky past, Coats therefore expanded semi-product manufacture at the
mill. In periods of reduced home demand, they agreed to, or even actively
encouraged, the use of spare capacity for local loan spinning orders, or the
production of weaving yarn for the local market, although maintaining a
vigilant eye to the possibility of future competition – refusing orders which
might eventually have been used by competing manufacturers of sewing
thread.[27] The main stress was however placed on the integration of Łódź
semi-products into Coats' European manufacturing network, an arrangement made additionally attractive by low labour costs. From November
1921, 'half the mill' was to be employed regularly in spinning grey thread for
the Home Mills at Ferguslie, in quantities varying from 6,000 to 9,000 lb
weekly. From February 1922, grey thread was further directed to other Coats
Central European mills as required: in addition to the Paisley order,
quantities (initially 7500 lb weekly) were sent periodically to the Harland mill
at Wilhelmsburg in Austria, and from October 1923, the Paisley thread was
occasionally diverted to the Coats mill at Bratislava. From July 1924,
although consignments to these two mills continued intermittently, Łódź
mainly supplied the Strasdenhof mill at Riga, an old partner from the
Nevsky stable.[28]

By 1923–4 these arrangements were being given some priority over the
Łódź mill's own finished thread orders[29] – a fact which must be examined in
the context of the Polish inflation, compounded, especially following
Władysław Grabski's reform measures of 1923–4, by Polish exchange
control regulations. Throughout its post-war operation, the Łódzka Fabryka
Nici T.A. was theoretically working simply as a loan spinning mill for Coats,
who supplied raw materials and paid a spinning allowance – a purely formal
arrangement which provided some leeway in evading the impact of controls.

J. & P. Coats Ltd in Poland 141

In 1923, when the Warsaw Treasury Department had questioned this structure, Coats wrote to Łódź:

As according to your letter the new Devisen regulations permit you to utilise for the payment of foreign debts the sterling placed at your disposal, we presume you will have no difficulty in arranging that your invoices covering the manufacturing allowances should be purely formal documents. If the authorities require that the sterling should be utilised at all, it should be utilised ... for the manufacture of thread sold in Poland and whose proceeds should be remitted to this country.[30]

Later, Paisley suggested that in view of 'the present difficulty in having the Polish collections remitted home', payments due from Łódź to the parent company should be used to purchase coal in Poland for the Harland mills in Austria.[31] Thus, although in local currency the formal indebtedness of the Łódź company to Coats inevitably soared during the inflationary post-war years (the lending being partly capitalised in the new share issues of 1922 and 1924), the mill was probably able to reduce its debt somewhat in sterling.[32] None the less, the kind of profits to which Paisley had been accustomed from the Nevsky operation were evidently a thing of the past.

NOTES

1 Abbreviations used throughout: WAPŁ – Wojewódzkie Archiwum Państwowe w Łodzi; ŁFN – Łódzka Fabryka Nici T.A., archive in WAPŁ; CAW – Centralne Archiwum wojskowe; FO – Public Record Office, Foreign Office.
2 See E. E. Kruze, 'Tabaczni i nitocznii tresti' – iz istorii imperializma v Rosii', in *Iż Istorii Imperializma v Rosii*, Akademia Nauk SSSR, Trudy Leningradskogo Otdelenija Instituta Istorii, Vypusk 1 (Moskva–Leningrad, 1959), pp. 68 ff.; ŁFN 27, 28, 29, 30, 33, *passim*.
3 ŁFN 30; FO 371–3936, 202703, 8.VI.1920, letter from W. H. Coats to Lord Curzon.
4 FO 371–3894,no. 17710, 21.1.1919; MUN 4/6360, 62341, App. I, p. 15; FO 371–3936, 202703, 8.VI.1920, letter from W. H. Coats to Lord Curzon.
5 ŁFN 27, M14, 8.XI.1919; ŁFN 27, 21, 24.XI.1919; ŁFN 27, 11, 21.1.1921; ŁFN 27, M145, 20.XII.1920; ŁFN 27, 94, 17.V.1921.
6 ŁFN 143, employment records in twisting mill; ŁFN 144, employment records in spinning mill.
7 ŁFN 27, 6, 15.1.1920; ŁFN 27, M86, 24.IX.1920.
8 ŁFN 27, M, 6.VII.1920.
9 ŁFN 27, 66, 23.VII.1920; ŁFN 27, 70, 5.VIII.1920; ŁFN 27, 89, 1.X.1920.
10 ŁFN 27, M, 18.XI.1920
11 ŁFN 27, unnumbered, 'Minutes of a meeting held in Glasgow on 19th October 1920...'.
12 ŁFN 27, 11, 21.1.1921; ŁFN 27, 94, 17.V.1921.
13 ŁFN 27, M10, 30.V.1921.
14 ŁFN 27, M112, 21.VI.1921; ŁFN 28, 3.X.1921.
15 ŁFN 28, no. 6, 12.XI.1920; ŁFN 28, 37, 9.VII.1921 ff.; ŁFN 30, Ch. no. 4, 21.II.1922 ff.
16 WAPŁ, Zwiazek Przemysłu Włókienniczego 7, no. 52, p. 32.

142   Emma Harris

17 ŁFN 28, 29.IV.1922.
18 ŁFN 28, 268, 5.X.1922 ff.; ŁFN 33, 309, 30.I.1923.
19 ŁFN 27, M16, 22.I.1921; ŁFN 27, M10, 30.V.1921; ŁFN 33, 369, 6.VII.1923; ŁFN 33, 373, 20.VII.1923.
20 FO 371–3936, 202703, 8.VI.1920, letter from W. H. Coats to Lord Curzon.
21 ŁFN 27, M111, 5.XI.1920.
22 CAW I.300.54.79; ŁFN 28, 170, 30.III.1922; CAW I.300.54. 77, LDG 48119/22V KM, 14.VI.1922; CAW I.300.54.132; ŁFN 33, 489, 6.VI.1924; ŁFN 33, 604, 2.X.1924.
23 CAW I.300.54.79, Dep. VII, Liczba 24251 KMV; CAW I.300. 54.79, Protokuł nr 30, Dep. VII, Komisja Mundurowa 15.III.1923.
24 ŁFN 28, 214, 16.VI.1922; CAW I.300.54.79, Dep. VII, Liczba 4130/OA, Eksp. 1-sza; CAW I.300.54.79, Dep. VII, Liczba 21273/23 KMV to SAA 21.III.1923; CAW I.300.54.79, SAA L6081/OA/WA/Tj. to Dep. VII.
25 CAW I.300.54.79, Dep. VII, Ldz. 12783/Zaop./23/ZP, 11.X.1923 to SAA.
26 ŁFN 30, 'Protokuł. W dniu 18-ego lutego 1924r....'
27 ŁFN 28. 231, 1.VII.1922; ŁFN 28, 134, 13.II.1922; ŁFN 28, 140, 22.II.1922; ŁFN 28, 261, 22.IX.1922; ŁFN 28, 262, 26.IX.1922; ŁFN 28, 277, 20.X.1922.
28 ŁFN 28, 130, 7.II.1922; ŁFN 28, 157, 18.III.1922; ŁFN 28, 184, 28.IV.1922; ŁFN 33, no. 537, 4.VIII.1924; ŁFN 33, no. 557, 29.VIII.1924; ŁFN 33, 424, 16.I.1924; ŁFN 33, 458, 14.IV.1924.
29 e.g. ŁFN 33, 468, 30.IV.1924; ŁFN 33, 462, 18.IV.1924.
30 ŁFN 33, 375, 27.VII.1923.
31 ŁFN 33, copy of letter from William George to company headquarters, 19.VIII. 1923.
32 ŁFN 30, 'Protokuł. W dniu 18-ego lutego 1924r....'

Summation

In this collection of essays, we have moved from the surveys to pioneering contributions, to new perspectives, to case studies of particular firms, and concluded with a few essays on the history of multinationals in individual host countries.

The Introduction indicated that what has been presented here is only a tiny selection from the vast quantity of publications in this field. While this collection seeks to be representative, there are nonetheless some egregious omissions. One set not mentioned in the Introduction cannot be ignored. I had hoped to include a last section on the historical aspects of politics and the multinational enterprise. Many of the books and articles cited in the Introduction as well as some of the essays included herein do deal with political issues and matters of national security. A number of students of the history of multinationals have been interested in diplomacy and multinational enterprise behaviour over time. Many authors that deal with multinationals in particular host countries have been concerned with their impact on national political conditions. Alas, to have included even a sample of the sizeable literature on multinationals and their political interactions would have made this volume far too lengthy. It is, however, necessary to point out that multinational enterprises operate – by definition – under more than one national sovereignty. They are influenced by and, on occasion, influence governmental rules, regulations, legislation and attitudes. Their relationships through time with governmental bodies are in some cases important determinants of their profitability and durability. Home and host governments can close the door to multinationals: the home country can prevent them from making investments in a foreign country – or any foreign countries; a host country can forbid them from entering or expropriate their existing operations. Governments can also use taxation as a means of discouraging or encouraging multinationals. They can foster business abroad and the entry of foreign business by providing a range of other benefits, special or general. Likewise, multinationals often negotiate with governments, negotiations that can be crucial to the success (or lack of success) of projects. A number of books and articles have dealt with the history of home and host governmental policies towards multinationals. In this summation, I do not have space to provide a bibliography but want to point out that these topics are highly significant aspects of the history of multinational enterprise.

Furthermore, because of space constraints, there are no essays in this volume by D.H. Fieldhouse, Charles Wilson, William Reader, Peter Hertner, Fred Carstensen, William Wray, Raj Lundström, Alice Teichova, Charles Harvey, R.T. Davenport-Hines, Clive Treblicock, Sherman Cochran, Irving Anderson, T.A.B. Corley, Jean-François Hennart, Patrick Fridenson, Stephen Randall, Nobuo Kawabe, nor by many other individuals who have made important contributions to the growing field of the history of multinational enterprise. Hopefully, however, despite these and many other omissions, the reader of this volume will have obtained some sense of the many issues which relate to the history of multinational enterprise and will, moreover, see the relevance of such studies to the economic history of nations worldwide and to today's world economy.

Name Index